THE GREAT DECEPTION

THE GREAT DECEPTION

The True Story of Britain and the
European Union

Revised and updated fourth edition

CHRISTOPHER BOOKER
and
RICHARD NORTH

BLOOMSBURY CONTINUUM
LONDON • OXFORD • NEW YORK • NEW DELHI • SYDNEY

BLOOMSBURY CONTINUUM
Bloomsbury Publishing Plc
50 Bedford Square, London, WC1B 3DP, UK
29 Earlsfort Terrace, Dublin 2, Ireland

BLOOMSBURY, BLOOMSBURY CONTINUUM and the Diana logo are trademarks of
Bloomsbury Publishing Plc

First published in paperback 2003
Revised and updated fourth edition 2021

A catalogue record for this book is available from the British Library

ISBN: TPB: 978-1-4729-8465-4; eBook: 978-1-4729-9372-4;
ePDF: 978-1-4729-9373-1

2 4 6 8 10 9 7 5 3 1

Typeset by Deanta Global Publishing Services, Chennai, India
Printed and bound in Great Britain by CPI Group (UK) Ltd, Croydon CR0 4YY

To find out more about our authors and books visit www.bloomsbury.com
and sign up for our newsletters

CONTENTS

Foreword and Acknowledgements   vii

1   The Early Days: 1918–1945   1
2   Try, Try and Try Again: The First Attempts at European
    Integration: 1945–1949   24
3   The Rocky Road to Rome: 1950–1957   51
4   'A Triumph for Monnet': 1958–1961   74
5   Why de Gaulle Kept Britain Out: 1961–1969   91
6   The Real Deceit of Edward Heath: 1970–1972   123
7   Britain Stays In: 1973–1975   151
8   The Awkward Partner: 1975–1984   176
9   Enter Mr Spinelli: 1979–1986   202
10   Decline and Fall: 1986–1990   230
11   'At the Heart of Europe': 1990–1993   260
12   The Single Market: A Tale of Three Halves   289
13   Odd Man Out: 1993–1997   311
14   Towards 'Political Unity': 1997–1999   342
15   Hearts and Minds: 1999–2001   367
16   The Crowning Dream: 2002–2004   396
17   Downfall: 2004–2005   429
18   The Road to Lisbon: 2006–2009   459
19   The Euro Crisis: 2010–2012   491
20   Countdown to Referendum: 2012–2013   525
21   The Impossible Dream: 2014–2016   549
22   End Game: 2016–2020   574

    Conclusion: End and a Beginning   609

    Index   635

FOREWORD AND ACKNOWLEDGEMENTS

The sovereign nations of the past can no longer solve the problems of the present: they cannot ensure their own progress or control their own future. And the Community itself is only a stage on the way to the organised world of tomorrow.

Closing words of Jean Monnet's *Memoirs*

Europe's power is easy to miss. Like an 'invisible hand' it operates through the shell of traditional political structures. The British House of Commons, British law courts and British civil servants are still here, but they have become agents of the European Union, implementing European law. This is no accident. By creating common standards that are implemented through national institutions, Europe can take over countries without necessarily becoming a target for hostility.

Mark Leonard, Centre for European Reform, 2005

Since this book was first published in 2003, the story it tells has moved on to the point where – with the end of the transition period on 31 December 2020 – we can decently draw a line under an extraordinary and lengthy chapter in Britain's history. This was something Booker and I always intended to do together, but sadly he passed away in July 2019 – at least having seen the outcome of the referendum but before the UK had actually left the European Union, on 31 January 2020.

It falls to me, therefore, as the survivor of a working partnership that reached back to 1992, to finish the story that, in the second and third editions, we left in the middle of 2005. The book now covers some of the most tumultuous years of our relationship with the EU, encompassing not only the referendum on 23 June 2016 and the campaign that preceded it, but also the subsequent years devoted first to negotiating the Withdrawal

Agreement and then the 'future relationship' with the EU, culminating in the Christmas Eve deal labelled the Trade and Cooperation Agreement.

Something that yet again became painfully apparent, this time in the referendum campaign, and even more so afterwards, was how remarkably little the protagonists in the debate seemed to understand of the very thing on which they were focused. For 48 years Britain had been in the thrall of this vast, amorphous new system of government centred in Brussels. Again and again, it became clear how astonishingly ignorant the politicians were about the working of the European Union and, when it came to the crunch, how we could manage successfully to extricate ourselves from it.

When we first began researching for this book, we had already long been learning how the European Union worked and reporting on the extremely damaging effects it was in so many ways having on British life. But when we got seriously to work, we were continually amazed by how much about the history of the 'European project' had never been properly uncovered before, and how often we came across crucial episodes in the story that had been quite deliberately misrepresented.

No one before, it turned out, had tracked down how the core principles that were to shape the evolution of the project from the early 1950s onwards had originated in the minds of two men back in the 1920s. No one had really uncovered how their real purpose was to create a wholly integrated 'United States of Europe', ruled by an unelected 'supranational' government – or how in the 1950s it was deliberately decided to disguise that ultimate goal, and only to work towards 'ever closer union', step by step, starting with the pretence that what was being set up was only a trading arrangement, a 'common market'.

We were able to tell, more fully than ever before, the story of how, when Britain applied to join in 1961, the Macmillan government deliberately decided to go along with the same deceit. Although he and his 'minister for Europe' Edward Heath had been briefed that the real aim was full political and economic union, they decided, for what they called 'presentational' reasons, to conceal this from the British people behind the same pretence that we were only joining a 'common market'.

We told for the first time the real story behind the French president de Gaulle's veto of Britain's application to join, that he wanted first to get firmly in place the financial arrangements for the Common Agricultural Policy, which would require Britain to hand over huge sums to subsidise his French farmers and to buy in return some of their resulting surpluses. Only when this had finally been put in place in 1969 was Britain allowed to join, which Heath was desperate to do when elected prime minister the next year. And throughout the negotiations, Heath followed that same policy of deception, hiding what he well knew was the real aim – full political and economic union – by repeatedly claiming that our membership would involve 'no essential loss of sovereignty'.

Even while the accession negotiations were continuing, Heath learned that there were already plans in Brussels for a single currency, and had to send over his Europe minister to implore them to keep this under wraps until Britain was safely in: just as his ministers deliberately lied to Parliament about the extent to which we had given away the richest fishing waters in Europe as part of our price of entry.

So the deceptions continued – into the early 1980s with secret plans for further moves towards integration, which were so ambitious that it was agreed that the treaty they proposed needed to be split in two. The first part, the Single European Act in 1986, was sold to the British people as the setting up of a 'Single Market', when in reality it was much more than that and just what its title should have indicated: a further giant step towards creating a 'Single Europe'.

The second part was signed in 1992 as the Maastricht Treaty, completing the task of transforming the 'European Community' into the 'European Union'. It launched the single currency and much more, including the first serious moves towards giving the fast-emerging 'government of Europe' its own foreign and defence policies – further supported after 1997 by Tony Blair, who was also enthusiastic for giving the now vastly expanding European Union its own 'constitution' after 2001.

Not once in all those years did any British prime minister, with the exception of Mrs Thatcher, try to explain what had always been the project's real goal, any more than we were ever told the truth by David Cameron when he staged his referendum in 2016. It was for this and so much more that we had no hesitation in calling this book *The Great Deception*.

When we wrote the original edition, our aim was unashamedly to produce a Eurosceptic manual, better to inform those who were seeking to leave the European Union of the nature of the construct against which they were campaigning. Now that we have left, where the process of our leaving could hardly have been worse managed and the problems attendant on our newly restored status have yet to be resolved, there are siren voices calling for us to re-join. Possibly, as our difficulties multiply, those voices will intensify.

The purpose of this book, therefore, has subtly changed. While the aim is still to write a proper history of the 'European project', right up to the point of the UK's full departure, the purpose is graphically to recount the 'nature of beast' and Britain's experience of it, in order to warn current and future generations against seeking to repeat the experience. To that extent, the book erects a 'fence' around a metaphorical 'Chernobyl', to mark a point beyond which we as a nation should never pass.

With that, this is not and never has been an 'insider's' book. We cannot tell you what Jean Monnet had for breakfast on the morning of 9 May 1950 when his Schuman Plan was about to be announced, nor do we trouble our readers with the pallor of the then Chancellor of the Exchequer just before he met the prime minister on 15 March 2017. Rather, the book is the product of meticulous research, drawing on thousands of books, documents, academic papers and other sources, augmented by interviews and tempered by long personal experience of EU issues, working with many of the personalities who later feature in the story. Most crucially though, it is the product of informed analysis and synthesis, filtering out extraneous material to get to the essence of over a hundred years of history, in a way that is accessible, readable and informative.

To that effect, as time has passed and new perspectives have been acquired, some issues that seemed (and were) important in previous editions seem less so now, enabling me with judicious editing to cut some fifty thousand words from the original text, despite adding a considerable amount of new archival and other material. New writing amounts to about a third of the text, without adding to its overall length.

Our work (that of Booker and I in the first three editions and my solo efforts in this current edition) reveals a picture of the story so radically different from any previous accounts – even up to date with the account of the referendum campaign – that anyone remotely concerned with this hugely important subject might find it both startling and illuminating. Certainly, when our first edition appeared, that view was confirmed by the private responses of a number of well-informed readers. These ranged from historians and respected commentators to a retired senior diplomat who had been intimately involved in some of the episodes we described. They commended the book for having reconstructed the story in a way that at last made sense of so much that had previously been confusing, and brought to light so much that had remained previously hidden.[1]

---

[1] Among the many people who privately gave the first edition a fulsome welcome were the historian Sir John Keegan, Lord Rees-Mogg, Sir Oliver Wright, formerly HM Ambassador to Washington and Bonn, and Ruth Lea of the Centre for Policy Studies. Bill Jamieson, executive editor of the *Scotsman*, generously wrote 'I have been reading *The Great Deception* every night for the past week, and am so enthused and inspired by its detail and thoroughness ... not just a must read but a truly monumental achievement'. We were particularly pleased to have an equally generous letter from Dr Richard Vaughan, formerly Professor of History at Leyden, who in the 1970s had written what up to that time was the fullest historical account of how the 'European project' had been launched on its way. Although he had begun with rather more sympathy for the 'project' than ourselves, he kindly described our work as 'surely the best and most readable book on the EU so far written'.

The public response to the first and successive editions could not have provided a greater contrast. Not a single national newspaper found space to review them. Only the *Spectator* (ed. Boris Johnson) published a spectacularly jaundiced 'non-review' of the first edition, by the author of an earlier book on the subject whose views he believed we had failed to treat with sufficient respect. This silence was broken months later by the columnist Peter Hitchens, who, in the *Mail on Sunday*, expressed surprise at how comprehensively the book had been ignored, and urged that it should be read by 'every MP, every senior civil servant, every journalist with any claim to understanding the current state of the country'.

Despite such lack of publicity, the three editions have sold more than fifty thousand copies, including those generously sent by a businessman, Paul Sykes, to every British member of the Westminster and European Parliaments (there was no evidence, alas, that most of them ever bothered to read it!).

That the book ever came into being is in no small measure due to those many people who helped us in the early days, such as Richard Balfe MEP, who shed light on the hugely significant part played in relaunching the 'project' in the early 1980s by Altiero Spinelli, which was to lead to the transformation of the European Community into the 'European Union'.

Another reason why it was possible to write this book has been the crucial part played in our researches by the internet. This has made it infinitely easier and quicker than before to track down myriad sources, ranging from books long out of print to obscure documents on European integration. The internet has also proved invaluable in reconstructing the history of recent years, for which it is not yet possible to draw on the evidence of historical accounts or political memoirs, especially during the period of Covid-19 restrictions when many physical archives were closed and travel was difficult.

For the first edition, we owe a great debt to Dr Helen Szamuely (sadly deceased) for casting her customary shrewd eye over many passages of the text while the book was in preparation. For particular insights, documents and other help, we also owe thanks to Charlotte Horsfield, Dr Saul Kelly, John Ashworth, Derek Bennett, Jens-Peter Bonde MEP, Nicholas Booker, Heather Conyngham, Nigel Farage MEP (for underlining the significance of Verdun), Jim McCue, Bill Jamieson, Lord Pearson of Rannoch, Dr Anthony Coughlan, and the readers of the *Sunday Telegraph*.

We also owe a special debt to Brigadier Anthony Cowgill of the British Management Data Foundation (also deceased), not least for his unique consolidated and annotated editions of the various European treaties, producing texts before they were officially available. We were also grateful to Mary and Peter North for their tireless quest through Yorkshire's second-hand bookstalls, for ever more obscure old books that might shed a further chink of light on one of the most labyrinthine political stories the human mind has yet produced.

My special thanks to Peter Troy (also sadly deceased), who arranged the interviews of the Norwegian actors who feature in this edition. Our thanks, and mine separately, are also due to our publisher Robin Baird-Smith for his unfailing encouragement, and to his staff at Bloomsbury. Finally, no one but ourselves (and especially myself as the final author of record) can be blamed for any mistakes that will inevitably have crept into such a complex narrative.

1

The Early Days: 1918–1945

Europe is being liquidated, and the League of Nations must
be the heir to this great estate.

Jan Smuts (1918)[1]

The United States of Europe must be a political reality or it
cannot be an economic one.

Arthur Salter, *The United States of Europe* (1931)

On 22 September 1984, two portly middle-aged men stood holding hands in
front of the largest pile of human bones in Europe. One was the president of
France, François Mitterrand; the other the chancellor of Germany, Helmut
Kohl. The reason why the two most powerful political leaders in western
Europe were staging an act of reconciliation before tens of thousands of
graves was that the site of this ceremony was the ossuary at Douaumont,
overlooking Verdun in eastern France.

And if there was one historical event that more than any other inspired
what was eventually to become the European Union, it was the battle
that had raged around Verdun in the First World War. For the British
the defining battle of that war was the Somme in the summer of 1916.
For France and Germany, it was the colossal battle of attrition launched
in February the same year, when the French commander, General Philippe
Pétain, pronounced that the fortresses on the hills overlooking Verdun on
the River Meuse were where the advance of German armies into his country
would be brought to a halt. His legendary words '*Ils ne passeront pas*' were
endorsed the same day by France's prime minister, Aristide Briand.

[1] Quoted by Lloyd George, David (1938), *The Truth About The Peace Treaties* (London: Victor
Gollancz), Vol. 1, p. 80.

For nearly a year, the French and German armies battered each other to destruction in the most intense and prolonged concentration of violence the world had ever seen. French artillery alone fired more than twelve million shells, the German guns considerably more. The number of dead and wounded on both sides exceeded seven hundred thousand. So deep was the wound Verdun inflicted on the psyche of France that the following year her army was brought to mutiny. Its morale would never fully recover. And from this blow were to emerge two abiding lessons.

The first was a conviction that such a suicidal clash of national armies must never be repeated. The second was much more specific and immediate. It came from the realisation of the degree to which the war had been shaped by industrial power. As the battle for Verdun had developed into a remorseless artillery duel, trainloads of German shells were arriving at the front still warm from the factories of the Ruhr. The battle, and the war itself, became a contest between industrial systems. And the French system had been found sorely wanting.

Particularly inferior had been the heavy guns, many dating back to the 1870s, able to fire shells at only a seventh of the rate of their German counterparts. More and better guns became vital. But manufacturing them and their ammunition was beyond the capacity of an industry that compared poorly with Germany's. In the summer of 1916, therefore, a crisis-stricken French government turned to an industrialist, Louis Loucheur. Before the war, he had been an early pioneer in the use of reinforced concrete, and, in a national economy dominated by artisan manufacture, he was one of the few French technocrats familiar with mass-production techniques.

Loucheur built new factories to make the guns. But improved production brought shortages of steel and coal, made worse by the German seizure in the first weeks of the war of around half of France's north-eastern industrial base.[2] Supplies from Britain and then the USA filled the gap, but the consequential demands on shipping required unprecedented economic co-operation between the Western Allies. This led Loucheur to observe that success in modern warfare demanded industrial organisation, from which he concluded that removing key industries, above all coal and steel, from national control and vesting them in a 'higher authority' might be the means of preserving peace.[3]

---

[2] Carls, Stephen Douglas (1993), *Louis Loucheur and The Shaping of Modern France 1916–1931* (Baton Rouge: Louisiana State University Press), p. 33.
[3] Carls, op. cit., p. 264.

BUILDING THE WORLD ANEW

When the fighting stopped on 11 November 1918, much of the pre-war world that had brought it about had already slipped into history. Four great empires had fallen: that of Germany itself, and those of Austria-Hungary, Russia and the Ottoman Turks who had ruled over so much of the Middle East. There followed a general sense that the world must be rebuilt, in a way that might ensure that such a catastrophe could never be repeated. But this determination took two competing forms: one was idealistic, the other vengeful.

Post-war idealism was symbolised by US president Woodrow Wilson, whose country's intervention in the last year of the war had finally tipped the military balance against Germany. Wilson's famous 'Fourteen Point Declaration', supporting the right of peoples to self-determination, guided the post-war settlement agreed at the Paris Peace Conference in 1919. New nations arose in the former lands of now-defunct empires, their borders supposedly guaranteed by a League of Nations that would keep the peace.

This mood of idealism was quickly undermined. Following opposition from the US Senate and Woodrow Wilson's succession by President Harding, the US withdrew from the League. America's retreat into isolationism left the new international forum largely a European body, dominated by Britain, France and Italy (neither Germany nor Russia, now locked in the civil war that followed the 1917 Bolshevik revolution, were initially admitted as members). Then France decided to wreak vengeance on Germany, the country it held chiefly responsible for the war, seeking to ensure that it would never again be strong enough to endanger the peace.

Largely as a result of French pressure, therefore, the 1919 Treaty of Versailles imposed on defeated Germany fearsome punishments. She lost more than an eighth of her land area and all her overseas empire. Alsace and Lorraine were returned to France in perpetuity, along with the Saar, rich in coal and iron, pending a plebiscite after 15 years. The Rhineland was to remain under Allied occupation. Germany's army was limited to 100,000 men and she was prohibited from producing heavy guns, tanks or military aircraft. Additionally, she was required to pay crippling reparations, amounting eventually to £6.6 billion.

In January 1923, the screw was tightened further. Taking as excuse the late delivery of a small quantity of timber for telegraph poles due under the reparations settlement, followed by a default on deliveries of coal (at a time when coal was plentiful), France and Belgium sent 70,000 armed men to occupy the Ruhr, Germany's industrial heartland. The French contingent included a large number of colonial troops who were allowed to run amok, triggering a widespread campaign of non-cooperation and sabotage. The French countered by deposing or imprisoning the ringleaders and expelling nearly 150,000 people from the district, including over 46,000 German officials and their families. They also resorted to hostage-taking and collective fines, to aggressive house searches, identity checks and summary executions.[4]

Few details of this episode survive in modern textbooks on European history, but it was clear that the French were seeking to destabilise the German nation.[5] The occupation force actively interfered in German civil administration, in violation of the Versailles Treaty, and sponsored the deliberate wrecking of Germany's infrastructure, particularly its railway system.

These interventions caused industrial output to collapse, creating mass unemployment. When the German government guaranteed the wages of dispossessed workers, hyper-inflation ensued. By November 1923, this had so devalued the currency that a single US dollar could buy 4.2 trillion German marks. The resulting turmoil saw attempts at revolution, an unsuccessful *putsch* in Bavaria by Adolf Hitler and his followers, and moves to create a separate Rhineland republic, the latter financed by French agents using money stolen from German municipalities.

Despite this, Germany recovered, and remarkably quickly, largely due to the leadership of one man, Gustav Stresemann, chancellor of a coalition government, from 13 August 1924 until 23 November. So highly regarded was he that his successor as German chancellor in November 1924 chose him as foreign affairs minister, an office he was to hold with distinction under four governments. He established a warm friendship with Aristide Briand, now France's foreign minister. With him in 1925, he became co-author of the Locarno Treaty, supported by Britain, Italy and Belgium, which guaranteed mutual security for France and Germany. For this achievement, the two men were awarded the Nobel Peace Prize. Thus did western Europe emerge into what Winston Churchill was to describe as 'the pale sunlight of Locarno'.[6]

The following year, 1926, Germany was admitted to the League of Nations. A week later, Stresemann and Briand, celebrating over a private lunch, 'waxed expansive over Stresemann's favourite theme of Franco-German

[4] Marriott, Sir John (1941), *The Tragedy of Europe* (London: Blackie and Son Ltd), p. 87.
[5] In the later decades of the twentieth century, after the 'European idea' had become the prevailing ideology, it became noticeable how books mentioning the occupation presented only a heavily sanitised version of events, scarcely acknowledging that it had taken place.
[6] Churchill, W. S. (1948), *The Second World War:* Vol. I – *The Gathering Storm* (London: Cassell), p. 63.

economic collaboration'.[7] It was no accident that both men had become active supporters of a movement that had lately become remarkably fashionable, calling for a 'United States of Europe'.

VISIONS OF EUROPE

By the mid-1920s there was a heady sense that the shadows of the previous decade had receded. Amid what became the euphoria and idealism of the period, leading politicians, businessmen and intellectuals became seized by the vision of a united Europe.

Even before the war had ended, in 1918, the Italian industrialist Giovanni Agnelli, founder of the Fiat empire, had published a book entitled *European Federation or League of Nations*, arguing that the only effective antidote to destructive nationalism was a federal Europe. But the young man who truly caught the mood of the moment was Count Richard Coudenhove-Kalergi, born in Tokyo in 1894 to a diplomat in the Austro-Hungarian embassy and a Japanese mother.

In 1922, still in his late twenties, he published his book *Pan Europa*, launching a movement under the same name. Like Louis Loucheur, he sought peace by merging the German and French coal and steel industries into a single 'pan-European' industry. They would form the basis for a federal 'United States of Europe' on the American model. Two years later he developed this idea by supporting the suggestion of a French economist, Charles Gide, that Europe should form a customs union.[8] However, Coudenhove was emphatic that his federation would not eradicate national identities or reduce the sovereignty of its members, but celebrate the 'spirit of Europe' by providing a framework in which they could co-operate for the common good.

The speed with which Coudenhove attracted the support of many of Europe's leading cultural figures was remarkable. Among them were Albert Einstein, Pablo Picasso, Sigmund Freud, and writers such as Thomas Mann, Paul Valéry, Guillaume Apollinaire and St John Perse. Businessmen and left-wing thinkers joined the cause, including, in Italy, Giovanni Agnelli and Professor Luigi Einaudi, a left-wing lawyer who had formerly edited *La Stampa*; in Holland, Edo Fimmen, chairman of the International Transport

---

[7] New Cambridge Modern History, op. cit., p. 467.

[8] In the same year, 1924, Sir Max Waechter, a German-born British industrialist, published *How To Abolish War: The United States of Europe*, in which he independently proposed a customs union or 'common market', not least because this would be the only way for Europe to continue competing economically with America and, before long, Japan. He founded a European Unity League to advance his ideas, but this made little impact.

Workers' Federation; and in Germany, Karl Tucholsky, one of the leading left-wing intellectuals of the Weimar Republic.[9]

Among Coudenhove's most significant converts were European politicians, including the mayor of Cologne, Konrad Adenauer, who would play a crucial role in shaping Europe in the future. Stresemann was another, and French prime minister Edouard Herriot, who had briefly been munitions minister during Verdun, also joined. In 1931 he was to publish a book, *The United States of Europe*. Another convert later to become prime minister was Léon Blum, but the most committed supporter was France's foreign minister, Aristide Briand. Prime minister 11 times, he was now, with Stresemann, the co-author of the Locarno Pact.

It was these two major figures supporting the 'pan-European' vision that, on 24 June 1925, inspired Winston Churchill, then Chancellor of the Exchequer, to tell members of the House of Commons, as he later recalled, how 'ending the thousand-year strife between France and Germany seemed a supreme object'. By weaving the Gaul and Teuton closely together 'economically, socially and morally ... Europe would rise again'.[10]

In October 1926, Coudenhove enjoyed his greatest moment of triumph when, at the age of 32, he staged a European Congress in Vienna. Among the 2,000 who attended was Briand, who in 1927 became Pan-Europa's honorary president. In the same year, as a fervent supporter of the League of Nations, he proposed to US Secretary of State Kellogg a 'non-aggression pact', whereby their two countries would renounce war as an instrument of policy for ever. The outcome was the 'Kellogg–Briand Pact', under which, in 1929, 15 nations, including France and Germany, signed up to similar terms.[11] On 7 September that year, following discussions with Stresemann, at which he cited the 'menace of American economic power' as one of the greatest threats Europe now faced, Briand presented the League of Nations with a dramatic new proposal. 'I think', he said,

---

[9] Like many supporters of a 'United States of Europe', Tucholsky regarded narrow-minded, aggressive nationalism as the real threat to peace. In 1928 he was to write of the 'triumph over the nationalistic German and petty Bavarian thoughtlessness'. Two years earlier, in an essay on 'Foreign and Domestic Policy' in the pacifist journal *Friedenswarte*, he wrote: 'We no longer live in the individual fortresses of the Middle Ages. We live in a house and the name of that house is Europe.' (King, Ian, 2001, *Kurt Tucholsky as Prophet of European Unity*, European Paper 5/2001, London: South Bank University.)

[10] Churchill, W. S. (1948), op. cit., pp. 40–41.

[11] In 1929 Coudenhove-Kalergi adopted the theme of the last movement of Beethoven's Ninth Symphony as Pan Europa's 'anthem'. He was to organise further congresses in Berlin (1930), Basel (1932) and Vienna (1935), but none had the impact of his first Vienna congress in 1926.

that among peoples who are geographically grouped together like the peoples of Europe there must exist a kind of federal link ... Evidently the association will act mainly in the economic sphere ... but I am sure also that from a political point of view, and from a social point of view, the federal link, without infringing the sovereignty of any of the nations taking part, could be beneficial.[12]

On 20 May 1930, three days after French troops began their final evacuation of the German Rhineland (under the Young Plan), Briand circulated the governments of Europe with a memorandum 'on the organization of a system of European Federal Union.'[13] He proposed that, 'in the interests alike of the peace and of the economic and social well-being of the continent', Europe should be given 'something in the nature of a federal organisation'. Implemented within the framework of the League of Nations, it would 'respect national sovereignties', centring on 'the conception of European political co-operation'. It would subordinate 'the economic to the political problem', and would be concerned with co-operation on 'economic policy, transport, finance, labour, health and intellectual co-operation'.

Briand's proposal had already received its warmest welcome from Winston Churchill, now out of office, who told readers of the New York *Saturday Evening Post* on 13 February 1930: 'the mass of Europe once united, once federalised or partly federalised, once continentally self-conscious, would constitute an organism beyond compare ...' Then, as later, Churchill saw no place in such a federation for his own island, with its worldwide empire. Speaking for Britain, his article went on:

We are with Europe but not of it. We are linked but not comprised. We are interested and associated but not absorbed. And should the European statesmen address us in the words which were used of old, 'Wouldest thou be spoken for to the King, or the captain of the Host?' we should reply with the Shunamite woman. 'Nay sir, for we dwell among our own people.' We must build a kind of United States of Europe. Great Britain, the British Commonwealth of Nations, mighty America must be friends and sponsors of the new Europe.

Of the responses eventually received from 26 European governments, almost all 'expressed full agreement with the idea of closer European cooperation'.

[12] Gladwyn, Lord (1966), *The European Idea* (London: Weidenfeld & Nicolson), p. 43.
[13] The full text, in the original French, can be found here: http://fondationsaintjohnperse.fr/en/la-programmation-culturelle/archives/europe_documentation/texte-du-memorandumintroduction/.

Only Britain rejected Briand's proposals outright, possibly because he proposed the formation of a customs union, abolishing internal customs and raising 'more rigorous barriers' against states outside the union. But all the states except Holland insisted that such an association must be 'on the plane of absolute sovereignty and of entire political independence'.[14]

It was to no avail. The mood in Europe was changing. The previous autumn, only weeks after the death in October of Briand's closest ally, Stresemann, the Wall Street crash had heralded the greatest slump in history. In Germany's elections of 14 September 1930, fuelled by soaring unemployment and continuing nationalist resentment at the humiliations of the Versailles Treaty, votes for the National Socialist Party had soared from 810,000 to six and a half million. Hitler won over a hundred seats in the Reichstag. The following year the Japanese invasion of Manchuria was to expose the League of Nations as no more than a talking shop.

Those brave dreams of the 1920s were fading rapidly. But all this time a much smaller group of men, watching the events of the 1920s at close quarters, had begun to think that, if the goal of a United States of Europe was ever to be achieved, it would require a different strategy altogether.

ENTER THE SUPRANATIONALISTS
From the League of Nations, to Pan Europa and Briand's European Federal Union, the visions of the 1920s all had in common the idea of nations co-operating on an 'intergovernmental' basis. This was the road to universal peace: governments should learn how to work willingly together for the common good, but without abandoning their sovereignty.

Curiously enough, this posed a problem that had already exercised one of the finest minds Europe has ever produced, six centuries earlier. In 1318, exiled from his native Florence, the poet and statesman Dante Alighieri had, in his treatise *De Monarchia*, addressed the question of how Europe might overcome the endless wars and conflicts produced by a multitude of nations and city states. As an admirer of the Holy Roman Empire, he suggested that there must be one 'empire' above them all, with the power to control their actions in the common interest.

Over the years, many thinkers offered proposals for the political unification of Europe, from Leibniz, Kant and the Dutch lawyer Grotius, to Rousseau, Jeremy Bentham and Victor Hugo. The French King Henry IV's minister, Sully, suggested that Europe should be split into 15 states, governed by a council, and with an army of 100,000 men to keep the peace. William

[14] Salter, *The United States of Europe*, op. cit., p. 123.

8

Penn, who gave his name to Pennsylvania, proposed an 'Assembly of the United Europe', taking its decisions by a form of qualified majority voting, weighted accorded to national population sizes and economic importance.

In the eighteenth century, the French Abbé de Saint-Pierre suggested rule by a 'European Senate', also with a form of qualified majority voting according to size and the power to summon a European army. In the nineteenth century the Comte de Saint-Simon proposed a political union of Europe based on the union of England and France, with a bicameral parliament, the upper chamber chosen by governments, the lower elected by universal suffrage. The French revolutionary Proudhon, at the end of his life, published *The Federal Principle* (1863), attacking nationalism as the supreme evil that leads inevitably to war, and arguing not only that nation states should be welded together in a European federation, but that the states themselves should be broken up into regional governments.[15]

The element common to these proposals, to a greater or lesser extent, was the 'supranational' principle, an authority above the nation state, relegating national governments to a subordinate role. In the period after the First World War, the first to suggest such a structure for Europe was Louis Loucheur. During the Paris Peace Conference of 1919, when acting as chief economic adviser to French prime minister Clémenceau, he urged that peace would only come by integrating the economies of France and Germany, particularly those industries central to waging war: coal and steel.

It took until September 1926 for Loucheur's vision to be given practical expression. Emil Mayrisch, head of the giant Luxembourg-based steel combine ARBED, brokered an 'International Steel Cartel', the Entente Internationale de l'Acier (EIA), covering the steel industries of France, Germany, Belgium, Luxembourg and the Saar.[16] This was hailed by Gustav Stresemann as 'a landmark of international economic policy, the importance of which cannot be overestimated', not least because it had the power to reduce over-capacity by imposing production quotas for each member country. It also had a central 'treasury' with power to levy surcharges on members that broke the rules.[17]

Mayrisch's EIA had created Europe's first, albeit embryonic 'supranational' authority. He hoped it would be a model for similar schemes. It would

[15] For historical summaries of proposals for a united Europe, see Gladwyn, op. cit., pp. 33–42 and Vaughan, Richard (1979), *Twentieth Century Europe: Paths to Unity* (London: Croom Helm and New York: Harper & Row).
[16] Benham, Frederic (1934), Special Memorandum No. 39: *The Iron and Steel Industry of Germany, France, Belgium, Luxembourg and the Saar*, London & Cambridge Economic Service.
[17] Hexner, Ervin (1943), *The International Steel Cartel* (Durham, NC: University of North Carolina Press), cited in Carls, op. cit., p. 266.

certainly later be remembered by Konrad Adenauer and others as the model for the European Coal and Steel Community that was to be the embryo of the European Union. Loucheur himself, before his death in 1931, would in 1927 propose the setting up of an 'economic League of Nations' based on a customs union or 'common market'. But it was not Loucheur who would one day be remembered as 'the Father of Europe'. That title would be reserved for a younger man who alone would crack the secret of how to get that 'United States of Europe' finally launched on its way.

ENTER MONSIEUR MONNET

Among the senior figures in the League of Nations at its foundation were two who were already close friends. One was Arthur Salter, the British civil servant who was head of the League's economic and financial section, and also acted as general secretary of the Reparations Commission. His friend Jean Monnet, younger by seven years but appointed aged only 31 to be the League's deputy-secretary general, was a small, self-effacing Frenchman with a moustache, who decades later would be described as looking like Hercule Poirot.[18]

Monnet was born in Cognac in 1888, the son of a wealthy brandy-maker, leaving school at 16 to work in his father's firm, J. G. Monnet. From 1906 to 1914 he represented the firm abroad, spending more time overseas than in France, returning to his home country for the start of the war. While fit enough for his globetrotting adventures, he was found unfit for military service. Through the good offices of his family lawyer, who was a friend of France's prime minister, René Viviani, he managed to meet directly with Viviani, the outcome of which was to get himself sent to London, working for the French minister of commerce. His duties included buying and shipping wheat for the civilian market in France.[19]

At some point, Monnet returned to France, possibly in late 1915, to work for France's economics minister Clémentel, a friend of his father.[20] When the British decided to cut the amount of shipping they had allocated to the transport of French goods, at a time when they were carrying 48 per cent of their supplies, Monnet was despatched to London in an attempt to get the decision rescinded.[21] There, he first met Salter, who had been transferred from working on Lloyd George's national insurance scheme to a

[18] Sampson, Anthony (1968), *New Europeans* (London: Hodder & Stoughton), p. 7.
[19] Monnet, Jean (1978), *Memoirs* (London: Collins), pp. 49–52.
[20] Duchêne, François (1994), *Jean Monnet: The First Statesman of Interdependence* (New York: W.W. Norton and Co.), p. 35.
[21] Monnet, op. cit., p. 55.

new Ministry of Shipping, as director of ship requisitioning. Salter reported to John Anderson (of bomb shelter fame), then secretary to the Ministry, who was to become Churchill's right-hand man in the Second World War. Anderson and Monnet were to meet many times.[22]

Subsequent events are described at length by Salter in two of his books.[23] They culminated in the creation of the Allied Maritime Transport Council, with Loucher as one of two French ministerial representatives on the Council.[24] Monnet was a French representative on the Executive until the end of the war. He claims a significant role in creating these organisations, their official tasks being 'to watch over the general conduct of Allied transport' and then to make 'the most advantageous allocation and disposition of the tonnage under their control in accordance with the urgency of war needs'.[25]

Based in London, the Executive's secretariat comprised representatives of the four governments of the United Kingdom, the United States, France and Italy, eventually reaching 300 in number. Salter, who had been appointed secretary to the Council, noted that although members of the secretariat were of different nationalities, 'they divested themselves of any national point of view'.[26] Monnet thus was keen to talk up the 'supranational' role of the Council, an idea he found particularly appealing. To him, it was an example of what nations could achieve through co-operation, even though he had pressed for the Council to have full authority (*pleins pouvoirs*) – a proposal that had been rejected.[27]

It was, however, even less influential than Monnet thought. As Salter pointed out, Britain was the only one of the Allies that could meet her own essential military and civilian requirements with less than the total of her national tonnage and thus have some to spare for her Allies. The result was that, behind all Allied discussions, there was an ultimate power of decision in a single authority, the British government. Although this power was kept in the background, the fact that the power was there, and known to be there, must be taken into account in estimating the character of the Allied achievement.[28] When the idea of a conference to discuss the management

---

[22] Wheeler-Bennett, John (1962), *John Anderson, Viscount Waverley* (London: Macmillan & Co. Ltd), pp. 41–42.

[23] *Memoirs of a Civil Servant*, published in 1961 by Faber, and *Slave of the Lamp*, published by Weidenfeld & Nicolson in 1967.

[24] Loucheur took an intense dislike to Monnet, and tried to arrange his transfer to the front. After intense lobbying by Monnet, at Cabinet level, he retained his position. Monnet, op. cit., p. 63.

[25] National Archives, CAB 24/47/45, Minutes of the First Session of the Allied Maritime Transport Council.

[26] National Archives, CAB 24/65/55, Allied Maritime Transport Council, General Report.

[27] Fransen, op. cit., p. 24.

[28] Salter, *Slave of the Lamp*, op. cit., p. 83.

of Allied shipping had been first mooted back in August 1917 , the British government was reluctant to hold the conference. There was a risk, the secretary to the War Cabinet had written, 'that the Allies may insist on the pooling of British shipping among all the Allies, with a consequent loss of British control'.[29]

In the structure that was agreed, in Paris in December 1917, the British never gave up that control, a lesson that was apparently lost on Monnet. Nevertheless, he had gained his spurs as an accomplished behind-the-scenes operator, making alliances with others to help advance his projects. Salter was one such ally and, when the war was over, and the statesmen and civil servants of the victorious powers gathered in Paris for the peace conference, Monnet made many more. Among those was a young American lawyer, John Foster Dulles.

After tireless lobbying, the young Frenchman became a deputy-secretary-general in the new League of Nations, under Sir Eric Drummond. Working closely with his old friend Salter, now administering German reparations, for three years Monnet was at the centre of the new organisation. With its Secretariat, its Council, its Assembly and a Court of International Justice, he was initially highly optimistic that the League could impose its benevolent will on the world 'by its moral force, by appealing to public opinion and thanks to customs which would ultimately prevail'.[30] He admired the internationalist idealism of his colleagues (Drummond had decided from the outset that the secretariat of the League ... was not to consist of national delegates but of international servants loyal to the League).[31]

Increasingly, Monnet became frustrated by one particular feature of the League: every member state had the power of veto, so decisions could only be taken unanimously. As he was later to put it, 'the veto is the profound cause and at the same time the symbol of the impossibility of overcoming national egoism'.[32] Otherwise, he felt that the League of Nations 'was a disappointment'. He resigned in 1923.

It was left to Salter, therefore, to carry the flame of supranationalism. In 1931, he published a collection of papers under the title *The United States of Europe*, in which he addressed the possibility of adapting the largely Europe-orientated League of Nations to provide a framework for a politically united

---

[29] National Archives, CAB 24/24/99, The Proposed Inter-Ally Transport Conference.
[30] Jean Monnet, *A Short Biography* (Altiero Spinelli Institute for Federalist Studies).
[31] New Cambridge Modern History, op. cit., p. 477.
[32] This is the version given in Jean Monnet, *A Short Biography*, op. cit., The English translation of Monnet's *Memoirs* (op. cit., p. 97) is rather more pedestrian: 'the veto was at once the cause and the symbol of this inability to go beyond national self-interest'.

Europe. He drew on the nineteenth-century idea of German unification, which employed a *Zollverein* or 'common market', so his 'United States' would thus finance itself through a common tariff on imported goods. Like Germany, it would need 'a political instrument' to manage the distribution of funds. As these would be a 'central and substantial a part of their revenues', the common political authority would be almost as important as, or even more important than, the national governments, reducing them to 'the status of municipal authorities'.[33]

'In other words,' he went on, 'the United States of Europe must be a political reality', borrowing from the structure of the League of Nations, with its Secretariat, Council of Ministers, parliamentary Assembly and Court of Justice. But there was a crucial proviso. The authority in this new body, Salter urged, must be reserved for a 'Secretariat', a cadre of international civil servants, loyal to the new organisation, not to the member countries. The problem with giving too much power to a Council of Ministers was that they would always remain motivated by national interest:

> In face of a permanent corps of Ministers, meeting in committees and 'shadow councils', and in direct contact with their Foreign Office, the Secretariat will necessarily sink in status, in influence, and in the character of its personnel, to clerks responsible only for routine duties. They will cease to be an element of importance in the formation or maintenance of the League's traditions.[34]

'The new international officer needed for the League's task', he wrote, 'is something new in the world's history'.[35] It would adopt precisely the 'supranational' principle that nearly three decades later Monnet would apply to the European Economic Community, deliberately intended as an embryonic 'United States of Europe'. Salter even envisaged that another way to erode nationalism might be to split member states into regions. The only term in his blueprint that would eventually need to be changed was 'secretariat'; and as it happened, in describing reactions to Briand's proposal in 1930 for a 'European Federal Union', he was able to record that the League of Nations had already established a 'European Commission' to enquire into how this should be set up.[36]

[33] Salter, Arthur (1931), *The United States of Europe* (London: George Allen & Unwin), p. 92.
[34] Ibid., p. 134.
[35] Ibid., p. 136.
[36] Ibid., p. 124.

By now, however, as Europe plunged into the Great Depression, the shadows were gathering over such dreams: 1932 saw the death of Briand himself, the most distinguished champion a 'United States of Europe' had yet won to its cause. The next year brought the rise to power of Adolf Hitler. His idea of how Europe might be united was very different.

THE NAZI CUL-DE-SAC

In the late 1990s, it became fashionable in some Eurosceptic circles to assert that the European Union had Nazi origins. The thesis was mainly based on the publication by Reich economic minister Walther Funk in 1943 of his *Europäische Wirtschaftsgemeinschaft*.[37] As this term translates as 'European economic community' and the scope overlapped with some of the attributes of the EEC – such as industrial production, agriculture and a single currency – a common origin was assumed.[38] Yet there are few similarities in the structures of the two organisations and their governance. The former merely brought the economies of the occupied territories into the economic sphere of Greater Germany, segmented on racial lines.

The initial aims were set out in a set of lectures delivered by Funk in Berlin in 1942. These elaborated on a meeting on 22 July 1940 at the Reich Economic Ministry on the reorganisation of the European economy, chaired by the minister, and a speech by him on 25 July.[39,40] Notwithstanding that the structure of what was to become the EEC and then the EU had already been set out by Arthur Salter, what Funk sketched out was a command economy, relying on strong state intervention in industry and labour markets. As to the detail, Funk himself noted: 'One difficulty of planning lay in the fact that the Führer's aims and decisions were not yet known and the military measures against Britain were not yet concluded.' The assumption was that the British economy would continue to exist, but if that assumption was altered, 'other proposals would have to be worked out'.[41]

There is no evidence of any systematic attempt to put Funk's ideas into practice. Indeed, a European single currency would have caused Germany

---

[37] University of Luxembourg archives.

[38] There was also a confusion in terminology. Funk's *gemeinschaft* describes a community that has a sense of 'belonging together', sharing values, loyalties and perhaps kinship. This aptly describes what the Nazis had in mind, bringing together the Aryan peoples in a Germanic empire, with the outer regions pressed into service as vassals. The later 'European Economic Community' was more of a *gesellschaft*, a rule-based society of equals.

[39] Translation of the 1942 speech here: https://campaignforanindependentbritain.org.uk/wp-content/uploads/2017/04/EEC_EWG-1.pdf.

[40] Lipgens, W. (1985), *Documents on the History of European Integration, Volume 1* (Berlin and New York: De Gruyter), pp. 60–71.

[41] Ibid., p. 63.

serious problems. The occupied countries were being charged for the costs of their occupation: in the case of France twenty million Reichsmarks per day. Repayments were calculated at a much-devalued exchange rate, magnifying the debt to such an extent that 42 per cent of the total foreign contribution to the German economy came from France.[42] Whatever the rhetoric of some of his followers, therefore, Hitler had not the slightest intention of giving up control. As Goebbels put it: 'It is only right and just that we take the leadership of Europe definitely into our hands ... The German people ... have actually won the hegemony of Europe and have a moral right to it.'[43]

In fact, the Nazis only paid lip-service to European unity, largely for propaganda purposes, especially after the invasion of Russia when volunteer soldiers from occupied nations were encouraged to believe that they were fighting for 'Europe' against the Bolshevik hordes.[44]

A more prosaic appeal appeared in an article the *Catholic Herald* on 1 November 1940, at the height of the London Blitz. Headed, 'Axis plan: "Europe for the Europeans"', the article came in the wake of the Italian invasion of Greece. In the name of 'European solidarity', the Axis powers were seeking to bypass the strength of the British Empire east of Suez, the conquest of which was deemed 'impossible'. The aim, therefore, was to win strategic victories and seize strategic points such as Egypt and Gibraltar, and possibly Iraq, thereby setting the stage for 'a grand council of European solidarity to force peace on Great Britain'. The whole tone of Axis propaganda, the *Herald* said, was moving along these lines of 'Europe for the Europeans without British interference'.

'FEDERALISM' MOVES TO BRITAIN AND AMERICA

Rather than Nazi Germany taking on the role of champion of European political integration, that mantle was progressively assumed by the free democracies of the United Kingdom and the United States of America.

In the UK, the idea of international federation had been influential among certain strands of elite British opinion for some decades. Since 1910 the 'Milner group', largely made up of senior civil servants, had been advocating federalising the British Empire, arguing its case through the journal *Round Table*. Its editor, Philip Kerr (later to become Lord Lothian), saw this as a

---

[42] Burleigh, Michael (2000), *The Third Reich: A New History* (London: Macmillan), p. 478.
[43] Lochner, Louis P. (editor and translator) (1948), *The Goebbels Diaries 1942–43* (New York: Doubleday & Company Inc.), p. 83.
[44] Lipgens, op. cit., p. 9.

step towards world federalism.[45] Other notable figures, including Bertrand Russell and H. G. Wells, had long been expounding the need for world government, organised on a federal basis.[46]

A key member of the group was Lionel Curtis. As a British diplomat at the Paris Peace Conference in 1919, he had launched the idea of an organisation 'to foster mutual understanding of and between nations through debate, dialogue and independent analysis'. Originally proposed as a single body with branches in London and New York, what emerged was two 'think-tanks', each destined to play important roles in lobbying for European integration. The first was the London-based Royal Institute of International Affairs, known as Chatham House, set up in 1920. Its US counterpart was the Council on Foreign Relations (CFR), established initially in New York, later opening an office in Washington.[47]

In 1940, when Coudenhove escaped from Nazi-dominated Europe to America, the CFR arranged a position for him at New York University, where he held seminars on the problems of European federation. Through CFR contacts, he was given regular coverage in the *New York Times* and *Herald Tribune*, whereby the idea of a 'United States of Europe' was during the war years to become increasingly familiar to influential American opinion.[48]

In the immediate pre-war years, the idea of federalism as a means of preserving the peace had already entered a brief but intense vogue, particularly in Britain. Much of this had been tied in with a rising tide of pacifism. As early as 1933, the Socialist academic Harold Laski published a tract, *The Intelligent Man's Way to Prevent War*, arguing that peace could not be 'built on a system of separate sovereign states'. In 1935 Lord Lothian published a pamphlet entitled *Pacifism is Not Enough, Nor Patriotism Either*.[49] In this, he argued that the cause of war was 'the division of humanity into sovereign states'. Pacifists, he declared, would fail unless they worked for a federal constitution and a federation of nations.

A spate of similar tracts followed, notably, at the time of Munich in 1938, a best-selling book by Clarence K. Streit, an American living in Geneva, called

---

[45] Quigley, Carroll (1981), *The Anglo-American Establishment* (New York: Books in Focus). See p. 117 *et seq.*
[46] Summarised from Mayne, Richard and Pinder, John (1990), *Federal Union: The Pioneers: A History of Federal Union* (London: Macmillan), pp. 8–9.
[47] Chatham House website: https://www.chathamhouse.org/about/history#. The history of the CFR has been published online at: https://cdn.cfr.org/sites/default/files/book_pdf/Continuing_The_Inquiry.pdf.
[48] Jasper, William F. (1989), 'United States of Europe', *New American*, 5 (8), 10 April.
[49] See http://www.federalunion.org.uk/acrobatfiles/pacifism_is_not_enough.pdf – reproduction by the Federal Union.

Union Now. This advocated a federation of the 'North Atlantic democracies', to include the United States, Great Britain and the other democratic nations of western and northern Europe, plus Australia, South Africa and New Zealand. He suggested that its constitution should include sections on 'The Rights of Man', a common defence policy and a single currency.

The Munich agreement inspired the setting up in Britain of the Federal Union, which won the support of Curtis, Lothian and the historian Arnold Toynbee, then director of studies at Chatham House. In July 1939 Toynbee wrote an unpublished memorandum, 'First Thoughts on a Peace Settlement', arguing that, after the war that now seemed imminent, Britain and France should seek full political union.

He was not the first to propose such a union. In Paris in December 1938, Alfred Duff Cooper gave a public lecture that argued for the two countries to pool their resources.[50] In February 1940, the Comte Jean de Pange gave a talk to Chatham House on an Anglo-French federation, which would include a common air force.[51] Following up on his pamphlet, Toynbee wrote to the secretary general of the Centre d'Etudes de Politique Etrangère suggesting that the ties between Britain and France should be strengthened, making them the nucleus of a powerful European union. The secretary general, M. M. E. Dennery, was agreeable, and the two institutes set up a joint study group to explore the idea.[52]

Shortly after war began in September 1939, the now fast-growing membership of the Federal Union was given a further boost by the publication of *The Case for Federal Union*, a 'Penguin Special' by W. B. Curry, headmaster of the progressive school Dartington Hall. It sold over a hundred thousand copies in six months. This closely echoed the arguments of Streit's book the previous year. Such became the momentum of this movement that, on 24 February 1940, 2,600 people packed the Queen's Hall London to hear Barbara Wootton and other speakers. By April, the Federal Union had a hundred thousand members.

Meanwhile, other League of Nations insiders who had been enthusiastic for a 'United States of Europe' in the 1920s had remained in close touch. Salter, who continued to work for the League until 1930, became in 1934 the Gladstone Professor of Politics at Oxford and a fellow of All Souls. In 1937, he had been elected an independent MP for Oxford University. One close friend, since they had met at the Paris Peace Conference of 1919,

[50] Cooper, Alfred Duff (1939), *The Second World War: First Phase* (London: Jonathan Cape), p. 228.
[51] Cited in Slaim, Avi (1974), 'Prelude to Downfall: The British Offer of Union to France, June 1940', *Journal of Contemporary History*, Vol. 9, No. 3, pp. 29–30.
[52] Ibid.

was the economist John Maynard Keynes. Salter was later to recall how they had both been members of a 'small and secret committee' of leading economists that continued to advise successive prime ministers up to the outbreak of war.[53]

When the war began, Keynes held weekly meetings at his house, where they were joined by William Beveridge, the civil servant who was to shape the post-war expansion of the welfare state, and the economist Walter Layton, who in the early 1920s had worked alongside Salter in the League of Nations' economic and financial section.[54] From 1923 to 1939, Layton, a Liberal, had been an influential editor of *The Economist* and remained a fervent enthusiast for a federal Europe, a cause he was to continue to champion into the post-war era.

Another old friend with whom Salter was reunited shortly after the outbreak of war was Monnet, who had been appointed chairman of the Franco-British Economic Co-ordination Committee, with the task of arranging contracts for war supplies in America and their shipment across the Atlantic.[55] Salter, as parliamentary secretary to the new Ministry of Shipping, became his vice-chairman. Just as in 1914, the outbreak of war had brought the two men together in London and again for a very similar purpose.

In March of the following year, a month after Comte Jean de Pange's talk to Chatham House, Toynbee and Sir Alfred Zimmern travelled to the Centre d'Etudes de Politique Etrangère – the 'opposite number' of Chatham House – to hear Senator Honnorat, a former French minister of education, propose an Anglo-French union. In a memorandum to the Foreign Office, Toynbee described how Honnorat wanted the two governments, without delay, to conclude a 'treaty of perpetual association'. It would pool defence, foreign policy and the economic resources of the two countries. This, it was felt, would 'deeply discourage the Nazis', because 'it would show them that, even if Hitler's Greater Germany were to survive the war intact, it would henceforth be confronted by another European Power of still greater calibre and staying power'.[56]

R. A. Butler, the Foreign Office parliamentary under-secretary, asked Toynbee and Zimmern to develop their thoughts, whence Zimmern in consultation with Toynbee produced a 'draft Act of Perpetual Association'

---

[53] Salter, Arthur (1967), *The Slave of the Lamp* (London: Weidenfeld & Nicolson), p. 85.
[54] Op. cit., p. 88.
[55] National Archives, CAB 85/18, Letter of appointment: PM to Monnet (copy).
[56] National Archives, CAB 63/143, Memorandum: 'Some French views on Franco-British relations and on the time-factor in war', Arnold J. Toynbee.

between the two countries.[57] In parallel, Halifax had been thinking about post-war Anglo-French collaboration and 'the experiment of Anglo-French union'. On 8 April 1940, he wrote to Maurice Hankey, then a minister without portfolio in Chamberlain's administration, asking him to form an inter-departmental committee to examine the administrative implications of post-war Anglo-French collaboration.[58]

On examining Zimmern's draft Act at its very first meeting on 30 April 1940, the committee complained that the document was 'somewhat academic'. It planned a second meeting for 7 May.[59] Before then, on 5 May – five days before German forces crossed the border of neutral Holland – the outline of the 'secret' plan was leaked to the press.[60] The second meeting of the committee did not take place until 21 May, a day before Hitler's 2nd Panzer Division arrived on the outskirts of Calais and the British Expeditionary Force was in headlong retreat. The Zimmern draft was again explored, with the discussion enlivened by a comment from Treasury representative, Mr T. K. Bewley. He noted that a common currency 'had never been possible historically without a common government'.[61]

Although Hankey's committee was never to meet again, the Honnorat/Zimmern plan was not entirely dead. Towards mid-June, when the French collapse was imminent, Monnet seized on the crisis to propose immediate implementation of a 'Franco-British Union'. With Salter, he prepared a text that was sent to Sir Robert Vansittart, formerly the permanent head of the Foreign Office, and thence to Lord Halifax who, with Charles de Gaulle and others, put the plan to Churchill.

On 16 June, the War Cabinet discussed the draft and Churchill made only one substantive change, striking out a reference to 'a common currency'. However, the initiative came too late. On 14 June, the Germans entered Paris and the French government was back in Bordeaux. On 16 June, Prime Minister Reynaud read the text of the declaration of 'indissoluble union' to his Cabinet, which unanimously rejected it. Pétain, hero of Verdun, described it as 'fusion with a corpse'. Reynaud resigned, to be succeeded by Pétain, who promptly sued for a humiliating peace with Germany.

Monnet's proposal proved to be the high-water mark for the hopes of federation during the war. It was not quite the end of the affair though. Paul

---

[57] The seven-page text, marked 'secret', can be found in CAB 85/18.
[58] National Archives, CAB 63/143, Letter from Halifax to Hankey, 8 April 1940.
[59] National Archives, CAB 85/18, Hankey Committee, 1st Meeting, Minutes.
[60] *Reynolds News*, 5 May 1940, 'Plans to Join Britain & France'.
[61] National Archives, CAB 85/18, Hankey Committee, 2nd Meeting, Minutes.

Reynaud, like Monnet, became committed to the cause of European unity. In 1951, he wrote of the British offer:

I have continued to think that a Franco-British Union, as Churchill proposed it, could have served as the basis for the unification of all Europe, And I become more and more convinced, during my years of enforced reflection, that after the Allied victory, it would be necessary, in order to win the peace, to take up again the offer Churchill made to win the war.[62]

As for Monnet, appointed a member of the British Supply Council in Washington, he threw himself into transferring French contracts with America to the British. In 1941, Salter was asked by Churchill to head a British mission to Washington, allowing him to continue liaising with Monnet.[63] Based in Washington until 1943 (and again in 1944–1945), Monnet's talent for 'networking' soon won him influential friends in the US establishment, from Justice Felix Frankfurter of the Supreme Court to Dean Acheson, later US Secretary of State. Both men would lend active support to his post-war campaign for European integration.

While in Washington in 1941, Monnet met Paul-Henri Spaak, the pre-war prime minister of Belgium. To him, he expounded his underlying philosophy for a united Europe and explained in rough outline plans for a European coal and steel union.[64] It marked the beginning of another personal alliance that was to become hugely influential.

At the end of February 1943, after the Allies had retaken French North Africa, Monnet was sent by President Roosevelt to Algiers, nominally to arrange for arms shipments to the Free French forces. Here he found bitter rivalry developing between the two French generals who could claim to act as leader of the Free French, de Gaulle and Giraud. In his efforts to resolve this dispute, Monnet formed a close alliance with Churchill's political representative in the Mediterranean, Harold Macmillan.[65]

Macmillan records extensive conversations with Monnet about the future of France and post-war Europe. Despite reservations, they agreed that de Gaulle was the only man of sufficient stature to lead a government in exile. Between them they laid the foundations for what amounted to a provisional French government, the Comité français de libération nationale (CFLN),

[62] Cited in Shlaim, op. cit., p. 61.
[63] Salter, Arthur, *Memoirs of a Civil Servant* (London: Faber), p. 269.
[64] Spaak, Paul-Henri (1971), *The Continuing Battle: Memoirs of a European* (Boston: Little, Brown and Company), p. 213.
[65] Macmillan, Harold (1967), *The Blast of War* (London: Macmillan & Co. Ltd), p. 92 and pp. 297–298.

to be led by de Gaulle.[66] As a co-opted member, Monnet then, on 5 August 1943, produced a memorandum declaring that there would be 'neither peace, prosperity nor vital social progress until the nations of Europe formed a federation of a "European entity", forged into a single economic unit'. This would, he wrote, include an 'inventory of heavy metallurgy'. Interestingly, he excluded Britain from his grouping.[67]

Again, Monnet was developing his vision of a Europe that could achieve lasting peace only if organised under a supranational authority sufficient to overrule the fractious impulses of national sovereignty.

FASCISTS AND COLLABORATORS

Had the war gone the other way, of course, Europe would have looked very different. Despite that, some Nazi allies in the occupied countries nurtured dreams of European unity that were superficially similar to those in the free world. In their rhetoric were two persistent themes. The first was a desire to proclaim the end of the nation state and its absorption into a greater European identity; the other a sense that the emerging 'New Europe' could now recover its old self-confidence and compete with any power in the world.

In 1941, Mussolini's finance minister Alberto de Stefani wrote in such terms, arguing that 'nationalities do not form a sound basis for the planned new order'. Nations should be subordinate to a continental policy. A European Union, he said, 'could not be subject to the variations of internal policy that are characteristic of liberal regimes'.[68] Another Fascist opponent of the nation state, Camillo Pellizzi, editor of the magazine *Civiltà Fascista*, wrote that the Axis could be 'the first definite step towards surmounting ... that typically European phenomenon which we call the nation'.[69]

Many politicians and intellectuals who had advocated the cause of European unity since the 1920s now convinced themselves that working with the Nazis was the way to achieve it. These included one of the leading collaborators in Vichy France, Jacques Benoist-Méchin, secretary of state for Franco-German relations from June 1941 to September 1942, and the writer and philosopher Pierre Drieu La Rochelle.[70]

In Belgium, Pierre Daye, a leader of the Fascist Rexist movement, wrote a tract in 1942, *Europe for the Europeans*, in which he saw Nazi Europe as

[66] Ibid.
[67] University of Luxembourg archives.
[68] Alberto De Stefani, 'The Reorganisation and Pacification of Europe', *Ravista Italiana de Scienze economiche*, October 1941, pp. 989–992. Reproduced in Lipgens, op. cit., pp. 187–190.
[69] Lipgens, op. cit., pp. 190–193.
[70] Werth, op. cit., p. 126.

a bastion against Communism and the divisive foreign policies of Great Britain. Vidkun Quisling, the Norwegian collaborationist leader, argued that Europe would be strong and peaceful only if united: 'We must create a Europe that does not squander its blood and strength in internecine conflict, but forms a compact unity. In this way it will become richer, stronger and more civilised, and will recover its old place in the world.' He wanted to see a Pan-Germanic Federation with a federal flag and the Führer as president.[71]

Nothing of this would spill over into the movement for European integration that was to develop in the post-war years. Nazi thinking was an ideological cul-de-sac. The practical steps to realise the dream of a 'United States of Europe' would be inspired by those who, during the war, regarded themselves as the Nazis' sworn enemies, at odds with everything Nazism and Fascism stood for.

THE RESISTANCE

Many supporters of European unity, caught in the occupied territories, joined resistance movements. If they had any unifying philosophy, it was a determination to build on the concept of a united Europe. In common with the pre-war 'Pan-Europeanists' (and that of the Nazis when it suited them), they held nationalism and national pride to be responsible for past European wars, and supported the creation of new structures to transcend historical boundaries. This much was openly declared, long before the end of the war, by resistance groups in Czechoslovakia, France, Italy, the Netherlands, Poland and Yugoslavia, and even in Germany itself. But the most strident supporters of European unity were the Italian Communists, who were at the core of the anti-Fascist movement.

From this group emerged the Italian Altiero Spinelli, who was eventually to make a very significant contribution to the birth of the European Union. Born in 1907, he joined the Communists at the age of 17 and had been active in opposing Mussolini. In 1928, he was arrested and imprisoned, spending 12 years in jail before being exiled to the Mediterranean island of Ventotene, 30 miles west of Naples. In prison, he broke with Communism and embraced the cause of European unity. With the help of a fellow prisoner, Ernesto Rossi, he composed in 1941 what became known as the 'Ventotene Manifesto', under the title *Towards a Free and United Europe*.[72]

[71] Vidkun Quisling: 'Norway and the Germanic task in Europe', *Zeitschrift für Politik*, No. 12, pp. 789–804. Reproduced in Lipgens, op. cit., pp. 103–107. Quisling was, incidentally, utterly contemptuous of Coudenhove-Kalergi and his 'utopian ideas'.
[72] Menéndez, Agustín José (2007), *Altiero Spinelli: From Ventotene to the European Constitution* (Centre for European Studies, University of Oslo). The full text of the Manifesto (in English) is published on the Union of European Federalists website.

This was to become one of the basic texts of European federalism, echoing the language used by the British federalists. The similarity was no accident. His co-author, Rossi, was a friend of Luigi Einaudi, a liberal economist who was to become the first president of the post-war Italian Republic. Einaudi had sent him a number of books by English federalists, which Spinelli subsequently translated.

His thinking was devoted to exploiting post-war chaos as a means of securing 'the definitive abolition of the division of Europe into national, sovereign states'. To achieve this, he called on his followers to foment revolution. From there, a 'dictatorship of the revolutionary party' would give birth to a new state in which a 'new, genuine democracy would grow'. Popular assent would be sought only when the project was all but complete. At that moment of their 'crowning dream' a 'constituent assembly' would 'decide upon the constitution they want' as the final act in the emergence of the 'United States of Europe'. Only then, within the framework of the new state that had been brought into being, would 'democracy' be permitted to resume.

In July 1941, the manifesto was smuggled to the Communist-dominated Italian Resistance, leading to the formation in 1943 of the European Federalist Movement. This spread the message to groups in other countries, culminating in a major conference in Geneva in July 1944, attended by activists from Italy, Denmark, France, Norway, the Netherlands, Poland, Czechoslovakia and Yugoslavia. There, representatives produced a 'Draft Declaration of the European Resistance Movements', largely written by Spinelli, now freed from prison.

The post-war world, it proclaimed, 'must be based on respect of the human individual, on security, on social justice, on the complete utilisation of economic resources for the benefit of the whole and on the autonomous development of national life'.[73] But these aims could not be fulfilled 'unless the different countries of the world agree to go beyond the dogma of the absolute sovereignty of the state and unite in a single federal organisation', a European 'Federal Union'.[74]

It would be another 40 years before Spinelli would make his central contribution to the shape of the Union as it would finally emerge. But the ideals on which this was based were in the declaration of 1944, originating from the pages he had scribbled in his island prison, at a time when Hitler's 'Thousand Year Reich' had seemed the undisputed master of Europe.[75]

---

[73] Vaughan, Richard (1976), *Post-war Integration in Europe* (London: Edward Arnold), p. 17.
[74] Vaughan, Richard (1979), *Twentieth-Century Europe: Paths to Unity* (London: Croom Helm), pp. 54–55.
[75] See also Altiero Spinelli, *Battling for the Union*, European Parliament (31 December 1988).

2

Try, Try and Try Again: The First Attempts at European Integration: 1945–1949

> More than ever, we are convinced that we are right in
> proclaiming the necessity for complete European Union.
> But … it is a disgrace that Europe had to wait for a word
> of command from the other side of the Atlantic before she
> realised where her own duty and interest lay.
>
> Dr Henri Brugmans, Chairman of the European
> Union of Federalists, August 1947[1]

Official histories of the European Union invariably begin with the period immediately after the Second World War. Most often they start with the historic speech made by Winston Churchill in the Great Hall of Zurich University on 19 September 1946, where he declared that 'we must build a kind of United States of Europe'. The former prime minister (as he was then) was to renew his message in three more major speeches in the years that followed, in London in 1947, at The Hague in 1948, and in Strasbourg in 1949.

These rallying calls by Europe's only statesman at that time of world stature would later be claimed as having been the inspiration for the steps that eventually led to the European Union. In every respect this is based on a misreading of the facts. Not least, when he delivered his Zurich speech, Churchill proclaimed that the 'constant aim' must be to build and fortify the United Nations organisation. It was 'under and within that world concept', he said, that 'we must recreate the European family in a regional structure.

---

[1] Brugmans, Dr Henri (1948), *Fundamentals of European Federalism*, foreword by Lord Layton (London: The Federal Union), p. 4.

It may be the United States of Europe, and the first practical step will be to form a Council of Europe.'[2] He continued:

> Much work has been done upon this task by the exertions of the Pan-European Union, which owes so much to the famous French patriot and statesman Aristide Briand. There is also that immense body which was brought into being amidst high hopes after the First World War – the League of Nations. The League did not fail because of its principles or conceptions. It failed because those principles were deserted by those states which brought it into being, because the governments of those states feared to face the facts and act while time remained. This disaster must not be repeated. There is, therefore, much knowledge and material with which to build and also bitter, dearly bought experience to spur. There is no reason why a regional organisation of Europe should in any way conflict with the world organisation of the United Nations. On the contrary, I believe that the larger synthesis can only survive if it is founded upon broad natural groupings.

A year later, in 1947, at the Albert Hall in London, he returned to the theme, telling his audience: 'We accept without question the world supremacy of the United Nations organisation'. In the UN Constitution, he reminded them, 'direct provision was made for regional organisations'. A United Europe would be one of his regional entities. The United States, the Soviet Union and the British Empire and Commonwealth would be the others – pillars of the 'World Temple of Peace'.[3]

When he spoke in The Hague in 1948, his aim was still 'nothing less than the union of Europe as a whole'. Reiterating his Zurich message, he stated that nothing we do or plan 'conflicts with the paramount authority of a world organisation of the United Nations'. On the contrary, he said, a 'Council of Europe' was 'a subordinate but necessary part of the world organisation'. Furthermore, he added 'there should be several regional councils, 'august but subordinate', the 'massive pillars' upon which the world organisation would be founded 'in majesty and calm'.[4]

In three seminal speeches, therefore, Churchill had sketched out his vision of a 'United Europe'. It would be a regional organisation, 'august but subordinate' to the United Nations. But 'Europe' was only a means to an

---

[2] The text of the speech is widely available, for instance on the Council of Europe website: https://rm.coe.int/16806981f3.

[3] W. S. Churchill archive.

[4] Luxembourg University archives.

end: 'We do not of course pretend that United Europe provides the final and complete solution to all the problems of international relationships', he had said in his Albert Hall speech:

> The creation of an authoritative, all-powerful world order is the ultimate aim towards which we must strive. Unless some effective World Super-Government can be set up and brought quickly into action, the prospects for peace and human progress are dark and doubtful. But let there be no mistake upon the main issue. Without a United Europe there is no sure prospect of world government.[5]

As to the structure of his 'regional organisation', from his references at Zurich to a 'pan-European union', to that 'famous French patriot and statesman Aristide Briand', and to the League of Nations, it would seem that Churchill was essentially looking back to that internationalist idealism of the 1920s, an 'intergovernmental' alliance of sovereign states. This could not be further from the structure of the European Union that has emerged.

THE FIRST ATTEMPTS: THE MARSHALL PLAN

For the supporter of European integration even to think that Churchill had opened the way for a 'supranational' body of the type they were later to find requires a major leap of faith that cannot survive rational analysis. Nevertheless, Monnet was nothing if not an opportunist. And even as Churchill was touring Europe – a war leader out of office making a victory lap in front of adoring crowds – an opportunity was emerging in the form of a plan by the United States. This was to become known as the Marshall Plan, after its author US Secretary of State George Marshall.

The immediate driver of the Plan was US fear of insurrection in Italy and France, where the Communists were making significant electoral gains. Its roots lay in the economic dislocation caused by the war, exacerbated by the unusually severe winter of 1946–1947. These had undermined the initial post-war optimism about the recovery of western Europe's economies.[6]

Ironically, the first country to run into real economic crisis was Britain: over-stretched by her still enormous military commitments and by six years of war, sustained by huge American loans under the wartime 'Lend-Lease' programme. When that ended abruptly in August 1945, the impact was compared by John Maynard Keynes to that of 'a financial Dunkirk', only

---

[5] Churchill archive, op. cit.
[6] Vol. I of the General Report of the Committee of European Economic Cooperation, released in September 1947 by the State Department. Available online.

partly mitigated by a US loan of $3.75 billion and a further $1.25 billion from Canada. When the cost of supporting the British zone of Germany in the financial year 1946–1947 was estimated at over £80 million, the only remedy was economic integration of the occupation zones.[7] The British and US authorities had already begun the rebuilding of German self-government centred on the *Länder*, the regional divisions of Germany dating back to the Weimar Republic. Now they fused the British and American zones, creating the so-called 'Bi-zone' from 1 January 1947, with the US paying three-quarters of its financing.[8]

Further burdened by the costs of her military and political responsibilities in the eastern Mediterranean, Britain informed Washington on 21 February 1947 that she could no longer continue financial aid to Greece and Turkey (in addition to her substantial military commitment to Palestine).

This precipitated emergency meetings between members of Congress and State Department officials, which had Truman's Under-Secretary of State Dean Acheson propounding what would later become known as the 'domino theory'. Facing the possibility of a Communist takeover in both Greece and Turkey, he declared that more was at stake than just those countries. If they fell, Communism might spread south to Iran and even perhaps to India.

A support package was hastily devised and, addressing a joint session of Congress on 12 March 1947, Truman asked for approval of $400 million assistance for Greece and Turkey. 'It must be the policy of the United States,' he declared, 'to support free peoples who are resisting attempted subjugation by armed minorities or by outside pressures.' He thus established the 'Truman Doctrine', which was to guide US diplomacy for the next 40 years.

This also marked the beginning of America's Cold War foreign policy, at a time when the fragile détente between the western allies and the USSR was visibly crumbling. The events of 1947 were to mark a decisive turning point. As local Communist parties registered significant electoral gains in Romania, Hungary and Czechoslovakia, it had become clear that Stalin was intent on creating a new Soviet empire. In October a Warsaw conference was to set up the 'Cominform' (Communist Information Bureau), to co-ordinate the activities of all Europe's Communist parties. The so-called 'Big Three' negotiations between America, the Soviet Union and Britain on the future of Germany were getting nowhere.

---

[7] Approximately £2 billion at 2003 values.
[8] Woodhouse, C. M. (1961), *British Foreign Policy Since the Second World War* (London: Hutchinson & Co.), pp. 16–18 and 110–112.

Against this background of a rapidly polarising Europe, George Marshall early in 1947 called together a team of officials, led by one of his most senior advisers, George Kennan. Its task was to map out an ambitious new aid strategy for Europe. Kennan, and two other key figures, Dean Acheson and Will Clayton, were members of the Council of Foreign Relations.[9]

Clayton, at the time, was Under Secretary of State for Economic Affairs and, on 27 May, he sent his now famous memorandum on 'The European Crisis' to Dean Acheson.[10] 'It is now obvious', he wrote, 'that we grossly underestimated the destruction to the European economy by the war.' As a result, Clayton wrote, 'Europe is steadily deteriorating. The political position reflects the economic. One political crisis after another merely denotes the existence of grave economic distress.'[11] Recommending a grant of six or seven billion dollars-worth of goods a year for three years, he went on to call for an economic federation, adding: 'Europe cannot recover from this war and again become independent if her economy continues to be divided into many small watertight compartments as it is today.'[12]

From this emerged the fully-fledged 'Marshall Plan', announced by Marshall himself on 5 June 1947 in a speech at Harvard University. Taking a cue from Clayton, he couched the offer of help in these terms:

> It is already evident that, before the United States government can proceed much further in its efforts to alleviate the situation and help start the European world on the way to recovery, there must be some agreement among the countries of Europe as to the requirements of the situation and the part those countries themselves will take in order to give proper effect to whatever action might be undertaken by this government. It would be neither fitting nor proper for this government to undertake to draw up unilaterally a programme designed to place Europe on its feet economically. This is the business of the Europeans. The initiative, I think, must come from Europe.[13]

This vividly illustrated the crucial aspect of the plan: the US was turning away from a system of bilateral aid and forcing the Europeans to make a collective request to Congress, having agreed an amount between themselves. Whether this would necessarily require the creation of a new organisation

[9] Bundy, William P., www.foreignaffairs.org/generalInfo/history.html.
[10] FRUS, https://history.state.gov/historicaldocuments/frus1947v03/d136.
[11] Ibid.
[12] Ibid.
[13] www.marshallfoundation.org/about_gcm/marshall_plan.htm.

to administer the funding, however, was not a foregone conclusion. Behind the scenes, regional organisations of the United Nations, which Churchill had so enthusiastically embraced, were being developed. The first was the UN Economic Commission for Europe (UNECE), established on 27 March 1947.[14] Although it had been created to tidy up an alphabet soup of different UN bodies dealing with European recovery, the possibility of using it to administer the Marshall Plan was considered.

A supporter of its involvement was an adviser to Dean Acheson, economics professor Walt Roscow. He had been Assistant Chief of the State Department's Division of German and Austrian Economic Affairs, and his chief recalled that in early 1946, he had 'had a revelation that the unity of Germany could not be achieved without the unity of Europe, and that the unity of Europe could best be approached crabwise through technical cooperation in economic matters, rather than bluntly in diplomatic negotiations'.[15] In 1947, Roscow was assistant to the Executive Secretary of UNECE.

However, within UNECE, the Soviets had voting rights, which complicated matters after foreign secretary Molotov rejected Soviet involvement in the plan. And, although the French foreign minister, M. Bidault, was in favour of its involvement, the British felt that the Commission had yet to develop a secretariat capable of dealing with the initial response to the plan, and therefore should not be used.[16]

The British view was to prevail, consigning UNECE to the backwaters of European politics – ironically occupying the former League of Nations building in Geneva – where it concentrated on the technical aspects of the recovery plan. It never became a forum where ministers of finance and economy could meet regularly to address the problems facing the region, as had been intended.[17] Nevertheless, in decades to come, it was to develop a powerful alliance with the EEC and its successor organisations, developing the regulatory agenda and facilitating its global reach.

With the UN bypassed, 16 European nations agreed to attend a conference in Paris on 12 July 1947, intent on setting up a 'temporary organisation' to

[14] Berthelot, Yves and Rayment, Paul (2007), *Looking Back and Peering Forward: A Short History of the United Nations Economic Commission for Europe, 1947–2007* (New York and Geneva: United Nations). The other Commissions are: Economic Commission for Africa (ECA); Economic and Social Commission for Asia and the Pacific (ESCAP); Economic Commission for Latin America and the Caribbean (ECLAC); and Economic and Social Commission for Western Asia (ESCWA).

[15] Kindleberger, Charles P., Washington, 22 July 1948, Memorandum for the files: Origins of the Marshall Plan, FRUS, 1947, The British Commonwealth; Europe, Vol. III, p. 241.

[16] Office of the Historian, Letter from the British Ambassador (Inverchapel) to the Secretary of State, Washington, 19 June 1947, https://history.state.gov/historicaldocuments/frus1947v03/pg_262.

[17] Berthelot, Yves and Rayment, Paul, op. cit., p. 23.

deal with the Marshall proposal. They called it the Committee for European Economic Co-operation (CEEC). Deliberately limited in scope, its terms of refence prohibited it from intervening in the internal affairs of those states. No action was to be taken that might be regarded as implying a violation of their sovereignty and there was to 'no restriction to the beneficial development of European trade'.[18]

The chairman was a British civil servant, Oliver Franks, and, representing the second-largest economy in the group, was Jean Monnet, appointed as vice-chairman. His deputy, Robert Marjolin, became chief of staff. At the time, Monnet had been working directly for de Gaulle, now president, on a reconstruction plan for France. This was the so-called Plan de modernisation et d'équipement, named after its author, the Monnet Plan, heavily reliant for its success on the post-war annexation of Germany's coal-rich Saar region – France's own version of European economic integration. Although the area lay in the British zone of occupation, the UK government had in April 1946 agreed that the ownership of the Saar mines should be transferred to France, with the territory included in the French customs and currency system. French military forces were to be stationed permanently in the territory, and the territory itself transferred to French administration pending a final settlement. The assets transferred were to be debited to France on reparation account.[19] In March 1947, with the Saar's steel production representing a fifth of France's total production, business interests were even proposing a customs and monetary union.[20]

France supported Clayton – a former cotton broker and free-trader by conviction – in his call for a European customs union. He believed that this form of economic integration would unleash market forces and stimulate recovery in Europe. His enthusiasm spilled over into a speech to the initial meeting of UNECE on 2 May 1947, when he had urged European nations to work together in the process of reconstruction, rather than attempting isolated action.[21] The UK, though, was firmly opposed to the idea, and, in the event, the State Department did not insist. On 10 July 1947, Robert Lovett, in Washington, wrote to Clayton agreeing that a customs union was a 'desirable long-term objective' – reflecting a more general view held by the

[18] Luxembourg University Archives.
[19] National Archives, CAB 129/8, Memorandum CP (46) 139, 15 April 1946. See also CAB 128/5, Cabinet Conclusions, 17 April 1946.
[20] Long, Bronson (2015), *No Easy Occupation: French Control of the German Saar, 1944–1957* (London: Camden House), pp. 25 and 28.
[21] Healy, Timothy, 'Negotiating the Marshall Plan and European Economic Integration', *Diplomatic History*, Vol. 35, No. 2 (April 2011), pp. 229–256. Published by Oxford University Press.

State Department. But, he told him: 'an attempt to work it out now would bog Europe down in details and distract from the main effort'.[22]

Nevertheless, the Europeans were able to construct a plausible case for funds – sufficient to satisfy a not wholly sympathetic Congress. This was in no small part due to Monnet, who enlisted his former Washington lawyer, George Ball, to advise him on how the CEEC case could most effectively be presented to Washington.[23] The bid from 16 nations was $19.1 billion to cover the period 1948–1951. On 19 December, after making provision for emergency aid to France, Italy and Austria, President Truman submitted to Congress his 'European Recovery Bill', requesting $17 billion over four years.

Despite his immediate path having been blocked, Monnet still nurtured hopes that a permanent organisation that was to evolve from the CEEC might provide a platform to further his ambitions – an idea favoured by the State Department.[24] The purpose and scope, in its view, went 'far beyond trade relationships', and had 'as [an] ultimate objective [the] closer integration of Western Europe'.[25] But the matter was settled at a plenary meeting of the CEEC on 15 March 1948 when, despite French proposals, the British insisted on a scheme that placed no limits on their sovereignty nor had 'middlemen meddling in their relations with the United States'. The Organisation for European Economic Cooperation (OEEC) that emerged was 'predictably intergovernmental', controlled by a 'Council of Ministers' making decisions on the basis of unanimity.[26]

Monnet's comment to George Ball could not have been more withering: 'the OEEC's nothing: it's only a watered-down British approach to Europe – talk, consultation, action only by unanimity. That's no way to make Europe.' He nonetheless ensured that his deputy, Marjolin, became its secretary general.[27] With that, the first serious attempt to set up a large-scale supranational European organisation had failed.

Monnet was not the only one to be disappointed. Anticipating failure, in September 1947, Kennan had written that 'Europe is only partially capable

---

[22] FRUS, 1947, The British Commonwealth, Europe, Vol. III. p. 325.
[23] Ball, op. cit., pp. 77–78.
[24] For example: Memorandum by William T. Phillips, 4 March 1948, FRUS, 1948, Western Europe, Vol. III, p. 387. See also Ball, op. cit., p. 78. Clayton hinted that the Marshall Plan funding might depend on the establishment of a permanent organisation.
[25] Telegram: Lovett to Ambassador Murphy, 6 March 1948, FRUS, 1948, Western Europe, Vol. III, p. 389.
[26] Duchêne, op. cit., p. 168.
[27] Hoffmann, Stanley and Maier, Charles (1984), *The Marshall Plan: A Retrospective* (Boulder and London: Westview Press). See also Brugmans, Dr Henri (1948), *Fundamentals of European Federalism*, foreword by Lord Layton (London: The Federal Union), p. 4.

of making [decisions] on her own behalf', the Paris conference reflecting 'in short, all the weakness, the escapism, the paralysis of a region caught by war in the midst of serious problems of long-term adjustment, and sadly torn by hardship, confusion and outside pressure'. He added: 'But glaring deficiencies will remain. No bold or original approach to Europe's problems will be forthcoming. No startling design will emerge here for the removal of the pitiful dependence of much of this great peninsular area on overseas supplies for which it cannot pay.'[28] It was perhaps as well that the report in which he wrote had been marked 'secret'.

Meanwhile high-level politics continued to dominate the stage, with European politics focused on the 'Big Three' talks on the future of Germany. By 1948, it was clear that they had broken down and relations between 'East' and 'West' in Europe seemed to be worsening by the month.

Less than a month after the Prague Coup, on 17 March 1948, Britain, France and the three 'Benelux' countries had signed the Treaty of Brussels, a mutual defence treaty known as the Western Union, or sometimes the Brussels Treaty Organisation (BTO). Collectively, the members were referred to as 'the Five'.[29] Their role in the next drama was to prove pivotal. But, before that, in June, the great powers were to be plunged into their most serious crisis since the end of the war, which was to culminate in the year-long Berlin blockade.[30]

THE NEXT ATTEMPT: THE COUNCIL OF EUROPE

The Marshall Plan had been greeted with particular excitement by many of the advocates of European unity, who immediately recognised it for what it was. One such was Dr Henri Brugmans, Chairman of the European Union of Federalists. Addressing a congress of his federalists at Montreux in August 1947, he praised it in the terms reproduced in the epigram at the beginning of this chapter. Józef Retinger, a Polish émigré, who early in 1947 had formed an Independent League for Economic Co-operation (ELEC), had been present, as had Duncan Sandys, Winston Churchill's son-in-law.[31]

Brugmans' group was one of several campaigning for European unity, but there was no overarching organisation – an odd omission under the

[28] FRUS, 1947, The British Commonwealth; Europe, Vol. III, pp. 397–398.
[29] Luxembourg University archives.
[30] The crisis was provoked by the decision of the three Allied powers to introduce the deutschmark into West Berlin. The Soviet authorities imposed a blockade, cutting off road and rail access to the three western zones, fearful that the new currency would soon come to be used throughout the city, and aware that control of a currency brought economic control. This was a lesson the advocates of a European 'single currency' were quickly to learn.
[31] Brugmans, op. cit., pp. 3–4.

circumstances. In remedying that lacuna, however, campaigners were about to set in train a three-stage drama that would culminate in another failed attempt to unify Europe, the first stage being the creation of a Europe-wide umbrella group.

One of the most recent groups to have been formed had been in Britain itself. On 14 May 1947, Churchill had launched at the Albert Hall an all-party United Europe Movement, with Sandys as president. Its committee included two members of the Labour Cabinet and several future Conservative Cabinet ministers, among them Macmillan. In July 1947, Sandys met Retinger in Paris, along with Paul van Zeeland, more than once Belgium's prime minister, under the aegis of the ELEC. Alongside Brugmans, on 20 July 1947, they set up a Liaison Committee of the Movements for European Unity which, on 11 November 1947, was transformed into the much larger International Committee of the Movements for European Unity (ICMEU). Sandys presided and Retinger was secretary general.[32]

The ICMEU was then to lead to the next stage of the drama, when Retinger, Brugmans and Sandys together set out to organise a major event in The Hague. This was to be a vast 'European Congress', chaired by Sandys's father-in-law Winston Churchill.

On 7 May 1948, the thirteenth-century Ridderzaal or 'Hall of the Knights' was packed with 713 delegates, nearly half from Britain and France. They included more than twenty former and future prime ministers, such as Paul Reynaud (who had supported the Anglo-French union proposal in June 1940), Alcide De Gasperi of Italy, Paul van Zeeland of Belgium, Robert Schuman of France and Harold Macmillan of Britain; 29 former foreign ministers; and even a 51-strong delegation from West Germany, led by the man soon to become its first chancellor, Dr Konrad Adenauer. Others included Bertrand Russell, the English philosopher, Salvador de Madariaga, the Spanish historian, and Denis de Rougemont, the eminent Swiss intellectual and fervent 'federalist'.[33] Reflecting divisions within the ranks of the activists, the Congress was sharply split between the 'federalists' and the 'confederalists', such as Churchill, who wished only for closer co-operation. Easily the more numerous and vocal were the 'federalists', who cheered Brugmans' declaration that called for setting up 'a European government and a European parliament'.

[32] Biskupski, M. B. B. (2017), *War and Diplomacy in East and West: A Biography of Józef Retinger* (London: Routledge), pp. 241–243.
[33] An online record of the proceedings was published jointly by the European Parliament and the Council of Europe in 1999.

Delegates were presented with a report calling for 'common citizenship, without loss of original nationality'; the creation of a 'Single European Defence Force'; a 'unified economic system' and 'a complete federation with an elected European Parliament'. Echoing Spinelli, they voted for a 'constituent assembly' to draft a constitution for a European 'union or federation'. But the more cautious intergovernmentalists, co-ordinated by Sandys, managed to water down these demands. During the proceedings, which lasted four days, tempers may have been cooled (or not) when each of the participants received a souvenir packet of cigarettes bearing the official colours of the event as a gift from the Dutch authorities and the organising committee.[34]

One interesting intervention came from Arthur Salter, who had been invited to speak. He thought 'a much closer and more expansive political union of Europe' should be achieved, 'not by means of a sudden surrender of all our sovereignties, but by the development of the financial and economic organs and others created for the purpose of dealing with their immediate tasks'. As they developed, Salter said, they would gradually acquire 'by a delegation of sovereignty and authority from the constituent members so much power as will, without any sudden break, enable international authorities to be constituted'.

This 'softly, softly' approach, Salter felt, would 'enable a coordinated financial policy to be carried out, and coordinated economic development, and without us having made anything like a revolution'. He anticipated 'an international authority' would emerge that pooled an enlarged sovereignty. If not a federal state, it would constitute something that had its advantages, able to secure sufficient co-ordination of policy in all the different 'spheres' relevant to economic progress, without interference.[35]

At its conclusion, the Congress produced resolutions running to 12 pages in the original French.[36] The most important part was the 14-point political resolution, calling for a 'European Assembly'. Its purpose would be to 'stimulate and give expression to European public opinion; advise upon immediate practical measures designed progressively to bring about the necessary economic and political union of Europe; and to examine the juridical and constitutional implications arising out of the creation of such a Union or Federation and their economic and social consequences'. With that, it was to prepare the necessary plans to bring about this part of the resolution.[37]

---

[34] Luxembourg University archive.
[35] Proceedings, op. cit., pp. 176–177.
[36] Proceedings, op. cit., pp. 408–418. English summary: Luxembourg University archive.
[37] Ibid.

Immediately after the Congress, the International Committee assumed responsibility for implementing the resolutions, setting up the third and final stage of the drama. Crafting a European Assembly was delegated to former French prime minister Paul Ramadier, who had been Chairman of the Political Committee at the Congress. His plan called for the establishment of an Assembly with a strictly deliberative and consultative role.

At this point, several moving parts were coming together, one of which was the Brussels Treaty Organisation, which had been brought into being earlier in the year. As well as joint defence, its aim was also to strengthen economic and cultural ties.[38] And in that guise, it was to perform as the Trojan Horse for the final stage of this drama.

The supreme body of the BTO was its Consultative Council, comprised of five foreign ministers, including Bidault for France, Spaak for Belgium and Bevin for the UK. It was to this, on 23 November, that the European Movement submitted a memorandum with detailed recommendations for a European Consultative Assembly and a European Council of Ministers.[39] In response, Bidault proposed an economic and customs union and a European parliament. But his colleagues – even Spaak – thought this premature. This led a frustrated Sandys to dash off a letter to the Five, on behalf of the International Committee, saying that if they did not wish to assume the responsibility of convening a European Assembly, the Committee would do so itself.

The 28 July, however, brought something of a breakthrough. The Foreign Affairs Committee of the French National Assembly invited the French government to open negotiations with a view to convening a European Assembly. Then Spaak, speaking in Brussels, agreed that the Congress resolution on a European parliamentary assembly was 'a good idea' and 'achievable'. He asked the International Committee to put a proposal to the governments, whence he hoped 'to be able to adopt that proposal and thereby assist in bringing it about'.[40]

On 18 August the ICMEU sent a proposal, not only to the Five but also to the governments of the OEEC states. Additionally, it sent a memorandum concerning the method for the convening of an Assembly, the text drawn up by Ramadier. Without delay, the French Council of Ministers decided to 'give this proposal its active support and take whatever initiatives seemed appropriate in this respect'. François Mitterrand, junior information minister and a member of the French delegation to the Hague Congress,

---

[38] NATO website: The Origins of the North Atlantic treaty.
[39] Luxembourg University archives, op. cit.
[40] Luxembourg University archives.

promised that the French government would liaise as appropriate through normal diplomatic channels and that the first governments to be consulted would be those of the United Kingdom, Belgium, the Netherlands and Luxembourg.[41]

On 2 September 1948, the Belgian and French representatives formally presented to the Western Union the ICMEU proposal and, on 8 September, the Five announced officially that it was being considered. It then received the further boost of overt support from the United States and when the Italians and the Dutch gave their backing, it was evident the wind had changed. Predictably, the UK's Labour government viewed the initiative with considerable reservations. But, after a conference of the prime ministers of the Dominions at the Commonwealth Conference on 10 October came out in favour of an association, resistance weakened. The Five thus formed a 'Committee for the Study of European Unity' to examine 'the measures to be taken with a view to achieving a closer union among the peoples of Europe'.

On 25 October 1948 in Brussels, the International Committee decided to change its name to the European Movement. Based initially in London and then Paris, it did not find its permanent home in Brussels until 1951.[42] In the meantime, it reinforced its status by electing former French prime minister Léon Blum; Winston Churchill; the Italian prime minister, Alcide De Gasperi; and the Belgian prime minister – previously foreign minister – Paul-Henri Spaak, as its honorary presidents. Their ranks were soon to be strengthened by Robert Schuman, Coudenhove-Kalergi and the German chancellor, Konrad Adenauer.[43]

When a delegation from the European Movement was received at the Quai d'Orsay by the Five, the game was all but over. From 25 to 28 February 1949, in Brussels, the first political Congress of the European Movement focused on setting up the future European Assembly and a European Political Authority. Despite last-minute backtracking from the British, with attempts to relabel the body a 'conference', at meetings on 27 and 28 January the Five decided to establish a Council of Europe. It would consist of a Committee of Ministers, which would meet in private, and a consultative body that would meet in public. The latter would be made up of national delegations appointed by member states.[44]

---

[41] Ibid.
[42] Luxembourg University archive.
[43] Ibid.
[44] Schuman, Frederick L. (1951), 'The Council of Europe', *The American Political Science Review*, Vol. 45, No. 3, pp. 724–740.

The task of finalising arrangements was entrusted initially to a Conference of Ambassadors meeting, and then to a legal committee of ten nations, comprising the Five and Denmark, Italy, Norway, Sweden and Ireland. On 6 April 1949, a delegation from the European Movement was again invited to put its views on the composition and organisation of the Assembly. On 5 May 1949, the deed was done, one year almost to the day after the Congress. Its Statute was signed in London by the ten governments that had attended the preparatory conference. On a proposal from Ernest Bevin, who saw it as a symbol of Franco-German reconciliation, the Council would have its seat in Strasbourg.

Its first session began on 10 August 1949, attended by senior politicians from each of the participating countries, including leading members of the British and other governments. The star was indisputably Churchill, who was given the freedom of the city and made a memorable speech to a rapturous crowd of 50,000 in Strasbourg's main square (telling his fellow delegate Harold Macmillan 'this is the best fun I've had for years and years').[45]

The first president was Spaak, who had resigned as Belgian prime minister after a defeat in the general election only a week before the first session. He took his seat to preside over a series of discussions on how the Council could further the cause of integration, keen on the one hand to promote integration but, on the other hand, anxious not to lose touch with the British.[46] With the exception of Richard Mackay, an Australian-born Labour MP, none of the British delegation advocated British entry into a federal Europe.[47]

In the second session, the 'federalists' launched a 'major offensive', seeking to establish supranational authorities in the 'key sectors' of defence, human rights, coal, steel and power. This provoked sustained opposition to integration from British and Scandinavian delegates. Macmillan, then one of the Conservative delegates, explained that the British opposition was, above all else, 'a matter of temperament', a preference to work empirically when dealing with practical problems, rather than setting out 'general principles' that were then applied to practical issues.

The coolness towards the Council was reflected in Attlee's government. On 23 October 1950, the Cabinet considered whether ministers should attend the Assembly. Members were impressed by the arguments 'that Ministers had

---

[45] Horne, Alistair (1988), op. cit. p. 315.
[46] Spaak, op. cit., p. 209. See also, Aldrich, op. cit., pp. 355–356. Mackay's activities were funded generously by the American Committee on United Europe (ACUE), with CIA approval.
[47] Urwin, Derek W. (1995), *The Community of Europe: A History of European Integration Since 1945* (London: Longman, 2nd edn), p. 35.

in the past found themselves embarrassed by the course of the discussions in this forum and that the Government would be more free to ignore its decisions if Ministers were not part of the UK delegation'. It was then agreed that the government should 'make it clear that they would not regard themselves as bound by the Assembly's decisions'.[48] Unsurprisingly, at around that time – as Spaak was later to recall – the idea first took shape of a 'little Europe' of six, comprising France, Germany, Italy and the Benelux countries.[49]

By the third session, in the autumn of 1951, when the Conservatives had succeeded Labour and Churchill had replaced Attlee, there were some hopes of a more 'Europe-minded' Britain. But, in power, the Conservatives proved no keener on integration than their predecessors. Sir David Maxwell Fyfe (later to become Lord Kilmuir) broke the news. The Churchill government was ready to give its friendly support to the movement for European integration, but there was no question of taking an active part. Spaak finally concluded that the Council would never be anything more than a talking shop and came to realise that 'we must do without Britain's support if we were to make any headway'. He resigned as president on 11 December 1951, by then sharing Monnet's view that Britain would not consider joining until a united Europe was created.[50] Already, though, a third bid to give Europe a supranational government was under way. This one, for very different reasons, would succeed.

MONNET'S 'ALMOST MYSTICAL CONCEPTION'

Through the late 1940s, one man had stood more or less apart from the abortive efforts to set up a 'government for Europe'. Monnet was now nearing the end of implementing his four-year plan for the 'modernisation' of France. But, as he was to recall in his memoirs two decades later, he had watched what he considered to be the successive failures of the OEEC and the Council of Europe with a sense of resigned detachment, only too certain that neither of them could

> ever give concrete expression to European unity. Amid these vast groupings of countries, the common interest was too indistinct, and common disciplines were too lax. A start would have to be made by doing something more practical and more ambitious. National sovereignty would have to be tackled more boldly and on a narrower front.[51]

[48] National Archives, CAB 128/58, Cabinet Conclusions, 23–24 November 1950.
[49] Spaak, op. cit., pp. 211–212.
[50] Spaak, op. cit., pp. 219–220 and 225.
[51] Monnet, op. cit., pp. 273–274.

If Monnet was sure that something much 'more practical and ambitious' was needed to achieve the desired goal, however, then events in the late spring of 1950 conspired to create precisely the opportunity he was looking for.

During 1949, West Germany had finally emerged to self-government under the chancellorship of Konrad Adenauer. Under its Basic Law, passed on 8 May 1949, the new Federal Democratic Republic, or FDR, was based on 11 highly decentralised *Land* governments, which, on British insistence, retained considerable power, guaranteed by a constitutional court. In crucial respects the federal government, centred in Bonn, could not act without the consent of the *Länder*. In particular, all international treaties had to be ratified by them, through their legislative assembly, the Bundesrat. The largest and most powerful *Land*, Bavaria, had actually voted against the new constitution, for not reserving them even greater power.

Economically, the new Germany, under the guidance of Ludwig Erhard, was already showing signs of a remarkable recovery. This raised the question of how the new nation should be assimilated into the western European community. At the Council of Europe in August 1949, Churchill had shocked many delegates by proposing that she should be given the warmest of welcomes. Two of the western occupying powers, the USA and Britain, wanted to see her continue on the road towards full economic recovery and nationhood as soon as possible. But this had provoked a deep rift with France, which wanted to keep control over Germany's economy, for fear that she might once again become too strong a political and economic rival.

The argument centred on that old bone of contention, the coal and steel industries of the Ruhr, heartland of Germany's economy and former arsenal of her war machine. From the end of the war, France had been calling for her security to be guaranteed by means of the internationalisation of ownership of Germany's mines and steel industry. This proved unacceptable to the British and Americans and, when in November 1947 they established in their newly formed Bizone, a German administration, the Deutsche Kohlenbergbauleitung, was given the task of managing the Ruhr mines. This, in turn, proved unacceptable to the French.[52]

Eventually, after difficult diplomatic negotiations, an uneasy compromise was reached. The representatives of the United States, France, the United Kingdom and the three Benelux countries met in London to discuss the creation of a separate regulatory body for the area.[53] A detailed

[52] Luxembourg University archives.
[53] Ibid.

agreement was reached on 28 December 1948, creating what was to be called the International Authority for the Ruhr (IAR). It was charged with regulating steel and coal production and trade practice, in co-operation with the OEEC, providing the French with the security guarantees they thought so necessary.[54] Based in Düsseldorf, it became operational in September 1949.

From November 1949, the Germans were allowed to send delegates to the IAR, but they did not feel adequately represented. Konrad Adenauer, soon to become chancellor, was particularly incensed. The Authority, in his view, was 'no less than the rape' of a major industrial area of the Ruhr.[55] His protests, however, were ignored, although the dangers of mishandling the occupation had been recognised. In February, Lewis Douglas, the US Ambassador to London, had written to Acheson warning that rigid controls over the Ruhr could drive a German regime to ally itself with the Soviets, especially as the Ruhr had previously had strong Communist leanings.[56]

Even earlier, Robert Murphy, the political adviser to General Lucius Clay, the military governor of American-occupied Germany, had sent his observations to Acheson. He noted that, after two years of occupation, there had been no organised sabotage of US policy, but, with a keen grasp of history, warned that 'continued hopelessness and absence of incentive may at a future point develop passive resistance to that of the 1923 period'. In cautious tones, Murphy suggested that this 'would militate against European recovery'.[57]

Clearly, the Ruhr situation had the potential to disrupt the Marshall Plan, in which the Americans had invested so much, but in what was being freely referred to by the Americans as 'the Saar problem', the situation was even worse. A partial solution was a proposal to admit both West Germany and the Saar as associate members of the newly formed Council of Europe, but before that could be progressed, the French sought agreements with the Saar government, which were to become known as the Saar Conventions. These would recognise the Saar mines as the property of the Saar government and award the French 50-year leases on them.[58]

This left Adenauer 'furious' and soured relations between him and the then-French foreign minister, Robert Schuman.[59] It also alarmed

[54] FRUS, 1948, Germany and Austria, Vol. II, pp. 577–581.
[55] Williams, Charles (2000), *Adenauer: Father of the New Germany* (London: Little, Brown and Company), p. 332.
[56] FRUS, 1948, Germany and Austria, Vol. II, p. 98.
[57] FRUS, 1947, Council of Foreign Ministers; Germany and Austria, Vol. II, p. 982.
[58] Long, op. cit., pp. 136–137.
[59] Williams, op. cit., pp. 358–359.

the Americans, who did not want to see separate agreements that might prejudice a final peace settlement. A flurry of telegrams ensued between Acheson and his Europe-based officials, culminating in one to the Embassy in France, firmly rejecting the French 'solution'.[60] Despite this, the French went ahead with their Conventions.[61] Adenauer retaliated by hinting that the Federal Republic would not seek membership of the Council of Europe. Schuman, fearing that if Germany didn't join, Saarland's application would be rejected, suggested that membership was a necessary condition of German participation in the Marshall Plan.[62]

At this point, it is not clear whether Adenauer was ready to burn his bridges. That month, during an interview with a journalist, he proposed that France and Germany should unite as one nation with their economies managed as one, their parliaments merged and their citizenship held in common.[63] Earlier, at the Hague Congress, he had openly supported European integration, declaring: 'European nations must transfer and merge some of their sovereign rights so as to secure common political and economic action'. Afterwards, Adenauer had observed: 'In truth, in [the unification movement] lies the salvation of Europe and the salvation of Germany'.[64]

Nevertheless, tensions were rising and the European recovery programme was looking ever more fragile. On 10 May 1950, however, there was to be a tripartite meeting of the French, British and US foreign ministers in London, so Schuman placed 'Germany' on the agenda.[65] In Delphic terms, he wrote to Acheson suggesting that 'certain new proposals' could be examined, but he did not elaborate. The British suggested that Germany should be the first item on the agenda.[66]

This is where Monnet saw an opportunity to pursue his dream of building a 'United States of Europe'. Knowing that Schuman 'had no constructive proposals to take with him' to London, he decided to offer him his own.[67] From this emerged what Monnet later described as 'the first step of a European federation'.[68] This was to become the Schuman Plan.

---

[60] FRUS, 1950, Central and Eastern Europe; The Soviet Union, Vol. IV, pp. 935–936.
[61] Luxembourg University Archive.
[62] Long, op. cit., p. 137.
[63] Williams, op. cit., p. 358.
[64] Schwarz, Hans-Peter (1981 and 1983), *Die Ära Adenauer, 1949–1957* and *Die Ära Adenauer 1957–1963*; Vols II and III of *Geschichte der Bundesrepublik Deutschland* (Stuttgart: Deutsche Verlags-Anstalt). Cited in Williams, op. cit., pp. 331–332.
[65] FRUS, 1950, Western Europe, Vol. III, p. 837.
[66] FRUS, op. cit., p. 834.
[67] Monnet, op. cit., p. 292.
[68] Fransen, op. cit., pp. 96–97.

Once his 'plan' was ready, Monnet addressed the 'question of timing'. He was convinced that the tripartite meeting on 10 May was not be the right place for the proposal he had in mind. To achieve a result, he wrote in his memoirs, a totally new situation had to be created: 'the Franco-German problem must become a European problem'.[69] Schuman, he felt, was precisely the man to deliver the 'plan'. Born in 1886 in Luxembourg to a German mother, he was fluent in both German and French, having read law at the universities of Berlin, Munich and Bonn. He had then moved to Alsace Lorraine when it was under German rule, which meant that in 1914 he had been recruited into the German army. Yet in the Second World War, when Alsace Lorraine was again part of Germany, he had, as a French citizen, been arrested by the Gestapo. He was thus a perfect witness to the need to resolve the Franco-German conflict.

The French foreign minister was easily convinced that the 'plan' offered a way out of his immediate difficulties, whence his office passed the text in great secrecy to Adenauer, in the hope of securing his provisional agreement. Other governments, especially the British, were not told. According to Professor Bernard Lavergne, a prominent political commentator of the time, who was to publish a highly critical study of the plan:

The curious thing was that M. Bidault, the Premier, was – at least, at first – not at all favourable to the Plan which, in early May, was suddenly sprung on him by his Foreign Minister, M. Schuman. And oddly enough – though this was typical of M. Schuman's furtive statesmanship and diplomacy – neither was M. François-Poncet, the French High Commissioner, nor the Quay d'Orsay, nor even the French Government, properly informed of what was going on during the days that preceded the 'Schuman bombshell' of 9 May.[70]

Weeks previously, Acheson was 'considering' stopping in Paris on his way to London, to speak to Schuman. He did that, on 8 May, the day before the 'Schuman bombshell'. Monnet claims he was present at their meeting, whence he says, 'courtesy and honesty obliged us to take Acheson into our confidence'.[71] On the day itself, at 1 p.m., Acheson flashed off a 'top secret', 'eyes only' telegram to his under-secretary James E. Webb, back in Washington. He referred to a 'conversation' and warned him that 'tomorrow

[69] Monnet, op. cit., pp. 293–294.
[70] Lavergne, Bernard (1952), Le Plan Schuman (Paris: Librairie de Médicis), pp. 14–15. Cited in Werth, op. cit., pp. 479–480.
[71] Monnet, op. cit., p. 301.

or soon afterwards', the 'French Government may propose important approaches towards Germany in the economic field'. We have not, he added, been consulted or involved in the proposals, if made, in any way. The matter, he wrote, 'may be in the embryonic stage' and, prior to Cabinet consideration, may not materialise at all.[72]

Later, Acheson sent another telegram to Webb, telling him that the French Cabinet had approved the proposal and that Schuman was planning to make an announcement in the afternoon, without really knowing what it was all about. Schuman made his 'announcement' at 4 p.m. that afternoon. He later repeated it on France's state radio. To safeguard 'world peace', he declared:

> the French Government proposes that action be taken immediately on one limited but decisive point ... it proposes that Franco-German production of coal and steel as a whole be placed under a common High Authority, within the framework of an organisation open to the participation of the other countries of Europe. The pooling of coal and steel production should immediately provide for the setting up of common foundations for economic development as a first step in the federation of Europe.

After describing how 'the solidarity in production thus established will make it plain that any war between France and Germany becomes not merely unthinkable, but materially impossible', he went on to say that this would help simplify and speedily achieve 'that fusion of interest which is indispensable to the establishment of a common economic system'.

The Plan was immediately greeted with great excitement by the press, although one historian noted that literally nobody knew exactly what it was about, not even Schuman.[73] Mostly, though – to judge from contemporary newspaper cartoons, the Plan was seen as a Franco-German rapprochement. On 12 May 1950, for instance, British cartoonist David Low, alluding to the Scottish tradition of couples going to blacksmiths' forges in Gretna Green to exchange their wedding vows over an anvil, illustrated Acheson in such a scene presiding over a wedding between Adenauer and Schuman, representing Germany and France.[74] Other cartoonists depicted the same couple, but with a baby labelled 'Saar'.

---

[72] FRUS, 1950, Western Europe, Vol. III, p. 691.
[73] Werth, op. cit., p. 478. The 'excitement' was not universal. Journalist Raymond Aron, in the *Manchester Guardian*, wrote: 'One may ask how it is that an idea as banal as this should now be accepted as something vital and new' (30 May 1950).
[74] See https://www.cvce.eu/en/obj/cartoon_by_low_on_the_schuman_plan_12_may_1950-en-f5aa7683-68f2-47f8-a30e-115123ec46b5.html.

The cartoonists had assessed Adenauer's response correctly, although his initial enthusiasm cooled somewhat when he learned that Monnet was behind the Plan, fearing that the real aim was to promote French interests at the expense of Germany. However, during a meeting between the two men on 23 May, Monnet assured him of absolute equality between nations. Only then did Adenauer relax, declaring, 'I regard the implementation of the French proposal as my most important task. If I succeed, I believe my life will not have been wasted.'[75]

As to the British reaction, Prime Minister Clement Attlee was said to have 'received the French proposal with ill-grace'.[76] In fact, he did not 'receive' it at all. His government had been sent a summary only hours before the public broadcast and learned of the full text only from the broadcast. Attlee was extremely annoyed, and had every right to be. Not only was France's behaviour wholly undiplomatic; he had also specifically asked that no decisions involving Germany be taken before the tripartite conference on the 10th.[77] Furthermore, when he heard that Acheson had been informed in advance, he suspected that the Americans and French were colluding – as indeed they were.

For instance, although Schuman had only mentioned it 'quite causally' and in 'general terms' to Acheson, John McCoy, the US High Commissioner for Germany, had talked with Monnet the night before the announcement. It was these talks that had prompted his warning telegram to Webb. Through this, it was 'evident' to Acheson that 'Monnet has been the mainspring of this proposal'.[78] This did not prevent the myth developing that the Plan had originated with Schuman, who has thus become honoured as one of the 'Founding Fathers of Europe'.

With the proposal out in the open, the French imposed a deadline of 1 June for governments to agree to participate in the talks. But, as this deadline approached, Attlee and his chancellor, Sir Stafford Cripps, were out of London and could not be contacted. Herbert Morrison, as acting prime minister, was tracked down to a restaurant after having spent the evening at the theatre. Asked for a decision, he famously remarked: 'The Durham miners won't wear it.' A thinly attended Cabinet, held specially on the Friday afternoon to discuss the Plan, confirmed Morrison's reaction.

---

[75] Monnet, op. cit., p. 311.
[76] Denman, Roy (1996), *Missed Chances: Britain and Europe in the Twentieth Century* (London: Cassell), p. 187.
[77] Duchêne, op. cit., p. 201.
[78] FRUS, 1950, Western Europe, Vol. III, p. 694.

Bevin, at this time in poor health, was absent from Cabinet.[79] The presentation was made by his deputy, Kenneth Younger, intriguingly under the heading: 'Integration of French and German Coal and Steel Industries'. There was no sense that they were witnessing the birth of 'Europe'. But Younger's appraisal was damning. In spite of the numerous diplomatic exchanges over the past few days, he told the depleted Cabinet, it had proved impossible to reach agreement with the French government about the terms on which the UK could join in the talks.

'The French Government,' Younger continued, 'were insisting that all Governments participating in the proposed examination of this proposal should commit themselves in advance to accepting the principle of the scheme before it was discussed in detail.' Attempts had been made 'to overcome the French scruples' by seeking agreement for the UK to 'participate in the proposed conversations in a constructive spirit in the hope that, as a result of the discussions, there would emerge a scheme in which they would be able to join'. However, Younger said, it was made clear that, the UK government 'could not at this stage enter into any more precise commitment'.

This suggestion, Younger went on to say, had been rejected by the French government, which insisted that all participating governments 'set to themselves as an immediate aim the pooling of their coal and steel production and the institution of a new high authority whose decisions would be binding upon them'. It was also known, Younger informed his colleagues, that the French government desired that a treaty embodying the general principles of their plan should be concluded and ratified before the participating countries proceeded to the detailed examination of a practical scheme. Furthermore, 'the French Government had stated that, if we were unable to assure the basis which they now proposed, they would feel compelled to go forward without United Kingdom participation'.[80]

Morrison, in response, said that he and Kenneth Younger had talked through the position with Bevin. He had agreed that 'this latest French proposal must be rejected', asking for the French to be told that the UK government were unable to accept it, 'since they were still without any information about the practical details of the scheme and were therefore unable to estimate its possible effects on their programmes for economic development and defence'.[81] It took until 13 June before matters had settled sufficiently for Attlee, back in harness after the break,

[79] Bevin was to die on 14 April 1951 from a heart attack, aged 70.
[80] National Archives, CAB 128/17, Cabinet Conclusions, 2 June 1950.
[81] Ibid.

to give a comprehensive statement to the House of Commons. Essentially reaffirming the government's view expressed at the 2 June Cabinet meeting, he told MPs:

> It became perfectly clear in the course of informal discussions between M. Monnet, the Chief Planning Officer of the French Government, and British officials that while the French Government had not worked out how their proposal would be applied in practice, their views on the procedure for negotiations were definite. They were that Governments should accept at the outset the principles of the pooling of resources and of a high authority whose decisions would be binding on Governments, and the next step should be the conclusion of a treaty in which these principles would be embodied. Shortly thereafter the French Government secured the agreement of the German Government to the proposed basis on which the negotiations should proceed. This fact naturally determined the course of the subsequent exchanges of view between the two Governments and made difficult the achievement of His Majesty's Government's desire to play an active part in the discussion of the French proposal but without commitment to the acceptance of its principles in advance.[82]

Monnet had, therefore, 'Britain-proofed' the Plan by making joining the talks conditional on accepting the supranational principle. To make things even more difficult, he set an impossibly short deadline of 1 June, during the Whitsun holiday, for agreeing to this condition.

Not unreasonably, the British government had also pointed out that the fundamental change the French proposal would bring about was 'the elimination of the age-old antagonism between France and Germany'. The inclusion of other governments in the negotiations 'in itself begins a new phase by enlarging the scope of the discussions, which are thus placed from the outset on a European basis'.[83] In other words, Monnet's proposal was essentially a Franco-German affair; bringing in other countries was not strictly necessary.

In that context, only the previous year Britain had nationalised its iron and steel industries. It was not prepared to hand over control to another body that did not necessarily have Britain's national interest at heart. Furthermore, Manny Shinwell, then defence minister, was concerned about relying on pooled western European resources, some of which might be

---

[82] HC Deb, 13 June 1950, Vol. 476, cc35-47.
[83] FRUS, 1950, Western Europe, Vol. III, p. 712.

lost to an invader.[84] Thus, the central objective of the Plan that made it so attractive to its advocates – eliminating the independent war-making capability of member states – was anathema to the British.

However, there was one British MP who was unequivocally in favour of British involvement. A day after Communist North Korea's armies swept over the frontier into South Korea on 25 June, thus precipitating another major Cold War crisis, the new young Conservative Member for Bexley gave his maiden speech in the House of Commons. Ignoring convention that such speeches should avoid controversy, Edward Heath averred that British abstention would be a grave error. By standing aside, he said, 'we may be taking a very great risk with our economy in the coming years – a very great risk indeed'.[85]

What Heath did not appear to recognise was the skill with which Monnet had deliberately managed to exclude the British from the negotiations. It was regarded by many of his colleagues as one of his greatest triumphs.[86] But many British 'Europeanists' argue to this day that Britain made a fundamental and tragic error in not joining the negotiations, thereby seeking to influence them. Acheson himself was later to describe it as 'the greatest mistake of the post-war period'.[87] The author of the British official history of the period disagreed. He wrote:

> The conversations and correspondence with French officials and with Schuman between 9 May and 2 June can lend some credence to the idea that the United Kingdom might have obtained an acceptable treaty, meaning one with no subjugation to a High Authority as a promise of closer union ... Nevertheless, the outcome of the negotiations suggests that there was no treaty which would have given Britain the economic and political advantages identified by officials, without a supranational authority as embryo and symbol of a European federation. Acceptance of Monnet's non-negotiable principle did require a change of national strategy ... It would have meant a commitment of political support ... to a reconstruction of the pattern of political power in Europe in which the United Kingdom ... could not share.[88]

[84] Milward, op. cit., pp. 41–42 and 52–53.
[85] *Hansard*, 26 June 1950, col. 1959.
[86] Fransen, op. cit., p. 100.
[87] Horne, Macmillan, op. cit., p. 319. See also Denman, op. cit., p. 188; George, Stephen (1990), *An Awkward Partner: Britain in the European Community*, 3rd edn (Oxford: Oxford University Press), p. 5; and Dell, Edmund (1995), *The Schuman Plan and the British Abdication of Leadership in Europe* (Oxford: Clarendon Press).
[88] Milward, op. cit., pp. 61–62.

This confirmed that UK involvement was precisely what Monnet had wanted to avoid. Correctly reading the psychology of the British government, he had created an offer it could only refuse.

MONNET'S 'ONE-MAN SHOW'

Launching his plan was only the start of Monnet's achievement. Invitations to discuss it had also been extended to representatives of the three Benelux countries and Italy. By 3 June they had all agreed to take part. Particularly enthusiastic was Italian premier Alcide De Gasperi. Thus the 'Six' came together.

As the talks began, Monnet engineered another coup. Not only did he get agreement that he should chair the negotiations; he had also managed to convince a French inter-ministerial committee that he should be France's representative, with power to appoint his own advisers.[89] In what was to become one of the most important negotiations in its history, therefore, France was represented by a man who was not even a member of its government.

To get the negotiations under way, Monnet produced a *document de travail*, which meant that, in addition to organising the talks, chairing the sessions and representing France, he also set the agenda. The 'one-man show' was to continue. Nevertheless, it was July before he could produce a working draft for consideration by the governments of the Six, not least because of the incoherence of his original document. Belgian prime minister Paul van Zeeland described that as 'so vague on essential details that it was impossible to speak definitely about it'.[90] When it was ready, a summary of Monnet's July text was given to the press, in which he was 'careful to include the following stipulation':

> The withdrawal of a State which has committed itself to the Community should be possible only if all the others agree to such withdrawal and to the conditions in which it takes place. The rule in itself sums up the fundamental transformation which the French proposal seeks to achieve. Over and above coal and steel, it is laying the foundations of a European federation. In a federation, no State can secede by its own unilateral decision. Similarly, there can be no Community except among nations which commit themselves to it with no limit and no looking back.[91]

[89] Duchêne, op. cit., p. 209.
[90] Ibid.
[91] Monnet, op. cit., p. 326.

After that, wrote Monnet, 'no one could any longer doubt our ambition and our determination'. Nevertheless, each of the representatives involved sought to extract the maximum advantage for their nations. Part of the price was a 2 per cent turnover tax imposed on German collieries to support the decrepit Belgian coal mines; and a preferential ore supply arrangement for Italy, with subsidies for the importing of coal, and special tariffs and quotas to protect its steel industry.[92] These concessions breached Monnet's original concept of 'equal treatment' but they were needed to get agreement.

There were other concessions. At the behest of the Belgians, a Court of Arbitration was added, to adjudicate in case of disputes. The French finance minister had then proposed the inclusion of an Assembly, which would retain the ultimate power to dismiss the High Authority, much as a shareholders' meeting has the power to dismiss a board of directors. The Dutch chief negotiator, Dirk Spierenburg, then called for an intergovernmental 'watchdog' to supervise the High Authority. Monnet reluctantly accepted this so long as there was majority voting and no 'veto'. The 'watchdog' would be a 'forum' through which the High Authority could 'play an educating role *vis-à-vis* the governments'.[93]

So was born the 'Council of Ministers', which, with the court and Assembly, brought the structure into line with Salter's pre-war template. Monnet then set about devising a voting formula that prevented the combined power of Germany and France outvoting the remaining members, a system that was to become known as 'qualified majority voting'. Finally, he secured a crucial agreement that, although the Council of Ministers could take part in decision-making, it could not instruct the High Authority. Monnet's 'Authority' was to remain supreme, immune from the interference of nation states. Supranationalism had survived its greatest challenge.

In the first months after the launch of Monnet's Plan, among those who had praised it was Macmillan. To the Council of Europe Assembly on 15 August 1950, he described it as being 'not just a piece of convenient machinery'; it was 'a revolutionary and almost mystical conception'.[94] As someone who had enjoyed lengthy discussions with Monnet during their time together in Algiers in 1943, Macmillan perhaps had a shrewder understanding than most of the intentions that lay behind it. However, in

---

[92] Gillingham, John (1991), 'Jean Monnet and the European Coal and Steel Community: A Preliminary Appraisal', in Brinkley, Douglas and Hackett, Clifford (eds), *Jean Monnet: The Path to European Unity* (New York: St Martin's Press), p. 144.
[93] Fransen, op. cit., pp. 106–109.
[94] Horne, *Macmillan 1894–1956*, op. cit., p. 319. It is not clear whether Macmillan was being ironic. Horne portrays his subject as being a more enthusiastic supporter of European integration than other sources.

the same speech, he made it clear that it was not for Britain. 'Our people will not hand over to a supranational authority the right to close down our pits and steelworks,' he told delegates.[95]

Then, after the negotiations had meandered on for some months, several British delegates to the Council of Europe, including Macmillan, sought to reassert the intergovernmental agenda. They put to the Assembly that the Coal and Steel Community be made an agency of the Council rather than an independent, supranational authority. Monnet reacted sharply. In a letter to Macmillan, he strongly denounced the proposal, complaining that it would not offer the creation of a new economic community, 'but merely a mechanism for coordination among nation states' – precisely what he was most anxious to avoid.[96]

But, by then, the momentum of the Six was unstoppable. Final agreement was reached and formalised by the Treaty of Paris, signed on 18 April 1951, creating the European Coal and Steel Community. Not until December, though, was the treaty ratified, 'in an atmosphere of doubt and resignation, and a good deal of indifference'.[97] The Gaullist deputy Jacques Soustelle thought the Plan was not 'European' but 'anti-European'.[98] But Monnet had got his great project. Unsurprisingly, he was also appointed president of the High Authority, based in Luxembourg. As for where it might all lead, he himself left little room for doubt. Addressing the inaugural session of the Community's assembly, he told the delegates that they were participating in 'the first government of Europe'.[99]

[95] Cited in Spaak, op. cit., p. 216.
[96] *Archives Nationales*, Paris, 8 August 1950, 81/AJ/158, 36. Werth, op. cit., p. 481.
[97] Werth, op. cit., p. 481.
[98] Débats, AN, 6 December 1951, p. 8881. Cited in Werth, op. cit., p. 550.
[99] Duchêne, op. cit., p. 235.

3

The Rocky Road to Rome: 1950–1957

Our Community is not a coal and steel producers' association.
It is the beginning of Europe.

Jean Monnet[1]

Nobody after the first two years of Monnet's presidency at the
High Authority would again talk of it or its equivalents as 'a
European government' ... the idea of a Europe in some sense
above the nations was no longer stated in the open.

François Duchêne[2]

One remarkable feature of Monnet's triumph was that, despite the protracted
arguments about how his 'government of Europe' should be constructed,
what finally emerged was almost identical to that outlined by Salter 20
years earlier. Yet, in previous accounts of the 'European project', this has
been overlooked. In vain does one look for any reference to Salter. There
is scarcely a mention of the crucial developments in the 1920s, when the
key ideas emerged. There may be perfunctory references to Coudenhove-
Kalergi. And, as with Salter, the name of Loucheur has vanished.

By this means, the 'project' has evolved its own foundation myths, the
most important of which is that it started after 1945. This allows the claim
that it had put an end to European wars, characterising it as a progressive
creation of the modern world rather than as a failed dream of the 1920s.[3]

---

[1] *Memoirs*, p. 392.
[2] Duchêne, op. cit., p. 288.
[3] One unintended by-product of this rewriting of the official chronology was that it would help to
reinforce the 'Nazi origins' myth', in that the ideas behind it could then be shown to have followed
those of the Nazis about European integration rather than having preceded them.

The official hagiography would also have Monnet as a visionary whose only concern had been to achieve lasting peace. Spinelli, for all his talk of dictatorships and revolution, would be the man who made the EU democratic. Schuman would be honoured as the 'Father of Europe', despite his most prominent contribution being to act as Monnet's 'front-man'.

Some British historians were keen to rewrite the events surrounding Britain's involvement in the project. Two accounts, in particular, were published in the 1990s, one by journalist Hugo Young, who died in 2003, and the other by Sir Roy Denman, a former Foreign Office mandarin.[4] Their narratives portrayed the founders of the project as reasonable and open to ideas, contrasted with an 'obdurate' Britain, lacking in vision. Their implicit message was: 'Europeans – positive, forward-looking, good; British – negative, backward-looking, bad'.[5]

As for Monnet, despite having brilliantly pulled off the first step of his grand design, he was now to overreach himself. Consequently, the next six years were to prove a rocky road. He would not achieve his goal until his allies had impressed on him the need for their most daring strategy yet: to cloak the *projet* in deceit.

MONNET TAKES A FALL

When the president of the new European Coal and Steel Community first came before its Assembly, he told the 'deputies' it was 'the beginning of Europe'.[6] For all his triumphalism, though, Monnet then made a near-fatal mistake. The cause of his near-nemesis was the Korean War, which had broken out on the Sunday after ECSC negotiations had opened. He feared that possible Soviet aggression in Europe might lead the Americans to strengthen their demands for German rearmament. Adenauer might even lose faith in the Schuman Plan, as this key objective lay within reach without having to place Germany's coal and steel under the control of the High Authority.

To regain the initiative, Monnet had decided to widen the scope of the Schuman Plan to include a European Defence Community (EDC), launching a European Army. It would be run by a European minister of defence and a council of ministers, with common budgeting and arms

---

[4] Young, Hugo (1998), *This Blessed Plot: Britain and Europe, From Churchill to Blair* (London: Routledge; Denman, op. cit.).

[5] Young even mocked the 'British *idée fixe*, that the Schuman Plan would lead to a European Federation' (*This Blessed Plot*, p. 60). Such an analysis, he wrote, 'turned out to be premature, if not something of a hallucination'. Young thus completely missed the Plan's central purpose (cf. for instance, Monnet's *Memoirs*, p. 326).

[6] Monnet, op. cit., p. 392.

procurement. While all other members would be allowed separate forces, for colonial and other purposes, Germany's troops would be embedded in this army.

For his advocate this time, Monnet bypassed Schuman, who was strongly opposed to German rearmament, seeking out a former assistant – René Pleven, now France's prime minister. The familiar deception was repeated. Although the proposal was entirely Monnet's, it became the 'Pleven Plan', which the prime minister outlined to the French Assembly on 24 October 1950, winning approval by 343 votes to 220. Nevertheless, during the debates, Pleven made clear that negotiations would not start until the Coal and Steel Treaty had been concluded, thus safeguarding Monnet's original scheme.[7]

Unlike the Schuman declaration, this plan was not well received abroad. Acheson noted inconsistencies in the French proposals and feared conflict might arise with future NATO plans. A determination to integrate German troops into French cadres, keeping them at battalion strength or less, was seen as 'wholly unworkable'. The German people, Acheson felt, would not participate in a plan where they were labelled as inferiors.[8]

The Germans preferred their forces to be part of NATO, and were highly suspicious – with good reason. Monnet intended his EDC to be 'a government capable of taking the supreme decisions in the name of all Europeans'. Yet that was precisely why Italian premier, De Gasperi, proclaimed his support. 'The European Army is not an end in itself,' he said. 'It is the instrument of a patriotic foreign policy. But European patriotism can develop only in a federal Europe.'[9]

Nevertheless, on 15 February 1951, the ministers of the Six met in Paris to start negotiations, which progressed in a rather desultory fashion. The British Labour government once again decided not to participate. On 8 May, in a written report to the Cabinet, Herbert Morrison gave the Foreign Office view, predicting that 'an agreement of some sort will be reached'. But, he wrote, 'there seems no reason yet for Her Majesty's Government to reconsider their decision not to join the European Army and to attend the Conference only as an observer'.[10]

At this point, the Korean War, following the intervention of Communist China, had entered a critical phase. As anticipated, American pressure for German rearmament had intensified, giving Adenauer considerable

---

[7] Luxembourg University archives.
[8] FRUS, 1950, Western Europe, Vol. III, p. 410.
[9] Monnet, op. cit., p. 382.
[10] National Archives, CAB 129/45/53 (circulated on 10 May).

leverage. He chose to exploit it, offering in return for his support of the EDC a 'general treaty'. This would recognise West German sovereignty, accept German contingents into the EDC on an equal footing, allow West Germany into NATO, end the remnants of allied occupation of his country, and conclude a peace treaty. Ambitious though this proposal was, it was quickly agreed by the Allies. By the end of November 1951, a draft treaty was ready.[11]

During the final stages of the treaty negotiations, Labour lost a general election to the Conservatives. From 25 October 1951, Churchill was once again prime minister. Anthony Eden was foreign secretary. In opposition, Churchill had favoured the idea of a European army, but now aware of its supranational element, he brushed it aside. At a Cabinet meeting on 11 December 1951, he read out a letter from Field Marshall Montgomery dismissing the idea as 'impracticable'. He did not recommend UK participation. Churchill told the Cabinet he was 'in general agreement with these views'.[12]

Nevertheless, the new Conservative government did its best to be constructive. At a meeting with Schuman in February 1952, Eden assured him that British forces on the continent would co-operate very closely with 'European forces'.[13] In a further effort to be helpful, Eden proposed in March 1952 that the two Communities of the Six should come under the aegis of the Council of Europe. Monnet, predictably, saw this as a challenge to his supranationalism.[14] Nothing came of the initiative.

By then, the French were beginning to worry about the possibility that Germany might, after beginning rearmament, secede from the EDC. Eden had recommended his government authorise 'some sort of British guarantee'. Schuman, on the other hand, wanted an assurance from the US and the UK that they would both keep troops in Germany as long as necessary. Truman, however, could not go beyond Congress authorisations, especially in what was a presidential election year.[15]

---

[11] Williams, op. cit., pp. 372–373. US enthusiasm for European integration was now at its height. On 11 August 1952 the USA was the first non-member country to give international recognition to the ECSC. Monnet's friend Dean Acheson, as Truman's Secretary of State, sent Monnet a personal message declaring: 'All Americans will join me in welcoming the new institution and in expressing the expectation that it will develop as its founders intended …' (published on the EU's Washington website, 2004).

[12] National Archives, CAB 128/23/16.

[13] Calvocoressi, Peter (1955), *Survey of International Affairs – 1952* (London: Oxford University Press), pp. 93–94.

[14] Documents on British Policy Overseas, Series 2, Vol. 1, doc 484, 29 August 1952.

[15] FRUS, 1952–1954, Western European Security, Vol. V, Part 1, p. 40.

Under the 1948 Brussels Treaty, Britain had already pledged to give assistance to France and the Benelux countries in the event of war. The Six now asked for that guarantee to be extended to West Germany and Italy. Britain agreed – an offer that was well received by the Six. In Germany it was hailed as 'one of the most important political developments of recent times'.[16] However, this was not an Anglo-American guarantee, for lack of which the French Cabinet refused to sign the agreements. The *impasse* was eventually resolved by the US and Britain agreeing to regard any action that threatened the integrity of the EDC as a threat to their own security.[17] It was enough. The European Defence Treaty was signed on 27 May 1952, along with a general treaty that effectively restored German sovereignty.[18] It was far from what Monnet had envisaged, with the budget subject still to national veto. Even so, there was still so much opposition in France that her new prime minister, Antoine Pinay, signed the treaty without intending to seek immediate ratification.

It was over ratification that Monnet's scheming began to unravel. Opposition in the French Assembly had been hardening. The Socialist group wanted a 'more democratic' EDC, with a European Assembly elected by universal suffrage. This was to prompt Monnet's most daring initiative so far, in concert with the man who over the next few years would be his closest ally, Paul-Henri Spaak. He proposed setting up a European Political Community (EPC), as a 'common political roof' over the Coal and Steel and Defence Communities, creating 'an indissoluble supranational political community based on the union of peoples'. In September 1952, this proposal was jointly endorsed by the foreign ministers of the Six, along with the assemblies of the ECSC and the Council of Europe. The ECSC Assembly was asked to study the question of creating a 'European Political Authority'. The result, from an ad hoc committee under Spaak's chairmanship, was a 'Draft Treaty Embodying the Statute of the European Community'.

This was nothing less than the first formal attempt to give 'Europe' a constitution. It was submitted to the foreign ministers of the Six on 9 March 1953 and to the ECSC Assembly the following day, which approved it by fifty votes, with five abstentions. Introducing his draft to the ECSC Council, Spaak began with the opening words of George Washington's address in presenting the American Constitution to Congress in 1787, going on to

---

[16] Calvocoressi, op. cit., p. 94. See also Foreign Office Press Release, 15 April 1952, and *The Times*, 16 April 1952, *Le Monde* and *Neue Zeitung*, 17 April 1952.
[17] Ibid., p. 103.
[18] Ibid., p. 126.

express his conviction that, 'with the same audacity', Europe could hope for the same success.[19]

Although discussion of this draft continued through the following months, it could not progress while the EDC itself was still arousing opposition.[20] Part of the Plan was to apply supranational controls on any production of nuclear weapons, which caused the French Atomic Energy Commission, Gaullist in sympathy, to wake up to the implications for France's nuclear ambitions.[21] By October, deputies in the National Assembly were worried lest the treaty gave too many advantages to Germany. Objections were also raised that they were being presented with a *fait accompli*.[22]

Thus, while the rest of the Six went on to ratify the Defence Treaty, the French process stalled, collapsing the Pinay government. René Mayer, with Gaullist support, took over. The 'Europe of Jean Monnet' became almost a term of political abuse. Then, after four months, Mayer was replaced by Joseph Laniel. In the despairing words of Monnet, the latter 'did nothing'. Despite intense pressure from the United States, with Secretary of State John Foster Dulles threatening to cut US aid, France's ratification process ground to a halt. Outside Parliament, opposition was at least as strong. Army leaders were against it, intellectual groups detested it and de Gaulle, in November 1953, declared himself implacably hostile to it. In a bitter parody of Monnet, he declared, 'Since victorious France has an army and defeated Germany has none, let us suppress the French Army.'[23]

What finally brought matters to a head was a quite separate event: the fall on 7 May 1954 of Dien Bien Phu. The disaster ushered in yet another government, led by Pierre Mendès-France, the radical nationalist. He immediately sought to dilute the supranational element of the EDC. Adenauer rejected the idea out of hand and Spaak made an almost hysterical plea to Mendès-France to support the treaty, clasping him by the arm while telling him that France would be 'completely isolated' unless he supported 'the integration of Europe'.[24]

Brushing aside Spaak, Mendès-France also ignored entreaties from the Americans and even Churchill, from whom he sought, unsuccessfully,

[19] Griffiths, Richard T. (2000), *Europe's First Constitution: The European Political Community, 1952–1954* (London: Federal Trust), p. 93.
[20] On the day of Queen Elizabeth II's Coronation, 2 June 1953, a lead item on the main news page of *The Times* reported that Dr Adenauer had 'decided to attend the conference in Rome of the Foreign Ministers of the six members of the Coal and Steel Community which opens on June 12', its original purpose 'to consider the draft of a constitution for the proposed political community'.
[21] Duchêne, op. cit., p. 233.
[22] Calvocoressi, op. cit., p. 127.
[23] Werth, op. cit., pp. 646–647.
[24] Ibid., p. 696.

guarantees of British involvement in the EDC. He thus brought the treaty before a hostile Assembly on 30 August 1954 without endorsement. After a stormy debate, in which the supranational issue predominated, it was rejected by 319 votes to 264 on a technical motion. Mendès-France's government abstained. The triumphant majority burst into the Marseillaise.[25] The EDC was dead. The idea of a Political Community soon faded into obscurity. Monnet's supranationalism had suffered a resounding defeat.

Still the problem of German rearmament remained. Eden proposed an extension of the 1948 Brussels Treaty, bringing Germany and Italy into its scope, to become the intergovernmental Western European Union (WEU).[26] With that, it seemed that the supranational adventure had been all but blocked. Intergovernmentalism had triumphed. In December that year, to complete her success, Britain signed an agreement of 'association' with the ECSC, committing her to no more than friendly co-operation.

THE NEW STRATEGY: DECEIT

The effect of the EDC rejection was profound and long-lasting. Quite simply, the 'project' went underground. According to Duchêne:

> Nobody after the first two years of Monnet's presidency at the High Authority would again talk of it or its equivalents as a 'European government' ... Awareness that the French would have to be coaxed into further progress introduced caution into the European vocabulary. The word federal was reserved as the political equivalent of Latin for the rare religious occasion. Even supranational ... tended to be used only when another fig-leaf could not be found. The idea of a Europe in some sense above the nations was no longer stated in the open.

From then on, therefore, Monnet set the tone of the 'project', relying on a necessary but short-term stratagem. It would become an elite project, denied popular assent, thereby lacking long-term democratic legitimacy. If it had ever been a peoples' project, its character had irrevocably changed. However, his more immediate reaction to his crushing defeat was to resign as president of the ECSC. This meant that arrangements

---

[25] Duchêne, op. cit., p. 256.
[26] US Secretary of State Dulles, a supporter of the EDC (and Monnet's friend since 1919), wrote dismissively to Eden about the plans for WEU that he would regard 'any solution which did not provide for the creation of a supranational institution as makeshift'. Eden, Anthony (1960), *Memoirs: Full Circle* (London: Cassell), p. 159.

had to be made to fill his post, requiring a meeting of the foreign ministers of the Six. Originally set for 8 February, in the interim, Mendès-France's government fell, delaying the meeting. The new French government was led by Edgar Faure, less hostile to European integration.

Somewhat encouraged, Monnet settled on his earlier strategy of building 'Europe' through the progressive integration of other economic sectors. In late 1955, from various options, he had picked the nascent nuclear industry as his target. It seemed to offer distinct advantages. Coal and steel represented the past. The 'power of the atom' could position 'Europe' as forward-looking and modern. Furthermore, the scale of investment required to develop the industry was so huge that Europe-wide co-operation was eminently logical.

To present his new plan for what was eventually to become 'Euratom',[27] Monnet needed another front-man, particularly since he had now made so many enemies. His choice was Spaak, his closest ally. The new French prime minister Faure proved receptive to his overtures. On 4 April 1955, Spaak sent Monnet's proposals to Adenauer. They encompassed not just nuclear but all forms of energy and also transport. Pinay – now France's foreign minister – and Italy's foreign minister, Gaetano Martino, were copied in. In an accompanying letter, Spaak suggested the time had now come for a 're-launch' (*relancer*) of the 'European idea'.[28] There was one highly significant omission from Spaak's letter: the possibility of a 'customs union' or 'common market' among the Six. Monnet feared that to raise it so soon after the collapse of the EDC might be going too far.

The German response was not encouraging. Rather than pooling resources through Euratom, Erhard thought Germany's advantage lay in buying technology from the US or Britain. France's reaction was even less positive. In a message delivered orally to Spaak via the Belgian Ambassador, her foreign minister replied that to 'supranationalise energy and transport might produce another EDC in France'. He added: 'Take care! Edgar Faure does not like Monnet.'[29]

Only the Dutch foreign minister, Johan Beyen, responded positively. He proposed the very idea Monnet had not dared broach: a 'common market'. Crucially, he suggested that this would be a customs union. Duties levied on goods traded between member states would be progressively reduced, then abolished, while a common external tariff would be erected against

---

[27] So far-reaching was this change that, in 1965, when the 'Merger Treaty' was agreed between the Six, combining the executives, councils and assemblies of the three 'Communities' – ECSC, EEC and Euratom – any reference to the 'supranational character' of the Commission's duties was omitted.
[28] 'Archives of the Ministry of Foreign Affairs, Paris, Europe, 1944–…', *Generalities*, Vol. 110, pp. 109–111.
[29] Duchêne, op. cit., p. 271.

non-members. All this precipitated an internal battle between senior political figures of the 'Six', from which three options emerged. One, favoured by Erhard, was a broader free trade area, using the infrastructure of the intergovernmental OEEC. The second was Beyen's 'common market'. The third was Monnet's strategy of sector-by-sector integration.

Quite how this issue was resolved is not clear.[30] But on 18 May 1955, the Benelux foreign ministers jointly offered a document they called the 'Benelux Memorandum', linking the Beyen and Monnet strategies. For what became known as the *junktim*, they suggested a working group to draft treaties for a 'common market'.[31] It would embrace transport, energy – including nuclear – and social legislation.[32] Erhard's free-market views had been ignored.

The memorandum had been composed by Spaak, based on a draft prepared by himself and Monnet. After Spaak had amended Monnet's version, he sent it back with the note '*Ici votre bébé* ('Herewith your baby').' The most significant change from Monnet's original was the exclusion of the words 'United States of Europe'. Instead, Spaak had been careful to emphasise the idea of an 'economic community'.[33] So was the central deception established. Political integration was to be disguised as economic integration. Building 'Europe' was to be presented as a matter of trade and jobs.

MESSINA: A CLOSE-RUN THING
France was attracted to Euratom, which would facilitate control of Germany's nuclear industry. It might also assist in the as-yet undeclared objective of producing a French nuclear bomb. On the other hand, with the highest tariffs of the Six and many other protectionist rules, she was hostile to the common market. Nevertheless, she agreed to 'exploratory discussions' of the Benelux Memorandum, during planned talks on who should fill Monnet's vacated position as head of the ECSC. The Germans had considerable reservations as to whether to proceed at all.

The venue chosen was Messina, on 1–2 June 1955, in deference to Italy's foreign minister Gaetano Martino, who was facing an election in Sicily. A British representative was invited, but the location was

---

[30] Ibid., p. 274.

[31] European Parliament (2002), *The European Parliament and the Euratom Treaty: Past Present and Future* (Luxembourg: Directorate General for Research), Working Paper, Energy and Research Series, ENER 114EN, p. 9.

[32] Bruylant, E. (1987), *Pour Une Communauté Politique Européenne, Travaux Préparatoires – Tome II: 1955–1957* (Bruxelles: Paul-Henri Spaak Foundation), pp. 25–29.

[33] Monnet, op. cit., p. 403.

deemed too distant for what was, ostensibly, only a meeting of ECSC ministers. Beforehand, Monnet learned that the French were preparing to submerge the Memorandum in pious resolutions.[34] Conscious that his presence might inflame the situation, he decided to let Spaak chair the discussions. Even then, they went badly at first. Monnet was on the telephone constantly, seeking to instruct Spaak. Max Kohnstamm, the Dutch secretary to the High Authority, was eventually driven to tell his old boss: 'Please understand, they are not here to make Europe. They are here to bury you.'[35]

But late at night, Spaak had gone to the hotel room of the French foreign minister Pinay. By the early hours, some kind of agreement had been reached, enough for Spaak to order a bottle of champagne and greet the dawn with a rendition of 'O sole mio'.[36] That morning, ministers adopted a resolution incorporating much of the Benelux Memorandum, some of it word for word. However, this only committed the Six to study how to implement the Memorandum.[37] The future was far from certain. The French, for instance, had simply agreed 'not to oppose a continuation of talks'.[38] Luxembourg's representative, Joseph Bech, said the most significant thing about the meeting was its lack of any 'smell' of a High Authority, Schuman-style, to ruffle French concerns over sovereignty.[39] The deception was continuing.

A translation of the Messina communiqué was despatched to London by the British Embassy in Rome on 11 June. In an accompanying letter, assistant under-secretary John Coulson observed: 'it looks as though the Ministers had difficulty in reaching agreement on any specific action', adding:

> The Germans were keenly interested in transport, while Benelux wanted to expand the scope of the authority. The Italians went all out for a common market, while the French views were not clear. It is evident that the final communiqué went as far as possible to repeat the views of all the participants without taking any decisions of principle. It will be noticed that all the questions are to be 'studied', but there is no indication of how this is to be done.[40]

[34] Duchêne, op. cit., p. 280.
[35] Ibid.
[36] Duchêne, op. cit., p. 281.
[37] European Parliament, Selection of texts concerning institutional matters on the Community from 1950 to 1982. Luxembourg, Committee on Institutional Affairs. pp. 94–100.
[38] Duchêne, op. cit., p. 282.
[39] Young, op. cit., p. 81.
[40] National Archives. FO371/11640, pp. 7–9. Letter from J. E. Coulson Esq. to Ashley Clarke.

The Foreign Office, in fact, had considerable difficulty in finding out what had happened. In a letter to the new foreign secretary, Harold Macmillan, on 15 June, the UK Ambassador in Paris referred to the communiqué as 'lengthy but not very informative', suggesting that it had accurately reflected the vagueness of the conference. 'There is some evidence for the theory that the six Ministers were unable to get to real grips with the problems they discussed', he wrote, continuing:

> the Europeans are having to proceed very cautiously. Their opponents on the other hand, or many of them, do see advantages in some of the schemes now being considered. The practical differences between the two camps are therefore much narrower than the ideological differences. Therefore when M. Pinay says that the new schemes are to be supranational and the Gaullists say they are not, both sides are using contradictory words to express roughly the same issues. M. Boegner, when asked to explain M. Pinay's language, said that he might well be thinking of organisations which had powers of decision (and were therefore supranational) but whose decisions would be reached unanimously (and were therefore intergovernmental). I am aware that this is a quibble. But this sort of double talk does seem to keep the Europeans quiet and if it serves to quieten a largely useless quarrel it has some justification.[41]

Press coverage was meagre. The Italian newspaper, *Il Tempo*, described the communiqué as 'another unnecessary document' and *Le Monde* reported 'the governments have implicitly abandoned the idea of supranationality'.[42] Macmillan later observed 'the official view seemed to be a confident expectation that nothing would come out of Messina'.[43]

This was to reckon without Monnet. He was about to launch the 'Action Committee for the United States of Europe', with funding from the Ford Foundation, arranged by ACUE. It published its inaugural manifesto on 15 October 1955, the immediate objective being 'to ensure that the Messina resolution ... should be translated into a genuine step towards a United States of Europe'. An important adjunct was to give Monnet a 'permanent visiting card' to any head of government. This new platform would provide him:

[41] National Archives, FO371/116040, pp. 38–43. Letter from Gladwyn Jebb to Harold Macmillan, 15 June 1955.
[42] National Archives, Coulson, op. cit.
[43] Macmillan, Harold (1971), *Riding the Storm – 1956–1959* (London: Macmillan), p. 73.

with the advantage of being able to influence political élites directly without having to face the disadvantage of public scrutiny. Europe was being constructed by a remarkably small élite; while public support was welcomed, it was never a prerequisite for Monnet's Europe.[44]

And while Monnet worked in the shadows, Spaak was to bask in the limelight.

THE SPAAK COMMITTEE

The complex drama just beginning essentially involved two separate plots. One was the discussions in Brussels directed by Spaak, mainly conducted through the work of four 'preparatory' committees. The other centred on the response of Britain, still Europe's most powerful nation but not directly involved.

By this time the principal roles in the British government had changed. Churchill had retired, succeeded by Anthony Eden, who led his party to electoral victory in May 1955. Macmillan became foreign secretary. Eden's Cabinet considered the Six's invitation to join the talks just beginning in Brussels. Despite rejecting participation, it decided on 30 June to send Russell Bretherton, an under-secretary of the Board of Trade. Much would later be made that only a civil servant rather than a minister was sent, but only technical talks were involved.

When the talks began, Bretherton, under instructions from London, attempted to steer the Six towards a limited alternative, under the aegis of the OEEC, warning that there was much duplication of the OEEC's work. This, Spaak dismissed. It 'offered no prospect of a European political union'.[45]

OEEC representatives were also present. Alarmed at the way the meetings were being handled, the head of its UK delegation, Hugh Ellis-Rees, complained to Macmillan that warnings of a conflict with the OEEC's work had not been heeded. The Secretary General has been made to feel most unwelcome, he wrote, and: 'All the evidence here suggests that the OEEC's position will not be considered.'[46] His seven-page letter gave numerous examples of how the committee's objectives might duplicate the OEEC's work or cut across it, suggesting 'political' objectives. French and German representatives had no 'object in view' other than European integration.[47]

---

[44] Holland, Martin (1993), *European Integration: From Community to Union* (London: Pinter Publishers), p. 9.
[45] Spaak, op. cit., p. 236.
[46] National Archives, T 232/433, 11 October 1955, pp. 49–55.
[47] Ibid.

Spaak confirmed these suspicions, writing: 'we realised the political implications of our goal and knew that what we were about to achieve was nothing short of a revolution'.[48] Yet it was clear the British were not alone in their concerns. German finance minister, Hans Schäffer, took the view that:

> partial or functional integration in the style of the Iron and Steel Community [sic] should not go further, since it was necessarily bound up with supranational authorities. Instead, one should aim for a gradual process towards full integration, making progress, if possible, on many subjects but in every case by co-operation between governments and without developing any further supra-national authorities.[49]

The note added that it was not possible to judge what sort of agreement was likely on the common market. There were clear 'signs of conflicting interests':

> The Germans, who have been very active in Brussels in supporting the movements towards further integration, have nevertheless been unwilling to make many concessions in the field of agriculture, which, of course, must be a matter of prime concern to the Dutch and the French. There are also signs that the French will be extremely reluctant to go very far very fast in the direction of true integration through dismantling of tariffs ... and may try to create a diversion by suggesting integration in particular sectors, notably in transport, energy and the development of atomic energy.[50]

In parallel with the common market talks, details of an 'Atomic Community' were being discussed, and it emerged that the new organisation would require all fissile materials, including supplies of uranium, to be placed in a common 'European pool' under Euratom's full control and ownership. The intention was to limit military use, a restriction wholly unacceptable to Britain as Europe's only nuclear power. On 7 September 1955, therefore, she withdrew from the Euratom talks. Spaak was formally notified in a letter from the British Ambassador in Brussels, George Labouchère. The UK government recognised 'the strong impetus towards multilateral co-operation in Europe', he wrote, but Britain's civil and military nuclear

---

[48] Spaak, op. cit., pp. 230–231.
[49] National Archives, T 232/433, 10 October 1955, pp. 2–4.
[50] Ibid.

programmes were so closely integrated that there would be 'overriding difficulties in the defence field'.[51]

As discussions ground on, Spaak laid out his plan for the final stages of the preparatory committees' activities. In late October, there would be a meeting of delegations to hear reports from the committees, restricted to the Six. A small drafting group would then write the final report, from which Britain would be excluded. Her presence 'might in some way act as a brake on the others'.[52] But there would be an open meeting of the full steering committee, held on 7 November 1955, to which Britain was invited. There, reflecting the inevitable, Bretherton announced Britain' withdrawal from the common market talks.

This is echoed by a Treasury memorandum dated 17 November 1955, which recording notes of a meeting with Spaak. It stated 'we cannot join Euratom' and then observed *vis-à-vis* British membership of the common market that, until Spaak had produced his report, 'it would be impolitic for us to take a formal position'. It concluded: 'It would indeed be a major reversal of UK policy to say that we should join a common market and the Europeans would be very surprised if we did.'[53]

The departure of the UK subsequently became a legendary episode in the history of Britain's relations with 'Europe', subject to bizarre claims that Bretherton had walked out after delivering a declamatory speech.[54] Nevertheless, there is no documentary evidence that anything so exciting occurred.[55] Furthermore, the British departure was expected. Spaak is said to have commented that some governments could not understand the new context for European integration created by the Messina Conference, but separation would be peaceful – as long as Britain refrained from torpedoing the Messina initiative.[56] In fact, Britain made clear her wish to continue with co-operation. On nuclear power, Spaak was told that the UK was fully prepared to conclude a separate agreement with the European organisation.[57]

In October 1955, the UK Atomic Energy Authority had already proposed an Anglo-German joint civil nuclear programme and, largely at the behest

---

[51] National Archives, FO 371/116054, pp. 61–63.
[52] National Archives, T 232/433, 14 October 1955, pp. 56–57.
[53] National Archives, T 234/181, 17 November 1955.
[54] See, for instance: Denman, Roy, op. cit., p. 199; and Grant, Charles (1994), *Delors: Inside The House That Jacques Built* (London: Nicholas Brearley), p. 62.
[55] Young, op. cit., p. 93.
[56] Kaiser, Wolfram (1996), *Using Europe, Abusing the Europeans: Britain and European Integration, 1945–63* (London: Macmillan Press), p. 47.
[57] National Archives, FO 371/116054.

of Britain, the OEEC had set up a working party on the possibilities of wider nuclear co-operation. Labouchère stated that this body:

> seems likely to recommend a flexible system of multilateral co-operation ... the working party may well propose that within the organisation there should be room for agreement on specific projects or for specific purposes between groups of countries which would be neither binding on other countries in the organisation nor subject to their veto. Under such a scheme the countries more advanced in atomic energy could co-operate closely on joint research projects ...

The working party reported in December.[58] It advocated the establishment of an OEEC directorate for nuclear energy, to co-ordinate national research and prepare joint projects. A key proposal was to build a plant to give Europe self-sufficiency in enriched uranium. But this was to be an intergovernmental venture, as opposed to Monnet's supranational plan and, although welcomed by Erhard, it created a crisis for Spaak. The combination of Britain's departure, the OEEC proposals and splits in the German delegation put not only the Messina agenda at risk but also Monnet's supranational ambitions.

Nothing better illustrates the gulf between intergovernmentalism and supranationalism than Monnet's response. Instead of welcoming Britain's generous offer, he called on his 'Action Committee' in January 1956 to emphasise the supranational nature of Euratom and call on the parliaments of the Six to give it their support. Adenauer also intervened. Unlike Erhard, he strongly favoured the customs union aspect of the common market. Less keen on Euratom, he saw this as necessary to gain French support for the market. To counter the opposition of Erhard and others, he, on 19 January, demanded from all his ministers 'a clear, positive attitude to European integration', stating that the Messina resolution had to be implemented without alteration and delay.[59]

On Monnet's advice, the US had kept a friendly distance from Euratom, to avoid upsetting the French government. But, on 22 February 1956, at Monnet's request, President Eisenhower announced that the US would release 20 tons of enriched uranium (equivalent to 40 million tons of coal) for peaceful use by friendly states. It would be offered on more preferential terms to Euratom than to any individual state, as long as it had 'effective communal

[58] Nelsen G. R. (1958), *European Organisation in the Field of Atomic Energy* (European Yearbook IV), pp. 36–54.
[59] Schwartz, H. (1997), *Konrad Adenauer: German Politician and Statesman in a Period of War, Revolution and Reconstruction*, Vol. 2: *The Statesman, 1952–1967* (Oxford: Berghahn), p. 231.

authority and could undertake duties and responsibilities similar to that [sic] of national governments'.[60] Again America had backed supranationalism.

Even in Washington, though, signs of division were appearing: there was now more enthusiasm for European integration in the State Department than among US economic policy-makers, who feared the new common market might discriminate against imports from the dollar area.[61] Yet, for the moment, Monnet's supporters continued to prevail.

FRANCO-GERMAN MUSICAL CHAIRS

Through the first ten months of 1956, the two main players in the drama, France and Germany, lumbered through elaborate shifts of policy, ending in each reversing the positions they held at the start of the year. The resultant impasse threatened to bring the whole process to a halt.

The year began with a major upset in French domestic politics when the Gaullists lost 100 of their 120 seats in the Assembly and most of their influence. The new Socialist prime minister, Guy Mollet, was a committed supranationalist, having been president of the Council of Europe assembly, a delegate to the ECSC assembly and an active member of Monnet's Action Committee. His foreign minister, Christian Pineau, was of like mind. Despite this, the new French government, also preoccupied with the rebellion in Algeria, still believed it would have difficulty selling a common market to its public. On 7 February, Pineau told the American Ambassador that it would not be possible 'without a great deal of education in France'.[62] The pair therefore agreed that the two 'communities' should be separated, allowing Euratom to proceed. This, they thought, would better serve French interests. Germany, however, although still unenthusiastic about Euratom, favoured the common market.

On 21 April, the Spaak Committee finally published its report.[63] Running to 84 pages on the common market and 24 on Euratom, it largely followed the lines of the Messina resolution. Crucially, the elements of Euratom that would have made British acceptance impossible remained. At Monnet's insistence, in the wake of the EDC debacle, the report made no mention of a 'High Authority', or 'supranational'.[64] It proposed that the new authority

[60] Goldschmidt, B. (1982), *The Atomic Complex: A Worldwide Political History of Nuclear Energy* (Grange Park, Illinois: American Nuclear Society), pp. 293–294.
[61] National Archives, FO 371/116054, pp. 83–84. Letter from J. H. A. Watson, British Embassy, Washington, to A. J. Edden, Mutual Aid Department, Foreign Office, London, 10 November 1955.
[62] Duchêne, op. cit., p. 290.
[63] Intergovernmental Committee created by the Messina Conference, *Report of the Heads of Delegation to the Foreign Ministers* (Brussels: Secretariat), 21 April 1956, pp. 9–135.
[64] Duchêne, op. cit., p. 257.

should be given the more neutral title of 'commission'. According to Miriam Camps, a former State Department analyst:

> great care had been taken to present proposals which could be accepted by the French government without, at the same time, abandoning any of the points of principle to which the 'Europeans' attached real importance. Words and phrases such as 'supranationalism', which in the post-EDC atmosphere were certain to generate unfavourable emotional responses, were abandoned in favour of phrases that were neutral emotionally and logically defensible. Thus, on the most difficult aspect of them all, that of institutions, the Benelux memorandum side-stepped the acrimonious 'intergovernmental-supranational' argument but, at the same time, firmly established the central point, that is, that an institution endowed with real power would be required.[65]

One highly significant new element in the package, added on French insistence, was a common agricultural policy. 'One cannot conceive the establishment of a general Common Market in Europe', said the report, 'without agriculture being included.' The rationale was that farming still accounted for a quarter of France's workforce and was over-represented in parliament.[66] A policy offering farmers new outlets for their increasing surpluses of grain and sugar beet might be vital.

Nevertheless, France remained opposed to a common market in principle. Her government thus pushed for the two treaties to be 'decoupled', hoping that the common market negotiations could stagnate. Germany would not agree. On 9 May, Adenauer's Cabinet confirmed that the two treaties must be linked.[67] At a foreign ministers' meeting in Venice at the end of May, the Germans, with Italy and Benelux, reiterated that the treaties were interdependent and must be negotiated together. The *junktim* became a central feature of the talks, with the reluctant agreement of the French.[68]

France then insisted on another 'linkage' – between the reduction of tariffs in a common market and the harmonisation of social costs: overtime, length of paid holidays, equal pay for men and women.[69] Pineau further proposed that the treaty's scope should be extended to member

[65] Camps, Miriam (1964), *Britain and the European Community 1955–1963* (London: Oxford University Press), p. 66.
[66] Duchêne, op. cit., p. 291.
[67] Stirk, Peter M. R. (1996), *A History of European Integration Since 1914* (London: Pinter), p. 142.
[68] Camps, op. cit., p. 66.
[69] Ibid., p. 65.

states' overseas territories. These proposals seemed calculated to provoke disagreement. It was an early example of a French negotiating tactic that was to become only too familiar in the decades ahead whereby, if France wanted to stop something – in this case the common market – it would make demands it knew to be unacceptable.

These would provoke a breakdown of negotiations, for which others could be blamed. Nevertheless, the foreign ministers agreed to start the negotiations. They would be held at the Château Val-Duchesse near Brussels, and Spaak's report would provide the basis for discussion. In the record of these discussions, Euratom tends to get glossed over. But, as a study by the European Parliament put it:

> This neglect is unwarranted. Its tactical pairing with the EEC was a crucial factor in initially persuading and eventually convincing a sceptical French government to engage with European integration after the embittering experience of the aborted European defence community ... At the time, in 1955 and early 1956, however, it was widely believed in many quarters that the Euratom proposal held the greater promise of success, while the EEC negotiations faltered.[70]

Yet it was the Euratom talks that got bogged down, mainly over fears that it would halt the French military nuclear programme. This prospect so angered France's nationalists that Euratom looked destined to follow the EDC.[71] By early July, therefore, Mollet was forced to reassure the National Assembly that Euratom would not block French nuclear ambitions. But a favourable vote strengthened a growing lobby against Euratom in Germany, which now believed it could allow France to restrict Germany's own nuclear ambitions. This supposed discrimination put ratification by the Bundestag at risk.[72]

The German situation was complex. In June, rumours that Soviet leaders would be invited to Washington DC by Eisenhower had fuelled German fears of a US–Soviet détente, the neutralisation of West Germany and the withdrawal of American troops from Europe. On 13 July, the *New York Times* revealed a plan to replace 800,000 US forces in Europe with tactical nuclear weapons. Adenauer, already nervous about American intentions, had become determined that Germany should have its own 'nukes'. Despite the opposition of some of his Cabinet, led by Erhard, he welcomed Euratom as a means of acquiring them.

[70] Directorate General for Research, op. cit., p. vii.
[71] Duchêne, op. cit., p. 295.
[72] Ibid., p. 297.

To Adenauer's frustration, the majority of his Cabinet supported Erhard's wish for a wider free trade association rather than a customs union. Erhard was now a highly respected figure, identified with his country's *Wirtschaftwunder* (economic miracle). Adenauer, therefore, had to make tactical concessions. He retreated from Monnet's 'common market' concept in favour of Erhard's preference. Perversely, Monnet was also trying to ditch the idea. At a meeting in Bonn on 12 September, he told Adenauer that the French Parliament might not accept it. Therefore, on 20 September, he instructed his Action Committee to call for Euratom's ratification by the end of the year, ahead of any treaty on the common market.[73]

On 5 October, however, Adenauer muddied the waters, telling his Cabinet that Euratom would allow West Germany access to nuclear technology, but the only way to get Euratom was to agree to Erhard's free trade area.[74] Almost simultaneously, though, the French were rooting for a full customs union, after the leaders of France's farmers and key French industrialists had come out in favour of one. But they demanded a price. If high social welfare standards were to be imposed on employers, as France had originally suggested as a 'wrecking' tactic, they must be 'harmonised' throughout the new 'community', to avoid the other five member states, especially Germany, gaining a competitive advantage. Predictably, this was entirely unacceptable to the Erhard faction.

Thus, from the beginning of the year, the two main players had almost wholly reversed their positions. The ensuing crisis was so serious that, at a meeting of the foreign minister of the Six in Paris on 19–20 October, no way forward could be found. Euratom looked doomed. With an impasse on the harmonisation of social policies, it seemed the common market would follow. Erhard, for one, was confident that the 'distasteful common market project' was dying.[75] At that very moment, however, great events would come to the rescue. Ironically, the country to put it firmly back on the rails was Great Britain.

BRITAIN'S 'DESTRUCTIVE EMBRACE'
Despite Britain's seemingly confident refusal to get drawn into any supranational experiments, some in her government were becoming alarmed that a successful 'customs union' of the Six, based on common tariffs, might be used to exclude British trade.

Following the collapse of the attempts to set up 'Defence' and 'Political' Communities, it had not been unrealistic for the British government to believe that the Messina initiatives would fail. The French Fourth Republic

[73] Ibid.
[74] Williams, op. cit., pp. 439–440.
[75] Schwartz, op. cit., p. 240.

was already a byword for political and economic instability, with 20 changes of government in ten years. The value of the franc was plummeting. There was the humiliating failure in Indochina and the running sore of Algeria. In Germany, Adenauer and Erhard were at loggerheads.

Furthermore, following the failure of the EDC, Eden had brought off his triumphant intergovernmental solution with the WEU, enthusiastically accepted by the Six. If the Euratom and common market negotiations failed, there was no reason to believe that British alternatives, based on intergovernmental structures, might not also be accepted. Nevertheless, the British government had given serious thought to membership of a common market, having in June 1955 asked a working group under a senior Treasury civil servant, Burke Trend, to assess its advantages and disadvantages. The group's findings, submitted in October 1955, reflected the dominant British view that a free trade area was preferable to a customs union. Only this option allowed Britain to retain national autonomy in foreign trade policy and to safeguard its Commonwealth preferences.

Conscious of the danger of British exclusion from a 'customs union', the report suggested that 'the disadvantages of abstaining would, in the long run, outweigh the advantages'.[76] The Foreign Office batted this aside: membership would be incompatible with Britain's role as a world power.[77] But it also believed that, as with the EDC, the Messina initiative would founder through French obstruction.[78]

Macmillan accepted the Foreign Office view. But in the autumn of 1955, with the prospect of a more 'Europe-friendly' regime in France, there seemed an increasing chance of a common market succeeding. Civil servants of the economic ministries became more concerned about the dangers of exclusion from 'Europe'. In October 1955, just as the Spaak talks were drawing to a close, it was agreed they could no longer 'count on the project collapsing of its own accord'. It should therefore, if possible, be 'frustrated'.[79]

To spearhead this change of policy from 'benign neglect', a diplomatic offensive was to be launched, intending to divert the Six into the orbit of the OEEC, where the British government could dilute their plans into something more intergovernmental. The term given to this strategy was 'destructive embrace', taken from a note appended to a memorandum by Gladwyn Jebb, Britain's Ambassador to France.[80] To that effect, Macmillan

[76] National Archives, CAB 134/1030/201, 24 October 1955.
[77] National Archives, CAB 134/1030/200, 24 October 1955.
[78] National Archives, CAB 134/889, 17 October 1955.
[79] National Archives, CAB 134/1026, 27 October 1955.
[80] Harold Macmillan Archives. Quoted in Horne, op. cit., p. 363. Gladwyn Jebb appended to a brief on the Common Market the words 'embrace destructively'.

wrote to the US and German governments, stressing British displeasure with the Messina initiative and particularly the plan for a customs union. On 14 December 1955, while he was on a visit to Paris to attend a WEU ministerial council and then a North Atlantic Council meeting, Macmillan was still convinced the Messina initiative would fail.[81]

Inevitably, Macmillan was roundly attacked by the Six, led by Spaak. Nobody had expected British participation, he said, but neither had they foreseen a frontal assault.[82] When, on 12 December, Secretary of State Dulles affirmed support for the Europeans, Macmillan aborted his offensive. British embassies were instructed to back the common market, to avoid conflict with Washington.[83] All this 'attempted sabotage' had achieved was 'the creation of justified suspicion among the Six as to the British motives in Western Europe ... and to raise among the Six the traditional unpleasant spectre of perfidious Albion'.[84]

On 21 December 1955, Macmillan was, somewhat unwillingly, transferred to the Treasury, although he kept some control of the European agenda. By then he was seriously worried that the common market might succeed.[85] Despite the failure of his 'destructive embrace', therefore, he again attempted to regain the diplomatic initiative. In the spring of 1956, a working group was set up to explore options, chaired by Richard Clarke, number three in the Treasury. It produced seven plans: A to G. Plan G was chosen, a free trade area (FTA) for manufactured goods only.[86] Parliament was told what was happening in July 1956 and, on the European front, approaches were made to the OEEC. Its Council set up a working party to study possibilities for association with the Six, including a Europe-wide free trade area.

The European reaction was broadly sympathetic. Erhard was enthusiastic about something closer to his own ideas than any *dirigiste* common market. Macmillan reported that Washington was 'surprisingly positive'. Even Commonwealth leaders were not hostile, seeing in it an opportunity for increased trade with Europe. Duchêne conceded that it was 'a genuine attempt to adapt British interests to the Common Market'.[87]

Work on 'Plan G' continued through the summer and, to minimise the institutionalisation involved, it was proposed that the FTA be integrated into the existing structures of the OEEC. Formal OEEC negotiations were launched

[81] Harold Macmillan diaries. Quoted in Horne, op. cit., p. 362.
[82] National Archives, FO 371/116057/384, 15 December 1955.
[83] National Archives, FO 371/116057/390, 31 December 1955.
[84] Kaiser, op. cit., p. 53.
[85] National Archives, T 234/100, 1 February 1956, Macmillan to Sir E. Bridges.
[86] National Archives, BT 11/5715, 10 May 1956.
[87] Duchêne, op. cit., p. 320.

in Paris in October 1956. By that time, common market negotiations looked irretrievably stalled. Erhard was confidently predicting the death of the idea. The Six were in disarray. At that moment, the great events intervened.

SUEZ: THE WATERSHED

On 26 July 1956, Egypt's new leader Colonel Nasser had nationalised the Suez Canal, removing it from its Anglo-French owners. Amid a crisis atmosphere, Britain and France assembled a military task force to recover it. To avoid it being seen as an act of 'colonialist aggression' by the international community, including the US, a ruse was devised. On 23 October, in great secrecy, Eden – now prime minister – sent his foreign secretary to rendezvous in a French villa at Sèvres with Mollet, Pinay, Israel's prime minister Ben Gurion and his chief of staff, General Dayan. Between them they hatched a plan. Israel would invade Egypt. Anglo-French forces would then 'intervene' to separate the combatants. While there, they could reclaim the Canal and Nasser would be toppled.

As planned, on 29 October Israel invaded Egypt, but the deception failed. When Britain and France issued their ultimatum, demanding a ceasefire, it provoked a storm of international protest, only complicated by a crisis over the Soviet Union's invasion of Hungary. This explosive situation convinced Adenauer more than ever that Germany must have nuclear weapons. In Cabinet on 31 October, he put to Erhard that Euratom was now vital to West Germany's security interests. He then added that the only way this treaty could be agreed was if Germany accepted the common market. As Soviet tanks rolled into Budapest, he invoked his constitutional right as chancellor to make policy on matters of national interest, bludgeoning his Cabinet into agreeing that he should go to Paris to negotiate, on his own terms, a final settlement on both Euratom and the common market.[88]

Through one of those accidents of history, Adenauer was on the overnight train to Paris as the news broke of the Anglo-French landings. When he arrived in the early hours of 6 November, he found half the French Cabinet waiting for him at the station. He immediately gave his unconditional approval to the action. As that day unfolded, however, the British had to confront massive selling of sterling, leading to a collapse in her currency reserves. Washington was furious at Britain and so were the Soviets. Prime minister Nikolai Bulganin threatened to shower London and Paris with nuclear missiles. Unilaterally, Eden decided to abort the action. To a furious Mollet, Adenauer suggested: 'make Europe your revenge'. Monnet mooted, only half-jokingly, that a statue should be erected to Nasser, 'the federator of Europe'.[89]

[88] Williams, op. cit., p. 441.
[89] Monnet, op. cit., p. 422.

Progress was now rapid. The contentious issue of social harmonisation became a mere trifle when Adenauer agreed 'in principle' to the French demands. On 24 January 1957, the Germans also agreed to exclude military installations from Euratom control, clearing the way for the French nuclear weapons programme. Adenaur had already satisfied his nuclear ambitions when, in December, a NATO military committee had stipulated that 12 *Heer* divisions could be equipped with US-supplied nuclear weapons.[90]

However, the way for the common market was still not entirely open. Two more issues had to be resolved: overseas territories and the decision-making mechanisms. The key was the overseas territories question. Bled dry by wars in Indochina and Algeria, France could not afford vital modernisation programmes in its territories without German money. Post-Suez, Adenauer was willing to contribute nearly half the needed funds.[91] Final agreement was reached in February, when any restrictions on the use of fissile material supplied by Euratom were removed.

The Euratom and Common Market treaties were signed by representatives of the Six on 25 March 1957, at a venue carefully chosen for its symbolic significance: the Capitol in Rome, the city which for two thousand years under the Roman Empire and the Papacy had stood at the centre of European history. Monnet was not invited for the signing.

The recitals of what was to become known as the Treaty of Rome opened with the 'High Contracting Parties' determined to 'lay the foundations of an ever-closer union among the peoples of Europe'. The text was not so much a treaty as a constitution, defining the institutions of a new type of government. It centred on a European Commission, a combined executive and civil service that alone had the right to initiate legislation. Alongside was a 'Council of Ministers', representing member state governments; an 'Assembly', made up of delegates from their national parliaments; and a 'European Court of Justice'. Salter's structure had survived intact. Crucially, national vetoes had been heavily circumscribed.

Both the Bundestag and the Assemblée Nationale ratified the treaties in the first week of July. Mendès-France voted against. When Italy ratified in the following December – the last to do so – the 'European Economic Community' was finally born. But it had been a close-run thing.

---

[90] Williams, op. cit., p. 442.
[91] Stirk, op. cit., p. 145. He cites: *Küsters, Fondements de la Communauté économique européen*, pp. 257–268.

4

'A Triumph for Monnet': 1958–1961

Great Britain has lost an empire and not yet found a role.
Dean Acheson, speech to West Point Military
Academy, 5 December 1962

No matter how much Macmillan privately asserted that entry into Europe was an act with wide-ranging political consequences, he presented it to the British people as an economic move dictated by commercial imperatives.
George Ball, The Past Has Another Pattern[1]

The first declared aim of the new European Economic Community was to establish among its six members a common market, based on what were known as the 'four freedoms': the freedom of movement, within its boundaries, of goods, services, people and capital – four principles that were to become the central tenet of the entire project. But this new 'internal market', behind tariff walls to protect its interests against the outside world, was never intended to be a 'free trade area'. The four 'freedoms' would be enforced internally by an ever more extensive system of regulation.

Behind these declared principles, what had been set up by the Treaty of Rome was never regarded by its founders as anything other than an embryonic government of Europe. Their ultimate goal was full political integration. The means by which this would be achieved, drawing inspiration from the tactics already pioneered by Monnet and Spaak, came to be known as *engrénage*, or 'gearing'. But it was also a rachet. Powers ceded to the supranational authority were never returned.

[1] Ball, op. cit., p. 217.

Engrénage would be applied through three main strategies. The first was to use the powers ceded through the treaty to make laws, reinforced by the judgements of the new European Court of Justice. This was crucially important, because each time a power or 'competence' agreed in the treaties was exercised in passing a new law or regulation, that policy area would pass from nation states to the supranational authority. The second strategy would be to pressure national governments into extending the integration process into areas not covered by the Rome Treaty. The third, in due course, would be 'enlargement', whereby the Community would seek to widen its membership from the original Six, by taking new nations into its fold.

During its first dozen years of existence, all these strategies would be called into play. But the first task was simply to get 'Europe's' new 'government' established and on its way.

BUILDING A GOVERNMENT

According to one historian, the governing bodies of the new 'Economic Community' started work in Brussels on New Year's Day 1958.[2] This hardly seems likely, and not just because it was a bank holiday. In what was to become a characteristic of the Community's decision-making process, the foreign ministers of the Six, meeting in Paris on 20 December, had failed to reach an agreement on nominations for the key post of president of the Commission and had adjourned their meeting. By the time ministers reconvened on 6 January, they had decided on Walter Hallstein, the law professor who had been West Germany's foreign minister.[3] His priority was to turn the Commission, comprising nine members, into an executive body that would 'breathe economic and political life into the product of the Treaty authors'.[4]

The choice of Brussels as headquarters was accidental. Monnet had hoped for a single site on the lines of the USA's District of Columbia. Giving 'Europe' its own capital would make it tangible and real to people. One idea was Compiègne, near Paris, where the 1918 armistice had been signed, and where Hitler humiliated the French government in 1940. In the event, Luxembourg's foreign minister partly decided the issue. He insisted that ECSC staff stay in his country while refusing to accept any more Eurocrats

---

[2] Duchêne, op. cit., p. 309.

[3] Hallstein had been Adenauer's representative at the Schuman Plan talks. He was the second German to hold a senior international post after the war, following the appointment of General Hans Spiedel as commander of NATO land forces in Europe in 1957.

[4] Narjes, K. H. (1998), 'Walter Hallstein and the Early Phase of the EEC', in Wilfried Loth, *et al.*, *Walter Hallstein: The Forgotten European?* (London: Macmillan Press), p. 109. Each country had one Commissioner, plus a second for each of the three largest states – France, Germany and Italy.

apart from the new European Court of Justice. Brussels ended up as a 'provisional' site for the rest. In the manner of things, 'provisional' was to become permanent.

Initially, the Commission was financed by a loan from the High Authority of the ECSC, which gave it freedom to develop its own agenda. Briefs to individual Commissioners were allocated in ten weeks, the key agricultural portfolio going to a Dutchman, Sicco Mansholt. A crude organisational structure emerged three weeks later and, by the end of 1958, a thousand officials were at work. Hallstein was very much in charge, insisting on the right to choose his own staff. He enjoyed the trappings of power, receiving emissaries from foreign governments in royal style. One visiting American, Clarence Randall, was heard to complain that Hallstein's officials were 'getting a little stuffy', addressing each other as 'Your excellency'.[5]

One problem was the demand for support staff for the Council of Ministers – not foreseen in the treaties. On 26 January 1958, therefore, the Six decided to create the Committee of Permanent Representatives (Coreper) to prepare the work of the Councils. This body was soon a powerful Brussels institution, examining and discussing Commission proposals and preparing decisions. Initially, its meetings absorbed much of Hallstein's time until he was able to delegate this work to his own directors-general. The bureaucracy had developed a life of its own.

Then there was the language problem. It had been agreed that the languages of the member states should be used, although the Commission had refused to treat Dutch and Flemish as separate languages. The very first Council regulation, on 15 April 1958, established French, German, Italian and Dutch as the official languages. French soon became dominant. But this multilingual approach came at a price. Translation accounted for about 30 per cent of the entire staff expenditure.[6]

On 19 March 1958, the 142-member European Assembly, made up of delegates from national parliaments, convened for the first time, electing Robert Schuman as its president. Lacking its own base, it used the Council of Europe building in Strasbourg.[7] During those early days of the EEC, Monnet avoided direct involvement in its affairs. But he was far from idle. Through his Action Committee, he searched for ways to extend the scope

[5] Winand, Pascaline (1993), *Eisenhower, Kennedy and The United States of Europe* (New York: St Martin's Press), p. 130.

[6] Narjes, op. cit., p. 112.

[7] Another 'Community institution' launched at the same time was the European Investment Bank (EIB). Drawing on substantial funds guaranteed by member state governments, this was set up to provide low-interest loans to a vast range of projects that might serve the purposes of 'integration'.

of his 'Communities', in pursuit of his 'United States of Europe'. One idea that particularly excited him was monetary union. The trigger for his interest had been France's continuing financial crisis, and the plummeting value of the franc, exacerbated by the Algerian war. As always, the solution had to be within a 'European framework'. 'Via money', as Monnet had put it in September 1957, 'Europe could become political in five years.'[8] The following year he wrote to a Dutch politician, suggesting that: 'the current communities should be completed by a Finance Common Market which would lead us to European economic unity. Only then would ... the mutual commitments make it fairly easy to produce the political union which is the goal.'[9]

Monnet had already suggested a common financial policy to one of France's many prime ministers of the period, Félix Gaillard, yet another of his former assistants from 1945. But Gaillard was to last only five months in office, so no progress was made. Monnet was undismayed. 'There are no premature ideas', he wrote. 'There are only opportunities for which one must learn to wait.'[10]

He would have to wait a little longer. The Fourth Republic was in its death throes, torn apart by insurrection in Algeria. On 1 June 1958, in a legal *coup d'état*, brought on by rumours of a deal with the Algerian independence movement, de Gaulle returned to power.[11] By Christmas, he had imposed a series of crisis measures, one of which was to convert every 100 francs (then standing at 1,300 to £1) into one. The psychological boost given by the 'New Franc' and other measures transformed France's economy with remarkable speed. By this time, Monnet had already found another focus for his energies. With his 'supranational government' in place, he felt the need to tackle the only major power in Europe that he thought could pose a threat to it, with its unrepentant belief in 'intergovernmentalism'. He wanted to solve the 'problem' of Britain.

THE SUPRANATIONALISTS' REVENGE

The political disaster of Suez had dealt Britain's self-confidence a shattering blow, fatally weakening Eden, who resigned, pleading ill-health, to be succeeded on 10 January 1957 by Macmillan. By the time the new prime minister was able to refocus on European affairs, the situation had changed irretrievably. Britain's prestige had been badly damaged and

[8] Duchêne, op. cit., p. 312.
[9] Ibid.
[10] Monnet, op. cit., p. 428.
[11] *Hansard*, House of Lords, 2 August 1962, col. 430.

the reorientation of European politics was well advanced. This was not immediately appreciated by Macmillan, who later conceded that he failed to recognise the depth of Franco-German reconciliation.[12]

Despite this, he did make adjustments. With the Common Market and Euratom now looking inevitable, the OEEC had been asked to research options available for Britain's proposed Free Trade Area. In late January, a working party reported that such an area would be technically feasible, including the Six as a single bloc. Thus, Macmillan, previously having seen the FTA as an alternative to the Common Market, began to think of it as a 'trade roof' over all the OEEC countries, including EEC members.

After the signing of the Rome treaties, however, Britain's FTA was viewed by the Six without enthusiasm. London therefore offered substantial concessions, not least in allowing the 'supranational' principle of 'majority voting'. Then, in October 1957, the other OEEC members agreed to set up an intergovernmental committee to develop the project further. However, suspicion of the British verged on paranoia and, by February 1958, the French were demanding wholly unacceptable conditions, not least that Britain end its preferential trading agreements with the Commonwealth.[13]

With the accession of de Gaulle, things got worse. While Erhard had sympathised with the idea of a free trade area, de Gaulle brokered a 'non-intervention' deal with Adenauer, as a result of which, on 14 November, France was able to reject the British plan.[14] The Times thundered 'France the Wrecker', but to no avail. The initiative had collapsed.

The collapse rocked British industry. Leaders of the Federation of British Industries (later to become the Confederation of British Industry or CBI) feared they might also be excluded from a second customs union taking shape in Scandinavia. They called on the government to set up a separate European Free Trade Association (EFTA). A plan was rapidly conceived, creating what became known as the 'outer seven', with a format remarkably similar to the abortive 'Plan G'. Negotiations were wrapped up by November 1959, with the initialling of the Stockholm Convention. Great Britain, Denmark, Sweden, Norway, Austria, Portugal and Switzerland had their own free trade association. Europe was now, literally, at sixes and sevens.

Meanwhile, Monnet turned his attention to his remaining rival, the OEEC: the jewel in the crown of European intergovernmentalism. As long as it existed, under British chairmanship, it could provide a rallying point for further dissident schemes. It had to be destroyed. Monnet set about this task

[12] Horne, op. cit., p. 364.
[13] Duchêne, op. cit., p. 321.
[14] Wallace, William, 'Walter Hallstein: The British Perspective', in Loth, et al., op. cit., p. 189.

in his usual meticulous and devious way, devising as neat an assassination as can be imagined.[15] For a start, Monnet used Hallstein to draft a paper on the EEC's policy on external economic relations, stating that there should be no 'regional' association with the FTA. Instead, the EEC should treat all non-member groups and countries on an equal basis, thereby enabling members to be played off against each other, minimising the chances of Britain mobilising yet another coalition against the Common Market. The Council of Ministers adopted the paper on 16 March 1959.

On 27 May, Monnet was in Washington to attend the funeral of his old friend John Foster Dulles. He took the opportunity to see another friend, Douglas Dillon, now Under-Secretary of State for Economic Affairs.[16] Next day he lunched with Eisenhower. Back in Paris on 9 June, he had a long talk with John Tuthill, economics minister at the US embassy. The ground had been prepared. What Monnet had in mind was a 'reform' of the OEEC, by which he meant its neutralisation or abolition. To dilute Britain's influence, he suggested to Tuthill that the US and Canada should become full members, upgrading from their 'associate' status.[17] Then, in his own version of 'shuttle diplomacy', Monnet crossed the Atlantic again, to give Dillon a paper entitled *A New Era in Atlantic Relations*. In July he learned that the US and Canada would join the OEEC. Back in Paris, Monnet saw Tuthill again, this time with a plan to replace the 'discredited' OEEC altogether.

On 27 July, Monnet handed a revised version of his original paper to Pinay, now finance minister, omitting any reference to the OEEC. He simply proposed an organisation for 'permanent consultations', including the Common Market, the US and Great Britain. True to form, he chose proxies for his idea, suggesting that this proposal be put jointly by de Gaulle and Adenauer. In December everything came together. Dillon arrived in Europe for a North Atlantic Council meeting. While in Europe, he 'informed himself' first-hand of current thinking on European trade.[18] The impression gained in London was that he was 'cool to an OEEC-wide free trade area', and 'becoming increasingly concerned at the prospect of friction between the two European groups'.[19] However, he seemed to have agreed with British officials that the OEEC 'was the right forum for discussions on European trade', although, without knowing the background, Camps wrote: 'it seems

---

[15] Reconstructed from Duchêne, op. cit., pp. 321–323, with additional detail from Camps. Despite his detailed account of this episode, Duchêne does not seem fully to have appreciated the wider significance of what he had uncovered.

[16] Dillon had been US Ambassador to France in 1956 when Monnet first met him.

[17] Duchêne, p. 321.

[18] Camps, op. cit., p. 241.

[19] Ibid.

clear that the Commission of the Community, M. Monnet, and the French government all made it plain during his subsequent discussions with them that they disliked the OEEC as a forum, particularly as a forum for the discussion of European trade questions'.[20]

Coincidentally, the leaders of the four Western powers – Eisenhower, de Gaulle, Adenauer and Macmillan – held a summit in Paris on 19–21 December 1959, at the end of a NATO council. Unknown to most parties, Monnet had written to Eisenhower suggesting a committee to establish a new 'Organisation for Economic Co-operation and Development' (OECD). He stressed how important it was that the Commission be represented on that committee.

Thus, the ambush was prepared. During a meeting supposedly about East–West relations, Camps reported that, 'rather unexpectedly', trade questions were introduced, 'particularly in the corridors'. She noted that the subsequent communiqué had 'all the marks of a highly negotiated document'.[21] The result was that, on a US initiative, a 'Special Economic Conference' was held in January 1960. Before it had even started, the balance had been tilted against the OEEC. Nearly half the OEEC's representatives were excluded, yet the Commission, United States and Canada were included. Furthermore, Dillon took the chair, annoying the British with his 'obvious support for the French'.[22] When business turned to the real reason for the meeting, Dillon suggested that:

The twenty governments who were members or associates of the OEEC should examine the question of whether there should be a 'successor' organisation to the OEEC which should continue those functions of the OEEC that still seemed important, take on appropriate new functions, and be so constructed that the United States and Canada could become full members.[23]

With the ambush sprung, Dillon suggested that the OEEC itself should not examine the question. The task should be delegated to a group of three experts, one each from the EFTA countries, the EEC and the USA. Not surprisingly, because of the 'similarity' in the views between the US and the EEC, the Seven thought this group would be 'unbalanced' – even 'rigged'. Thus, Dillon did not wholly get his way. The committee convened with a Frenchman,

[20] Ibid., pp. 241–242.
[21] Ibid., p. 243.
[22] Ibid., p. 246.
[23] Ibid., p. 247.

an Englishman, an American and a Greek. The conference communiqué, however, gave testament to the underlying power struggle. Wrote Camps:

> To the more ardent 'Europeans', the OEEC was the embodiment of the British concept of European unity: co-operation without political commitment. This kind of unity they believed to be inadequate and they feared that if it were allowed to flourish it would undermine the European Community.[24]

Unsurprisingly, when the expert committee reported, as Camps put it, 'it had not been easy for the Four to find a common view'. The upshot was another committee, chaired by the secretary-general designate of the OEEC's replacement organisation, the OECD. The major US objective, 'fully shared by the French and to a considerable extent by the Six', had been achieved. The OEEC, together with Britain's power base in Europe, had been destroyed. Monnet's revenge was complete.

EFTA – THE *COUP DE GRÂCE*

One of the myths assiduously fostered about Britain's post-war attitude towards Europe, before she supposedly showed herself to be more 'outward looking' by joining the Common Market, is that until that time she had somehow remained condescendingly aloof from continental affairs. The record shows the very opposite. Even after the Second World War, Britain had remained profoundly involved in the affairs of Europe, mainly seeking to assist and co-operate with her neighbours in every conceivable way.

The only reason why this myth of her insular lack of concern later came to be promoted was that it reflected the divergence between those two sharply opposed views of how international co-operation in Europe should best be pursued. Britain's opposition to 'supranationalism' stemmed from a different vision of how Europe should be brought together. Favouring the alternative of 'intergovernmental' co-operation, that was why she had consistently supported or led the way in setting up every kind of intergovernmental organisation, from NATO and the WEU, to the Council of Europe and the OEEC itself.

Another area in which Britain showed tireless zeal for intergovernmental co-operation was civil aviation, where her aircraft industry was still a world leader. She was active in setting up the European Civil Aviation Conference in Strasbourg in 1953, which led to the Europe-wide system of air navigation safety known as Eurocontrol (agreed in 1960). In 1956, through the setting

---

[24] Ibid., p. 248.

up of a Supersonic Transport Aircraft Committee, she laid the foundation of Franco-British co-operation that led to *Concorde*.

To 'supranationalists', these forms of co-operation were suspect because they depended on preserving that principle of national sovereignty. This was why they viewed with particular suspicion the idea of 'free trade', as expressed in the new European Free Trade Area. And the final step in sabotaging Britain's attempts to maintain European co-operation on an intergovernmental basis came in 1960 when Hallstein masterminded what was to become in effect EFTA's *coup de grâce*.

The Treaty of Rome had laid out a programme for harmonising external tariffs between the Six in three four-year stages, during which time duties on what was called 'intra-community trade' would be abolished. The first stage was due to end on 31 December 1961. But Hallstein proposed that the process should be speeded up. This would mean that low-tariff countries of the Six would have to levy much higher duties on their imports from the outside world, including the EFTA members with whom they did substantial trade.

Decided unilaterally, this threw EFTA into disarray, as it had planned to phase its own tariff reductions in line with the EEC. Member states had difficulties in agreeing to match the cuts and, compared with the EEC, the Seven were seen as weak and unco-ordinated. Eventually, the EFTA members came into line, but not until six months after the EEC changes had come into force, and after Britain had fruitlessly invested considerable diplomatic capital in trying to get Hallstein to reverse the programme. The delay was a major defeat for the British, who were perceived to be unable to match the cohesion of the EEC.[25] The very future of EFTA seemed in doubt. Relations between Britain and the Six sunk to an all-time low.

BRITAIN'S CRISIS OF CONFIDENCE

At the start of the 1960s, Macmillan and his colleagues were having to think hard about Britain's position in the world. In the 15 years since the end of the Second World War, this had changed dramatically. In 1945, politically, economically and militarily, she had still been unmistakably a world power. But, in the post-war years, her financial and political standing had deteriorated. While she still took her place at international conference tables as one of the world's 'Big Three', all across her empire and spheres of influence troubles were multiplying.

[25] Kaiser, op. cit., p. 105.

Then came Suez, which finally brought home to Britain that she was no longer a 'Big Power', scarcely even a power of world rank. In 1957, by granting independence to Ghana, she launched the process of abandoning her remaining colonies. Within little more than a dozen years, the transformation of the old British Empire into a Commonwealth was complete. At home, the British discovered 'affluence', and their new prime minister, hailed as 'Supermac', won a landslide election in 1959. But behind the seeming façade of economic well-being, people were beginning to wake up to some uncomfortable realities about their place in the world.

THINKING THE UNTHINKABLE

In the early months of 1960, Macmillan's thinking began to move in a direction that even six months before would have seemed incredible. Shortly after the speech in Cape Town on 3 February, when he spoke of 'the wind of change' beginning to blow through Africa, he decided to re-examine the validity of the Churchillian doctrine of three interlocking circles, and the assumption that too close a relationship with Europe would necessarily weaken Britain's relationships with the Commonwealth or the US.

As part of the process, he instructed that the committee originally set up to supervise the FTA negotiations should be renamed the 'European Economic Association Committee'. Macmillan took the chair. Changes were also made to the Whitehall committee structures, from which emerged an Economic Steering (Europe) Committee, chaired by the joint permanent Under-Secretary to the Treasury, Sir Frank Lee. This was to be exclusively responsible for matters of European integration. In March 1960, a supporting committee was set up called the European Economics Questions (Official) Committee, comprised of middle-ranking civil servants. It was to conduct a wide-ranging review to cover a whole spectrum of possibilities, from abandoning attempts to find accommodation with the Six to joining them.

The workhorse of the process was Lee's Economic Steering Committee. On 23 May 1960, on the basis of its deliberations, Lee made a presentation to a special sub-committee of the Cabinet, chaired by Macmillan. His analysis was largely neutral. There were both political and economic advantages in joining the Community, and they would better be obtained by joining the EEC than by some form of 'association', which in any case was unlikely to be offered.[26] A memorandum was circulated to the Ministerial European Economic Association Committee, appraising the options, including joining the Community or 'near identification' with it, and the consequences that

---

[26] Bell, Lionel (1995), *The Throw That Failed* (London: New European Publications), p. 17.

might arise from each. This was discussed at the Committee on 27 May 1960, when Macmillan summed up by saying:

> The basic choice for the government … was between initiating a dramatic change in direction in our domestic, commercial and international policies, and maintaining our traditional policy of remaining aloof from Europe politically while doing all we could to mitigate the economic dangers of a divided Europe. This would be another of the historic moments of history and would need much careful thought.[27]

The officials were then instructed to consider further questions 'to be indicated by the prime minister'.

There was another reason why Britain might now be reconsidering her involvement with the new 'European Economic Community'. Since the appearance of France's new president in 1958, it seemed the character of the new 'Europe' might be evolving away from dogmatic emphasis on supranationalist technocracy.[28] Furthermore, in 1958 and 1959 a serious international problem had been developing over the future of Berlin, still occupied by the four powers. The Soviets, under their new leader Nikita Khrushchev, seemed determined to use the city as the central pawn in his desire to make permanent the separate existence of its puppet state, the German Democratic Republic.

This confounded the 'Hallstein doctrine' – named after the Commission president from the days when he was Adenauer's foreign minister – under which West Germany claimed to speak for all Germans, in the hope of eventual reunification. As tension mounted over this issue, at the end of a NATO council meeting in Paris, de Gaulle organised a meeting on 19 December 1959 between himself, Eisenhower and Macmillan, representing the three Western occupying powers, to discuss Berlin. West Germany's exclusion infuriated Adenauer, his displeasure intensifying when his three supposed allies agreed to meet Khruschev at an East–West summit the following May, to settle this question over his head.

Two weeks before the arranged summit, on 1 May, an American U-2 'spy plane', flying at 80,000 feet over Sverdlovsk in the heart of the Soviet Union, was shot down by a SAM 2 missile. Amid the resulting furore, an apoplectic Khrushchev demanded the summit be postponed until Eisenhower had left the US presidency.

[27] National Archives, CAB 134/1820/29.
[28] See Milward, op. cit., p. 443. Foreign Office officials used de Gaulle's repeated denunciations of the federal Europe concept to justify 'the lack of discussion about sovereignty'.

The delay did nothing to improve Franco-German relations, which were not helped further by France's explosion of her first nuclear device on 13 February 1960. Already at an all-time post-war low, with both countries threatening to withdraw from NATO, they dropped another notch when de Gaulle at Grenoble in October declared that the only reality in Europe was that of the nation state. This coincided with a visit to Bonn by France's prime minister and foreign minister. Such was the *froideur* that an official banquet at the Palais Schaumburg had to be delayed for an hour by a blazing row. During the ensuing dinner, hosts and guests were scarcely on speaking terms.[29]

This frigidity created an opportunity for Britain. Amid intense secrecy, Macmillan and his colleagues meditated on whether to take Britain into 'Europe'. A clue as to his intentions came in a Cabinet reshuffle in July when he appointed the Earl of Home as his foreign secretary, moving his chief whip Edward Heath to a new post at the Foreign Office, with responsibility for 'European affairs'. Ever since entering Parliament in 1950, Heath had been a committed 'Europeanist' and an enthusiast for supranationalism. Two other enthusiastic 'Europeanists' were appointed to posts that would be important if Britain applied to join. Duncan Sandys, former president of the European Movement, became Commonwealth Secretary; Christopher Soames, minister of agriculture.

A key question was how far they should commit Britain to a 'supranational' form of government, over which Britain might have influence but ultimately no control. When, following the Lee Report, civil servants responded to Macmillan's further questions, they qualified their answers with two reservations. The first was that many of the policies of the Six were not yet settled, 'notably on matters left open in the Treaty of Rome'. Second, if the UK joined the Six, this would 'undoubtedly influence ... the development of these policies', although, they added, 'it is not possible to judge how great our influence would be'. They did, however, note that in choosing between 'joining' and a 'close association', in the latter event 'we should not be members of the inner councils of the Six, and would thus not solve the political difficulties which we think will arise if we remain outside'.[30]

So much about where this European project might lead was inevitably unknown. Thus, while some argued that there would be economic advantages to Britain in joining it, these rested on unpredictable factors. At the time, contributions to the EEC budget could not be estimated. What

[29] Williams, op. cit., p. 485.
[30] National Archives, CAB 129/102/7.

was to become the Community's biggest single expense, initially accounting for over 90 per cent of that budget – the Common Agricultural Policy – had yet to be defined. For similar reasons, it was impossible to predict the effects on British agriculture or trade.

Yet Macmillan and his colleagues were in no doubt what was involved. Even before the Treaty of Rome was signed in 1957, the Foreign Office had been briefed that its six signatories intended 'to achieve tighter European integration through the creation of European institutions with supranational powers, beginning in the economic field … the underlying motive of the Six is, however, essentially political'.[31] In the summer of 1960, Sir Roderick Barclay, head of the UK delegation to the European Commission in Brussels, sent a despatch to the Foreign Office stressing that the aim of the Community was not merely harmonisation but 'the unification of policies in every field of the economic union, i.e., economic, social, commercial, tariff and fiscal policy. That this was not just "pie in the sky" needed to be made clear to the politicians.'[32]

When Heath, as minister of state for Europe, visited Hallstein in November 1960, his report on the meeting noted how the Commission president had emphasised that joining the Community was not just a matter of adopting a common tariff, 'which was the essential hallmark of any "State" (and he regarded the EEC as a potential State)'. It would be necessary, Hallstein had insisted, for any new entrant to accept that the EEC was intended to evolve into something much deeper, 'some form of Federal State'.[33]

Particularly revealing in this context was the reply given in December 1960 by the Lord Chancellor, Lord Kilmuir, to a request from Heath for an opinion on the constitutional implications of signing the treaty for Britain's sovereignty. Kilmuir responded that loss of sovereignty would in several respects be considerable: by Parliament; by the Crown in terms of Britain's treaty-making powers; and by the courts, which to an extent would become 'subordinate' to the European Court of Justice.[34] On the making of laws, Kilmuir said it was clear that:

> the Council of Ministers would eventually (after the system of qualified majority voting had come into force) make regulations which would be binding on us even against our wishes … it would in theory be possible for Parliament to enact at the outset legislation which would give automatic

[31] National Archives, FO 371/150360.
[32] Bell, op. cit., p. 22.
[33] National Archives, FO 371/150369.
[34] National Archives, FO 371/150369, cited by Bell, op. cit., pp. 36–39.

force of law to any existing or future regulations made by the appropriate organs of the Community. For Parliament to do this would go far beyond the most extensive delegation of powers, even in wartime, that we have ever experienced and I do not think there is any likelihood of this being acceptable to the House of Commons.

As for the subordination of Britain's courts to the ECJ, Kilmuir wrote:

I must emphasise that in my view the surrenders of sovereignty involved are serious ones, and I think that, as a matter of practical politics, it will not be easy to persuade Parliament or the British public to accept them. I am sure that it would be a great mistake to underestimate the force of the objections to them. But these objections should be brought out into the open now because, if we attempt to gloss over them at this stage, those who are opposed to the whole idea of joining the Community will certainly seize on them with more damaging effect later on.

It is thus manifestly clear that Macmillan and his Cabinet were fully aware of the political implications of the decision that lay before them. But there was still one other consideration that might have to outweigh everything else: her 'special relationship' with the United States of America. It was on that, and on the fact that, since detonating her first H-bomb in 1957, she had become the world's third thermonuclear power, that Britain's dwindling prestige and influence in the world now rested. If she were now to throw in her destiny with 'Europe', would all this have to be thrown away?

That question had suddenly become more acute than ever, brought to a head by the same incident that brought such an abrupt end to the East–West summit, and had provoked such bitter feuding between Germany and France: the shooting down of Gary Powers's U-2.

AMERICA LETS MACMILLAN OFF THE HOOK

To no one did this come as more of a shock than Britain's defence planners. Britain's nuclear deterrent had since 1956 depended on her force of high-altitude V-bombers. If the Soviets were now capable of intercepting aircraft at 80,000 feet, any deterrent value had vanished. The only alternative would be a missile, and Britain had been developing two. But the first, Blue Streak, had been cancelled only three weeks before the U-2 incident. The other, Blue Steel, would be cancelled later in the year. This left Britain with only one hope of preserving her 'independent' deterrent: to buy missiles from the USA – either the air-launched Skybolt or the new Polaris, which would require building a fleet of nuclear submarines. Either solution required Washington's agreement.

With 1960 nearing its end, Macmillan's old friend President Eisenhower was soon due to leave office. His successor, elected in November, was the charismatic young senator John F. Kennedy, to whom Macmillan was related by marriage. As the new administration prepared to take office, Macmillan's most urgent priority was to discuss with the new president the two issues at the top of his agenda: 'Europe' and Britain's deterrent.

Talks were fixed for 4 April 1961, but, before they took place, much behind-the-scenes groundwork was necessary. In Washington this centred on a man who had now become one of Kennedy's most trusted advisers, George Ball, his Under-Secretary of State with special responsibility for European affairs. Kennedy had picked him as a key member of his team after hearing him address a conference in New York in January 1960, when Ball spoke of the need for further progress towards political integration in Europe.

Ball was, of course, one of Monnet's closest and most committed allies, and was now at the heart of the new administration, guiding a president who knew little of contemporary European politics. What was just as significant was that Monnet had become convinced that de Gaulle's brand of nationalism required the counterweight of Britain's membership in his fledgling Community. With this in mind he visited America twice in the early months of 1961, when he met Ball and other members of the new administration. At Ball's instigation in the March, he 'had a long talk with the President'. They were said to have liked and respected each other.[35]

Ball was now actively pushing for British membership. Prior to the Macmillan–Kennedy talks, he flew to London where, on 30 March, at the suggestion of Sir Frank Lee, he met Heath. The three met in the house of the Earl of Perth, son of Sir Eric Drummond (later the 16th Earl of Perth), who had been Monnet's boss when he was the first general secretary of the League of Nations. Ball intended to encourage Britain to take the plunge, but Heath began by confirming that, provided an overall settlement could be found to take care of the Commonwealth, agriculture and EFTA problems, the UK was 'ready to accept a common, or harmonised, tariff'.[36] When Heath temporarily absented himself, Lee put the direct question, 'does the United States want the United Kingdom to join the Common Market?' Ball, in his reply, emphasised that the EEC's institutions should

[35] Bill, James (1997), *George Ball: Behind the Scenes in US Foreign Policy* (New Haven, CT: Yale University Press), p. 120.
[36] Ball, op. cit., p. 211.

not become mere technocratic bodies, they should continue to develop politically. If Britain joined the EEC, it should be on the understanding that the present institutions did not form a completed edifice, but would continue to evolve and that the Rome Treaty was not a 'frozen document' but a 'process'.[37]

When Heath returned to the meeting, Lee summarised what had been said. Heath 'seemed impressed'. Ball 'emerged exhilarated' that 'both Heath and Lee had gone much further than I expected'.[38] Five days later, Macmillan arrived in Washington for his talks with Kennedy. When the two met, 'almost the first question Macmillan asked the President', according to Ball who was sitting with Kennedy, was 'how he and the American government would react if Britain applied to join the European Community'.[39]

Macmillan states that Kennedy 'repeated how anxious the Americans were for us to get into the Six'.[40] At a dinner in the British Embassy next evening, Ball recalls that the prime minister twice took him privately aside, seeming 'excited'. 'Yesterday was one of the greatest days of my life,' he said with apparent emotion. 'You know, don't you, that we can now do this thing and that we're going to do it. We're going into Europe.' The only obstacle left was de Gaulle, but Macmillan was convinced 'we're going to do it'.[41]

The last hurdle was the Cabinet. Back in February Heath had warned Macmillan that its earlier opposition had been so pronounced because, in July 1960, the prime minister had allowed a free debate. Instead, Heath advised, he should now organise the policy-making process in such a way that the EEC application was seen as 'inevitable'.[42] In the last days of June, therefore, Macmillan opened his Cabinet discussions by pointing out that the first question they needed to consider was that 'if we were to sign the Treaty of Rome we should have to accept its political objectives, and although we should be able to influence the political outcome we did not know what this would be'.[43]

He conceded that a decision to enter would 'raise great presentational difficulties'. Britain would not only have to convince the Six that 'we

[37] Ibid., p. 212.
[38] Ibid., pp. 212–213. Ball quotes 'one of the ablest men in the American Embassy in London upbraiding me for encouraging Britain to move towards Europe'. Despite what had been said, this man implied, with some prescience, 'that he did not believe Britain would ever play more than a foot-dragging role in Europe, resisting any move towards political unity'.
[39] Ibid., p. 214.
[40] Macmillan, Harold (1972), *Pointing the Way* (London: Macmillan), p. 350.
[41] Ball, op. cit., p. 214.
[42] National Archives, FO 371/158264/12 (7 February 1961), letter from Heath to Macmillan.
[43] Bell, op. cit., pp. 59–62.

genuinely supported the objectives of the Treaty', but also 'to satisfy public opinion in this country that the implementation of the objectives of the Treaty would not require unacceptable social and other adjustments'. But for every problem there was a solution: to stay as quiet as possible about 'political objectives' and to sell British membership of the 'Common Market' as a matter of economics: improved trade, more jobs, greater prosperity. The great deception would continue.

The Cabinet voted for entry and, on 28 July, Macmillan wrote to President Kennedy telling him that 'after long and earnest consideration' his government had concluded that it would be right for Britain to apply to join the EEC.[44] To general astonishment, on 31 July 1961, Macmillan made that public.[45] According to Duchêne, citing a conversation with Camps, the key part played by the US president in bringing about this *volte face* had been no accident. 'There was a "Monnet effect" on Ball and then a "Ball effect" on Kennedy, and then a "Kennedy effect" on Macmillan. It was a triumph for Monnet.'[46]

---

[44] FRUS, 1961–1963, Vol. XIII, Western Europe and Canada. Document 14.
[45] HC Deb, 31 July 1961, Vol. 645, cc928-42. See also Macmillan, Harold (1973), *At the End of the Day – 1961–63* (London: Macmillan), p. 1.
[46] Duchêne, op. cit., pp. 325–326. Curiously, Britain would not be the first country to apply to join the 'Six'. Turkey had applied to join in July 1959. The EEC's response was to suggest the forming of 'an association' until Turkey's circumstances permitted its accession. Negotiations led to the Ankara Agreement of 12 September 1963, aimed at securing Turkey's full eventual membership.

5

Why de Gaulle Kept Britain Out: 1961–1969

> The French did not wish the British to be at the table taking part in the formative discussions on the CAP, for fear that we might disrupt the very favourable arrangements they otherwise had every reason to expect.
>
> Edward Heath[1]

It is a familiar fact of history that, during the 1960s, de Gaulle was to slam the door against Britain's entry to the Common Market, not just once but twice. Why he chose to do so is still hotly debated, although his motives were undoubtedly far more nuanced than the simplistic accounts will allow.

From a British point of view, the generally accepted version begins with the formal acceptance of Britain's application to join on 26 September 1961. Over the next year, as this version has it, Heath showed himself highly skilled in negotiating Britain's terms of entry. But, after the talks became mysteriously bogged down in January 1963, de Gaulle then startled the world by announcing his veto. This came as a great blow to Macmillan, at the beginning of a year that was to see his government disintegrating amid a welter of scandals.

In 1965, after a Labour government had taken over under Harold Wilson, Heath became leader of the Conservative Party: not least thanks to the reputation he had won as Britain's negotiator in Brussels. When Wilson made a second bid to join the Common Market in 1967, de Gaulle again blocked British entry. Only when, in 1969, de Gaulle departed from the stage and was succeeded by Georges Pompidou, this version concludes, did France's attitude change. Largely thanks to the 'personal chemistry' between

[1] Heath, Edward (1998), *The Course of My Life* (London: Hodder & Stoughton), p. 222.

Pompidou and Heath, when he became prime minister in 1970, Britain's third application proved successful.

This construction, at best, is incomplete. It is true that the key role in the EEC throughout the 1960s was played by de Gaulle. But what most historians tend to overlook is the central underlying reason why France could not yet afford to allow Britain into the Common Market. But no sooner was this problem resolved than she then needed Britain to join as soon as possible for reasons, it turns out, to which the personal views of Heath and Pompidou were irrelevant.

'THE COMMONWEALTH PROBLEM'

On 16 October 1961, Heath went to Brussels to make his opening statement on Britain's entry to the Common Market. Three weeks later, on 8 November, negotiations began. Heath was in no doubt that the greatest difficulty would be in securing transitional arrangements for the Commonwealth. Addressing the Six, he told them, 'I am sure you will understand that Britain could not join the EEC under conditions in which this trade connection was cut, with grave loss and even ruin for some of the Commonwealth countries.'[2] Already, when announcing his decision to join back in July, Macmillan had pledged to the House of Commons that this would be subject to satisfactory arrangements for the special needs of the UK, the Commonwealth and EFTA.[3]

By far the greatest problem was the system of 'imperial preference', which had been in place for 60 years and more. The effect was significant. In 1961, 43 per cent of British exports went to the Commonwealth, as against only 16.7 per cent to the Six and 13.1 per cent to her EFTA partners.[4] In 1960, Britain had taken more than half of New Zealand's exports and a quarter of those from several other Commonwealth countries, including Australia and India.[5] Inside the EEC, Britain would have to erect tariff barriers against their goods, while allowing tariff-free trade with her new partners.

This posed difficulties that none of the Six had faced. Prior to announcing Britain's intention to join, therefore, Macmillan sent several of his Cabinet ministers, led by Duncan Sandys, round the Commonwealth capitals, pleading for their assent to his action. These were countries that, less than 20

---

[2] For some reason, this was not reported by *The Times* and other newspapers until 28 November 1961.

[3] Macmillan, *At the End of the Day*, op. cit., p. 22.

[4] Figures taken from speech by Hugh Gaitskell to Labour Party Conference, 1962. Holmes, Martin, ed. (1966) in *The Eurosceptic Reader* (London: Macmillan), p. 15.

[5] *Britain and the European Communities* (London: HMSO, 1962).

years before, had sent some four million of their citizens to fight alongside Britain in the Second World War. Now they were to be dealt a mighty economic blow, which most were to see as an incomprehensible betrayal. The response from Ottawa typified the sentiment. Canadian ministers expressed 'grave concern' about the political and economic effects of British EEC membership on Canada and on the Commonwealth as a whole.[6]

The main task confronting Heath as he began formal negotiations in November was to ensure that the damage inflicted on Commonwealth partners was at least softened. His top priority was to persuade his prospective new partners to grant 'derogations'. These would extend for as long as possible the period in which imports from the Commonwealth could continue, allowing its producers time to search for new markets. But, as he got down to detail, it soon became evident that his prospective partners were prepared to make few concessions. The reason was simple. For the Six this was precisely the test of Britain's willingness to abandon her old, traditional role in the world and to demonstrate her willingness now to develop new loyalties.

What Heath did not realise, however, was that one member of the Six was not only reluctant to make any concessions at all but was actually opposed to Britain's entry even before the talks began.

DE GAULLE PLAYS HIS OWN GAME

President de Gaulle was unlike any other post-war European leader. He saw himself as the man who had saved his country twice, the first time at the end of the Second World War and the second in 1958, when he had rescued France from the chaos of the Fourth Republic to set up his new Fifth Republic. But with the continuing threat of internal instability spreading from the fearful civil war in Algeria, he was aware that any time France might be again plunged into violent chaos. In his 11 years in office he faced no fewer than 34 assassination attempts, more than any other statesman in history.

For these reasons, de Gaulle also saw the 'European Communities' and his country's place in them very differently from other leaders. One of his first acts on becoming France's president in July 1958 had been to arrange a meeting with Adenauer, which took place in September at de Gaulle's home in Colombey-les-Deux-Églises. They announced that close co-operation between France and Germany was the foundation of 'all constructive

[6] Mansergh, Nicholas (1963), *Documents and Speeches on Commonwealth Affairs, 1952–1962* (London: Oxford University Press), p. 635.

endeavour in Europe', and that this should be put on an organised basis.[7] In 1959, de Gaulle's prime minister Michel Debré took this idea forward in a speech proposing that the Six should be aiming not only at economic but also at political union. The way to this should be paved by frequent consultations between their leaders.[8]

By 1960, both publicly and privately, de Gaulle canvassed the idea not merely of regular meetings of the Six heads of government but of 'standing commissions' to co-ordinate policies on political, defence and cultural issues, with their own secretariat.[9] He was pursuing his own vision of a new kind of integration among the Six, shaped on intergovernmental lines: his vision of what he was to call a '*Europe des Etats*'.[10] De Gaulle had never been an enthusiast for what he regarded as Monnet's supranational obsessions. As he once remarked: 'we are no longer in the era when M. Monnet gave the orders'.[11] Not only did he seem unsympathetic to Monnet's ideas; his prime minister Debré so detested them that he would allegedly pass Monnet with averted gaze. A commentator remarked: 'the European reformation had scarcely begun, and the counter-reformation was installed in Paris'.

The impression thus conveyed in 1960 – that 'Europe' might now be moving away from supranationalism towards a more intergovernmental approach – had a significant impact on Macmillan and his advisers. It held out the possibility that, by skilful negotiation of her terms of entry, Britain might use her influence to help redirect the EEC onto the path of intergovernmentalism.[12]

In February 1961, de Gaulle's proposals for 'closer political co-operation' were discussed at a meeting of the Six in Paris, which set up a committee under Christian Fouchet to consider them. These talks had been preceded by a private meeting between de Gaulle and Adenauer, intended to patch up their bitter disagreements the following year over the abortive East–West summit on Berlin. Adenauer had wanted to clear the air about de Gaulle's

---

[7] Royal Institute of International Affairs (1959), *Documents on International Affairs, 1958* (London: Chatham House), p. 445. These will subsequently be referred to just as Documents, with relevant dates.
[8] Documents (1959), pp. 508–509.
[9] See for instance his press conference on 5 September 1960, and Documents (1960), pp. 157–158.
[10] This came often to be misrepresented as a 'Europe des Patries', a phrase that de Gaulle himself went out of his way at a press conference to explain that he never used. The misunderstanding arose through a reverse translation back from his original words.
[11] This and the two following sentences come from Duchêne, op. cit., p. 315.
[12] As the Foreign Secretary Lord Home put it: 'if we act quickly now we can go into Europe and help shape the political structure in the way which suits us best. De Gaulle doesn't want a tight European Federation, a Federal Europe. He wants a union of independent states. If we go in now, that is what it will be' (interview in the *Observer*, 23 September 1962).

seeming desire to emasculate the Community, and also to discuss France's plans regarding NATO. He appeared sufficiently satisfied to agree to de Gaulle's wish for more 'political co-operation'.

At the subsequent meeting with their EEC partners, despite a Dutch protest that the rest of the Six should not always be bound by what was agreed between Germany and France, it was resolved that the Fouchet committee should report on further political union. This would not, however, involve any further supranational elements, and would respect national sovereignty with full rights of veto. Fouchet's recommendations were considered at two more heads of government meetings in Bonn, one in May, the second in July. Under discussion were two rival proposals: a 'Union of States', proposed by the French, and a 'union of peoples' preferred by the rest of the Six. Monnet himself had high hopes that the first steps towards a European currency would be practicable.[13] His optimism was misplaced, and he plaintively asked why at this time France should be trying 'to bring back into an intergovernmental framework what had already become a Community'.[14]

Nevertheless, the Six did agree on what became known as the Bonn Declaration, announcing on 18 July their decision 'to give shape to the will for political union already implicit in the Treaties establishing the European Communities'.[15] This was just 13 days before Macmillan announced Britain's decision to apply for entry.

FRANCO-GERMAN RAPPROCHEMENT
For the next 17 months, two quite different dramas were to unfold simultaneously: in public, it seemed, wholly unrelated, but behind the scenes, in important respects, linked.

The first drama, little understood in Britain, was the coming together of de Gaulle's France and Adenauer's Germany in a new and much closer alliance. It was based on a sense that they shared a European identity in a way that set them apart from the British and even more from the Americans. A powerful trigger for their new sense of common identity was the immense international crisis that blew up on Sunday 13 August 1961, when East Germany sealed off West Berlin's borders with the GDR and began to build the 'Berlin Wall'. The long-simmering East–West tension over Berlin had at last come to a head. When the initial response of the Kennedy government was slow and uncertain, as was that of the British, this reinforced the

[13] Monnet, *Memoirs*, op. cit., p. 439.
[14] Ibid., pp. 439–440.
[15] Documents (1961), pp. 187–189.

suspicions of Adenauer and de Gaulle that Anglo-US support could not be relied on.

On 19 October 1961, the French delegation on the Fouchet committee presented a draft treaty to establish a union between the countries of the Six. This proposed severing of Europe's dependence for military security on the Atlantic Alliance and the USA, reflecting de Gaulle's wish for a more self-reliant Europe, centred on a Franco-German alliance. De Gaulle further proposed a radical reconstruction of the EEC, turning it into a voluntary union of independent states. Its secretariat would be based in Paris and there would be extensive national veto powers over all common policies. He envisaged a drastic dilution of the powers of the Commission and Council of Ministers, and the subjection of Community law to national law. This was the supreme expression of his vision of a '*Europe des Etats*'. Predictably, the reaction of the other five governments was hostile.

Early in the New Year, on 18 January 1962, tensions were further exacerbated when the French put forward 'a revised draft treaty' that, far from taking account of the objections of the others, seemed in many respects to be worse.[16] The amended plan had been drawn up in de Gaulle's own hand.[17] Shortly afterwards, on 9 February, de Gaulle asked for an urgent meeting with Adenauer to discuss his 'Fouchet proposals' and European security. The chancellor had only recently suffered a heart attack, although his illness had been kept secret, even from de Gaulle. They met in a hotel in Baden-Baden, where Adenauer refused to support the idea of a looser EEC structure. But the meeting marked a distinct warming in the relationship between the two leaders, not least as they were able to agree on their mistrust of American and British attitudes towards the Soviet Union, and the absolute necessity of avoiding another Franco-German war. Most importantly, de Gaulle was completely at one with Adenauer on the importance of not making deals with the Soviets on Berlin. They shared concern that the Americans and British might placate Khrushchev. Adenauer was beginning to look to France as his only reliable ally.[18]

DE GAULLE'S REAL AGENDA

During this time, the negotiations for Britain's entry into the EEC were continuing in Brussels as if none of these fundamental shifts in thinking about the future of the 'European project' were taking place. Yet, at the

[16] Camps, op. cit., p. 418.
[17] De Gaulle, p. 34. For the original text see https://www.cvce.eu/en/obj/draft_treaty_fouchet_plan_ii_18_january_1962-en-c9930f55-7d69-4edc-8961-4f12cf7d7a5b.html.
[18] Williams, op. cit., pp. 498–499.

very time when it seemed de Gaulle was seeking to move away from the concept of supranationalism, he was in fact looking to the supranational mechanisms of the EEC to solve a problem that threatened the very stability of the Republic. That problem was agriculture, already a vital issue in France's relationship with the Communities. According to Maurice Couve de Murville, de Gaulle's minister of foreign affairs, without the promise of a common agricultural policy, the Treaty of Rome would never have been ratified by the French Parliament.[19]

By 1962, however, French agriculture was in crisis, described by de Gaulle himself as a 'gigantic and predominately national problem'. While other countries had been able to rationalise and modernise the sector, in France it still accounted for around 25 per cent of total employment, while three-quarters of the farms were too small to be viable.[20] In the years immediately after the war, all European countries had introduced state subsidies to their agriculture, to avoid any repetition of the food shortages of the wartime period or the farming depression of the 1930s.[21] But in no country had the subsidy system come to be as important as in France. State spending on agriculture had more than tripled between 1958 and 1962, confronting the Fifth Republic with the need 'to provide subsidies so enormous that they would cripple its finances'.[22]

Although these subsidies had hugely boosted output, this had led to persistent downward pressures on prices, which in turn further threatened the economic viability of many farms. For France's politicians, this presented a nightmare: the thought of millions of small farmers being displaced from the land and gravitating to towns and cities that could offer them neither jobs nor housing.

Little of this was appreciated outside France, but one widely cited example of the turmoil was the so-called 'artichoke affair'. From 1959 to

[19] Cited in Webber, Douglas, *The Hard Core: The Franco-German Relationship and Agricultural Crisis Politics in the European Union* (European University Institute, Working Paper RSC No. 98/46, December 1998).
[20] Compared with, for instance, 4 per cent in the United Kingdom.
[21] A widespread subsequent 'myth' about post-war European agriculture was that it was the Common Agricultural Policy that boosted production and made farming prosperous. Decades later, a 'Fact Sheet' on the European Parliament website ('The Treaty of Rome and Green Europe') would, typically, claim that 'the CAP produced spectacular results: the Community was soon able to overcome the food shortages of the 1950s, achieving self-sufficiency and then generating cyclical and structural surpluses'. In fact, it was in the 1950s, long before the CAP, that the combination of subsidies and technological innovation had already led to over-production of food, which the CAP only helped to exacerbate.
[22] De Gaulle (1972), *Memoirs of Hope: Renewal and Endeavor* (New York: Simon & Schuster), pp. 155–159; See also Keeler, John T. S., 'De Gaulle and Europe's Common Agricultural Policy: The Logic and Legacies of Nationalistic Integration', *French Politics and Society*, Vol. 8, No. 4 (Fall 1990), pp. 62–77.

1962, over-production of Breton artichokes caused prices to plummet, threatening growers with bankruptcy, driving them to organise as a political constituency. In June 1961, thousands of farmers gathered in the tiny town of Morlaix, Brittany, where they set fire to surplus piles of artichokes and potatoes, cut telephone wires, overturned vehicles and set up roadblocks. Some occupied government buildings, and arrests by the police sparked even more street violence.[23] In the following days, the revolt spread to the whole of Brittany.[24]

What made this affair politically significant was the support from the intellectual elite of the 'university set' in Paris, which helped promote an artichoke boycott among its like-minded, liberal, urban friends.[25] This was a foretaste of the politics of radical economic protest that were to climax in 1968. Highly politicised local groups of famers were set up, under the umbrella of a parent organisation, the Federation Nationale des Syndicats d'Exploitants Agricoles (National Federation of Exploited Farmers).[26] At a Cabinet meeting in August 1962, with the Algerian crisis now largely over, de Gaulle was to call the 'stabilisation' of agriculture the 'most important problem' facing France. If the problems were not resolved, he declared, there was a potential 'second Algerian question on our own soil'.[27]

De Gaulle and his advisers concluded that the answer was a European agricultural policy that would open access to external markets and tap into new funds, primarily from Germany, balancing the advantages that would accrue to Germany through free trade in manufactured goods. Thus, despite his overt dislike of supranational institutions, de Gaulle came to regard the EEC as the most essential instrument in furthering France's national interest.[28]

The idea of a 'Common Agricultural Policy' went back to the Spaak Report in 1955, and an outline policy had been included in the Rome Treaty. But the detail had to wait for agriculture Commissioner Sicco Mansholt to produce his famous 300-page 'Mansholt Plan'. He proposed replacing direct national subsidies with a system of variable levies and support prices, under the control of the Commission, financed from the Community budget. For the next two years, though, Adenauer consistently blocked the Plan. He feared that negative repercussions on cereal prices could cost his

---

[23] Peters, Annie Loring, 'The Breton Case for Regional Autonomy: Centuries of Struggle in Brittany, France' (1986), University of Nebraska at Omaha, Student Work, 405.

[24] *Breton News*, 15 June 1961, 'Breton Farmers Revolt'.

[25] Ibid.

[26] Ibid.

[27] Peyrefitte, op. cit., p. 302.

[28] See also Webber, op. cit.

party, the CDU, its absolute majority.[29] Only on 14 January 1962, after what Hallstein famously described as '137 hours of discussion, with 214 hours in sub-committee; 582,000 pages of documents; three heart attacks', did the Germans finally agree to give legal effect to the CAP. The clock was 'stopped' for two weeks and the conclusions back-dated to meet the symbolic 31 December deadline.[30]

For all that, the agreement was a fudge. Mansholt's plan set up the EAGGF (European Agricultural Guidance and Guarantee Fund – also known by its French initials, FEOGA – Fonds Européen d'Orientation et de Garantie Agricole). France wanted the policy financed by levies on imported goods. Her imports – especially if her overseas departments were included – were minimal.[31] However, the Regulation agreed by the Council on 4 April 1962 allowed only for a phased transition lasting until the end of the financial year of 1964/1965, with a complicated funding formula. For the first financial year, 100 per cent of the funding would come from member contributions, set according to the scale agreed in the Treaty of Rome. By the 1964/1965 period, this would drop to 80 per cent, and 20 per cent would be levied in proportion to net imports from third countries.[32]

The effect of this Regulation was to defer the final decision on the structure of CAP funding, which the Council decided should be taken before 1 July 1965. Even though it had been agreed in principle that the EAGGF should be funded by levies, this was not locked in stone. At stake was a fundamental principle. Some member states thought it important that the financial burden should be evenly shared between the Six. Others, including France, sought to apply the principle of 'common financial responsibility': those who imported most paid most.[33] Britain had much to lose from the latter option, and within the Community could side with other member states to block it. At all costs, de Gaulle believed, she had to be excluded from membership until final agreements were in place.[34] Therein lay the explanation for the dramas to come.

DE GAULLE PREPARES TO VETO
By the spring of 1962, de Gaulle had three issues to address. The first was his 'Fouchet proposals' for political union of the Six. On the grounds that these

[29] Ibid.
[30] Hallstein, Walter (1973), *Europe in the Making* (New York: W. W. Norton & Company), p. 65.
[31] Milward, op. cit., p. 424.
[32] Regulation 25 on the financing of the Common Agricultural Policy (OJ 991/62).
[33] The issues are discussed in the Commission Newsletter on the CAP, No. 25, December 1964. Archive of European Integration: http://aei.pitt.edu/6331/1/6331.pdf.
[34] Milward, op. cit., p. 424, and National Archives, CAB 134/1821.

would seriously influence the nature of the union Britain was seeking to join, Heath had made a belated bid for British involvement in the discussions. At a WEU meeting on 10 April, he made plain Britain's assumption that the existing Communities would be the foundation on which 'Europe would be built', but that he hoped their work could be 'knit together with the new political structure in a coherent and effective whole'. There was little need for his concern, because shortly afterwards the proposals collapsed, when France's partners could not agree a way forward.[35]

De Gaulle's second issue was his new alliance with Adenauer. In the same month of April, the chancellor's fears about American policy seemed to be confirmed when the US Secretary of State Dean Rusk came up with a new plan for Berlin, which seemed to propose de facto recognition of the GDR. Given only 48 hours to respond, Adenauer had no option but to reject it and, at his request, de Gaulle followed. When Kennedy endorsed Rusk's action and criticised Adenauer, affirming that negotiations with the Soviet Union over Berlin would continue, relations between Adenauer and Kennedy became frigid. Exploiting this rift, de Gaulle moved in to cement the Franco-German axis. He invited Adenauer to make a state visit to France two months later, in July.

The third item on de Gaulle's agenda was Britain's application to join the EEC. By now he was certain Britain would have to be kept out. Thus, on 19 May, Macmillan was noting the impressions of the British Ambassador in Paris, Sir Pierson Dixon, that de Gaulle 'has now definitely decided to exclude us'. Macmillan forlornly noted: 'others (and I am one) do not feel that de Gaulle has definitely made up his mind'.[36]

Throughout, Macmillan remained oblivious to de Gaulle's hidden agenda. He convinced himself that the key to changing the General's mind lay in easing his path to acquiring nuclear weapons: perhaps by talking the Americans into assisting the French (although it had already been made clear to him that this was very unlikely). An alternative was an Anglo-French arrangement for 'joint targeting of nuclear forces', without the direct involvement of the United States.[37] In pursuit of his fantasy, on 2 to 3 June Macmillan met with de Gaulle in a beautiful small château near

[35] On 15 May 1962, de Gaulle gave a press conference to explain the collapse, in which he reiterated his view that 'only the States, in this respect, are valid, legitimate, and capable of achieving it [political union]. I repeat that at present there is and can be no Europe other than a Europe of States – except of course for myths, fictions, and pageants.' This particularly rankled with Monnet, who castigated de Gaulle's comments in his *Memoirs* as having 'travestied' his beloved Community and all that supranationalism stood for.
[36] Horne, op. cit., p. 326.
[37] Letter from Macmillan to Lord Home on 16 May, quoted in Horne, op. cit., pp. 326–327.

Paris, Champs, once the home of Madame de Pompadour. He described his host as playing 'the role of a stately monarch unbending a little to the representative of a once hostile but now friendly country'. But de Gaulle 'repeated his preference for a Six without Britain; first, because British entry would entirely alter the character of the Community'. Only second did de Gaulle offer the view that 'Britain was too tied to America'.[38]

The French Ambassador to London, de Courcel, present at the discussions, recorded that Macmillan made a direct offer of Franco-British nuclear collaboration as an implied *quid pro quo* for France supporting British EEC entry. Contrary to British expectations, de Gaulle did not react. Instead, he emphasised France's absolute need to export her agricultural surpluses and insistently raised the issue of Commonwealth imports, which he insisted was the 'most fundamental' issue.

Throughout the discussions, Macmillan completely failed to understand what was at stake. Responding to de Gaulle's demand that Commonwealth imports should be limited to tropical products only, he insisted on transitional arrangements, confirming de Gaulle's fears. When Macmillan tried to shift the conversation away from agriculture, de Gaulle kept returning to it.[39] Coming away without the first idea of what had transpired, Macmillan later reported to the Queen that 'the danger of the French opposing a resolute veto to our application has now been avoided, at least for the time being'.[40]

The following month Adenauer paid his state visit to France, the first by a German chancellor since the war. The six-day visit culminated on 8 July with the leaders attending High Mass in Rheims cathedral, after having taken the salute at a parade of French and German troops outside the city. It was the first time since the Battle of Leipzig in 1813 that French and German troops had marched together. In private discussions, de Gaulle expressed doubts about Britain joining the EEC. When Adenauer did not disagree, the General knew he had his backing. This had been de Gaulle's real purpose in so assiduously cultivating his alliance with Adenauer. With his flank secure, he now felt able to instruct his negotiators in Brussels to take a harder line with the British.

---

[38] Horne, op. cit., p. 328. Adenauer had also by this time made clear, in a speech in West Berlin on 11 May, his view that Britain could not possibly join any 'political union' of the Six. In a broadcast on 29 May, he reiterated this, saying that even if Britain did join the Common Market, her interests were so different from those of the Six that she could not join a political union.

[39] National Archives, PREM 11/3775, pp. 7–9. Record of a conversation at the Château de Champs, 2–3 June 1962.

[40] Horne, op. cit., pp. 328–329.

There were now only four weeks left before the marathon talks in Brussels broke up for the summer. Already the negotiators for the Six had been startled by how many concessions Heath had been prepared to make on Britain's behalf, particularly over Commonwealth imports and even on issues formerly thought to be 'non-negotiable'. This had provoked a joint statement by the prime ministers of Australia and New Zealand, on the eve of Macmillan's visit to Champs, highly critical of Britain's new readiness to abandon imperial preferences.[41]

It was all to no avail. At the final session of the talks, during the night of 4–5 August, when everyone was exhausted, the chairman from Luxembourg, Eugène Schaus, had collapsed at two in the morning. Yet the session had continued with Spaak in the chair and, as Heath was to record:

> A little before 4am, the French unexpectedly demanded that we should sign a paper on financing the CAP, committing us to an interpretation of the financial regulation favourable to the French. They wanted a new tariff arrangement on imports from outside the EEC which would maintain the price of domestic produce. The action was self-evidently dilatory in intent, and I refused to be bounced into a snap judgment on such a complex matter. I was supported in this by the Germans and the Dutch, who were as interested as I was. The French redrafted the document twice, but this only hardened my resolve. This was no way to carry on such an important negotiation, and I was having none of it. In response, Couve de Murville said that he would reserve his position regarding food imports from the British Commonwealth, a matter which I had thought to be fully resolved.[42]

It was a classic negotiating ambush, of a kind that in the years ahead was to become only too familiar. With no agreement possible, the talks had to be adjourned until the autumn. Then the French would make it clearer than ever that they had no intention of allowing Britain's application to succeed.[43]

---

[41] Ibid., p. 327.
[42] Heath, op. cit., p. 222.
[43] See Milward, op. cit., pp. 438–441. He takes the view that, had de Gaulle not eventually vetoed Britain's application, the British government would have been forced to break off negotiations over precisely this issue. This view is shared by another historian. He claims that Couve de Murville was convinced that France was within 'striking distance' of forcing Britain to withdraw its application, and was thus reportedly furious with de Gaulle for invoking the veto. (Ludlow, Piers, 1997, *Dealing With Britain: The Six and the First UK Application to the EEC* (Cambridge: Cambridge University Press), p. 210.

The following month, on 5 September, de Gaulle began a triumphant state visit to the German Federal Republic, regarded as even more successful than his host's visit to France. In their private talks, they confirmed that Britain must be excluded. De Gaulle continued the courtship with a six-page memorandum, suggesting a solemn agreement between the French and German governments to co-ordinate their foreign policy and defence. Without referring to his own Cabinet, Adenauer signalled that such an agreement would be his first priority.[44]

THE DENOUEMENT APPROACHES

In Britain that autumn the Common Market issue briefly moved to the centre of the political stage. Although the Brussels negotiations had been dragging on for a year, they had never attracted much public interest. Now, as one historian put it, they seemed to be 'inexplicably dragging out as if scripted by Kafka. Hours and even days were being taken up by discussion of the tariffs on Indian tea or Australian kangaroo meat.'[45]

Belatedly the newspapers published turgid supplements, trying to explain in laborious detail what joining the Common Market would entail, most to be thrown away unread. Apart from the super-patriotic, right-wing titles owned by the ageing Canadian Lord Beaverbrook, a long-standing champion of the 'Empire', most of the press supported British entry, without showing any understanding of its deeper implications. As the government wanted, the issue was presented almost entirely in terms of economics and the supposed benefits that would follow from British industry being exposed to the 'icy blasts of competition' from the more 'dynamic' economies of the Six.[46]

The greatest enthusiasm for Britain's involvement with 'Europe' was expressed by a group of younger writers and politicians representing what came to be dubbed the 'What's Wrong With Britain School of Journalism'. These publicists, such as Michael Shanks, author of a best-selling paperback *The Stagnant Society*, or the Labour MP Anthony Crosland, a regular contributor to the intellectual monthly *Encounter*, enjoyed contrasting what they saw as a stuffy, tradition-bound, class-ridden, obsolete, inefficient Britain, lost in nostalgia for the days of Empire, with the newly energetic, innovative, efficient 'Europeans'. These paragons of virtue did not have licensing laws that prevented drinking after 10.30 at night and

---

[44] Williams, op. cit., p. 506.
[45] Booker, Christopher (1969), *The Neophiliacs* (London: Collins), p. 183.
[46] Or, as Macmillan himself termed it, 'the cold douche of competition' (Ball, op. cit., p. 217).

had discovered the secret of economic 'dynamism', which Britain had so obviously lost.[47]

This mindset in turn reflected a much deeper shift in social attitudes that was now evident at all levels of British society. Politically it expressed itself in the striking change that had come over the image of Macmillan, who, at the time of his election victory in 1959, had been identified with the social changes that were carrying Britain into a new age. But in 1961, with his languid aristocratic style, he had quite suddenly come to be seen as a tired, Edwardian grandfather-figure, particularly when measured against the young and 'dynamic' new President Kennedy across the Atlantic. By a new generation of satirists, in the revue *Beyond the Fringe*, in the new magazine *Private Eye*, and in the BBC's television show *That Was The Week That Was*, Macmillan was made an object of ridicule. He was an antediluvian relic of a past age, out of touch with the 'exciting', 'irreverent' new world now taking shape around him.[48]

Then, in early October, the Labour leader Hugh Gaitskell electrified his party's conference at Brighton with a speech wholly dedicated to the Common Market. Lasting 105 minutes, it was arguably the most remarkable speech made to a party conference in the post-war era. He began by observing that the level of debate in the media over this 'crucial, complex and difficult issue' had not been high. He then ranged in magisterial fashion across all the individual issues raised by Britain's application, analysing each in turn, putting the arguments on both sides with devastating clarity, lit by flashes of humour.

He began by discussing at length the economic implications of joining a protectionist trading bloc and abandoning the Commonwealth and EFTA, although, as he noted, these were now showing a more impressive rate of economic growth than the Six. He pointed out that, as even Heath was now being forced to admit, as an 'essential part of the Common Market

[47] The 'What's Wrong With Britain' vogue had also caught on with the two leading 'trendsetting' glossy magazines of the time, *Queen* and *About Town* (owned by a new young publisher, Michael Heseltine). According to a contemporary history: 'It was no accident that it was just these papers which were on the crest of a wave of young, upper-middle class popularity, with their antennae out for any new excitement that happened to be in the air, whether joining the Common Market or candy-striped shirts, economic 'growth' or 'ton-up kids'. (Booker, op. cit., p. 158.)

[48] It was in a full-page strip cartoon in *Private Eye* on 2 November 1962 that Edward Heath was first portrayed as 'Grocer Heath', a nickname that stuck. The sequence of images (drawn by William Rushton to a text by one of the present authors) showed Heath and a senior civil servant, Sir Brussels Sprout, going off to Brussels to negotiate with 'the evil Hallstein gang'. By shouting 'Euratom!', Sprout is transformed into 'Supermarketeer'. He and Heath start laying about them and win 'the Concessions!', such as '2d. off Indian tea' or '4d. off New Zealand butter' (hence 'the Grocer'). Returning home, they are acclaimed as heroes, but the final frame records how their 'great victory was nothing more than the graceful surrender that had been inevitable all along'.

agricultural policy' now taking shape, Britain would be obliged 'to import expensive food from the continent of Europe in place of cheap food from the Commonwealth'.

He addressed the by-now familiar claim that, by joining the EEC, Britain would have a 'home market of 220 million people', pointing out that some of Europe's most successful economies belonged to small countries, such as Switzerland and Sweden, which did not have large home markets. He dismissed the more extravagant claims being made for the economic benefits of joining the EEC as 'rubbish', explaining that Britain would not find a solution to her economic malaise simply from joining the Common Market. Ultimately, she would only be able to solve it by her own internal efforts.

Gaitskell then turned to the political aspects of merging Britain's destiny with Europe. Here he challenged Macmillan for being nothing like frank enough with the British people. 'We are told,' he said, 'that the Economic Community is not just a customs union, that all who framed it saw it as a stepping stone towards political integration.' But Macmillan was keeping remarkably quiet about the 'serious political obligations' this might imply. What the move towards 'political' or 'federal' union meant, Gaitskell explained, was that powers would be taken from national governments and handed to the new federal government. If Britain was to become part of this, she would be 'no more than a state … in the United States of Europe, such as Texas and California'. If this process was ultimately to lead the British people to hand over all the most important decisions on economic and foreign policy and defence to a 'supranational system', to be decided by a Council of Ministers or a 'federal parliament', Britain would become no more than 'a province of Europe'. It was this that prompted Gaitskell to the most famous passage in his speech, where he said:

> We must be clear about this; it does mean, if this is the idea, the end of Britain as an independent European state … it means the end of a thousand years of history. You may say 'let it end'. But my goodness, it is a decision which needs a little care and thought.

In conclusion, Gaitskell pointed out that Macmillan had no mandate for his proposals. Indeed, it ran contrary to everything the government had told the British people during the 1959 election campaign. Yet they were now, in effect, being told that they were 'not capable of judging this issue – the government knows best, the top people are the only people who can really understand it … the classic argument of every tyranny in history'. The

Labour Party proposed that the only honest, democratic way to proceed was to see what terms emerged from the negotiations, then put the most important decision the British people had ever faced to the test of an election.[49] His speech received a tumultuous ovation.

However, Denis Healey thought the argument exaggerated. He found it 'inconceivable' that the Common Market would acquire supranational powers in any major area, still less become a federation. He did not share Gaitskell's 'romantic chauvinism' and thought the whole issue 'a futile distraction'. In any case, 'it was certain that de Gaulle would veto Britain's entry'.[50]

Macmillan's response when the Conservatives met for their own conference at Llandudno the following week was to ridicule Gaitskell's analysis. Referring to his fears of political union, he said: 'Mr Gaitskell now prattles on about our being reduced to the status of Texas or California. What nonsense! ... there can be no question of Britain being out-voted into some arrangement which we found incompatible with our needs and responsibilities and traditions.'[51] But the headlines were reserved for Macmillan's quotation of an old music hall song, in which he sought to contrast his own decisiveness with Gaitskell's lack of courage: 'She wouldn't say "yes", she wouldn't say "no". She wouldn't say "stay", she wouldn't say "go". She wanted to climb but she dreaded to fall. So she bided her time, and clung to the wall.'

The 4,000 Tory delegates, most of whom sported 'Yes' badges handed out by party managers, rocked with laughter and gave Macmillan a standing ovation, so backing a policy that all but a handful of them two years earlier would have rejected as unthinkable. The irony was that, although none of those hearing these speeches were aware of it, the die against British entry had already been cast. The day after Macmillan's speech, pictures taken by an American U-2 identified nuclear-capable Soviet missiles on the island of Cuba, only 90 miles off the Florida coast. So began the 'Cuban Missile Crisis', which by 25 October had escalated to the point where nuclear war seemed imminent. What emerged was evidence of America's willingness to pursue her own interests, irrespective of the effects on her allies. One effect was to cement the Franco-German relationship.

On 15 December 1962, Macmillan met de Gaulle at Rambouillet. Six weeks after the end of the Cuba crisis, Macmillan was more determined than ever to keep Britain's independent nuclear deterrent, but he had just learned that the US had cancelled the missile he hoped to buy, Skybolt. He told de

---

[49] Gaitskell's speech is published in full in *The Eurosceptic Reader*, op. cit., pp. 15–37.
[50] Healey, Denis (1989), *The Time of My Life* (London: Michael Joseph), p. 211.
[51] *The Times*, 15 October 1962.

Gaulle that, as a replacement, he planned to ask Kennedy for Polaris. But the French president seemed preoccupied with the Brussels negotiations. 'In the Six', as he was later to reflect, France could say 'No', even against the Germans; she could stop policies with which she disagreed, because of the strength of her position. Once Britain and all the rest joined, 'things would be different'.[52]

De Gaulle's negative attitude came as a shock to Macmillan. With 'indignation', he accused the French president of putting forward 'a fundamental objection to Britain's application'.[53] He was right. And de Gaulle had already decided to turn this 'fundamental objection' into a veto, which he explained to his own Cabinet a few days later, on 19 December 1962:

> If Great Britain and … the Commonwealth enter, it would be as if the Common Market had … dissolved within a large free trade area … Always the same question is posed, but the British don't answer. Instead, they say, 'It's the French who don't want it' … To please the British, should we call into question the Common Market and the negotiation of the agricultural regulations that benefit us? All this would be difficult to accept … Britain continues to supply itself cheaply in Canada, New Zealand, Australia, etc. The Germans are dying to do the same in Argentina. The others would follow. What will we do with European, and particularly French surpluses? If we have to spend 500 billion [francs] a year on agricultural subsidies, what will happen if the Common Market can no longer assist us? These eminently practical questions should not be resolved on the basis of sentiments. [Macmillan] is melancholy and so am I. We would prefer Macmillan's Britain to that of Labour, and we would like to help him stay in office. But what can I do? Except to sing him the Edith Piaf song: *Ne pleurez pas, Milord.*[54]

Still failing to recognise de Gaulle's real concern, Macmillan pursued the acquisition of Polaris during a bilateral summit with Kennedy at Nassau on 18 to 21 December 1962, when he asked Kennedy to make the missile available to both Britain and France. Kennedy was only prepared to say, Delphically, that the two countries might be given Polaris on 'similar terms'. He knew that Britain was in a position to make her own thermonuclear warheads while France was not; which meant that, even if Congressional approval was forthcoming, there was no way France could be given the missiles.

[52] *Memoirs*, pp. 353–354.
[53] Ibid.
[54] Peyrefitte, Alain (1994), *C'était de Gaulle*, Vol. 1: *La France redevient la France* (Paris: Fayard), p. 333.

On Boxing Day, Macmillan wrote to Heath, evaluating his own performance at Rambouillet and ruminating over whether this or Nassau had complicated the negotiations. But, from what he described as a 'rather shrewd analysis', the Official Historian noted there was missing one important ingredient. 'Macmillan', he wrote, 'with his strategic view of the sweep of history, almost certainly underestimated the extent to which France's agricultural interests were prominent in de Gaulle's political calculations, as they have been in every one of his successors since.'[55]

Macmillan was about to get an object lesson on de Gaulle's real concerns. On 14 January 1963, under crystal chandeliers in the Élysée Palace in Paris, and without warning his partners in the Six, de Gaulle announced that he intended to veto Britain's entry. In the most-quoted passage of his 1,500-word statement, he declared:

> England, in effect is insular. She is maritime. She is linked through her trade, her markets, her supply lines to the most distant countries. She pursues essentially industrial and commercial activities and only slightly agricultural ones. She has, in all her doings, very marked and very original habits and traditions. In short England's nature, England's structure, England's very situation differs profoundly from those of the Continentals.

This part of the text has often been interpreted as a nationalistic attack on Britain. Commentators have used it to argue that de Gaulle vetoed the British application because of Macmillan's deal with Kennedy over Polaris. This is cited as evidence of Macmillan's 'Atlanticism' and his preference for the 'special relationship' with the United States. Certainly, this weighed heavily with de Gaulle, as he saw the whole philosophy of the British and the Americans as quite different from that of the 'Europeans', characterised above all by France and Germany.

However, in his memoirs, Alain Peyrefitte, then de Gaulle's information minister, recalls a conversation with the General on the veto, while the press conference was being prepared. De Gaulle stressed that he intended to clear up the matter of England's (sic) entry into the Common Market, explaining why she could not enter. It was not because we don't want her, de Gaulle said. Rather, she was not yet ready to subscribe to the obligations

---

[55] Wall, Stephen (2013), *The Official History of Britain and the European Community: Volume II – From Rejection to Referendum, 1963–1975* (Abingdon, Oxon: Routledge), p. 18. Wall cites: National Archives PREM 11/4412.

of the treaty. First, he declared, we build the Common Market. When the construction is 'irreversible', 'then we will see'.[56]

In that context, the preceding paragraphs of de Gaulle's speech, rarely quoted, could hardly have revealed his real underlying concern more clearly. Referring to the vagueness of the Treaty of Rome on agriculture, he stated that, for France, this had to be 'settled':

It is obvious that agriculture is an essential element in our national activity as a whole. We cannot conceive of a Common Market in which French agriculture would not find outlets in keeping with its production. And we agree further that, of the Six, we are the country on which this necessity is imposed in the most imperative manner. That is why when, last January, consideration was given to the setting in motion of the second phase of the Treaty – in other words a practical start in its application – we were led to pose the entry of agriculture into the Common Market as a formal condition. This was finally accepted by our partners, but very difficult and very complex arrangements were needed and some rulings are still outstanding.[57]

In this de Gaulle signalled his concern for the consequences of Britain being allowed to take part in the negotiations before detailed arrangements for the CAP had been finalised. This is confirmed by his own memoirs. Referring to Britain's initial antagonism to the Common Market, and her attempt to set up a rival in EFTA, he says that, by the middle of 1961, the British had 'returned to the offensive':

Having failed from without to prevent the birth of the Community, they now planned to paralyse it from within. Instead of calling for an end to it, they now declared that they themselves were eager to join, and proposed examining the conditions on which they might do so, 'provided that their special relationship with their Commonwealth and their associates in the free trade area were taken into consideration, as well as their special interests in respect of agriculture'. To submit to this would obviously have meant abandoning the Common Market as originally conceived ... I could see the day approaching when I should either have to remove the obstruction ... or extricate France from an enterprise which had gone astray almost as soon as it had begun.[58]

[56] Peyrefitte, op. cit., p. 598.
[57] In Salmon, Trevor and Nicoll, Sir William (1997), *Building European Union: A Documentary History and Analysis* (Manchester: Manchester University Press), p. 88.
[58] De Gaulle, op. cit., pp. 41–42.

The inescapable inference is that de Gaulle was convinced that Britain's entry would have meant 'abandoning the Common Market as originally conceived', threatening the very core of his survival strategy. She could not be permitted to join until the financial details of the CAP had been settled. At last, it seems, Macmillan was beginning to understand what he was up against. In Cabinet discussions on 22 January, he concluded that the intervention 'had been due not to his conviction that the Brussels negotiations had failed but to his realisation that they were within sight of success'. However, he attributed this to de Gaulle's 'ultimate purpose' of creating a Franco-German partnership that would dominate Europe to the exclusion of any Anglo-Saxon influence.[59]

Later, on 11 February 1963, Macmillan repeated his observation to the Commons, telling MPs: 'The end did not come because the discussions were menaced with failure. On the contrary, it was because they threatened to succeed.'[60] In his memoirs, though, Heath did recognise that agriculture had been crucial, noting that:

the Community had agreed, largely under pressure from the French, to sort out the framework of the new policy before entering into serious discussions with us on the arrangement for our entry. The French did not wish the British to be at the table taking part in the formative discussions on the CAP, for fear that we might disrupt the very favourable arrangements they otherwise had every reason to expect from their partners.[61]

Despite this, Heath never acknowledged that this lay at the heart of the French veto. After the first three months of negotiations, he expressed his suspicions to one of his senior civil servants that the French seemed to want to drag out the talks as long as possible. He gave three reasons:

The French expected that opposition would grow in the UK the longer the negotiations progressed; that our own desire to reach an agreement would weaken; and, finally, that something else would turn up to prevent the negotiations being successfully concluded.[62]

The third reason, he suggested, was to prove crucial. The French suspected that our position was becoming progressively weaker economically,

[59] National Archives, CAB 128/37/5.
[60] HC Deb, 11 February 1963, Vol. 671, cc943-1072.
[61] Memoirs, 1961–1963. pp. 216–217.
[62] Ibid., p. 220.

politically and militarily, *vis-à-vis* both the Six and the US. In their view, the longer matters were drawn out, the greater the opportunity for securing better terms for the Community and themselves in particular.

Heath's view of the negotiations was wholly Anglocentric. To be fair, wrapped up in the narrow, sterile world of the Brussels negotiating circuit, he could hardly have been expected to have grasped the bigger picture. For that, he was reliant on his officials. Yet they were no better informed. A report on the negotiations prepared by the UK delegation was to admit that, during the period between Britain's application and the start of the negotiations, contacts with the Six and the Commission had been minimal, and confined only to 'questions of procedure':

> there was very little knowledge in London of the manner in which the Member Governments, and the Institutions of the Community, were interpreting the provisions of the Treaty of Rome. It is at least possible that, if we had initiated during this period preliminary consultations on matters of substance with Member Governments, and still more with the Commission, we might have acquired information on which we should have been able to base a more informed judgment.[63]

The real failure, therefore, lay with the Foreign Office. Informed analysis would have indicated that a British application could not succeed. The signals were there. But entirely lacking from the tortuous analyses presented to Macmillan and the Cabinet by officials was any recognition of the true French agenda. At heart though, the civil servants (and many of the subsequent commentators) were 'little Englanders'. Like Heath, they viewed the continent from an entirely Anglocentric perspective, assuming that, just because Britain wanted to join, the Six would roll over to admit her, wholly failing to grasp why French rejection was inevitable.

When Britain's application was finally rejected, these 'little Englanders' put the blame on the politicians (though not on Heath, whose 'negotiating skills' continued to win admiration). Yet the failure to understand the vital importance of agriculture to France, and how the CAP was then to be weighted so massively in France's favour, led all those responsible for Britain's application to overlook how greatly disadvantaged Britain would be when she was finally to enter. At their door must lie a great deal of the responsibility for the eventual problems in British farming, which by the

[63] O'Neill, Con (2000), *Britain's Entry into the European Community: Report on the Negotiations of 1970–1972* (London: Frank Cass), p. 49.

late 1990s had led to a major social and economic crisis. The fabled 'Rolls-Royce minds' of the Foreign Office and the Home Civil Service had failed.[64]

As for one of the other items on de Gaulle's agenda, only a week after he had shocked the world with his veto, Adenauer arrived in Paris for the final negotiations on their planned Franco-German treaty. On 20 January, while Adenauer was dining at the German Embassy, Monnet, Hallstein and the Dutch Commissioner, Blankenhorn, burst in to plead with him to link the Franco-German treaty with an assurance that negotiations with Britain should continue. Here de Gaulle's courtship paid off. Adenauer refused. On 22 January the two men signed their treaty, in the same Élysée Palace where de Gaulle, nine days earlier, had announced his veto.

This grand symbol of reconciliation was to be Adenauer's swansong. He had initiated what became known as the Élysée Treaty without consulting his Cabinet and, when it was presented to the Bundestag for ratification, it had been accepted only with the addition of a long, rambling preamble – written by Monnet – which effectively nullified the treaty.[65] This was the last straw for his Christian Democrat Party, which, supported by the Free Democrats under Erhard, forced Adenauer to announce his retirement. The following October, at the age of 87, he reluctantly handed over the reins to the minister who had presided over West Germany's 'economic miracle'.

De Gaulle, when told of this response to the treaty, was reported to have greeted it with a verbal shrug: 'Treaties are like maidens and roses, they each have their day,' he said.[66] In securing Adenauer's support for his veto, the treaty had already served its original purpose.[67] But its longer-term consequences in placing a Franco-German alliance at the heart of the Community were to be profound.

The Six formally confirmed Britain's rejection on 28 January 1963. The news came as Britain was enduring the harshest winter of modern times. Much of the island was covered by deep snow from the beginning of January to March. For weeks London was obscured under a thick freezing fog. This helped bring on the sudden death of Gaitskell, from a rare chest disease, at only 56. He was succeeded by Harold Wilson leading a Labour Party that

---

[64] Milward (op. cit., pp. 425–426) also remarks that, 'In retrospect, the Ministry of Agriculture's optimism about the role Britain would play in shaping the CAP is hard to explain ... their reports and briefings seemed sometimes wilfully to minimise the problems involved ...' and they were 'not based on a full consideration of the way the CAP would also be shaped by political pressures within the Six'.
[65] www.weltpolitik.net/regionen/europa/frankreich/943.html.
[66] Duchêne, op. cit., p. 330.
[67] Spaak confirms de Gaulle's cynicism: Adenauer, he writes, 'failed to resist de Gaulle's deliberate bid to seduce him'. The carefully stage-managed rapprochement at Rheims 'was enough to confuse a man whose advanced age had already weakened his powers of judgement' (Spaak, op. cit., p. 342).

in October 1964 scraped into power on the promise of creating a 'dynamic' and 'classless' 'New Britain'. Scarcely noticed but with almost frenzied speed, Britain was now freeing herself of almost all her remaining colonies across the globe.

When in January 1965 Churchill died at the age of 90, his spectacular state funeral seemed like the nostalgic requiem for a Britain that had already faded into history.

THE CAP: THE BATTLE CONTINUES

The Council, having 'kicked the can down the road' on CAP funding with the 1962 Agriculture Regulation, was now having to confront the 30 June deadline for resolving the issue that it had imposed. In anticipation of its decision, on 31 March 1965 Hallstein submitted a proposal to the Council. But rather than dealing with the funding of the CAP as a separate issue, he decided to link it with contentious proposals to establish the Community's own resources, and stronger powers for the Assembly, all in one package.[68]

Although this strengthened the supranational nature of the Communities, and would therefore attract the hostility of de Gaulle, the Commission calculated that the French government would be prepared to sanction a widening of the EU's powers in exchange for a CAP financing regulation that would be in France's financial interests. The Commission also calculated that, on the eve of presidential elections, de Gaulle would refrain from any action that could jeopardise the CAP for fear that this would alienate French farmers on whose electoral support he depended.[69]

However, not only was French antagonism stronger than anticipated, Hallstein made the tactical error of submitting the package to the Assembly before sending it to the Council. When it was presented to the Council on 28 June, it was rejected. The French then demanded immediate agreement on CAP funding, to allow it to be adopted by 30 June, as originally agreed. But, in the 72 hours left for negotiation, nothing could be agreed, whence the French representative, Couve de Murville – then president of the Council – declared the meeting a failure.[70] De Gaulle ordered his permanent representatives to leave Brussels, and announced a French boycott of all

---

[68] The full text of the proposal is here:
https://www.cvce.eu/en/obj/commission_proposals_concerning_the_financing_of_the_cap_own_resources_and_the_powers_of_the_european_parliament_31_march_1965-en-d4e4ba9d-4d02-4899-aa3a-320a96c46e68.html.
[69] Webber, op. cit.
[70] Spaak, op. cit., pp. 481–482.

EEC meetings concerned with new policies. The Community had entered what became known as the 'empty chair' crisis.

As France's presidential elections approached, Monnet turned openly against de Gaulle, announcing he would vote against him. The combined pressures put de Gaulle in the humiliating position of winning less than 44 per cent in the first round. Monnet then endorsed Mitterrand, the opposition candidate, and de Gaulle only scraped home with a margin of 55 to 45 per cent, far short of the huge majorities he was used to.[71]

Once re-elected, however, de Gaulle set out an ambitious price for France's co-operation with the Community. His government called for the Council to have at least the same powers as the Commission; it should abandon diplomatic missions; cease criticising member states' policies in public; submit proposals to the Council before publicising them; and draft vaguer directives. Most of all, de Gaulle demanded explicit recognition of the right of member states to veto any decision arrived at by qualified majority voting when they considered their 'vital interests' to be at stake.[72]

Yet, despite de Gaulle's overtly nationalistic stance through the crisis, it was significant that his officials only boycotted discussion on new policies. They continued to participate in the EEC's work on existing policies, including the negotiations on the CAP. The effect of the 'empty chair' policy was to draw the Community more tightly together. Consensus, hitherto elusive, suddenly became easier, and the impasse on QMV was resolved in January 1966 with an agreement known as the 'Luxembourg Compromise'. This acknowledged that any government that considered its 'vital interests' threatened by EEC legislation could prevent a decision being taken.[73]

Another price extracted for de Gaulle's return to co-operation was the resignation of Hallstein. But his real victory was the protection of 'vital interests', because the particular vital interest de Gaulle had in mind, as he confirmed in his memoirs, was France's agriculture. He made clear his conviction that, without a settlement designed to suit France's needs, her agriculture 'would constitute an incubus which would put us in a position of chronic inferiority in relation to others'. Thus, he felt obliged to put up

---

[71] Duchêne, op. cit., p. 332.

[72] EEC Commission. Note on the proceedings of the extraordinary meeting of the Council held on 17 and 18 January 1966 in Luxembourg, Strasbourg, 20 January 1966.

[73] Spaak (op. cit., p. 471) was surprised to hear de Gaulle insist that 'the European Community, as established under the Treaty of Rome, must be maintained'. He added, 'De Gaulle tends to adopt this rigid stance to prevent Britain's entry into the Common Market; on the other hand, he is apt to disregard the Treaty altogether when it is a matter of respecting the powers of the EEC Commission or of submitting to a majority vote.'

'literally a desperate fight', sometimes going so far as to threaten to withdraw membership.[74]

BRITAIN'S SECOND REBUFF

By 1967, the 'project' seemed to be making steady progress. By the so-called 'merger treaty', signed in 1965, the EEC, Euratom and the Coal and Steel Community were now brought together as 'the Communities'. In Brussels the new Berlaymont building was opened and immediately filled by 3,000 Commission officials. On a French initiative, the EEC agreed to adopt a new form of indirect taxation, value added tax or VAT: a percentage of which would be passed to the Commission to provide an additional source of revenue for the CAP. And the output of EEC legislation was quickening. In the early years of the decade, the annual production of new directives and regulations had been around 25 a year. By the middle of the decade, the total had reached 50. Now it was topping 100.[75]

Then, quite unexpectedly, came a new British application to join the 'Common Market'. In March 1966, Wilson, hitherto a supporter of his predecessor Gaitskell's opposition to entry, had won a landslide election victory over the Conservatives, now led by Heath. So unlikely was it that the Wilson government would apply to join the EEC that, during the election campaign, Nigel Lawson, then editor of *The Spectator*, commented: 'Europe is the supreme issue at this election ... no one who genuinely believes in a European Britain can vote Labour.'[76] Wilson's parliamentary secretary, Peter Shore, later recalled that he still seemed as hostile to British entry as Gaitskell.[77]

In July 1966, however, only four months after Wilson's election victory, Britain's chronic balance of payments problem came to a head. In the eight years between 1956 and 1964, Britain's economic performance had been lamentable compared with her continental neighbours. The annual increase in her industrial production had averaged just 2.8 per cent, against West Germany's 7.3, Italy's 8.2 and France's 6.2 per cent. The growth of national *per capita* income had shown Britain similarly lagging behind, her 26.2 per cent increase dwarfed by West Germany's 58.2 per cent, Italy's 58.3 per cent and France's 47.5 per cent.[78]

---

[74] De Gaulle, Charles (1971), *Memoirs of Hope: Renewal 1958–1962* (London: Weidenfeld & Nicolson), p. 159.
[75] *Official Journal of the European Communities: Directory of Community Legislation in Force and Other Acts of the Community Institutions*, Vol. II, *Chronological Index*.
[76] *The Spectator*, 25 March 1966.
[77] Shore, Peter (2000), *Separate Ways: The Heart Of Europe* (London: Duckworth), p. 68.
[78] *Britain and Europe: The Future* (1966), London, p. 47, cited in Maclean, Donald (1970), *British Foreign Policy Since Suez 1956–1968* (London: Hodder & Stoughton), p. 80.

With the pound now under extreme pressure, Wilson introduced panic counter-measures, including a surcharge on imports, which threatened to bring even this modest growth to a halt. His familiar cheery optimism vanished. He began to look around in desperation for some more dramatic solution. Another factor in his thinking was the growing frustration of his dealings with the Commonwealth. Since the white supremacist regime in Rhodesia had unilaterally declared independence from Britain in 1965, relations with his fellow Commonwealth leaders had become increasingly painful.[79] In addition, as Peter Shore recalled, Wilson had been 'got at' by some of his closest advisers, who were fervently 'pro-European', notably his private secretary Michael Palliser and his Home Secretary Roy Jenkins, who in the summer of 1967 Wilson was to make Chancellor of the Exchequer.[80]

In face of all these pressures, Wilson made a remarkable *volte face*. By October 1966 he had decided that Britain should make a new application.[81] Although his Cabinet was sharply divided, with ministers such as Denis Healey, Barbara Castle and Douglas Jay strongly opposed, a majority supported his change of policy, on the promise that Wilson and his new foreign secretary George Brown would make a 'Grand Tour' of the capitals of the Six to sound out opinion.

The tour started on 15 January 1967, when Wilson was described by his Eurosceptic backbencher Michael Foot as trotting round Europe 'like Don Quixote, his Sancho Panza at his side'.[82] Yet there was far more to this tour than Foot could even have imagined. The Italians and the Germans supported British entry, but, on the Wednesday afternoon of 25 January 1967, the pair met the French prime minister, Georges Pompidou, and foreign minister Maurice Couve de Murville, at the Hotel Matignon in Paris.[83] After George Brown had talked about the problems for the UK in adapting to the CAP, Pompidou noted that the difficulties 'were not secondary ones'. They 'went to the heart of the Common Agricultural Policy and concerned precisely

[79] Shore, op. cit., p. 70.
[80] Ibid., p. 71.
[81] US views were no longer a serious factor. Washington was now almost wholly preoccupied with the Vietnam War. Most of the 'Europeanists' in Kennedy's Cabinet had either departed or were otherwise engaged. Even George Ball was now devoting much of his time to Vietnam policy (and was eventually to resign over President Johnson's handling of the war). The State Department's economic bureau was actually hostile to British entry, because it believed that this could threaten the successful conclusion of the 'Kennedy Round' of GATT (Department of State telegram 186605, 2 May 1967, Administrative History of the Department of State, LBJL, cited in Winand, op. cit., p. 362).
[82] The Times, 9 May 1967.
[83] National Archives, CAB 129/128 c33. Record of a meeting between the Prime Minister and the Foreign Secretary and the French Prime Minister and the French Foreign Minister at the Hotel Matignon, Paris, on Wednesday 25 January 1967, at 3 p.m.

those points on which it has been most difficult to reach agreement between the Six partners in the Common Market'.

Pompidou went on to say that it had been 'necessary to construct the Common Agricultural Policy on a basis that would enable the Community to become self-sufficient, and to impose penalties on imports of food from outside the Community, hence the high prices and the system of protecting the least competitive elements in the Community'. While he agreed with Brown that the UK's difficulties were not 'insuperable', Pompidou felt 'bound to point out that it was precisely the three points he had mentioned, i.e., imports from third countries (e.g., from the Commonwealth), the level of prices, and the financial regulations, on which the Community had found it most difficult to reach agreement'. If these issues were reopened, the French prime minister said, 'major problems would arise for the Six'.[84]

Wilson and his foreign minister then went on to meet President de Gaulle at the Élysée Palace. In a short preliminary meeting, before the rest of his ministers joined him, de Gaulle immediately raised the issue of agriculture, only then to raise it again in the broader meeting, stressing that it was of 'special importance to the French Government'.[85] If he had flagged it up in neon lights at the top of the Eiffel Tower, he could not have made himself clearer. In terms of detail, Wilson later told his Cabinet that General de Gaulle 'did not of course commit himself', but Pompidou did. He emphasised that 'the Common Agricultural Policy had given rise to very serious problems within the Community itself before the Six finally succeeded in reaching agreement on it, and it would be very unwise, therefore, to underrate the difficulties which would arise if it now had to accommodate British entry into the Community'.[86]

Despite this, Wilson and Brown came away from meetings optimistic. They thought they had convinced de Gaulle and his ministers that the UK was not only 'entirely serious' in its determination to enter the Community, but also 'that the stock French excuses for obstructing our entry would no longer serve their purpose'. The prime minister recommended to Cabinet that entry should be pursued.[87] At Adenauer's funeral on 26 April,[88] Wilson had admitted to the then-German chancellor Dr Kiesinger that there were: 'economic disadvantages in entering the Common Market but they are

[84] Ibid.
[85] Ibid. Record of a conversation between the Prime Minister and the President and the Prime Minister of France at the Élysée Palace on Wednesday 25 January 1967 at 4.15 p.m.
[86] Ibid.
[87] Ibid. The Approach to Europe, Memorandum by the Prime Minister and the Foreign Secretary.
[88] Adenauer died on 19 April 1967.

being overlooked by the British Government because of the tremendous political advantages'.[89] On 30 April, the Cabinet voted to apply for entry, by 13 votes to eight. Wilson described the application as 'a great turning point in history', stating that he believed, on balance, 'it will be right economically, but the political argument is stronger'. Britain's role was 'to make Europe stronger, more independent, more decisive in world affairs'.

Monnet's Action Committee had already declared itself 'unanimously in favour' of British entry.[90] In Strasbourg on 9 May, when the European Parliament discussed Britain's application, Fernand Dehousse, a Belgian Socialist, declared that it had 'rejoiced our hearts'. The Gaullists were silent. When, on 10 May, after Britain's entry had been considered by the French Cabinet, Georges Gorse, the minister of information, said:

> France in the past has sufficiently deplored British insularity not to rejoice over any trend in the opposite direction. I think General de Gaulle will speak about this at his press conference and will be in a position to express the satisfaction provoked in French public opinion by the movement which is pushing Britain towards Europe – a movement we have always hoped for – and the difficult problems raised by a candidature of this importance with everything that implies.[91]

But de Gaulle still had not secured his financing system for the CAP. It could hardly have been a coincidence, therefore, on 16 May, that he delivered his verdict: *Le Grand Non*. His statement included the widely cited declaration that Britain's entry would only be possible when 'this great people, so magnificently gifted with ability and courage, should on their own behalf and for themselves achieve a profound economic and political transformation which could allow them to join the Six continentals'. But perhaps more significant was the long earlier passage in which, by referring to 'the agricultural regulations', de Gaulle gave another indication of his real motives. Britain, he said, 'nourishes herself, to a great extent, on foodstuffs bought inexpensively throughout the world and, particularly, in the Commonwealth'. If she was to submit 'to the rules of the Six', then her 'balance of payments would be crushed' by the duties on her food imports. She would then be forced to raise her food prices to continental levels, causing her even greater problems. But, de Gaulle continued,

[89] Crossman, Richard (1976), *The Diaries of a Cabinet Minister*, Vol. II (London: Hamish Hamilton), p. 330.
[90] Monnet, op. cit., p. 487.
[91] *The Times*, 11 May 1967.

if she enters the Community without being really subjected to the agricultural system of the Six, the system will thereby collapse, completely upsetting the equilibrium of the Common Market and removing for France one of the main reasons she can have for participating in it.[92]

Just as in 1963, de Gaulle had laid out with consummate clarity for those with eyes to see why British entry at this stage was out of the question. Wilson, like Heath and Macmillan before him, showed no signs of understanding de Gaulle's objections, tabling Britain's application in July 1967. If there was any doubt, though, it must have been dispelled in November, when Couve de Murville addressed the French National Assembly. He told the deputies that Britain's acceptance of the Treaty of Rome did not resolve membership issues. 'The questions which immediately come to mind', he argued, 'are those concerning the CAP and, in the first place, the financial regulation because it constitutes the framework.' He went on:

Everyone knows it will have to be completed before 1 January 1970 in order for this to become a definitive regulation. As things are at present, we can envisage that there will be no insurmountable difficulties. But what would it be like if Britain participated in the discussion? In any case, we cannot imagine that, prior to a negotiation, the Six would not adopt the definitive regulation ... even if subsequently other arrangements might form the subject of discussion.[93]

Commenting on this, the official historian wrote: 'There could not have been a clearer signal that France would not allow negotiations with Britain to begin.'[94] Predictably, on 27 November 1967, at a news conference in the Élysée Palace, attended by more than a thousand diplomats, civil servants and ministers as well as journalists, de Gaulle formally vetoed Britain's application. Shore records how Wilson then instructed that preparations should be made for another application in the summer of 1970.[95]

THE FINAL BATTLES
Before de Gaulle could finally secure the ultimate prize of his financial regulation, he unexpectedly found himself facing a major crisis. In May

[92] De Gaulle, Charles, fifteenth press conference, 16 May 1967. Text supplied by the French Press and Information Service, New York.
[93] Cited in Wall, op. cit., p. 245.
[94] Ibid.
[95] Shore, op. cit., p. 70.

1968, Paris was taken over by crowds of rebellious students, triggering a wave of strikes and unrest that paralysed the French economy. De Gaulle fled his capital, appealing for support from his army. Invoking fears of a Communist revolution, he called a snap election and won an overwhelming victory.

In Brussels the same year, agriculture commissioner Dr Sicco Mansholt had become seriously disturbed by the way the half-formed version of the CAP was running out of control, with subsidies continuing to soar and food surpluses increasing. As a Dutch free-trader, he had originally wanted a liberal, market-orientated CAP. In particular, he sought to encourage major structural changes to the sector, leading to greater productivity and a substantial drop in employment. What had so far emerged had been the opposite: high support prices with no spending limits and maximum protection. Prices were harmonised at the highest levels, bolstered by subsidised exports of surpluses that were flooding world markets.

In desperation Mansholt decided to work on a major CAP reform, the first of what would be many, producing in 1969 the 'second Mansholt Plan'. This concluded: 'The Community is now having to pay so heavy a price for an agricultural production which bears no relation to demand that measures to balance the situation on the market can no longer be avoided ...'[96] He proposed halving the number of farmers, slaughtering millions of farm animals and turning over 7 per cent of all agricultural land to forestry. Hundreds of thousands of farmers rioted in Brussels and other capitals and two died. Mansholt's own life was threatened. The Six's agriculture ministers, led by Germany, rejected his proposals out of hand. De Gaulle had now almost completely got his way. The Community, and eventually Britain, would pay the price.

In April 1969 de Gaulle held a referendum asking for the French people to approve a tranche of radical reforms. When he lost, he retired from office, to be succeeded by his prime minister, Georges Pompidou. Valéry Giscard d'Estaing became the new premier. It was this succession that was later to be credited for the shift in French policy that allowed Britain, after Heath's victory in the 1970 general election, to make her third and successful application to join the EEC. Another factor attributed to Heath's eventual success was the arrival of Willy Brandt, a supporter of British entry, as the new German chancellor.

---

[96] Commission of the European Communities, 'Memorandum on the Reform of Agriculture in the European Economic Community', Supplement to Bulletin No. 1–69, 1969.

But there was still that vital detail to be settled before Pompidou could allow a further application from Britain or the other three potential applicants – Ireland, Denmark and Norway. He, like de Gaulle, needed that guarantee on CAP financing. At his first presidential press conference on 10 July 1969, he declared that he had no objection in principle to British accession, but the Six first had to 'reach agreement amongst themselves'. At the same press conference, Pompidou agreed to a summit that had been called for by Brandt and other leaders of the Six, to be held at The Hague in December. There, Pompidou hoped, the arrangements would be finalised.

There was also another important issue on the Six's agenda – a sharp revival of interest in economic and monetary union, first mooted by Spaak in his report setting out the framework for the Treaty of Rome. In the early 1960s this had again been advocated by Monnet and Luxembourg's prime minister, Pierre Werner; then again by the European Assembly and the Commission in 1965. Furthermore, the Council of Ministers had already laid the foundations for a common economic policy, by setting up various committees to discuss monetary and economic issues. The most important was Ecofin, at which the finance ministers of the Six held monthly meetings.

In January 1968 Werner formally proposed that the Six should move to full economic and monetary union. This was followed by proposals from Giscard d'Estaing and the Commission.[97] Momentum had now built up to such a degree that Pompidou proposed that the Hague Summit, fixed for 1–2 December, should link negotiations on the budget and the CAP with talks on monetary integration and 'enlargement'. When the summit began, Brandt immediately turned the tables on Pompidou, with a thinly veiled threat that, unless there was 'fair play' for the applicant countries, there would be no agreement on the budget. Piet de Jong, the Dutch prime minister, proposed that the Six should discuss enlargement. Pompidou, in pained surprise, countered that farming must come first. This was agreed. Everyone knew by this time that that was France's price for lifting the veto.[98]

Thus, the Six agreed to deal with the budget and CAP package first. Farm subsidies would be funded not only from levies on imports from outside the EEC but also from a percentage of member state VAT receipts.[99] By 21 April 1970, the replacement funding system had been agreed, with a 1 per cent

---

[97] The Barre Proposals, named after the then-president of the Commission.
[98] Kitzinger, Uwe (1973), *Diplomacy and Persuasion: How Britain Joined the Common Market* (London: Thames & Hudson), p. 71.
[99] 'Communiqué of the meeting of Heads of State or Government of the Member States at The Hague (1 and 2 December 1969)', in *Bulletin of the European Communities* (Luxembourg: Office for Official Publications of the European Communities), 01-1970, no. 1, pp. 11–16.

VAT levy imposed.[100] This was augmented on the same day by a Council Regulation on financing the CAP.[101] To regularise the budget procedure, and to give the Assembly (soon to become the European Parliament) a veto, a new treaty was drawn up and signed on 22 April 1970 in Luxembourg. In the manner of such things, this became the Luxembourg Treaty.[102]

With these matters settled, France could at last agree to the Six opening negotiations with the four would-be applicants, led by Britain, subject to the crucial condition that they would not be allowed to alter the terms of that all-important financial package.[103] In other words, the transition from de Gaulle to Pompidou made no difference to French policy. There could be no enlargement until the CAP financial arrangements were in place. Nevertheless, the budgetary arrangements were not the only unfinished business. The summit's other aim was to plan for further integration: to which effect the heads of government recognised that the Community had now reached a turning point.[104]

If there had ever been any question as to where the Six intended to go, there now could be none. To help it on its way, they commissioned two reports. The first, by Pierre Werner, would be on 'economic and monetary union'. The subject of the other, by the Belgian foreign minister Étienne Davignon, was 'political union'. All this was in train before Heath applied for entry to what he would consistently describe to the British people as merely a 'common market'.

[100] Council Decision 70/243 of 21 April 1970 on the Replacement of Financial Contributions from Member States by the Communities' own Resources. OJ No. L 94/19.
[101] Regulation (EEC) No. 729/70 of the Council of 21 April 1970 on the financing of the common agricultural policy.
[102] https://eur-lex.europa.eu/legal-content/FR/TXT/PDF/?uri=CELEX:11970F/TXT&from=EN.
[103] O'Neill, op. cit., p. 169.
[104] Summit communiqué, *Bulletin of the European Communities*, 1–1970: para. 4.

6

The Real Deceit of Edward Heath: 1970–1972

There are some in this country who fear that in going into
Europe we shall in some way sacrifice independence and
sovereignty. These fears, I need hardly say, are completely
unjustified.

Edward Heath, prime ministerial TV broadcast,
January 1973

The bedrock of European union is the consent of the people.

Edward Heath, The Course of My Life[1]

In April 1970, a Gallup poll showed that only 15 per cent of the British
electorate were in favour of a further bid to join the Common Market.
Nearly three in five voters were opposed. A month later Wilson called
a general election which, on 15 June, unexpectedly resulted in Heath
becoming prime minister.

The Common Market played virtually no part in the campaign. Sixty-
two per cent of Conservative candidates made no reference to the EEC in
their election addresses. Only 2 per cent declared strong support for British
entry.[2] Even Heath devoted only 3 per cent of his speeches to it.[3] His party's
manifesto contained only a one-line promise 'to negotiate, no more, no
less'.[4] In television and radio coverage, the Common Market did not even

---

[1] Heath, op. cit., p. 359.
[2] Butler, David and Pinto-Duschinski, Michael (1971), *The British General Election of 1970* (London: Macmillan), p. 440.
[3] Ibid., p. 444.
[4] Conservative Party (1970), *A Better Tomorrow: The Conservative Programme for the Next Five Years*, p. 28.

rate among the top 12 issues.[5] It might therefore have come as something of a surprise to most voters to learn that, within two weeks of the election, two of Heath's senior ministers would be in Brussels to begin negotiations for entry and that, within three years, without any electoral mandate, Britain would have become a full member of the EEC.

'SWALLOW IT WHOLE, AND SWALLOW IT NOW'

The two ministers handling the negotiations were foreign secretary Alec Douglas-Home and his colleague Anthony Barber. On 30 June 1970, they were in Brussels. In the presence of delegations from the three other applicant countries, Ireland, Denmark and Norway, Barber explained that Britain was now ready to accept the Treaties establishing the three European Communities, and all 'the decisions that have flowed from them', in their entirety. As Sir Con O'Neill, the civil servant leading Britain's negotiating team, was to record, this 'had far-reaching implications'.[6]

It was true that, as in 1961, Britain had little choice but to accept the *acquis communautaire*, but the situation had 'fundamentally altered'. In 1961, the *acquis* had consisted of little more than the treaties themselves. Since then, an 'almost inconceivable flood' of new laws had been enacted, amounting to some 13,000 pages, for many of which the official translations would not be completed until after the treaty of accession had been signed.[7] This, O'Neill was to recall, 'haunted us throughout the negotiations':

> Everything, beginning with the Treaties themselves, on which any of the three Communities, through any of their institutions, had ever reached agreement in any form, even if it had never been published, was, provided it had not clearly lapsed or been rescinded, a part of it. And we were asked to endorse, accept and be bound by it all.[8]

O'Neill himself summed up Britain's policy: 'swallow the lot, and swallow it now'.[9] The negotiations, therefore, were no more than a façade, to conceal

[5] Butler and Pinto-Duschinski, op. cit., pp. 159 and 210.
[6] O'Neill, op. cit., p. 434. As an FCO Under-Secretary, O'Neill was in charge of Britain's negotiating team between 1970 and 1972. When the negotiations were concluded, he was commissioned to write a full internal report of 475 pages, which was only published in 2000. Between 1935 and 1946 O'Neill was a Fellow of All Souls, with Arthur Salter, and served in Brussels as British Ambassador to the European Communities, 1963–1965.
[7] Ibid., p. 38.
[8] Ibid.
[9] Ibid., p. 40.

the fact that Heath was determined on entry at almost any price. As in 1961, Britain could only seek transitional concessions or 'derogations'. These centred on the amount Britain would contribute to the Community budget; arrangements for Commonwealth exports, and what Barber tactfully called 'certain matters of agricultural policy'. Barber himself was not to lead the British delegation much longer because, following the death in July of Iain Macleod, Heath appointed him Chancellor of the Exchequer. His place was taken by Geoffrey Rippon QC, who led the top-level negotiations. Detailed day-to-day work was conducted by officials.

The issue dominating the first months of negotiations was Britain's budgetary contribution. The way agricultural funding had been devised would ensure that her contribution to the £3 billion annual budget was disproportionately high. And with the CAP funding soaking up 91 per cent, the largest share of the payments would go to France. For political reasons, it was agreed that Britain would not pay her full share immediately, particularly since the shift to more expensive European food imports would be increasing prices in Britain. As Heath himself put it:

> We resolved that we should assume our obligations gradually, because too large a contribution at the beginning, before the dynamic benefits of membership had come through, would have damaged both Britain and the Community as a whole. It would have jeopardised the smooth passage upon which the enlarged Community's successful progress in the first few years would depend.[10]

Initially, Britain would pay 11.5 per cent in the first year, rising to 21.5 per cent after five years. This the British thought excessive but, as expected, initial Community responses to complaints were 'slow and stiff'.[11] It was not until Christmas 1970 that they came back with counter-proposals. Thus ended the first phase of the negotiations, in which little had been achieved.

'A FEDERAL STATE WITH A SINGLE CURRENCY'
Elsewhere in Brussels, as agreed at the Hague Summit, work had continued on Werner's report on 'economic and monetary union' and Davignon's on political union. As their findings emerged, they threatened to cause Heath considerable embarrassment. There was no doubt that the target of the

---

[10] Heath, op. cit., p. 364.
[11] National Archives, PREM 15/062, W. A. Nield to Robert Armstrong, 16 October 1970.

final Werner Report, published on 8 October 1970, was an immense leap forward in political integration.[12]

Monetary union would mean an irreversible freezing of exchange rates between the EEC's currencies. A 'sole Community currency' was optional but 'considerations of a psychological and political nature' militated in favour of its adoption, confirming 'the irreversibility of the venture'.[13] Economic policies would be centralied in stages, to be completed by 1980, which would also mean centralised co-ordination of regional and structural policies. Werner himself was explicit about implications. The 'centre of decision for economic policy' would be supranational and be able to 'influence' national budgets. A new 'Community institution' (foreshadowing the future European Central Bank) would be 'empowered to take decisions, according to the requirements of the economic situation, in the interests of monetary policy as regards liquidity, rates of interest, and the granting of loans to private and public sectors. In the field of external monetary policy.' It could also intervene in the foreign exchange market and the management of the monetary reserves of the Community.[14]

Werner conceded that such a massive 'transfer of powers to the Community level from the national centres of decision' would raise 'a certain number of political problems'.[15] These were not lost on Whitehall. The Foreign Office (now the Foreign and Commonwealth Office or FCO) produced an urgent note for Heath, copied by the Treasury, pointing out that the Plan had 'revolutionary long-term implications, both economic and political'. It could imply the ultimate creation of a European federal state with a single currency. All the basic instruments of national economic management (fiscal, monetary, incomes and regional policies) would ultimately be handed over to the federal authorities, to be accomplished within a decade.[16]

Monetary union, the FCO feared, could become a central point of negotiations over entry, since it would arouse strong feelings about sovereignty and provoke vigorous discussions of its implications for future

---

[12] Council – Commission of the European Communities (1970), *Report to the Council and the Commission on the Realisation by Stages of Economic and Monetary Union in the Community* (The Werner Report), Supplement to Bulletin 11.

[13] Ibid., p. 10.

[14] Ibid., p. 13.

[15] Ibid.

[16] As reported in the *Guardian*, 1 January 2002: 'Treasury Warned Heath that EMU Plan Could Herald European Superstate'. The Treasury text is essentially the same as the FCO briefing. National Archives, FCO 30/789 (undated).

policy. In some areas, such as taxation, Britain might find it hard to make more compromises than other countries. Nevertheless, the FCO argued, 'we see no real reason why UK interests should significantly suffer'. Any problems, it added optimistically, 'ought not to be incapable of agreed solutions within the community'. But it had to be faced that EMU would lead to the UK and the other EEC countries becoming as

> interlocked as those of the states of the US. Indeed, it could be argued that the independence of the members would be less than that of the (US) states, for the latter have more autonomy over their budgets. The degree of freedom which would then be vested in national governments might indeed be somewhat less than the autonomy enjoyed by the constituent states of the US. There would be relatively little surrender of national sovereignty in the economic field, though as the first stage (of EMU) progressed, sovereignty would pass steadily towards the centre. At the ultimate stage economic sovereignty would to all intents and purposes disappear at the national level and the Community would itself be the master of ... economic policy.[17]

Crucially, the FCO warned, 'there must be no mistake about the final objective; the process of change is "irreversible", and the implications, both economic and political, must be accepted from the outset'.

For Heath and his advisers privately to accept such a plan was one thing. But at a moment when the British people were being assured that the Common Market was little more than a trading arrangement, this could be political dynamite. Geoffrey Rippon hurried over to Luxembourg for a personal interview with Werner on 27 October. He congratulated him on his report but, alarmed at how such a radical step might be received by the British public, asked that political and economic union be achieved through a 'step by step approach'. It was 'natural for people to be afraid of change' and 'part of his problem in Britain was to reassure people that their fears were unjustified'.[18]

If Werner's proposals were not enough, three weeks later the foreign ministers of the Six adopted Davignon's report, on 'the problems of political

---

[17] Ibid.
[18] From minutes to the meeting recorded by Rippon's private secretary Crispin Tickell (National Archives, CAB 164/771). When these were released under the 30-year rule on 1 January 2000, Tickell admitted in a BBC television interview that worries over Britain's loss of sovereignty had been 'very much present in the mind of the negotiators', but that the general line had been 'the less they came out in the open the better'.

unification', in what became known as the 'Luxembourg Agreement'.[19] This too was radically integrationist in tone, proposing a single European foreign policy. To express 'the will for a political union' it was necessary 'to bring nearer the day when Europeans can speak with one voice'.[20] Ministers agreed to hold twice-yearly meetings, while a committee of senior officials would confer at least four times a year to lay the groundwork for them. Governments undertook to consult on all major foreign policy issues and to 'pursue work on the best way to achieve progress towards political unification'.[21] In view of the revolutionary contents of the two reports, it must have come as a relief to Heath that they were barely noticed in Britain.[22]

A COUP DE THÉÂTRE

The resumed negotiations in January 1971 continued to move with glacial slowness, the focus remaining on Britain's budget contribution. At a press conference on 21 January, Pompidou was asked his opinion of the British position. He replied: 'One must admit that the British have three qualities among others: humour, tenacity and realism. I have the feeling that we are slightly in the humorous stage.'[23] So little had been achieved that O'Neill found it necessary to convey to the officials with whom he was negotiating his 'concern at the pace at which this conference is proceeding'.

Several reasons were adduced for this delay.[24] However, the consensus seems to be that French 'intransigence' was to blame, with Pompidou insisting that Britain should move to full Community preference from the beginning.[25] Frustration was shared by other member states. Davignon, then *chef de cabinet* to the Belgian foreign minister, suggested that Pompidou 'had the mentality of a small trader who wished to sell his overcoat for as

---

[19] European Parliament (1982), *Selection of Texts Concerning Institutional Matters of The Community from 1950–1982* (Luxembourg), pp. 146–151.

[20] Ibid., p. 147.

[21] Ibid.

[22] A rare exception was the response to the Werner proposals by a former city editor Nigel Lawson in the *Sunday Times* on 22 November 1970, observing that 'a national currency lies at the very heart of national sovereignty. A common currency is something that can only properly follow political union: it cannot precede it.' In later years Werner was to be described as 'the father of the single currency'.

[23] National Archives, FCO 30/789, op. cit.

[24] Con O'Neill, for instance, hypothesised that the French were waiting for ratification of the 1970 Luxembourg Treaty to secure the CAP financing package. This can hardly have been the case. The move to own resources had been foreseen in the Treaty of Rome (Art. 201) and did not need a treaty change to bring it into effect (op. cit., p. 172).

[25] Wall, op. cit., p. 382. See also National Archives, PREM 15/062, Letter from W. A. Nield, permanent secretary at the Cabinet Office, to the Prime Minister, dated 30 December 1970. Neild refers to the French having 'again demonstrated their capacity for intransigence'. He also wrote of the need for 'a summit about April/May to break a deadlock in the negotiations arising from French intransigence'.

much as possible. The only way to persuade him that it was hardly worth selling at all was to put the British arguments directly to him at a meeting with the Prime Minister.'[26]

In late February 1971, Christopher Soames had a long talk with Pompidou's right-hand man, Michel Jobert. He came away persuaded that such a meeting would be useful. But, on 25 February, Soames met Pompidou himself. The French president said nothing about a possible meeting but stressed that the UK must pay a higher percentage of the Community budget after the end of the transitional period than it had so far proposed, and that 'Community preference' must apply from the first day of UK accession. These were France's 'priorities'.

Through Jobert, Pompidou was then told that a meeting between himself and Heath 'would be an important element in the negotiations'. By similar circuitous means, the principle of a meeting was agreed. The great 'summit' itself finally took place on 20 and 21 May in the Élysée Palace. Heath was to wax lyrical in his memoirs about the venue. Yet to the actual contents of their discussion he gives just a few lines, amid two and a half pages of description:

> Pompidou had stressed that what he felt was needed was an historic change in the British attitude. Britain was really determined to make this change, France would welcome us into the Community. He regarded his own country and Britain as the only two European countries with what he termed a 'world vocation' and said quite explicitly that, if the political and intellectual prestige and authority of Britain were added to those of the Six, the Community would be greatly enriched. My task was to convince him that this was also what we wanted to see ... Our purpose was a strong Europe, which could speak with one voice ... and could then exert effective influence in different parts of the globe.[27]

Such was narrative of the time that Heath had managed to convince Pompidou that 'Britain was genuine in its desire to enter the European family'.[28] At a press conference on the Friday evening, Pompidou gave his own version:

> Many people believed that Great Britain was not and did not wish to become European, and that Britain wanted to enter the Community only so as to destroy it or to divert it from its objectives. Many people thought

[26] Op. cit., p. 386.
[27] Heath, op. cit., p. 370.
[28] Ibid., p. 372.

that France was ready to use every pretext to place in the end a fresh veto on Britain's entry. Well, ladies and gentlemen, you see before you this evening two men who are convinced to the contrary.[29]

For Heath, this was a 'wildly exciting moment', rounded off by the pair seated together at a table in the Salle des Fêtes – the same room in which, eight years before, de Gaulle had pronounced his first veto on Britain's application. There, Pompidou had declared: 'It would be unreasonable to think that agreement between Britain and the EEC will not be reached in June.'[30]

THE NEGOTIATIONS ARE 'SUCCESSFUL'

Following the summit, French support for British entry was now assured. Considering how little had been achieved in the first nine months, the speed with which all outstanding issues were resolved seemed almost miraculous.[31] But the timing of this had nothing to do with the Heath–Pompidou summit. The most important factor had been the agreement of an 'own resources' decision in the January, which had paved the way for CAP payments.[32] Now the formerly intractable problem of Commonwealth imports could be resolved, with special concessions given for New Zealand butter, although O'Neill reckoned that the terms on which these were granted would add an extra £100 million a year to Britain's budgetary contribution (at 1972 prices). No concessions at all were made for Australia and Canada, although some Caribbean sugar and bananas would still be allowed into Britain under preferential arrangements.

The key meetings took place between 21 and 23 June, when agreement was finally reached on New Zealand dairy products and Britain's budgetary contribution. The 'back of the negotiations was broken' and, after two all-night sessions, when the last meeting ended a little before 5 a.m. on 23 June, 'all were convinced that the negotiations would succeed'.[33] The price was extremely high, but to Heath the agreement was a 'favourable compromise'. Britain was to pay 8.64 per cent of the Community budget in

---

[29] Ibid.

[30] National Archives, PREM 15/371.

[31] Spaak (op. cit., p. 237) was to remark that a lesson he had learned from earlier negotiations was that, 'Where there is a political will, there are no surmountable technical obstacles. Where such a political will is lacking, every technical obstacle becomes a pretext for those out to wreck whatever negotiations are in progress.' This episode seems to have borne out his view.

[32] Regulation No. 2/71 of January 1971 implementing the Decision of 21 April 1970 on the replacement of financial contributions from member states by the Communities' own resources.

[33] O'Neill, op. cit., p. 75.

year one, rising to 18.92 per cent after the transitional period. After that, there would be no limit.[34] Britain's massive disadvantage was now locked in, leaving her the second-highest net contributor after Germany. Recognising this, Heath's answer was a 'regional policy', through which Britain might claw back some of her deficit through subsidies to the regions. Initially this would fall on deaf ears.

'FAIR AND REASONABLE' TERMS

With one crucial exception, negotiations were concluded at the June meeting of the Council of Ministers. Heath had achieved the goal on which he had set his heart. The cost to Britain had been enormous. She had been saddled with an enormously expensive CAP, already costing as much each year as the Americans were spending on reaching the moon, with its in-built bias in favour of France.[35]

She had agreed to comply with 13,000 pages of legislation that she had no part in framing, and was now committed to enact all future legislation passed by the Community, whether or not in her interest. She had agreed to subordinate her courts to a higher court against which there was no appeal. In anticipation of economic and monetary union, Heath had undertaken to undermine sterling's position as a reserve currency. And, while securing minimal concessions for a few Commonwealth countries, he had committed Britain to make a hugely disproportionate contribution to the budget.

None of this prevented the government setting out to sell its 'achievement' to the British people. The first move came in July 1971 with the publication of a White Paper.[36] A shortened version, after going through innumerable drafts to ensure that its message was crafted as persuasively as possible, was distributed to every household in the country. Although the 16-page booklet claimed to set out 'the difficulties as well as the opportunities' of joining, its tone was relentlessly upbeat, starting with a boast that Britain's negotiations had been 'successful'. The essential choice offered was between better security and more prosperity, against having 'in a single generation ... rejected an Imperial past and a European future' and 'found nothing to put in their place'. Membership 'would enable Britain to achieve a higher standard of living'.

Many of the document's claims would become only too familiar in future decades, such as that membership of the Community 'would mean that British manufacturers will be selling their products in a home market

[34] Ibid., pp. 186–187.
[35] *Guardian*, 14 December 1970.
[36] *The United Kingdom and the European Communities* (Cmnd 4715).

five times as large as at present'. Not mentioned was that their continental competitors would have free access to the British market. As for British industry, it was claimed simply that 'the effects of entry will be positive and substantial'.

Despite Heath having discussed with Pompidou at the May summit the progress towards economic and monetary union, and reaffirmed the readiness of Britain to participate fully 'and in a European spirit in this development', there was no mention of this subject or of the commitments made.[37] It was, however, claimed that there would be no loss of national identity. Britain's monarchy, parliament and courts would not change. The legal system would 'continue as before', apart from 'certain changes under the treaties concerning economic and commercial matters'. And in a sentence often quoted later, it was stated that: 'There is no question of Britain losing essential national sovereignty; what is proposed is a sharing and an enlargement of individual national sovereignties in the economic interest.'[38]

Nowhere in the document was there any mention of the word 'supranational', nor that the idea of joining the 'Common Market' was just the start of a long process of political integration.

THE GREAT FISHERIES SCANDAL

There was a further anomaly in the White Paper. No fewer than three times, it made reference to one issue on which final agreement had still to be settled. Under 'Fisheries', the people of Britain were told: 'The Government is determined to secure proper safeguards for the British fishing industry. The Community has recognised the need to change its fisheries policy for an enlarged Community of Ten, particularly in regard to access to fishing grounds.'

[37] This was discussed in Heath's autobiography, op. cit., p. 375, and raised in the House of Commons shortly after the summit. See HC Deb, 10 June 1971, Vol. 818, cc1235-44.
[38] Despite the ambiguous use of the word 'essential', the government was fully aware that signing the treaty would involve an immense loss, not so much of 'sovereignty' as of power. A confidential FCO paper in 1971 concluded that EEC entry would result in very substantial restraints on Britain's powers of self-government, and that over the years this would become ever more obvious. Presciently, the paper also predicted that people would become increasingly alienated from government as it became more bureaucratic and remote, with ever more decisions being taken in Brussels and ever more power being exercised by unelected officials. While recognising this, the paper's chief concern was with how these 'public anxieties' masquerading as concern for 'loss of sovereignty' might be allayed. Various remedies were suggested, such as giving more power to the European Parliament, creating new mechanisms whereby Parliament could scrutinise Community legislation, and strengthening 'regional democratic processes'. It was also suggested that these problems would only become fully evident many years into the future, possibly not until 'the end of the century' (National Archives FCO 30/1048, undated).

This was untrue. The Community had 'recognised' no such thing. On fishing, as the Heath government was already uncomfortably aware, Britain had been badly caught out. Indeed, with disarming candour, O'Neill was to record that 'when our negotiations opened on 30 June 1970, the problem of fisheries did not exist. It came later the same day. From then on fisheries was a major problem.' At first, he wrote, 'we did not realise how difficult it would prove to solve, or how strong the political passions would be which it was to arouse'.[39]

Whether or not the negotiators should have been so unprepared is debatable. Had O'Neill been aware of the views of the 'father' of the Common Agricultural Policy, Dr Sicco Mansholt, he might not have been forgiven for taking a relaxed view. Back in May 1962, speaking in Vlaardingen, a Dutch fishing port near Rotterdam, Mansholt had called for immediate conferences between the EEC and Great Britain, Norway and Denmark on a common fisheries policy – 'a matter which the European Community has not yet undertaken'. These conferences, he said, would be independent of negotiations for their membership in the European Community. But, he added, 'it would be impossible for the Community countries to formulate a meaningful fisheries policy without prior consultation with Great Britain, Norway and Denmark, which fish the same North Sea waters'.[40]

When, in 1966, the Wilson government had applied to join the EEC, there was no discussion about a common policy. Broadly, for the fishing industry, entry was seen as beneficial. Because the EEC was a net importer of fish, the authors of a paper written in September 1966 suggested that the UK fishing industry should gain from access to the markets of the Six. But, wrote Official Historian Stephen Wall in 2013: 'The paper could not, and did not, foresee that Britain's future partners would fix a Common Fisheries Policy on the eve of British accession, deliberately so as to maximise their relative advantage at British expense, thus creating a commercial advantage for themselves and provoking a source of political friction which has persisted to the present day.'[41]

Wall was, perhaps being too generous to the authors of the paper. Already, on 22 June 1966, the Commission had lodged a detailed proposal for a Common Fisheries Policy (*une politique commune*). Central to the 512-page document was the very issue that was to cause such turmoil in the final accession negotiations: the principle of equal access (*L'égalité d'accès*) to a

---

[39] O'Neill, op. cit., p. 245.
[40] European Community Information Service, 'Common Market Vice-President calls for Immediate Meetings on European Fisheries Policy', 23 May 1962.
[41] Wall, op. cit., p. 134.

common resource.[42] Although the proposal was published only in the four community languages, an English explanatory memorandum was produced a month later, making it clear that there could be no decision until the Economic and Social Committee and the European Parliament had been consulted. And spelt out with unmistakable clarity was the fundamental principle that would guide the policy: the aim of 'ensuring equal access to Community resources for all fishermen in the EEC without discrimination'.[43]

The proposal re-emerged in the form of three *actes préparatoires* presented to the Council on 6 June 1968, grouped under the heading of 'Politique commune de la pêche'. There, as a formal proposal for legislation, was the principle enshrined that 'Community fishermen must have an equal access to fishing grounds and their exploitation in waters under the sovereignty or jurisdiction of the Member States.'[44] Although published in the *Official Journal* on 13 September 1968, the timing was perhaps unfortunate. Coming after de Gaulle's second veto of Britain's application and before the Heath government had reopened the issue, British official interest in community affairs might have been at its lowest.

As before, though, there was an English-language 'information memo', this one published by the Commission 'Spokesman's Group' in June 1968. It noted that, 'to a great extent, the proposals are in line with the basic principles for a common policy submitted by the Commission in June 1966'.[45] Already, therefore, the proposals were two years old.

The *actes préparatoires* were, in accordance with procedure, submitted to the European Parliament, with its Agriculture Committee publishing its report on 30 September 1968.[46] This was approved by the full parliament in its session of 24 October, with the proceedings published in the *Official Journal* on 8 November 1968.[47] The paper trail was getting longer and longer, extended even further when the Social and Economic Committee gave its opinion on 26 March 1969, the nine-page document being published on 17 June in the *Official Journal*.[48] All the procedural steps had

<hr/>

[42] *Report on the Situation of the Fishing Sector in the Member States of the EEC and the Basic Principles for a Common Policy*, COM (66) 250 final, 22 June 1966.
[43] Information Memo, Main outlines of a Common Fisheries Policy for EEC, July 1966.
[44] *Official Journal*, C 91/1, 13 September 1968.
[45] Information Memo, Common Fisheries Policy, Brussels, June 1968, http://aei.pitt.edu/29925/1/P_36_68.pdf.
[46] Rapport fait au nom de la commission de l'agriculture (doc. 78/68), 30 Septembre 1968, http://aei.pitt.edu/65847/1/WD3183.pdf.
[47] *Official Journal*, C 116/1, 8 November 1968, https://eur-lex.europa.eu/legal-content/FR/TXT/PDF/?uri=OJ:C:1968:116:FULL&from=GA.
[48] Consultation du comité economic et social sur trois propositions de règlement du Conseil relatives à la politique commune de la pêche 26 March 1969, OJ No. C 76/11, 17.6.69.

now been completed, requiring only Council approval for the proposals to become law.

At that point, according to O'Neill, the proposals should in theory have been approved by the end of 1969, but, in his words, 'nothing much happened'. In fact, he has them coming before the Agriculture Council in the December, delayed until then by French resistance to the Commission's proposals. At that Council, the French secured agreement that the basic regulation should be adopted before April 1970.

Asking what had changed, O'Neill answered his own question, noting that, by December 1969, the Hague Conference had taken place, the enlargement of the Community had been agreed in principle and the Community was about to embark on its preparations for a common negotiating position. 'There can be no reasonable doubt', O'Neill wrote, 'that what led to the Community's Common Fisheries Policy and its provisions (with very limited exceptions only) for common access to each other's waters, "right up to the beach" was the approach of the candidates.'[49]

Furthermore, there was already international pressure for a major revision of the international law of the sea, to extend national control of fisheries to 200 miles (or the 'median line' between two nations). When this took place, the waters of the four applicants would contain well over 90 per cent of western Europe's fish, some 80 per cent in seas controlled by Britain.[50] The deadline of 30 April was not observed. After further Council meetings of 27 and 28 April, the decision was deferred to the Council of 25–26 May, whence the French minister of transport (responsible for fisheries) urged agreement by 30 June, declaring that it would not be a good thing if the enlargement negotiations started in the twilight of unfinished business. But no decision was taken then, nor at a further Council on 8–9 June, leaving the matter to a meeting of 29 June.[51]

By 22 June, the British delegation in Brussels had become aware that an agreement on a Common Fisheries Policy might be reached by 29 June, but 'fears were much allayed' by a Dutch official who told the Embassy that this was unlikely. Although the French were by then pushing for completion, the official thought it 'bad timing' to reach an agreement a day before the

[49] O'Neill, op. cit., p. 251.
[50] Following declarations of a 200-mile limit by South American countries in 1964 and a 50-mile limit by Iceland, the 200-mile extension was agreed by the United Nations Conference on the Law of the Sea (UNCLOS) between 1972 and 1975. Britain formalised her right to a 200-mile limit in the Fisheries Limits Act 1976, even though by then she had ceded control of fisheries to the EEC. See http://www.fao.org/3/s5280T/s5280t0p.htm.
[51] O'Neill, op. cit., p. 253.

negotiations started. 'It would look like a kind of insult to the candidate countries,' he said.[52]

Only days before the negotiations were due to be opened, the Cabinet was still discussing the draft of the statement that was to be delivered by the Chancellor of the Duchy of Lancaster in Luxembourg. By then, the word had reached the highest level that something was in the offing regarding fishing. In the discussion, it was suggested that 'the tone of the draft Statement was perhaps too elevated and diffuse', and that it would be 'desirable' to make a reference to fisheries (at that point absent from the statement):

> in order to anticipate the possibility that the Council of Ministers of the European Communities at a meeting on 29 June would make some move towards the development of a common fisheries policy which, by leading to changes in international fishery limits, could be seriously damaging to United Kingdom interests.[53]

From this, it was evident that that nature of the policy had not been fully understood and, while a reference to fisheries was inserted into the final version of the statement, it was vague and thereby weak, simply noting that developments in the Community since July 1967 could affect the position of the British government, and 'fisheries policy may prove to be one such development'.[54]

The statement, of course, had no impact whatsoever. The very day it was made, the fisheries decisions were 'forced through' the Agriculture Council by the French, albeit in outline form only. The Dutch, having undertaken to block the proposals, failed to do so. They offered the 'rather shamefaced, and indeed shameful, explanation' that the instructions to their delegation only required them to block agreement before the opening session of the enlargement negotiations.[55]

The regulations were finally agreed at the Council of 20 October, coming into force on 1 February 1971, before the UK had formally joined the EEC.[56] Contrary to Mansholt's original warning that 'it would be impossible for the Community countries to formulate a meaningful fisheries policy without prior consultation with Great Britain, Norway

---

[52] Ibid.
[53] National Archives, CAB 128/47, Cabinet Conclusions, 25 June 1970.
[54] National Archives, CAB 129/150, Membership of the European Communities: Opening statement for 30 June.
[55] O'Neill, op. cit., pp. 256–257.
[56] Regulation (EEC) No. 2141/70 of the Council of 20 October 1970 laying down a common structural policy for the fishing industry. OJ No. L.236/1.

and Denmark', the Community had agreed an instrument that would have a profound effect on the UK industry, without the slightest attempt to consult on the issue. It is hard to describe that in any other terms than as an egregious act of bad faith.

What was also true was that the legal base, on which the new regulations relied, was extremely slender, where the main provisions in the treaty, Articles 39–43, were on agricultural policy. Only Article 38 of the treaty made any reference to fish, and that was in relation to 'fisheries products'. In October an FCO briefing for the Permanent Under-Secretary, who was due to meet Heath at a top-level Sunningdale conference, claimed that the legal basis for the CFP was 'Article 38 of the Treaty'.[57] This was despite the recital to the regulation showing the 'judicial base' as Articles 7, 42, 43 and 235 of the treaty. There was no mention of Article 38. Nevertheless, the canard that this Article was the legal basis for the Common Fisheries Policy became lodged firmly in the official mind and was repeatedly cited over the years by authorities ranging from Con O'Neill to Heath himself.[58]

Initially, the only country fully alive to the implications of the move was Norway. For months the Foreign Office did not seem to focus on the issue, or make any efforts to ascertain what its consequences might be for Britain's fishermen. Internal notes in July recorded there was 'real doubt about the right of the Community ... to regulate access to fishing grounds'. There was 'nowhere any indication that it was the intention ... [to] vest in the Community the right to exercise extra-territorial competence'.[59] The Ministry of Agriculture and Fisheries told Con O'Neill they could 'not believe the equal access proposals are serious' and suggested they 'must be a basis for bargaining'.

The first warnings were sounded by a trickle of letters from MPs for coastal constituencies, alerted by their local fishermen. Kent and Essex fishermen were warning that, 'if Britain joins the Common Market and French fishermen are given access to inshore waters, they will clean them out'. Throughout the summer such letters continued to arrive, to be side-stepped by Geoffrey Rippon with replies such as 'there is as yet no Common Fisheries Policy in the European Community', or 'we made our interest clear at the start of negotiations on 30 June' (even though a note from O'Neill

[57] National Archives, FCO 30/656.
[58] O'Neill quotes it in his book. Edward Heath, when challenged on the illegality of the CFP in the 1990s, referred to article 38 in the *Sunday Telegraph* (18 February 1996, '*J'Accuse Booker*'); in his memoirs in 1998 (op. cit., p. 70) and in the House of Commons (*Hansard*, 25 January 2001). Either he had never read the regulation that was the basis of the CFP, or he had not grasped one of the most elementary principles of the way European law is drafted.
[59] National Archives, FCO 30/656–659 and FCO 30/954–978.

dated five days earlier had said 'we see no requirement for a special marker to be put down as regards fisheries policy').

By now, the MPs' letters were becoming increasingly aggressive in tone. Patrick Wolridge-Gordon, an Aberdeenshire MP, wrote to Rippon on 30 October that there was 'not a fisherman who does not think that if territorial limits are to be abandoned, it means the end of an extremely successful and worthwhile industry for the whole coastline of Scotland. It is indeed unacceptable.' Robert Maclennan, MP for Caithness and Sutherland, wrote that the only major herring stocks left in European waters would be 'swept away within a few weeks by their so intensive methods of fishing that have cleaned out the stocks from their own waters'. Jo Grimond, leader of the Liberal Party, MP for Orkney and Shetland, and a keen 'Europeanist' wrote:

> I am perturbed to say the least of it about what is happening over the fishing policy of the Common Market and the curious light it sheds on British diplomacy. I went to Brussels a year ago and was told that there was no final policy on fishing but that the Commission would be receptive to the needs of Britain, Norway, Denmark etc. Since then I have been questioning both the Labour and Conservative governments ... all I got was flannel.[60]

The government's response was to work out a formula whereby the protests might be defused. In a memo drafted by D. K. Rowand of the Scottish fisheries department on 9 November, he admitted that the damage to Britain's fishermen would be considerable but argued that Britain could not afford to spend its 'limited negotiating capital' on resisting. He therefore suggested that replies to further letters or parliamentary questions should indicate that the government was 'aware of the anxieties of the fishing industry' and would 'bear them in mind in the negotiations'. But it was vital not to go into any detail: 'The more one is drawn into such explanations, the more difficult it is to avoid exposing the weaknesses of the inshore fisheries position, the only answer to which may be that in the wider context they must be regarded as expendable.'[61]

---

[60] O'Neill is particularly scathing about Grimond (op. cit., p. 247). He and Lord Boothby, he wrote, 'were rather typical of a number of European enthusiasts in public life who had always imagined that entering the Community would be an easy, pleasant and comfortable process. They had never bothered to discover how intensely technical and difficult the process was bound to be, and had relied too much on mere idealism and good fellowship to do the trick'.

[61] Also referred to by Alex Salmond in a House of Commons debate about fishing in 2004, with reference to Wolridge-Gordon. HC Deb, 02 March 2004, Vol. 418, cc756-8. The MP is said to have seen the paper (a handwritten note) during a meeting with a 'minor mandarin'.

From then on, replies to letters by Rippon and others repeated the same formula: 'I can assure you that the Government will take proper account of the importance of the inshore fishing industry to the British economy as a whole.' By this means it was concealed from the public that Britain's fisheries were indeed 'expendable'.

Through the spring of 1971, while the negotiations were still being stalled by France, the FCO was dealing with other issues. But by June, as the deadline to complete the negotiations approached, O'Neill and his team suddenly realised the seriousness of the problem. Ministers took the view, O'Neill was to record, that the ideal solution would be for the Community to suspend its fisheries policy, pending agreement on a suitable regime after British accession. This was ruled out, so Britain sought a compromise, suggesting that the Community could control waters between six and twelve miles off the coast, as long as British fishermen could enjoy exclusive fishing rights out to six miles. Again, the Community insisted on control right up to the beaches, offering only a temporary derogation, whereby all member states could keep an exclusive six-mile zone for five years, possibly to be extended to ten, with 'a review' thereafter.

It was on this basis that, with all other issues agreed, the government put out its White Paper in July claiming that 'the Community has recognised the need to change its fisheries policy ...' Not for the last time on fisheries, the British public was being seriously misled.

THE 'GREAT DEBATE'

Having already agreed to join, without revealing the details of what was involved, the Heath government's next objective was to launch a massive publicity campaign on the merits of entry. Ostensibly this was a campaign to sell the 'Common Market' to the British people, advertised as 'the great debate'. Its real purpose, however, was not to win over the people. In the words of the official appointed as the campaign's co-ordinator, it was 'to convince Members of Parliament that the tide of public opinion was moving in favour of joining the EEC', and thus to 'win approval for the entry terms from Parliament'.[62]

The first serious move in this campaign was the shortened White Paper, circulated at a cost of £2 million to every home in Britain (anti-market Labour MPs asked how taxpayers' money could be spent on what they described as mere 'propaganda'). Ministers were despatched all over the

---

[62] Hugh-Jones, Sir Wynn (2002), *Diplomacy to Politics* (Spennymoor, Durham: The Memoir Club), p. 411.

country to sell the 'benefits' of the Common Market on any platform that could be arranged. Between July and October 1971 nearly three hundred such speeches were made. Rippon alone made over fifty.

One novel feature of the operation was the way pro-market lobby groups were co-ordinated under the umbrella of the European Movement, part-funded by the European Commission, to act as an integral part of the government campaign. Government 'information' services, funded by taxpayers, thus co-ordinated activities with the Trade Union Committee for Europe, the Conservative Political Centre, the Labour Committee for Europe, the CBI and many other organisations, including the National Farmers Union, the Associated Chambers of Commerce and the British Council of Churches.

A key part was played in the campaign by weekly 'media breakfasts' held at the Connaught Hotel, presided over by Geoffrey Tucker, a senior advertising man who had helped to 'sell' Heath and the Tory Party during the 1970 election. Funded by the European Movement, these meetings enabled politicians, representatives of industry, Foreign Office civil servants and influential sympathisers in the media to develop suitable tactics and 'story lines' for the campaign. Journalists were invited to meet the men 'who were actually negotiating in Brussels' and offered 'exclusives' to promote the cause.[63]

> The journalists were able to tell the European Movement and Whitehall frankly what they thought of their public relations efforts and how they could be improved – that such and such a line of argument was too airy-fairy, or that it needed quite a different speaker to put it over if it was ever to get across. Party politicians and industrial representatives would suggest lines of argument for the press to explore.[64]

Another strategy was a carefully organised campaign based on letters to *The Times*, then still regarded as Britain's most influential newspaper. Pre-written letters were circulated, to be signed by 'top name' individuals or groups of businessmen, to be sent in as if they were the signatories' own work. Particular efforts were made to woo the BBC. One regular breakfast guest was Ian Trethowan, a former political correspondent, then head of BBC Radio. Another was Marshall Stewart, editor of the *Today* programme. Tucker himself later claimed that he had engineered the dismissal of the

---

[63] BBC Radio 4, Documentary: *A Letter to The Times*, 3 February 2000. Based on interviews of Geoffrey Tucker. Transcript supplied by the British Management Data Foundation.
[64] Kitzinger, op. cit., p. 205.

programme's popular chief presenter, Jack de Manio, a Eurosceptic, to be replaced by the more sympathetic Robert Robinson. 'Nobbling was the name of the game,' as he later put it.[65]

For all this campaigning, the European Movement needed money. In the year ending 31 March 1972, it had disbursed £550,000, more than five times its normal budget.[66] But its income, mainly from unnamed donors, reached £915,904, helped by an assurance that the government would increase its annual grant from £7,500 to £20,000.[67] No attempt was made to give the public objective or factual information. Instead, the Movement used market research to identify issues that might sway public support in favour (the technique later associated with 'focus groups'). The aim was to discover what people wanted to hear, then use it to shape the campaign's propaganda.[68]

THE PARLIAMENTARY CAMPAIGN

Having negotiated the terms of entry, all Heath wanted was a rubber-stamp from Parliament. He even considered asking it to endorse membership before the summer break. However, Francis Pym, the Conservative chief whip, counselled against being seen to rush MPs. Heath thus settled for a 'take note' debate before the summer recess, followed by a full debate and vote in October.

In what was again to become a familiar pattern, the 'pro-Marketeers' went to great lengths to present support for their cause as an issue that transcended party divisions and loyalties. Thus, in defiance of normal practice, Rippon maintained informal contacts with prominent 'pro-Europeans' in the Labour Party, pre-eminently its deputy leader, Roy Jenkins. Labour was deeply divided. Wilson had initially equivocated but, in May, the issue was forced by Jim Callaghan, who famously declared '*non, merci beaucoup*'. To avoid a disastrous split in his party, Wilson finally had to take a stance. Despite a private lecture from Jenkins on the advantages of sticking to the 'pro-European position' he had taken in government, Wilson chose to not challenge the principle, but merely the terms of entry.[69]

The Conservatives, with an overall majority of only 25, also included a sizeable number of dissenters. After calculating that at least 38 of his MPs could not be relied on, Heath decided on the tactical device of a free vote,

[65] Ibid.
[66] Kitzinger, op. cit., p. 208.
[67] Ibid., p. 212.
[68] Ibid., p. 216.
[69] Jenkins, Roy (1991), *A Life at the Centre* (London: Macmillan), p. 319. Jenkins advised Wilson that sticking to the pro-European position would kill his damaging reputation for being 'devious, tricky, opportunistic'.

hoping to recruit Labour pro-marketeers. His resolution was reinforced by the Conservative conference at Brighton on 13 October 1971. Enoch Powell, the most eloquent Tory Eurosceptic, had pleaded with delegates to reject entry:

> I do not believe that this nation, which has maintained and defended its independence for a thousand years, will now submit to see it merged or lost. Nor did I become a member of a sovereign parliament in order to consent to that sovereignty being abated or transferred.[70]

His speech prompted Heath to call for a vote, which resulted in a huge majority of 2,474 to 324 in favour of entry.[71]

The Commons debate itself was scheduled for six days, culminating in a vote on 28 October. Opening for the government was Foreign Secretary Sir Alec Douglas-Home, who asked the House to approve the decision to join, 'on the basis of the arrangements which have been negotiated' (even though MPs had still not been given a chance to examine the terms). He reminded the House how twice before it had instructed Conservative and Labour governments to negotiate entry, and suggested that, if it were now to change its mind, the international community would look at Britain askance.[72]

Addressing fears of a 'federal Europe', he acknowledged that 'some people might still like to pursue this idea', but claimed that 'political change' in the Community had to be unanimous, and that there was no way any country could be 'dragooned or coerced into a pattern of political association' it did not like.[73] As before, there was no mention of economic and monetary union, and nothing of committing to work for a common foreign policy. Instead, Douglas-Home offered the prospect that, once she was in, Britain could play a part in shaping a new regional policy, which could bring lavish subsidies to boost the poorer areas of the country.

Denis Healey led the attack for Labour, but his speech betrayed a naiveté that was to become familiar. He limited his case purely to economic arguments, on the grounds that the Common Market was 'after all an economic community and nothing more'.[74] Wilson also steered firmly away from the political implications of entry. He stuck to attacking what was

---

[70] *The Poisoned Chalice*, authors' transcript.
[71] *Daily Telegraph*, 14 October 1971, 'Tories vote 8–1 for Europe'.
[72] HC Debates, 28 October 1971, Vol. 823, cc2076-217.
[73] Ibid.
[74] Ibid.

known of the terms Heath had negotiated, giving notice of how a Labour government would respond if it came into office after accession:

> What we should do ... would be immediately to give notice that we do not accept the terms negotiated by the Conservatives and, in particular, the unacceptable burdens arising out of the CAP, the blows to the Commonwealth, and any threats to our regional policies. If the Community then refused to negotiate ... or if the negotiations were to fail, we should sit down amicably with them and discuss the situation [laughter]. We should make it clear that our posture, like that of the French after 1958, would be rigidly directed towards the pursuit of British interests and that other decisions and actions in relation to the Community would be dictated by that determination, until we had secured our terms. They might accept this, or they might decide that we should agree to part; that would depend on them. That is our position.[75]

After six days of debate, Heath wound up on 28 October. To their intense frustration, none of the leading Labour pro-marketeers had been allowed by the Speaker (in consultation with party managers) to take part. As Roy Jenkins commented later:

> This was supposed to be the great debate of the decade (at least) and we were leaders of one-eighth of the House of Commons ... and, because we were the hinge, were going to make the biggest difference ... Yet of more than one hundred speeches which filled the six days we were not allowed to contribute one.[76]

Just before the vote, Heath was able to announce that the House of Lords had endorsed his terms by 451 votes to 58, a majority of almost 400. Jenkins led 69 Labour MPs through the 'Aye' lobby and, with 20 abstentions, Heath amassed 356 'Ayes' against 244 'Noes', an unexpectedly large majority of 112. Without the support of the Labour pro-marketeers, entry would have been rejected by 36 votes. The result was greeted with pandemonium. Teddy Taylor recalled this as the only time he ever heard bad language openly used in the House. After Jenkins had been called a 'Fascist bastard' by a Labour MP, friends advised him to depart quickly for his own safety.[77] That

[75] Ibid.
[76] Jenkins, Roy, op. cit., p. 330.
[77] *The Poisoned Chalice*.

evening he had the dubious pleasure of reading the *Evening News* front-page headline: 'Witch hunt for Labour traitors'.

After the vote, Heath called in briefly on a private party, where he received warm congratulations from his friend and mentor, Jean Monnet, who had been watching the vote from the public gallery. He then returned to his private sitting room at Number 10, where he played the First Prelude from Book 1 of Bach's *Well-Tempered Clavier* on his clavichord. That night, Macmillan presided over the lighting of a bonfire on the cliffs of Dover. Next morning, the *Sun* proclaimed in bold capitals on its front page: 'IN WE GO'.

FISHERIES: THE LIE DIRECT

Before Heath could fly to Brussels to sign the Treaty of Accession, there remained the issue of fisheries. Having accepted Community control over the fishing waters between six and twelve miles from Britain's coast, Heath still hoped to retain exclusive rights to the six-miles zone. On 18 June, Ireland declared their refusal to accept the Community's proposals. The Norwegians followed suit three days later. Having given away so much, Britain's negotiators feared that the Community might now offer the other countries concessions it was too late for her to ask for.

The situation became increasingly fraught as Norway passed a law limiting the size of vessels allowed within her six- to 12-mile limit, excluding British deep-water trawlers from one of their most lucrative fishing grounds.[78] Iceland had unilaterally extended its limits to 50 miles, excluding British vessels from another lucrative ground. Pressure began to build for Britain to seek concessions similar to those demanded by the Norwegians. But the political situation was becoming so explosive that O'Neill's team decided to defer further demands until after the parliamentary debate, lest awkward questions were put by Labour frontbenchers. Because the fisheries problem had only come up since Labour's application in 1967, it was an issue over which Labour spokesmen felt no inhibitions in attacking the government.

By the time negotiations were resumed, they became 'so intense, intricate and continuous', according to O'Neill, that he gave up trying to record a step-by-step account.[79] Fisheries had been raised briefly in the debate,

---

[78] A question that inevitably arises when looking back at the fisheries episode is why Britain and the other applicant countries did not band together to insist that the 'equal access' rule was unacceptable. It is clear from the FCO papers that this was rejected because Britain's distant-water fishing companies, then the biggest players in the fishing industry, saw in 'equal access' a chance to win greater access to Norwegian waters. In the end, of course, Norway did not join and within a few years most of those companies disappeared.

[79] O'Neill, op. cit., p. 270.

prompting Rippon to make the misleading claim that there was now 'a clear understanding' that there would either have to be a wholly new fisheries regulation or the Community would have to accept 'the *status quo*'.[80] On 9 November, the Community came up with another minor variation on its earlier proposal, offering member states a 'derogation' adding control up to their 12-mile limits in certain geographical areas.

These arrangements would still be subject to review after ten years, but the decision as to whether they could continue would have to be unanimous. Although O'Neill described this as 'in many respects entirely unsatisfactory', it was to be the basis on which agreement was eventually reached.[81] The Norwegians were even less happy. Meeting with Rippon, they rejected any solution that was only temporary, insisting that national limits must be permanent. They were unimpressed by his remark that 'it was better when dealing with the Community to go round a problem rather than deal with it head on'. O'Neill regarded the Norwegians as 'stubborn'. Their stance was to bring their relations with the Community to crisis point.[82]

By now Rippon was under almost continuous fire in the Commons, to which he could only respond with evasive or ambiguous answers. As he and his colleagues tried to extract further minor concessions from the Six, centred on those areas where they wanted to retain a 12-mile limit, the Norwegians remained adamant that they must have a permanent 12-mile limit for the whole of their coastline.[83]

Heath was now worried that, unless the issue could be resolved, his timetable for entering the Community on 1 January 1973 would have to be abandoned. On 29 November, as ministers were due to arrive in Brussels for a final marathon session, he sent an urgent message to the Norwegian prime minister, Trygve Bratteli. 'You will know', he wrote, 'that it is very important that we present this question in a manner that will appear satisfactory to our fishing interests.' But Heath went on to say that he was now 'seriously concerned' by the way negotiations were dragging on. If Norway kept up its 'stiff' and 'intransigent' attitude, the Community might lose patience.

It was only because he believed it was of 'the utmost importance' that Norway should join the European Community, wrote Heath, that, 'I dare send you this message today'. It was a great mistake, when dealing with the EEC, he suggested, to make demands 'of a permanent nature', because this 'touches a principle which the EEC considers as fundamental'. If

---

[80] HC Deb, 25 October 1971, col. 1243.
[81] O'Neill, op. cit., p. 272.
[82] Ibid., p. 273.
[83] Ibid., p. 275.

Mr Bratteli could only accept a time-limit, 'subject to revision', Heath suggested, then in practice he would surely find that the EEC would be understanding, and 'will give you the essential concession which you expect'. In other words, so long as the Commission got what it wanted on paper, Heath was sure it would privately allow Norway the de facto permanence she wanted. After pleading with Bratteli to instruct his negotiators to give way, Heath ended by threatening, 'with very much regret', that, unless Norway conceded, the other candidate countries would have to join without her.

When this message was received in Oslo, its contents were swiftly leaked.[84] Word of Heath's intervention reached Brussels just as the crucial meeting was beginning. From the high-handed attitude of the French foreign minister, Maurice Schumann, it was more obvious than ever that the real driving force behind the policy was France. The Six had all at different times privately indicated unhappiness at the ruthless way it was being forced on the applicants. The evening after the Brussels talks ended, the German Ambassador to London confessed to Rippon's secretary Crispin Tickell that Schumann's behaviour in Brussels and France's subsequent blocking tactics had been 'deplorable'. 'As seen from here,' he said, 'the Community had behaved at its worst.'[85]

After the fiasco of the Brussels talks, a further meeting was scheduled for Saturday 11 December. Cynically, the British government's only real concern was to get a formula covering the 12-mile limit that would somehow enable it to defend the policy in Parliament.[86] By Sunday morning, wrote O'Neill, 'we got almost everything we wanted'.[87]

The following day, 13 December, Rippon made a statement to the House on the outcome of the final meeting. He claimed that 'the United Kingdom together with the Republic of Ireland and Denmark have now reached agreement on the outstanding problems'. The Community had been persuaded of the need to protect Britain's vital interests, both by conserving fish stocks and by protecting 'the livelihoods of our fishermen'. He then said, 'it is clear that we retain full jurisdiction of the whole of our coastal waters up to 12 miles.'[88]

This was untrue. Under the Fishing Regulation as set out by the EEC in 1970, British vessels would only have exclusive rights out to three miles,

[84] The full text of Heath's letter appeared in the Oslo newspaper *Aftenposten* on 7 December 1971.
[85] Note from Tickell dated 2 December 1971 in the FCO files, op. cit.
[86] Telegram from Douglas-Home to Soames, 6 December, FCO, op. cit.
[87] O'Neill, op. cit., p. 277.
[88] HC Deb, 13 December 1971, Vol. 828, cc51-65.

limited to five years.[89] What the British delegation had done was negotiate a further derogation – which had Community-wide effect – allowing member states to restrict fishing within the six-nautical-mile limit until 31 December 1982, and special arrangements for some areas up to 12 miles.[90] Crucially, Britain had conceded to the Community the right to control her fishing waters, eventually right up to the beaches. Even inshore fishermen would have to comply with Community rules. And when the 200-mile limit took effect, the world's richest fishing waters would have been given away *in toto*.

Desperate to hide how much had been given away, Rippon then said: 'I must emphasise that these are not just transitional arrangements which automatically lapse at the end of a fixed period.'[91] This claim drew a fierce challenge from Denis Healey and Peter Shore, both of whom suspected he was lying.[92] But neither had sight of the accession treaty, which would not be shown to MPs until after it had been signed a month later.[93] Only then did it become clear that Rippon had told a blatant lie. The Norwegians were unmoved by the concessions offered. Still further concessions brought a reluctant agreement by them on 15 January 1972, but these provoked the resignation of their fisheries minister. When the accession deal was put to the Norwegian people in a referendum on 25 September 1972, they rejected it, by 53.5 per cent to 46.5.

PARLIAMENT HANDS OVER ITS POWER

On 20 January 1972, Labour MPs led by Peter Shore made a last-ditch bid to stop Heath signing the treaty until Parliament had been given a chance to read the full text. Rippon asserted that there was 'no constitutional or other limitation upon the power of the Crown to conclude on behalf of the United Kingdom an internationally valid treaty'. The conclusion of treaties, he stated, 'is an exercise of the Royal Prerogative in the conduct of foreign affairs'. With blunt finality, he added: 'Parliament's rôle arises in the period between signature and ratification.' When the House divided, the government won the vote, 298 votes to 277.[94] Two days later, as Heath's memoirs record, he was given 'a huge ovation' as he entered the great hall of the Palais d'Egmont in Brussels to sign the accession treaty, watched by

---

[89] Regulation (EEC) No. 2141/70, op. cit.
[90] This additional 'concession' became part of the 198-page Accession Treaty (Article 100). In Article 103, provision was made for further derogations.
[91] HC Deb, 13 December 1971, op. cit.
[92] Ibid.
[93] Article 100, Fishing Rights.
[94] HC Deb, 20 January 1972, Vol. 829, cc677-809.

'many of those who had played a part in founding and building the European Community', including Monnet and Spaak.[95]

The next great task was to frame the legislation needed to enact the *acquis* into UK law. This seemed an awesome prospect, with 13,000 pages of directives and regulations already in force and an unknown number yet to come. Heath's Solicitor General, Geoffrey Howe, was given the task. To work himself into the job, he recalled that he spent a weekend re-reading Enoch Powell's arguments against the legitimacy of the whole exercise. 'Did we,' he asked himself, 'really have the authority of the British people to effect such a change. Had we been sufficiently candid about the implications?' In the end, he concluded that these had been fully explained, in documents beginning with those published by the Wilson government in 1967. Apparently ignoring the fact that the British people had been offered no choice in the matter at the 1970 general election, he concluded that the electorate had endorsed the principle of membership. Thus, he believed, the final, crucial stage could properly be entrusted to Parliament.[96]

Only then did Howe address himself to how this was to be done. Already there had been speculation that any Bill might have to run to thousands of clauses. Tony Benn claimed it would never get through Parliament in time for Britain to join. However, with the help of his senior parliamentary counsel, John Fiennes, Howe produced what he himself described as a *coup de théâtre*: a 'European Communities Bill' of just 12 clauses and four schedules, in a mere 37 pages.

At its heart was one short passage that used a long-standing device in British law-making: the 'enabling Act' whereby Parliament delegated to ministers the power to enact law directly. This would allow any relevant minister to enact into British law any item of Community legislation. In purely constitutional terms, it represented by far the greatest accession of power to the executive in history. As that internal Foreign Office paper on 'sovereignty' had predicted, it would place unprecedented powers in the hands of unelected officials, both in Brussels and Whitehall. In effect, they were being given the right to make laws with only a semblance of democratic accountability.

Howe's next challenge was to persuade Parliament to accept what to a great degree was its own redundancy ticket. Heath's chief whip, Francis Pym, knew that even one amendment could negate the whole accession treaty, putting Britain's entry in jeopardy. In addition, Heath's government

[95] *Memoirs*, op. cit., pp. 381–382.
[96] Verbatim account from *The Poisoned Chalice*.

had by now become highly unpopular. Inflation was rising rapidly. Wracked by industrial unrest, Britain was in crisis over the miners' strike that was to make Arthur Scargill famous. Trade union power had become one of the most conspicuous features of national life. 'The stakes,' Pym declared, 'couldn't have been higher.'[97]

The second reading vote was held on 17 February after three days of debate, and not before Wilson had accused Howe of imposing, 'literally at a stroke', an alien system of law. With his unrivalled understanding of the constitutional implications, Enoch Powell added a careful analysis of how the Commons was about to lose its supremacy.[98] Heath knew he was in trouble. The Labour Party was officially committed to oppose the Bill, and he could not rely on his own backbenchers. In closing the debate, therefore, he threw down a gauntlet: if the House did not agree to the Bill, he said, he and his colleagues were 'unanimous that in these circumstances this Parliament cannot sensibly continue'.[99]

Faced with the collapse of their government, most Conservative 'anti-marketeers' gritted their teeth and walked through the 'Aye' lobby. Despite that, 15 Tories voted with the opposition. But Heath still got his vote, if only by a wafer-thin margin: 309 to 301. The issue had been decided by the four Labour MPs and five Liberals who voted with the government. The hardest part, however, was still to come, as the House embarked on the Committee stage, debating amendments that would involve 92 divisions. Again, defeat of any one might negate the treaty.

The story of how the government came through this ordeal was not to emerge for more than twenty years, when several of the MPs involved took part in a BBC documentary. They recounted an unprecedented secret collaboration between the Conservative whips and Labour 'pro-marketeers', who arranged, when necessary, to find pressing engagements elsewhere that would mean their absence from the division lobby. In the words of Shirley Williams:

> people disappeared. They went to the films, they just didn't show up, and so forth ... There was quite a bit of quiet understanding that there were certain amendments where it was better for people to just find themselves ... you know, speaking at a meeting at Little Ainsborough or something, so they wouldn't be there.[100]

[97] Ibid.
[98] HC Deb, 17 February 1972, Vol. 831, cc629-761.
[99] Ibid.
[100] *The Poisoned Chalice.*

At the heart of the plot was a red book kept by Labour whip John Roper, a 'committed European'.[101] He guaranteed there would be just enough Labour abstentions for the government to win every vote. But to stop the vote-rigging being noticed, and creating embarrassment for the Labour Party, he varied the abstentions. Francis Pym recalled, looking somewhat uncomfortable: 'it was a secret arrangement. Everybody knew it was happening. How it was happening, nobody quite knew. And that seemed to me very satisfactory.'[102]

After 39 days of debate, the Bill passed its third reading on 13 July by a majority of 17 – 'Ayes' 301, 'Noes' 284.[103] The European Communities Act 1972 would soon be law, the way clear for the UK to join the EEC. For Howe and Heath, it was a triumph. Enoch Powell despaired. 'I don't think people understood,' he said. Tony Benn was more forthright. 'It was a *coup d'état*,' he declared, 'by a political class who did not believe in popular sovereignty'.[104]

[101] Heath, op. cit., p. 384.
[102] Ibid.
[103] HC Deb, 13 July 1972, Vol. 840, cc1862-988.
[104] Both quotations from *The Poisoned Chalice*.

7

Britain Stays In: 1973–1975

Do you think that the United Kingdom should stay in the
European Community (the Common Market)?
   Referendum question put to the British people, 5 June 1975

The result showed conclusively that the British people …
whole-heartedly backed the decision taken in 1971 by the
British Government, over which I presided, to join the
Community.
                                    Edward Heath, *The Course of My Life*[1]

In 1975 I campaigned as a Conservative parliamentary
candidate for a 'yes' vote in the referendum that kept us in
the EC. In retrospect it is abundantly clear that I campaigned
on a prospectus that was sufficiently false to ensure that, if
the issue had been a public offer in securities, I would face
prosecution under the provisions of the Companies Act and
I would lose.
                           Tom Benyon, letter to *The Times*, 29 May 2003

To celebrate 'the entry of the United Kingdom into the European Community'
on 1 January 1973, the lawyer Lord Goodman, a former chairman of the
Arts Council, was invited by his friend Mr Heath to organise a series of
nationwide events under the title 'Fanfare for Europe'.
   At a gala evening at the Royal Opera House, Covent Garden, prosperous
bankers were regaled with operatic hits and guffawed at snippets about

---

[1] Heath, op. cit., p. 549.

foreigners read by actors, while a special arrangement of Beethoven's 'Ode to Joy' modulated into a piece of pseudo-jazz by Michael Tippett. In a darkened room, the Victoria and Albert Museum put on show a tastefully lit selection of art objects from each member state, such as a pair of Bronze Age wind instruments from a Danish bog. A concert was given in York Minster by the Great Universal Stores Footwear band. The Whitechapel Art Gallery staged an exhibition of sweet-wrappers. Gas and electricity showrooms across the country featured demonstrations of continental cookery.[2]

For many, however, their first experience of 'belonging' to the Common Market came with the arrival of VAT, possibly the most bureaucratic tax system ever devised – and notoriously prone to fraud. Introduced by the EEC in 1967, it now replaced purchase tax in Britain's shops, with the rules set by Brussels, requiring a net increase of 'some 5,400 to 5,900 in civil service staff' to administer it.[3] For the moment, it did not apply to 'essentials' such as food and children's clothes, or books and newspapers, but a constant concern was that the tax would soon extend to them, as it did in many European countries. As a reflection of the new system of government, under which the British people were about to live, it was a foretaste of much that was to come.

THE PARIS SUMMIT AND BEYOND

Before even the three enlargement countries had formally become part of the 'Communities', however, the integrationalists were planning their next steps towards a fully functioning government of Europe, complete with its own currency, foreign policy and most of the attributes of a central government.

The first of these steps began with the elaborate Paris Summit on 19–20 October 1972, held at the international conference centre in the former Majestic Hotel, starting the day after Heath's European Communities Bill received Royal Assent. Monnet claims the idea was his, organised to celebrate the 'enlargement' to the 'Nine', and that President Pompidou, who was to host the summit, feared it would be merely a public relations exercise. According to a somewhat folksy rendition in his memoirs, Heath assured him that it would be a serious occasion where real decisions could be taken. For example, 'there could be substantial progress towards economic and monetary union'.[4]

---

[2] *Daily Telegraph*, 20 January 1973, 'Lord Goodman's Cultural Circus'.
[3] National Archives, CAB 129/153, Memorandum by the Chancellor of the Exchequer, 30 October 1970.
[4] Heath, op. cit., p. 387.

According to the European Commission's narrative, the Summit Conference (as it was called), was a long time in the planning, with a number of preparatory Foreign Minister's Conferences held throughout the year, all attended by the Commission – for the first time acting as an equal partner with the member states. These meetings were held on 29 February, 20 March, 24 April, 26 and 27 May, 26 June, 19 July and 12 September (the last one was preceded by a meeting of the finance ministers on 11 September, both held at the picturesque town of Frascati, just outside Rome). The conferences of 19 July and 12 September were prepared by an ad hoc committee made up member states' Permanent Representatives, the ambassadors of the new members, and Commission representatives.[5]

The preparations also involved many bilateral meetings either between ministers or government leaders, after several member state representatives had expressed a reluctance to attend unless the summit 'could be expected to yield practical results'. After the Frascati conferences on 11 and 12 September, the governments were persuaded that this condition had been met.[6]

The proceedings themselves were a major event, diplomatically and politically, held in crowded conference rooms with media from all over Europe in attendance. In an atmosphere of growing excitement, the last sessions extended well into the early hours of 21 October. When the bleary-eyed leaders emerged, they were resolved to give 'a new dimension to the enlarged Community'. In a 16-point declaration, they committed to move irrevocably to Economic and Monetary Union. They would take the required decisions during 1973 to allow transition to the second stage of the EMU on 1 January 1974, with a view to completion by 31 December 1980 at the latest. Additionally, they assigned themselves 'the key objective of converting, before the end of the decade and in absolute conformity with the signed Treaties, all the relationships between Member States into a European Union'.[7]

At a press conference immediately afterwards, German chancellor Willy Brant praised the moves that would lead to 'the European Union envisaged in Paris' by the end of the decade. But, he said, the leaders were also taking the first steps of what could be called the 'social union'. For millions of European workers, he declared, it must finally be realised that this is not

---

[5] Archive of European Integration (AEI), http://aei.pitt.edu/1919/2/paris_1972_communique.pdf.
[6] Ibid.
[7] Ibid.

just a 'Europe of business'. It was also a Europe of working people and their quality of life.[8]

Within the framework of the summit, Heath claims he had additional objectives to deal with: the imbalance of the Community budget in favour of agriculture, and the rundown of Britain's traditional heavy industries, such as shipbuilding. Germany and other countries had used their Marshall Plan aid after the war to modernise and re-equip, which was one reason why their economies were now so obviously outperforming Britain's. An answer to both problems, he thought, would be a Community 'regional policy', whereby Britain could receive subsidies on a scale commensurate with what other countries, such as France, gained for their agriculture.[9]

When he received Pompidou's draft declaration for the summit, he replied that he 'had always admired the lucidity and clarity of French literature'. He agreed with Chancellor Willy Brandt that Germany and the UK 'would meet Pompidou's wish to underline progress towards monetary integration, provided that the French accepted our wish to give priority to regional and social problems'.[10] On 18 October, he met Pompidou before the summit to ask for his support for a 'regional development fund':

> He listened to what I had to say and then remarked that it was not a cause he wished to espouse, because France did not need help. 'Moreover', he added, 'you have sent me a map showing where the funds would go. I immediately turned my eyes to my own country and looked at my own home, Auvergne, only to find that it would not be getting a penny or a franc. So there is nothing in it for us.'[11]

Heath's recollection of the summit is somewhat egocentric (to say nothing of Anglocentric) for what was such a major event. In his opening speech, he states that he dealt with 'those issues to which we [the British government] had attached great importance'. Thus, in addition to 'a clear timetable for economic and monetary union', he called for commitments on the Community's regional policy and 'a common foreign policy'.[12] He was pushing at an open door. The assembled leaders were quite happy to

[8] *Bulletin of the Federal Government's Press and Information Office*, ed. Press and Information Office of the Federal Government, 24 October 1972, no. 148. Bonn: German Federal Publishing House, Declaration by Willy Brandt on the Results of the Paris Summit Conference (22 October 1972), pp. 1761–1762. Via University of Luxembourg archives.
[9] Archive of European Integration, op. cit.
[10] Heath, op. cit., p. 389.
[11] Ibid., p. 390.
[12] Ibid., p. 391.

give 'top priority to correcting the structural and regional imbalances in the Community', as the communiqué read. These, they considered, 'could hinder the achievement of the Economic and Monetary Union'. The problem, as Heath's successors would find, was in the financing – something on which the summit failed to agree.[13]

As to a common foreign policy, the heads of state and government affirmed that their efforts to construct their Community would 'only take on their full meaning to the extent that the Member States succeed in acting together to meet Europe's growing responsibilities in the world'. They also agreed that 'a European Parliament, elected by universal suffrage, would have to be associated with the development of the European construction'.[14] With the commitment to EMU and a 'European Union', the summit was to set the agenda for the next 30 years.

Nevertheless, Monnet – who is not mentioned in the official account of the preparations – was dissatisfied. He felt the summit had lacked focus and, more importantly, mechanisms for carrying its resolutions forward. It had embraced too much, too ineffectively. The long-term goals it had set were binding on everyone in general and no one in particular. His great regret was that it had not established 'a supreme body to steer Europe through the difficult transition from national to collective sovereignty'.[15]

By the end of August 1973, therefore, he produced another of his plans, this one outlining a structure for a 'Provisional European Government'. To carry forward the Paris programme, this body would draw up an outline for 'European Union', to include a 'European Government' and an elected European Assembly. This 'provisional government' would meet regularly and those taking part would keep its deliberations secret.[16]

Monnet came over to England to discuss his proposal with Heath at Chequers on 18 September, telling him 'we must give public opinion the feeling that European affairs are being decided: today, people have the impression that they're merely being discussed'. Heath readily agreed, but had a reservation about making the proposal public. 'Let's just do it,' he told Monnet.[17] He also worried about the term 'provisional government'. 'That would get me into great difficulties,' he said.

When Monnet approached Pompidou and Brandt, he claims they were equally enthusiastic. Neither shared Heath's reservations about the term

[13] AEI, op. cit.
[14] Ibid.
[15] Monnet, op. cit., p. 503.
[16] Ibid., p. 504.
[17] Ibid.

'provisional government' and Pompidou particularly warmed to the name 'European Union'. One of Pompidou's staff was heard to enquire what it meant. The reply came: 'nothing ... but then that is the beauty of it'. In late September, Pompidou mentioned Monnet's proposal at a press conference. Heath took up the baton at the Conservative Party Conference on 13 October. 'I believe,' he said:

> that already some of my colleagues as Heads of Government feel the need for us to get together regularly without large staff so that we can jointly guide the Community along the paths we have already set. I would like to see the Heads of Government of the member countries of the Community meeting together, perhaps twice a year, as I have said, alone and without large staffs, with the president of the Commission being present, as he was at the Summit ... our purpose in meeting together would be to lay down the broad direction of European policy.[18]

But he failed to mention that he was talking about a 'provisional government', and said nothing about it being intended to steer Europe through the 'transition from national to collective sovereignty'.

Two weeks later, on 31 October, Pompidou told his Cabinet that regular meetings of heads of states were needed 'with the aim of comparing and harmonising their attitudes in the framework of political co-operation'. He wanted the first meeting to be held before the end of 1973.[19] Monnet was now confident that, despite the turmoil into which the world had suddenly been plunged by the Yom Kippur War in the Middle East, his plan was back on track. Then, as he was to recall, 'when all seemed well, everything was thrown into turmoil'.[20] In the wake of the war, the price of oil quadrupled, threatening chaos to Western economies. The governments of the Nine rushed to strike individual deals with the oil sheikhs.

Heath was later to write that, at this moment, the Community 'lost sight of the philosophy of Jean Monnet: that the Community exists to find common solutions to common problems'. Each member state, he wrote, had 'drifted back to seeking its own, unilateral solutions. So we all had to relearn painfully that there is no solution if we act on our own.'[21] By then, in the 'big three' of the Six, there were changes at the top. In Germany, Brandt had retired under a cloud, over a high-profile spy scandal. He was replaced in

---

[18] Cited in Monnet, op. cit., p. 507.
[19] Monnet, op. cit., p. 508.
[20] Ibid., p. 510.
[21] Heath, op. cit., p. 395.

May by Helmut Schmidt. Georges Pompidou had died on 2 April and, in the month that saw a new German chancellor, Valéry Giscard d'Estaing became French president.[22] The old Pompidou and Brandt alliance effortlessly transformed into Schmidt and Giscard.

Britain's national politics had also been through turmoil. In the winter of 1973–1974, her ailing economy had been plunged into chaos by industrial unrest and a second miners' strike, leading to major power cuts and the 'three-day week'. Soaring wage demands and the quadrupling of world oil prices had led to galloping inflation. Heath called an election for 28 February, on the slogan 'Who Governs Britain?' (not, of course, meaning 'Westminster or Brussels' but himself or the unions), whence the electorate decided 'not you'. Although Heath and Wilson were both unpopular, Labour edged ahead, by 301 seats to 297. Heath did not resign immediately, instead opening coalition talks with Jeremy Thorpe. His Liberal Party held 14 seats, but Thorpe demanded electoral reform as a condition. Unwilling to accept his terms, Heath resigned, leaving Wilson to form a minority government.

WILSON'S 'SHORT PARLIAMENT'

Throughout its election campaign, the Labour Party had fought on a wide-ranging manifesto, which had included a long section on the Common Market. A profound political mistake made by the Heath government, it asserted:

> was to accept the terms of entry to the Common Market, and to take us in without the consent of the British people. This has involved the imposition of food taxes on top of rising world prices, crippling fresh burdens on our balance of payments, and a draconian curtailment of the power of the British Parliament to settle questions affecting vital British interests. This is why a Labour government will seek a fundamental renegotiation of the terms of entry.[23]

If renegotiations were successful, the Party pledged that the people should decide whether to stay in the EEC through a general election or a referendum. Only with successful renegotiations and popular approval

---

[22] Giscard had been born at Koblenz in Germany in 1926, because his father was finance director of the civil administration by which France ran the occupied Rhineland. The family name was Giscard, but 'd'Estaing', borrowed from an eighteenth-century French admiral, had officially been added in 1922, to suggest aristocratic origins (*Daily Telegraph*, 19 May 2003, *The Times*, 20 May 2003).

[23] http://www.labour-party.org.uk/manifestos/1974/Feb/1974-feb-labour-manifesto.shtml.

would a Labour government 'be ready to play our full part in developing a new and wider Europe'.[24]

Holding a referendum had been first mooted by Tony Benn in 1970, but Wilson had flatly rejected the idea. Asked on 27 May 1970 whether he would ever change his mind, he was unequivocal. 'The answer to that is no,' he said.[25] Benn's cause, however, was aided by the unlikely figure of Pompidou who, on 16 March 1972, gave France a referendum on EEC enlargement. Reasoning that the British should be given equal treatment, Benn took his proposition back to the NEC, winning on 22 March 1972 a majority of two for a referendum.

Wilson still opposed the idea. But faced with the Shadow Cabinet favouring the idea, not for the first time on a major issue he changed his mind. A referendum option was approved by eight votes to six. Jenkins resigned as deputy leader. 'This was no way to run an opposition,' he said later, 'chopping and changing from ... week to week ... on grounds purely of opportunistic politics.'[26]

In his memoirs, Wilson admitted his party was 'sharply divided', but nonetheless was more or less united over Heath's lack of mandate. The 1970 Conservative manifesto had said: 'Our mandate is to negotiate; no more ... no less.' In his 13 years as Leader of the Party, Wilson confided in his memoirs, 'I had no more difficult task than keeping the Party together on this issue.'[27] The formula that, so far, had held the party together had been crafted by Judith Hart, only the fifth woman Cabinet minister. An influential member of the Labour left, and a member of the NEC, she had in 1973 prepared what was to become the definitive Labour Party position, later a settled part of the February 1974 manifesto.[28]

Once in office, although barely in power, Wilson and his new government were immediately embroiled in a balance of payment crisis. This was a time when a 50 mph speed limit had been imposed on motorways to save fuel, reinforcing the sense of crisis.[29] Beset by the aftermath of the Yom Kippur War, spiralling oil prices and runaway inflation, Wilson also had to deal with an uncontrolled property boom, declining industrial productivity and the very issue that had brought the Labour Party to office – untrammelled union power. Nevertheless, the Cabinet 'moved quickly' to prepare for

[24] Ibid.
[25] Cited in Heath, op. cit., p. 540.
[26] *The Poisoned Chalice*, authors' transcript.
[27] Wilson, Harold (1979), *Final Term – The Labour Government 1974–1976* (London: Weidenfeld & Nicolson), pp. 50–51.
[28] Ibid., pp. 52–53.
[29] Not lifted until March 1974.

negotiations in the Council of Ministers, due on 1–2 April 1974. Wilson had chosen Jim Callaghan as his new foreign secretary, with whom he had numerous meetings in the first weeks of the government, crafting a working policy.[30]

In terms of a renegotiation 'shopping list', seven issues emerged: the structure of the CAP; the Community budget; economic and monetary union (EMU); the powers of Parliament to deal with regional, industrial and fiscal policies; capital movements; safeguards for Commonwealth and developing countries; and the right to exclude 'essentials' (such as food) from VAT.

When Callaghan arrived at the Council of Ministers in Luxembourg on 1 April, he read a prepared statement on the government's position[31] – 'substantially as it had been put before the people at the General election', setting out the points of contention.[32] Referring directly to the Paris Summit of October 1972, he expressed his government's deep concern that the resolutions 'seemed to lay down a rigid programme under which Economic and Monetary Union, including permanently fixed parities, would be achieved by 1980'. This, he said:

> seemed to us to be dangerously over-ambitious: over-ambitious because the chances of achieving by 1980 the requisite degree of convergence of the rates of growth of productivity and wages rates, of investment and savings, seemed to us to be very small: dangerous because of the impossibility for any country, particularly a country with a relatively low growth rate, to manage its own economy efficiently and provide for full employment if it accepted permanently fixed parities without such convergence having been achieved.[33]

The *Financial Times* described the statement as 'blunt to the point of rudeness'.[34] Challenged subsequently in the Commons by Sir Alec Douglas-Hume, then opposition foreign affairs spokesman, as to his lack of 'good diplomacy', Callaghan retorted: 'If good diplomacy led to the nature of the bargain that was struck by the previous government, then perhaps a little

[30] Wilson, op. cit., p. 54.
[31] Luxembourg University Archive.
https://www.cvce.eu/content/publication/1999/1/1/49bcefb2-4a53-4fbd-a33b-144e566699e4/publishable_en.pdf.
[32] Wilson, op. cit., p. 55.
[33] Luxembourg University Archive, op. cit.
[34] Cited by Wall, op. cit., p. 320.

rougher diplomacy will not come amiss.'[35] The Luxembourg statement was subsequently published as a White Paper.[36]

This was taken as the first step of the renegotiation process. Callaghan told the Commons on 3 April that they were 'now preparing for the second step', when the UK would submit detailed proposals. With that, he declared: 'Renegotiation has begun.'[37] In a report to Cabinet the next day, he remarked that, although the French foreign minister had made a hostile statement and other member governments had reacted adversely in public, his private conversations 'had revealed willingness to seek a satisfactory solution'. However, it had been made clear to him that there would be 'difficulty' if any attempt were made to renegotiate the treaties. The Germans were 'generally inclined to be helpful', but even they told him they would oppose that route, not least because 'such changes would set a precedent for any other country which was dissatisfied with Community arrangements'.[38]

These reactions convinced the government that the best approach would be to attempt to modify Community policies rather than go for treaty change.[39] That led to what Callaghan was to describe as 'some collapse in the Labour Party's confidence in the Government's determination to carry through the fundamental renegotiation'. He warned: 'If the Government's supporters felt that this objective had been modified in order to make renegotiation easier, there would be serious political consequences and the likelihood of a renewed split.' This was not helped by the president of the Commission declaring that he did not regard the Community as being engaged in any 'renegotiation'.[40]

Because of the death of Pompidou, and the need for French presidential elections, talks were delayed, along with the rest of EEC Council business. When they were eventually set for 4 June, they were limited to procedural matters. There would be further work during the summer, but serious negotiation could not be expected until the autumn.[41] Before there could be any further developments, domestic politics intruded. Heath, now leading the opposition, mounted an attack on Labour's plans for industry in the Commons, defeating the government by 11 votes.[42] This sealed the fate of what Wilson called 'The Short Parliament', setting in train the second

[35] HC Deb, 03 April 1974, Vol. 871, cc1257-67.
[36] Cmnd. 5593.
[37] HC Deb, 03 April, op. cit.
[38] National Archives, CAB 128/54, Cabinet Conclusions, 4 April 1974.
[39] Ibid.
[40] Ibid., 4 July 1974, Confidential Annex.
[41] Ibid., Cabinet Conclusions, 2 May 1974; 16 May 1974.
[42] HC Deb, 20 June 1974, Vol. 875, cc689-769.

general election of the year.[43] There could now be no real progress on the negotiations until the votes were in.[44]

Before that, on 24 June, Callaghan delivered a lengthy memorandum to the Cabinet on the renegotiations 'and related European Economic Community questions'. Shining through this was his view that the march of political integration had ended. In an attempt to reassure colleagues, he told them that the agreement at the 1972 Paris Summit to have 'European Union' by 1980 'turns out on investigation to have been completely without content'. 'European Union by 1980', he said, 'is a slogan or a banner to which many Europeans attach great importance and which the German and other Governments need for internal political reasons to hold out to their people as a long-term aim.'

From his talks with the other foreign ministers, he had concluded that none of them (not even the Dutch, who claimed to be the most 'federalist') seriously expected the Community to change the present basis for its decision-making in the foreseeable future. With that, he said, 'When further discussions of "European Union" take place I shall hold to the view that all important decisions should continue to be taken by unanimous consensus in the Council of Ministers and I believe the other member states will agree.'[45]

Such reassuring words had little effect on Labour's union allies. With an autumn election impending but the date not yet decided, the Common Market issue – in Wilson's words – was 'brutally and dangerously re-opened' at the annual TUC conference in early September. Although the TUC's annual report, endorsed by Congress, had committed to staying in the EEC but on better terms, a resolution calling for withdrawal was moved from the floor and carried. When the party conference looked as if it would also support withdrawal, Wilson had to threaten 'a leadership crisis'. He reasoned that the last thing the party would want, in the last conference before a general election, was for it to be dominated by 'speculation and direct canvassing over the new leadership'.[46]

THE FINAL TERM

Parliament adjourned for the summer on 31 July, although it was not officially dissolved until 20 September, with polling on 10 October. In the Labour manifesto, there was no equivocation. Within 12 months of the

[43] Wilson, op. cit., compiled from Part I.
[44] National Archives, CAB 128/54, op. cit., 2 July 1974.
[45] National Archives, CAB 129/177.
[46] Ibid., p. 53.

election, Labour pledged to hold a binding referendum. The electorate would have the choice of accepting the renegotiated terms and staying in, or rejecting them and coming out.[47] In the event, Labour gained 319 seats, taking 18 from the Conservatives who held 301, leaving Wilson with an overall majority of four, including the Speaker. It was enough for what was his final term.

Progress on the negotiations was slow. On 19 November, Callaghan had discussions with the new French president Valéry Giscard d'Estaing and his foreign minister Jean Sauvagnargues in Paris. Reporting back to Cabinet two days later, he gloomily observed that he had 'explained our case on the budget issue, but had not convinced the French'. Discussion on the CAP had been similarly unproductive: 'President Giscard had given nothing away.'[48]

The following week, on 27 November, the Labour Party Conference started in Central Hall in Westminster. The anti-marketeers narrowly carried a resolution laying down eight conditions for Britain's continued membership, including 'the right of British Parliament to reject any European Economic Community legislation, directives or orders, when they are issued, or at any time after'.[49]

Next day, however, the German chancellor, Helmut Schmidt, was guest speaker. Overcoming the hostility of delegates, he managed to charm them with a plea for Socialist solidarity, calling on them not to leave the Community. In what then turned out to be something of a breakthrough – for Wilson, at least – Schmidt then spent the weekend at Chequers with him. With Callaghan mediating, Wilson was able to explain with greater clarity what precisely he needed from the renegotiations. Schmidt, in turn, pledged to help him achieve his objectives, thereby keeping Britain in the Community. Here, a key stage in the negotiations would be a 'summit' in Paris on 9–10 December, chaired by Giscard d'Estaing. Schmidt telephoned him from Chequers and arranged a pre-Council meeting between him and Wilson.[50]

The pre-meeting was held in Paris on 5 December. Wilson described it in his memoirs as 'worthwhile'.[51] To his Cabinet colleagues, he called the talks 'useful'. He found it 'noteworthy' that the French government spokesman had been authorised after the meeting to stress the good climate in which

[47] http://www.labour-party.org.uk/manifestos/1974/Oct/1974-oct-labour-manifesto.shtml.
[48] National Archives, CAB 128/55, Cabinet Conclusions, 21 November 1974.
[49] Cited in Butler and Kitzinger, op. cit., p. 36: *Report of the Seventy-Third Annual Conference of the Labour Party, 1974* (London), pp. 249–260.
[50] Based on an interview with Schmidt, *The Poisoned Chalice*; PREM 16/77 Record of conversations at Chequers, 30 November 1974; PREM 16/101 Henderson to FCO, 4 December 1974; and Wilson, op. cit., p. 88.
[51] Wilson, op. cit., p. 88–89.

the talks had taken place. As for President Giscard, he had been at pains to give nothing away and had defended well-known French views in familiar and somewhat 'theological' terms. 'We should be ready to allow the French some degree of "theology",' Wilson observed tartly, 'provided that we secured the concrete results we required.'[52]

MONNET'S LAST GREAT COUP

Above the fray, Monnet was still working on his plan for a 'provisional government'. In March 1974, he had circulated yet another paper calling for more collective action. 'The existing European institutions are not strong enough today to do it on their own,' he warned.[53] The two new Franco-German leaders soon agreed that there should be 'no more separate national actions, only European actions'. They accepted Monnet's 'provisional government', using the title 'European Council' for its meetings.[54] The new body was formally approved at an informal meeting of heads of government at the Élysée on 14 September 1974.

Now the Plan was coming to fruition: Monnet's 'European Council' was taking shape. Ironically, its first meeting – set for 9–10 December – was to be in Paris, home of the 1972 Paris Summit. Setting the pattern for the future, it adopted a two-day format. Monnet's main concern was to make it a permanent institution, in which he had an ally in Giscard, who pointed out that there had only been three 'summits' between the heads of government in five years. These needed to be 'more organised' and regular, as Monnet had proposed.[55] When Giscard brought the proceedings at Paris to a close, he declared: 'The Summit is dead. Long live the European Council.'[56] Monnet had won the day.

Despite this landmark, journalists and others would continue to refer to the meetings as 'summits'. Even today, few realise the significance of what had happened. Monnet, however, had no doubts:

the European institutions were in charge of immense sectors of activity, over which they exercised the share of sovereignty that had been delegated to them. But if they were to work effectively, the governments had to have

---

[52] National Archives, op. cit., Cabinet Conclusions, 5 December 1974.
[53] Monnet, op. cit., p. 511.
[54] Not to be confused with the Council of Ministers, which had been one of the central components of the EEC structure since 1958 (as of the Coal and Steel Community before that). By institutionalising the earlier 'summits', the European Council was an entirely new concept, which would come to play an increasingly dominant role in Community affairs.
[55] Wilson, op. cit., p. 92.
[56] Monnet, op. cit., p. 514.

the same European will and be prepared, acting together as a collective authority, to transfer the additional sovereignty required to achieve a true European Union. The creation of the European Council supplied the means for reaching that essential decision. A major step had been taken.[57]

It was, effectively, Monnet's last great coup. Retiring to write his memoirs, he was called back to the public stage only once more when, in April 1976, by resolution of the European Council in Luxembourg, he was awarded the title 'Honorary Citizen of Europe'.

RETURN TO THE PARIS SUMMIT

Notwithstanding Monnet's concerns, the 1974 Council had addressed a remarkably full agenda, the leaders noting that 'internal and international difficulties' had slowed progress towards EMU. Crucially – and despite Callaghan's bland reassurances that the march to political integration was over – they affirmed the original Paris Summit objective. In respect of EMU, 'their will had not weakened and their objective has not changed'. Wilson was then in the unfortunate position of having to endorse the joint communiqué. And still the Council had not finished. Proposing even more integration, it confirmed its determination to work towards a common foreign policy and agreed to 'renounce' the practice, based on the Luxembourg Compromise, of making agreements conditional on unanimous consent. And, in a move that was to have endless repercussions, it launched a working party to assess the feasibility of a uniform passport for Community citizens.[58]

For Wilson, with the election behind him, this had been his first opportunity to demonstrate that he was looking after the national interest. Before leaving London, he had made strong statements about how he 'would accept no nonsense from other member states on the two vital issues yet to be agreed'.[59] But, when discussion turned to the budget, Giscard would not yield. At dinner that evening, however, he 'softened', thanks to the mediation of Schmidt, honouring his Chequers promise. He persuaded his fellow ministers to examine a formula suggested by British civil servants for a 'correcting mechanism' in relation to the EEC budget.[60]

Suffering from heart trouble, Wilson was not a well man, but he nonetheless attended Cabinet on 12 December to report back. There,

[57] Ibid., p. 515.
[58] European Parliament (1982), *Communiqué: Meeting of the Heads of Government of the Community*, Paris, 9–10 December 1974, para.14.
[59] George, op. cit., p. 86.
[60] Donoughue, op. cit., p. 196.

he had to defend himself from suggestions that certain passages in the communiqué, and particularly that on EMU, were incompatible with the February Election Manifesto and would weaken the government's stance. Wilson dismissed the complaint about EMU, saying that, 'it was fully clear' that no country regarded it 'as anything other than an ideal but distant goal'. The reference to it, he said, should be seen in the same light as the commitment to 'general and complete disarmament', to which governments were always ready to subscribe.[61]

THE PEOPLE MUST DECIDE

Opinion polls had for some time shown sizeable majorities in favour of Britain leaving the EEC. But, by November 1974, they were beginning to show a significant shift. According to Harris, 53 per cent of the electorate said they would be happy to remain in the Community 'on the right terms'. In January 1975 this was even more dramatically confirmed by Gallup. Although a simple majority was still in favour of leaving, when respondents were asked whether 'new terms ... in Britain's interest' would make a difference, 71 per cent preferred to stay in. With that, on 23 January, Wilson announced his intention to hold a referendum, even though the negotiations were not over.[62] The working assumption was that it would be held in June.

The same day, the Cabinet discussed information policy for the referendum and concluded that 'further thought should be given to the limitation of expenditure on propaganda activities by outside organisations'. Ministers also proposed an 'informal consultation with the BBC and the Independent Broadcasting Authority on the arrangements they would be making in order to maintain a fair balance'.[63]

However, just over three weeks later, on 17 February, Cabinet was presented with a draft White Paper on the referendum, setting out the government's ideas on how it should be run. Attached was a memorandum from the Lord President of the Council (Ted Short). Passages that were 'important and possibly controversial' were emphasised, one of which stated that there should be: 'No limit on total expenditure by the two sides.' The government had approached 'this difficult area' with no desire to limit traditional freedom of speech, but rather with 'a desire to see that both sides of the case are known to the public and that public interest in the issues is stimulated'.[64] The implications of this were clearly understood because, on

[61] National Archives, op. cit., Cabinet Conclusions, 12 December 1974.
[62] HC Deb, 23 January 1975, Vol. 884, cc1745-64.
[63] National Archives, CAB 128/56, Cabinet Conclusions, 23 January 1975.
[64] National Archives, CAB 129/181/c19.

20 February, Short warned the Cabinet that 'great care should be taken to prevent subsequent resentment' over the result because one side had greater resources than the other.[65]

The warning was not heeded. The government was to allow the campaign to be skewed by disproportionate spending on the 'Yes' side, something that was to rankle for a generation. Yet it scarcely provoked any public comment at the time. One lone MP, John Peyton, representing Yeovil, branded it 'sloppy thinking'.[66]

On 27 February, a major issue of regional policy was resolved. The Cabinet had already decided in September 1974 that Community rules for the co-ordination of national regional aids 'were in our interest', subject to satisfying 'five specific principles'. After intensive discussions with the Commission, the government's view was that new EEC rules would not interfere with the regional policies it needed to pursue, and therefore, the manifesto aim had been met.[67]

By 6 March, Wilson could confirm that there were only two issues outstanding: access to New Zealand dairy products and the budget contribution. These would go to the Dublin European Council on 10–11 March.[68] As regards the budget, the Treasury had estimated that by 1979, if nothing changed, Britain's share would increase to 21 per cent, against her 14 per cent share of Community GNP. However, the Commission declined to endorse these calculations and would not consider any estimate of future contributions. The French refused to recognise levies and tariffs as national contributions, on the grounds that the EEC was a customs union. All such duties had to be regarded as the Community's 'own resources' (even though the bill would have to be paid by British consumers in higher prices for imported goods). A rebate was out of the question.[69]

With so much to achieve, on top of disagreement about New Zealand produce, Wilson was gloomy about Dublin.[70] The first day was spent discussing 'a complex and incomprehensible German proposal for implementing the budget correcting mechanism', followed by a second of similarly arcane talks on import quotas for New Zealand dairy products.[71] The Belgian prime minister complained about heads of government being

[65] National Archives, CAB 128/56, Cabinet Conclusions, 20 February 1975.
[66] HC Deb 11, March 1975, Vol. 888, cc409-56.
[67] National Archives, CAB 128/56, Cabinet Conclusions, 27 February 1975.
[68] National Archives, CAB 128/56/11.
[69] George, op. cit., p. 83.
[70] National Archives, CAB 128/56, Cabinet Conclusions, 6 March 1975.
[71] Butler, David and Kitzinger, Uwe (1976), The 1975 Referendum (London: Macmillan), p. 41.

reduced to the level of auditors of a supermarket chain.[72] Nevertheless, after the French had backed off from their objection on inclusion of 'own resources' in the budget calculations, a semblance of agreement was reached.

On 13 March, the Cabinet continued preparing for the referendum, agreeing to provide grants of £125,000 for each of the two main campaigning organisations, Britain in Europe and the National Referendum Campaign. Ministers also finalised the referendum question. It would read: 'Do you think that the United Kingdom should stay in the European Community (the Common Market)?' The text in brackets had been a last-minute addition.[73] Cabinet next met over the period of 17–18 March and, to inform the discussions, Callaghan's office had prepared a lengthy report entitled *EEC: Renegotiation Stocktaking*. Significantly, it included an eight-page annex on the 'Consequences and implications of withdrawal from the Community', which made sombre reading. Even though the UK had only been in the EEC two years, and the level of integration was relatively modest, it found that:

A considerable number of complex issues would have to be settled in the withdrawal negotiations. The scale and difficulty of the operation could not be assessed until we could discuss the problems with the Community. Some time would elapse before the withdrawal was completed, but we could hardly take a full part in normal Community business during that period. The Community might be reluctant to negotiate before our formal withdrawal, about permanent post-withdrawal arrangements, for example on tariffs. The Community's main concern would be with its own continued cohesion. There would be bound to be bitterness about our withdrawal. The withdrawal negotiation could not avoid taking on the character of a confrontation between the Community and ourselves, on different sides of the table.[74]

The prescience of this warning was not to be tested for over forty years, and by a different generation of politicians. Wilson was not to be troubled by it. He was able to tell his Cabinet that the negotiating objectives had been 'substantially achieved'. The Community had changed de facto and de jure and the attitude of the Commonwealth had also changed: it 'wanted us to stay in'.[75] On the vexed question of EMU, Callaghan, bolstered by his 'stocktaking'

---

[72] Ibid.
[73] National Archives, CAB 128/56, Cabinet Conclusions, 13 March 1975.
[74] National Archives, CAB 129/182.
[75] Benn, Tony (1995), *The Benn Diaries* (single-volume edition) (London: Random House), p. 313.

report, assured colleagues that there had been a major shift in attitude on the 1980 target set by the Paris Summit. The programme 'had been tacitly abandoned', he said, even if it 'remained a long-term Community goal'.

The Cabinet voted 16–7 for staying in. This opened the way for Wilson to announce to the Commons, on 18 March, that his objectives had been 'substantially, though not completely, achieved'. In a downbeat address, he continued:

> It will be seen from what I have said that the Government cannot claim to have achieved in full all the objectives that were set in the manifesto on which the Labour Party fought and won two elections last year. Some we have achieved in full; on others we have made considerable progress, though in the time available to us it has not been possible to carry them to the point where we can argue that our aims have been completely realised. It is thus for the judgment now of the Government, shortly of Parliament, and in due course of the British people, whether or not we should stay in the European Community on the basis of the terms as they have now been renegotiated.[76]

In late March, the government published its White Paper on the renegotiations, and in a debate on 7–9 April asked Parliament to approve Britain's continued membership on the new terms. Wilson won by 396 to 170 but 145 of his MPs, including 38 ministers, had voted against their own government. The day was carried by Conservative MPs, including Heath, only eight voting against. Then, on 10 April, the Referendum Bill had its Second Reading in the Commons, winning its passage with 312 votes, to 248 against. Heath opposed the Bill, joining with most of the Conservative frontbench, now led by Margaret Thatcher, who had taken over the reins on 11 February.[77] When the Bill received Royal Assent on 8 May, the final decision was in the hands of the British people.

BATTLE LINES ARE DRAWN
Swallowing his objection to the referendum, Heath announced on 19 March that he planned to play a full part in the campaign, on behalf of a new 'all-party' organisation called Britain in Europe (BiE), publicly launched on 26 March. In December 1974, the long-established European Movement had put its own campaign into abeyance, placing all its resources

---

[76] HC Debates, 18 March 1975, Vol. 888, cc1456.
[77] HC Deb, 10 April 1975, Vol. 889, cc1418.

at the disposal of BiE. The new title was chosen because it seemed 'crisp' and 'fresh', and because it emphasised that the campaign favoured remaining with the status quo.[78]

BiE was designed as an umbrella organisation, encompassing separate Conservative, Labour and Liberal campaigns, along with a Trade Union Alliance for Europe. Its Labour president was Roy Jenkins, with several senior staff seconded from the party. The chairman was Con O'Neill, who had retired from the Foreign Office in 1972. Heath was a vice-president, along with the former Liberal leader Jo Grimond, William Whitelaw MP, Lord Feather, former general-secretary of the TUC, and Sir Henry Plumb, president of the NFU.

As the referendum approached, the Labour Party's fragile unity had begun to unravel. Left-wing MPs, led by Joe Ashton, Tony Benn's PPS, and Ian Mikardo had strongly criticised the terms of the renegotiation and were even calling for withdrawal from the EEC.[79] On 22 March, the Scottish Labour Party voted against staying in by 346,000 to 280,000, with Mikardo and others making speeches that bordered on personal abuse of leading members of their own party. Next day, five Cabinet ministers, Benn, Barbara Castle, Michael Foot, Shore and John Silkin, openly opposed the government line. Having anticipated this problem, Wilson released his ministers from their obligation of collective responsibility.

One bewildering feature of the battle was that, in addition to the official 'Yes' and 'No' campaigns, there were also 'Yes' campaigns for each party. Labour's 'Campaign for Europe' was launched on 8 April, with Shirley Williams as president. It included 88 MPs, 21 peers and 25 trade unionists.[80] The Conservative 'Yes' campaign was launched by Thatcher on 16 April, at a dinner at the St Ermin's Hotel. She could not have spoken more fervently for the cause.

Despite the Tories having a separate campaign, BiE relied heavily on its electoral machinery for implementing theirs.[81] It was nevertheless at pains to present itself as an all-embracing body, run by a council of 37 well-known names, including every living ex-prime minister, every ex-foreign secretary (barring Selwyn Lloyd, who, as Speaker of the House, had to stay neutral), and other public figures ranging from the television mogul Lew Grade to the

---

[78] Butler and Kitzinger, op. cit., p. 72; see also fn. 39 on p. 205.
[79] Ibid.
[80] The depth of division in the Labour Party was shown by a special conference organised by Labour's NEC in Islington on 26 April, when a motion to approve leaving the EEC was passed (under block voting) by 3.7 million votes to 1.98 million (Donoughue, op. cit., p. 202).
[81] Butler and Kitzinger, op. cit., p. 78.

former Archbishop of Canterbury, Michael Ramsey. The church was heavily involved, thanks to the efforts of a young Conservative would-be MP, John Selwyn Gummer, who claimed to have the support of over one-quarter of all clergy of all denominations, including almost every Anglican bishop.

'Prayers for Europe' were said in many Anglican churches and supportive items were placed in parish magazines. Mammon was also well represented, notably by the enthusiastic support of the CBI. A *Times* survey on 9 April showed 415 out of 419 chairmen of major companies supporting continued membership. The CBI set up its own European Operations Room, distributing over a million documents.[82]

As during the 'great debate' four years earlier, raising money proved to be no problem for the 'Yes' campaign. But the sources have remained a well-guarded secret, although, in 2005, one organiser of the 'Yes' campaign, Caroline de Courcey Ireland, spoke openly about her experience. She had been asked to charter British Caledonian airliners to fly 'nearly 1000' pro-European speakers to Brussels for briefings by top-level Commission officials. When asked who had provided the money for this, she replied: 'from the European Commission: it was a sort of special dispensation. I don't know how they fixed it, because one didn't ask too much. One just said "Thank you very much" and got on with organising it.'[83] The 'Yes' campaign's treasurer Alistair McAlpine admitted that, 'when the campaign started, money rolled in. The banks and the big industrial companies put in very large sums of money.'[84]

Together with the European Movement, BiE were to spend some £1,850,000 on the battle, completely dwarfing the mere £133,000 available to the ramshackle 'No' campaign, run by the National Referendum Campaign (NRC). As most anti-Market groups came from extremes of left and right, it represented an uneasy coalition. Many were at odds with one another, as when Tony Benn refused to appear in public with Enoch Powell. Tory anti-marketeers were notably absent from the campaign. Of the 41 who had defied the whip to vote against EEC entry, only five played an active role. The few other prominent activists included the historian Sir Arthur Bryant; journalists Paul Johnson and Peregrine Worsthorne; Patrick Neill QC, a future Warden of All Souls; the economists Lord Kaldor and Robert Neild; and a recently retired permanent secretary of the Ministry of Agriculture, now director of the National Trust, Sir John Winnifrith.

They could scarcely hope to compete with the galaxy of public figures supporting the 'Yes' bandwagon, which was now ready to roll.

[82] Ibid., p. 83.
[83] Ibid., pp. 82–83.
[84] Cockerell, Michael, *How We Fell for Europe*, BBC2, 4 June 2005.

THE CAMPAIGN

A feature of the campaign often overlooked is that it coincided with the worst economic crisis Britain had faced since the war. In June 1975 the inflation rate hit 27 per cent, the highest level ever recorded. Public spending was out of control and government borrowing was heading towards a record £11 billion. Britain's trade deficit had also reached record levels, not helped by the imbalance with Common Market partners, running at a yearly rate of £2.6 billion, against the modest pre-entry surplus. None of this impinged on the campaign, which was generally low-key. The most tangible sign of a campaign in progress was the three official booklets sent to every household in the country: two, from BiE and the government, calling for a 'Yes' vote; the third putting the case for a 'No'.

The 'No' leaflet listed benefits that had been promised if Britain joined the Market, from a rapid rise in our living standards and higher investment to more employment and faster industrial growth. In every case, it claimed, government figures showed the opposite result. It tried to evoke the dangers facing Britain from having handed over 'the right to rule ourselves', as her laws increasingly came to be made by 'unelected Commissioners in Brussels'. It claimed that the Market's 'real aim' was eventually to become 'one single country', in which Britain would be a 'mere province'. It rejected the 'scaremongering of the pro-Marketeers', who claimed that British withdrawal would lead to economic disaster, and called for Britain to negotiate a free trade agreement with the EEC, like that now enjoyed by Norway, Switzerland and the other members of EFTA.

The BiE case began with simple bullet points summing up the 'real advantages' of staying in. It made 'good sense' for 'our jobs and prosperity', for 'world peace', and 'for our children's future'. But it was the emotional pitch of the BiE case that stood out. It dwelt on how lonely and isolated Britain would be if she were foolish enough to withdraw. Everyone else in the world, it claimed, wanted Britain to stay in, from the USA and the Commonwealth to 'our friends' in the European Community. Outside, 'we should be alone in a cold, harsh world'. Claims that the Community was undemocratic and wanted to eliminate national identities were ridiculous. 'All decisions of any importance must be agreed by every member.'

Apart from a few new laws needed for 'commercial and industrial purposes', Britain would still retain the rest: 'Trial by jury, presumption of innocence remain unaltered.' The leaflet ended by quoting Heath: 'Are we going to stay on the centre of the stage where we belong, or are we going to shuffle off into the dusty wings of history?'

The government leaflet, *A New Deal in Europe*, emphasised how the renegotiations had brought 'significant improvements' in Britain's terms of membership. Under the heading 'Will Parliament Lose Its Power? What are the Facts?', voters were again assured 'we cannot go it alone in the modern world'. Membership of 'groupings like the United Nations, Nato and the International Monetary Fund' had not deprived the British of their national identity. It was 'the Council of Ministers' that took all the 'important decisions' in the Common Market, not officials. 'Inside the Market', it concluded, 'we can play a major part' in deciding policies that will 'affect the lives of every family in the country'; 'outside we are on our own'.

The press almost unanimously supported a 'Yes' vote, but, inevitably, television set the pace. Public meetings, although numerous, were relatively sparsely attended, their role being to provide news 'hooks' on which media coverage could be based. This helped to give the campaign an air of suffocating unreality, where 'debate' was reduced to little more than slogans and soundbites. This was a process deliberately encouraged by 'Yes' camp tacticians, who were far more effective than their opponents in setting the level on which the battle was fought. As one commentator observed:

> On both sides, the committed would have liked a political debate about patriotism, sovereignty and federalism, which is what had moved them to work hard for many years to get Britain into Europe, or keep it from the clutches of Brussels. But, especially on the pro-Community side, practical politicians and campaigners moved in to steer the debate in which prices, income levels and economic security dominated ... The familiar bread and butter issues of a British general election took top place in the minds of the publicity men and in the answers pollsters obtained about what the referendum question meant.[85]

At the centre of the 'Yes' campaign was a unit set up by Jim Callaghan in the Foreign Office, holding daily meetings with his team. As a senior civil servant, Sir Michael Butler, was later to recall, it included Shirley Williams, head of the Labour 'Yes' campaign, and the Head of the No. 10 News Department, plus one or two other ministers, together with officials. The daily strategy for the campaign was decided at these meetings.[86]

This unprecedented use of civil servants to promote what was essentially a propaganda exercise marked a fundamental break with the strict

[85] Steed, Michael (1977), 'The Landmarks of the British Referendum', *Parliamentary Affairs*, 30, pp. 130–131. Cited in George, op. cit., p. 93.
[86] Churchill College, oral archive, op. cit.

tradition of civil service impartiality (Butler himself called it 'an interesting innovation'). But this was excused by the assumption of those involved that 'Europe' was an issue transcending partisan politics.

Another 'regular' at Callaghan's meetings was the market researcher Bob Worcester, head of Mori International, who played a key role in guiding tactics. In a memorandum to Callaghan on 16 May, his advice was to focus on prices and the cost of living. With inflation heading for 27 per cent, the message should be 'that the government will have a better chance of keeping prices down if we stay in the Common Market than if we get out'. He concluded:

> We must not scatter our shots – let the Opposition talk about sovereignty, independence, Britain's role in the world, defence, etc. If they spend two days on this and three days on that between now and the 5 June (polling day), this is the best thing that could happen to us.[87]

In Worcester's subsequent analysis, he attached great importance to the public perception of each side's leading figures, where the 'No' campaign had suffered a marked handicap. Based on subtracting the percentage of the public who liked each figure from the percentage who disliked them, only one of the six leading 'anti-marketeers' registered a small plus rating: Enoch Powell. Those with minus ratings included Tony Benn, Michael Foot and the trade union leaders Jack Jones and Hugh Scanlon, with Rev. Ian Paisley on minus 59.

All six leading 'Yes' campaigners, including Wilson, Heath, Jenkins, Whitelaw, Maudling and Jeremy Thorpe, scored big plusses. With the pro-marketeers occupying the centre ground, there were few figures in the 'No' camp who could be presented as moderate, establishment figures. The media, anyway, liked to focus on the two figures who, to middle-ground opinion, seemed most extreme: Powell and Benn.[88] After the poll, a Conservative campaigner who had been in the thick of the action, commented on this effect:

> What was notable was the extent to which the referendum … was not really about Europe at all. It became a straight left versus right battle with the normal dividing line shifting further over than in general elections – hence

---

[87] Worcester, op. cit., pp. 14–15.
[88] As public concern mounted at the growth in trade union power, Benn and his anti-market Labour colleagues were seen by many as left-wing bogeymen. This was exacerbated by the extraordinarily high profile given to Benn by the media. Between 1 May and 4 June, he appeared in feature programmes or principal news items 52 times, followed by the almost equally controversial Powell at 23 times. The most prominent 'Yes' campaigner was Jenkins, who appeared 27 times, while Heath equalled Powell on 23 (Worcester, op. cit., p. 194). The media also highlighted attempts to break up 'No' campaign meetings by far-right National Front supporters, who had been excluded from the campaign by the NRC.

the Labour split and their discomfiture. In all the speeches I made to Conservative audiences the trump card was always – 'beware of Benn, Foot and Castle'. It was this, more than anything, which ... increasingly negated the efforts of the anti-EEC Conservatives.[89]

The 'antis' were never going to succeed. The greatest strength of the 'pros' was the status quo: 'If we leave, Britain will be isolated' was their central theme. In addition, there was the near-unanimity of establishment opinion in favour of staying in. The opposition was fatally split and the leading figures of the 'Yes' campaign were vastly more credible than their opponents.[90]

Unsurprisingly, when 5 June came, the public voted to stay in. When the results were declared the following day, the 'Yes' vote had gained a 2:1 majority. On a 64.5 per cent turnout of 29,433,194 electors, 67.2 per cent voted 'Yes', 32.8 'No'. Every part of mainland Britain registered a 'Yes' majority, the only exceptions being Shetland (where 56.3 per cent voted 'No') and the Western Isles (70.3). After the result had been announced, Thatcher declared: 'The message of the referendum for the government is that the people have looked at the really big issues ... They have looked at what really counts and they have voted that way.'[91] Heath was jubilant. 'The British people have now shown conclusively that they accept and endorse the historic decision taken by Parliament under my premiership to join the European Community. Once again, they have shown their true sense of vision and destiny. We must now play a major and constructive role in the development of the European Community,' he purred.[92]

The next day, the *Daily Express* paraded the front-page banner headline, 'Europeans!', telling its readers: 'Britain's Yes to Europe rang round the world last night louder, clearer, and more unanimous than any decision in peacetime history.' But there were voices, not all of them Eurosceptic, who would come to question the outcome. Roy Hattersley, years later, thought it had been 'wrong for us to deal superficially with what Europe involved'. 'We've paid the price for it ever since,' he said, 'because every time there's a crisis in Europe, people say, with some justification, "well, we wouldn't have been part of this if we'd really known the implications."'[93]

The really significant lesson of that referendum vote, though, was reflected in the fact that, only six months earlier, the opinion polls had

---

[89] Butler and Kitzinger, op. cit., p. 287.
[90] For a detailed analysis, see Worcester, op. cit.
[91] *The Times*, 7 June 1975.
[92] *Daily Express*, 7 June 1975.
[93] BBC Radio 4, Document: *A Letter to The Times*, 8 p.m., 3 February 2000.

consistently been showing majorities in favour of Britain leaving the EEC. What undoubtedly swung public opinion, as the pollsters themselves discovered, was that so many people genuinely believed Wilson had won a better deal. The campaign itself was in this sense wholly irrelevant.

The result on 5 June reflected almost exactly what the polls had been showing back in March, after voters had first started telling the pollsters that, if the government now assured them it was in Britain's interest to stay in, they would change their minds. Wilson had swung them round with renegotiations that many thought were a 'sham'.[94] A more nuanced view might be that Wilson, although generally supportive of EEC membership, genuinely wanted change. Having underestimated the difficulty involved in securing a new treaty, he settled for what he could get. The verdict of the referendum suggests that the British public were sufficiently impressed by his efforts to support him. The debate, however, had not been resolved.

On 22 November 1974, a piece of history was made in a British court, when for the first time a case had been decided entirely on the basis of the Treaty of Rome. Lord Denning had ruled in favour of a German company that had demanded an English customer should settle his disputed bill in deutschmarks. In a lower court the company had already been given judgement in sterling, this being previously the only currency in which an English court could legally make an award. But the German firm had appealed because, by then, sterling had been substantially devalued against the mark. Finding for the plaintiff, Denning said: 'This is the first case in which we had actually to apply the Treaty of Rome in these courts. It shows great effect. It has brought about a fundamental change ... It has already made us think about our own laws.'[95]

The trouble was that very few others were doing any serious thinking. Britain was sleepwalking into an entirely new situation, the nature of which her people could not yet begin to comprehend.

---

[94] Heath, op. cit., p. 542. Among those close to the negotiations also later to describe them as a 'sham' was Sir Michael Alexander (at the time Callaghan's assistant private secretary, later ambassador to NATO). Interview recorded for British Diplomatic Oral History Programme, Churchill Archives Centre, Cambridge. The most glaring omission from the issues submitted for renegotiation was the fisheries policy. Sir Oliver Wright, at the time deputy under-secretary for European Affairs in the FCO (later ambassador to Washington), suggested this was because it would have been impossible to win enough changes to the CFP 'to be able to declare the re-negotiations a success' (Churchill Archive).
[95] Schorsch Meier GmbH v. A R Hennin [1975] 1 All E.R. 152.

8

The Awkward Partner: 1975–1984

> Our decline in relation to our European partners has been so
> marked that today we are not only no longer a world power,
> but we are not in the first rank even as a European one.
>
> Sir Nicholas Henderson, UK Ambassador to
> France, June 1979[1]

> I must be absolutely clear about this … I cannot play Sister
> Bountiful to the Community while my own electorate are
> being asked to forego [sic] improvements in the fields of
> health, education, welfare and the rest.
>
> Margaret Thatcher, 19 June 1979[2]

The British people emerged from the referendum campaign to a bleak
prospect. Twenty-five years earlier Britain had been the second richest
country in the world, but in the mid-1970s her industries were inefficient,
over-manned and strike-ridden, kept afloat only by annual injections of
billions of pounds of taxpayers' cash.

Nightly familiar on the nation's television screens, trade union leaders
such as Jack Jones, Hugh Scanlon and Joe Gormley were viewed as the
most powerful men in Britain. Within a year Chancellor Denis Healey
would be calling on the International Monetary Fund for the largest loan
to which he was entitled. In economic terms, Britain was being scornfully
dismissed as 'the sick man of Europe'. To all these problems, membership
of the EEC seemed irrelevant. Although the British people had voted to

---

[1] Henderson, Nicholas (1987), *Channels and Tunnels* (London: Weidenfeld & Nicolson), p. 143.
[2] Thatcher, Margaret (1992), *The Downing Street Years* (London: HarperCollins), p. 79.

stay in the Common Market, many imagining that this meant little more than a free trade area. Its activities could scarcely have seemed more remote, and 'Europe', after the flurry of interest during the referendum, virtually disappeared from the headlines. The overriding concern of the politicians and the media was now again with domestic affairs.

Behind the scenes, though, Britain's already strained relationship with her European 'partners' was to deteriorate further, cementing her reputation as the Community's 'awkward partner'. This was the term that most commonly described that relationship in the post-referendum period, capturing the imagination of the British people in the early 1980s when Margaret Thatcher became prime minister. After she embarked on a seemingly interminable battle over Britain's budget contributions, it became a dominant theme, shaping much of the UK media coverage of EEC affairs. A prominent chronicler of this theme was Stephen George, a Jean Monnet Professor of Politics at the University of Sheffield, whose book first published in 1990 described in detail the troubled relationship.

George asserts that the relationship was more or less doomed from the moment Wilson arrived in Brussels on 16 July 1975 to attend the first European Council after the referendum – only the second formal Council to be held. The prime minister had announced that he would stand up for British interests 'no more and no less than our EEC partners', an apparently innocuous statement intended for domestic consumption. Nevertheless, it was seen in Brussels as 'alarmingly negative'.[3] Yet all Wilson might have been doing was suggesting that Britain intended to follow the example set most conspicuously by France. But while such statements were acceptable from the Fifth Republic, when British politicians indulged in anything like the same rhetoric, Britain, and Britain alone, became the awkward one.

Nevertheless, it seems unlikely that Wilson sought to give offence. In fact, he and his foreign secretary were barely engaged. The day before travelling to Brussels, the meeting was mentioned in Cabinet only in passing, without discussion. Wilson's main preoccupation was public expenditure and inflation.[4] On his return, the House of Commons was informed only briefly of the meeting by way of a Written Answer.[5] There is no reference to it in Wilson's memoirs, so his reaction is not recorded. The agenda, however, cannot have been to his liking. Issues included elections to the European

[3] *The Spectator*, 'Unanswered questions at Wilson's summit', 26 July 1975, cited in George, Stephen (1990), *An Awkward Partner: Britain in the European Community* (Oxford: Oxford University Press, 3rd edn), p. 96.
[4] National Archives, CAB 128/57, Cabinet Conclusions, 15 July 1975.
[5] HC Deb 22, July 1975, Vol. 896, cc109-10W.

Parliament by direct universal suffrage, the setting up of a Passports Union and giving special rights to the citizens of the nine member states as members of the Community. Nor can he have been particularly at ease with the lengthy consideration of the technical problems of floating Community currencies.[6]

Of far greater importance to the British government was the third stage of the Conference on Security and Co-operation in Europe. Held in Helsinki from 30 July to 1 August, representing 33 European states, with the participation of the United States and Canada, it happened to coincide with a crisis in Portugal. The fact that, in each case, the UK took an independent line – a largely unthinking habit redolent of its imperial past – almost certainly ruffled the sensitivities of the 'colleagues', and particularly the French.

ODD MAN OUT

It was not only in high-profile issues, though, that the UK was having trouble adapting to the 'Continental' regime. With little input from British officials, Brussels had been engaged in a programme of technical legislation that was to have a profound impact on the way certain matters in the UK were regulated, with considerable cost implications.

For instance, in 1975 the Community issued a new Directive – what was to be the first of a long series – harmonising controls over effluent discharges into rivers.[7] However, the exacting standards foreseen by the Directive were based on continental norms, designed to deal with problems associated with such rivers as the Rhine. When it was pointed out that, for the shorter, faster-flowing rivers of the UK, such costly standards were not necessary, this was seen as another example of British exceptionalism. Furthermore, if Britain was allowed to adopt relaxed standards, her industries would gain an 'unfair' advantage – the defining concept of the 'level playing field'.[8]

Then, in October 1975, just before the Commission was due to approve the first Regional Development Fund grants, amounting to 160 million 'units of account', the British Commissioner, George Thomson, found himself in the embarrassing position of having to warn member states – including the UK – about how they should be used. It was 'essential', he said,

---

[6] European Council, 'Summary of the Conclusions of the Meeting of the European Council held in Brussels on 16 and 17 July 1975'.
[7] Council Directive 75/440/EEC of 16 June 1975 concerning the quality required of surface water intended for the abstraction of drinking water in the member states.
[8] George, op. cit., p. 96.

that the grants were treated as 'additional to the national effort and not just a part-replacement of them' – the so-called principle of 'additionality'.[9] Given Heath's intention that regional funding should help compensate Britain for the budgetary imbalance, the Treasury automatically took the view that the funds could subsidise projects that would otherwise have been paid for by UK taxpayers. Britain's 'failure' to accept the rules was cited as evidence of a lack of good faith.

A more general charge against the British centred on the attitude shown by Callaghan. According to a contemporary comment:

> The Foreign Secretary's hectoring manner in the Council of Ministers would conspire to lose even a cast-iron case. He's a man to whom rudeness comes naturally in formal negotiations, and is much resented for it. In presentational terms, his arguments in the Council are frequently disastrous.[10]

But this mix of Community sensibilities and supposed British 'awkwardness' took a more serious turn when the Community set out to adopt a 'common policy' on energy in the wake of the Yom Kippur War, when dealing with the petroleum cartel, OPEC.

The problem for Britain was the recent discovery of North Sea oil. When US Secretary of State Dr Henry Kissinger had called a conference of 13 major oil-consuming nations in Washington, including the newly established EEC Nine, the British thought it only natural to assume the role of an equal player in the group. When, in the subsequent proceedings, Britain joined with the US position, the French (despite the agreement of seven of the Nine) angrily accused the temporary Anglo-US alliance of 'condominium'.[11]

In fairness, it was not only the British who were having trouble. When discussing the issue with President Ford in December 1974, Giscard talked of France being 'humiliated by the travails of its political system after World War II'. When de Gaulle came in, the French president said, 'he wanted to restore French dignity. That required antagonising the major powers.' Kissinger intervened with a disparaging comment about 'the complexity of the French mind'. Giscard retorted: 'We have this compulsion for

---

[9] See European Communities Commission Press Release of 19 October 1975, and Address by George Thomson to the Conference of Local and Regional Authorities of Europe, 14 October 1975. Both Archive of European Integration.

[10] *New Statesman*, 'The Odd Man Out of Europe', 24 October 1975.

[11] FRUS, 1969–1976, Vol. XXXVII, Energy Crisis, 1974–1980, Doc 16. This unusual term is taken to mean the joint control of a state's affairs by other states. The French, therefore, were complaining that the United States and the UK were seeking to control French affairs.

independence and self-esteem.'[12] To the British (Callaghan), Kissinger later remarked: 'They [the French] tend to use the conference as a substitute for any other kind of action.'[13]

This was what Britain had to confront in June 1975 when the French attempted to set up another energy conference. As before, they refused to take account of Britain's new status and instead agreed directly with the OPEC oil producers that the rich oil-consuming nations should be represented at the conference only by Japan, the USA and the EEC acting as a single entity. Callaghan, not having been consulted, immediately declared that Britain, with her separate interests, could not be represented by the EEC, with its different interests. Professor George records that 'the incident caused annoyance'.[14]

Another critic, Ian Davison, accused Britain of playing to the domestic gallery.[15] But the foreign secretary was merely reiterating the British line that a display of European solidarity might be seen as an attempt to frustrate the Arab embargo, provoking them to reduce supplies of oil to Europe still further, thereby increasing the Community's economic difficulties.[16] Nevertheless, this still aroused the ire of her EEC partners. Despite France having blocked the original US-inspired initiative, having set up its own conference, and then having negotiated arrangements without referring to Britain, the UK was the 'awkward partner'.

In the event, it was Wilson who compromised, agreeing that the Community could be represented by the Council and Commission presidents. The UK and Luxembourg (as the country due to succeed to the presidency at the end of the year) would be able to 'present additional statements'. This arrangement was not as satisfactory as a separate seat, Wilson conceded, but he had secured from the French in exchange for a minimum floor price for oil an agreement on emergency sharing arrangements for oil stocks. What we had gained for the UK, the Cabinet minute read, 'represented a good compromise. We could not have obtained more and what we had secured had only been got by tough and sustained negotiation on the part of the Prime Minister.'[17]

This deal was endorsed by the European Council, but not before – as Professor George noted – Wilson had come 'under heavy fire' from

---

[12] Op. cit., Doc. 24, as an example of strained relations between the French and the US.
[13] Op. cit., Doc. 38.
[14] George, op. cit., p. 102.
[15] Cited by George, op. cit., p. 103.
[16] Wall, op. cit., He cites PREM 14/2041.
[17] National Archives, CAB 128/57, Cabinet Conclusions, 4 December 1975.

Chancellor Schmidt. He was reported to have shouted at him that a country with one of the weakest economies in the Community was not in a position to negotiate on such issues without heed to the consequences.[18, 19] In the end, George claims, Wilson 'gave way'. Britain's stance had cost even more of her diminishing goodwill with her partners. 'The whole episode had been handled badly', he wrote, 'and it is difficult to see any good reason for this other than stubbornness.'[20]

While at the European Council, Wilson had also been updated on the progress of the Passports Union. His Cabinet colleagues were not enthused. They argued that the proposal that the Community passport should have the words 'European Community' at the top was likely to arouse 'nationalist reactions' in the country.[21] They were not wrong.

Closer to home, there was other trouble brewing. On 15 January 1976, the Lord President (still Ted Short), warned that there was 'increasing dissatisfaction with the way in which Parliament operated'. Members, he said, 'were driven very hard, long hours were worked, and recesses were short, allowing Members insufficient time with their families'. In particular, there was great pressure on Parliament. Debates on EEC matters were now taking up considerable time; it was difficult to fit in general debates; and, despite all efforts, the present session was now becoming overloaded. New and able younger members were frustrated by what they saw as the absence of a sufficiently constructive role. 'Unless radical changes were made', he warned, 'there was a danger of Parliament falling into increasing disrepute.'[22] He was not wrong.

FISHING FOR A COMMON POLICY

Energy was not the only issue now straining relations between Britain and the rest of the Community. There was also the contentious problem of fishing, given fresh impetus on 1 January 1977 when, after the Third United Nations Conference on the Law of the Sea (UNCLOS), the new 200-mile fisheries limit was adopted by most of the world's fishing nations, including the members of the EEC.[23]

The declaration of 200-mile limits by other countries meant that vessels from Community member states would now be excluded from rich fishing

[18] https://www.consilium.europa.eu/media/20809/1975_december_rome__eng_.pdf.
[19] George, op. cit., p. 103.
[20] Ibid., p. 104.
[21] Op. cit.
[22] National Archives, CAB 128/58.
[23] Bulletin of the European Communities 7/8-1976, points 2434 and 2440.

grounds off Norway and Iceland. This was of particular relevance to Britain's fishing industry, because a large part of her fleet was made up of 'distant water' trawlers, based in ports such as Hull and Fleetwood, fishing across the North Atlantic, from Norway to Iceland and Greenland.

One reason why many British fishermen had accepted the Common Fisheries Policy was that they assumed this deep-water fishing could continue. But now, it seemed, these waters could be barred to them. Already 1975 was seeing the height of the so-called 'Cod Wars', with British vessels being forcibly expelled from Icelandic waters by armed gunboats. The UK's deep-water fishermen therefore turned their attention to waters nearer home, where, under international law, Britain was about to extend her own limits to 200 miles through the 1976 Fisheries Limits Act. At a meeting in Edinburgh in April 1975, British fisheries organisations urged that all non-EEC members should be excluded from the new 200-mile limit, with a 100-mile limit to be reserved for British vessels only. But the government agreed only to press for the establishment of exclusive national zones of at least 50 miles. Predictably, the French and the Dutch demanded 'equal access'.

At this point the full implications of what Heath had given away finally began to dawn on UK fishermen. In February 1976, the Commission proposed that it should manage the fishing resource in all but inshore waters, to be parcelled out on the basis of national quotas.[24] Despite protests from the British and Irish governments, at a final meeting in The Hague in November 1976 the Council agreed a common 'conservation policy'.[25] The seas around Europe would be split into fishing areas, in each of which would be fixed the 'Total Allowable Catch', or TAC for each species of fish. This would then be allocated between member states on a quota system.[26]

After fierce argument as to how this should be decided, it was eventually agreed that the divisions should be based on 'historic catches', measured over

[24] Commission of the European Communities, COM(76) 59 final, 18 February 1976. Problems which the introduction of economic zones of 200 miles poses for the Community in the sea fishing sector. See also Information Note.
[25] Commission of the European Communities, COM(76) 500 final, 23 September 1976, 'Future External Fisheries Policy: An Internal Fisheries System'.
[26] There were several instruments, making up a package of measures. Among them was Council Regulation (EEC) No. 100/76 of 19 January 1976 on the common organisation of the market in fishery products. This was followed by Council Resolution of 3 November 1976 on certain external aspects of the creation of a 200-mile fishing zone in the Community with effect from 1 January 1977. Then there was Council Decision 79/1033/EEC of 3 December 1979 under the Treaties, concerning fishery activities in waters under the sovereignty or jurisdiction of member states, taken on a temporary basis pending the adoption of permanent Community measures.

a specific 'reference period'. This was modified by an additional allowance for areas that particularly depended on fishing for employment, known as the 'Hague preferences'. It was finally agreed that, once national shares of the catch for each species had been established, member states would continue to receive the same proportionate share by a principle known as 'relative stability'.[27]

Bitter squabbling over how all this could be implemented was to continue until 1983. But it was already obvious that the biggest loser would be Britain, which had thus suffered a double blow. Not only was the new 200-mile limit now forcing her deep-water fishing fleet out of business; she was also now discovering that, under the same rule, she had lost to the Community waters containing four-fifths of western Europe's fish. They were to be allocated to her 'partners' under the 'equal access' provisions that Heath had conceded and Wilson had made no effort to regain.

'A LOUSY DEAL'

On 13 April 1976, Wilson resigned suddenly. He was succeeded by Jim Callaghan, who made Anthony Crosland his foreign secretary. Among the problems they had to confront was the need to create a fully elected 'European Parliament'. When the 'Assembly' was set up in 1958, it was made up, like its predecessor in Monnet's Coal and Steel Community, of delegates nominated by national parliaments. But the Treaty of Rome had committed member states to a parliament 'elected by the people of Europe'.

When Giscard d'Estaing became president of France, he put this on the agenda. At the European Council in September 1974, it was agreed that the first elections should be held in 1978. Giscard's conversion to this project, reversing his party's previous policy, stemmed more from political calculation than conviction. For domestic reasons, he needed help from the smaller independent parties in his National Assembly, for whom 'commitment to European integration was an article of faith'.[28] Offering an elected Parliament for Europe was enough to woo them into his governing coalition. Wilson had agreed in principle and Callaghan felt obliged to abide by this commitment. He therefore asked a parliamentary committee to look into the mechanics of any election, which duly concluded that a Bill would have to be introduced by the start of 1977 if elections were to be held on the time-scale proposed.

[27] This Commission bulletin provides a useful overview. See p. 30 et seq., http://aei.pitt.edu/44029/1/A7583.pdf.
[28] George, op. cit., p. 118. He cites Jean-Louis Burban (1977), 'La Dialectique des élections européenes', Revue française de science politique, 27, pp. 377–406.

While Giscard had won domestic political advantage by this proposal, it soon became clear that the same was not true for Callaghan. At his first Labour Party Conference, in October 1976, the left-dominated NEC had tabled a resolution rejecting the idea, on the grounds that it would compete with national parliaments. This would strengthen the Commission, increasing the power of 'Brussels bureaucrats'.[29] Conference passed the resolution and, to avoid a damaging row with his own Party, Callaghan put the matter on the back-burner.

It was thus not until late 1977 that a Bill was introduced to permit direct elections, making it impossible to meet the timetable of 1978. There was no time for the Boundary Commission to define the new Euro-constituencies. Callaghan attempted a short-cut, but this brought threats of resignation from left-wing Cabinet members. Thus, when the Bill came to Parliament, Labour MPs were allowed a free vote. The Conservative opposition, combined with the votes of 115 Labour 'rebels', defeated it. Callaghan was forced to tell his EEC 'partners' that Britain could meet the 1978 deadline. 'Because of the priority given to domestic political considerations', George was to write, 'Britain again appeared to be in breach of the spirit of the Community.'[30] That it was only French 'domestic political considerations' that had set the timetable in the first place, passed him by.

With Britain thus coming under increasing fire, the next chance for her politicians to shine came with their first rotating presidency of the Council. Scheduled from January to June 1977, it began well enough. On 12 January, Crosland wowed the European Parliament with assurance that his government took the co-ordination of foreign policy seriously – a process that had acquired the title of European Political Co-operation (EPC).

Crosland's deputy was a rising star in Labour's ranks, the 38-year-old Dr David Owen. He later recalled that his first task had been to brief himself on the European Community. As he did, he found:

> that the UK really did have a lousy deal. The Agricultural Policy, which we had always known worked against our interests, was out of control – big surpluses were building up in milk products, olive oil and wine and costs were soaring. It was also clear that in a few years' time the UK budgetary contribution would rise so much that we were quite likely to find ourselves the nation making the largest contribution. We also had to cope with a

---

[29] Ibid., p. 118.
[30] Ibid., p. 121.

Fishing Policy which had been cobbled up by the Six members on the eve of the Community's expansion and which could hardly have been more unhelpful to UK fishing interests.[31]

In the early weeks of his new role, as Owen confronted the reality of Britain's membership of the Community, he was tempted to think that Wilson had been right in 1972, and that the terms had been unacceptable.[32] His main problem, however, was his own senior civil servants officials. With 'notable exceptions', he despaired of them being able to develop a tough negotiating stance.[33] 'Too many', he wrote, 'were reluctant to embark on any course which put us at serious loggerheads with the majority of Community members.'[34] They were intelligent people but they lacked the tenacity of French diplomats when it came to fighting for the national interest.

The most contentious issues to be handled by the British presidency were in front of the Agriculture Council, presided over by Britain's new agriculture minister, John Silkin. At the time, Labour had only a small majority, haemorrhaging through by-election losses, and many fishing constituencies were Labour marginal seats.[35] Silkin, therefore, was eager to show that he was defending Britain's interests: when the French led opposition to British and Irish demands for exclusive 50-mile fishing zones, he would not compromise. But all this did was ensure that no lasting deals were made during the British presidency, not least because of what other member states considered was biased chairmanship.

Again, Britain, in defending her national interests, was not being *communautaire*. Just as contentious was Silkin's refusal to accept a proposed 1.5 per cent increase in CAP funding, which, because of the distortions in the system, would have translated into a 3 per cent increase in British food prices. This was at a time when the government was struggling to contain price increases through a voluntary pay freeze policy. Blocking the increase, most of which would go to French farmers, caused further resentment.[36]

However, in the fifth month of the presidency, another milestone in Britain's relationship with the Community arrived, one not mentioned by George. On 28 May 1977, the Cabinet committee dealing with Common Market issues was told that the Commission had successfully appealed to

---

[31] Owen, op. cit., pp. 245–246.
[32] Ibid., p. 246.
[33] Ibid.
[34] Ibid.
[35] George, op. cit., p. 123.
[36] Ibid., pp. 123–124.

the ECJ to have ruled 'out of order' pig meat subsidies paid by the British government, and had instructed that they be stopped 'forthwith'. Tony Benn was present at the meeting. He asked whether this was the first time that a European Court decision had been taken against the British government and was told it was. In his diaries, he wrote:

> Then I asked what would be the political effect of this on pig producers in the UK. John Silkin said it would mean in effect the destruction of our industry, the mass slaughtering of pigs and the abandonment of our processing plants in favour of the Danes ... I wanted to be told explicitly – as I was – that I was a member of the first British Government in history to be informed that it was behaving illegally by a court whose ruling you could not alter by changing the law in the House of Commons. It was a turning point ...[37]

Unsurprisingly, following the British presidency, Callaghan set out to the 1977 Labour Party Conference a six-point plan for British policy towards the EEC, rejecting any increase in powers for the European Parliament, improving the 'scrutiny' procedures of the UK Parliament, and asserting the dominance of national, regional and industrial policies. However, this only added further fuel to the fire. When he asked the Community to admit Greece, Spain and Portugal because 'the dangers of an over-centralised, over-bureaucratised and over-harmonised Community will be less with twelve than with nine', Britain's disgrace in the eyes of her partners seemed complete.[38]

TOWARDS 'EUROPEAN UNION'

The British problem aside, the Community itself was again concerned with its real agenda: ever greater integration. As had been the case ever since the Werner and Davignon reports of 1970, this centred on what were now the Community's two chief aims: to establish economic and monetary union (EMU), and a common foreign policy.

In 1971, the United States had abandoned the 1944 Bretton Woods agreement, which had thrown international currencies into disarray. In response, most nations had allowed their currencies to 'float' freely against each other on the international markets, but this risked the destabilising effect of excessive fluctuations.

[37] Benn, op. cit., p. 417.
[38] In the 1990s Conservative Party policy on further enlargement would be making exactly the same points.

To tackle this, Europe's central bankers had met at Basel in 1972 to create a European Exchange Rate Agreement. This was to be known as the 'snake', which would limit European currency fluctuations to a band of ± 2.25 per cent. In addition to the Six, Britain, Sweden, Norway, Denmark and Ireland took part. The reptile did not prosper. Britain lasted six weeks before speculation forced her out. Italy followed shortly afterwards. France left in 1974, rejoined the following year and finally left in 1976. Only West Germany, Benelux and Denmark managed to keep within the margins, creating in effect an expanded deutschmark zone. By the mid-1970s, therefore, there was little hope of implementing Werner's EMU proposals.

Once an idea has entered the collective mind behind the 'European construction', however, it will always re-emerge. In early 1974 the Commission set up another study group to examine the prospects of achieving EMU by 1980, the objective of the Paris Summit. Chaired by Monnet's former close associate, Robert Marjolin, the group included two British representatives, Sir Donald MacDougall, the British government's chief economic adviser, and Andrew Shonfield, now director of the Royal Institute of International Affairs. Their report in March 1975 stated uncompromisingly that 'national and economic policies have never in twenty-five years been more discordant, more divergent, than they are today'.[39] This had led to a succession of monetary crises, and the problem, the group argued, was a lack of political will by the Community to take advantage of these crises. 'Like all crises', the report said, 'they could have been the occasion of progress, by provoking a crystallisation of latent wills. Great things are almost always done in crises. Those of recent years could have been the occasion for a leap forward.'[40]

This was an early exhortation to take advantage of the 'beneficial crisis'. Again and again some headline-making crisis would be exploited to justify an extension of integration. In this instance, the problems arising from floating exchange rates were used to revive the idea of economic and monetary union.

Marjolin's committee was in no doubt that the supranational institutions needed 'all the instruments of monetary policy and of economic policy' currently held by national governments. These would be exercised 'for the Community as a whole'. The 'common institutions' would have need of a Community budget and a central banking system, all of which would have

---

[39] Commission of the European Communities, *Report of the Study Group 'Economic and Monetary Union 1980'* (EMU – 63), Brussels, March 1975.
[40] Ibid., p. 4.

to act 'in a comparable way to those of a federal state'. Community taxes would be vital, so money could be given to less developed regions.[41]

In the manner of buses, though, no sooner had this report arrived than another one came along behind. Its author was Belgian prime minister, Leo Tindemans, published on 29 December 1975, with the beguilingly simple title of 'The European Union'. He regretted that 'the construction of Europe' seemed to have 'lost its air of adventure'. If it was to become a 'European Union', he intoned, it needed a common economic and monetary policy, and foreign and defence policies, complete with a 'European armaments agency'.

Significantly, the economic policy would need large-scale transfers of funds from the richer to poorer areas of the Community. That in turn would need a full-scale 'regional policy', with much of its funding directed through the Community budget. Tindemans also recommended a policy for forging a 'People's Europe' through 'concrete manifestations of the European solidarity in everyday life'. And he wanted to replace both the Council of Ministers and the Commission with a new supranational body.[42]

This 'government of Europe' would be responsible to and elected by a more powerful European Parliament, which would include a chamber directly elected by the 'peoples of Europe' and a 'Chamber of States' appointed by national governments. His final proposal, to speed up the process of integration, was a two-speed 'Europe', with an inner core moving faster towards political union than those states that were less committed. But this, he stressed, did not mean a *Europe à la carte*. Every country would have to work towards the same final objective.[43]

Wilson dismissed the report. When it came before the Luxembourg European Council on 1 April 1976, only days before he resigned as prime minister, he recorded that the discussions 'led us nowhere'.[44] Nevertheless, the proposals were to remain on the table.

ENTER ROY JENKINS

With talk of a single currency again in the air, a central role in what happened next was about to be played by another British politician,

[41] Ibid., p. 33.
[42] *Bulletin of the European Communities*, S/1-1976.
[43] Ibid.
[44] Wilson, op. cit., p. 238. One British MP who welcomed the report was Douglas Hurd, then Conservative spokesman for European affairs. He welcomed the single 'European foreign policy', emphasising that foreign ministers 'should accept an obligation to reach a common view' (*Hansard*, 17 June 1976, col. 870). However, it did not seem that Hurd grasped the logic of what he was saying, since he went on to observe that this did not mean 'removing the veto by some constitutional piece of surgery. It means creating the habit of agreement.' This was not what the integrationists had in mind. They wanted subordination, not co-operation.

whose view of European integration was very different from Wilson's. When, on Wilson's retirement, Roy Jenkins was heavily defeated by Callaghan in his bid to become prime minister, and refused the post of foreign secretary, he accepted an invitation to become president of the Commission. Curiously, this fervent 'Europeanist' was singularly unprepared for his new post. As he wrote in his memoirs, his 'conviction was complete, but my experience was negligible'. He was 'an enthusiast for *les grandes lignes* of Europe but an amateur within the complexities of its signalling system'.[45]

Having started work on 1 January 1977, Jenkins was later to admit that his first six months as president were not a success. In July 1977, after reading criticism to this effect, he decided a new initiative was necessary. As to the direction it should take, he concluded that he should throw his weight behind monetary union. In December 1977 the Brussels European Council supported him and agreed to commission various studies on monetary co-operation.[46] One was produced under the chairmanship of Sir Donald MacDougall, head of the British government's economic service. His report, produced in April 1977, was notable for its suggestion that, if the Community was to assume the kind of economic responsibilities suggested by the Marjolin Report, it would need, on the model of the federal government in America, to control between 20 and 25 per cent of the Community's GDP.[47] In the absence of any Community action, early in 1978 Giscard and Schmidt decided to back Jenkins. The outcome was to be the European Monetary System (EMS) within which was the Exchange Rate Mechanism (ERM), a more complicated version of the 'snake' (and eventual nemesis of the Conservative Party).[48]

The two leaders outlined their ideas to the Copenhagen European Council of 7–8 April 1978, but no formal decisions were taken. Instead, secret discussions took place between personal representatives of Giscard, Schmidt and Callaghan – whose support was being canvassed – in order to forestall opposition from central bankers, finance ministries and, most importantly, the Bundesbank. According to one commentator:

[45] Jenkins, Roy, *European Diary*, cited in Jenkins, op. cit., p. 446. Another 'Europeanist', Lord Carrington, was similarly to recall that, when he became foreign secretary in 1979 under Mrs Thatcher: 'I had no great knowledge of the other European statesmen with whom I would be dealing, no detailed knowledge of Europe or Community affairs. I had, however, conviction' (Carrington, Lord (1988), *Reflections on Things Past* (London: Collins), pp. 314–315).

[46] https://www.consilium.europa.eu/media/20779/bruxelles_december_1977__eng_.pdf.

[47] Commission of the European Communities (1977), *Report of the study group on the role of public finance in European integration*, Vol. 1.

[48] Jenkins, op. cit., p. 475.

The other six national chief executives, their finance ministers, and central bank presidents, as well as senior officials meeting in the Monetary, Central Bank and ECOFIN committees, were left in complete ignorance. The Danish prime minister, responsible for setting the Council agenda, heard nothing and assumed plans had been abandoned.[49]

Schmidt was unable to convince Callaghan that Britain should join the EMS. Having just weathered a major sterling crisis, Britain was geared to stimulating economic growth, whereas the German plan was deflationary. In addition, Callaghan was more interested in taking intergovernmental action through existing institutions such as the IMF.[50]

At the Bremen European Council in July, therefore, after a series of bad-tempered meetings, Callaghan pulled out altogether. He was by no means alone in his reservations. Former president of the Bundesbank, Karl Klassen, was concerned that *Europa Begeisterung* (Euro-fanaticism) did not lead his government into sacrificing the control they still had over their money. He was particularly wary of the French. If the EMF was once established, he claimed, 'we would not be dealing with M. Giscard d'Estaing but with the French bureaucracy. And if there is one thing I admire it is the French bureaucracy: it has been trained to the highest level by centuries of experience and is vastly superior to us in the diplomatic pursuit of national interest.'[51]

Nevertheless, by promising additional funds for regional development, particularly to the Italians and the Irish, Schmidt won agreement from the rest of the member states. Jenkins left Bremen 'in a high state of morale' but 'with substantially diminished hope of Britain at last learning its lesson and participating in a European initiative with enthusiasm and from the beginning'. His interest, he wrote, 'became increasingly that of avoiding Britain holding up the advance of others'.[52]

Even without the British, agreement on the details of the new system was reached only with considerable manipulation. Its complexities defy description in a non-technical briefing, replete as they were with such terms as 'parity grid system', 'asymmetrical obligations' and 'variable geometry'. What was significant, however, was that the final details of the agreement, during a bilateral summit between Giscard and Schmidt, were kept secret.

[49] Ludlow, Peter (1982), *The Making of the European Monetary System: A Case Study of the Politics of the EC* (Oxford: Butterworth-Heinemann Ltd), pp. 35.
[50] Ibid.
[51] Ibid., p. 137.
[52] Jenkins, op. cit., p. 481.

This meeting, in September 1978, was held at Aachen, where Charlemagne had been both born and buried as the first Holy Roman Emperor. Press officials of both governments stressed the historical reverberations of this joint visit to the throne of Charlemagne, evoking memories of the historic meeting between Adenauer and de Gaulle at Rheims, nearly two decades earlier. Giscard remarked that: 'Perhaps when we discussed monetary problems, the spirit of Charlemagne brooded over us.'[53] The details were agreed at the Brussels European Council on 4–5 December 1978. From 1 January 1979, the ERM would come into being. Currencies in the system could join the 'narrow band', in which they would be permitted to keep within a maximum margin of fluctuation of 2.25 per cent. When this margin was reached, there would be 'automatic intervention with no limit as to amount'.[54] Member states with floating currencies could opt for a 6 per cent margin, the so-called 'broad band'.

Obscured by the technicalities, it took the communiqué to make the political objective of the ERM clear. It would give 'fresh impetus to the process of European Union'.[55] The heads of government and the Commission president made it clearer. The ERM was vital 'for the future of the building of Europe'.[56]

Predictably, Britain's refusal to join the ERM had rankled with Giscard. His revenge was to demand that France be given the same share of a planned increase to the Regional Fund as Britain.[57] This effectively blocked any increase whatever, leaving Britain again uncompensated for the disparity of CAP funding. Furthermore, Britain's budget contribution was due to rise by 9 per cent, threatening within five years to make her the Community's largest net contributor. Of these events, Jenkins later recalled, 'It still seems to me impossible to explain what had come over Giscard.'[58] He should have consulted Professor George: Britain was the 'awkward partner', to be treated as such.

---

[53] Originally in *Corriere della Sera*, 16 September 1978. Now cited in multiple publications, including Connolly, Bernard (1995), *The Rotten Heart of Europe: The Dirty War for Europe's Money* (London: Faber and Faber), p. 17. It would later be pointed out by Connolly, a senior Commission economist and the first of the Commission 'whistleblowers', that all this was based on a deliberate deception. Although designed primarily to meet German needs, the EMS had been carefully dressed up to look more as if it served French interests. This explained the choice of word ECU (European Currency Unit) for the new unit of accounting, because it was reminiscent of the écu, a French coin from the time of the Valois.

[54] *Bulletin of the European Communities*, 12-1978, point 1.1.7.

[55] Ibid., point 1.1.10.

[56] Ibid., point 1.1.12.

[57] Jenkins, op. cit., p. 485.

[58] Ibid., p. 486.

THE 'BLOODY BRITISH QUESTION'

The problem of Britain's disproportionate contribution to the Community budget was now of serious concern. Known as the BBQ (British Budgetary Question), Jenkins and many others took to calling it the 'Bloody British Question'.[59] It was now poisoning relations between Britain and the Community more than any other issue.

By the end of 1976, even while transitional arrangements still applied, Britain was already the third-largest net contributor to the budget – after Germany and Belgium. Soon she would be the second-largest contributor, and within a few years, it was calculated, she would be the largest of all, paying subsidies to French farmers while the French blocked increases to regional funds. And now her politicians had the temerity to complain.

Complain they did. At a speech at the Lord Mayor's banquet in the Guildhall in London, on 13 November 1978, Callaghan made it clear Britain as the largest net contributor, with *per capita* income ranking only seventh out of nine, was unacceptable.[60] David Owen, who had taken over as foreign secretary after Crosland's untimely death, told the House of Commons the next day that even the current situation could not 'be good for the Community, any more than it is for the United Kingdom'.[61]

Predictably, Britain's complaints got short shrift. For sure, she had not been party to the original budgetary negotiations. But had she not accepted the arrangements as part of the *acquis communautaire*? Had there not been renegotiations? Yet now the British were saying, 'no, we still do not like the rules; you must change them to suit us yet again'. The French simply blamed Britain for importing food from the Commonwealth, on which levies had to be paid. They could buy Irish, French or Danish produce. Not to do so was wilfully anti-Communitarian. If they wished to reduce their contributions, all they had to do was to exercise Community preference.[62] So it was all Britain's fault. She was, after all, the 'awkward partner'.

'I WANT MY MONEY BACK!'

March 1979 saw an event that was to transform the politics of Britain and Europe. After the disastrous 'winter of discontent', when Britain had been paralysed by an avalanche of industrial disputes, the Callaghan government was defeated on a vote of confidence in the Commons by just one vote. The general election brought the Conservatives a clear majority of 44 seats. On

[59] Ibid., p. 489.
[60] *The Times*, 14 November 1978. Cited in George, op. cit., p. 133.
[61] *Hansard*, 14 November 1978, col. 214.
[62] George, op. cit., p. 134.

4 May 1979, Thatcher walked into 10 Downing Street, where she was to remain for 11 years.

Shortly after she took office, the first direct elections for the European Parliament were held. During the campaign, Thatcher emphasised her 'vision' of the Community, in her words, 'as a force for freedom'. Community institutions, she said, 'must not be permitted to dwindle into bureaucracy. Whenever they fail to enlarge freedom the institutions should be criticised and the balance restored.'[63]

Yet a smaller percentage of the electorate turned out to vote than anywhere else in the Community and the results simply mirrored the voting pattern of the general election, giving the Conservatives 60 of 78 seats. The Conservatives' apparent enthusiasm for 'Europe' was seen as 'positive' by many pro-Marketeers. Very quickly, however, Thatcher was thrust into the maelstrom of EEC politics, attending her first European Council on 21 to 22 June 1979. France hosted the talks, choosing Strasbourg as their venue in recognition of the new importance of the European Parliament. Already, there were signs that one issue above all was going to dominate the early days of Thatcher's relationship with the EEC: the budget.

From the first, Thatcher's policy was 'to seek to limit the damage and distortions caused by the CAP and to bring financial realities to bear on Community spending'. She had already told Chancellor Schmidt that she would be seeking 'large reductions' and was hoping he would pass the message on to Giscard, who was chairing the Council. Her short-term objectives were to have the budget question raised. She wanted an acceptance of the need for action, with a firm assurance that, at the next Council meeting in Dublin, the Commission would bring forward proposals to deal with the problem.[64] But, as an indication of what was to come, she observed:

> I knew that Chancellor Schmidt was keen that we should commit sterling to the ERM; but I already had my doubts about the wisdom of this course, which were subsequently reinforced. In any case, my announcement of our intentions as regards the 'ecu' swap did not receive much visible welcome from the others: like other such concessions to the *ésprit communautaire*, it appears simply to be pocketed and then forgotten.[65]

Her disillusionment was quickly reinforced. She knew the budget issue had to be raised on the first day, because the final Council communiqué was

[63] Thatcher, op. cit., p. 61.
[64] Ibid., pp. 62–63.
[65] Ibid.

always drafted overnight by officials, for discussion on the second and last day. During lunch, she had gained a 'strong impression' from Giscard that he would deal with the budget early on. But, when the meeting resumed, it became clear that he was intent on following the set agenda. By the end of the formal session, almost everything had been discussed, except the one thing Thatcher wanted to talk about. With that:

> President Giscard proposed that as time was getting on and we needed to get ready for dinner, the matter of the budget should be discussed the following day. Did the Prime Minister of the United Kingdom agree? And so at my very first European Council I had to say 'no'.[66]

However, the lateness of the hour worked in her favour: dinner beckoned. She won agreement that the Commission would be instructed to prepare a proposal for the next Council. Nevertheless, even Jenkins conceded that Thatcher had been 'very oddly treated'.[67]

The Dublin Council was not due until late November and, in the interim, Thatcher was determined to let the member states know she was serious about the budget. On 18 October, delivering in Luxembourg the Winston Churchill Memorial Lecture, she warned that she could not accept the present situation on the Budget. It was demonstrably unjust and politically indefensible: 'I cannot play Sister Bountiful to the Community while my own electorate are being asked to forego [sic] improvements in the fields of health, education, welfare and the rest,' she declared.[68]

In meetings with Schmidt and Giscard, she returned to the topic. Then, after a friendly lunch at the Irish president's official residence, in the historic setting of Dublin Castle, Thatcher set out the British case. But there was no meeting of minds. Some – for example, the Dutch prime minister, Mr Andries van Agt – 'were reasonable', she said, 'but most were not'. It was quite shameless: they were determined to keep as much of our money as they could.'[69]

By the time the Council broke up, Britain had been offered a £350 million rebate, leaving Britain's net contribution at £650 million. This was simply not enough. Thatcher was not going to accept it. She agreed that

---

[66] Ibid., p. 64.
[67] Jenkins, op. cit., p. 494.
[68] Thatcher, op. cit., p. 79.
[69] Ibid., p. 81. By now Thatcher was becoming known for the phrase 'We want our money back!', and was even sometimes heard to call it 'my money', according to the UK's Commissioner Christopher Tugendhat. (Young, Hugo (1990), *One Of Us* (London: Pan Books), p. 187.)

there should be another Council to discuss it, but was not over-optimistic that resolution would be reached. Even the influential *Guardian* columnist Hugo Young – and a consistent critic of Thatcher – had to concede, of the others, that:

> in response to her unsubtle demands for a fair deal, they were rude and derisive, and determined not to meet her anywhere near halfway. Roy Jenkins, a witness, writes that Schmidt feigned sleep during one of her harangues. At another point, Giscard had his motorcade drawn up at the door, engines revving, to signal that he would delay no longer. 'I will not allow such a contemptible spectacle to occur again', he said as he departed.[70]

Young did, however, note that Thatcher had 'broken all the rules': 'the smootheries of conventional diplomacy, the spirit of give-and-take on which the whole European edifice depended, were plainly values she could never be relied on to observe'.[71] But Thatcher was finding that 'give-and-take', in European terms, meant, 'you give, we take'. She could at least take some comfort from *Le Figaro*, which commented: 'To accuse Mrs Thatcher of wishing to torpedo Europe because she defends the interests of her country is to question her underlying intentions in the same way that people used to question those of de Gaulle in regard to French interests'.[72]

So the battle continued into 1980. To begin with, Francesco Cossiga, the prime minister of Italy, which had now assumed the rotating presidency, seemed to be working for a solution. On 25 February, Schmidt was back in London for talks, which again centred on the budget question, but with him repeating his wish to see sterling within the ERM. By the next Council, on 27–28 April, its venue moved to Luxembourg, Cossiga, after breakfasting with Giscard in Paris, believed the French were willing to offer a solution: a ceiling on Britain's net contributions for a period of years, subject to a final review. Thatcher was suspicious. On closer examination 'it became clear that what the French really wanted were decisions on their most politically sensitive topics – farm prices in the CAP, lamb and fishing rights – before dealing with the budget'.[73]

It gradually emerged that, as so often before, the French proposals were less helpful than appeared. After the agriculture ministers had given

[70] Young, op. cit., p. 314.
[71] Ibid.
[72] Thatcher, op. cit., p. 82.
[73] Ibid., p. 84.

the French more or less what they wanted, the *quid pro quo* was merely a modest rebate on Britain's net contribution, for one year only.[74] Thatcher had already made it abundantly clear that she wanted a permanent solution. Exercising some restraint, she did not dismiss the French response as an insult, although by any reckoning it was. She did nevertheless reject the 'offer', prompting Jenkins to call the meeting a 'fiasco'.[75]

Thatcher still expected a solution, not least because both the French and Germans wanted higher agricultural prices and the British could veto them. If she did, the Community would run out of money by 1982. The French response was to consider abolishing the 'Luxembourg Compromise', to prevent Thatcher using it – ironic, considering it was de Gaulle's innovation to protect France's 'vital interests'. By now it was clear there was going to be no quick solution. Her next move was to send her foreign secretary, Lord Carrington, with his colleague Ian Gilmour, both 'convinced Europeans', to Brussels on Thursday 29 May. After a marathon 18-hour session with the other foreign ministers, they reached what they considered an acceptable agreement, but Thatcher would not have it. Only after Gilmour contacted various Sunday newspapers, spinning the outcome as a 'Thatcherite triumph', did she agree to it, 'through gritted teeth'. In a Cabinet reshuffle soon afterwards, Gilmour was dropped.

For continuity, it is as well to stay with the story of the rebate battle, because the compromise agreed by the Carrington/Gilmour duo was far from the final solution. The issue would continue to fester on through 1982 into 1983, until it again became the central bone of contention at a Stuttgart Council on 17–19 June. By then there had been significant changes at the top table. Following her victory in the Falklands War in 1982, and the beginnings of economic recovery after Britain's deep recession of 1981, Thatcher led the Conservatives to a landslide election victory on 15 June. Giscard and Schmidt, the two dominant figures of the Franco-German alliance, had now been replaced by Mitterrand and Kohl. From Dublin, where Thatcher had been the tyro, she was now the senior figure.

At Stuttgart, Chancellor Kohl was anxious to make a success of his first Council in the chair, but for Thatcher there was only one issue: the need to make progress on the budget question. This, she had decided, meant full-scale reform of the Community's finances:[76]

---

[74] Ibid.
[75] Jenkins, op. cit., p. 504.
[76] Young, op. cit., pp. 312–313.

the Community was on the edge of bankruptcy: the exhaustion of its 'own resources' was only months away and it was possible to increase them only by agreement of all the member states to raise the one percent VAT 'ceiling' ... The requirement of unanimity gave me a strong hand and they knew that I was not the person to underplay it.[77]

Thatcher thought the Community could easily have lived within the discipline imposed by the 1 per cent VAT ceiling, if only it would cut out waste, inefficiency and corruption. But she judged that the will was lacking.[78] In the event, the Council did postpone a decision on financial reform, agreeing only to further negotiations. The results would be presented to the Council in Athens in December 1983, under the Greek presidency. At that Council, Thatcher was ready. But, from the start, things went badly awry. At the first session, Mitterrand seemed unprepared and Kohl was unwilling or unable to make much effective contribution.[79] Neither was the Greek prime minister, Papandreou, helpful.

Thus, on the first day, nothing was achieved, and it was to get worse. On the Monday morning, to Thatcher's astonishment, Mitterrand announced that his position on the budget had completely changed. He was no longer prepared to support Britain's fight for a long-term budget settlement. Instead, he would sanction only a series of ad hoc refunds of 1,000 million ecu per year for five years. As Geoffrey Howe was to point out later to the Commons, the final offer 'did not represent a systematic, equitable and lasting approach to the problem'.[80] Thatcher response was to block an increase in the Community's 'own resources' unless CAP spending was contained and its overall proportion of the budget reduced. She then demanded that member state contributions should be 'fair and in line with their ability to pay'. 'The argument continued,' Thatcher wrote, 'but I was clearly getting nowhere.'[81]

No communiqué was issued at the end of what was generally regarded as 'a fiasco'.[82] Much has been made of Thatcher's supposed 'anti-European' stance, but, as she was to recall, she genuinely believed that, once the budget contribution had been sorted out, Britain would be able to play a strong positive role in the Community. She considered herself a 'European

[77] Ibid., p. 313.
[78] Ibid.
[79] Thatcher, op. cit., p. 337.
[80] HC Deb, 22 March 1984, Vol. 56, cc1186-270.
[81] Thatcher, op. cit., p. 338.
[82] Ibid.

idealist', imbued with a vision of a free-enterprise *Europe des patries*.[83] Even Professor George concedes that the fault lay almost entirely with Mitterrand. His intervention, he writes, 'was either a terrible error, or an indication of more Machiavellian thinking'.[84] Yet, despite what Howe had seen at Athens, he was later to write that everything was now 'up to France, which took over the presidency of the Community [sic] for the first half of 1984'.[85] The French, he observed,

> were ideal negotiating partners for this closing stage of the battle. For they, better than most, could recognise the strength of our determination in defence of national interest. Moreover, they had the intellectual agility to identify, and argue with skill, the points where negotiation could oblige us to temper the strength of our case. We were aiming together to find an answer which the French Presidency could then sell to the other partners and table for acceptance at the Brussels meeting of the European Council on 19th to 20th March 1984, *en route* for the Fontainebleau Summit [sic] in June.[86]

Despite Howe's eulogy, the 'intellectually agile' French failed to table any proposals for the Brussels Council. They were not even properly prepared for it. Thatcher was. She had already discussed the issue with Mitterrand, at meetings in January in Paris, and in March at Chequers. In February she talked it over with Kohl at Number 10. She was thus confident that the Brussels Council, at last, would deliver a lasting solution to the 'BBQ'.[87]

When the meeting began, on 19 March, Mitterrand at least started proceedings with a discussion of the budget. Then officials were sent away to work on a text while Mitterrand turned to the Community's 'own resource'. His real agenda now became clear. He wanted to hike contributions from VAT receipts to 1.6 per cent, thus increasing CAP funds, from which France would benefit most. The Irish, now the Community's largest *per capita* net beneficiary, thanks to the size of their farming sector, wanted an even larger increase.[88]

For once, Thatcher and Kohl had something in common. Both set 1.4 per cent as their limit, making even that dependent on satisfactorily resolving

---

[83] Thatcher, op. cit., p. 536.
[84] George, op. cit., p. 153.
[85] Howe, op. cit., p. 398.
[86] Ibid., p. 399.
[87] Thatcher, op. cit., p. 538.
[88] Ibid.

the Community spending plan. That was the limit of the day's progress. Next day, to Thatcher's frustration, the session began with 'a gush of Euro-idealism'. Kohl and Mitterrand became 'quite lyrical on the subject of getting rid of frontier controls', followed by Mitterrand's urging that Europe should not be left behind by the USA in the space race.[89] When, at last, the Council got down to business, 'the high-mindedness quickly disappeared'. The Irish prime minister, having failed to win a special exemption from proposed milk quota limits aimed at trimming the Community's vast milk surplus, invoked the Luxembourg Compromise and walked out. Only after a long adjournment to discuss the text of the Council communiqué did business resume.

What happened then left Thatcher dumbstruck. Despite their earlier agreement, the Italians and Greeks refused Thatcher her permanent reduction. Mitterrand seemed to side with them. When she protested that she had been fighting for five years for a fair and lasting settlement, Kohl, possibly in concert with Mitterrand, offered her 'a 1,000 million ecu rebate for five years'. Even Howe dismissed this as 'half-baked'.[90] Almost immediately, France and the rest agreed with Germany. Naturally Thatcher rejected the 'offer'. The Council broke up without issuing a communiqué, whence France and Italy blocked payment of Britain's 1983 refund (worth about £440 million).[91]

Back in Britain, Thatcher decided she would stop British payments to the Community if she had the backing of her MPs. But, she wrote, 'there was a hard core of Euro-enthusiasts … who instinctively supported the Community in any dispute with Britain'. Reluctantly, she abandoned that 'nuclear option'.[92]

Clearly though, the arguments had to end. The next European Council, to be held at Fontainebleau on 25–26 June 1984, would be chaired by Mitterrand on his home ground. It had to be 'le grand showdown'. On the day, once again, Thatcher was forced to cool her heels. After the obligatory opening lunch, Mitterrand asked her to sum up the results of a recent economic summit in London. Others then joined in to give their views. Two hours passed. Only then did the French president turn to the budget and, no sooner had Thatcher given her views on a formula, he 'remitted' the matter to the foreign ministers for discussion later that evening, and moved on to other business.[93]

[89] Ibid., p. 539.
[90] Howe, op. cit., p. 400.
[91] National Archives, CAB128/78, Cabinet Conclusions, 22 March 1984.
[92] Thatcher, op. cit., p. 539.
[93] Ibid., p. 542.

Throughout the whole budget saga, there had been a central sticking point. Britain had insisted that its contributions included income from tariffs and levies as well as the VAT element. The French, on the other hand, still argued that customs charges constituted the Community's 'own resource'. At Fontainebleau, they produced a paper setting out how the calculation should be made. Once again, only VAT payments were included.

After the foreign ministers had churned over the same ground, Thatcher wearily conceded the point, as long as the VAT-based formula delivered a permanent rebate. All that remained was to agree the percentage. Thatcher had in mind 70 per cent, but Howe brought news that between 50 and 60 per cent would be offered, with a 'sweetener' bringing the rebate up to 1,000 million ecus for the first two years – no different from the Athens figure. 'How Geoffrey,' Thatcher wrote, 'who had been splendidly staunch in the negotiations so far, had allowed the foreign ministers to reach such a conclusion, I could not understand.'[94]

In the event, Thatcher held out for 70 per cent, Mitterrand stuck at 60 and Kohl settled for 65. When Thatcher went for two-thirds, a round 66 per cent, Mitterrand caved in, telling her, of course, 'you must have it'.[95] With that agreement, France and Italy lifted their block on the 1983 payment.[96] Immediately, however, Kohl announced that, since German money had made the settlement possible, he would pay his farmers extra money from Federal funds. Although against the rules, no one had the stomach to oppose him.[97] But this was not the end of the story. Tied up in the small print was a 'correction mechanism' for dealing with the continuing budgetary imbalances of a complexity that was 'outside the comprehension of every normal European citizen'.[98] Even the Commission itself was to admit that it 'inhibited transparency in the financial relationships between the Member States and the Community budget'.[99]

In 1988 at the Brussels European Council, further revisions were made to the funding system where what became known as the 'Own Resources Decision' was made. This laid down that VAT would henceforth play a reduced role in funding the Community, and introduced a new, fourth form of 'own resource' whereby each member state would make an additional payment representing a proportion of its Gross National Product (GNP).

[94] Ibid., p. 543.
[95] Ibid., p. 544.
[96] National Archives, CAB 128/79, Cabinet Conclusions, 28 June 1984.
[97] Ibid.
[98] Young, op. cit., p. 323.
[99] Commission of the European Communities (1998), Bulletin EU 10-1998 – Agenda 2000. 'Financing of the European Union (1998)', Luxembourg.

This, in turn, created new distortions and required a new mechanism to calculate Britain's rebate. So complicated was the calculation that, according to the Commission's own reckoning, '*it produced the somewhat surprising result that the United Kingdom appears to participate in the financing of its own rebate*' [our emphasis].[100]

While the Commission suggested that this 'self-financing' involved only 'very small amounts', the cumulative effects of the Fontainebleau agreement and the Brussels 'adjustment' were to be substantial. They created a situation whereby, whenever the UK applied for CAP funds over and above a threshold level agreed in 1984, the Commission, through its 'correction mechanism', was (and is) able to 'claw back' a substantial proportion of the funds paid. By 2003 this equated to 71 per cent.

Because this meant that, in applying for certain funds from Brussels, the Treasury would end up paying for most of them itself, the UK government decided that, having won her rebate, Britain should take maximum advantage from it. Therefore, wherever possible, the UK would refuse to apply for such funds, even though other member states were doing so. This further meant that other countries were able to draw on considerably more money for their farmers from Brussels than was available to British farmers, whose ability to match the prices of their EEC competitors was thus significantly reduced.

Fifteen years later this disparity in subsidy levels would help to bring about one of the most severe crises ever faced by British agriculture. Thatcher's 'victory' would turn out to be a very mixed blessing.

[100] Commission of the European Communities, *Financing the European Union: Commission report on the operation of the own resources system* (1998), Luxembourg. In 1992, summarising the formula for calculating the UK rebate, a Treasury minister, Sir John Cope, explained that it was necessary to:
(a) Calculate the difference between: (i) on the one hand, the UK's percentage share of member states' total VAT-based contributions to Community resources as if pre-1988 'uncapped VAT' arrangements were still in place, and (ii) on the other hand, the UK's percentage share of total 'allocated expenditure' – i.e., the total share of intra-Community budget expenditure, excluding aid;
(b) Apply the percentage difference obtained (the 'VAT expenditure share gap') to total allocated expenditure;
(c) Multiply the result by 66 percent;
(d) Deduct the benefit for the UK arising from the new own-resources structure agreed in 1988 (calculated by multiplying (1) the percentage difference between the UK's share of uncapped VAT and its share of capped VAT and fourth resources payments by (2) member states' overall capped VAT and fourth resources payments). (*Sunday Telegraph*, 4 October 1992.)

9

Enter Mr Spinelli: 1979–1986

I recall one low point when nine foreign ministers from the major countries of Europe solemnly assembled in Brussels to spend several hours discussing how to resolve our differences on standardising a fixed position of rear-view mirrors on agricultural tractors.

James Callaghan[1]

The Heads of State or Government, on the basis of an awareness of a common destiny and the wish to affirm the European identity, confirm their commitment to progress towards an ever closer union among the peoples and Member States of the European Community.

Solemn Declaration on European Union,
Stuttgart, 19 June 1983

On 16 March 1979, Monnet, the first and at the time only honorary 'Citizen of Europe', died at his home in the French countryside 30 miles outside Paris, at the age of 90 years and four months. Four days later Chancellor Schmidt joined Giscard in the nearby medieval church of Montfort-l'Amuary for his funeral, along with friends from all over Europe and several of his long-time allies from Washington, led by George Ball. The music chosen for the service included pieces by French, German, Italian and English composers, culminating in a recorded version of all five verses of 'The Battle Hymn of the Republic'.[2] As

---

[1] Callaghan, James (1987), *Time and Chance* (London: Collins), p. 304.
[2] Ball, op. cit., pp. 98–99.

this rousing American chorus rang through the nave, Giscard mused that a Frenchman almost felt left out.[3]

In his brief retirement, according to his biographer, Monnet had 'come to question his life's work'. 'Was European union too narrow for a changing world? Had the Common Market really added to growth?' He hoped Europe had 'at least secured peace between France and Germany'. But even there, it might be argued, 'the American presence in Europe had mattered more than a European Community reduced, it seemed, to a customs union'.

It was true that, in the years immediately preceding Monnet's death, the great advance towards 'ever closer union' seemed to have lost much of its impetus. Those brave dreams of the earlier 1970s, the proposals for full economic and monetary union by 1980, for political union and a common foreign policy, still seemed as far away as ever. The only place where the momentum of the 'European construction' seemed unflagging in the late 1970s was on what might be described as the level of 'low politics', where the Commission, allied with the European Court of Justice, had now become more active than ever in extending its supranational powers, in the name of 'completing the internal market'.

The removal of internal tariffs, though, served to highlight 'non-tariff barriers', by which individual states were still able to frustrate the emergence of a true 'common market'. Barriers ranged from national rules and standards that could be used to exclude imports from other countries, to 'state aid' by which governments could give their own producers financial advantage over their competitors. It was on these barriers that the Commission now launched an assault, and it did so on two main fronts.

First, using its monopoly right of proposal, the Commission 'harmonised' or 'approximated' the laws of member states, thereby replacing them. By the late 1970s, the output of new Community laws had risen to some 350 a year. Reflecting the fact that the CAP was still responsible for 90 per cent of the Community budget, it generated more law than any other sector, ranging from a long succession of directives that restricted the sale of plant varieties, to complex and lengthy regulations on market organisation. On its second front, in its efforts to stamp out 'illegal state aid', the Commission intervened to eliminate 'unfair competition' in all kinds of economic activity, from

---

[3] Duchêne, op. cit., p. 340. Duchêne records how, in 1988, to mark the centenary of Monnet's birth, Mitterrand arranged for his ashes to be transferred to the grandiose neo-classical setting of the Pantheon in Paris, to lie alongside the remains of such legendary French heroes as Rousseau, Voltaire, Victor Hugo and Émile Zola. Mitterrand addressed a torchlit ceremony on the steps, attended by Chancellor Kohl and many other European dignitaries, who stood for a performance of the 'European anthem' adapted from Beethoven's Ninth Symphony. Monnet's home at Houjarray was bought by the European Parliament as a shrine to his memory.

shipbuilding to textiles. It did this partly through legislation, but also in alliance with the Community's 'Supreme Court', the ECJ.

In 1977, the ECJ confirmed that the Treaty of Rome amounted to the 'internal constitution' of the Community, which member states were bound to obey.[4] One measure of the importance of the Court's 'constitutional' role was its growing workload. In the ten years before 1979, the average number of cases heard was 113. For the following five years, the case rate more than quadrupled, to 514. A significant landmark was the so-called Cassis de Dijon case in 1979. With the Commission's support, a German firm challenged its own state authorities for refusing to allow the import of a French blackcurrant liqueur on the grounds that its alcohol content of 15–20 per cent was lower than the 32 per cent prescribed by German law. The ECJ ruled that, in the absence of any specific Community law, goods could be imported from any member state as long as they conformed with the law of their originating states. So was born the doctrine of 'mutual recognition'.[5]

Amid this frenzy of activity, the role of the Council of Ministers seemed strangely marginal. Ministers spent much of their time approving a constant stream of incomprehensible legislation, presented to them by officials.[6] In 1977, for instance, Britain's minister of agriculture, John Silkin, found himself by the accident of Britain's 'presidency' having to sign into law the Sixth VAT directive, a complex attempt to harmonise taxation rules in each member states. As a farming minister, it was unlikely that he was fully *au fait* with the contents, but it is his signature on the directive.

Worthy though all these efforts to extend the supranational tentacles of the Community might have seemed, they also gave justification to Monnet's fear that his great dream was petering out in a sea of humdrum technocracy. This had been a time of 'Eurosclerosis', where the Community had struggled with seemingly endless internal wrangles, culminating in the battle for the budget, in which Mrs Thatcher had played such a prominent part. The 1980 deadline set by the Paris Summit had come and gone. The lofty idea of a 'European Union' remained a distant aspiration. Then momentum was

---

[4] CJEC, opinion 1/76 of 26 April 1977, ECR 741.
[5] Rewe-Zentral v. Bundesmonopolverwaltung für Branntwein, Case 120/78 [1979] ECR 649 [1979]3 CMLR 494. See also Weatherill, Stephen and Beaumont, Paul (1995), *EC Law: The Essential Guide to the Legal Workings of the European Community* (London: Penguin Books, 2nd edn), pp. 490–542.
[6] Callaghan was to record his frustration at this in the passage from his memoirs quoted at the head of this chapter, preceded by recalling his bafflement at finding himself having to correspond with his 'Chancellor, Denis Healey about import levels of apricot halves and canned fruit salad' (op. cit., p. 304).

restored. And, although the wind of change that seized the Community is generally linked with the arrival of Jacques Delors as Commission president in 1985, there was another player: Altiero Spinelli, author of the *Ventotene Manifesto*.[7]

THE 'CROCODILE CLUB'

After the war, Spinelli had worked briefly with Monnet on the abortive European Political Community. In June 1970 he had been nominated as one of Italy's two Commissioners, taking on the industry and technology portfolio, to which was added 'environment'. During his time with the Commission, he had become convinced that the role of the European Parliament should be expanded, and, in particular, that it should control the Community's budget. His opportunity came after the European Council in 1975 had agreed to direct elections.[8] When in 1979 the first elections had been held, he got himself – at the age of 72 – elected as an independent MEP attached to the Communist group.

He first showed his hand on 25 June 1980, when the Parliament refused to adopt the Council's draft Community budget. The Council came under fire from several speakers, but none so aggressive as Spinelli. He told his fellow MEPs that they must now take the destiny of the Community into their hands: 'I do not address the Council of Ministers', he told them, 'because it has demonstrated its total impotence.'[9] The action was to convince more MEPs that Parliament should initiate fundamental reforms of the Community. Thus, in July 1980 – with his assistant Pier Virgilio Dastoli – Spinelli invited his fellow MEPs to support a concerted move to further integration.[10]

Eight 'eager members' responded to his call, meeting at the prestigious Crocodile restaurant in Strasbourg. These included a German and an Italian Christian Democrat, an Italian Communist, and two British Labour MEPs. One of those was Richard Balfe, the other a lone Conservative,

---

[7] See Chapter 1.

[8] https://www.consilium.europa.eu/media/20809/1975_december_rome__eng_.pdf.

[9] From Palayret, Jean-Marie (2003), *Entre cellule Carbonara et conseiller des Princes: Impulsions et limites de la relance européenne dans le projet Spinelli d'Union politique des années 1980*', in Gérard Bossuat and Georges Saunier (eds), *Inventer l'Europe: histoire nouvelle des groupes d'influence et des acteurs de l'unité européenne* (Bruxelles/New York: PIE Lang, 2003), pp. 355–382, augmented by interviews with Richard Balfe MEP.

[10] Dastoli had been *chef de cabinet* for Spinelli when he was president of the 'Independent Left' group in the Italian parliament. From July 1979 to June 1983, he became Spinelli's parliamentary assistant in the European Parliament. By 2003 he was a senior official of the European Parliament, had been secretary-general of the international European Movement since April 1995 and was a professor of the History of European Integration at Rome University.

Stanley Johnson, father of Boris.[11] So was born the 'Crocodile Club', a cross-party group convinced 'of the need for European political reform of great width'. Spinelli aimed to outflank the existing party groupings, which he feared would block his initiative. As he explained later in a letter to a colleague:

> The European Parliament is elected using party electoral machines geared to national elections, which do not have European political programs but a vague trans-national background … their members were divided substantially into three groups: innovators, eager to advance the union; 'immobilists', eager to hold it where it was and to even make it regress; the swamp … composed of those which do not know what they want. The innovators are conscious that they must rally around a common policy and, by ignoring party loyalties, they would conquer the prevailing influence of 'the swamp'.

The club was to be the catalyst for 'awakening the innovators'. The established forum for promoting new ideas was the Political Affairs Committee, but this was dominated by the centre-right European Peoples' Party (EPP), hostile to Communists. Spinelli predicted that it would only give his project a 'first class burial'. Instead, he planned an ad hoc 'constitutional working group', which he could control. For this he needed a parliamentary resolution, to prepare the ground for which, in October 1980, he launched a 'semi-official periodical', *The Crocodile*.[12]

As expected, his resolution was treated with disdain by the established groups. Even the Communists were reluctant to back him, and only did so when Spinelli made a direct appeal to Italy's national Communist leader, Enrico Berlinguer. The Christian Democrats, however, proved to be the main obstacle, using a procedural device to delay a vote on Spinelli's resolutions, hoping that support would collapse. Here, a British MEP, Richard Balfe, acting as Spinelli's 'tactical adviser', took the initiative, launching a covert operation code-named 'Keep Silent'.[13] He gradually enlisted support from his Socialist colleagues. The 'Club' attracted heavyweight support from the Italian prime minister Bettino Craxi, and several leading Social Democrats, including Willy Brandt and Erwin Lange (president of the Parliament's

[11] Johnson had between 1973 and 1979 been a senior official of the European Commission as head *inter alia* of its Prevention of Pollution and Nuisances Division. In 1984, he resumed his career in the Commission, becoming Director for Energy Policy in 1990.
[12] The magazine survives to this day.
[13] Interview with authors, 2 December 2002.

powerful budgets committee). They were joined by the Liberal group under its German leader Martin Bangemann, later a commissioner.

With their help, on 9 July 1981, Spinelli set up a 'standing committee for the institutional problems charged to work out a modification of the existing treaties'. Working towards the establishment of the 'European Union', he then launched his ad hoc committee, formed on 22 January 1982, with himself as its co-ordinating *rapporteur*. Mauro Ferri was its president. It then set up a steering group to hold hearings for a wide range of politicians, trade union leaders and academics to give their views. The European Movement was recruited to mobilise public support.

THE GENSCHER–COLOMBO PLAN

By this time, some senior national politicians were becoming alarmed at Spinelli's activities. At a national conference of the German Free Democrat party in 1981, Germany's foreign minister, Hans-Dietrich Genscher, put forward a 'gradualist' alternative. He joined forces with Italy's foreign minister, Emilio Colombo, to produce what became known as the 'Genscher–Colombo Plan'. This included a proposal for a new treaty, to be known as the 'European Act'. It would formalise 'political co-operation' on foreign policy, binding on all member states, and a 'declaration' on economic integration.[14] But they did propose that member states should work towards a European defence policy, independent of NATO.

To justify a common foreign policy, Genscher and Colombo referred to a little-publicised meeting of foreign ministers that had taken place in London on 13 October 1981, under the chairmanship of Lord Carrington. The ministers had formulated new rules for political co-operation, building on the original agreement in Luxembourg in 1970, which they said had 'contributed to the ultimate objective of the European union'.[15] In London the ministers had already agreed to formalise their co-ordination of foreign policy through what were termed 'Gymnich-type meetings', taking place in private, without officials present, the contents of which would remain secret.[16] It was also at this London meeting that arrangements were agreed for the so-called troika structure, to become famous during the Yugoslav crisis nine years later, whereby the government acting as president of the

[14] European Parliament (1982), *Selection of Texts Concerning Institutional Matters of the Community from 1950–1982* (Luxembourg), pp. 492–499.
[15] Reproduced in *Selection of Texts Concerning Institutional Matters of the Community from 1950–1982*, pp. 539–542.
[16] Named after Gymnich Schloss, a palatial German Federal Government guest house near Cologne, used for informal, confidential meetings of foreign ministers. The British equivalent is 'Chatham House Rules'.

Council on the six-monthly rota system would act in concert with those that came before and after.

The Genscher–Colombo plan, incorporating the London agreement, was presented to the European Parliament on 19 November 1981, supported by the EPP. Colombo told the MEPs:

> We are calling for a revival of European integration, we want the institutions strengthened and the decision-making process improved and we want to encourage and extend to a greater degree the pragmatic process whereby political co-operation is achieved among our ten countries. In this way, co-operation will become more widespread on matters ranging from security to culture and law, which will bring us closer to the basic aims of a European union. We will achieve this by adopting a flexible approach and through the mutual support of political, economic and social aspects in turn, and as we gradually progress, it will be possible to set ourselves, and meet, new targets.[17]

In coded form, the Plan's purpose was to pre-empt Spinelli's much bolder initiative by deliberately watering down its 'constitutionalist' agenda. However, when it was presented to the London European Council of 26–27 November 1981, it received no immediate support and, by being referred back to the foreign ministers, was effectively kicked into touch. However, the ideas were not abandoned. They were incorporated into another document given the grandiose title of a 'Solemn Declaration on European Union', presented to the Stuttgart European Council on 17–19 June 1983.[18] It opened with this statement:

> The Heads of State or Government, on the basis of an awareness of a common destiny and the wish to affirm the European identity, confirm their commitment to progress towards an ever closer union among the peoples and Member States of the European Communities.[19]

The 'Solemn Declaration' was approved by the heads of government, including Thatcher, now so preoccupied with her battle over the budget rebate that she merely noted it in her memoirs as having been just 'one other aspect' of the Stuttgart meeting.

---

[17] Debates of the European Parliament, No. 1 289/237.
[18] Commission of the European Communities, European Bulletin, EC 6-1983, points 1.6.1 to 4.3.
[19] Ibid., point 1.1.

Only four days earlier, on 15 June, Thatcher had won a landslide election victory over a Labour Party led by Michael Foot, which had fought on a manifesto pledge to leave the EEC. Among the few new Labour MPs to be elected was the young member for Sedgefield, Tony Blair, who had promised in his election address that 'We'll negotiate a withdrawal from the EEC, which has drained our natural resources and destroyed jobs.'[20] In a dismissive comment on the 'Declaration on European Union', Thatcher noted the 'grandiloquent language' that 'had been used about the subject since before the UK had joined the Community'. But she took the view that she 'could not quarrel with everything, and the document had no legal force'. Therefore, she 'went along with it'.[21] When later questioned about the Declaration in the Commons, she replied, 'I must make it quite clear that I do not in any way believe in a federated Europe. Nor does that document.'[22] Her new foreign secretary, Geoffrey Howe, also gave the Declaration only a cursory mention in his memoirs, devoting more space to his visit afterwards to Stuttgart's art gallery. He recalled that 'we attached less importance than most of our colleagues – less than we should have done – to this blueprint of the future'.[23]

Thatcher was certainly right about the 'grandiloquent language' and much of the Declaration's text was in fact taken up with restating principles already agreed elsewhere. Its only real purpose was to head off Spinelli's draft treaty, now in active preparation. For precisely that reason, Spinelli was angry. His committee president Ferri exploded that, for the Parliament, 'no form of consultation with the Council and the Commission is possible'.[24] If only Thatcher and Howe had been better briefed as to the hidden reason for the Declaration, they might have been better prepared for what was to hit them at the Milan Council two years later.

THE FIRST 'FEDERAL POLICY'

Just at this moment when the Community was about to take a further giant step towards integration, there had emerged its first example of a fully-fledged 'federal' or supranational policy. In January 1983, after long and bitter argument, the Community had finally agreed how to apply the rules it had laid down for its Common Fisheries Policy.

---

[20] Blair's 1983 election address was published in facsimile on the No-Euro website, www.no- euro. com.
[21] Thatcher, op. cit., p. 314.
[22] HC Deb, 23 June 1983, Vol. 44, cc145-54.
[23] Howe, op. cit., p. 307.
[24] Debates of the European Parliament, No. 1/289: 261–262.

After The Hague conference in 1976, when the Community had agreed the broad principles of the CFP, fishing ministers had to decide how the principle of 'equal access' was to work in practice. A 'free-for-all' could not be allowed, otherwise the resource would be quickly exhausted, so a conservation strategy had to be devised. The first step was to determine the proportion of the Total Allowable Catches (TACs) for each of the main species of fish that would be allocated to each country, under a system of national 'quotas'. In doing this, the ministers opted to base the divisions on historical records, taking account of where national fleets had fished previously, and the tonnages caught. The crude percentages would then be modified by reference to the 'Hague preferences', which were more or less arbitrarily defined by subtracting parts of various countries' allocations in order to give them to others.

Predictably, this led to bitter arguments, first over which years should be picked as the historical 'reference points'. Eventually, the period agreed spanned 1973 to 1978, which was particularly disadvantageous to Britain. During that period, most of her fishing effort had been concentrated in North Atlantic waters now closed to her. On the other hand, the period was particularly advantageous to France, since most of her fishing effort in those years had been in waters now within the British 200-mile zone.

Then there were fights about the levels set for the TACs, which were to be agreed every year by fisheries ministers in the last Council of the preceding year. These fights became an annual ritual and identified a fatal flaw in the conservation system. Ministers, pursuing their national interests, would push the TACs higher than the data would bear, while continually resisting Commission attempts to take over the process. As a result, ministers often found themselves arguing about allocations of fish in excess of the quantities theoretically available.

As a 'conservation policy', there was a second flaw: although the rules were agreed centrally, their enforcement remained with member states, which meant that countries adopting a 'light-touch' regime would give their own fishermen a commercial advantage, and themselves short-term economic benefits. Lack of enforcement, and the relative severity of different national systems, became a constant source of aggravation, particularly to British fishermen who, with some justice, felt their own system was the most rigorous in the Community.

A problem also lay with the allocation of national quotas. This led to disputes so fierce and so prolonged that, even though the CFP was originally planned to begin in 1980, the start-date had to be delayed to 1 January 1983. Even then, the deadline was missed and final agreement was not reached until 25 January 1983. When the results of the negotiations were announced, Britain was allocated 37 per cent of the total catch. British fishermen were initially relieved that their country's contribution of four-fifths of the fish seemed at least to have been partially recognised. The detail, however, showed that the British allowance was very short on high-value species, such as sole, and weighted heavily in favour of lower-value fish, such as cod and haddock. In cash terms, the UK's share of the total catch was only 13 per cent.[25]

As would often be the case, other countries seemed to have won a very much better deal for their own fishermen, notably France, which secured, for instance, an 18,000-tonne cod quota for the English Channel, compared with the British 1,750 tonnes. Another flaw, in conservation terms, was the award of a huge 1,000,000-tonne quota to Denmark's 'industrial' fishing fleet, nominally to permit the harvesting of sand eels and pout for animal feed and agricultural fertiliser. But this fleet also caught other species, including juvenile cod, which it was allowed to use under the classification 'by-catch'.

The most serious flaw of all, however, was the very nature of the quota system itself. Dictating to fishermen the maximum quantities of each species they were permitted to land ignored the most basic realities of fishing. Fishermen unavoidably caught species for which they had no quota, having to 'discard' them, mostly dead, into the sea. This practice was to lead within a few years to an ecological disaster, as billions of fish every year were wasted.

The reason why 1 January 1983 had been set as the deadline for introducing the new system was in itself significant, in that this marked the end of the 10-year 'derogations' negotiated in the accession talks in 1971. Now those ten years were up, it lay with the Community to agree whether these 'transitional arrangements' could continue. The condition it imposed was that Britain must agree to the new CFP system.

But so intractable had the quota negotiations been that, on 1 January 1983, the derogations lapsed. Without the framework of quotas, the 'equal access' rule now prevailed without restriction. A Danish trawler skipper, Kent Kirk, also a Danish MEP, sailed into British coastal waters and began fishing. After being arrested, he appealed to the ECJ, which upheld his claim that, in the absence of a fisheries policy, he had been fully entitled to fish 'up to the beaches'. This incident, which caused a widespread stir, helped

---

[25] Figures confirmed by fisheries commissioner Frans Fischler in reply to a question from Charles Tannoch MEP in 2002.

concentrate the minds of the negotiators, and by 25 January the new quota policy had been agreed. Only then were Britain and other member states given back, for a further 20 years, the concession allowing them continued jurisdiction over their inshore waters. But Rippon's claim in 1971 that this was a permanent right had again been exposed as a lie.

It was not generally understood that even the CFP system introduced in 1983 was itself only intended to be a further 'transitional arrangement', based on 'derogations' that would run out on 31 December 2002. But in one respect this was becoming particularly evident in 1983, as negotiations continued over further 'enlargement' of the Community to admit two new entrants, Spain and Portugal.

These countries had applied for membership of the Community in 1977, following the deaths of the two dictators, Franco and Salazar, ending decades of isolation. Negotiations began in 1978 and the nine years of talks reflected the particular difficulties posed by the admission of two relatively impoverished states with mainly agrarian economies. An attempted military coup in Madrid in February 1981 lent particular urgency to Spain's entry, with the Community now anxious to strengthen her fragile new democracy. But despite this urgency, three central issues could not easily be resolved: agriculture, fisheries and the reduction of trade barriers for Spanish industrial goods.[26]

In some respects, the toughest challenge of the three was posed by fisheries, because, for domestic political reasons, Spain had built up her fishing fleet under Franco to become easily the largest in Europe. The accession of Spain and Portugal would increase the Community's total fishing capacity by three-quarters, while bringing little in the way of fishing resource. To allow these vessels immediate access to Community waters would be disastrous, not least because Spanish trawlers had already become internationally notorious for their predatory disregard of conservation rules.

To accommodate this 'cuckoo in the nest', ministers of the Ten decided that Spanish and Portuguese access to Community waters must be phased, starting with a limited number of vessels on 1 January 1995. Full integration would not be permitted until 31 December 2002. The newcomers were only persuaded to accept these conditions, however, in return for the Community

---

[26] There was also, in Community terms, the 'side-issue' of Gibraltar, and the opening of the land border that had been closed by General Franco since 1969. The border-crossing problem was partially resolved in February 1984 when, after 15 months of bilateral talks, Geoffrey Howe signed an agreement with Spain to reopen the border, on the promise of holding talks about Gibraltar's sovereignty. See Howe, op. cit., p. 407.

paying a heavy price. First, Spain and Portugal were given substantial aid from the Community's 'structural funds', to enable them to update and expand their fishing fleets. Second, the Community also undertook to pay out huge sums on buying fishing rights around the coasts of Africa and across the under-developed world. This largesse was to provoke an unintended consequence at the end of 1984. Thatcher recalled how, at the Dublin Council that December, just when the enlargement negotiations were nearing their conclusion,

> Mr Papandreou, the left-wing Greek prime minister, suddenly treated us to some classic theatre. A charming and agreeable man in private, his whole persona changed when it was a question of getting more money for Greece. He now intervened, effectively vetoing enlargement unless he received an undertaking that Greece should be given huge sums over the next six years.[27]

Other member states seemed 'curiously reluctant' to defend their financial interests, and the Greek Danegeld had to be met. The price eventually to be paid by British fishermen would be even higher.

A TREATY FOR 'EUROPEAN UNION'

During the second half of 1983, Spinelli and his team in the European Parliament were quietly at work on what become a 'Draft Treaty Establishing a European Union'. Among its innovations was a proposal that citizens of member states should, *ipso facto*, become Union citizens, and that they 'shall take part in the political life of the Union', enjoying the rights granted to them by the legal system of the Union while being subject to its laws. A central objective of the European Union, Spinelli declared, should be:

> The attainment of humane and harmonious development of society based principally on endeavours to attain full employment, the progressive elimination of the existing imbalances between the regions, protection and improvement in the quality of the environment, scientific progress and the cultural development of its peoples.

If Spinelli was at odds with Monnet, he nevertheless recognised his brainchild, the European Council, which his proposed treaty incorporated as a fully-fledged Community institution. The role he envisaged for it was

---

[27] Thatcher, op. cit., p. 545.

straight out of the Monnet playbook: its main role should be to manage the transition of power from national to supranational authority, a process that must be one-way only. Spinelli's draft also proposed a major expansion of the Parliament's competences, giving it supervisory powers over the Commission, with the right to veto its political programme.

In addition to the 'internal market', the Community was to assume the responsibility for co-ordinating national laws 'with a view to constituting a homogenous judicial area'; the full co-ordination of economic policy; and the harmonisation of taxes. All member states would be required to participate in the European Monetary System and a law should be enacted governing 'procedures and stages for attaining monetary union', complete with a European central bank.

The Union would have 'concurrent competence' over all social and regional policies, and those governing health, consumer protection, the environment, education and research, culture and information. It would have competence in certain aspects of foreign policy, and exclusive competence to make trade deals with third countries. There was provision for the Union to set up its own revenue-collecting authorities and mechanisms for creating new sources of revenue. Finally, should any country fail to ratify such a new treaty, the rest could carry on without it, creating a 'two-speed Europe'.[28] The draft was finally adopted by the Parliament on 14 February 1984 with 237 votes in favour, 31 against, with 43 abstentions. It was addressed directly to the governments and parliaments of the member states, to prevent the Council from blocking it.

FRANÇOIS MITTERRAND TAKES A HAND

Despite the support of the Parliament, Spinelli knew his treaty stood little chance of being accepted without heavyweight support. He therefore sought Mitterrand's aid, not least because France was then holding the presidency of the Council. Thus, in his speech to the Parliament – in the debate that resulted in his draft treaty being adopted – he exhorted France to take the initiative in winning support for it among other member states.

A month later, on 24 March, Spinelli told the European Movement congress in Brussels: 'too many times we have heard the heads of State and governments make solemn statements and then we see the intergovernmental and diplomatic machines practically crushing them, reducing them to nothing'. He handed a personal note to Mitterrand during a short audience in Paris on 16 April, telling him that he hoped the presidency

---

[28] Published in February 1984. Publications Office of the EU.

would contribute to advancement of the project, obliging all member states 'to assume their responsibilities'. In particular, he recommended that such an initiative should be taken 'apart from the Council of Ministers, to circumvent the rule of the unanimity'.[29]

Spinelli got his answer on 24 May. Mitterrand 'made the choice for Europe'. Speaking in Strasbourg, he declared himself in favour of the proposals. A new situation demanded a new treaty, and France was open to such a prospect.[30] He suggested 'preparatory discussions' that could lead to a conference of interested member states.[31]

Mitterrand's positive response was not entirely unselfish. France was nearing the end of her presidency, and with her economy in recession, fast-rising unemployment, widespread demonstrations and his party's failure in the European elections, he needed a dramatic gesture before his tenure ended. In the spring of 1984, therefore, he conducted a marathon tour of eight European capitals and judged that there was strong support for a new European initiative. The moment had come 'to leave the humdrum routine of technical questions' and to give 'the political impetus which could solve Europe's crisis'.[32]

However, his support was by no means unconditional. His own foreign ministry had been strongly opposed, so his economic advisers suggested one of two options. The first would be to split the treaty. Its economic proposals could be put forward as a first step, and discussion of its more ambitious institutional components could then be deferred for 'five years', when it was already envisaged that the Community would re-examine the Solemn Declaration on the European Union. The second option would be for France to advance her own proposals.[33] In the event, Mitterrand came up with a mixture, starting with an invitation to heads of government to take part in an 'informal meeting' in Paris in the autumn, to discuss 'political and institutional questions', the application of the Treaty of Rome and any other proposals that might be put forward.

The real significance of the advice given to Mitterrand at this time would only become apparent as events unfolded over the next seven years. It was this advice that first sowed the idea that the next great step forward in the integration of Europe should be in two stages, beginning with a major

[29] Spinelli, Altiero, *Diario Europeo*, pp. 976 and 998.
[30] See Palayret, op. cit., He cites official documents.
[31] Ibid., citing Mitterrand, F. (1985), *Réflexions Sur La Politique Extérieure De La France. Introduction à 25 discours, 1981–1985* (Paris: Fayard), pp. 261–262 and 281.
[32] Ibid., citing Dépêche Agence France-Presse, 21 February 1984, in AN. 5 AG (4) PM 12.
[33] AN AG 5 (4) PM 12. Direction économique et financière, service de coopération économique. Fiche sur 'Présidence française: réforme des institutions (projet Spinelli)', 20 December 1983.

'economic reform', then continuing, five years later, with more ambitious 'institutional reform'. Herein lay the genesis of the two treaties that would become known as the 'Single European Act', ratified in 1986, and the 'Treaty on European Union' agreed at Maastricht five years later. All this was eventually to flow from Spinelli's 'draft treaty' and from his decision at a timely moment to invite Mitterrand to act as its main sponsor.

One feature of Spinelli's project that particularly appealed to Mitterrand was the idea of a 'two-speed Europe' that could not be blocked by the veto of any country. He had in mind Britain, which might be reluctant to move to much fuller integration. Mitterrand was to confirm this by his actions at the closing European Council under France's presidency, scheduled for Fontainebleau on 25–26 June 1984.

At the start of June, Thatcher was almost entirely focused on what was to be the 'showdown' in the battle to win her rebate, but she was also to make very public her views on the 'unification of Europe'. In an 'exclusive' interview for the *Daily Express*, spread across two pages, she was asked about the pressure coming from Mitterand and Kohl 'for a new treaty and political union'. The prime minister's scorn came over clearly in her response:

> We haven't yet got a common market and we're a very long way from it. I must tell you that I do not believe in what I would call a United States of Europe. I do not believe in a federal Europe and I think to ever compare it to the United States of America is absolutely ridiculous.[34]

When it was put to her that the French and the Germans 'might go ahead with a new treaty in 1988', that again was 'absolutely ridiculous'. Ramming home her view, she added: 'Just to sit down and create a new treaty is ridiculous.'[35] The exchange provoked a pained telegram from Sir Christopher Mallaby, then ambassador to Germany. Her comments had been referred to 'with regret' in diplomatic circles, although her views about the Common Market had been 'recorded'.[36]

THE DOOGE COMMITTEE
Neither Mitterrand nor Kohl were deflected from their aim by Thatcher's comments. After 'very discreet meetings' between their advisers, the day before the Council meeting, Mitterrand slipped into the agenda a proposal

[34] *Daily Express*, 4 June 1984, pp. 8–9.
[35] Ibid.
[36] National Archives, PREM 19/1482, Telegram: Mallaby to FCO, 6 June 1984.

for a 'committee of experts' to consider future institutional reform. Each head of government would nominate a personal representative. Mitterrand himself already saw this as the equivalent of Spaak's 1955 committee, which had drafted the Treaty of Rome. A former Irish foreign minister, James Dooge, was chosen as chairman, for what would soon become known to insiders as the 'Spaak II Committee'.

In her account of Fontainebleau, Thatcher does not refer to this committee.[37] Had she understood the reasons for its informal title, this might have warned her of the ambitions of her partners. She also failed to note another decision at Fontainebleau, in the wake of the June elections to the European Parliament that had produced a 'disappointingly low' poll across the Community, with Britain's 31.8 per cent lowest of all. Concern at this apathy moved the Council to set up a committee on how to build 'a people's Europe', to be chaired by Italian MEP, Pietro Adonnino.

Mitterrand had anticipated the possibility that Thatcher might veto the Dooge Committee, by planning to convene a new 'Messina conference'. With additional members about to join, he was convinced that a larger Community needed stronger institutions.[38] If Mitterrand had been forced down this route, though, he planned to work with a Franco-German document comprising 'a draft treaty for the creation of the European Union'. Its starting point would be the solemn declaration of Stuttgart, taking account of the 'Spinelli project'.[39] But since Thatcher had now given her approval, this 'nuclear option' was not necessary.

Mitterrand ensured that he kept a guiding hand on the committee's work by nominating as his representative Maurice Faure, a 'convinced European', as the *rapporteur*. The committee was essentially controlled by its French and German members, who met in Bonn on 19 September 1984. Their objective was no more and no less than 'the realisation of the European Union'. The majority, in any case, recognised the value of Spinelli's project. They were in favour of a 'true political entity' and wanted an intergovernmental conference (IGC) to prepare a new treaty. This should take as its starting point 'the spirit and the method of the project voted by the European Parliament'.[40]

---

[37] Thatcher, op. cit., p. 546.
[38] Mitterrand, *Réflexions*.
[39] Saunier, G. (2001), 'Prélude à la relance de l'Europe. Le couple franco-allemand et les projets de relance communautaire vus de l'hexagone 1981–1985', in Bitsch, M. T., *Le couple France-Allemagne et les Constitutions européennes* (Bruxelles: Bruylant), pp. 464–485.
[40] AHCE; AS 365, document PE 94.568: 'Note établissant un parallèle entre le rapport du Comité Dooge et le projet de Traité instituant l'Union européenne', 13 December 1984.

FOG IN CHANNEL, CONTINENT CUT OFF

Thatcher was to say that, once the rebate issued had been resolved, she was determined that Britain should reunite with her partners to play a 'strong and positive role in the Community'. Looking back on how events unfolded during the ten months after the Fontainebleau Council, however, it seems as though Britain and her partners were operating on different planets. Immediately after Fontainebleau, Geoffrey Howe recalled that he had attended the Queen's birthday banquet in honour of the Diplomatic Corps, which he had arranged: an 'impeccably British function'. The Irish had now taken over the presidency of the Community, for what Howe reported as 'a quiet six months'. One of his few recollections of this period was 'an enjoyable day in Germany' in September, inspecting some of the 60,000 soldiers serving with BAOR (the British Army of the Rhine), who were taking part jointly with the Bundeswehr in NATO exercises.

Later that month, he returned to make 'an important speech in Bonn', where he stated that Britain's commitment to Europe was 'profound and irreversible'. Evidently oblivious of the most recent dealings between the French and Germans, he was seeking to demonstrate 'the range of Britain's European commitment' and, by implication, 'to suggest that the Franco-German relationship should not be seen as the only cornerstone of the European Community'.[41] This, as we will see, was to be the cornerstone of British policy, as successive British governments sought to interpose themselves between the French and the Germans. Thus, as others were to do after him, Howe argued that Britain should be 'a strong voice in the Community', as one of its leading members. 'We have brought to Europe a considerable dowry', he said: 'our markets for agricultural and industrial goods, our fishing grounds, our major contribution to the defence and security of the continent.' He continued:

> It is because we have so much at stake in the Community, because we depend so much on its healthy development and because we believe so wholeheartedly in its future that we have devoted so much effort to the reform of its internal arrangements; to building a better foundation for the future of Europe.[42]

So important did he consider this speech, along with others he was to deliver in similar vein over the months that followed, that he would eventually publish them in a book entitled *Europe Tomorrow*.

[41] Howe, op. cit., pp. 403–404.
[42] Cited in Hillman, Judy and Clarke, Peter (1988), *Geoffrey Howe: A Quiet Revolutionary* (London: Weidenfeld & Nicolson), p. 172.

Meanwhile, Mitterrand was pursuing plans to establish a European 'defence identity' independent of NATO, effectively continuing a French policy objective that stretched back to the time of de Gaulle. The opportunity had been presented by the general European alarm over the announcement by US president Ronald Reagan on 23 October 1983 of his Strategic Defence Initiative (SDI), the proposed anti-ballistic missile system dubbed 'Star Wars'. This had raised the spectre for some of America's European allies of the USA finding a way to make herself immune from the Soviet nuclear threat, and thus becoming less willing to commit her own nuclear deterrent on behalf of her allies.

By February 1984, therefore, Mitterrand felt he could use this opportunity to convince the Community to seek its own independent military capability: independent, that is, of the USA. To achieve his aim, he fastened on the moribund Western European Union. With a view to reactivating it, he had sent a memorandum to all its other members. The initial response was lukewarm. Thatcher predictably rejected the idea outright.

However, Howe and Michael Heseltine, now her Secretary of State for Defence, both fervent 'Europeanists', had felt 'a strong instinct towards strengthening our European defence linkage', presumably unaware or heedless of the French agenda. It was, they argued, in America's interest as well as Europe's that Europe should pull its weight.[43] By October 1984, the Community members had been sufficiently won round to Mitterrand's idea for a meeting of foreign and defence ministers to take place in Rome within the WEU framework. On 27 October they agreed a 'founding text' for reactivating the WEU, the 'Rome Declaration', the objectives of which included the establishing of a 'European security identity' and the gradual harmonisation of member states' defence policies.[44]

Two weeks later, on 11 November, there took place the ceremony with which this book began, when Mitterrand and Kohl met to hold hands at Verdun, solemnly to reaffirm that indissoluble alliance between France and Germany on which they saw that the whole future of 'European construction' must ultimately be centred.

While all these events were unfolding, the Dooge Committee produced an interim report for the Dublin European Council, favouring an 'intergovernmental conference' to prepare a new treaty. The UK, Denmark and Greece immediately tabled reservations. But agreement was reached on another matter. With strong backing from Mitterrand, Jacques Delors,

[43] Howe, op. cit., p. 386.
[44] www.weu.int.

a leading French *fonctionnaire*, was formally appointed as the new Commission president.[45] On the interim Dooge proposals, Mitterrand could not have made his position clearer. At the press conference immediately after the Council, he declared that 'the institutional debate may now take precedence over the others'.[46]

The significance of this clearly escaped Thatcher, but then she had other things to concern her. Only weeks previously she had survived a massive IRA bomb attack on her hotel at the Brighton Conservative Party Conference, and she was still dealing with the tense closing stages of the long-drawn-out 1984 miners' strike. But there was also an element of refusal to engage. In a speech in Avignon in October, she had claimed not to know what 'European Union' meant, preferring 'practical unity' in policies.[47]

A month later, in his New Year message to the German people, Kohl made no secret of his determination, with his ally France, 'to give decisive impetus to the European Union concept' during 1985. This was reinforced by the incoming president of the Council, Italy's foreign minister Giulio Andreotti, who had begun his political career as a protégé of Alcide De Gasperi. Setting out to the European Parliament his programme, he declared, 'no effort will be spared in seeking agreement by June on a date for convening an intergovernmental conference with the task of negotiating the Treaty on European Union'.[48] Therein lay the genesis of the 'ambush at Milan'. Howe, aided by the 'Rolls-Royce minds' of the Foreign Office, should have picked this up. He did not.

By the time of the Brussels Council, on 29–30 March 1985, the Dooge Committee's final report was ready. Starting with the assertion that the EEC answered 'the complex and deeply felt needs of all our citizens', it referred back to the summit in The Hague in 1969 and then to the Paris Summit in 1972. 'Europe', the Committee complained, was 'now in a state of crisis and suffers from serious deficiencies'. Member states had become caught up in differences that had 'obscured the considerable economic advantages which could be obtained from the realisation of the Common Market and for

---

[45] A *fonctionnaire* in France is much more than a civil servant. Most of the *fonctionnaire* class that came to rule France in the closing decades of the twentieth century were educated at the Ecole Nationale d'Administration (ENA), set up by Michel Debré in 1946, and known as 'Enarques'. The Enarques may play the role of politician and senior official interchangeably. Prominent Enarques included Giscard d'Estaing, Jacques Chirac, and several French Commissioners, such as Pascal Lamy and Yves Thibault de Silguy, responsible for setting up the single currency. Delors, though unmistakably a *fonctionnaire*, was not an Enarque. He did not attend the ENA.

[46] Agence Europe, No. 3984. 6 December 1984, p. 7.

[47] Corbett, Richard (2001), *The European Parliament's Role in Closer EU Integration* (London: Palgrave), p. 205.

[48] Debates of the European Parliament, 16 January 1985, No. 2-321, pp. 105–106.

Economic and Monetary Union', and, unlike Japan and the United States, it had not achieved a growth rate sufficient to reduce the disturbing figure of almost fourteen million unemployed.[49]

The Committee's answer was that 'Europe' must 'launch itself on a new common venture – the establishment of a political entity based on clearly defined priority objectives coupled with the means of achieving them'. Crucially, in arguing that institutional reform was essential, the Committee proposed that the national veto must in general be abandoned in favour of QMV. It urged member states to demonstrate their 'common political will' by creating 'a genuine political entity', namely 'a European Union', which would include a 'European social area' and a 'homogenous judicial area'. The Committee also wanted measures to promote 'common cultural values' and 'an external identity': i.e., a common foreign policy. These were to be augmented by 'developing and strengthening consultation on security problems as part of political co-operation'. Predictably, to achieve these radical changes, it called for a major revision of the treaties and thus formally proposed an IGC.[50]

Thatcher's representative on the Committee was Malcolm Rifkind, then a junior minister at the FCO. Although given the opportunity to comment on the report, he scarcely made any input and failed to warn his prime minister of what the Committee had in mind.[51] But when the Dooge Report was presented to the Brussels Council, no decision was taken. The 'high noon' of political integration would have to wait for the next Council, to be held in Milan on 28–29 June 1985.

SPLITTING THE TREATY

At the Brussels Council, Thatcher had nominated for the post of British Commissioner Arthur Cockfield, formerly the 'prices commissioner' under Heath's government. During the Council, she spoke animatedly about preventing the Community from being 'driven helter-skelter towards European federalism'. The thrust of the Community, she averred, 'should be

[49] Ad Hoc Committee for Institutional Affairs, *Report to the European Council*, SN/1187/85 (SPAAK II), Brussels, 29–30 March 1985.

[50] Ibid.

[51] As Thatcher's 'personal representative', Rifkind was later keen to emphasise that he was not authorised to 'support or oppose any proposal without the express agreement of Number Ten' (personal communication with authors). The countries whose representatives registered the greatest number of objections or reservations to the Dooge proposals were Greece (14) and Denmark (11). Britain came well behind with only four (one of which proposed even greater integration, with an increased role for the European Parliament). On the committee's final recommendation, that there should be a new IGC to negotiate a 'European Union Treaty', Britain and Greece proposed that this should be left to negotiation between governments, for discussion at the Milan Council.

towards achieving a genuinely Common Market envisaged in the original treaty, a force for free trade, not protectionism.[52]

The European Council had endorsed Mrs Thatcher's views, instructing the Community to pursue 'in a concerted manner … action to achieve a single large market by 1992, thereby creating a more favourable environment for stimulating enterprise, competition and trade'.[53] The newly appointed Delors took the hint. He worked closely with Thatcher's own Commissioner and, by 14 June – in time for the Milan Council – had produced a 92-page report on *Completing the Internal Market*.[54] This document identified nearly three hundred measures by which the Community could by 1992 achieve the 'completion' of its 'internal' or 'Single Market'.

The enthusiasm displayed by Delors for this task was by no means motivated solely by Mrs Thatcher's response. At the meeting of foreign ministers on 18–19 June, his fears had been confirmed by Geoffrey Howe, who told the assembled ministers that the UK was 'continuing to move opinion in the Community towards its position and away from support for Treaty amendment and for an open-ended intergovernmental conference'.[55]

Delors has anticipated this problem, as had Mitterrand his former boss when he had been France's finance minister. Mitterrand, no less than Delors, was aware of Thatcher's long-standing resistance to a new treaty and, despite his enthusiasm for further integration, was also aware of internal divisions in Germany's Federal government that could make agreeing a comprehensive treaty difficult. He thus felt that 'ambition would have to be moderated'.[56] It was better to go for a bottom line that everyone could agree on. That 'bottom line' was the completion of the Single Market.[57]

Mitterrand was also aware that expectations of a French success at the Milan Council were high, and a public row would play badly at home. Accordingly, he decided to take a long view, confiding to his adviser, Jacques Attali: 'France's objective is to create a European Union in the long term; the task is now to define the substance and the stages. If we do not agree [at Milan], nothing will be done.'[58] Thus, a start would be made on 'the

[52] Thatcher, op. cit., pp. 547–548.
[53] https://www.consilium.europa.eu/media/20653/1985_march_-_brussels__eng_.pdf.
[54] COM(85) 310 final, White Paper from the Commission to the European Council (Milan, 28–29 June 1985).
[55] National Archives, CAB 128/81, Cabinet Conclusions, 20 June 1985.
[56] Palayret, op. cit., He cites AN. 5 AG (4) EG 13, Note pour le Président (E. Guigou) a/s. 'Votre rencontre avec le chancelier Kohl: Que faire pour l'Europe?, 20 May 1985.
[57] Favier, P. and Martin-Rolland, M., *La décennie Mitterrand*. T. II, Les épreuves (1984–1988), p. 215.
[58] Attali, Jacques, verbatim account, cited in Palayret, op. cit.

construction of a political Europe', and the remaining objectives would be dealt with later.[59]

Spinelli got early warning of Mitterrand's change of heart, and was extremely disturbed by it. But he had undergone a major cancer operation on 22 May 1985 and was unable to travel until October. When he could travel, he went to Bonn, where he was well received at the Bundestag. But when he met Delors in Brussels, he was told that splitting the treaty was the only option. Not only Britain but France and also Germany were opposed to pursuing the full version of his treaty. Delors later told the Parliament that what had been agreed was not enough, but it was a significant step.[60]

All roads now led to Milan. The Commission, France, Germany and all the other member states, with the exception of Britain, Denmark and Greece, were determined that there should be a new treaty. The three main players, Kohl, Mitterrand and Delors, had reached the same conclusion: that the only proposal that all ten governments would support would be the completion of the Single Market. Further moves would have to be channelled through this project.[61] And to secure the support of Mrs Thatcher, the most prominent of the refusniks, for a new treaty, the Single Market was to be the 'bait'.

AMBUSH AT MILAN

As the participants arrived in Milan, the scene was set for a classic confrontation. The Italian 'presidency' had already announced the setting of a date for an IGC as its main objective. Kohl, Mitterrand, Delors and the Benelux countries were similarly determined. Against them were ranged the British, the Danes and the Greeks, with the Irish undecided. Thatcher and Howe in particular were intent on blocking an IGC. With 50,000 activists mobilised by the European Movement parading through the Milan streets, their banners proclaiming 'down with frontiers', Italy's Socialist prime minister Bettino Craxi was in the hot seat.

At first, he tried for a 'common position', but Thatcher argued strongly that the Community should rely on 'political co-operation'. A new treaty was not necessary.[62] Her arguments were to no avail. She found herself being bulldozed by a majority that 'included a highly partisan chairman'.[63]

---

[59] Attali, in Palayret, op. cit.
[60] Pinder, John (2007), 'Altiero Spinelli's European Federal Odyssey', *The International Spectator*, 42:4, pp. 571–588.
[61] Grant, op. cit., pp. 66–67.
[62] Thatcher, op. cit., p. 559.
[63] Ibid., p. 550.

To her astonishment, Craxi invoked his right as president to call for a vote – a highly unorthodox move. Thatcher and Howe were startled to hear that, contrary to their understanding of the rules, only a simple majority was needed to carry the day.[64] An IGC was agreed by a vote of seven to three.[65] In the presidency conclusions, Craxi noted that 'the required majority as laid down in Article 236 of the Treaty had been obtained' for the convening of a Conference.[66] The Portuguese and Spanish governments would be invited to take part in it. Delors was relieved: 'at least we know where we stand; if we had waited another year or two, we should not have made any progress,' he told journalists. Belgium's prime minister said the Council had been a 'turning point marking the end of Europe's opposition to progress'. The IGC would pave the way for the adjustments that would undoubtedly be necessary in a twelve-member Community.[67]

Returning home, Thatcher morosely addressed the Cabinet on 4 July, telling her ministers that the Milan Council 'had been the worst-chaired international meeting she had attended'. Furthermore, she had met Kohl at Chequers on 18 May; had let him have the United Kingdom's proposals for agreement on political co-operation, improved decision-making and the completion of the internal market; and had sought his views. The proposals had also been circulated to all member states by Howe, at the foreign ministers' meeting, and 'had been generally well received'.[68]

Mitterrand had said to her that he was 'not in favour of deferring decisions' to an IGC. Yet, one day before the European Council, Germany, with French support, had announced their proposal for a Treaty of European Union. Apart from the new title, this had been, 'almost verbatim', the British text on political co-operation. However, Thatcher concluded: 'In reality, the United Kingdom wished to move faster than many other member states on the completion of the internal market.' When there was talk of a two-speed

---

[64] The European Council, at this stage, was not a formal EEC institution and therefore worked to its own rules. By convention, decisions were made by 'consensus', which was usually 'divined' by the president without a vote. The FCO had assumed 'consensus' to mean unanimity, but Craxi, self-evidently in a premeditated move, chose to interpret it as a simple majority. With the Council being established outside the treaty framework, there was no 'higher authority' to which Thatcher could appeal.

[65] *Bulletin of the European Communities*, EC 6-1985, point 1.2.10.

[66] See https://www.consilium.europa.eu/media/20646/1985_june_-_milan__eng_.pdf. This was a further oddity. Article 236 allowed for the government of any member state or the Commission to submit to the Council proposals for the amendment of the Treaty of Rome. If the Council then delivered an opinion in favour of calling for an IGC, the Article then required that 'the conference shall be convened by the President of the Council'. The reference to 'Council' was the Council of Ministers, not the European Council, which was not recognised in the Treaty.

[67] Council conclusions, ibid.

[68] National Archives, CAB 128/81, Cabinet Conclusions, 4 July 1985.

Europe, she added, 'it was important that it should be seen that on such substantive matters the United Kingdom was in the fast lane'.[69] Following the foreign ministers' meeting on 22–23 July, Howe announced that the IGC would start on 9 November, with the UK present.[70] The 'bait' had been swallowed whole.

THE SINGLE EUROPEAN ACT

So it came to pass that, over the next six months, an unwilling Britain for the first time took part in negotiations for a new 'European' treaty.[71] The IGC, which negotiates the treaty, is not so much a single event as a process, lasting many months, encompassing scores of meetings between both ministers and officials (known as 'Sherpas'). Only after the contents of the treaty have been endlessly thrashed out does the process conclude at a final 'summit', where the heads of government settle outstanding issues. The final text is then prepared for signing at a later date, after which the treaty is ratified by each of the member states.

A striking feature of this IGC was the role of the Commission. Although it had no formal status, Delors attended the meetings of foreign ministers, where much of the work was done, while his secretary-general, Emile Noël, worked with officials. Delors, Noël and François Lamoureaux, Delors' institutional expert, then saturated delegates with proposals that 'helped define the agenda, dissuading governments from putting forward their own ideas'.[72] All proposals were drafted by these three, without reference to other Commissioners.

With considerable subtlety, Delors steered the negotiations in his direction, not least by linking the UK objectives, notably the Single Market, to institutional reform.[73] To get what they wanted, the British were being forced to concede that which they least wanted: an extension of qualified majority voting.

Once the mass of paperwork had been distilled to its essentials, the substantive issues emerged. The first two were acceptable to the British:

---

[69] Ibid.

[70] Ibid., 25 July 1985.

[71] Contrary to general understanding, the Single European Act was not to be the first treaty since the Treaties of Rome. There had also been the Treaty of Brussels in 1965, merging the three 'Communities'; the Luxembourg Treaty of 1970 on budgetary procedures, and the 1975 Brussels Treaty (which introduced the Court of Auditors). In addition, there were the accession treaties each time there was an 'enlargement', which could themselves be used to establish new principles of policy that might have repercussions wider than those affecting the applicant countries alone (as in the details of fisheries policy established in 1972).

[72] Grant, op. cit., p. 73.

[73] Corbett, op. cit., p. 219.

the completion of the Single Market, based on Cockfield's White Paper, and strengthened co-operation on foreign policy. Delors had also inserted 'chapters' on environmental policy, research and 'cohesion' (the so-called 'structural funds' providing regional aid). These were important policy areas in which the Commission had already become active with no legal base. The proposed new competence on environmental policy also brought an arcane new principle described as 'subsidiarity', the ramifications of which few at the time could have predicted.

The British agreed to these 'chapters', as they did to a modest extension in the role of the European Parliament. But the price Thatcher would have to pay was a significant extension in majority voting.[74] The final version of the treaty added 12 policy areas to the maw of QMV, including the 'internal market' measures, occupational 'health and safety', decisions relating to regional development and an extension of Community competence to air and sea transport.[75]

Yet, despite being fully aware of the implications of this expansion, Thatcher seemed determined to believe that it would only be used to promote the Single Market. What the British could not accept at all was Delors' vision of 'space without frontiers', which would effectively mean ceding some powers on immigration policy to the Commission. There were two other battles, one with proposals put forward by Cockfield over tax harmonisation and the other on EMU.

The crucial battle was on EMU. Delors insisted that it be included as a new 'chapter' in the treaty. This, Thatcher resolutely opposed, right up until the last summit of the IGC, held in Luxembourg in December. On this, she thought she could rely on German backing and she certainly had the full support of Lawson. He stressed that it would be essential that the language used should contain no obligation on us to join the ERM. It should also make it clear that exchange rate policy is the responsibility of national authorities, minimise any extension of Community competence and avoid any treaty reference to EMU.[76]

At a preparatory meeting of foreign ministers on 25–26 November, however, Delors protested at the changes proposed to his cherished 'space without frontiers', saying that they left his texts with 'more holes than Gruyère'. He stormed off to see Kohl and Mitterrand, with spectacular results.

---

[74] With the accession of Spain and Portugal in 1986, the number of votes in Council rose to 76: the four biggest countries, France, Germany, Britain and Italy each with ten votes; Spain with eight; Belgium, Greece, the Netherlands and Portugal with five; Denmark and Ireland with three; and Luxembourg with two.
[75] A 'qualified majority' would require 54 of the 76 votes, thus preventing the 'big four' ganging up on the smaller states, but leaving Britain with only just over one-seventh of the vote.
[76] Thatcher, op. cit., p. 554.

By the next ministerial meeting, his proposal had been reinstated.[77] Worse still for Thatcher, the new-found Franco-German axis had also reached an accommodation on monetary union. A triumphant Delors inserted into the treaty preamble a reminder that 'the Heads of State or Government, at their Conference in Paris from 19–21 October 1972, approved the objective of the progressive achievement of Economic and Monetary Union'. Two technical articles were then added to the treaty text, authorising work on 'convergence of economic and monetary policies'.[78]

At the summit in Luxembourg on 2–3 December, Thatcher considered using her veto, but the Foreign Office assured her that the statement had no legal significance. With the new articles embedded in the treaty, that was not strictly true. When the treaty was signed in February 1986, she thought 'long and hard' before affixing her own name to the text.[79] But when the deed was done, Delors had his treaty, an instrument that took the Community further down the road to 'a European Union'. The spirit of Paris 1972 was very much alive.

Almost as an afterthought, the heads of government also signed an intergovernmental treaty on 'co-operation' in foreign policy, enshrining the London agreement of 1981. As a Council, they agreed that regional and development funds would be 'significantly increased in real terms', and to co-operation in research and the funding of technological development (the so-called 'Eureka' programme). Finally, they decided that the 'EEC' should formally become the 'European Community', a term already informally used for several years.

For the few British journalists interested, one of the main points of concern was EMU. Thatcher dismissed the text as 'meaningless'; otherwise, she told them, she would not have signed it.[80] Delors had different ideas: 'It's

---

[77] Grant, op. cit., p. 73.

[78] Texts resulting from the European Council in Luxembourg, 2–3 December 1985, p. 12, ʰttps://www.consilium.europa.eu/media/20433/1985_december_-_luxembourg__eng_.pdf.

[79] Thatcher, op. cit., p. 554.

[80] Having in June the previous year recorded Thatcher as dismissing the idea of a treaty as 'absolutely ridiculous', to coincide with the first day of the summit the *Daily Express* published a page 6 'World News' report. Loyally, it reported: 'Maggie backed in battle to beat Europe terrorist threat'. The text recorded: 'MRS THATCHER won backing last night against Common Market plans which could have flooded Britain with terrorists and drug smugglers. The Prime Minister is flying to Luxembourg today for a crucial summit after Euro Ministers were persuaded to keep tough border controls. The proposals would have forced Britain to open its doors to visitors and goods from EEC countries. The idea, dreamed up by Brussels bureaucrats and backed by many Continental Euro MPs, was to create a barrier-free Europe without travel restrictions. But British officials feared it would have led to an invasion of terrorists, drugs, illegal immigrants and rabies into this country.' Mrs Thatcher's main objective at the summit, the paper went on to say, 'will be to preserve Britain's veto over EEC reforms' (2 December 1985).

like the story of Tom Thumb lost in the forest, who left white stones so he could be found,' he said. 'I put in white stones so we could find monetary union again.'[81] Spinelli was downbeat. He had wanted so much more, and thought 'the mountain' had given 'birth to a mouse'.[82] BBC television news mistook the new treaty for 'a few modest reforms of the Treaty of Rome'.[83] The *Guardian* considered Britain had been the victor. *The Economist*, redolent of Spinelli, called the treaty a 'smiling mouse': it was well intentioned but too diminutive to make much difference.[84]

And although the Single European Act would be presented as a measure to complete the 'internal market', in reality it was much more. Crucially, it paved the way for the next treaty, which would comprise the second half of a unitary whole, implementing the agenda agreed in Paris 13 years previously. Of all this, though, Thatcher seemed sublimely unaware. On her return from Luxembourg, she was challenged in the Commons by Tony Benn on the 'long-term objective of political union within a fully federal united states of Europe'. She replied:

I am constantly saying that I wish they would talk less about European and political union. The terms are not understood in this country. In so far as they are understood over there, they mean a good deal less than some people over here think they mean.[85]

If Thatcher, unlike Benn, had not yet got the message, neither had the rest of Parliament. When the treaty came to be ratified, the necessary Bill amending the European Communities Act 1972 was pushed through an often thinly attended Commons in just six days. The main debate was started on a Thursday, knowing that MPs would want to get away for the weekend. After only three sessions of the committee stage, the government abruptly curtailed further discussion with a 'guillotine'.

For the final reading, so few MPs turned up that the Bill passed by a mere 149 votes to 43. Peter Tapsell, an unrepentant Eurosceptic who within a few years would be prominent in opposing the Maastricht Treaty, later spoke for not a few of his colleagues in recalling how they had eventually

[81] *Interview with Delors.* Grant, op. cit., p. 74.
[82] Palayret, op. cit.
[83] *The Poisoned Chalice.*
[84] Grant, op. cit., p. 74.
[85] HC Deb, 05 December 1985, Vol. 88, cc429-39. In her statement to the House, Mrs Thatcher seemed to have difficulty separating the IGC – which had agreed the treaty – and the European Council, which had no powers in this respect. Although the two bodies comprised the same people, technically and legally they were very different. The confusion was evident in other heads of government.

become 'ashamed' at having voted for it. 'We didn't give it the attention we should have done,' he said.[86] The real irony was that, in accepting the treaty as an economic measure, Thatcher had unwittingly placed herself in exactly the same situation as the people who had been deceived by Macmillan and Heath into accepting something that was 'political' as just a matter of economics (of which she had been one). But Milan was the start of a learning curve that was eventually to prove her downfall.

On 23 May 1986, Altiero Spinelli died in Rome in his eightieth year, his dream not yet fully achieved, but his life's work done. In his honour, when the European Parliament completed its vast new building in Brussels, opened in 1998, it named it the Alterio Spinelli Building.

[86] *The Poisoned Chalice.*

10

Decline and Fall: 1986–1990

> The British economy has been transformed in the past twelve years. In the 1960s and 1970s we were the sick man of Europe, at the bottom of the league tables for growth, investment and productivity. In the 1980s we were at the top.
>
> Conservative Campaign Guide, 1991

One cannot understand the second half of Thatcher's 11-year reign as Britain's longest-serving prime minister of the twentieth century without appreciating just how significant was the part played in it by 'Europe'. In the years after Milan, she found herself increasingly at odds, not just with her Community 'partners' but with her most senior Cabinet colleagues, until they worked to bring about her downfall.

The first signs of this division came from an unexpected direction. Early in 1985, her chancellor Nigel Lawson, known as a robust 'Thatcherite', became persuaded that the key to imposing monetary discipline on Britain's economy was to join the Exchange Rate Mechanism. He was soon supported by Howe, although his motives were quite different. Lawson regarded himself as something of a 'sceptic' on European issues. He saw linking the pound to the deutschmark-dominated ERM simply as an economic tool, on the grounds that Germany had become a byword for maintaining price stability.[1] The move would signal to the markets that the UK had no intention of devaluing her currency, so he genuinely believed the ERM was a way of co-operating to serve a common economic

[1] Lawson, Nigel (1992), *The View from No. 11: Memoirs of a Tory Radical* (London: Bantam Press), p. 419.

purpose.[2] Howe, on the other hand, was well aware that the ERM's real purpose was not economic but political: a mechanism designed to pave the way to EMU.

Thatcher disagreed with both her colleagues. Under the influence of her economic adviser Professor Alan Walters and others, she was convinced that, if Britain tried to confine the exchange rate of sterling to the levels allowed by the ERM, this would expose the pound to speculative pressure.[3] By the summer of 1985, however, as she became increasingly worried about inflation, all Lawson could offer was his obsession with entry to the ERM. Unable to persuade him to moderate his enthusiasm, Thatcher arranged a seminar at Number 10, attended by not only Lawson and Howe but also Willie Whitelaw, her deputy prime minister, Norman Tebbit, party chairman, John Wakeham, chief whip, and John Biffen, as leader of the House. Also present were Treasury officials, all of whom favoured entry, alongside Robin Leigh-Pemberton, governor of the Bank of England.

Apart from Biffen, all ministers spoke for entry, even, to Howe's surprise, Tebbit. Whitelaw thought the verdict was clear and the question was settled. It was not. The lady said 'no', and meant it. She brought the meeting quickly to a close. Lawson invited Whitelaw, Tebbit and Howe to join him at Number 11. They were 'downcast and dumbfounded'. According to Howe, they asked themselves what had been the point of the meeting if the prime minister had been unwilling to heed the collective judgement. Lawson's first instinct had been to resign, but he was dissuaded. For the moment, the topic had been removed from the agenda.[4]

Attention, meanwhile, had been distracted by a major political spat, occasioned by Michael Heseltine, then Defence Secretary. As a fervent 'Europeanist', he was aware of the growing pressure from the continent, expressed in the 'Rome Declaration' and the Dooge Report, for integration of the Community's defence industries. His enthusiasm embraced Britain's

---

[2] In this respect, Lawson shared the view originally held by the economist Bernard Connolly, who joined the European Commission in 1978, just when Schmidt and Giscard were finalising the deal that brought the ERM into being. As Connolly recalled in *The Rotten Heart of Europe*, he had also believed that the Community's purpose was to promote international co-operation. But, as head of the unit responsible for monitoring the ERM's performance, he soon became aware that its real purpose was to undermine the political and economic independence of the nation states (Connolly, op. cit., pp. xi–xii).

[3] Including, famously, Patrick Minford, then professor of economics at the University of Liverpool. See National Archives, PREM 19/2162. For a flavour of the public debate, see the Commons debate on 29 January 1986, led by Roy Jenkins moving a motion: 'That this House urges the Government to bring the United Kingdom into the Exchange Rate Mechanism of the European Monetary System forthwith'. HC Deb, 29 January 1986, Vol. 90, cc979-1009.

[4] Howe, op. cit., p. 450.

participation in the biggest joint-defence project so far, the 'European Fighter Aircraft', later called the Typhoon by the RAF. But, in what was to become known as the Westland Affair, he became embroiled in supporting a takeover of Britain's leading helicopter manufacturer by a Franco-German-Italian consortium, despite the company's wishes to align itself with US builder Sikorsky.

The matter came to a head in Cabinet on 9 January 1986, when, after lengthy exchanges, Heseltine 'withdrew from the meeting', thence to resign as Defence Secretary.[5] The effect was to weaken Thatcher. In her colleagues' eyes, she was no longer quite the impregnable leader. Nor had she heard the last of Heseltine.

A NEW ENEMY

Having made one enemy, Thatcher now made another. In the second half of 1986, Britain held the 'rotating presidency' of the Council of Ministers. Almost the only progress made by the Community during this period was the passing of 47 new Single Market directives, including the 13th VAT Directive. This was the sort of progress, Thatcher argued, that the Community needed, rather than 'flashy, publicity-seeking initiatives which came to nothing or just caused bad feeling'.[6] Howe records the same 'notable achievement' but adds a chilling detail:

> We had been able, in other words, to exploit the full steps agreed at Luxembourg for the enlargement of the Community authority at the expense of 'sovereign parliaments'. It was an achievement worth recording, not least under this presidency.[7]

But the most remembered incident of these six months came at the end of its concluding London Council, when Thatcher and Delors gave a press conference. Howe records how, with Delors and himself on the podium, Thatcher did most of the talking, leaving Delors little opportunity to speak.[8] Then, suddenly, she ended one answer by inviting him to comment. Howe has it that Delors had 'switched off': his concentration had faltered. The chancellor then quoted Thatcher's own memoirs, recording how she

---

[5] National Archives, CAB 128/83. See also Thatcher's lengthy account of the affair (*Downing Street Years*, op. cit., pp. 424–427) and Heseltine, M. (2000), *Life in the Jungle* (London: Hodder & Stoughton), pp. 293–333 and pp. 535–542.
[6] Ibid.
[7] Howe, op. cit., p. 521.
[8] Ibid., p. 521.

complained that he 'had refused to say anything, even when I asked him to comment on one of my answers'. She eventually remarked, to the laughter of the press corps, 'I had no idea you were the strong silent type.'[9] According to his biographer, Delors felt 'snubbed and patronised' and thought Thatcher had tried to humiliate him.[10] Howe records that 'Neither side really forgave the other for the "offence" which neither of them had wittingly committed.' It was another step along the road to deeper misunderstanding.[11]

More revealing perhaps were Thatcher's comments about Delors' behaviour during the Council. This was a new kind of European Commission president, she wrote, a major player in the game … a new breed of unaccountable politician.[12] She still had not quite understood what the Community was all about. With the 12 member states in the EC, there were 13 governments, the Commission being the 13th. In status, Delors was a 'head of government', but Thatcher saw him as some kind of 'top civil servant' and treated him accordingly. No wonder Delors bridled at her treatment of him.

Thatcher's education was to continue. On 9 December 1986, she reported on the presidency to what she insisted on calling the 'European Assembly' in Strasbourg. Her speech, she claims, could not have been 'more *communautaire*'.[13] When she sat down, 'a quite new M. Delors whom I had never seen or heard before', began to speak, cheered on by members.[14] 'It was Euro-demagogy,' she wrote, 'designed to play to the prejudices of his audience, to belittle the British presidency and to ask for more money.'[15] A combative Thatcher demanded a right of reply. This was something apparently unknown in this 'Parliament'. Speaking off the cuff, she answered Delors' points, as she had done so many times in wind-up speeches in the Commons. And she did not fail to observe that the Commission president had said nothing of what he told the 'Parliament' when he had had the chance at the press conference after the Council.[16]

Afterwards, at lunch in the Orangerie restaurant in a park opposite the Parliament, she sat next to Cockfield and is said to have fulminated against Delors in language that brought blushes to the Commissioner's cheeks.[17]

[9] Thatcher op. cit., p. 558.
[10] Grant, op. cit., p. 77.
[11] Howe, op. cit., p. 521.
[12] Thatcher, op. cit., p. 558.
[13] Grant, op. cit., p. 77.
[14] Ibid.
[15] Thatcher, op. cit., p. 558.
[16] Ibid.
[17] Grant, op. cit., p. 77.

Delors himself came in late, and took his place beside Thatcher. She told him how, again and again in the Commons, she had supported his position, even though under intense pressure. 'Of one thing he could be sure,' she told him, 'that would never happen again.'[18] She had come a long way from her launch of the 'Yes' campaign for the Conservatives 11 years earlier. In addition to noting the determination of the 'Franco-German bloc' to set the Community's agenda, she observed that the Commission 'was now led by a tough, talented European federalist'. She also recorded how easily the officials of her own Foreign Office seemed to be 'moving to compromise with these new European friends'.[19]

TAKING ON THE COMMUNITY

In the early months of 1987, the British people suddenly began to wake up to the extent to which, in the seven years since Thatcher came to power in 1979, their country's economy had been transformed.

The brooding presence of trade union power, which had cast such a shadow over British life in the 1970s, had been vanquished. One after another, state industries that for so long had been draining billions of pounds out of the economy, from British Steel and British Leyland to British Airways and British Telecom, had been sold off by her government. The result of these 'privatisations' had been an extraordinary boost in productivity. British Steel, by cutting its workforce by two-thirds while maintaining the same output, was on the way to becoming by 1988 the most efficient steel company in the world. A similar revolution, after the 1984 miners' strike, was taking place in the coal industry. The newspaper industry was similarly able to cut its workforce by two-thirds, after the power of the printing unions was broken in 1986.

After years of decline, the City of London had just been through its own electronic revolution, in the 'Big Bang', which was re-establishing it as one of the three leading financial centres in the world. Across the globe, from oil and pharmaceuticals to civil engineering and telecommunications, Britain was showing itself capable of taking on any competition. A rebirth of inventiveness and enterprise was creating thousands of new small and medium-size businesses. When Lawson came to present his budget in March 1987, no chancellor in living memory had been able to deliver such an upbeat message. Britain was in the midst of the 'Lawson boom'.

In that same month, Lawson embarked on a daring initiative. Still smarting from the frustration of his wish 15 months earlier to take Britain

---

[18] Ibid.
[19] Thatcher, op. cit., pp. 558–559.

into the EMS, he decided to do the next best thing, by secretly allowing the pound to shadow the deutschmark. He would use his power over interest rates and Britain's reserves to keep the levels of sterling and the deutschmark as closely linked as possible. Even the governor of the Bank of England and Thatcher herself were not taken into his confidence. She was left to discover it only months later, when she was told what Lawson was up to by 'journalists from the *Financial Times*'.[20]

Long before this, however, she had been encouraged by the effects of the 'Lawson boom' to call an election on 9 June 1987. After winning for the third time in succession, by an improved margin, she felt ready to take on the rest of the Community, in which she was now the longest-serving head of government, with a new confidence.

THE BUDGETARY CRISIS

In the determination to deal with the Community, there was no time to waste. The Commission's 'budgetary situation' was now 'characterised' as being on the brink of bankruptcy. In February, Delors had published what became known as the 'Delors package', proposing a multi-annual budget, spanning five years, and a curb on CAP. But structural or regional funds would be doubled over the next five years. A massive increase in funding would be needed, not just from increasing the Community's share of VAT proceeds to 1.6 per cent, as agreed at Fontainebleau, but also from a 'fourth resource', representing 1.4 per cent of member states' gross national product (GNP).[21]

Thatcher certainly shared Delors' concerns. The lack of effective budgetary discipline and runaway spending on the CAP – by far the most expensive item in the budget – had left a legacy of inefficiency, fraud and excess. Huge surpluses had been created: beef and butter 'mountains', milk and wine 'lakes' – much of which were then dumped on third countries or sold at cut price to Soviet Russia. These caused considerable embarrassment, undermining the lofty ideals of the European *projet*.[22]

Seemingly unworried by such concerns, the European Parliament had in the first half of 1987 launched a new drive to reactivate Spinelli's 'draft treaty on European Union', winning support from the national parliaments of Belgium, Italy, Holland and Ireland.[23]

---

[20] Thatcher, op. cit., p. 701.
[21] Commission of the European Communities, COM(87) final, Brussels, 28 February 1987, *Report on the Financing of the Community Budget*, http://aei.pitt.edu/1370/1/Finance_Budget.pdf.
[22] Ibid., p. 728.
[23] See Corbett, op. cit., pp. 276–284.

In response to this relentless obsession with further schemes of integration, Thatcher decided 'to stake out a radically different position', raising the flag 'for national sovereignty, free trade and enterprise'. In this, she knew she was isolated in the Community, but 'taking the wider perspective' she thought the federalists were the real isolationists, 'clinging grimly to a protectionist, artificial mega-state, when truly global markets were emerging'.[24] But her vision was to mark the start of a war of attrition that was to dominate her remaining three years in office. That war started just three weeks after her election victory when, with Howe at her side, she attended the Brussels Council on 29–30 June 1987.

Prior to the Council, Delors had written personally to every head of government, drawing attention to the parlous state of the Community finances. Thatcher's views were mixed. She strongly favoured tighter financial discipline and a curb on CAP spending, but felt the Commission's proposals were nothing like 'tough enough'. She was also profoundly irritated that the Commission's 'traditional answer' to any financial problem was to demand more money. When Delors linked his plans to changes to Britain's rebate, she suspected he was trying to whittle it away. And although the 'structural funds' increase was strongly backed by Ireland, Spain, Portugal and Greece, she hoped France and Germany might support her in rejecting it. Yet she opposed a 'blatantly protectionist' French proposal for an 'oil and fat' tax, designed to exclude US imports of oilseed, for which Britain was the largest customer.

The Brussels discussions started badly and got worse, bogged down in impenetrable detail. By the second afternoon, as the leaders sat round the uncleared lunch table, with the air conditioning having failed, Howe recorded that impatience grew as the temperature rose. When a vote was called, it was eleven to one for the package, blocked by Thatcher.[25] Inevitably, she was blamed for the Council's 'failure', although she thought the complexity of some of the matters under discussion was 'absurd'. It was unreasonable to expect that, with such a large number of contentious and complicated matters on the agenda, agreement would be reached on the first serious attempt.[26]

In September, three months before the Copenhagen Council, due on 4–5 December, Thatcher had private meetings with two of the main players in the coming drama, while she was in Berlin attending an IDU conference:

[24] Thatcher, op. cit., p. 728.
[25] Thatcher, op. cit., pp. 729–730.
[26] Ibid.

Jacques Chirac, Mitterrand's new prime minister, and Chancellor Kohl.[27] With Chirac, she had a working breakfast at the British Ambassador's residence. Kohl she was to meet later for afternoon tea in the German government guesthouse. She did not come away from either meeting any more optimistic about the likely outcome of the Council.[28]

At the previous Council in Brussels, Chirac had dismissively referred to Thatcher as 'a housewife', an epithet picked up by George Robertson, the Labour spokesman for Europe. Writing in *The Times* on the first day of the Copenhagen Council, he turned the 'Iron Lady' into 'the abrasive housewife'. 'Momentous issues' faced the EEC leaders, he wrote, but instead of dealing with them, they 'will swirl around in a sea of acrimony, bogged down in cereal prices, quotas and the minutiae of the EEC budget. And orchestrating that acrimony will be Mrs Thatcher, isolated and alone.' Asserting that: 'The bitterness she leaves in her wake now seriously threatens the British rebate,' he concluded: 'The violence of the rhetoric underlines the poverty of vision of the Prime Minister's approach to Europe.'[29]

Copenhagen fared little better than Brussels. British officials reported that: 'A build-up of intractable problems – with the French and the Germans on cereals, the southerners on their structural funds and the Italians on their fourth resource – made it obvious that there was no prospect of agreement at this Council.'[30] At Cabinet on 10 December, Thatcher remarked that Kohl and Mitterrand 'had not even been prepared to discuss the draft conclusions tabled by the Danish presidency'. Instead, they had wanted an agreement on 'general principles', even though these had already been agreed at Brussels, the previous June.[31]

Part of Thatcher's problem was that neither Kohl nor Mitterrand, both facing crucial elections at home, could afford to upset their farmers.[32] But it was not to get better. With no final resolution at Copenhagen, the leaders decided to hold an additional, special meeting in Brussels on 11–12

---

[27] The International Democrat Union, a forum for centre-right parties, formed in 1983. Thatcher had been a founder member, along with George Bush, Chirac and Helmut Kohl. Party leader meetings were held every three or four years.

[28] Thatcher, op. cit., pp. 730–731.

[29] *The Times*, 4 December 1987, p. 12.

[30] National Archives, PREM 19/2158.

[31] National Archives, CAB 128/87.

[32] Kohl had given very early warning of this. At the European Council dinner on 5 December 1986, he went so far as to buttonhole the Cabinet Secretary, Charles Powell. In a note to the prime minister, Kohl was recorded as having said: 'he hoped it was absolutely clear that there was no question of Germany being able to take major decisions on agriculture before his elections. He would not say this openly but he assumed he understood it', PREM 19/2154. The French presidential elections were to be held on 24 April (first round).

THE GREAT DECEPTION

February 1988, under the German presidency. The day before the event, Howe briefed the Cabinet, remarking that Chirac's conduct was 'difficult to predict'. He warned that there were 'a number of tactical issues that would have to be addressed by the Council'. For example, he said, 'at present, it was proposed, quite illogically, that the level of own resources should be discussed before agriculture'.[33]

After the event, Howe commented that, even by the standard of European Councils, it was 'a gruelling and bafflingly complex' negotiation. Agreement seemed to have been reached, but, as Thatcher recorded, 'anyone who imagined that it would all be plain sailing ... under-rated the French'. To general astonishment, Mitterrand and Chirac refused the deal, wanting to go back over ground that had been agreed at Copenhagen. Four hours of heated argument ensued. Eventually, the Danes suggested referring the final points of detail to a foreign ministers' meeting scheduled for 22–23 February. Thatcher agreed.[34]

No communiqué was published after the Council. The prime minister nevertheless reported to the Commons on 15 February that the meeting had 'concluded a major and far-reaching review of the Community's finances and policies'. There followed a welter of detail on 'stabiliser measures', price thresholds for agricultural commodities and the new 'guideline base'. Thatcher then reported that the Commission's proposal for the own-resources ceiling to be raised from 1.4 per cent of VAT to 1.4 per cent of GNP, equivalent to 2.3 per cent VAT, had been beaten down to 1.2 per cent GNP, an increase of some 25 per cent. This ceiling was expected to last until 1992, at the least. On top of this, there was more funding for the Community's structural funds – regional, social and agricultural. Up to 1992, they were to get an increase equivalent to 80 per cent over 1987, permitting a doubling of payments for less developed regions. However, the UK rebate had been kept intact and, Thatcher declared, 'the way is now clear for the Community to concentrate on its most important goal – the creation of a genuine single market by 1992'.[35]

Roy Hattersley, answering for the opposition, cited 'the ultra-loyal *Daily Telegraph*' describing the settlement as 'A British retreat on several fronts', with *The Times* warning that, even allowing for the vaunted rebate, Britain's net contribution would increase, thus forcing Thatcher to confirm that, for all her 'triumph', there would be an annual increase in contributions of £300 million.[36] In 'European terms', even when she 'won', she lost.

[33] National Archives, CAB 128/89.
[34] Thatcher, op. cit., pp. 736–737.
[35] HC Deb, 15 February 1988, Vol. 127, cc705-17.
[36] Ibid.

238

On 18 February, the prime minister herself reported to Cabinet, and received the congratulations of all present.[37] The next day, the Council presidency published an unusually long note, running to 44 pages, confirming the details of the settlement.[38] When the foreign ministers met on 22 February, business was quickly concluded. Howe was thus able to report to Cabinet on 25 February that the Council 'had been able to dispose quickly of the agenda'.[39] The budget crisis was over – for the time being. Delors was later to claim, though, that the increase in the structural funds was his most important single achievement.[40] It gave the Commission power to control substantial transfers of money within the Community – vital to the ultimate success of economic and monetary union.[41] Thus, in the final analysis, what Thatcher described as 'better than a draw' had turned out to be a major extension of integration.

AT ODDS WITH EVERYONE

In the summer of 1988, Trade and Industry Secretary Lord Young launched a major marketing campaign to sell the idea of '1992' and the completion of the Single Market. He used the slogan: 'Make no mistake: Europe is open for business'.[42] However, while the Single European Act was still being sold to the British people as a triumph for Thatcher, the 'colleagues' were planning the next stage in their agenda: the single currency. Lawson realised that it could only be a matter of time before a move was made to realise this objective.[43] To the fore, of course, had been Delors, backed by Mitterrand, whose motivation, according to Lawson, was no less than to seize 'the political and intellectual leadership of Europe which France regarded as her birthright'.

> That was threatened by the superior economic strength of Germany and, in particular, the Bundesbank, in the crucial field of economic policy. The only way the French could see of trumping the Bundesbank was to subsume it into a central bank responsible for a single European currency.[44]

[37] National Archives, CAB 128/89.
[38] https://www.consilium.europa.eu/media/20614/1988_february_-_brussels__eng_.pdf.
[39] National Archives, CAB 128/89.
[40] Delors, Jacques (1991), *Le Nouveau Concert Européen* (Paris: Odile Jacob), p. 81.
[41] Gren, Jörgen (1999), *The New Regionalism in the EU* (Stockholm: Fritzes Offentliga Publikationer), pp. 16–23. Not least of the 'new regionalism' approach was the insistence on multinational co-operation, bypassing member state central governments, thus breaking down national barriers. This process was given the name 'perforated sovereignty'.
[42] Young, Lord (1990), *The Enterprise Years: A Businessman in the Cabinet* (London: Headline), pp. 262–264.
[43] Lawson, op. cit., p. 901.
[44] Ibid.

Kohl, Delors' other co-conspirator, under the influence of his foreign minister, Hans-Dietrich Genscher, took the view that a strong Germany aroused too much fear for her to be able to exercise the political power and influence warranted by her economic strength. That strength had to be restrained. In a coincidence of interest with the French, therefore, he too saw merit in a single currency and a central bank, which would serve to reassure his neighbours that the German dragon had been tamed.

The opportunity for the triumvirate to pursue their objective came when Germany assumed the rotating Community presidency on 1 January 1988. The Germans let it be known that they would propose at the Hanover European Council, scheduled for 27–28 June, a committee of 'wise men' to pursue EMU and, in particular, the idea of a central bank. The decision was confirmed at the Council, the committee's task defined as one of 'studying and proposing concrete stages leading towards economic and monetary union'. It was to report in time for the Madrid Council in 1989.[45]

Delors was also formally proposed as the Commission president for an unprecedented second term. After his name had been put forward, Thatcher somehow found herself seconding him. Nevertheless, there was one casualty. Cockfield had tried Thatcher's patience too often. She replaced him with Leon Brittan, who went native even faster than Cockfield, and immediately started pressing Thatcher to join the ERM.

Curiously, Karl Otto Pöhl, head of the Bundesbank, was highly disconcerted by Delors' appointment to head the committee of 'wise men', seeing in it a move to a central bank. He 'raged' that Kohl had reneged on an agreement not to commit Germany to EMU, and, for a time, he considered resigning.[46] Also far from pleased was Lawson. When, the day after the Council, Thatcher conveyed to him her achievement in getting 'them' to drop all reference to the European central bank, Lawson told her she had achieved nothing: 'there is no way that a committee with those terms of reference can possibly do anything else than recommend the setting up of a European central bank,' he told her. To Lawson, as an unqualified opponent of monetary union, the Council had been a disaster. Of Thatcher, he felt that the very least she could have done was to have prevented Delors becoming the committee's chairman.[47]

The following day, when Thatcher was reporting on the Hanover Council to the Commons, Lawson was troubled by her apparent confusion

[45] https://www.consilium.europa.eu/media/20606/1988_june_-_hannover__eng_.pdf.
[46] Grant, op. cit., pp. 120–121.
[47] Lawson, op. cit., p. 903.

over what she had conceded. Neil Kinnock, as leader of the Opposition, reminded her that she had said many times that a European central bank was 'not on the cards'. Her reply was that monetary union would be the first step, but progress towards it 'would not necessarily involve a single currency or a European central bank'.[48] Lawson thought this answer 'mind boggling'.[49]

> Unlike economic union, monetary union had a clearly defined meaning, which had been established in the Community context by the Werner Report in 1970 and which I had spelled out to her on the eve of the 1985 European Council. Now she appeared to be implying that it meant something completely different and relatively trifling, even though she had not the slightest idea what that might be.[50]

Thatcher continued to reject the idea of a European central bank in her lifetime. As she told journalists in Italy in October, this could only mean 'surrendering your economic policy to that banking system'.[51] Lawson, however, could see the writing on the wall. When the Delors committee started work in September, he could read copies of the working papers emerging from it. It was only too clear that the committee and the UK government were on a collision course.[52]

There was something of Monnet in the way Delors worked. For his *rapporteur* he nominated an Italian economist who had long been an ardent advocate of a single currency. Then, he restricted the committee's terms of reference. It was not permitted to consider whether EMU was desirable, only how it could be made to work. Finally, he formed alliances with two enthusiastic supporters of a single currency: the governor of the Bank of Italy and a Danish professor of economics who had been co-opted onto the committee by Delors himself. The Commission president then arranged for his two allies to speak to his agenda during the committee sessions, thus enabling him to maintain the appearance of an independent chairman. Before each session, though, he had spent a day with them and other

---

[48] HC Deb, 30 June 1988, Vol. 136, cc525-35.
[49] Lawson, op. cit., p. 904.
[50] Ibid., One feature of the German presidency that pleased Lawson was France's agreement to abolish exchange controls. There was a hiccup when a new French finance minister argued that this would lead to a massive loss of tax revenues as savings flooded abroad. He proposed that all the member states should adopt a 15 per cent 'withholding tax' on savings. At the time nothing further came of this, but later events were to confirm that, once a proposal has been made in the Community, it never goes away.
[51] *Independent*, 22 October 1988, cited in George, op. cit., p. 193.
[52] Lawson, op. cit., p. 906.

advisers, debating tactics.[53] Small wonder Lawson was alarmed at what was being produced.

Delors was also busy elsewhere. On 6 July 1988, shortly after his second term as president had been confirmed, he had addressed the European Parliament at Strasbourg. There, he noted with satisfaction that the Community had 'taken more decisions in the previous six months than in the whole of the time from 1974 and 1984'. He told MEPs that he found it 'extraordinary' that most national parliaments had failed to realise what was going on. He went on to predict that in ten years, 'eighty percent of economic legislation, and perhaps our fiscal and social legislation as well, will be of Community origin'. His own feeling, he said, was that 'we are not going to manage to take all the decisions needed between now and 1995 unless we see the beginnings of a European government in one form or another'.[54]

Thatcher was outraged. She felt Delors had 'slipped his leash as a *fonctionnaire* and become a fully-fledged political spokesman for federalism'. The time had come, she decided, 'to strike out' against what she saw as 'the erosion of democracy by centralisation and bureaucracy' and to set out an alternative view of Europe's future. She commissioned a paper from her officials to spell out in precise detail how the Commission was now pushing forward the frontiers of its competences into all sorts of new areas, including culture, education, health and social security.

It used a whole range of techniques. It set up 'advisory committees' whose membership was neither appointed by, nor answerable to member states and which tended therefore to reach *communautaire* decisions. It carefully built up a library of declaratory language, largely drawn from the sort of vacuous nonsense that found its way into Council conclusions, in order to justify its subsequent proposals. It used a special budgetary procedure, known as *actions ponctuelles*, which enabled it to finance new projects without a legal base for doing so. But most seriously of all, it consistently misused treaty articles requiring only a qualified majority to issue directives which it could not pass under articles which required unanimity.[55]

Delors, was to pull off another coup. On 8 September 1988, he addressed the annual congress of the TUC in Bournemouth, selling them the

[53] Grant, op. cit., pp. 121–123; McAllister, op. cit., pp. 201–202.
[54] Publications office of the EU, Debates of the European Parliament, No. 2-367/138, 6 July 1988.
[55] Thatcher, op. cit., pp. 742–743.

'social dimension' of Europe. In what was clearly intended to be a highly provocative challenge to the very basis of Thatcherism, he told delegates that the internal market should be designed to benefit each and every citizen of the Community. Therefore, it was necessary to improve workers' living and working conditions, and to provide better protection for their health and safety at work.[56] Historically hostile to 'Brussels', the union delegates embraced the message with enthusiasm. Responding to Delors' closing words, 'Europe needs you', Ron Todd, general secretary of the Transport Workers' Union, told delegates there was not 'a cat in Hell's chance' of getting recognition in Westminster. The 'only game in town at the moment', he said, was in a town called Brussels. The game was 'poker' and the unions had to learn the rules very fast.[57]

Peter Shore later noted: 'It had a very remarkable effect on the trade union leaders. Reviled and rejected' by their own government, they had been 'treated with respect and welcome, even with affection, by the rulers of Brussels'. Thatcher's reaction, in the words of Charles Powell, was 'volcanic'. 'What really bugged her was seeing the president of the Commission trying to play a political role.' She did not realise at the time that the visit had been arranged with the assistance of her own Foreign Office. 'Somewhat cackhandedly', Lawson recalled, the FCO officials had thought this was a way of improving relations with the French.[58]

The FCO was also responsible, as it happened, for setting up a speaking engagement for Thatcher less than two weeks later, on 20 September 1988, in the Great Hall of the College of Europe in Bruges, the very heart of Eurofederalism. There she told her audience that there was no better place to talk about the future of Europe 'in a building which so gloriously recalls the greatness that Europe had already achieved over six hundred years ago'. To emphasise that, she talked about European civilisation in a rather larger sense, both historically and geographically, than the narrow sense in which the word 'Europe' had commonly come to be used.[59]

Emphasising the broad nature of the 'European identity', she went on, 'the European Community is one manifestation of that European identity. But it is not the only one.' She reminded her listeners that Europe in its proper sense also included the countries east of the Iron Curtain. 'We shall always look on Warsaw, Prague and Budapest as great European cities.' Moreover,

---

[56] McAllister, op. cit., p. 203; *Independent*, 9 September 1988.
[57] *The Poisoned Chalice*.
[58] Ibid.
[59] Thatcher Foundation website: https://www.margaretthatcher.org/document/107332.

she told her audience there were powerful non-economic reasons for the retention of sovereignty:

> Willing and active co-operation between independent sovereign states is the best way to build a successful European Community ... Europe will be stronger precisely because it has France as France, Spain as Spain, Britain as Britain, each with its own customs, traditions and identity. It would be folly to fit them into some sort of identikit European personality.[60]

In 'Europeanist' circles, both in Britain and on the continent, the reaction was one of 'stunned outrage'.[61] Howe was firmly among those who were 'outraged'. The picture of a Europe being 'ossified by endless regulations' was 'sheer fantasy', he felt. The Community trying to impose on Europe some kind of 'identikit' personality was a 'caricature'. To hold out as an alternative the idea that decisions should be taken simply through 'willing and active co-operation between independent sovereign nation states' showed that Thatcher clearly had no understanding of what the Community was about.[62]

This was the beginning of the end for Howe. To be working alongside Thatcher while she continued to act outwardly as if she were a committed leader of the Community, he now realised, was 'like being married to a clergyman who had suddenly proclaimed his disbelief in God. I can see now that this was probably the moment at which there began to crystallise the conflict of loyalty with which I was to struggle for perhaps too long.'[63]

LAWSON MAKES HIS MOVE

The speech made little immediate impact on the British public. In the closing months of 1988 and the first half of 1989, interest in 'Europe' was far outweighed by concern over domestic issues. Political news was dominated by worries over NHS reform and water privatisation, by the impending 'poll tax', and by the 'food scare' set off by junior health minister Edwina Currie over salmonella and eggs. Inflation was creeping up, house prices soaring. Thanks to Lawson, interest rates were high and rising. Thatcherism, heavily reliant on the property-owning classes, was running into the sand; and with it the popularity of her government.

With a new round of elections to the European Parliament due in June 1989, Heath launched a sustained attack on Thatcher, beginning with

---

[60] Thatcher, op. cit., p. 745.
[61] Ibid.
[62] Howe, op. cit., p. 537.
[63] Ibid., p. 538.

a speech delivered in Brussels when she was in the same city at a NATO conference. Referring to Bruges, he said that the British public 'reject such false popularism and such distortions of the truth for the patronising and self-serving hypocrisy that they are'.[64] Although the Conservative Party tried to exploit the Bruges speech, 'Europe' never really registered. The electorate made its judgement largely on domestic issues, giving Labour 40 per cent of the vote, against the Conservatives' 35 per cent. It was Labour's first victory over the Tories in a national election since 1974.

Meanwhile, battles of epic proportions on the European front were being fought, of the nature of which only a few were even aware. The location for one of those was the offices of the Bank of International Settlements in Basel, Switzerland, borrowed by the Delors committee. During its eight sessions between September 1988 and April 1989, the launch of the euro was being planned. Anticipating the worst, Lawson, with his officials, drew up a plan to tone down its recommendations. Key to this plan was Pöhl, robbing Delors of support from the Bundesbank. But Delors had anticipated this. He worked on Pöhl, using a mixture of flattery and persuasion, and then turned the central bankers' heads 'with the prospect of a new, Super-Bundesbank at European level. It would be totally independent of governments and consequently able to exercise a degree of power beyond the wildest dreams of many heads of government.'[65]

Instead of blocking monetary union altogether, as expected, Pöhl therefore merely insisted on certain conditions. He asked for a commitment that the ECB could not 'bail out' Community governments in financial difficulties; tight limits on the size of budget deficits that countries would be allowed to run; and that all central banks must be made independent before monetary union took place. Delors was happy to oblige.[66] By Pöhl's failure to stand firm, Lawson and his all-important ally in the Bank of England, Leigh-Pemberton, were left isolated.[67] Unwilling to be the odd man out, Leigh-Pemberton prepared to put his name to the final report. This did much to undermine Thatcher's opposition to monetary union.[68]

Lawson now started 'to prepare the ground for what seemed Britain's inevitable rejection' of the report. But his other key objective was to draw a clear distinction between the ERM and EMU. On 25 January 1989, therefore, he told an audience at Chatham House that, while monetary union meant

[64] *The Times*, 30 May 1989.
[65] Connolly, op. cit., p. 78.
[66] Ibid., p. 79.
[67] Lawson, op. cit., p. 908.
[68] Connolly, op. cit., p. 79.

handing over control of key economic decisions to a European central bank, ERM was 'an agreement between independent sovereign states'.[69] Even at this late stage, Lawson still failed to understand that his European colleagues regarded the ERM primarily as the first step towards monetary union – it was a 'glidepath' to monetary union, not an alternative. His strange inability to see the political dimension of the ERM is all the more inexplicable when contrasted with his aversion to EMU.

Reading his own account of those years, it seems as though there were two separate sides to his brain: one that could see the perils of EMU, and the other that saw only merits in the ERM, neither able to communicate with the other. In this respect, Lawson was simply suffering from that same delusion that has afflicted generations of British politicians, especially those in the senior ranks of the Conservative Party. They continued to believe that the Community's central purpose was to promote co-operation. It was not and never had been. The agenda was subordination. Failing to grasp this, Lawson continued in his attempts to lead the UK down the path to ruin, and with it, Mrs Thatcher.

Indeed, while Lawson was carrying out his lone battle against the Delors committee of 'wise men', his personal battle with Thatcher over the ERM was also coming to a head. As ever, he had the ready assistance of Howe. Thus, the three most senior members of the British government were divided on the issue. Thatcher and Lawson were opposed to the idea of a single currency. Howe and Lawson agreed that membership of the ERM was desirable to aid monetary stability. Thatcher alone was opposed to the ERM, while only Howe wanted Britain to join the single currency.[70]

When the Delors Report was ready, it was first presented to Community finance ministers on 17 April 1989. It recommended that monetary union should be achieved in three stages. First, all countries should join the ERM in what was known as the 'narrow band'. Stage two should see the establishment of the institutions necessary to run the currency, headed by the European Central Bank. Stage three, with exchange rates irrevocably fixed, would see the central bank taking over responsibility for monetary policy. Confirming Lawson's and Thatcher's worst fears, the report also insisted that, by embarking on the first stage, the Community would commit itself irrevocably to eventual economic and monetary union.[71]

---

[69] Lawson, op. cit., p. 910.
[70] Howe, op. cit., p. 534.
[71] *Report on Economic and Monetary Union in the European Community*, http://aei.pitt.edu/1007/1/monetary_delors.pdf.

In Lawson's view, the report affected the question of sterling's membership of the ERM in two important ways. First, it gave the ERM a new lease of life, but, more importantly, 'it also fatally confused the essentially economic question of the ERM with the fundamentally political argument over EMU'.[72] It turned the economic mechanism of the ERM into a political instrument. Yet Lawson still persisted in his delusion that the ERM was an economic measure, pressing Thatcher to join.

To pursue this aim, Lawson and Howe together hatched a scheme: an attempt to use the Dutch prime minister, Ruud Lubbers, to convince Thatcher of the merits of the ERM. It misfired, but he did at least inject a note that became Lawson's main argument: joining the ERM would greatly strengthen Britain's case in resisting the recommendations of the Delors Report. At a meeting between himself and Thatcher early in May, Lawson expanded on his theory of how entering stage one of a three-stage process would help resist being drawn into the next two stages. He wanted to argue with the Community that there was no need for monetary union, as the ERM would be sufficient.[73] Thatcher would have none of such naiveté. Equally, Lawson was not going to give way. The ERM had become a battle of wills.

Howe made the next move, 'innocently' suggesting to Thatcher that, before the Delors Report was presented to the forthcoming Madrid Council, he and his co-conspirator should send her a joint analysis of the economics and politics of the ERM, 'in the context of the new situation created by our need to respond to the threat of EMU'. Lawson doubted the value of this, and their paper went through several drafts, reflecting the difference of view between himself and Howe.

Headed 'EC Issues and Madrid', the final version ran to 12 pages of dense typescript, signed jointly by the conspirators.[74] They argued that 'if we simply said "no" to EMU at Madrid, the others would go ahead without us, creating a two-tier Europe, which would be damaging to us'. Therefore, Britain should join the ERM (stage one) but then try to postpone any progression to stage three. This was a classic Foreign Office ploy, arguing that we should go along with something we did not want because it was the only way to pre-empt something worse.[75]

It also reflected what was to become a prominent theme in Europeanist rhetoric: the use of such metaphors as 'missing the bus', 'missing the train',

[72] Lawson, op. cit., p. 913.
[73] Ibid., p. 915.
[74] National Archives, PREM 19/2665.
[75] Connolly, op. cit., p. 78, fn 6.

'travelling in the slow lane' and many other such clichés, all intended to convey that Britain would be missing out on something, inevitably with dire consequences. No one ever seemed to ask why it was so important to catch this bus, train or whatever, when its ultimate destination was so uncertain.

Nevertheless, that was the plan. 'If it could be achieved,' wrote Lawson in his memoirs, 'this would head off the intergovernmental conference and subsequent amendments to the Treaty on which the French were so keen. But we could turn the trick only if we convinced a sufficient number of others of our sincerity.'[76] So that was what it was all about: sincerity. To prove her 'sincerity', Britain should give a 'non-legally binding' undertaking to join the ERM by the end of 1992.

At least Lawson had the decency to feel unease. 'I had an innate distaste for cabals and plots, and had never been part of one', he wrote later.[77] With what seemed cautious regard for his own self-protection, he also insisted on some amendments to the 'minute' and, crucially, that it was delivered to Thatcher on Foreign Office paper. Howe agreed and it was forwarded to Number 10 on 14 June with a request for a joint meeting. Lawson records that Thatcher's reluctance to talk was 'extraordinary'. Grudgingly, she agreed to see the conspirators on 20 June, just six days before the Madrid Council.[78]

The meeting was not a success. Thatcher disagreed completely with the Lawson/Howe analysis and was totally opposed to any commitment to joining the ERM by a particular date. The conspirators got nowhere other than an agreement from Thatcher that she would not 'close her mind' and would reflect further on what had been said.[79]

Thatcher had meanwhile received a paper from her adviser, Professor Walters, suggesting that a series of virtually impossible conditions should be met before Britain joined the ERM.[80] When the thrust of this was conveyed to Howe by Charles Powell, he immediately contacted Lawson, who considered it 'palpably absurd': it was merely another delaying tactic.[81] Together he and Howe began plotting what Thatcher termed 'the ambush before Madrid', for which purpose they demanded another meeting. The three met at Chequers at 8.15 a.m. on the Sunday morning before Madrid. Howe and Lawson stood each side of the fireplace in Thatcher's study. Having prepared their tactics beforehand, Howe urged his boss to speak first at Madrid, setting out her

[76] Lawson, op. cit., p. 929.
[77] Ibid., p. 930.
[78] Ibid., p. 931.
[79] Ibid.
[80] Thatcher, op. cit., p. 709.
[81] Lawson, op. cit., p. 932.

conditions for joining the ERM and announcing Britain's date of entry. He and Lawson had even worked out a precise formula for her statement. As before, they stood by their argument that this would stop the Delors process from moving to stages two and three. Then came the bombshell. Unless she acceded to their demands, they would both resign.

Even though the loss of two senior ministers in one go would be highly damaging, Thatcher would not be blackmailed into a policy she thought wrong. She refused point-blank to undertake to set a date, but would reflect further on what to say at Madrid. So, the 'nasty little meeting' ended.[82] Five hours later, Howe and Thatcher met again in an RAF VC10 to Madrid. But they travelled in separate compartments, a drawn curtain between them. On arrival, they went separately to their suites in the Ritz Hotel. When they met again, their conversation was 'brittle and businesslike', with neither the ERM nor EMU being discussed.[83]

Monetary union led the Council agenda. Thatcher was expected to 'handbag' Delors, but she let others speak, keeping everyone in suspense, including Howe. When she spoke, she was calm, quiet and measured, telling the meeting, 'we should be pragmatic'. It was 'right to go for a staged approach to EMU and its analysis was invaluable'. Speaking very deliberately, she then declared: 'I can reaffirm today the United Kingdom's intention to join the ERM.' But she did not give a date. The timing was for her government alone.

The effect, Howe recalls, was 'electrifying'. At lunch, a number of 'colleagues' commended the 'new, strikingly calm presentation of a much more positive position'. Delors was delighted. Having escaped a 'handbagging', he congratulated Howe 'on having won the intellectual argument within the British government'. Howe too was pleased. Although Thatcher had avoided giving an entry date to the ERM, 'we had made an essential breakthrough', he wrote.[84] In the context of his warm relationship with Delors, there can be little doubt as to the identity of the 'we' to which he referred. It was not his own government.

Thatcher was dismissive of the whole issue. 'I was, of course, opposed root and branch to the whole approach of the Delors Report,' she wrote later, 'but I was not in a position to prevent some kind of action being taken on it.'[85] Her greater concern had been Delors' second project, which he was pushing hard: his 'Social Charter'. From the moment he had arrived at the Commission, this had been a pet project, balancing the Single Market, as

---

[82] Ibid.
[83] Howe, op. cit., p. 581.
[84] Ibid., p. 583.
[85] Thatcher, op. cit., p. 751.

he put it, with 'an effort to improve the lot of workers'.[86] Reminiscent of the Paris Summit and Willy Brandt's 'social union', he had promised trades unions a series of Community labour laws, whence the term 'Social Charter' emerged. Thatcher felt this to be 'simply a socialists' charter'.[87] But when it came to the vote, she was again on her own.

THE END OF HOWE AND LAWSON

Once back in London, Howe was high on the list of unfinished business. In a July reshuffle, he was demoted to Leader of the House and the non-job of deputy prime minister. With no very visible qualifications for succeeding him, John Major took over as foreign secretary. Thatcher thought this comparatively unknown figure would be more malleable. Nevertheless, the balance of her new Cabinet, with John Gummer and Chris Patten taking over agriculture and the environment, had slipped towards the Euro-enthusiasts. This, she mused, did not matter as long as crises that threatened her authority could be avoided. But, 'they came not in single spies but in battalions'.[88]

The first crisis erupted next door, at 11 Downing Street. Following the ultimatum on the eve of the Madrid Council, tension between Thatcher and her chancellor had not abated. Shadowing the deutschmark had caused interest rates to soar and, just before the Conservative Party Conference on 10 October, following a rate rise by the Bundesbank, they reached a record 15 per cent. The *Daily Mail* savaged Lawson as 'this bankrupt chancellor', demanding his resignation. Relations were not helped by a series of critical statements from Walters, prominently reported by a media keen on exploiting personal differences.

Feeling his job was being made impossible, Lawson had by 26 October decided that either Walters should go or he would.[89] When Thatcher preferred her adviser, he sent round his resignation letter. To her chagrin, Walters also insisted on resigning. For her replacement chancellor, Thatcher chose Major, drafting in Douglas Hurd, another long-time Euro-enthusiast, as foreign secretary.

Predictably, the markets reacted adversely. The pound fell two cents against the dollar within ten minutes of Lawson's resignation becoming public. A further two cents were lost by the New York close. There was a similar dive against the deutschmark, with the pound falling through the psychologically important DM 3 barrier, bottoming out at DM 2.90. The

[86] Grant, op. cit., p. 83.
[87] Thatcher, op. cit., p. 750.
[88] Ibid., pp. 758–759.
[89] Lawson, op. cit., p. 961.

next day's *Daily Mail* splashed its front page with: 'Thatcher Day of Disaster', while the *Mirror* screamed 'Thatcher in Crisis'. Only the *Sun* took a contrary view, with the succinct comment on Lawson: 'Good Riddance'.

That weekend, Howe gave a speech, described by Thatcher as 'of calculated malice', praising Lawson's courage for his fight to get Britain into the ERM. At least, she thought, his replacement 'had not got personal capital sunk in past policy errors'. However, she soon found that her chancellor – a former whip – favoured ERM entry as a way to reduce internal strains within the party. With a heavy heart, she conceded the point, but on EMU she remained immovable. This 'went to the heart not just of the debate about Europe's future but about Britain's future as a democratic, sovereign state'.[90]

It was to no avail. The day before he resigned, Lawson – at the behest of Thatcher – had finalised a paper on what became known as the 'hard ecu', an arrangement whereby all currencies of the member states should become legal tender throughout the Community. The theory was that the most popular currency would drive out the others, leading to de facto monetary union, without loss of sovereignty. It fell to Hurd, the new foreign secretary, to unveil this idea to the foreign ministers at their Council in Brussels on 26 October 1989. It was immediately seen as a diversionary tactic, scorned by the French finance minister as 'illusory and unacceptable'. The French prime minister, Michel Rocard, warned, 'Britain is like a slow ship in a naval convoy. Sometimes, for the good of all, the last vessel must be abandoned to its tragic destiny.'[91]

DIVERSION FROM THE EAST

In the autumn and winter of 1989, Europe was shaken by its greatest political event for decades: the collapse of the Soviet Union. The influence of this event on the nascent European Union was to be enormous, but the most immediate impact came from the fall of the Berlin Wall on 9 November. At once this opened up the prospect of a united Germany, bringing together 60 million West Germans with the 20 million in the east, to make what would be easily the largest, richest and most powerful nation in the Community. It was a prospect the rest of Europe viewed with alarm.

For Kohl, however, this was the opportunity of a lifetime. On 28 November he announced a hugely ambitious plan to bind the two Germanies in a confederation, preceded by free elections in East Germany and a massive infusion of aid. Every weak East German mark would be exchanged for

---

[90] Thatcher, op. cit., p. 719.
[91] *Time International*, 20 November 1989, p. 42.

a strong deutschmark. Significantly, Kohl had consulted none of his allies in Washington, Paris or London, or even his own foreign minister. Nevertheless, he insisted that Germany's reunification must be embedded in the 'European' process and that this 'enlargement' would require the Community to be strengthened further.[92]

France now held the presidency. At the Strasbourg Council on 8 December 1989, Mitterrand set the scene by declaring: 'Rarely has a European Council confronted such major issues.'[93] He seized the moment to insist on an IGC on economic and monetary union before the end of 1990. Thatcher, recognising that the Germans had aligned themselves with the French, knew she could not block this. She decided to be 'sweetly reasonable'.[94]

Another agenda item was Delors' Social Charter. On this, Thatcher refused to budge, reinforced by her discovery that the Commission was proposing no fewer than 47 initiatives, including 17 directives, in this area of policy. From a British point of view, she wrote, that effectively ended discussion on the Charter.[95] Equally, Thatcher remained utterly opposed to 'political union'. Once more she was placing herself in the firing line.

THATCHER CAPITULATES

The year 1990 started with a dramatic proposal from Delors. Confident that the integration bandwagon was rolling in earnest, he told the European Parliament on 17 January that the Conference, under a single chairman:

> should conduct two parallel sets of discussions, one on Economic and Monetary Union and its specific institutional aspects, the other on the remaining questions, including additional powers and political cooperation, to draw up a full blueprint for the Community of the future, even if it takes us a number of years, and to strengthen its institutional and political structure.[96]

Then, on 23 January, he told French television viewers:

> My objective is that before the end of the millennium Europe should have a true federation. The Commission should become a political executive which can define essential common interests ... responsible before the

---

[92] McAllister, op. cit., p. 215.
[93] Cited in *Time International*, 18 December 1989, p. 17.
[94] Thatcher, op. cit., p. 760.
[95] Ibid.
[96] *Official Journal*, Annex No. 3-385, Vol. 38, 19 February 1990.

European Parliament and before the nation-states represented how you will, by the European Council or by a second chamber of national parliaments.

For the first time, Delors had openly used the word 'federal'. He later told his biographer that this could not work unless the Twelve had first 'delegated important powers of sovereignty to the centre'.[97]

In March 1990, his position was reinforced when the European Parliament adopted an interim report produced by its vice-president, the British Socialist MEP David Martin, calling for a 'European Union of federal type'.[98] Again the Parliament was acting as a driver of integration. Then the Irish, as holders of the presidency, convened a special European Council on 28 April to discuss German reunification and political union. Just before this, on 18 April, Kohl and Mitterrand jointly published their own ideas, effectively supporting the Parliament in calling for 'political union' to coincide with EMU, on 1 January 1993. The two leaders also called on the Community to 'define and implement' a common foreign and security policy.

Thatcher had to concede that, to go with monetary union, 'political union' was logical. The combination ultimately implied a single government. However, she was particularly cynical about the prospects for a common foreign policy. She noted that Kohl and Mitterrand had sent a joint letter to the president of Lithuania urging him to suspend his country's declaration of independence to ease the way for talks with Moscow, without consulting the rest of the Community, let alone NATO.[99]

In May, France further muddied the waters when the foreign ministers met in Ireland. Roland Dumas, the French foreign minister, talked of changing the European Council from a periodic gathering of heads of governments to an institution with its own secretariat. He also suggested that the Council presidency should be strengthened by appointing a president from one country for several years, rather than the six-monthly rotation. This was an idea to which the French were to return. Meanwhile, Delors, fearing that this 'intergovernmentalism' might wreck his own plans, began to refer to the next treaty in terms of an *Acte Unique Bis* – A Single Act Part Two – emphasising the need for institutional changes in order to forestall French ambitions.[100]

[97] Grant. op. cit., p. 135.
[98] Luxembourg University archives.
[99] Thatcher, op. cit., p. 761.
[100] Grant, op. cit., p. 142.

The 25 June brought the Dublin European Council. Against Thatcher's wishes, it declared that two IGCs would start immediately after the October Rome Council. Meanwhile, a committee of national officials would carry out preparatory work on 'political union'.[101] For the rest, Mitterrand and Kohl indulged in grandstanding, proposing a billion-dollar aid programme for the Soviet Union. Thatcher was again cast in the role of objector, arguing that without fundamental market reforms, the money would simply be wasted in propping up a decaying political structure. For once Delors agreed. The plan was shelved.[102]

Meanwhile, with the prospect of East Germany becoming an integral part of the Community, Austria and Sweden had tabled applications to join, followed by Malta and Cyprus. Britain favoured their entry on the basis that 'widening' would prevent the 'deepening' of the Community. This was to become a constant refrain, but the Community stood firm. There would be no further enlargement until after the completion of the Single Market in 1992. As for the central European countries, Delors argued that it would take 15 to 20 years of preparation before they would be ready to join.[103]

Back in the UK, the Conservatives were having their own troubles. The poll tax had become the focus of growing discontent and in May the party had performed dismally in local government elections. This had lent strength to an emerging 'Thatcher must go' caucus, balanced only by what some pundits were calling the 'Keep Calm Party' headed by Major.[104] He would keep Thatcher as leader but take the country into the ERM and generally make friendlier noises to the Europeans.[105]

Instrumental in Major's conversion to the ERM had been Hurd, who courted his younger, less experienced colleague over a series of breakfasts at his London residence in Carlton House Gardens. Thatcher was again confronted by an alliance between her two most senior ministers. With Howe also sniping in the background, a glowering Lawson on the backbenches and the broadsheet newspapers all pushing for ERM, encouraged by *ex cathedra* statements from the now totally 'native' Leon Brittan, the prime minister was becoming increasingly beleaguered. One constant friend was her trade and industry secretary, Nicholas Ridley. But, in an unfortunate interview for *The Spectator*, he equated integration with giving up sovereignty to Adolf

---

[101] https://www.consilium.europa.eu/media/20562/1990_june_-_dublin__eng_.pdf.
[102] Thatcher, op. cit., p. 763; Grant, op. cit., p. 143.
[103] Grant, op. cit., p. 143.
[104] Watkins, Alan (1992), *A Conservative Coup: The Fall of Margaret Thatcher* (London: Duckworth, 2nd edn), p. 131.
[105] Ibid.

Hitler. Such was the outcry that he was forced to resign, leaving Thatcher without support in her own Cabinet. Elsewhere, on 30 July, she lost a long-time friend and political ally, when Ian Gow was murdered by the IRA.

A few days later, on 2 August, while Thatcher was in Aspen, Colorado, to give a lecture, news broke of the Iraqi invasion of Kuwait. President George Bush was in the same town and the pair met. Thatcher immediately urged the strongest possible response, stiffening his resolve by promising large-scale British military support. This did little to increase her domestic popularity; nor did it strengthen her position with her own Cabinet. The eyes of her colleagues were still fixed on Brussels.

In the manner of an infidel embracing Christianity under threat of painful death, Thatcher now accepted that Britain should join the ERM. This was announced by a jubilant Major on 5 October 1990, days before his party conference in Bournemouth. The joining rate was DM 2.95, later held by ERM apologists to have been 'too high' and the reason why Britain would be forced into a humiliating exit in 1992. But it was backed by Labour, the Lib-Dems, the trade unions and the CBI. The one person who was furious was Delors. By now, his main concern was to be free of his most formidable enemy: the one leader who could upset all his plans for the new treaty. Joining the ERM, he feared, might give her a political lifeline. Thatcher had to be removed, quickly.[106]

An opportunity was to hand. A European Council, scheduled for Rome in late October under the Italian presidency, was supposed to clear the decks of other business, notably the GATT talks. The Council could then move on to what were seen as the really big issues: the aims and organisation of the forthcoming IGCs.[107] The GATT talks involved 125 countries. Hailed as 'the biggest negotiating mandate on trade ever agreed', they had reached a critical stage in the so-called 'Uruguay Round' that had started in September 1986. They aimed to achieve a drastic further reduction in tariffs on industrial goods across the world, and to open up new areas to freer trade, including agriculture and services, increasing the world's annual income by over $200 billion.[108]

According to his biographer, GATT brought out the worst in Delors: 'uncontrollable emotion, a Gallic view of the world and a deep mistrust of the Anglo-Saxons'.[109] The term 'liberalise' meant reducing subsidies and

[106] Connolly, op. cit., p. 104.
[107] Ibid., p. 105.
[108] Sandiford, Wayne, 'GATT and the Uruguay Round' (www.eccb-centralbank.org/Rsch_Papers/Rpmar94.pdf).
[109] Grant, op. cit., p. 171.

preventing 'Europe' from dumping her agricultural surpluses on the world market. French farmers, predictably, were implacably hostile to the proposed changes.

It was a measure of how far Britain had surrendered her powers that, although she was the world's second-largest overseas trader, she no longer had a seat at these talks. Instead, the Community negotiated as a single bloc, with the Council hammering out its position from a welter of conflicting interests among the Twelve, then giving the Commission the mandate to undertake negotiations. Any deal had finally to be approved by the Council. Britain, Germany, Holland and Denmark generally supported 'liberalisation'. France resorted to obstruction at every opportunity. The Commissioner responsible for the negotiations was a Dutchman, Frans Andriessen, disposed towards flexibility, but he was often blocked by the Irish Agriculture Commissioner, Ray MacSharry. When disputes broke out between the pair, Delors did nothing to resolve them.[110]

THE ROCKIER ROAD TO ROME

By the summer of 1990, the Community's inability to reach a common view had brought negotiations to an impasse. The sticking point was the EEC's refusal to accept US demands for a drastic cut in agricultural subsidies. The GATT secretariat suggested a compromise, but, at a meeting in July with James Baker, the US Secretary of State, Delors threatened to resign rather than accept it.[111] Community trade and agriculture ministers had then met six more times, but, almost entirely due to French intransigence, failed to agree. Again, Delors did nothing. With final negotiations scheduled for Brussels in December 1990, time was running out. Thatcher was therefore insistent that the issue had to be discussed in Rome.

The 'little Europeans', obsessed with their own plans, would have none of it. Orders were given within the Commission that at all costs a planned report called *One Market, One Money* must be rushed out in time for the October Council.[112] The 341-page report, when it arrived, conveniently claimed that a single currency would save the Community about 0.25 per cent of GDP a year in transaction costs.[113] Then, on 21 October, the Commission issued its 28-page opinion on 'political union'. It had adopted most of the Parliament's proposals, including majority voting for foreign policy and the notion of 'European Union citizenship', going on to say that

---

[110] Ibid.
[111] Ibid., p. 172.
[112] Connolly, op. cit., p. 105.
[113] https://ec.europa.eu/economy_finance/publications/pages/publication7454_en.pdf.

the new treaty would not produce the final shape of the European Union 'but should leave the door open to developments in a federal direction'.[114]

Now the strands were coming together. Shortly before the Rome Council, the Christian Democrat group, led by Italian prime minister Andreotti, decided Thatcher must be ambushed. The Council would refuse to discuss GATT and focus instead on monetary union. The thinking was that Thatcher would be forced out into the open. Either she would agree, conceding the game, or, more likely, she would have to refuse, leaving the door open for a strike by her British opponents.[115] Thatcher was unprepared for what happened. At the Council on Saturday 27 October 1990, Andreotti made clear that he had no intention of discussing GATT. Thatcher railed against the decision, hoping others would intervene.[116] But it was in vain. After bad-tempered discussion about a proposal from Delors that the Council should support the Soviet Union by declaring that its external borders must remain intact, thereby denying independence to the Baltic states, the agenda moved on.

In an increasingly tense atmosphere, the 'Eleven' were determined to insert into the communiqué a statement on political union, which only Thatcher refused to accept. What they were proposing, she told them, pre-empted the conclusions of the IGC.[117] The 'Eleven' then demanded that stage two of monetary union must start on 1 January 1994, a year later than initially proposed. Thatcher could not agree to this either.[118] The trap had snapped shut. A bewildered Thatcher wrote: 'they were not interested in compromise. My objections were heard in stony silence. I now had no support. I just had to say no.' She repeated that 'no' to journalists outside, telling them: 'We have made it quite clear that we will not have a single currency imposed on us.'[119]

Back home on 30 October, Thatcher told the House what had happened, expressing her regret at the refusal to discuss GATT. Kinnock, however, jeered that 'her tantrum tactics' would 'not stop the process of change or change anything in the process of change'.[120] His intervention provoked a reply that included one of the most famous lines of Thatcher's premiership.

---

[114] Commission opinion of 21 October 1990 on the proposal for amendment of the Treaty establishing the European Economic Community with a view to political union, COM(90) 600 final. Brussels: Commission of the European Communities, 23 October 1990.

[115] Connolly, op. cit., p. 106.

[116] Thatcher, op. cit., pp. 766–767.

[117] The UK objections were entered into the Council conclusions as a series of footnotes, https://www.consilium.europa.eu/media/20554/1990_october_-_rome__eng_.pdf.

[118] Thatcher, op. cit., p. 767.

[119] Cited in Watkins, op. cit., p. 142.

[120] HC Debates, 30 October 1990, Vol. 178, cc869-92.

Delors, she retorted, had said that he wanted the European Parliament to be the democratic body of the Community. He wanted the Commission to be the executive and he wanted the Council of Ministers to be the senate. Her response was: 'No! No! No!'[121]

Another commentator who showed no interest in GATT was Howe. He could only caricature Thatcher's performance in terms of its 'reckless' and 'crude' nationalism, drawing cheers from the 'anti-Europeans' on her backbenches.[122] If all this was 'nationalist crudity', one suspects that he heard what he wanted to hear. Even his own emollient presence, Howe mused, 'was no longer restraining her dangerous anti-Europeanism'.[123] With that, he claims, he resolved to depart and set about drafting his resignation letter. If his resolve needed strengthening, the subsequent front page of the *Sun* might have helped, with its famous headline: 'Up Yours, Delors!'

THE END OF THATCHER

It was not so much Howe's resignation that caused a stir as his statement in the Commons afterwards. His fellow Europeanist, Vernon Bogdanor, of Brasenose College, Oxford, had advised him to make his 'resignation count, really count'. That meant, in Howe's view, making it clear that 'he could no longer share the prime minister's view of the right approach to the European question'.[124] In his peroration, phrased with feline craft, he explained to a silent House that:

> The conflict of loyalty, of loyalty to my Right Honourable friend the Prime Minister – and, after all, in two decades together that instinct is very real – and of loyalty to what I perceive to be the true interests of the nation, has become too great. I no longer believe it is possible to resolve that conflict from within this government. That is why I have resigned. In doing so, I have done what I believe to be right for my party and my country. The time has come for others to consider their own response to the tragic conflict of loyalties with which I myself wrestled for perhaps too long.[125]

Just as important as the words was the timing. Under the Conservative Party's rules, the annual leadership election was in the offing. Normally uncontested, it was to present Thatcher with her ultimate test. Waiting in

[121] Ibid.
[122] Howe, op. cit., p. 644.
[123] Ibid.
[124] Howe, op. cit., p. 661.
[125] HC Deb, 13 November 1990, Vol. 180, cc461-5.

the wings was Howe's ally and the chief pretender to the throne, Heseltine, who had been conducting an unofficial campaign for the leadership ever since he walked out of the Cabinet three years before. When Heseltine launched his bid, it plunged the parliamentary Conservative Party into turmoil. For days the media feasted on the spectacle of Tory MPs queuing to plunge their dagger into the back of the woman whose force of personality and conviction had dominated them for so long. Particularly conspicuous were three of the most fanatical 'Europeanists', who seemed permanently available to the cameras on St Stephen's Green to contribute their drops of poison to a receptive BBC: Emma Nicholson, Hugh Dykes and Peter Temple-Morris. All three of them would, within seven years, have defected to other parties.

After beating Heseltine by only 204 votes to 185 on the first round, Thatcher felt she had no option but to resign, which she did on 22 November 1990.[126] When the news came though, Heath rang his office with the gleeful admonition, 'Rejoice, Rejoice.'[127] He celebrated by buying his staff champagne.[128] However, Heseltine, the wielder of the knife, did not gain the crown. That went to Thatcher's preferred successor, John Major. Howe had achieved precisely what he had hoped for. On the last page of his memoirs, he reveals how he wanted: 'to change the policies, not the leader. But if that meant the leader had to go, then so it had to be. I have no regrets whatsoever about resolving the conflict of loyalty in that way, however deeply I regretted the necessity for having to do so.'[129]

Although Delors had longed for Thatcher's downfall, when it came his feelings were mixed. She had been a unifying force in the Community. But the Italians were 'triumphant'. They immediately set about preparing for the second Rome Council, hoping to give a decisive push to 'political union'.[130] Representing Britain would be Major, determined to be 'at the heart of Europe'. His own education was about to begin.

[126] She had advised the Cabinet that morning, which took note 'with profound sadness' of the prime minister's statement, National Archives, CAB 128/97.
[127] The words Thatcher used on hearing of the liberation of South Georgia on 26 April 1982.
[128] Campbell, John (1993), Edward Heath: A Biography (London: Jonathan Cape), p. 787.
[129] Howe, op. cit., p. 692.
[130] Grant, op. cit., p. 150.

11

'At the Heart of Europe': 1990–1993

My aim for Britain in the Community can be simply stated.
I want us to be where we belong. At the very heart of Europe.
John Major, Bonn, 11 March 1991

Now we've signed it – we had better read it!
Douglas Hurd, Maastricht, 7 February 1992[1]

When Major became Britain's prime minister, as the least experienced holder of the office since Ramsay MacDonald in 1924, he was faced by three immense challenges. The first was that his country was about to go to war: 50,000 British servicemen were assembling in the Gulf, under overall American command, for the liberation of Kuwait. The second was that Britain's economy had entered its sharpest recession since 1945. The 'Lawson boom' had pushed inflation to 10 per cent, its highest level for more than a decade, and unemployment was soaring. The conventional remedy would have been to lower interest rates, but the need to maintain the value of the pound at a level required by the straitjacket of the ERM had driven them to record highs, at one point reaching 15 per cent.

The third challenge was the Rome European Council, poised to launch the two IGCs in preparation for the Treaty on European Union. High on the agenda were two proposals Major knew he would have serious difficulty in persuading his party to accept: the single currency and Delors' 'Social Charter', granting workers' rights that threatened to overturn the reforms by which Britain had in the 1980s curbed the power of the unions. 'Europe', he was to say later, 'is a gut issue for the Tory Party;

---

[1] Jamieson, Bill (1994), *Britain Beyond Europe* (London: Duckworth), p. 72.

260

it runs very deep amongst people; they take a view very sharply one side or very sharply the other.'[2]

While Britain's attention was focused on the drama surrounding the downfall of Thatcher, the European Parliament had staged a joint meeting with representatives of national parliaments. Calls were heard for the Community to be remodelled as a 'European Union', centred on a single currency, and for a constitution. This would confirm the Commission as the executive in a government of Europe, with the Council of Ministers and the Parliament itself as the two houses of its legislature.[3] One result of this initiative – a hybrid between Spinelli's Draft Treaty of 1984 and ideas more recently advanced by Delors – was that it persuaded Britain's Labour Party to support monetary union, completing its conversion to the 'European' cause.

Douglas Hurd, retained as foreign secretary, made his own pitch for further integration with a speech in Berlin where he called for a 'distinct European role' in defence. The WEU, he suggested, should represent the Community in NATO. This encouraged Delors to argue that a 'common foreign and security policy' run on an intergovernmental basis would lead national governments to hand more powers to the Commission.[4] Another piece of unfinished business was GATT. On 7 December 1990, 2,000 delegates from 107 countries accounting for 85 per cent of world trade gathered at the Heysel conference centre in the outskirts of Brussels. Outside, 30,000 angry, placard-waving farmers denouncing cuts in agricultural subsidies were greeted by armed riot police and clouds of tear gas, prompting them to run amok, smashing cars and buildings.[5]

Yet again the Community refused to agree to more than a limited subsidy cut, and the talks collapsed. 'Never have such hopes been so brutally dashed,' said Australian trade minister, Neal Blewitt, representing 12 southern hemisphere countries that had formed the Cairns group.[6] Delors blamed the United States, the country he saw as taking the lead in trying to undermine the CAP.[7]

THE GULF THAT DIVIDES

At his very first Cabinet meeting as prime minister, on 29 November 1990, Major had included a very specific item on the agenda: 'Handling European

[2] Interview 19 May 1993, http://www.johnmajorarchive.org.uk/1990-1997/mr-majors-comments-on-the-maastricht-treaty-ii-19-may-1993/.
[3] Corbett, op. cit., pp. 299–300.
[4] *Independent*, 13 December 1990, cited in Grant, op. cit., p. 151.
[5] *Time International*, 17 December 1990, p. 42.
[6] Ibid.
[7] Grant, op. cit., p. 172.

Community issues'. The 'new boy', determined to put the acrimony of the Thatcher years behind him, told his colleagues that 'it would be important to seek alliances with other member states to a greater extent than hitherto and to be active from an early stage of the debate'. This required, said Major, 'a wide-ranging programme for making contacts with key people in the Community'.

To the approval of his colleagues, the new prime minister then insisted that the UK 'needed to maximise its influence in decision-making within the European Community'. A 'fresh look across the board' was desirable. However, in an alarming display of naiveté, he also declared:

> It was questionable whether the Commission should retain the sole right of legislative initiative. If a group of member states had a united view on an issue, they should be able to put it on the Community's agenda for discussion. On the other hand, there were some areas, notably agriculture, where giving a right of initiative to individual member states would lead to worse decisions, as compared with the present situation in which the Commission could exercise a degree of control.[8]

Major had a great deal to learn about how the Community worked.

On his arrival at Rome on 14 December 1990 for the European Council – another first as prime minister – his fellow leaders went out of their way to be friendly, as if to show that previous differences had been the fault of Thatcher. But it did not take long for the new boy to provoke Delors. That occasion came immediately after the Council, when the finance ministers started to explore their options for EMU, in the first of their two IGCs.

Delors expected them to welcome a draft treaty, largely written by himself, allowing the single currency to begin when eight members were in favour, with no country being obliged to join. This was less warmly received than Delors would have liked, not least because the Dutch and the French suddenly found praise for Major's 'hard ecu'. A petulant Delors stormed at what he considered Major's attempt to sabotage his project. In what was taken as a dark reference to the part he saw himself as having played in the overthrow of Thatcher, he threatened 'if we have to provoke another crisis, we will'.[9] However, Major had more pressing concerns than Delors' tantrums. The eyes of the world were on the Middle East, where, after the expiry of a UN ultimatum to Saddam Hussein to withdraw from Kuwait

[8] National Archives, CAB 128/97.
[9] Grant, op. cit., p. 151.

by 15 January, the US-led coalition two days later launched its spectacular assault.

The Gulf War had already created serious strains within the Community. Initially, 'Europe' had put up a common front, with France joining Britain in contributing to the coalition forces. Public opinion in member states, however, varied sharply. Eighty per cent of Britons and 65 per cent of the French thought the war justified, but in Germany 80 per cent were opposed. Banners fashioned from bedsheets festooned windows across the country, proclaiming 'War in the Gulf is genocide! No blood for oil!' Germany refused not only to commit any troops to the Gulf but even to support its NATO ally, Turkey, which feared incursions from neighbouring Iraq. This drew a sharp rebuke from the Turkish president, Turgut Özal, when it was discovered that German firms had supplied Iraq with materials for making chemical and biological weapons.

Just before the UN ultimatum was due to expire, on 14 January, Major met Mitterrand in Paris for an 'amiable and enjoyable discussion', only to find that two hours later French diplomats had launched a separate peace initiative through the UN, linking Iraqi withdrawal from Kuwait with a Middle East peace conference. Neither Britain nor America had been informed.[10] Major was furious and said so. When Britain and America blocked the French move, any semblance of a common European foreign policy was again in tatters.

No one was more sensitive to this than Delors. In early February, with the Middle East land war still raging, he had addressed the European Parliament with ironic understatement: 'Public opinion senses that Europe has been rather ineffectual,' he told MEPs. 'We will have to face up to that lesson.' On leaving the chamber, he raised his hand like a pistol to his head, pulling the trigger as a sign of his frustration.[11] Alan Clark, Major's junior defence minister, was more forthright. 'One of the great arguments of the people plugging the whole Euro-unity notion was that we were going to move into common military policy, common foreign policy and common financial policy,' he said, but at the first major test, 'they ran for the cellars'.[12]

In March, Delors produced his response. It was time, he said, for 'Europe' to 'shoulder its share of the political and military responsibilities of our old nations'. He proposed that the WEU should be reactivated as a Community

[10] Major, John (1999), *John Major: The Autobiography* (London: HarperCollins), pp. 231–232.
[11] *Time International*, 11 February 1991, p. 46.
[12] Ibid.

institution, with its own multilateral forces: an embryonic European army.[13] To him, the Community's divisions had become a 'beneficial crisis' to justify further political union. This was 'the lesson of the Gulf War' he told an American journalist: 'its heart, its motor is the desire to shape a joint foreign and security policy'.[14] France and Germany endorsed the idea that the European Council should co-ordinate Community defence policies, with the WEU becoming the 'European pillar' of NATO.[15]

In the wake of the successful liberation of Kuwait, Major took an opportunity to rebuild relations with Germany. After meeting Kohl in late February, when he was invited to review a German guard of honour, he returned to Bonn on 11 March to give a lecture, organised by the British Ambassador and attended by Kohl. This was Major's moment to seize the initiative, outlining 'his vision of a free-market Europe, based on nation states, open to the new democracies of the east, a bulwark of peace as well as an engine of prosperity'.[16] The key word was 'co-operation': the code-word for doing business outside the 'straitjacket' of the Brussels institutions.[17] With this in mind, Major proclaimed what was to become the most familiar expression of how he wanted to see Britain's relations with 'Europe': 'My aim for Britain in the Community can be simply stated. I want us to be where we belong. At the very heart of Europe. Working with our partners in building the future.'[18]

Yet, this was the complete antithesis of the Community method. It harked back to those post-war days when Britain had so fervently embraced intergovernmentalism through the Council of Europe and the OEEC. Now, after the GATT fiasco, where the Community had shown itself the very opposite of a free-market organisation, and the Gulf War where it had shown itself so split, the idea of 'partners' working together in harmony was either wildly optimistic or profoundly self-deluding. Major was heading for direct conflict with Delors, the high priest of supranationalism.

Such was Major's innocence that he thought that his ambition to be 'at the heart of Europe' was an 'unexceptional objective'. He soon realised his error. 'Few sentiments in recent British political history', he was to write, 'have provoked such havoc or been so misrepresented.' To Eurosceptics at home, his ambition was seen as unabashed 'federalism'. Despite this, Major

[13] Grant, op. cit., p. 186.
[14] *Time International*, 22 April 1991, p. 24.
[15] Grant, op. cit., p. 186.
[16] Hogg, Sarah and Hill, Jonathan (1995), *Too Close to Call: Power and Politics – John Major in No. 10* (London: Little, Brown and Company), p. 78.
[17] Ibid.
[18] Major, op. cit., p. 269.

was determined to bring his own proposals to the IGC at Maastricht, since he 'didn't like what was on offer'.[19]

At that point, the Council presidency was held by tiny Luxembourg. A special European Council was convened on 8 April to discuss what was scathingly described by Belgium's foreign minister as a situation where the EC had shown itself to be 'an economic giant, a political pygmy and a military larva'. At the centre of the discussions was a common foreign and defence policy, but the only immediate outcome was an initiative by Major to create a UN 'safe haven' in northern Iraq, to protect hundreds of thousands of Kurdish refugees displaced by the Gulf War.

The main task of the Luxembourg presidency was to co-ordinate the proposals for the two IGCs. From over two thousand pages of submissions emerged a 'global draft' that, in the arcane vocabulary of the Community, was called a 'non-paper'.[20] Its proposal was a highly radical innovation: the new 'European Union' should rest on what were called three 'pillars'. The first, 'Community pillar', would be based on an extended version of the existing treaty. It would be concerned with the Community's core activities, with the Commission playing its classic supranational role. The other two 'pillars' would establish a wholly new legal framework, separately to cover foreign affairs and internal security. These would be handled on an intergovernmental basis.

The European Council considered the draft in Luxembourg on 28–29 June. It concluded that it formed 'the basis for the continuation of negotiations, both as regards most of the principal points and the state of play at the two Conferences', on the understanding that 'final agreement by the Member States would only be given to the Treaty as a whole'.[21]

Just before the Council, Westminster MPs discussed the draft in an adjournment debate. It was notable for Hurd's rejection of the idea that all European co-operation should ultimately be channelled through the institutions established by the Treaty of Rome. 'We do not accept such a model,' he said. When it came to areas such as foreign and security policy or the work of interior or justice ministers, 'there is nothing intrinsically more European about channelling all co-operation through the institutions of the Community rather than proceeding, where it makes sense, through co-operation between Governments directly accountable to national

[19] Ibid.
[20] Luxembourg University archive,
https://www.cvce.eu/en/obj/projet_de_traite_sur_l_union_de_la_presidence_luxembourgeoise_luxembourg_18_juin_1991-fr-dbebd2a6-a860-4915-8edf-0a228ecde976.html.
[21] https://www.consilium.europa.eu/media/20528/1991_june_-_luxembourg__eng_.pdf.

Parliaments'.[22] Before these ideas could be addressed, however, EU leaders were diverted by a grave new crisis, one that was to expose the Community's pretensions.

THE YUGOSLAV DEBACLE

On 25 June 1991, two small nations, Slovenia and Croatia, declared their independence from the Federation of Yugoslavia. Tensions between the seven nations making up Yugoslavia had been mounting ever since 1987, when Slobodan Milošević had gained control of the Serbian Communist Party, the ruling group in the Serb-dominated federation. As Communism crumbled across central Europe, the peoples of Slovenia and Croatia prepared to break loose from the Belgrade government, to set up free, democratic states on what they imagined was the western European model. Belgrade's response on 27 June was to order the Yugoslav People's Army (JNA), into Slovenia to put down the 'rebellion' by force.

As news of the fighting in Slovenia reached the Council, it was greeted as an almost heaven-sent opportunity to put the 'common foreign policy' in action. The Council immediately sent three of its number to mediate. This 'troika' – the structure agreed in 1981 – was led by Jacques Poos, Luxembourg's foreign minister. He was joined by Italy's foreign minister, Gianni De Michelis, the most recent past-president, and Hans van den Broek, chosen because Holland was about to take over the presidency.

For Poos, 'the hour of Europe' had dawned. In full flow, he crowed: 'If one problem can be solved by the Europeans, it is the Yugoslav problem. This is a European country and it is not up to the Americans. It is not up to anybody else.'[23] With the internal strains now breaking Yugoslavia apart, the Council of the Commission on Security and Cooperation in Europe (CSCE) met in Berlin on June 1991, where ministers declared their support for the 'territorial integrity of Yugoslavia'.[24] In late June, the troika met two of the major protagonists, Ante Marković, the Yugoslav prime minister, and Serbian president Slobodan Milošević. Poos conveyed the support of the European Council and, reflecting the CSCE phraseology, called for 'the preservation of the unity and territorial

---

[22] HC Deb, 26 June 1991, Vol. 193, cc1007-91.
[23] Almond, Mark (1998), *Europe's Backyard War: The War in the Balkans* (London: Heinemann), pp. 31–57.
[24] CSCE Council, Berlin 19–20 June. Statement on the situation in Yugoslavia, in *Summary of Conclusions*. The CSCE had been founded in 1973, a non-treaty organisation started to promote security and co-operation between East and West. It came into its own during the break-up of the USSR, but became a major player during the Yugoslav crisis.

integrity of Yugoslavia'.[25] Without equivocation, the preservation of Yugoslavia as a state was the initial policy of the Community.[26]

The Council was simply unable to grasp why the peoples of Slovenia and Croatia would do anything to break away from the tyranny of Belgrade, which had held them in its grip since 1945. Since the whole purpose of this Council was to discuss building a new federal government for 'Europe', the Twelve could hardly be expected to welcome the idea of another federation collapsing.[27] Luxembourg's prime minister Jacques Santer, speaking as president of the European Council, reflected the general view when he told journalists: 'We have to try all means to save the Federation.' Even Major joined in, saying, 'the great prize is to hold the federation together'.[28]

So opened the first stage of a tragedy that was to cast a shadow over Europe for 11 years. In the first Act, the troika flew to Yugoslavia in their role as mediators. The peoples of Slovenia and Croatia decked their streets and villages with 'ring of stars' flags, imagining that envoys of the European Community were coming to support their wish for freedom, democracy and self-determination. When the three arrived in Belgrade on 28 June, however, their only purpose was to reassure the Federal authorities of their desire to see Yugoslavia held together. Already the Community had agreed to give the Federal government a huge loan of 700 million ecus. As Poos himself put it, 'the idea of national self-determination is dangerous as a basis for international order ... It would release an explosive development.'[29] He poured scorn on tiny Slovenia's aspirations to survive as an independent nation, even though its population was six times greater than Luxembourg's.

With that, the troika demanded that Slovenia should revoke its declaration of independence as a condition of a ceasefire, unaware that the Federation had already reconciled itself to Slovenia's secession. At midnight on 30 June, the moment when the EC presidency passed to Holland, van den Broek, now leader of the troika, raised a glass to the Federal politicians with whom he was sitting in Belgrade, pledging EC support for Yugoslavian unity.

By then, the Federal authorities had already lost control of the JNA in Slovenia, which was now running amok. As television pictures of the

---

[25] Rapport de la mission de la troïka ministérielle en Yougoslavie (1er juillet 1991) (Gouvernement luxembourgeois) (sous la dir.). Coopération politique européenne – Recueil semestriel des textes agrées par les Douze au titre de la coopération politique européenne pendant la présidence luxembourgeoise (1er Janvier–30 Juin 1991). Tome 1. Luxembourg: 1991, p. 204.
[26] Almond, op. cit., p. 42. Britain's Douglas Hurd proposed that the Community should look forward to welcoming the Yugoslav federation as a member.
[27] Ibid.
[28] Ibid., p. 33.
[29] Ibid.

fighting dominated the weekend news, cracks in the EC façade began to appear. On 3 July, Hurd told the Commons that the conflict appeared to be escalating 'out of control'. He conceded that 'it may no longer be possible to hold the whole country together'. Without apparent irony he declared, 'We have learnt that one cannot suppress nationalist feeling or force it into a framework against which it revolts.'[30]

On 4 July, the EC ministers convened a summit between the Serb and Slovene leaders on Brioni, Tito's luxury island retreat in the Adriatic. The intention was to broker a peace deal, but the Serbs and Slovenes had already made their own. The troika was 'kicking at an open door'. The 'Brioni Agreement' on 8 July, in effect, marked formal acknowledgement of the break-up of Yugoslavia.

Hailed as a triumph for 'European' diplomacy, the agreement was anything but. Not only did it leave the major issue of Slovenia's sovereignty unresolved; it opened the way for the JNA, now effectively a Serb army, to turn on Croatia, which, in April, had formed the Croatian National Guard (ZNG). By August, just when a popular coup in Moscow was marking the fall of Gorbachev and the imminent collapse of the Soviet Union, Serb artillery units were bombarding the Croatian town of Vukovar, followed by the even bloodier siege of Osijek, inflicting thousands of military and civilian deaths.

Nevertheless, the European Community continued its futile efforts at mediation, not least with a conference that opened on 17 September, chaired by Britain's former foreign secretary Lord Carrington. This aimed to create a new Yugoslavia in the form of a 'union of sovereign republics'.

By now, it was clear that the EC's intervention had been a shameful fiasco. On 25 September, the UN intervened, with a Security Council Resolution placing an arms embargo on the whole of the former Yugoslavia. On 8 October the UN Secretary-General appointed Cyrus Vance, once US Secretary of State, as his personal envoy to 'former Yugoslavia'. The tragedy still had years to run. But the idea that the European Community could play an effective part in its humane resolution had already been dispelled.

COUNTDOWN TO MAASTRICHT

Compared with such tumultuous events, the efforts of the 'little Europeans' to construct their next treaty might have seemed trivial. But they were not. The Commission's endeavours, currently under the tutelage of Delors, and the persistence of member states, driven by the Franco-German motor of

[30] *Hansard*, 4 July 1991, col. 328.

integration – most recently under the leadership of Mitterrand and Kohl – were now coming to a climax.

The agenda so confidently proclaimed at the Paris Summit in 1972 nearly twenty years previously, with its ambition to create a 'European Union' by 1980 bound by economic and monetary unions, all tied into a 'Social Europe', had been delayed. Spinelli's original plan for a 'Treaty of the European Union' had been diluted by Mitterrand in the interests of expediency, whence the integrationists had been content with their 'smiling mouse' of the Single European Act. But now the agenda was back on the table and hopes were high. Of one thing it could be reasonably certain: the new British prime minister had no clear idea of what he was confronting nor, at the conclusion of the Maastricht Summit, of what precisely he would be asked to agree.

It would not have helped Major's focus on the real issues when, in the run-up to Maastricht, the agenda was bogged down in a welter of excruciating detail that only European politics seemed to be able to produce. So far, it had been agreed at the Luxembourg Council that no country could be compelled to join economic and monetary union. Britain was safe in that respect, although she could not stop the project. Thus, Major at the summit would be focusing on the UK's 'opt-out', rather than *les grandes lignes* of which Roy Jenkins had been so fond.

The situation was further confused when, in September, the Council presidency was in the hands of the Dutch. They produced another version of the proposed treaty, one that could not have been more integrationist. It proposed a unitary structure for the proposed European Union, and brought foreign policy and internal affairs into the supranational maw of the Community. Fortunately for Major, he was not alone in his objections. The draft met with outright hostility from every country except Belgium, even France and Luxembourg, the latter taking offence because its own draft had been so unceremoniously dumped. The Dutch had no option but to revert to the Luxembourg text, proceeding with specific changes on an issue-by-issue basis. Despite two further foreign ministers' meetings in November, no agreement on a final text was reached.

Even with what was left, Major was still dismayed. Quite apart from his refusal to accept a single currency, there was also the 'Social Chapter'.[31] He felt this would reverse Conservative reforms to the labour market and increase unemployment. As regards foreign and home affairs, he was also adamant that these policy areas should not 'come under the control

---

[31] Major, op. cit., p. 271. As part of the new treaty, the 'Charter' became the 'Social Chapter'.

of Brussels'. Nor would he accept a Commission role in defence policy. As he put it later: 'It was evident that we were bound to play the abominable no-men in the negotiations, and that we would face a domestic cacophony of conflicting advice.'[32] That 'conflicting advice' was already becoming vocal from within his own party, not least from Thatcher, whose every whisper was passed on to the waiting media.[33]

To flush out parliamentary opposition, Major decided to hold a Commons debate on 20–21 November. It was a risky, but, if the Commons backed his position, this would lend weight to his negotiating stance at Maastricht. However, if it was an act of courage, it was also, according to an analyst who studied the Eurosceptic movement, 'an act of deception':

The motion was very weak and almost impossible to oppose unless MPs subscribed to the hard-line sceptical position. Major's commitments were remarkably open-ended, carefully constructed to allow him the maximum flexibility in finding a means to agree British support for the treaty. He also talked up his government's opposition to commitments that were neither in the draft treaties nor even a likely outcome. And he was vague on issues which still had to be decided.[34]

Reading the debate, which in *Hansard* ran close to 120,000 words, the length of a sizeable novel, it is hard to detect the passion that was to dog the later debates. The single currency was the chief preoccupation, mentioned 233 times, with 'federalism' getting 152 mentions and 'sovereignty' 113. However, it was also a debate that showed all three major parties in favour of a treaty of some kind, even though Labour and the Liberal Democrats were keener on the single currency. None of them seemed aware of the underlying integrationist agenda – those pesky *grandes lignes*.

A significant contribution came from Thatcher in one of her last appearances in the Commons. Picking up on a suggestion from Tony Benn that there should be a referendum on the single currency, she pointed out that if, in future, all three major political parties should agree to monetary union, the British people would have no say in the matter.[35] The constitutional implications would be so serious, she argued, quoting the great constitutional authority Dicey, that there should be a referendum. Otherwise, they would have no chance to pronounce on whether fundamental rights should be

[32] Ibid.
[33] Ibid., p. 274.
[34] Forster, Anthony (2002), *Euroscepticism in Contemporary British Politics* (London: Routledge), p. 97.
[35] HC Deb, 21 November 1991, Vol. 199, cc436-528.

taken away 'not only from them but from future generations, and which, once gone, could not be restored'.[36] 'We should let the people speak,' she concluded. Hurd, Kenneth Clarke and Michael Portillo disagreed.

If MPs were uncertain about what was to happen at Maastricht, they at least had that in common with Delors. Addressing the European Parliament on the same day as the second half of the Commons debate, he declared that the Dutch-brokered final draft of the treaty, due to go before the heads of government at Maastricht, was unworkable and 'crippling'. He was worried about the intergovernmental pillars. Because of the 'likelihood of politicians and bureaucrats striking deals behind closed doors,' he said, these components 'will pollute the European Community and roll it back'.[37] The plan for the EC to manage external economic relations and for member states to run foreign policy would lead to 'organised schizophrenia', he warned.[38]

Delors wanted all parts of the treaty to be brought into a 'single institutional framework', run by the 'Community method', with his Commission at the centre. But he found no backers. To compound his woes, his own headquarters in Brussels, the Berlaymont complex, had to be closed down, after 1,400 tons of asbestos in the building were ruled to be dangerous. More than three thousand displaced officials had hurriedly to be evacuated and re-housed across the city. Boris Johnson, then Brussels correspondent for the *Daily Telegraph*, was later to report that the building was to be blown up.[39]

MAASTRICHT: THE BIRTH OF EUROPEAN UNION

As the motorcade carrying Major and his colleagues arrived in the suburbs of the Dutch city of Maastricht on Sunday 8 December 1991, it was by no means clear that the integrationists would prevail. Delors had been addressing 'a thousand flag-waving, foot-stamping federalists' in the town square, in a last-minute appeal to the 'peoples of Europe', telling them: 'We have been focusing too much on a country which has said no, no, no!'[40] Major and his team admitted to 'low morale' and he put the chances of achieving an acceptable agreement only at 50/50. Politically, the position he faced was 'dire'. All he could achieve was a series of blocking moves that would reduce the effect of any new agreement on the UK. But he could not

[36] Ibid.
[37] Grant, op. cit., p. 197.
[38] Ibid., p. 198.
[39] Repeated in the *Guardian*, 14 July 2019. 'How Boris Johnson's Brussels-bashing stories shaped British politics', which noted that, three decades on, the building was still standing.
[40] Ibid., p. 200.

stop the treaty. If he tried, huge ill-will would be caused on the continent and his party at home would be split.[41]

That Sunday evening, as Major and Hurd were meeting with Ruud Lubbers, the Dutch prime minister who was to chair the summit, news broke that Boris Yeltsin, Russia's new president, had joined with the leaders of the newly independent Ukraine and Byelorussia to declare 'the Soviet Union has ceased to exist'.[42] It was curious that, just when one 'Union' had finally collapsed, Europe's politicians should be gathering to create a new one.

Next morning the summit convened in the Provincienhuis, an austere modern structure recently erected on 'Government Island' in the River Maas. Across the water, several thousand bored journalists waited for any titbits of news that might emerge from the conference room. Sealed from the outside world, the leaders assembled around the table were dominated by the 'big players', Kohl and Mitterrand, with Delors brooding in attendance but not permitted to contribute directly. The journalists, at least, were fortunate in not having to be present at the summit sessions. Possibly, if there was one thing more tedious than reporting these events, it was attending them. Despite his determination to be a conciliatory 'new broom', Major found himself at odds on EMU, which Kohl wanted in place by 1996 to 1997. Wilfried Martens of Belgium then wanted a common defence policy in the treaty, without a national veto, which would effectively mean that no country could act independently.

On the second morning, having worked through the night, the Dutch presidency presented its draft conclusions. Major and his team were horrified. Thanks to Belgian pressure, the intergovernmental 'pillar' structure was now to be regarded as a mere transitional stage, before its policy areas were handed over to full 'Community competence'. There was also the Social Chapter, the item that topped the day's agenda. The Dutch had only made minor concessions to the British, and when Mitterrand objected even to these, the rest supported him. Major was again on his own, but here he had no opt-out, leaving him forced to reject the Social Chapter. When Mitterrand countered that, without it, he would block the entire treaty, the issue was deferred for bilateral talks.

Meanwhile, there was drama elsewhere in the building, where, at a parallel meeting of finance ministers, the British unveiled the opt-out they were demanding on stage three of EMU, the single currency. Drafted in full legal form, this specified all the articles of the treaty that would not apply to the UK.

---

[41] Major, op. cit., p. 276.
[42] Cited in Major, op. cit., p. 277.

It was 'non-negotiable'.[43] As the hours dragged on in the main meeting, Lubbers even refused refreshment for the heads of government, assuming that this would speed consent. Gradually, agreement was reached on all outstanding points, until the only item left was the Social Chapter. Discussion took six hours, with Major doggedly refusing to allow it into the treaty. Unanimity it had to be, and 'eleven to one', as Major pointed out to a pleading Lubbers, was not unanimity.[44]

Eventually, the issue was resolved by a classic fudge. Lubbers proposed an agreement outside the treaty that would apply only to the Eleven, but with a protocol allowing Community institutions to be used for its implementation. By this formula, British Commissioners could take a hand in framing legislation under the Chapter and British MEPs could vote on it, but Britain would take no part in Council decisions and they would not apply in the UK. For Major, it was a real achievement.

His other achievement was to refuse Community control over immigration. A common form of visa had been agreed and Britain had already accepted the list of countries whose citizens must apply for them, including those of the Commonwealth, such as Australia and New Zealand. Furthermore, in 1990, Britain had already signed the Dublin Convention, an agreement for dealing with asylum seekers. It was due to come into force in September 1997 and would cause the UK immense problems. But Major would not accept Community control over who was or was not allowed to immigrate to Britain. The point was not pressed.[45]

On the Wednesday at 1.30 a.m., negotiations finally ended. For Delors, his major success had been the single currency. The treaty established a firm legal foundation and a timetable for its introduction, as well as setting up a European Central Bank (ECB). Rules were set out limiting government budget deficits to 3 per cent of gross domestic product (GDP) and overall government debt to 60 per cent of GDP (the so-called Maastricht criteria), together with an excessive deficit procedure.[46] There were also provisions to sanction defaulting states. Crucially, the treaty added a so-called 'no-bailout clause', which specified that member states would not be liable for, or assume, the commitments or debts of another member state.[47]

As for Major, he had succeeded in getting his opt-outs. But a huge amount had been conceded. For the first time, written into the treaty were common foreign, security and defence policies, and 'co-operation'

---

[43] Ibid., p. 284.
[44] Ibid., p. 287.
[45] Hogg and Hill, op. cit., p. 155.
[46] Originally Article 104c and Protocol 5, repeated in subsequent treaties.
[47] Article 104b.

on 'justice and home affairs'. The member states undertook to support 'the Union's external and security policy actively and unreservedly in a spirit of loyalty and solidarity'. And, in a declaration appended to the treaty, the WEU was recognised as 'an integral part of the development of the Union'. To all intents and purposes, it was now a Community institution.

In addition, the 300 million inhabitants of the Community, like it or not, became 'citizens of the European Community'. They would be allowed to participate in local and European Parliamentary elections, as voters or candidates, anywhere in the Community and would have a Parliamentary Ombudsman. There would also be a Court of Auditors to report on Community finances. In a major extension to the 'structural funds', necessary for the workings of the single currency, the treaty set up a 'cohesion fund', to transfer money from richer countries to poorer. A new Committee of the Regions would be established, made up of representatives from the Community's 111 'regions', which would have to be 'consulted' on legislation. The ECJ was given power to levy fines on member states that failed to implement its rulings.

The treaty had also greatly extended the areas of Commission 'competences', along with an extension of qualified majority voting to 30 more areas of policy – despite UK opposition.[48] Added to those already ceded under the Single European Act were 'broad economic guidelines', social policy, public health, consumer protection, telecommunications, energy, education, culture, vocational training and transport, including measures relating to the 'trans-European network'. There were also major extensions of Community control over environmental law, including, for the first time, 'town and country planning' and 'measures which significantly affect a member state's choice between different energy sources'.[49]

A final part of the treaty introduced the principle of 'subsidiarity'. Destined to become a major point of contention, this amounted to an agreement whereby the Commission would only take action in areas of policy where it did not already have exclusive competence, when it was considered that this could be done more effectively at 'Community' rather than national level.[50] As Major was to find out, this was as meaningless as it was obscure.

Such was the complexity of the overall treaty, however, that not even Major knew in detail what he had committed his government to signing. In the early hours of Wednesday, his first task was to instruct his officials to summarise

[48] In Cabinet on 5 December, Hurd told colleagues that, at a conclave of foreign ministers on 2–3 December, he and the Danish foreign minister 'had opposed majority voting in any form'. See National Archives, CAB 128/100.
[49] Cowgill, Anthony (1992), *The Maastricht Treaty in Perspective: The Consolidated Treaty on European Union* (Stroud, British Management Data Foundation), pp. xvii–l.
[50] Cited in Grant, op. cit., p. 203.

the 'bull points', as a guide to what had been agreed. It was to be months before a full printed version of the treaty became available. Even then, because so much would be shown only as 'amendments' to the existing treaties, it would be comprehensible only when cross-referred to earlier texts. Nevertheless, Major's 'bull points' were enough to be going on with. Exhausted, he returned to London, to tell the British people what he had agreed to in their name.

MAJOR'S 'TRIUMPH'

Considering how little anyone yet knew of what the treaty actually contained, it was perhaps small wonder that the British media took Major at his own estimation. On 11 December, *The Times'* front page carried the headline: 'Major wins all he asked for at Maastricht', and the newspapers were almost unanimous in praise of what the *Daily Telegraph* called 'Major's success at Maastricht'. The *Daily Express* was almost ecstatic. It splashed the headline across the front page: 'Major wins Euro deal', with the sub-heading: 'Triumph as social charter is dropped from political treaty'. A page-six story, headed 'MPs hail Major victory', had British officials 'throwing their hats in the air with delight' in Maastricht, 'after Mr Major's summit triumph'.

In London on Wednesday afternoon, Major made a statement to the Commons. It was received with acclaim and much waving of order papers. He told MPs:

This is a treaty which safeguards and advances our national interests. It advances the interests of Europe as a whole. It opens up new ways of co-operating in Europe. It clarifies and contains the powers of the Commission. It will allow the Community to develop in depth. It reaches out to other Europeans – the new democracies who want to share the benefits we already enjoy. It is a good agreement for Europe, and a good agreement for the United Kingdom.[51]

Yet Major cannot have been wholly unaware what an immense range of powers he had ceded, perhaps indicated by his response to one of his own backbenchers, who asked him to summarise them. His reply was evasive. Detailed information 'could be found in the Commons library'.[52] In fact, it was to be months before MPs or anyone else would find out just how much had been surrendered.

The next day, in Cabinet, it was 'sweetness and light', although Major conceded that 'he had had to make concessions on some points which

[51] *Hansard*, 11 December 1991, col. 862.
[52] Ibid., col. 873.

ideally he would have preferred to avoid'. Conversely, though, he had made 'more progress than expected'. This included 'preservation of the pillared structure of the new Treaty' as well as retaining 'the right to decide whether to opt into a single currency'.[53] However, Major also had to admit:

> The Commission's ability to continue to bring forward under the existing provisions of the Treaty, proposals for legislation which the United Kingdom found unpalatable, and which in some cases arguably amounted to misuse of the provisions in question, would remain. There could well be pressure to press ahead with such legislation during 1992, before the new Treaty entered into force at the beginning of 1993.[54]

Unaware of this detail, Conservative backbenchers rapturously received Major's ministers at their meetings. It was the modern equivalent of a Roman triumph, wrote Major, adding in hindsight 'soon it would all be very different'.[55] But that time had not yet come. In a two-day Commons debate a week later, Major moved his own motion, asking the House to support the treaty.[56]

Even then, there were some dissenting voices and the most passionate speech came from Conservative backbencher Richard Shepherd. He told the House he already belonged to a 'union', the United Kingdom of Great Britain and Northern Ireland, formed by people with one language and united by their will to make it work. He did not know how to relate to a 'union of Europe'. As to the treaty: 'Where is the mechanism whereby we may hold Ministers accountable?' he asked. Despite his intervention, and those of others, the government won the vote comfortably by 339 votes to 253.

After a 'successful' debate in the House of Lords on 18 December, the way was clear for Hurd, as foreign secretary, accompanied by Francis Maude as his minister of state, to return to Maastricht for the ceremonial signing. This they did on 7 February 1992. Along with representatives of 11 other heads of state, they formally inscribed their names on behalf of Her Majesty Queen Elizabeth II, to the strains of a Mozart string divertimento, K.136. Afterwards, Hurd joked to journalists, 'now we've signed it, we'd better read it'.[57] The 'European Union' had been born. All that was now left was the formality of getting the treaty ratified.

[53] National Archives, CAB 28/100, Cabinet Conclusions, 12 December 1991.
[54] Ibid.
[55] Major, op. cit., p. 288.
[56] Hansard, 18 December 1991, col. 275.
[57] Hurd's admission that he had not read the Treaty was later to be more famously echoed by his Cabinet colleague Kenneth Clarke.

THE RISE OF EUROSCEPTICISM

In the immediate aftermath of Maastricht, Major was advised that a snap general election might bring a Conservative victory. This was tempting, because Labour had been ahead in the opinion polls for more than two years. But he decided to wait for 9 April, giving time for a tax-cutting budget and the completion of legislation to abolish the unpopular poll tax.

The election campaign was strangely unreal. Britain was still in the grip of a recession, the jobless total had risen above two and a half million, and 75,000 homes had been repossessed from those unable to afford the mortgage payments, either because they were out of work or through crippling interest rates. Much of this agony was directly attributable to the constraints imposed by the ERM, yet the opposition parties could not make this an issue because they too endorsed membership. The big difference on 'Europe' between the parties was the Labour and Lib-Dem support for the single currency and the Social Chapter.

Despite the recession, the most emotive issue in the campaign was a proposal by Labour's shadow chancellor John Smith to raise £3 billion a year in taxes from the better-off. With polls still predicting a Labour victory, Kinnock also blundered by staging what seemed like a victory rally in Sheffield a week before polling day. When 9 April came, to general astonishment, the Conservatives took 14,092,891 votes, the largest number ever won by a party at a general election. Within weeks Kinnock was to resign as opposition leader, later to become a European Commissioner. He was replaced by the man who, more than anyone, had lost Labour the election: John Smith. Major remained at Downing Street. Despite the record vote, his majority had been cut to 21.

The first major Bill before the new parliament was the amendment to the European Communities Act, bringing into effect the Maastricht Treaty. Not the least remarkable feature of the second reading of this Bill on 20–21 May was that MPs were expected to approve the treaty without having seen the full text. Tristan Garel-Jones, the new Europe minister, believed it would be 'presumptuous' for MPs to have it 'until it had been approved by the House'. Fortunately, 1,500 copies of a consolidated edition of the treaty compiled by a tiny private organisation were made available to MPs and peers in time for them to study what they were voting on.[58]

On 20 May the debate ran on until 7.30 the next morning, marked out by the prominence of a new generation of Tory 'Eurosceptics', venomously

---

[58] It was produced by Brigadier Anthony Cowgill at the British Management Data Foundation. The 1,500 copies were bought by Sir Keith Joseph of the Centre for Policy Studies for distribution. A definitive version with analysis was published in October 1992, and distributed, *inter alia*, by HM Stationery Office, thus giving it semi-official status.

characterised as 'anti-Europeans' by their opponents. During the six months since the treaty had been agreed, an array of new organisations had also been formed, both inside and outside parliament, dedicated to fighting what was seen as its undermining of democracy. After a further year had elapsed, some 27 organisations had emerged.[59]

Within the Conservative parliamentary party, a 'Fresh Start Group' was led by Michael Spicer and Bill Cash, himself once an enthusiastic 'Europhile'. Spicer and Jonathan Aitken formed the European Reform Group. One recruit, who made his maiden speech in the debate, was Iain Duncan Smith, Tebbit's successor as MP for Chingford. Many of the new extra-parliamentary organisations were supported by Tory members in the constituencies. A rift was opening up between grass-roots activists, largely Eurosceptic, and the party leadership.

By now the extent to which Maastricht represented a further leap towards 'federalism' had begun to register with many Conservatives, despite the determination of Major and Hurd to pretend otherwise. Even the new 'pillars' promoting common policies on foreign and home affairs, although intergovernmental in character, potentially represented a major extension of 'Community' influence over the right of nations to run their own affairs. The fact they were to be run by the Council did not rule out the possibility that the powers would later be handed to the supranational Commission.

The central plank on which Major rested his claim of a reversal of 'centralism' was the inclusion of 'subsidiarity'. But if Major and Hurd honestly believed that Maastricht had 'reversed the tide of federalism', they can only have been monumentally self-deceiving. Yet, despite evidence that the 'Eurosceptics' were now becoming considerably sharper and better informed in their criticism, when it came to the crucial vote only 72 MPs voted against the Bill, including 22 Conservatives. By approving the Maastricht Treaty in principle, the oldest parliament in Europe had voted for what was potentially an even greater surrender of its powers than that implicit in the original European Communities Act 20 years before.

Scarcely two weeks later, on 2 June, the Danish people in a referendum rejected the treaty by 50.7 to 49.4 per cent. Although all the main political parties had favoured ratification, a poorly funded coalition of activists, led by the 'June Movement', had run a spirited *Nej* campaign, aided unwittingly by their own government, which had circulated 300,000 copies of the treaty, without explanation or summaries. Sight of this unreadable document had been enough to tilt the balance in a country that held its leaders in

[59] Forster, op. cit., p. 88.

healthy disrespect. Even Denmark's foreign minister admitted he did not understand it, 'and I negotiated it,' he said.[60]

The defeat sent shock waves across Europe. If any member state failed to ratify a treaty, it had to be declared void. But the Danish prime minister, Poul Schlüter, disowned the result. 'Can anyone seriously believe,' he said, 'that our small nation with five million people can stop the Great European Express of three hundred million?'[61] Other governments, supported by Hurd, immediately looked for ways to move the goalposts. The Danes were reviled in the most condescending terms.

Whatever else, the Danish vote presented Major with an immediate problem. Britain was about to take over the presidency, so his was the task of rescuing the treaty. And with his own Maastricht Bill about to go to its Commons committee stage and backbench opposition becoming more organised, something had to give. To allow him to focus on Denmark, he therefore postponed the committee stage. The response from France was rather more dramatic. Mitterrand announced that he would suspend parliamentary ratification and allow his people a referendum of their own. It was a serious gamble. Mitterrand at the time was unpopular. If French voters followed the Danish lead, Maastricht really would be dead.

SUBSIDIARITY TO THE RESCUE

The Community response was to convene a special Foreign Affairs Council on 4 June. Its decision was to continue with ratification. The door would be 'left open' for Denmark, but there would be no renegotiation.[62] Over the next few weeks, the Community evolved a more considered answer to the Danish problem, and also to the more general fear that the peoples of Europe were becoming concerned by the shift of power away from nation states. That answer was that magic word 'subsidiarity'. As Hurd explained to the Commons, the plan was to get the European Council to set limits to the powers of the Commission. 'We need,' he said, 'to make it clear to our constituents and others in the Community that matters will improve.'[63]

By the time the European Council met to consider this in Lisbon on 26 – 27 June, its members were in happier mood. The Irish referendum had endorsed the treaty with a 69 per cent 'Yes' vote. The Council welcomed this result. Denmark was not mentioned.[64] Nor was the hardly irrelevant fact

[60] *Time International*, 1 June 1992, p. 70.
[61] *Time International*, 15 June 1992, p. 10.
[62] *The Times*, 8 June 1992.
[63] *Hansard*, 8 June 1992, col. 37.
[64] *Bulletin of the European Community*, 'Presidency Conclusions', 29 June 1992, p. 3.

that the Irish were now the greatest beneficiaries of Community largesse, receiving £6 back for every £1 they paid in.

Nevertheless, a keynote of the Council was a long speech from Delors on the importance of subsidiarity. He had just been subjected to the ordeal of waiting to see whether he would be reappointed president for a further two years. Chastened but relieved, he made it clear that subsidiarity was now his 'big idea' for 1992.[65] Kohl and Major agreed that this was the way to reassure public opinion that the European Union was not bent on becoming a 'superstate'. This was echoed in the presidency conclusions, making the principle of subsidiarity' essential 'to ensure a direction of the European construction which is in conformity with the common wish of the member states and of their citizens'.[66] That left the Commission and Council to 'undertake urgent work' needed to implement the 'big idea', to be presented at Edinburgh in December, when Major would be in the chair.[67] A truer indication of the real agenda, however, was a resolution tucked away on page 14 of the presidency conclusions, calling for steps to be taken to set up 'Europol', eventually to provide the Union with a supranational police force.

Less than two weeks before, just as little public attention had been given to another dramatic leap forward in the integration process, when defence ministers of the WEU held a meeting in Bonn on 19 June. Although the Maastricht Treaty had yet to be ratified, they had already jumped the gun by moving to establish a common defence policy.

With Britain represented by Malcolm Rifkind, they drew up what was known as the 'Petersberg Declaration'. In light of 'the progress made in developing the role of the WEU as a defence component of the European Union', they agreed that it should move its secretariat from London to Brussels. It would also develop 'its operational capabilities' to allow it to undertake measures of 'conflict prevention and crisis-management'. This was the embryonic 'Rapid Reaction Force', the first step towards giving the European Union its own armed forces.[68] In addition, they asked for a report on the setting up of a European Armaments Agency.

Although there was careful emphasis that the WEU would operate in close co-operation with NATO, this was a very significant further step in creating a 'European Defence Identity'. Yet, although Rifkind advised the Commons that he was to attend the Bonn meeting, no report on what was agreed was

[65] Grant, op. cit., p. 217.
[66] Bulletin, p. 9.
[67] Ibid.
[68] WEU, Meeting of the Council of Ministers, Bonn, 19 June 1992.

made to the House afterwards. Again, the stealthy transformation of the WEU had slipped the net of parliamentary scrutiny.

'BLACK WEDNESDAY'
Long before the Edinburgh Council, the political landscape was to undergo a cataclysmic change. The cause of this was the precipitate departure of the UK from the ERM on 16 September 1992.[69] Strangely enough, the trigger for this explosive event was the Danish 'No' vote, which shattered any assumption that ERM would be a trouble-free glidepath to the single currency. Instead, EMU might be sunk completely, or the 'core' countries might form their own 'mini-Union', outside the framework of Maastricht. Anticipating such possibilities, the financial markets began to reposition themselves.

The first sign of trouble came when investors with exposure in Spain and Italy began to withdraw their money. When Spain made no move to support its currency, devaluation of the peseta was inevitable. Italy responded with drastic budget cuts, which temporarily stabilised its currency. But then Germany, faced with a massive bill for reunification, raised its interest rates, heedless of its effect on other ERM members. Money flooded into Germany, pressuring other countries to raise their rates. Italy took the heat, reluctantly raising its rate by 1.25 per cent. But that made it difficult for the government to finance its deficit, negating earlier budget cuts. The lira started to slide.

In Britain, the German rate rise also presented problems. Sterling had enjoyed a honeymoon flush after Major's unexpected re-election, but was now caught by the deutschmark interest hike. This called for a rate increase to bolster the value of the pound. But with the UK economy already in deep recession, and fearful of the effect on mortgages, Chancellor Norman Lamont chose instead to drop the rate. This sent an alarm signal to the money markets. As sterling fell to the bottom of its permissible ERM band, the rules demanded a rate rise. But Lamont and Major realised that this would be political suicide. Instead, in an attempt to stave off the inevitable devaluation, they resorted to bravado. The money markets were not impressed.

By late August, as the deutschmark rose to the top of the ERM band, the pound was at its lowest permissible level. The lira actually slipped below it. The rules required that the deutschmark should be 'realigned', to relieve the strain. But this was vetoed by EC finance ministers. Then, fatally, the UK Treasury announced that it had borrowed 10 billion ecu to finance intervention on behalf of the pound. This signalled that the government was

---

[69] This account was constructed from Connolly, op. cit., contemporary newspaper reports, and from Stephens, Philip (1996), *Politics and the Pound* (London: Macmillan), pp. 226–262.

now prepared to throw in any money it could find to avoid raising interest rates. Sterling was being set up as a speculators' target.

Despite that, the lira was the first to come under pressure, after fears of imminent devaluation prompted wholesale selling. As the deutschmark strengthened still further, wiping out gains made by sterling as a result of the borrowing announcement and driving the lira against its lower ERM limit, Italian interest rates went through the roof. At an Ecofin council, the head of the Bundesbank came under concerted attack by the finance ministers of Italy, Britain and France, pleading with him to reduce Germany's interest rates. Despite nine hours of heated argument, he refused.

At stake now was more than the ERM: the whole Maastricht treaty was at risk. In a televised debate days earlier, Mitterrand, in support of his 'Yes' campaign for the referendum, had effectively rewritten the treaty, claiming that the Council of Ministers could control the proposed European Central Bank. Now, as the world's media looked on, Ecofin was demonstrating its inability to control the Bundesbank – the natural model for the ECB. This would have told French voters that Mitterrand had no control and ensured a French 'No', consigning the treaty to perdition. For public consumption, therefore, a fudge had to be arranged. The Council declared that the Bundesbank had agreed not to raise interest rates further, something it had already decided.

Financial pundits soon penetrated the fudge, aided by 'unhelpful' statements from the Bundesbank, which also made it clear that Lamont had failed to extract a promise of lower interest rates. Sterling again dropped, and weaker currencies began falling out of the system altogether. First to go was the Finnish markka, which put pressure on the Swedish krona, forcing the Swedish central bank to push overnight interest rates to 24 per cent.

There were now eight days to go before 'Black Wednesday', and, after further unhelpful statements from the Bundesbank, the lira came under massive attack. On the Thursday, with one week to go, Major made a speech to a Glasgow dinner of the Scottish CBI that was finally to destroy any credibility he had left. He declared that realignment within the ERM was the 'soft option, the devaluers' option that would be the betrayal of our future and our children's future'. All too soon, he was to eat his words.

On Friday 11 September, as the lira closed below its permitted ERM floor, Kohl made a secret visit to the Bundesbank, hatching a deal that amounted to ditching the 'peripheral' currencies in order to protect the franc. A new Franco-German alliance had been forged, contravening all the ERM rules. Behind the scenes, George Soros, a soon-to-become famous hedge fund manager, had amassed a £10 billion 'war chest' with which to attack sterling. Its effect was soon felt. On the Tuesday, sterling closed at its lowest level since joining the ERM, a mere fifth of a pfennig above its ERM floor. After European markets closed, the pound ran into firestorm selling in New York, plunging below its ERM limit. The Bank of England intervened, but when European markets reopened the next day, its reserves were leaking at an alarming rate. Sterling remained nailed to the floor. By mid-morning, under ERM rules, there was only one course left. Lamont raised interest rates to 12 per cent – to no effect. At 2 p.m., he raised them another three points to 15 per cent.

The markets took this as a signal that the game was up. Sterling would have to leave the ERM. Selling increased until, by 4 p.m., the Bank surrendered. Sterling fell four pfennigs below the ERM floor. By mid-evening, after panic consultations with the ERM monetary committee, Lamont stumbled out of the Treasury to announce that sterling's membership of the ERM had been suspended. The Italian lira was also on its way out, as was the peseta.

Soros claimed a profit of more than £1 billion. The ERM was in tatters. So was the Conservative Party. Only five months earlier it had won the largest popular vote in Britain's electoral history. Over the next ten years it would never rise above Labour in the opinion polls.[70]

MAJOR'S NIGHTMARE BEGINS

Despite the ignominious collapse of one of their most ambitious experiments to date, the integrationists scarcely blinked. Four days after 'Black Wednesday', on 20 September, the French people went to the polls. Turnout at 70.5 per cent was unusually high, but the treaty was approved only by 51.05 per cent to 48.95. With just one vote in a hundred going the other way, the treaty would have been dead. Nevertheless, Kohl exulted, 'the positive result of the French referendum ... will give the European integration process a new boost in the other member states'.[71]

For Major, the victory was a mixed blessing. A French 'No' might have given him a way out of Maastricht. Now he had to confront a rebellious party, 71 of his backbenchers having signed an Early Day Motion calling for the government to abandon economic union. At the party conference in Brighton, the newly ennobled Lord Tebbit won a huge ovation for a defiantly Eurosceptic speech, telling Major to adopt 'policies for Britain first, Britain second, and Britain third'.[72]

The next step in Major's trial by fire was a Commons debate, triggered by a letter from Neil Kinnock in October, asking for a report on the significance

---

[70] The only freak exception would be September 2001, due to the fuel-tax protests.
[71] *Guardian*, Special Report, 22 September 1992.
[72] Gorman, Teresa (1993), *Bastards* (London: Pan Books), p. 100.

of Denmark's rejection of Maastricht. Major refused but unexpectedly offered a debate when Parliament resumed. What became known as the 'paving debate', on 4 November, gave the Fresh Start Group their chance. With seventy or so potential rebels, and an alliance with Labour and the Ulster Unionists, they could defeat the government. It was a threat Major took very seriously. One rebel, Teresa Gorman, recalls a massive 'dirty tricks campaign' by party whips aimed at forcing MPs into line.

Major's life was not made any easier by Baroness Thatcher, recently elevated to the Lords. She attacked him in a television interview for agreeing to re-appoint Delors and described Maastricht as 'a treaty too far'. On 2 July, in her maiden speech to the Lords, she again called for a referendum and declared that she would vote against ratification.[73]

The 'paving debate' in November thus became a battle between Major and the Thatcherites, with Major determined to save 'his' treaty. Parliament, he said, had supported, 'indeed acclaimed', the deal when it had first been laid before it.[74] He could not cope with the idea that his MPs had acclaimed it sight unseen, and that when they actually read the treaty they had not liked it. Many now believed they had been sold a false prospectus. Doggedly persisting in his claim that he had reversed the tide of federalism, and determined to resign if Parliament now overruled him, Major again stressed the value of subsidiarity.[75] This featured so prominently in the debate that it was mentioned 71 times. It was Major's shield, his 'proof' that Maastricht was a decentralising treaty.

What set this debate apart, though, was Labour's determination to use it as a stick to beat the government. In the event, with Liberal Democrat help, Major carried the day, but only by 316 votes to 313, a majority of just three. His 'success' was entirely the result of extraordinary pressures put on his rebels by his whips, prompting one commentator to record that the debate: 'was so unreal that it seemed to be taking place in a fairground hall of mirrors, punctuated only by the distasteful off-stage noises of government managers forcing MPs into voting against what they believed. It was a spectacle that degraded everyone.'[76]

DELORS' 'BIG IDEA'

In championing subsidiarity as his 'big idea' for 1992, Delors was drawing on his Catholic past, in particular the encyclical *Quadragesimo anno* issued

---

[73] *Hansard*, House of Lords, 2 July 1992, cols 895–901.
[74] Major, op. cit., p. 361.
[75] Ibid., p. 363.
[76] *Sunday Telegraph*, 8 November 1992.

by the Vatican in 1931.[77] This held that every task in society should be fulfilled by the smallest social unit capable of carrying it out, beginning with individuals and families, up through larger social units. Only when a task could not be fulfilled on a lower level should a higher unit step in and take over. But, crucially, the 'sub-units' had no veto. It was up to what Delors called the 'higher agencies' to decide when subsidiarity should apply.[78]

Herein yawned a gulf. Major imagined that, with subsidiarity, member states could reclaim power. Delors saw it as an instrument of integration. And when he told his officials to produce a list of competences that might be handed back, they failed to find any. As a gesture, Delors withdrew three proposals for directives.[79] Two were highly technical, concerning radio frequencies, and the third dealt with the 'compulsory indication of nutritional values on the packaging of food'. But a directive on this had already been issued three years earlier.[80] The Commission also considered withdrawing 11 other proposals, including one on 'the classification of documents of Community institutions'. No existing laws were scrapped. Yet the Edinburgh Council meekly accepted Delors' report. Such was Major's reversal of the tide of 'federalism'.

That hardly helped Major with his 'toughest and most vital' task of convincing the Danes to ratify Maastricht. His strategy was to get the Danish prime minister to 'declare' that the citizenship of the 'Union' did not replace national citizenship'; that Denmark would not enter the single currency, and that there would be no involvement in the common defence policy. Eleven leaders then happily turned this statement into a 'solemn declaration'. Even though the Danes had not been obliged to opt in either to the single currency or to the common defence policy, this sleight of hand was enough to turn the tide.

Another Major 'triumph' was the budget increase, from £51 billion in 1992 to £64 billion in 1999. He also kept 'Thatcher's' rebate, although this was nearly blocked by the Spanish, who had demanded a doubling of regional aid as the price of agreement. Delors did some swift creative accounting and found an extra seven billion ecus.[81] Also agreed was a start to accession

[77] Vatican website: http://www.vatican.va/content/pius-xi/en/encyclicals/documents/hf_p-xi_enc_19310515_quadragesimo-anno.html.

[78] Føllesdal, Andreas (1999), 'Subsidiarity and Democratic Deliberation', ARENA Working Paper 99/21 (www.arena.uio.no/publications/wp99_21.htm). See also lecture given by Delors in 1991 (Delors, Jacques, *Subsidiarité: defi du changement*, Institut européén d'administration publique, Maastricht, 1991, pp. 8–9).

[79] Bulletin, Annex 2 to Part A, p. 2.

[80] Council Directive 90/496/EC of 24 September 1990 on nutrition labelling of foodstuffs. OJ L276, 06/10/1990, pp. 0040–0044.

[81] Grant, op. cit., p. 229.

negotiations with Austria, Sweden and Finland in 1993, subject to Maastricht being fully ratified, and the candidate countries accepting the whole of the *acquis*. An application from Norway would also be considered. Germany got more MEPs, reflecting the addition of East Germany, and France gained recognition for Strasbourg as the official seat of the European Parliament.[82]

Major paraded these 'successes' in Parliament on 14 December, claiming that the Council had 'agreed a package of measures to reverse centralisation' and that the Commission had produced a list of laws that it believed 'must be simplified or abolished.'[83] This was simply untrue. The Commission had only undertaken to withdraw proposals for new laws. But no one challenged him.

PARLIAMENTARY RATIFICATION: ROUND TWO

'With the future of the treaty secured,' Major wrote, thinking of his 'success' with the Danes, 'the committee stage of the Bill could begin.'[84] It was taken on the floor of the House. Unlike Thatcher with the Single European Act, Major dare not guillotine these proceedings. They thus became a marathon, opposition being co-ordinated by the Fresh Start Group led by Bill Cash. Under his direction, the group submitted over five hundred amendments and a hundred new clauses. The debates took over two hundred hours, lasting 25 full days.

From Major's perspective, this was completely unproductive. Parliament could not amend the treaty. But the Fresh Start Group wanted to demonstrate the strength and intensity of British Euroscepticism, and perhaps influence the Danish to vote 'No' in their second referendum. Throughout, both sides allied themselves with opposition forces.[85] But there was no equality of arms. Major heartily approved of his whips contacting the Lib-Dems, but called the Eurosceptic's dealings with Labour 'trickery.'[86] The Fresh Start Group took a different view. None could have been considered as anything other than mainstream Conservatives. Teresa Gorman, who regarded the Maastricht Bill as 'the greatest threat to Britain's independence since the Second World War', explained that: 'confronted with a politician apparently willing to sacrifice ambition for principle ... our instinct was to band together to save democracy.'[87]

What nearly made the difference was Labour tabling an amendment at the committee stage making ratification of the treaty conditional on

---

[82] https://www.consilium.europa.eu/media/20492/1992_december_-_edinburgh__eng_.pdf.
[83] *Hansard*, 14 December 1992, col. 24.
[84] Major, op. cit., p. 372.
[85] Ibid., p. 373.
[86] Ibid., p. 372.
[87] Gorman, op. cit., p. xvii.

accepting the Social Chapter. Although accepted, voting was deferred until after the third reading of the Bill. It became a 'ticking time bomb' that would nearly destroy the treaty.

By late April the Bill had completed its committee stage, but before its third and final reading, three events took place. The first was a speech by Major on 22 April to the Conservative Group for Europe, in which he told his audience that Maastricht had been used as a scapegoat for the 'varied and nameless fears about Europe'. Going on to state what was now his party's chief official mantra, Conservatives, he declared, 'must have the confidence and the sharp-edged determination to stay in the heart of the European debate to win a Community of free, independent members'.[88]

Nevertheless, the speech was mainly remembered for its eulogy for an England long past, 'the country of long shadows on county grounds, warm beer, invincible green suburbs, dog lovers and – as George Orwell said – old maids bicycling to Holy Communion through the morning mist'. Major claimed he was simply reminding his audience that Britain's involvement in Europe did not threaten national distinctiveness, but it became a caricature of his political philosophy.[89]

Next came a by-election, the first since the ERM debacle, to be held at Newbury. On 6 May 1993, it saw a Tory majority of 12,367 turned into a Lib-Dem majority of 22,055. Also standing was an obscure academic from the London School of Economics, Dr Alan Sked, fighting under the banner of the Anti-Federalist League. This was to become the United Kingdom Independence Party (UKIP). Sked's 601 votes would blossom into millions. That time had not yet come, but still the election news was dire. In local government elections, the Conservatives lost a record 24 county councils. The Tories were paying the price for the ERM debacle.

The third event was the second Danish referendum, on 18 May, just two days before the third reading. The result was a 'Yes' for Maastricht, 57 to 43 per cent, marked by the worst riots Copenhagen had seen since the war. Protesters smashed shop windows, burnt cars and barricaded part of the city, declaring it an 'EC-free zone'. Eleven demonstrators and 26 police were injured.[90] How well the voters understood the arguments was questionable. In one post-referendum poll, only 17 per cent knew of the Edinburgh

---

[88] Ibid., p. 376.
[89] Ibid.
[90] *Time International*, 31 May 1993, p. 22.

'concessions'.[91] Others complained that the constitution prohibited holding two votes on the same issue.[92]

When, on 20 May, the Maastricht Bill went for its third reading, the crucial issue in the minds of many Conservative MPs was the defeat at Newbury. Labour had already indicated that it intended to abstain, and with the Tory backbenchers fearful for their seats, the result was pre-ordained. There was a majority of 180 for Maastricht: 'Ayes' 292 and 'Noes' 112.

The drama was not yet over. There was still Labour's amendment, the 'ticking time bomb' on the Social Chapter. For procedural reasons, there had to be two votes and, for Major to save his treaty, the government had to win both. It would be wrong, though, to dignify the proceedings on the night with the title 'debate'. As before, only more so, it was pure theatre, with the issues being decided on the fringes. Key to the outcome were the Lib-Dems, who had decided to swap sides, and the Conservative whips, who had been out in force, using every tactic they knew, short of physical violence, to bring members into line.

The whips' pressure carved out enough of the Fresh Start Group support to turn the result of the first vote – the opposition amendment – into a dead heat: 317 votes each. Speaker Betty Boothroyd, as tradition demanded, cast her vote for the government. Proceedings were being broadcast live on the late television news and, after that cliff-hanger, the next result, on the substantive motion, was cataclysmic. Amid pandemonium, the Speaker called: 'Ayes to the right, 316; Noes to the left, 324. The Noes have it.' The government had lost by eight votes.

Even before the vote, Major had decided to call a vote of confidence if he lost. For mysterious reasons, the Ulster Unionists, until then staunch opponents of the treaty, handed Major their eight votes. They were enough. The vote next day was of dubious constitutional propriety, as the confidence motion sought to overturn the vote of the previous night, technically against the rules. But, facing a general election if the government lost, and with the whiff of Newbury still in the air, the rebels caved in. Every Conservative MP, with the exception of Rupert Allason, voted with the government.

At 4.30 p.m., Major won the day by 39 votes. Around him, the product of 18 months of bitter fratricide, stood the wreckage of the Conservative Party.

[91] Cited in Franklin, Mark, et al. (1995), Referendum Outcomes and Trust in Government: Public Support for Europe in the Wake of Maastricht in West European Politics, Vol. 18, p. 15.
[92] Time International.

12

The Single Market: A Tale of Three Halves

> No longer is European law an incoming tide flowing up the
> estuaries of England. It is now like a tidal wave bringing down
> our sea walls and flowing inland over our fields and houses.
>
> Lord Denning[1]

For many British businesses, the much-heralded Single Market, with its
unasked-for 'benefits' of being able to trade freely across borders, was an
unmitigated disaster. For instance, in November 1992, Colman Twohig,
who ran a one-man business in Rochester, Kent, supplying electronic
devices for use in dredging work, received a letter from the Department
of Trade and Industry. It informed him that he would soon have to
comply with new regulations issued under the EEC's Electromagnetic
Compatibility Directive 89/336/EEC. His products would have to be
tested by a 'competent body' to ensure they did not cause interference with
other electrical items (in which case they would be given a 'CE' mark, for
Communauté Européen). Mr Twohig had no argument with the principle
behind the regulations. The problem was that the devices he assembled for
his customers were 'one-off', each designed for specific tasks, many priced
at £50 or less. Yet the cost of individual testing would be £1,000 a day,
making his business unviable.

Roger Brown, who ran a small garden centre near Appleby, Westmorland,
had for years used a disused quarry on his land as a compost heap. He was
now informed that, under new EEC waste regulations, his dead leaves and
other composting materials constituted 'controlled waste'. Since he did not
hold a waste management licence, he would have to hire an authorised

---

[1] H. P. Bulmer Ltd v. J. Bollinger SA (1974), Ch. 401.

contractor to remove them, costing £20,000. He also faced possible prosecution.

In Farcet, Huntingdonshire, Tom Chamberlain ran a butchery business, owned by his family for 100 years. In 1992 he was named Champion Sausage Maker at the East of England Show. Soon afterwards, he was informed by the Ministry of Agriculture, Fisheries and Food (MAFF) that, under the Fresh Meat (Hygiene and Inspection) Regulations 1992, implementing EC directive 91/497, he must make extensive structural changes to his premises. If he did not, on 1 January 1993 he would lose his licence, forcing him to close his business.

Although his butcher's shop was only just across the yard from his slaughterhouse, he would no longer be allowed to carry meat between them unless he built a refrigerated tunnel between the two buildings. Among many other requirements, he would also have to build a shower and rest room for 'visiting lorry drivers', even though most animals arriving at his slaughterhouse came from farms within a five-mile radius. Contemplating the cost of these changes, he concluded that he had no option but to cease trading.[2]

Through the closing months of 1992, many such examples began to come to light, from almost every sector of British industry, signalling a new phase in Britain's relationship with what many still called the Common Market. Until now, 'Europe' had seemed remote from their concerns. Occasionally the media would have fun with some 'crazy new EEC directive' (such as the one harmonising laws on jam in 1988, which classified carrots as a 'fruit'[3]) and the production of 'Euro-sillies' became a cottage industry.[4]

If 'Brussels' was still viewed as some faraway place of little relevance to ordinary life, this was by no small measure the result of events and developments in the EEC – then to become the EC and EU – being largely treated as foreign news, competing for space in newspapers and the broadcast media with global events. Most often, important developments were ignored as so many of the stories had all the appeal of a provincial council meeting on a bad day, or were so technical as to be beyond the capability of the average journalist to report. Yet, all of a sudden, people

---

[2] Hundreds of similar examples were reported on by Booker, Christopher and North, Richard (1994), *The Mad Officials* (London: Constable), and *The Castle of Lies*, op. cit.

[3] Council Directive 88/593/EEC of 18 November 1988 amending Directive 79/693/EEC on the approximation of the laws of the member states relating to fruit jams, jellies and marmalades, and chestnut purée. The Directive arose because the Commission wanted to rule that jam could only legally be made from fruit. The Portuguese objected that they also made jam from carrots. By a typical EEC compromise, the Commission's solution was to allow carrots to be called fruit.

[4] Not least Boris Johnson, the Brussels correspondent for the *Daily Telegraph*.

running every kind of business were disconcerted to be told they would now have to comply with new 'EEC regulations'. Largely (but not entirely), the reason for this was the 'completion' of the Single Market, scheduled for 1 January 1993.

But, if Single Market regulation was seen by many in the UK as an additional – and very often unnecessary – burden, in continental terms it made absolute sense. With multiple countries, cheek-by-jowl – some, as in Luxembourg, no bigger than an English metropolitan borough – the removal of borders was not a luxury that made the annual sojourn to the Costa Brava a little easier. It was a vital economic necessity.

When, in 1957, the Six agreed the Treaty of Rome, they established a customs union, the effect of which was to abolish tariffs at internal borders and set a common external tariff. The union was complete by 1968, two years ahead of schedule, but that did not mean the abolition of border controls. By the early 1980s, checks were still common, and by 1984, the European Commission was despairingly reporting:

Last year a Belgian journalist rented a van and loaded it up with some old furniture that he wanted to take to a holiday house that he had just bought in the South of France. He drove to the frontier and was eventually allowed to cross an hour and a half, 15 signatures and half-a-dozen forms later. The import of second-hand furniture into France for a holiday home ('Do you have proof of ownership, sir?') is perfectly legal, and not subject to any tax or duty. But all the old French customs procedures still exist. The red tape involved in transporting an old wardrobe is the same as for a load of computers or fifty barrels of poisonous dioxin waste from Seveso.[5]

Border checks were estimated to cost between 5 and 10 per cent of the value of goods crossing frontiers, and in February that year, a go-slow by customs officials on the Franco-Italian border brought the system to crisis point when French lorry drivers mounted a strike in protest, blockading roads and paralysing commerce. After two weeks, riot police and soldiers had to be mobilised to clear the roads.

At Community level, the response in June 1984 was for the Fontainebleau European Council to agree in principle the abolition of customs and police formalities at the Community's internal borders. On 13 July 1984, the French and German governments took the step towards attaining this objective, signing the Saarbrücken Agreement at the Saarbrücken–Forbach

---

[5] *Europe 84* (magazine), Commission of the European Communities, London. Via AEI.

border crossing point in the symbolic Goldene Bremm area. This bilateral treaty – outside the framework of the Treaty of Rome – committed the two nations to reducing checks and establishing joint control points.[6]

The following year, on 14 June 1985, Belgium, Luxembourg and the Netherlands joined with France and Germany to build on this initiative, signing the Schengen Agreement. The five countries committed themselves to the gradual abolition of checks at common borders and to facilitate the transport and movement of goods at those borders.[7] This, like the Saarbrücken Agreement, was outside the Community framework. Thus, when the Commission White Paper on the completion of the internal market was published, on the same day as the Schengen Agreement, its proposal to secure the complete abolition of frontiers was nothing new.

The resultant Single Market was not a 'British invention' and nor, as Margaret Thatcher liked to think, had 'Britain given the lead'.[8] As early as March 1968, the Commission had set out a programme for the elimination of technical obstacles to trade between member states, with a target for completion of 1 January 1971.[9] The 1985 White Paper was simply the extension of a policy line established with the Treaty of Rome and pursued ever since.

EMERGENCE OF THE EUROPEAN ECONOMIC AREA (EEA)

While the British were struggling with the concept of a border-free Europe, the EFTA states were concerned that the 'growing interdependence of the sixteen nations [of the EEC and EFTA] made it necessary to ensure that the advantages deriving from the free trade are not jeopardised as a result of diverging economic developments and policies'.[10] Furthermore, this was a long-standing concern, expressed most vividly at a meeting held in Vienna on 13 May 1977 at the invitation of the Federal Chancellor of Austria. From this emerged the idea of a European Economic Space (EES) as a way of 'satisfying the need to develop trade and economic co-operation with the EC on a pragmatic and practical basis'.[11]

Subsequent meetings culminated in the Luxembourg Declaration of 1984, where the parties committed to 'broaden and deepen' co-operation

---

[6] Luxembourg University archives.

[7] Luxembourg University archives.

[8] In her speech at Lancaster House on 18 April 1988, opening the Single Market campaign, Mrs Thatcher did indeed aver that Britain had 'given the lead'.

[9] http://aei.pitt.edu/29978/1/P_19_69.pdf.

[10] *Seventeenth Annual Report of the European Free Trade Association*, Geneva, September 1977.

[11] European Parliament, Working Papers, 'Agreement on the European Economic Area, Background and Contents'.

between the EC and EFTA.[12] While the Commission responded positively in May 1985, it had reservations on what was to become the core issue, noting that: 'Community integration and the Community's independent powers of decision must under no circumstances be affected'.[13] However, the need for more co-operation was pressing. A month later, the Commission had published its White Paper on the completion of the internal market, which had EFTA states worried about marginalisation and trade diversion effects from a more developed EC market.[14]

The somewhat glacial pace was transformed on 17 January 1989 when Delors made what was described as 'a visionary speech' to the European Parliament in Strasbourg. He referred to 'our close Efta friends', for whom he suggested 'a new, more structured partnership with common decision-making and administrative institutions'. These would make joint activities more effective and 'highlight the political dimension of our co-operation in the economic, social, financial and cultural spheres'.[15] Enjoining the MEPs not to forget 'the others who are knocking at our door', he referred to Mikhail Gorbachev's notion of a 'common European house', which had been articulated as early as 1987.[16]

As an alternative, Delors offered a 'European village', in which he saw a house called the 'European Community'. 'We are its sole architects; we are the keepers of its keys,' he said, 'but we are prepared to open its doors to talk with our neighbours.'[17] This was exactly what the EFTA states wanted to hear. On 14–15 March 1989, they responded with the 'Oslo Declaration', affirming their readiness 'to explore together with the EC ways and means to achieve a more structured partnership'. Predictably, they emphasised the need for common decision-making.[18] The houses in the village were to make up a community of equals.

An EFTA ministerial meeting on 20 March 1989 sought to bring this vision to life, with the establishment of a joint 'High Level Steering Group', which concluded its meetings in the October. There then followed a meeting between the EC and EFTA in the December, when ministers decided to open formal negotiations on expanded co-operation in the first half of 1990, with a view to concluding them as rapidly as possible.[19] What broke

[12] http://www.efta.int/sites/default/files/documents/about-efta/EFTA-EC-joint-declaration1984.pdf.
[13] COM(85) 206 final, 13 May 1985.
[14] COM(85) 310 final, 14 June 1985.
[15] Luxembourg University archive.
[16] http://www.rug.nl/research/portal/files/10431148/03_c3.pdf.
[17] Luxembourg University, op. cit.
[18] http://www.efta.int/sites/default/files/publications/annual-report/efta-annual-report-1989.pdf.
[19] European Parliament, Working Papers, op. cit. See also Luxembourg University archive.

the consensus though was the cataclysmic and unexpected fall of the Berlin Wall – to be followed by the collapse of the Soviet Union. The newly liberated Soviet satellites of central and eastern Europe were in flux, their relationship with the EU yet to be defined. Former French president Giscard d'Estaing sought to fill the gap, expanding on the Delors vision of a 'European village'. He suggested it could be made up of five 'homes' comprising the Community states (EC), the EFTA countries, the east European countries of the Warsaw Pact, the 'isolated' countries – Yugoslavia, Albania, Malta – and the European part of the Soviet Union.[20]

Embracing this idea, EFTA sources wrote enthusiastically about the 'new architecture of Europe' for all countries of the continent. They called for the EES to remain an 'open concept', allowing the countries of eastern Europe to join at a later date.[21] The 'village' concept was taking shape. Common decision-making remained on the agenda at the EFTA–EC ministerial meeting in Brussels on 19 December 1989 and the mood was optimistic. A high-level examination had finished in the October with an agreement that there was sufficient common ground for negotiations to continue. They were to be based on the idea that common rules and common decision-making were to govern the EES.[22]

At stake, according to Jón Baldvin Hannibalsson, Iceland's foreign minister, was 'a genuine participation in a joint EES decision process'. This was of 'crucial importance' for the political acceptability of an EC/EFTA agreement. Jean-Pascal Delamuraz, the Swiss economics minister, was equally firm. 'Let us be clear and state openly from the outset,' he said, 'there will be no new forms of co-operation between the European Community and the Efta States unless there exists the machinery to prepare and take decisions jointly.'[23]

Delors, however, had other ideas. He now wanted the former Soviet satellites to become full Community members in a 'big bang' enlargement, which, with Cyprus and Malta, would add another ten members to what was soon to be the European Union. A European Economic Space, a 'village of equals' with common decision-making and full membership of the Single Market, would have been more attractive than EU membership.[24]

[20] Cited in http://discovery.ucl.ac.uk/1349617/1/363021.pdf, pp. 143–144.
[21] Luxembourg University archive.
[22] Luxembourg University archive.
[23] Ibid.
[24] For instance, see: O'Neil, Patrick H., 'Politics, Finance and European Union Enlargement Eastwards', in Sperling, James, ed. (1999). *Two Tiers or Two Speeds? The European Security Order and the Enlargement of the European Union* (Manchester University Press), p. 82, *et seq.*

On 17 January 1990, therefore, exactly a year after he had offered joint decision-making, Delors resiled on his promise. 'There will have to be some sort of osmosis between the Community and Efta, to ensure that Efta's interests are taken into account in major Community decisions,' he told the European Parliament. 'But this process must stop short of joint decision-making.'[25] The EFTA Council was not impressed. In a declaration in Gothenburg on 13–14 June 1990, it reiterated that genuine joint decision-making had to be 'a basic prerequisite for the political acceptability and legal effectiveness of an agreement'.[26]

By October, the negotiations had centred on two key issues: a number of permanent derogations from the *acquis communautaire* and, crucially, the reluctance of the Community to enter into substantive talks on decision-making. In Geneva on 23 October, EFTA ministers offered a compromise. They would reduce to a minimum the number of derogations called for, in return for 'a genuine common decision-making mechanism'.[27] It was not to be. Delors stood his ground and by 19 December 1990, the battle was effectively over. An EFTA–EC ministerial meeting in Brussels conceded that 'the decision-making autonomy of the parties should be fully respected', leaving only a fig-leaf. There were to be 'procedures' to ensure that EFTA state's views were 'taken into account'.[28] This was limited to EFTA experts being given an equal opportunity of consultation in the preparation of new EC legislation, on matters of relevance to the EEA.[29]

The 'surrender' cleared the way for the final agreement in May 1992 with the signing of the European Economic Area Agreement, creating the European Economic Area or EEA. But that was not the end of it. By way of compensation for the lack of shared decision-making, EFTA states insisted on a 'general safeguard clause' that could be triggered unilaterally if serious economic, societal and/or environmental difficulties of a sectoral or regional nature arose.[30] In time, it became Article 112 of the EEA Agreement, on which EFTA member Liechtenstein was able to rely to exempt itself from some of the free-movement provisions of the treaty. Despite that, there was no disguising the unsatisfactory nature of the final outcome.

---

[25] http://europa.eu/rapid/press-release_SPEECH-90-1_en.htm?locale=en. See also AEI: http://aei.pitt.edu/8600/1/8600.pdf.
[26] Luxembourg University archives.
[27] http://www.efta.int/sites/default/files/publications/annual-report/efta-annual-report-1990.pdf.
[28] Luxembourg University archives.
[29] European Parliament, Working Papers, op. cit.
[30] http://www.efta.int/sites/default/files/publications/annual-report/efta-annual-report-1991.pdf. See also Luxembourg University archives.

A NEW LEGAL FRAMEWORK

While the EFTA states were embracing their own version of the Single Market, British businesses were having to come to terms with what amounted to a new legal order, succinctly explained by the first Commission president, Walter Hallstein:

> The Community's body of laws is neither a mere bundle of agreements between sovereign states nor is it something that somehow has been tacked on to existing national legal systems. What the member-states have done by founding the Community is surrender part of their separate national sovereignty, and to create an entirely new and independent legal system to which both they as states and their citizens are subject.[31]

Three things in particular were striking about this 'body of law'. One was the prescriptive way in which most of the laws were framed, which was widely perceived to have lost contact with common sense. A second was its draconian nature. Never in history had so many new criminal offences been put on the statute book in so short a time. Again, these often seemed to be related not to correcting genuine problems but simply to failing to comply with bureaucratic procedures, involving reams of paperwork. A third was what was commonly perceived to be a marked change in the attitude of the officials and inspectors responsible for enforcing the new laws.

Older people in Britain could remember the 1940s and early 1950s, when 'red tape', official 'snoopers' and state controls had been such a prominent feature of national life. But by the mid-1950s this tide had receded and for decades officialdom had generally been much less intrusive. Now, however, it seemed that a culture change had taken place. Inflated by their new powers, many of the officials regulating businesses seemed to have become almost routinely aggressive and confrontational.

This change appeared with such speed that, initially, many of those affected thought it was something happening only to them. Only gradually did it dawn that they were caught up in something much wider. Although few realised it, what they were experiencing were the first practical consequences of a dramatic change in the way their country was governed. Until now, the emphasis in the story of the 'European project' had been on 'high politics'; on the gradual construction of a new system of government. But this had only been, as it were, the theoretical end of the process. What

---

[31] Hallstein, op. cit., p. 33.

was becoming visible was how this new form of government operated in practice.

From a British point of view, the first thing this represented was a radical change in the way most of their laws were made. For centuries the chief form of law-making had been the Act of Parliament, debated and voted on in public by elected representatives of the people. Now, as ever more areas of law-making had passed into Community competence, laws were increasingly being made by quite different methods, representing a revolution in the nature of British government.

No one could hide the fact that the Community had become a law factory, every year churning out more directives and regulations. But no claim was more persistently made for this process than that it was 'democratic'. And this claim centred on the fact that, although only the Commission had the exclusive right to initiate these laws, the supreme legislative body in the Community was the Council of Ministers. It was the Council, made up of elected politicians answerable to national parliaments, which exercised ultimate democratic control over the whole project.

Such was the theory. As for the charge that power in the 'new Europe' lay with an army of 'unelected, faceless bureaucrats', the ritual riposte came back that this was absurd, since the Commission employed fewer officials than any large local authority.[32] As far back as 1975, Thatcher herself had used this argument, pointing out that there were 'only 7,000 officials' working for the Commission, mainly in Brussels. In later years, this number crept up to 'only 15,000 officials', then 'only 18,000', then 'only 22,000', then 'only 25,000'. It was true the number crept inexorably upwards. But to see just these officials as the source of the avalanche of legislation emerging from 'Brussels' was completely to miss the nature of the revolution.

What made this new Brussels-centric system unique was that, to assert its dominance, it did not need to eliminate the institutions of the governments whose powers it was taking over. Rather, they were left in place while the supranational power worked through them, controlling them and enlisting their active collaboration in a way that remained largely out of view.[33] 'Brussels', therefore, was a nexus, the centre of an immense and complex network, linking institutions and organisations throughout the Community: not least the administrations of all the member states. Officials in Brussels were reinforced by countless thousands more at work back home in each

---

[32] The European Commission, Representation in the United Kingdom (undated), 'A Glossary of Eurosceptic Beliefs: An Exposé of Misunderstanding'.

[33] The importance of this collaboration had long since been noted by Spinelli in *The Eurocrats*.

country, all participating in what had become the most complex legislative machine ever known.[34]

This was reflected in the bewildering variety of ways by which proposals for Community laws came about in the first place. As the Delors' study group on subsidiarity had reported in 1992, only 30 of 535 legislative proposals in the previous year originated with the Commission itself. The rest came from other sources, ranging from the civil servants of national governments to an array of anonymous committees, which might include professional consultants, academics, environmental pressure groups, NGOs or even commercially funded lobbyists acting on behalf of a particular industry or company. It would later be estimated that there were 3,000 such committees operating in Brussels, and beyond them 170,000 lobbyists of one kind or another across the EU, ranging from pan-European trade associations representing whole industries to the representatives of individual local authorities pleading for a share in regional funding.[35]

The second stage of the process came when the Commission formally made a proposal for legislation. Again, in many cases aided by professional consultants or academics from universities across the Community, who would produce the initial drafts, texts would be negotiated over months or years by a further array of committees, often chaired by officials from the Commission.[36] Some were made up of national officials from the relevant government departments of the member states, formally constituted as regulatory committees, often advised by representatives of interest groups. This was the system that had become known as 'comitology', operating by such arcane rules that few people understood it.

The contributions made to this legislative process by national civil servants would be co-ordinated through Coreper, the Committee of Permanent Representatives, which had been part of the Community's

---

[34] This point was latterly acknowledged by Thatcher in her book *Statecraft*, published in 2002. She notes that the figure given for the Commission staff – which by then had increased to 30,000 – 'leaves out the much larger number of national officials whose tasks flow from European regulations' (London: HarperCollins), p. 324.

[35] By no means all of these are formally classified as lobbyists. Later estimates of numbers of full-time lobbyists ranged between 25,000 and 30,000.

[36] The Commission made widespread use of academia to assist in the preparation of legislation. This was a useful device, since contracts were often issued under the 'research' budget, which automatically compelled member states to contribute 'co-funding'. By this means, not only was the Community able to increase its spending at the expense of member state taxpayers but it was able to call on the services of a much larger workforce than was represented by its own employees. Similarly, much of the technical harmonising legislation was now drafted by European standards institutes, particularly CEN (Comité Européen de Normalisation). Because these were funded mainly by national institutes and governments, this also provided the Community's integration process with an extensive hidden subsidy.

core structure since 1958. Made up of teams of officials from different government departments in each of the member states, Coreper exercised as much power as any institution in Brussels. Its officials were largely responsible for agreeing new laws on behalf of the Council. Only at this point was the proposal ready to move on to its final stage, its submission for approval by the relevant ministers sitting in the Council of Ministers; and it was here, according to the theory, that the whole legislative process would finally be given 'democratic' legitimacy.[37]

In practice, a close appraisal of the workings of the Council of Ministers revealed that there was nothing 'democratic' about it whatever. Its meetings took place behind closed doors, without any public record of what was said or how ministers had voted (as was wryly observed, almost the only countries with a legislative process as secretive as that of the Community were Cuba, North Korea and Iraq). Equally relevant was that more than 80 per cent of proposals that came before the Council had already been settled by Coreper officials. They were classified as 'A items' and approved as a package without discussion before the start of meetings.[38] Only the remainder were seen by ministers and, of those, only a tiny fraction, marked with a star, were regarded as so contentious that they might actually be discussed.

One of the few participants who ever publicly described the workings of the system was Alan Clark, who recorded in his diary his first Council as a junior trade minister in February 1986. This began with an account of how, before the meeting, he was coached on 'the line to take' by an official of Ukrep, the UK's permanent representation in Brussels, before she then set about rewriting the speech he had been planning to make. 'Not that it makes the slightest difference to the conclusions of a meeting what Ministers say', he went on: 'Everything is decided, horse-traded off, by officials at Coreper … The Ministers arrive on the scene at the last minute, hot, tired, ill or drunk (sometimes all of these together), read out their piece and depart.'[39]

Another minister described how, when he arrived at his first Council, he was startled to find that the first item on the agenda was the final

---

[37] At this stage there might be added what, also according to the theory, was a further element of 'democratic' accountability. Before the Council took its final decision, many legislative proposals would go for consideration by the European Parliament. The MEPs would go through their own show of examining and voting on the proposal. But in no conventional sense was this a legislature providing a democratic check on the executive. Hardly ever did the Parliament attempt to reverse a Commission proposal, except occasionally in detail. In those cases where, by the procedure known as 'co-decision' (now renamed the 'ordinary legislative procedure'), consent was required from both Parliament and Council. Even where their views differed and further complex procedures had to be invoked to achieve 'conciliation' between them, in practice a proposal was hardly ever significantly changed.
[38] https://www.consilium.europa.eu/en/council-eu/decision-making/.
[39] Clark, Alan (1993), *Diaries* (London: Weidenfeld & Nicolson), p. 139.

communiqué. When he protested to his officials that this should surely come last, after the rest of the agenda had been settled, he was condescendingly told, 'Oh no, Minister, all the other items have already been agreed at last week's Coreper.'[40] The volume of business transacted in this way was colossal. By 1998, it was estimated that more than three thousand Council meetings took place each year, an average of 60 a week.[41]

In Britain, this charade of democracy was further compounded by the pretence that no minister could approve an item of legislation in the Council of Ministers unless it had been 'scrutinised' in advance by Parliament. This scrutiny system had been set up under Heath in 1973, and on 24 October 1990 was formally confirmed by a Resolution of the House of Commons.[42] In practice, however, the system was little more than an empty ritual. MPs had no influence whatsoever over what went on in the Council. The 1990 Resolution was to be forlornly reprinted year after year in Commons reports, recording innumerable instances where ministers approved items without scrutiny, often because the MPs had not been supplied with the relevant documents in time.[43] The record of most other national parliaments, less than half of which even went through the pretence of examining legislation passed in their name, was even worse.[44]

Once a proposal had become Community law, there were still two more stages before the process was complete. In the case of a directive, it had to be 'transposed' into a form appropriate to the country, usually by means of the 'statutory instrument' mechanism devised by Howe in the European Communities Act. As we shall see, the civil servants would often add damaging requirements.[45] The officials would present these 'regulations' to the minister for his signature (only rarely did a minister read a statutory instrument before 'signing it into law', let alone query its contents).[46]

---

[40] Lord Hesketh, Minister of State DTI 1990–1991, in private conversation, 1995.

[41] The European Commission, op. cit.

[42] The scrutiny system is explained here: https://www.parliament.uk/documents/commons-committees/european-scrutiny/European-Scrutiny-Committee-Guide-May15.pdf.

[43] See, for instance, the *Twenty-Seventh Report of the Select Committee on European Legislation on The Scrutiny of European Business*, 18 July 1996; the *Select Committee on Procedure's Third Report on European Business*, 12 March 1997; the *Seventh Report of the Select Committee on Modernisation of the House of Commons on The Scrutiny of European Business*, 9 June 1998.

[44] See 'The Scrutiny of European Business', *Twenty-Sixth Report from the House of Commons Select Committee on European Legislation, Session 1995–96*, p. x.

[45] At this point a further curious element was added into the process whereby the proposed new law would be submitted for 'consultation' to organisations representing the industry and other interests that might be affected by it. That this was no more than a further sham of 'accountability' was demonstrated by the fact that in almost no case was the wording of the law ever changed by the 'consultation' process.

[46] Information based on interviews with ministers and ex-ministers.

As a formality, the instrument would be 'laid before Parliament', giving MPs the right to object. But again, this right was only theoretical. The chance of it being rejected was nil.[47] However, when it came to EU Regulations, these did not require transposition. They had 'direct effect', applying the moment they were 'done at Brussels' or on their designated commencement dates.[48] The effect was a huge transfer of power from politicians to officials.[49] The only useful role left to the politicians in this process was to lend it a veneer of democratic legitimacy. But there was still one final stage to come. This was the way in which these new laws came to be applied. In theory every country in the EC was subject to the same directives and regulations. However, it would soon emerge that the spirit in which different countries chose to enforce these laws would vary wildly between one member state and another.

It was on this basis that, towards the end of 1992, the British, whether or not they understood how their laws were now made, began to discover to an unprecedented degree what belonging to the European Community was really about.

THE UNLEVEL PLAYING FIELD

In London, at midnight on 31 December 1992, Major and Heath together lit a 'beacon' (no more than a puny, oil-fired flame sputtering in the rain), celebrating the launch of the 'Single Market'. For five years, millions of pounds had been spent on telling businesses how this would be the moment when all remaining trade barriers were finally dismantled, 'opening up a new market of 340 million consumers', providing an unprecedented boost to growth, jobs and prosperity.

In practice, as those running businesses had already been discovering for some months, the most obvious consequence was a huge increase in regulation. The new Single Market was a 'regulatory union', the most highly regulated economic zone in the world, the setting up of which had required the issuing of 1,368 EC directives.[50] Their chief purpose had been to integrate the member states by 'harmonising' their laws over almost every

---

[47] When in 1995 a rare attempt, backed by MPs of all parties, was made to halt a statutory instrument, setting up the Meat Hygiene Service to enforce EC rules on the meat industry, ministers merely transferred the 'debate' to a standing committee where it had an in-built majority. Government supporters passed the legislation without contributing to the discussion. One MP ostentatiously dealt with his constituency correspondence throughout the proceedings, before voting for the proposal (authors' observation).

[48] https://eur-lex.europa.eu/legal-content/EN/TXT/HTML/?uri=LEGISSUM:l14547&from=EN.

[49] All this had been foreseen by the anonymous Foreign Office official who in 1971 wrote the paper on 'Sovereignty' cited earlier.

[50] *Global Britain*, August/September 1998, p. 8.

aspect of economic activity, from the labelling of fire-extinguishers to the manufacture of teddy bears.

One of the most conspicuous features of this legislation was the way so much of it was portrayed as promoting causes to which no one could possibly object, notably those shibboleths of the modern age: 'safety', 'hygiene', 'consumer protection' and 'protecting the environment'. A flagship of the new regime was six directives on health and safety, governing anything from the prescribed height of office chairs to the number of minutes employees were allowed to spend in front of a computer screen. The purpose was supposedly to guarantee that all workers throughout the EU would now enjoy the same high standards of safety.

Another swathe of directives, again in the name of 'safety', introduced new 'harmonised' standards to regulate the manufacture of every conceivable type of product, from machine-tools to children's toys, from climbing equipment to gas heaters, from lifts to cricket pads. Every item that met the new standards of the 'Communauté européen' had to carry the 'CE' mark, as an outward sign of how the Community was now looking after its citizens.

One particular attempt to 'open up the market' that had excited British enthusiasts, such as the former trade minister Lord Young, was the policy designed to enable firms from any EC country to bid for all public contracts above a certain size. Under three 'procurement directives', covering utilities, services and public works, whenever a hospital wished to buy a scanner, a local council needed to replace its vehicles or a highways authority wanted to build a bridge, the contract would first have to be advertised in the Community's *Official Journal*, allowing firms across the EC to compete, with a requirement that the lowest tender must be accepted.

Almost all the laws bringing about this revolution had to be transposed into UK statutory instruments, so that, while Parliament was spending months on the Maastricht Treaty, debating whether to give away more power to the European Commission, civil servants were busy drafting an unprecedented quantity of secondary legislation based on the previous treaty, the Single European Act. All this was 'nodded through' Parliament without debate, using powers MPs had already ceded under the European Communities Act.

A measure of just how dramatically the use of this form of law-making had been expanded was the increase in the number of statutory instruments issued each year. In the mid-1980s, the annual average had been around 2,300, mostly concerned with routine matters of administration such as teachers' pay or road closures. By 1990 the number had risen to 2,667. In 1991, as the Single Market approached, this increased to 2,933. In 1992 the total for the first time soared past the 3,000 mark, to 3,359. At the same time, the number of Bills going through Parliament declined precipitately, from an average of 150 to 200 a year through much of the post-war period to just 41 in 1993–1994.

There was no more immediate example of the contrast between theory and practice in the Single Market than the Commission's constantly repeated boast that it would bring 'the scrapping of 70 million customs forms a year'. But the Commission still wished to keep statistical records, showing the volume of what it called 'intra-Community trade'. It therefore issued EC Regulation 3330/91 imposing a complex new system known as Intrastats. Responsibility for compiling the data was placed on the traders themselves. In return for the abolition of customs forms, the cost of the new system to UK companies alone was estimated at more than £1 billion a year.

Another significant problem that came to light in the run-up to the Single Market was what became known as 'gold-plating'. So zealous were Whitehall officials in transposing EC directives into British law that they frequently added onerous requirements not included in the original directive. An example was the toy safety directive, 88/378, which required all new toys made after 1990 to be tested, in order to qualify for a CE mark. When the legislation came to the DTI, however, it chose to extend its application to second-hand toys, which provided a significant source of income to charities. This 'gold-plating' meant that many old toys could no longer be sold, depriving charities of millions of pounds a year.

Yet, despite the much-hyped benefits of the Single Market, when British firms attempted to sell their goods and services to other EC countries, this proved remarkably difficult. The Single Market had far from succeeded in dismantling all protectionist barriers. All too often the promised 'level playing field' was in practice a mirage. French officialdom in particular proved tirelessly ingenious in ensuring that business would continue to be given only to French companies, as was demonstrated in particular by the chaos surrounding the 'procurement directives', intended to ensure that public contracts were thrown open to companies across the EC.

While the new system was rigorously enforced in Britain, adding greatly to the complexity and expense of tendering procedures, other countries were notoriously reluctant to allow contracts to go to outsiders. A 1995 analysis of engineering design contracts advertised in the EC's *Official Journal* showed that nearly half had been submitted from Britain. Not long after the market was 'opened up' in this way, Renault ambulances, BMW police cars and Volvo fire engines would be racing round British streets, the new Severn Bridge would be built from subsidised Spanish steel, and

French catering firms would be serving meals to council officials in English town halls. But many continental authorities found that British products and services never somehow matched their requirements.

Yet another problem in complying with this mass of new legislation was its cost. Not only had it called into being a whole new industry of regulatory consultants; there were bodies such as authorised 'testing houses', charging huge sums to certify that products could be given 'CE' marks. The cost of regulation was also exacerbated by the emergence of a new type of public regulatory body, the 'Sefra' or Self-Financing Regulatory Agency, empowered to charge fees for inspections and for the licences that were now becoming required by EC law for many firms to stay in business. These Sefras ranged from the Meat Hygiene Service and the Medicines Control Agency, financed from the millions of pounds it charged pharmaceutical companies to license their drugs, to the Waste Authorities, set up to enforce a thicket of new EC waste disposal rules, and the quaintly named Her Majesty's Inspectorate of Pollution (HMIP), set up to enforce EC directives supposedly designed to curb pollution by industry.

By the closing months of 1992, the concern aroused by this regulatory explosion was becoming so widespread that the government could no longer ignore it. The District Surveyors' Association estimated that the cost to businesses of just one proposed new set of fire regulations, supposedly implementing two short passages from EC health and safety directives, would be £8 billion, making them the most expensive law in British history. The regulations, as drafted by the Home Office, were 20 pages long, accompanied by 100 pages of guidance: 3,500 lines derived from just 34 lines of Commission text. At the last minute, following the public furore created by the revelation of their cost, they were withdrawn, but it was to take four more years and sixteen more drafts before the Home Office officials could be persuaded to come up with a more reasonable version.

In September 1992, when, for the first time, this practice of 'gold-plating' was exposed in a newspaper article, it so shocked Major's ministers that they discussed it at a Cabinet meeting, apparently unaware of their own officials' actions.[51] This prompted Major to call for a lightening of the burden of government regulation as the keynote of his party

---

[51] *Daily Telegraph*, 'Who's That Lurking Behind the Brussels Book of Rules?' by one of the present authors (CB) appeared on 14 September 1992, two days before Britain left the ERM. On 24 November, Hurd referred in the Commons to 'cases where officials in Whitehall take decisions made in Brussels and carry them through in excessive detail'. This was 'known in the jargon' he said, 'as "Bookerism", after the journalist who identified the ill'. See HC Deb, 24 November 1992, Vol. 214, cc758-843.

conference speech at Brighton two weeks later. Launching a 'deregulation offensive', he announced that he had appointed his trade and industry minister Michael Heseltine to: 'take responsibility for cutting through this burgeoning maze of regulations – who better for hacking back the jungle. Come on, Michael, out with your club, on with your loin cloth, swing into action.'[52]

Over the next four years, inspired by the gold-plating of EC directives, this was to remain a flagship policy. Yet during that time, when his government put its lengthy 'Deregulation Bill' through Parliament, not a single regulation implementing a directive was changed. The annual number of regulations issued, which only topped three thousand for the first time in 1992, never dropped below that figure. Only at the end of the Bill's passage through Parliament did a junior minister in the House of Lords finally admit that it was always intended to exclude regulation stemming from the EC.

CAP 'REFORM'

Not only industry was being engulfed in 'red tape' at this time. In 1993 the Commission's CAP reforms were taking effect, including compulsory set-aside and a new system of linking subsidy payments to the acreage under cultivation rather than to the quantity of crops grown. This brought a quantum leap in bureaucracy as the new 'Integrated Administration and Control System' (IACS) required British farmers to submit exact details of their field areas. Yet maps of the required precision were often not available and, even when they were, the timetable set for the submission of an accompanying 79-page form was impossibly short. In the days before the deadline, long queues of farmers formed outside shops selling maps. In Portugal and Ireland, the equivalent IACS form ran to just two pages. In France, the authorities accepted estimates of field areas provided by the local town hall.

In the fruit production sector, as a result of grants offered to fruit-growers to cut back their production, hundreds of British apple orchards were rooted up, while continental growers preferred to continue to exploit a system under which they were subsidised to grow fruit even if it had to be destroyed. In the year 1994 alone, this would result in the destruction of 77 per cent of the French apple crop and 73 per cent of Italian pears. Greek farmers would receive £89 million from the EC to destroy 657,000 tonnes of peaches. According to Commission figures, EC taxpayers in 1994 paid £439 million to remove millions of tons of fruit from the market, 94 per cent of

---

[52] Prime Minister's speech, Conservative Party Conference, Brighton, October 1992.

it going to just four countries: Greece, Italy, France and Spain.[53] The net result of compulsory set-aside, intended to take 15 per cent of arable land out of production, was that in the first four years of the scheme, costing EC taxpayers £4 billion, annual production of cereal crops rose by 10 per cent.

In addition to the labyrinthine subsidy system, Brussels poured out sheaves of law to assert its ever-growing control over almost every aspect of agriculture. The dairy industry alone was subject to more than 1,100 pieces of legislation, covering everything from the insemination of cows to the permissible chemical constituents of cheese. Sheep and goats each had to be given numbered ear tags, with written records of every movement off the farm. Vegetable seedlings could not be sold for commercial use without a 'plant passport' and, under a directive on 'Forestry Reproductive Materials', based on a Nazi forestry law of 1934 and designed to preserve the genetic purity of European oak trees, it became a criminal offence to sell acorns from 'hybridised' trees. The result was that by 1995 more than three-quarters of commercially grown oaks in Britain had to be imported from eastern Europe, to climatic conditions for which they were genetically unsuited.

One of the Commission's most ambitious schemes involved more than fifty separate directives designed to maintain the health of European vegetables. It became illegal to sell seed varieties unless they had each been registered at a cost of £3,000, plus a further £700 a year to keep them on the list. This resulted in the disappearance of thousands of traditional plant varieties, including more than 95 per cent of the 2,500 known varieties of tomato.

ONE SIZE FITS ALL – THE SLAUGHTER OF THE SLAUGHTERMEN

There was no more comprehensive instance of the way this tidal wave of EC legislation was imposed by the Major government than the devastation it wrought on Britain's meat industry. Before Britain joined the EEC, the Commission had issued Directive 64/433, to harmonise hygiene standards for the production of meat exported across national frontiers. When these rules, based on a nineteenth-century German code, had been challenged by non-EEC countries, including New Zealand, as being outdated, the Commission had then modified them, producing new, extra-legal guidelines called the 'Vade Mecum'.[54]

---

[53] HoL Select Committee on the European Communities, *Report on Reform of the EC Fresh Fruit and Vegetable Regime* (London: HMSO, 19 December 1995).

[54] Commission of the European Communities, Directorate General for Agriculture (1992), 'Guidelines for European Commission Inspections of Fresh Meat Establishments', VI/1111/92-EN Rev. 2. (Several versions were produced – this one was made available to the authors.)

In the 1980s, the UK Ministry of Agriculture, Fisheries and Food had imposed these 'EC export rules' only on those abattoirs that produced meat for export, also providing grants worth millions of pounds to enable them to comply with the 'structural standards'. The result reinforced the three-tier structure of the industry, which became split between some 80 large 'industrial' abattoirs, mass-producing meat for supermarkets and for export; several hundred medium-size abattoirs, mainly producing for family butchers; and hundreds of tiny local slaughterhouses, often serving a single adjoining butcher's shop.

As the Single Market approached, harmonised meat hygiene rules were included in the list of measures to apply even to those producers who did not export. The result was a new directive, 91/497, which was actually little different from the earlier directive, but still posed enormous difficulties for the hundreds of small and medium-size abattoirs. They would now have to make the same hugely expensive structural changes originally required only of industrial meat plants. But, unlike their larger competitors, they could expect no financial assistance.

What made the situation worse was that as early as May 1990, long before the new directive was finalised, MAFF veterinary officials began 'advising' abattoir owners on the supposed new legal requirements. These instructions were based not on the directive, which only emerged in July 1991, but on the *Vade Mecum*, which had no legal force. Bemused owners were then told that unless they complied with these standards by 1 January 1993, the start of the Single Market, they would be prohibited from trading. They were given just seven months to make often major and expensive structural changes without which they would be refused a licence to operate. Faced with what seemed impossible demands, between 1990 and 1992, 205 businesses – more than a quarter of all the abattoirs in Britain – shut their doors.

The survivors were immediately confronted with another problem. The new law also imposed a continental system of public health, requiring supervision by veterinary surgeons, to replace traditional local authority environmental health officers. These vets, however, were not qualified to inspect meat, so MAFF adopted a clumsy compromise of having meat inspectors supervised by veterinary officials. Abattoir owners had to pay for both, facing charges of up to £100 per hour for the 'services' of vets, many of them hired from Spain and with little knowledge of slaughterhouse practice. Hundreds of small operations closed, forcing some farmers to ship animals over a hundred miles to be slaughtered.

When agriculture minister John Gummer was challenged as to why the industry was being so damaged, he initially argued that the closures were necessary for 'hygiene reasons'. When this was disproved, he then repeatedly fell back, in letters to MPs and others, on the curiously disingenuous explanation that the owners had 'taken a commercial decision not to invest in the future of their business.'[55]

AN ECOLOGICAL DISASTER

As minister responsible for agriculture and fisheries, Gummer was also now presiding over the destruction of another British industry. For the first few years after the start of the 20-year transitional stage of the Common Fisheries Policy in 1983, the British fishing industry had not fared too badly, although in 1985 the people of Greenland, previously part of Denmark but now autonomous, became so frustrated at the depredation of fish stocks in their waters by EC trawlers that they withdrew from the Community. In return for allowing EC fishing boats to continue fishing her waters, under strict conservation rules, Greenland was paid £107 million a year by the EU.

What did anger British fishermen, as Spain's accession approached, was the practice whereby Spanish fishing companies registered their vessels as British and then bought up UK fishing licences. This entitled them to a share in UK quotas, even though they continued to sail from and land their catches in Spanish ports. Since these vessels operated under the Red Ensign, they became known as 'flag boats', or 'quota hoppers'. By 1988, two years after Spain's accession, the problem of these 'quota hoppers' prompted Parliament to pass the Merchant Shipping Act. To qualify for British quota, vessels had to be owned and crewed in Britain. In what was to become a historic demonstration of the impotence of Parliament, however, a number of Spanish-owned companies, headed by Factortame Ltd, brought an action under Article 7 of the Treaty of Rome, asking for the Act to be set aside as representing 'national discrimination'.

After hearings in the London High Court and the House of Lords, the case was referred to the ECJ, which ruled in 1991 that 'certain aspects' of the Act were 'not compatible with Community law'.[56] This left the Lords no option but to set aside the will of Parliament.

Meanwhile, the Commission had to come to terms with the failure of its fisheries policy. By 1991 fishing capacity in the Community had substantially increased. Since 1970, the total tonnage of the EC fleets had risen by 153 per cent, and fishing capacity by 420 per cent.[57] Worse still,

---

[55] Multiple copies passed to the authors.
[56] Case C-221/89 R v. Secretary of State for Transport, *ex parte* Factortame [1991] ECR I-3905, [1991] 3 CMLR 589.
[57] Porter, G. (1998), *Estimating Overcapacity in the Global Fishing Fleet* (Washington, DC: WWF).

the 'conservation' rules, which forced fishermen to 'discard' fish for which they had no quota, were causing an ecological crisis. Even the Commission estimated that North Sea discards of haddock for 1985 were 460 million individuals, whereas landings amounted to 500 million. In the Bay of Biscay/Celtic Sea, hake discards were estimated at 130 million individuals, for a landing figure of 110 million.[58] Yet in Norwegian waters, where the government was still able to impose its own rules, 'discarding' had been banned since 1987.[59]

The Commission's response was to propose reducing 'fishing effort' by 'decommissioning' vessels in each national fleet. Known as the Multi-Annual Guidance Programme (MAGP), the news of this was sneaked out by Gummer on 27 February 1992 by way of a written parliamentary answer. He then tried to claim that the UK fleet reduction would be only 12 per cent, but it eventually emerged that the Commission was demanding 19 per cent, equivalent to nearly a fifth of the fleet. Yet the cut demanded of the much larger Spanish fleet was only 4 per cent, much of it financed from EC structural funds. Of the £25 million allocated to the British scheme, however, £20 million would have to be repaid through the rebate 'claw-back'.[60] In other words, British taxpayers would be paying to make room for the Spanish to fish in British waters.

It had already been recognised by the Commission, however, that in view of the size of the Spanish fleet, more would be needed. It thus gave notice that further cuts might follow, unless member states made their own reductions. The UK government dutifully introduced the Sea Fish (Conservation) Bill, giving it unprecedented powers to dictate the terms on which fishermen were permitted to fish (the so-called 'days at sea' restrictions). This would enable it to squeeze thousands more fishermen out of business, by denying them the right to earn a living without having to pay compensation.

The Bill was rushed through Parliament, with the support of almost every Conservative MP, so fast that it had passed its second reading even before the deadline for industry 'consultation' had expired. Outraged fishermen challenged the scheme in the courts and it was eventually dropped. But the problem had not disappeared. The fishermen's victory had merely postponed their tragedy.

[58] Commission of the European Communities, *Report 1991 from the Commission to the Council and the European Parliament on the Common Fisheries Policy*, SEC(91) 2288 final, Brussels, 18 December 1991.
[59] Norwegian fisheries management, our approach on discard of fish, ʰttps://www.regjeringen.no/globalassets/upload/fkd/brosjyrer-og-veiledninger/fact_sheet_discard.pdf.
[60] *Hansard*, 3 June 1992, col. 52.

A WATERSHED MOMENT

What was now becoming uncomfortably clear was that, whatever the Community claimed it was trying to do, the result was invariably the opposite. A Single Market claimed to be a great act of 'liberation' and 'deregulation' had produced one of the greatest concentrations of constrictive regulation in history. A 'reform' of the CAP intended to cut back on over-production and misplaced expenditure ended up producing more unwanted food at even greater expense. The CFP, intended to 'conserve Europe's fish stocks', had resulted in an ecological crisis.

At least on balance, it might be argued that the Single Market must have achieved its intended purpose of stimulating economic growth and creating jobs. But even that was a mirage. In the three years preceding the launch, average EU growth had been an unimpressive 2.3 per cent per annum, while average unemployment had been 8.5 per cent. In the four years after January 1993, the growth rate was to slump to 1.67 per cent – the poorest performance of any economic bloc in the developed world – while EU unemployment would soar to 10.9 per cent, with nearly 20 million people out of work.

The significance of what was happening to the 'European project' in the early 1990s was that from now on, more than ever before, it was going to become increasingly possible to measure all those euphoric, long-familiar promises of the great things it was going to achieve in the indefinite future, against what it was actually achieving in practice. It was a watershed moment.

13

Odd Man Out: 1993–1997

Building the Single Currency is like building the mediaeval cathedrals. It will be as big. It will be as beautiful. It will last as much.

Chef de cabinet to Yves-Thibault de Silguy, Commissioner in charge of preparations for monetary union, August 1996[1]

An economic union will survive only if it is based on a political union.

Helmut Kohl, 1993[2]

As a former Chancellor, I can only say I cannot pinpoint a single concrete economic advantage that unambiguously comes to this country because of our membership of the European Union.

Norman Lamont, October 1994

Unemployment in this country is now the lowest of any major European competitor. We have created more jobs over the past three years than Germany, France, Italy and Spain – indeed, we have created more than Germany, France, Italy and Spain added together.

John Major to House of Commons, 24 June 1996

[1] BBC Radio 4, 24 August 1996.
[2] *Financial Times*, 4 January 1993.

It was a measure of the unease provoked by the Danish '*Nej*' and the narrowness of the French vote on Maastricht that Delors, late in 1992, felt it necessary to examine means of 'strengthening the image of Europe'. To do this, he appointed a '*Comité des Sages*', headed by Willy de Clercq, a Belgian MEP, working with some advertising executives. Their report was unveiled on 31 March 1993 to a press conference in Brussels. Nothing better demonstrated the gap between the political elites of Europe and the 'citizens' they purported to represent than this report. The 'wise men' suggested that 'Europe' should be treated as a 'brand', and marketed as such. The Maastricht Treaty was too complicated, so, instead of being allowed to read it, the 'citizens' should be fed slogans, such as 'Together for Europe for the benefit of us all' and the toe-curling 'Mother Europe Must Protect Her Children'.[3]

The 'wise men' also suggested financing 'pan-European television broadcasts' by Delors himself, including a programme 'directed at the women of Europe'. 'This will probably be the first time', the report intoned, 'that a statesman makes a direct appeal to women.'[4] Similarly, the media should be paid to take 'a more positive line' about the EU. History books should be rewritten 'to reflect the European dimension' and broadcasters should be funded to introduce that 'dimension' into television soap operas. Even for a normally quiescent Brussels press corps, this was too much. Amid a 'cacophony of protest', angry journalists walked out and the Greek president of the Brussels association of journalists, Costas Verros, accused the Commission of 'acting like a military junta'.[5]

This flight from reality presented a stark contrast with two other developments in Europe in 1993. First, there was the tragedy unfolding in Bosnia, where Croats, Muslims and Serbs, sponsored by the Belgrade government, were locked in a murderous civil war while those who claimed to represent 'Europe' had no means of stopping the carnage. On the economic front, the Community also seemed ineffective. Growth, which in the late 1980s had averaged 3–4 per cent, had slipped to 1 per cent in 1992, and was heading for zero. With German unemployment rising to 7 per cent

---

[3] Reflection on Information and Communication Policy of the European Community, March 1993.

[4] *Daily Telegraph*, 1 April 1993, 'De Clercq suggested that young people should be targeted because 'it is strategically wise to act where resistance is weakest'.

[5] Three years later a Belgian journalist, Gerard de Selys, described in the French monthly *Le Monde Diplomatique* (June 1996) how many of the 765 journalists accredited in Brussels were offered lucrative work, with generous expenses, either freelance or for one of the many publications produced essentially by the Commission. Some of them doubled or tripled their salaries. ('The Propaganda Machine of the Commission', June 1996.) Cf. *European Journal*, June 1996, p. 12.

and France's over 11, jobless totals had doubled over the decade to reach 18 million.

Yet, maintaining the air of unreality, Delors complained to the European Parliament in Brussels on 4 February that, 'there is a lack of willingness to co-operate', and 'a dangerous back-sliding from Europe's economic strategy: the next stage of economic and monetary union'. More integration was his answer, centred on three issues: preparation for EMU; enlargement; and the need to take on more supranational powers through the 'institutional reforms' enshrined in a new treaty.

WITHIN THE BUBBLE
The first European Council of 1993, meeting in Copenhagen on 21–22 June, also seemed to dwell in its own world. EU leaders applauded their 'success' in the second Danish referendum and set 1 January 1995 for the accession of Austria, Finland, Sweden and Norway.

Then on the horizon was entry of the former Communist countries of central and eastern Europe, a prospect not viewed with any enthusiasm. To avoid making a firm commitment to their early entry, the Council set out five so-called 'Copenhagen criteria'. Candidates would have to establish proper democracy and a free-market economy, protection for minorities, together with respect for the rule of law and human rights. Membership also presupposed the candidate's 'ability to take on the obligations of membership including adherence to the aims of political, economic and monetary union'.[6] The criteria were widely regarded as a delaying tactic.

Only briefly did the Council touch on the Community's worsening economic plight, asking Delors to prepare a White Paper on 'jobs, competitiveness and growth'. But they did confirm the finance ministers' decision to expand 'structural' funding. For the period 1994 –1999 this was to be increased to £30 billion a year, matching CAP levels and almost three times the size of the Marshall Aid programme. This was to be Delors' next 'big idea'.

Lower down the agenda was a ticking time bomb. 'To promote confidence in the construction of Europe', as the communiqué put it, the Council 'underlined the importance' of continuing to combat Community fraud, allegations of which were becoming persistent. When Antonio Quatraro,

[6] As was widely observed at the time, considering the undemocratic method whereby the Community made its own laws, it was not obvious that the EC itself met its own criteria for membership. France would have been disqualified in 1958 for her systematic use of torture in Algeria. A similar point was for different reasons made about Italy when she took on the presidency under Berlusconi on 1 July 2003.

the Commission official in charge of CAP tobacco subsidies, committed 'suicide' in mysterious circumstances, this added to the sense of unease. His department's handling of the £800 million a year in payments to Italian and Greek farmers was under investigation. For now, though, all the Council wanted were proposals for an 'anti-fraud strategy' by March 1994.

This was not the only crisis in the making. As the Council ended, Delors took the opportunity to crow about the healthy state of the ERM.[7] But it was then only seven weeks away from collapse, torn apart by the contradictory needs of different economies. The Bundesbank needed interest rates high, to aid Germany in financing reunification with borrowed money. France needed low rates to boost her ailing economy, yet was forced by the ERM to keep them high.

When in late July Germany ignored French pleas for a rate cut, the markets became convinced that France would have to devalue. In four days leading up to 1 August, 'Black Sunday', France committed $100 million to supporting the franc, before conceding defeat. ERM margins were relaxed from 4.50 to 30 per cent, effectively allowing the currencies to float freely. 'Stage one' in the 'glide-path' to a single currency existed only in name. For Delors, stricken by sciatica and forced to use a walking stick, the prospect of monetary union must suddenly have seemed remote.

At the same moment, Major was vacationing in Portugal, meditating on Britain's involvement with 'Europe'. It had been 20 years since the UK had joined the Community and Maastricht had proved the 'fork in the road':

> Our partners wanted a single currency. We did not. They wanted a social chapter. We did not. They wanted more harmonisation of policy. We did not. They wanted more Community control of defence. We did not. Increasingly they talked in private of a federal destination, even though in public they were reassuring about a Europe of nation states.[8]

Undaunted, in the autumn, Major contributed an article to *The Economist*, setting out his own 'vision' for 'Europe'. It should focus, he argued, on what its people wanted, not on the institutional reforms that so obsessed its leaders. Our prime concerns, he wrote, should be peace, growth, prosperity and employment.[9] But he soon discovered that his efforts were fruitless. 'I caused a stir,' he recalled, 'but wasted my ink.'[10] In 'Europe' he found himself

[7] Cited in Grant, op. cit., p. 262.
[8] Major, op. cit., p. 579.
[9] *The Economist*, 25 September 1993. p. 29.
[10] Major, op. cit., p. 587.

perpetually in a minority of one for not giving enough. When he returned home, he found himself harried by his backbenchers and even the 'bastards' in his own Cabinet for giving away too much.[11] Meanwhile, his party's standing in the opinion polls was at its lowest level in history.

THE BUBBLE CONTINUES

For Brussels, though, the autumn of 1993 brought a moment of celebration after Germany's constitutional court in Karlsruhe ruled that the Maastricht Treaty did not breach the country's Basic Law, thus allowing the treaty to come into force. On 29 October, the heads of state and government were summoned to an 'Extraordinary European Council', to declare that, as from 1 November, the European Community would now be known as 'the European Union'.[12] Outside the bubble of self-congratulation, unemployment had reached its highest level since the EEC was founded. As for bringing an end to 'bloody wars', the headlines were daily dominated by the chaos in Bosnia, which the Community had been unable to end.[13]

Unreality continued with the next European Council, again in Brussels, on 11–12 December.[14] The highlight was Delors' presenting his White Paper on how to cure 'Europe's structural unemployment'.[15] At its heart was a hugely ambitious programme. Delors wanted control of the Community's research and development policy, so that 'co-operation' directed by the Commission would 'gradually become a basic principle'. Even bigger was a scheme to build the 'trans-European infrastructure': interconnecting energy transmission systems and a series of cross-border road and rail projects, collectively known as the Trans-European Network or TEN. The 400 billion ecus cost would come partly from regional funds but mainly from member states, with private finance involvement. The aim was to boost employment by launching a neo-Keynesian public works programme, which would also promote integration.

---

[11] Having just finished a television interview at Downing Street and unaware that the microphone was still live, Major had launched into a tirade against three of his Eurosceptic ministers – not named, but almost certainly Michael Howard, Peter Lilley and Michael Portillo – calling them 'bastards'. *Guardian*, 'Major hits out at Cabinet', 25 July 1993.

[12] https://ec.europa.eu/commission/presscorner/detail/en/DOC_93_7.

[13] Almost the only decision the Community had been able to take over the Yugoslav conflict was to support the international embargo on arms sales to the combatants. This policy was summed up by Douglas Hurd's lofty pronouncement that selling arms would only create 'a level killing field'. Since the Serbs were already well armed, the Croats and Bosnian Muslims were seriously hurt by the embargo. Hurd would have been more honest to admit that he was arguing for an 'unlevel killing field'.

[14] https://www.consilium.europa.eu/media/21216/82736.pdf.

[15] Commission of the European Communities (1993), White Paper on 'Growth, Competitiveness, and Employment: The Challenges and Ways Forward into the 21st Century', COM(93) 700 final, Brussels, 5 December 1993.

The Council approved Delors' 'kind of road map' in such glowing terms that he described himself 'as proud as a peacock'.[16] When Major explained it to Parliament, no one could have guessed that he and his fellow heads of government had just agreed in principle a programme of state-subsidised public works, equal to the entire annual spending of his own government.[17]

'THE POODLE OF BRUSSELS'

By March 1994, after more than a year of negotiations, terms had been agreed for the accession of Austria, Finland, Sweden and Norway, although Norway was still insisting on protection for her fisheries. Spain, as always, demanded her ransom, which had Delors scraping up the money to buy fishing rights for the Spanish fleet from Russia.[18] This left a sombre mood in Brussels, as next in line were the former Communist states of central and eastern Europe.

Major, meanwhile, had been doing his arithmetic and had worked out that, with new countries in the Community, Britain's already minimal voting power would be unacceptably reduced. He decided to make an issue of this. Fully supported by his Cabinet, he gave notice that he would veto enlargement unless the Community retained its existing rule that, under the system of qualified majority voting, 23 votes were sufficient for a 'blocking minority'. In so doing, Major had touched a nerve. QMV was the defining characteristic of supranationalism. As Salter and Monnet had recognised in the 1920s, it could be used to force nations to accept decisions against their national interests. As long as they retained the veto, they could block new laws. But even QMV presented problems as long as a minority could still form blocking alliances. This was precisely what Major recognised: each 'enlargement' of the Union could be used to increase its supranational powers.

Initially, Major relied on support from Germany, France and Spain. But, as negotiations progressed, and after Spain's support was bought off by the Russian fishing deal, this evaporated. Again, Britain was on her own. Thus, when asked in the Commons which was more important to him, the status quo on QMV or enlargement, Major could only side-step the question. He was determined 'to fight Britain's corner' just as hard as any other nation, he declared. It was the Labour leader, Mr Smith, who 'would sign away our votes, our competitiveness and our money', which was why he should be described as '*Monsieur Oui*, the poodle of Brussels'.[19]

[16] See Grant, op. cit., p. 268.
[17] *Hansard*, 14 December 1993, col. 685.
[18] Grant, op. cit., p. 270.
[19] *Hansard*, 22 March 1994, col. 134.

It was a jibe soon to rebound on Major, as Hurd departed for three days and nights of continuous negotiation with his fellow foreign ministers at Ioannina in Greece. He ended up with a classic 'Euro-fudge'.[20] To save face, 23 votes might still be permitted to hold up a proposal for a short time. Otherwise, Britain was forced to concede her point. Smith charged Major with a 'humiliating climbdown'.[21] One of Major's own backbenchers, Tony Marlow, angrily denounced the 'so-called compromise', demanding that the prime minister should stand aside.[22]

For Major, it was a low point of his premiership. 'The mood in the party was fierce. The press was hideous. It was an appalling time, made worse by the knowledge that the wound was self-inflicted', he wrote.[23] On 30 March, the front page of the *Daily Mail* had a cartoon depicting Delors in the high heels and fishnet stockings of a Parisian prostitute, leading a dainty poodle on a leash, its head bearing the face of Major. Another prime minister was on his way to being destroyed by 'Europe'.

HUMILIATION CONTINUES

Rather less media attention was paid in Britain to the news from Marrakesh on 15 April 1994. After seven years of tortuous negotiations, the governments of 123 nations had signed the 'Final Act' of the Uruguay GATT Round. Its consequences would be felt all over the globe, not least in the damage it would inflict on the third world. It had been a 'stitch-up' between US and EU negotiators, who, by what was known as the 'Blair House Accord' in November 1992, had agreed to 'fudge' an agreement to reduce subsidies.

Under the 'MacSharry CAP reforms', many EU farm subsidies had indeed been reduced, but farmers were being paid more in 'compensation' for losing them than they had originally been paid. Similarly, the rich producer-countries could continue dumping forty million tons of subsidised wheat on the world market, driving down the world price. At the same time, GATT was forcing third-world countries to open their markets.[24] Unsurprisingly, 150,000 rioted in New Delhi, complaining that Western imports would ruin Indian farmers and force many industries out of business.

---

[20] Major, op. cit., p. 589.
[21] *Hansard*, 29 March 1994, col. 798.
[22] Ibid., col. 802.
[23] Major, op. cit., pp. 589–590.
[24] See CUTS Centre for International Trade, Economics and Environment, Briefing Paper: 'Overdue Reforms in European Agriculture: Implications for Southern Consumers', 6/1999 – www.cuts.org/no6-99.pdf; Howarth, Richard (2000), 'The CAP: History and Attempts at Reform', IEA Policy Paper, June.

In Britain, the nation was shocked by the unexpected death on 12 May of John Smith. He was succeeded as Labour leader by the young and still comparatively unknown Tony Blair. Smith's death delayed the start of the election campaign for the European Parliament and, when it began, the Conservatives ran on the ticket: 'A Strong Britain in a Strong Europe'. But Major's reputation as the 'poodle of Brussels' destroyed its credibility. The Conservatives' vote plummeted to 27.8 per cent, its lowest in a national poll in the twentieth century. Labour's 44.2 per cent increased its representation from 45 seats to 62. Britain's overall turnout, 36.1 per cent, was again the lowest in the EU.

Shortly after the elections, Major was 'bounced' by another incident. On the agenda of the Corfu European Council for 24–25 June was a successor to Delors, due to retire at the end of 1994 after a record nine years in office. Kohl and Mitterrand strongly backed a fanatical integrationist, the prime minister of Belgium, Jean-Luc Dehaene. Major's objections forced Dehaene's withdrawal, but, later in the year, at an emergency Council in Brussels, he accepted Luxembourg's prime minister, Jacques Santer, as a compromise. The president-elect promptly declared that, in his enthusiasm for integration, there was no difference between himself and Dehaene.[25]

So much did this episode preoccupy Britain's media that scant coverage was given to the rest of the Council agenda, which included endorsing Delors' ambitious 1994–1999 framework programme on scientific and technological research. This greatly extended the reach of the Union's budget, since the Commission's contributions had to be matched by national governments. The Council also gave the Commission extensive new regulatory powers over what it called the 'information society', covering use of computer networks for anything from air traffic control to health care.[26] It accepted a Franco-German 'initiative against racism and xenophobia', extending the reach of the 'Justice and Home Affairs' pillar of Maastricht. Finally, the Council agreed to set up a 'Reflection Group', to start work on a new treaty.[27] Monnet's 'provisional government' was beginning to flex its muscles in a way that was to have profound effects.

ODD MAN IN

It was in this summer of 1994 that another key aspect of Britain's separateness from the EU began to emerge. In the two years since she had dropped out of the ERM, her economy had begun to expand, faster than any other in

[25] George, op. cit., p. 262.
[26] Ibid.
[27] https://www.consilium.europa.eu/media/21207/corfu-european-council.pdf.

the EU. Many were now looking on 16 September 1992 as having been not 'Black' but 'White' Wednesday. The former 'sick man of Europe', with an economy that had ranked fourth behind Germany, France and Italy, was now moving rapidly back towards second place. In terms of *per capita* income, she had then been almost at the bottom of the European league. She was now moving towards the top.

Also evident was the remarkable extent to which Britain's burgeoning new prosperity was due, not to her trade with the EU, but to her world trade. Britain was actually trading with the rest of the EU at a huge loss, building a 20-year cumulative deficit of £87 billion. Added to her net contributions to the Brussels budget, this made an overall deficit of £108 billion. Fortunately, this was counter-balanced by a dramatic growth in her non-EU income, not least from her US investments, double those in the EU. The constant claim that EU membership was vital to her economic survival was false.[28]

However, it was still to be some years before the implications registered. And it was not until 1998 that, according to OECD figures, Britain's economy again became the fourth largest in the world, after those of the USA, Japan and Germany; and not until 2002 that her *per capita* income exceeded Germany's to become the highest in Europe. But already, a country becoming economically the most successful in the EU was at the same time becoming politically regarded by her partners, bent on ever greater integration, as no more than a tiresome irrelevance.

This was neatly illustrated in the autumn of 1994 by the startling contrast between two views of Europe's future: one from Germany; the other from Major. In a paper addressed to the forthcoming IGC Reflection Group on 1 September 1994, two leading German politicians, Wolfgang Schäuble, Kohl's heir apparent, and Karl Lamers, warned that the Union was in danger of reverting to 'a loosely knit grouping of states', amounting to little more than a free trade area. So great was this threat that they called for a redoubled drive for further integration, with a 'hard core' of six or seven states leading the way.[29]

Major responded in a speech in Leiden, Holland, on 7 September, offering 'flexibility' as an alternative. Nations, he said, should not be forced into the same mould, but should be able to opt out of specific policy areas. Only in areas such as the Single Market or the environment was there a

[28] Jamieson, Bill (1994), *Britain Beyond Europe* (London: Duckworth).
[29] Christian Democratic Union/Christian Social Union Group in the German Lower House (1994), 'Reflections on European Policy', Bonn, 1 September.

need for conformity.[30] As before, though, Major was ignored. Rather greater note was taken of a voice from the past, former French president Giscard d'Estaing. Forget political integration for the time being, was his message. Concentrate on EMU. Achieve this and political union would inevitably follow.[31]

ASSAILED FROM EVERY SIDE

Back home during that autumn of 1994, Major came under mounting pressure from both wings of his party. His conference in October saw a packed fringe meeting cheering Norman Lamont for the most outspoken attack ever heard from a senior Conservative politician on the EU. 'If Britain was not a member of the European Union today,' he said, 'I do not believe there would be a case to join.' But, displaying the deeply embedded schizophrenia within the Tory ranks, he did not advocate withdrawal, even if it was 'nonsense' to suggest that Britain could not survive outside the EU. 'The issue,' he warned, 'may well return to the political agenda.'[32]

From the 'Europhile' wing, in November, a carefully co-ordinated campaign was launched by a phalanx of senior political and business figures to pressure Major into joining the single currency. In the lead was the CBI, with support from such figures as Leon Brittan, the EU's trade commissioner. Major also faced a rebellious House when he presented the legislation needed to authorise increased UK contributions to the EU. Its budget was up 103 per cent between 1986 and 1994. At the Edinburgh Council, he had agreed to increase Britain's payments. Now, he had to resort to a threat of resignation if the House rejected the 'international commitment'.[33]

To make mischief, Labour tabled an amendment linking approval of the Bill to action on cutting EU fraud. This had lately been making more headlines. In July 1994 a House of Lords committee had reported that fraud, particularly in the CAP, was now taking place 'on a monumental and growing scale', amounting to £5 billion a year.[34] A book published across

[30] Cited in Salmon and Nicoll, op. cit., pp. 261–263. Major was favouring the term 'variable geometry' to describe his notion of a 'Europe of overlapping circles', describing how to a limited extent the Union was developing: different groups brought together by, say, the Schengen Agreement, monetary union and defence.
[31] Szukala, Andrea and Wessels, Wolfgang (1997), 'The Franco-German Tandem', in Edwards, Geoffrey and Pijpers, Alfred, The Politics of European Treaty Reform: The 1996 Intergovernmental Conference and Beyond (London: Cassell), p. 91.
[32] Lamont, Norman (1995), Sovereign Britain (London: Duckworth), p. 29.
[33] Major, op. cit., p. 599.
[34] 12th Report (Session 1993–94): Financial Control and Fraud in the Community, HMSO, 1994.

the EU by a French MP, François d'Aubert, put the total even higher.[35] The EU's Court of Auditors, in what was to become a yearly ritual, refused to approve the EU's 1993 accounts on the grounds that they contained too many 'irregularities'.

For the government, Chancellor Kenneth Clarke argued that the increased contribution was the necessary price Britain paid for the benefits of EU membership. 'Our economic well-being is dependent in huge part on our membership of the Single Market,' he intoned.[36] This was counterpointed by speeches from Eurosceptics, including Norman Lamont, who had tried to raise the issue of CAP fraud at a special meeting of finance ministers. A Court of Auditors report had been circulated, detailing various frauds, including a famous episode when a ship in Hamburg had been loaded and unloaded repeatedly with the same meat, for which export subsidies had been claimed several times. Italy had in 1992 claimed subsidies for 4.3 million acres of durum wheat, used for pasta, although satellite photography showed only 1.9 million acres grown. Yet, Lamont found:

> a number of the ministers did not turn up. I opened the discussion. A large number of ministers just read their newspapers. No one contributed a word to the discussion, then Mr. Delors attacked me for being political by introducing the subject of the Court of Auditors.[37]

At least there was compensation. The Norwegians for a second time rejected EC membership in a referendum, by 52.1 per cent to 47.9, on a 90.4 per cent turnout. Decisive again were the rural communities, some of which voted 80 per cent 'No'.[38] Another feature was the opposition of many young people, one of whom, a pretty blonde, explained to the BBC after the result: 'it is the lack of democracy in your system we don't like'. For some British viewers it was chilling to realise that, in speaking of 'your system', she meant one of which Britain was now part.

SPAIN: CUCKOO IN THE NEST
For Major, there was the European Council treadmill. However, when he went to Essen for the last Council of 1994, hosted by Kohl on 9–10

---

[35] D'Aubert, François, *Main basse sur l'Europe: enquête sur les dérives de Bruxelles*, quoted in *The European*, 4 November 1994.

[36] *Hansard*, 28 November 1994, col. 932.

[37] Ibid., col. 961.

[38] Saether, Arild (1995), 'Det norske nei! – Norwegians say no!' *EIPASCOPE*, 1995 (2), pp. 1–3. Via AEI. Based on a speech held at a Trade Union conference at Wakefield, November 1995.

December, he was to recall it as 'mercifully free' of petty wrangles.[39] The last Council attended by Delors and Mitterrand, it set 1999 for the launch of the single currency. It agreed that Malta and Cyprus should be allowed to apply to join the EU. And it approved the usual raft of integrationist measures, including five 'key areas' in which the heads of government hoped to tackle the mounting problem of Europe's unemployment.

They instructed themselves, for instance, to increase 'the employment-intensiveness of growth', with more flexible organisation of work 'in a way which fulfils both the wishes of employees and the requirements of competition'. They suggested a wages policy based on 'initiatives, particularly at regional and local level, that create jobs which take account of new requirements, e.g., in the environmental and social-services spheres'. They agreed to 'transpose these recommendations in their individual policies into a multi-annual programme'.[40]

When Major returned home to report to MPs on 12 December, he tried to portray these conclusions as evidence that his colleagues had accepted the need for 'labour market flexibility', 'deregulation' and the need to make Europe 'competitive'. 'Yet again', he claimed, policies pioneered by Britain were now accepted 'across the European Union'.[41] One item on which Major was questioned, however, was an opaque passage on fisheries referring to the Act of Accession of Spain and Portugal. On this, he reassuringly claimed that it meant 'no great change'.[42] He did not realise that, from 1 January 1995, Spain would have limited fishing rights to 70,000 square miles of waters around the Irish coast known as the 'Irish Box'. The Spanish demanded access for 220 vessels, threatening that, if this was refused, they would block the accession of Austria, Sweden and Finland.

The unfortunate fisheries minister, then William Waldegrave, was thus forced to fight a rearguard action at the Fisheries Council on 22 December. His only hope was to negotiate a tighter limit on the number of Spanish vessels allowed. Reporting to a crowded House after the Christmas recess on 10 January 1995, he had to confess that, against Britain's wishes, 40 Spanish boats would be permitted entry. Not explaining that these would be large, modern vessels capable of catching more fish than the Cornish and Irish fleets combined, he claimed that, 'had we not limited the number of ships', things could have been much worse, so 'we have made considerable

---

[39] Major, op. cit., p. 523.
[40] 'Presidency Conclusions', European Council, Essen, 9–10 December 1994, para. 9.
[41] HC Deb, 12 December 1994, Vol. 251, cc613-30.
[42] Ibid.

gains'.[43] As a sop to angry Conservative backbenchers, Waldegrave doubled funding to compensate British fishermen for 'decommissioning' their boats, to £53 million. Several hundred more British fishermen would be bribed to go out of business.

THE 'BENEFITS OF BRITAIN'S MEMBERSHIP'

Against this background, it was scarcely credible that, on 2 January 1995, Douglas Hurd chose to regale the British people with the 'benefits of Britain's membership of the European Union', urging his party colleagues to follow suit. For a man not known to be stupid, however, his catalogue of 'benefits' defied logic. 'First,' he said, 'the EU brings us jobs.' The EU, he claimed, 'now takes 53 percent of our exports' (government data for 1995 showed this figure as only 44.6 per cent).[44] 'The French,' he claimed, 'cannot block our lamb, or the Germans our beef' (he was shortly to discover to the contrary). 'The Italians and Spaniards pay hefty fines for breaking the rules on milk quotas' (the fines were never paid). The EU, and NATO, have brought us 'the priceless gift of nearly 50 years of peace on our continent' (the Bosnian tragedy was at its height).

He also claimed that: 'Membership has enabled us to take the European Commission to the ECJ over the French government's enormous subsidies to Air France' (when the court declared this £2.4 billion subsidy illegal, the Commission reformulated its permission, allowing the subsidy to continue). 'The new principle of subsidiarity enshrined in the Maastricht Treaty is helping to reverse the tide of new EU laws' (between 1993 and 1994, the total of new directives and regulations had risen from 1,602 to 1,800).[45] 'We have now persuaded our partners that jobs should be top of the EU agenda' (EU-wide unemployment was now higher than at any time since the 1930s).

Even against this catalogue of self-deceiving rhetoric, however, Hurd was driven to concede that, 'Not everything is rosy', acknowledging that: 'Often it is the image of a remote, interfering and wasteful EU which dominates.' But this was why, he said, 'we need to make real headway in correcting what goes wrong' and why 'we must win the argument for a flexible, decentralised Europe'.[46]

---

[43] *Hansard*, 10 January 1995, cols 26–27.
[44] *The United Kingdom Balance of Payments*, ONS, 1995.
[45] Figures taken from the Commission's CELEX database, quoted in a parliamentary answer by Lord Howe.
[46] Conservative Party News, published by Conservative Central Office, 2 January 1995.

DIVIDED LOYALTIES

On 9 March 1995 came a crisis that highlighted just how membership of the EU was straining Britain's traditional loyalties. After a four-hour chase, three Canadian fisheries protection vessels in international waters off the Canadian coast had arrested a Spanish trawler, the *Estai*, suspected of breaking conservation rules. Yet, even before the facts had been established, the EU's fisheries Commissioner Emma Bonino was accusing the Canadian government of 'piracy'.[47] She was supported by Leon Brittan, the UK's Commissioner, who accused the Canadian authorities of acting illegally.[48]

Although the *Estai* had been fishing in international waters, Canada had invoked international law on straddling stocks to defend rapidly declining stocks of Greenland halibut, with the Newfoundland fisheries minister Brian Tobin complaining that: 'We're down now finally to one last, lonely, unloved, unattractive little turbot clinging on by its fingernails to the Grand Banks.'[49] But what disturbed many in Britain was the automatic support their government gave the Commission, which had allowed the UK Ambassador to the European Union to support Brussels' action against Canada.[50]

When the *Estai* was arrested, she was found to have a secret fish room containing 25 tons of banned species, mostly undersized, which could only have been caught with illegal nets. As a rash of maple leaf flags spread across Britain, to show solidarity with the Canadians, Major belatedly changed tack, indicating that he would veto any move by the EU to impose sanctions against Canada. But the damage had been done. Spain was not amused. Said her prime minister, Felipe Gonzales, 'we are developing a common foreign policy. At some point there will come a time to remind Britain it has to show solidarity always, not just when it suits it.'[51]

THE MARCH OF INTEGRATION CONTINUES

Now moving rapidly to the top of the EU agenda was the next treaty, work on which began when the Reflection Group symbolically held its first meeting at Messina on 2 June 1995, the fortieth anniversary of the Messina Conference.

Back home, John Major had had enough. Faced with constant sniping from his Eurosceptic backbenchers, he decided to 'lance the boil', resigning on 11 June as party leader, and standing for re-election. His only rival was

[47] *Washington Post*, 29 March 1995, 'Canada's fish affair: diplomacy or piracy?'
[48] Inter Press Service, 17 March 1995.
[49] CBC News, 27 July 2005: 'Court backs Canada's seizure of trawler during "turbot war"'.
[50] HC Deb, 13 March 1995, Vol. 256, cc563-74.
[51] *Daily Telegraph*, 5 April 1995.

the Eurosceptic John Redwood, who left the Cabinet to stand against him. The result would be declared before the summer recess. Meanwhile, Major went off to Cannes for the European Council of 26–27 June, chaired by Jacques Chirac, now France's president (who had attended his first Council as prime minister in 1974). The most significant decision was an agreement to set up 'Europol', an embryonic EU equivalent of the American FBI.[52] By 1995 it had acquired 80 staff, with a budget of £2.8 million.

This raised barely a flicker of interest in the Commons when Major reported back. MPs were enthralled by the outcome on 4 July of the Conservative leadership contest. Although Major easily defeated Redwood by 218 votes to 89, to the last moment the vote might have been sufficiently close to force Major's resignation, until Heseltine offered to swing 20 of his own supporters behind Major in return for being given the new post of deputy prime minister and First Secretary of State. In a Cabinet reshuffle, a relieved Major replaced Hurd as foreign secretary with Malcolm Rifkind.[53]

A 'ROCK FOR EUROPE'

If Major's re-election raised his morale, it did little to improve his grip on reality. In September, he was off to a European Council in Majorca, where the leaders met in idyllic surroundings to debate Europe's economic strategy. As Major recorded:

> high taxation and public spending, state regulation, central planning, protectionism and other socialist and corporatist mantras were suddenly unfashionable. I argued for flexible labour markets, to help create real jobs, for less red tape, for affordable social costs and above all for making Europe a competitive, free-trading area ...[54]

Then, Major recalls, 'an unusual thing happened ... our partners dared to be seen agreeing with the British prime minister'. Speaker after speaker opened by saying, 'I agree with John.' 'For a brief moment,' he added, 'I knew what it must feel like to be Helmut Kohl.'[55] Yet, even as he was speaking, the

[52] https://www.consilium.europa.eu/media/21189/cannes-european-council.pdf.
[53] Rifkind almost immediately faced the crisis that arose when Serb forces massacred seven thousand Bosnian Muslims outside Srebrenica. Dutch troops ordered to guarantee the town as a 'safe haven' for Muslims had retreated when the Serbs attacked. The bloodiest incident Europe had seen since the Second World War eventually prompted US-led NATO air strikes on the Serbs, paving the way at last for a Bosnian peace settlement. As defence secretary, Rifkind had firmly opposed the use of air power, famously declaring 'no war in history has ever been ended by air strikes' (forgetting how history's greatest war was ended at Hiroshima and Nagasaki).
[54] Major, op. cit., p. 523.
[55] Ibid., p. 524.

Reflection Group was working on a report for the Madrid Council on 15–16 December that could not have been more diametrically opposed. The creation of jobs, they argued, would best be 'encouraged' by three things: more integration, economic and monetary union and the Social Chapter: the three features of the Union that Major was keenest to avoid. More generally, they wanted a 'single institutional framework', absorbing the three Maastricht 'pillars' into a single Community. If Europe was 'getting the message' it was certainly not Major's.

The Madrid Council agreed that the report provided a sound basis for the discussions of the IGC, to begin work in Turin on 29 March 1996. Of more immediate concern, however, was the single currency. Top of the agenda was its name and, with dreary predictability, it became the 'euro'.[56] Portuguese prime minister António Guterres was ecstatic. 'Just as St Peter was the rock on which Christianity was built, so the single currency will be the rock for Europe,' he gushed.[57] The Council then drew up a timetable for its introduction. On 1 January 1999, the currencies of member states would be irrevocably fixed. On 1 January 2002, notes and coins would be issued, and by 1 July the same year, existing currencies would cease to be legal tender. In March 1998 it would be decided which countries could join in the 'first wave', according to whether their figures for 1997 met the Maastricht 'convergence criteria'.

Already these 'criteria' were posing serious difficulties: not least the requirements that government borrowing should not exceed 3 per cent of spending, and that national debt should not exceed 60 per cent of a country's gross domestic product. The national debt of several would-be participants was well above 60 per cent. Those of Belgium and Italy were above 120 per cent. France was already wracked by strikes against drastic spending cuts designed to reduce her deficit to 3 per cent.

Major remained in his own world. Reporting to MPs on Madrid, he told them: 'the drive to promote subsidiarity was again strongly in evidence'. It was 'now widely recognised that the United Kingdom was right to reverse the trend towards greater intrusiveness by the Commission'; and increasing emphasis had been given 'to the need to cut the burden of red tape and over-regulation'.[58]

That same month the Commission was dealing with a score of new proposals for directives, including one 'amending Directive 93/16/EEC', which 'facilitates the free movement of doctors and provides for the mutual

[56] https://www.consilium.europa.eu/media/21179/madrid-european-council.pdf.
[57] *The Economist*, 23 December 1995, p. 61.
[58] *Hansard*, 18 December 1995, col. 1222.

recognition of their diplomas, certificates and other evidence of formal qualifications'. This alone was to cause outrage in years to come when it would be discovered that doctors applying to join the NHS from countries such as Spain and Greece could not be examined on their English-speaking skills, even if they could speak no English at all. On the other hand, applicants from Commonwealth countries such as New Zealand would be required to undergo compulsory tests.[59]

MORE STINKING FISH

To British eyes, two events in the autumn of 1995 cast the EU in a particularly unfavourable light. One, in September, was *The Times'* serialisation of a book by a senior Commission official, entitled *The Rotten Heart of Europe: The Dirty War for Europe's Money*. As head of the division responsible for monitoring the ERM, Bernard Connolly's insider's account of the progress towards monetary union gave an insight into the Commission's internal workings like nothing published before. As an economist involved with monetary policy at the highest level, he had finally lost patience with the pretence that the ERM and EMU were economic policies when their only real purpose was political.

The ERM, he wrote, was not just 'inefficient' but profoundly 'undemocratic', a 'confidence trick' designed to subordinate the 'economic welfare' and 'democratic rights' of Europe's citizens to the will of a political and bureaucratic elite, bent on creating 'a European superstate'.[60] As the first of a succession of Brussels whistleblowers, Connolly ended by describing the Commission's fanatical intolerance towards any divergence from its strict 'party line': 'dissent cannot be tolerated'. As if to prove his point, no sooner was his book published than Commission officials called him 'psychologically unstable'. He was quickly dismissed from his post.

Two months later, on 28 November, uproar broke out over an opinion from the European Court of Justice in the ongoing Factortame case. Spanish 'flag-boat' companies having been disbarred by the Merchant Shipping Act from fishing for 18 months, the court held that they were now eligible for compensation from the UK government. With at least ninety Spanish vessels claiming from £250,000 to £600,000 per boat, £100 million might have to be paid by British taxpayers. Eurosceptic media were incandescent, summed up in a *Daily Mail* headline: 'They fly our flag, take our fish – and now our money'.

[59] Ibid.
[60] Connolly, op. cit., pp. xiii and 65, p. 17.

The timing of the Advocate General's opinion was impeccable. In Brussels the annual haggling on quota allocations was due, and the Commission was again proposing that UK quotas should be drastically cut. In a debate before the Council, the government spokesman Michael Forsyth fell back on the well-worn mantra that the problem arose from 'too many people chasing too few fish'.[61] He did not, of course, admit that most of the fish were in UK waters and that, because of the CFP, too many Community fishermen were trying to catch them. Labour pulled out all the stops to exploit Tory divisions, resulting in a government defeat by 297 votes to 299. Ministers would have to negotiate in Brussels without parliamentary approval.

The cuts they were forced to accept were indeed savage: mackerel down 33 per cent, plaice 27 per cent, sole 23 per cent. But this was hailed by fisheries minister Tony Baldry as a 'famous victory', on the slender basis that he had negotiated slight reductions in the cuts originally proposed (which had been pitched high precisely to allow for face-saving 'concessions'). He boasted that he had secured 'the best possible deal' for British fishermen.[62]

LET THE PEOPLE DECIDE

On 28 February 1996, the Commission put forward its proposals for the IGC. Predictably, it wanted one 'with real ambitions'. This was the chance 'for a genuine debate on Europe'.[63] Delors, conscious that his brainchild, the single currency, was on its way to becoming a reality, was now ready for the next steps. But it was the same old shopping list. He wanted the Union to have a 'strong political and social identity', a common foreign policy, backed by the ability 'to project credible military force', and 'better integration of the armaments industry'. The treaty should establish an 'area of freedom and security', bringing the Schengen Agreement into Community law and transferring Justice and Home Affairs into the 'Community framework', to form the basis for an EU-wide judicial, legal and policing system.

On classic supranational lines, the Commission argued that, as a general rule, national vetoes must be eliminated in favour of QMV (even future amendments to the treaty). As long as the veto remained, the Union would be in danger of 'stagnating'. There should be a wholesale simplifying and restructuring of the treaties, to give the Union a constitution. Finally, the Union 'must not be for ever bound to advance at the speed of its slowest members'. 'Flexibility' must be 'organised', to permit some member states to

---

[61] *Hansard*, 18 December 1995, col. 1352.

[62] *The Times*, 23 December 1995.

[63] Commission of the European Communities, 'Reinforcing Political Union and Preparing for Enlargement', Bulletin 1/2-1996, point 2.2.1.

move ahead more quickly than others. But firmly rejected was Major's idea of a 'pick-and-choose' Europe. This was to 'fly in the face of the common European project and the links and bonds which it engenders'.

A curious situation was now emerging. The Commission, the European Parliament and nearly all member states were now looking to the IGC for a dramatic advance in integration. But when the British government set out its proposals in a White Paper on 12 March, they seemed to come from a different planet. Britain wanted to stem the integrationist tide; reduce the flow of Brussels legislation; curb the powers of the ECJ, which had become too 'political'; and reform the 'irrational' CAP.[64] She also wanted treaty changes to end the scandal of 'quota hopping' and no absorption of the two 'intergovernmental pillars' into the Community framework. Britain opposed any further erosion of the powers of national parliaments and the creation of a 'United States of Europe'.[65] Her view of 'flexibility' was that it would allow a country to be given permanent 'opt-outs', while the others saw the concept as allowing a 'two-speed' Europe.[66] On almost every issue the British government was at odds with the rest.

So determined was Major to avoid controversy that Commons debate was limited to three hours without a vote. Heath for once spoke for many, complaining that, when Britain entered the Community, Parliament had been given ten days of debate. He noted the White Paper's claim that it was 'crucial that national parliaments remain the central focus of democratic legitimacy'. 'Is "democratic legitimacy" what we have this evening,' he asked; 'three hours in which to discuss a White Paper containing ten vital subjects?'[67]

Major could afford to ignore Heath; but not so a challenge from the Anglo-French billionaire industrialist Sir James Goldsmith, who sat as a French member in the European Parliament. In October 1995 he had launched a 'Referendum Party' to fight the next general election. On 11 March, on the eve of the White Paper, he challenged Major in full-page newspaper advertisements to allow a referendum not just on the currency but on Britain's continued membership of the EU.

---

[64] The British government was irked by several other ECJ rulings that it considered 'political', by virtue of their support for Commission supranationalism. Particularly controversial was one upholding the Commission's right to use the 'health and safety' Article 118 of the Treaty to authorise its Working Time ('48-hour week') directive. This should have been issued under the Social Chapter, from which Britain had opted out, but the device was used to apply the directive to Britain as well. Major protested in a personal letter to President Santer, to no avail.

[65] White Paper (1996), *A Partnership of Nations*, Cm. 3181 (London: HMSO).

[66] See Rifkind, *Hansard*, 21 March 1996, col. 519.

[67] *Hansard*, 21 March 1996, col. 541.

On 4 April, Major tried to neutralise the threat to Tory marginal seats by conceding the demand for a referendum on the currency. The Conservatives would be committed not to join the euro without first asking the British people.[68] Seven months later, in November 1996, Gordon Brown would give the same pledge for Labour. These commitments were to play a more crucial part in Britain's future relations with the EU than anyone at the time was aware. More immediately, however, a crisis erupting out of nowhere had already brought Britain's relations with her partners to their lowest point since she joined the Common Market in 1973.

MAD COWS AND MADDER POLITICIANS

On 20 March 1996, Britain's health secretary Stephen Dorrell gave a statement to a packed Commons on the cattle disease Bovine Spongiform Encephalopathy (BSE). After years of denial and confusion about risks to human health, what appeared to be a new strain of the related human disease, Creutzfeldt-Jakob Disease (CJD), had emerged in a number of young people, their brains presenting lesions similar to those of BSE-infected cattle.

Warned by the government's Spongiform Encephalopathy Advisory Committee (SEAC) that this could represent the early stages of a major epidemic, Dorrell told MPs that, although there was still 'no scientific proof' that BSE could be transmitted to man by beef, SEAC had concluded that 'the most likely explanation' for new variant CJD was eating meat before the government had imposed strict regulatory measures in 1989.[69] His statement set off the greatest food scare in history. Media hysteria knew no bounds. The *Observer* revelled in an apocalyptic vision of Britain in 2015, with thousands of Britons dying from CJD every week, the Channel Tunnel blocked and Britain isolated from the world.[70] On *Newsnight*, SEAC's chairman agreed that there could be half a million victims. Beef sales plummeted, not just in Britain but all over Europe.

One European country after another imposed bans on British beef. On 25 March, the Commission's Standing Veterinary Committee (SVC) voted 14–1 for a worldwide export ban, not just of British beef and cattle but of all their derivatives, from skin creams to wine gums.[71] While Major declared the ban 'well beyond any action justified by the available scientific evidence',

---

[68] *Independent*, 4 April 1996.
[69] *Hansard*, 20 March 1996, col. 375.
[70] 24 March 1996: 'A conspiracy to make us all mad'.
[71] The SVC includes one senior veterinary official from each EU country.

MPs were outraged to discover that the EU had power to prevent Britain selling beef even to countries still willing to buy it.[72]

As the beef industry faced meltdown – exports alone were worth £550 million a year – the priority was to restore confidence. One option was to slaughter the entire 11 million-strong national herd, but that was rejected as too expensive. On the basis that older cows presented the greatest risk, SEAC recommended that cattle over 30 months old should be deboned before their meat was sold. This was seized on by supermarkets. NFU president David Naish advised agriculture minister Douglas Hogg that, as a confidence-building measure, these older animals should be removed from the food chain. Major agreed to a three-year plan to destroy an estimated three million cattle, at a cost of £2.4 billion.[73]

His next priority was to get the export ban lifted, and it was agreed that this should be left to the Agriculture Council in Luxembourg on 1 April.[74] In Britain's view, all necessary measures to minimise risk had been taken: the ban on the use of meat and bonemeal in animal feed; the removal of potentially risky materials at slaughterhouses and the destruction of every BSE-affected animal. But the other member states wanted more. Wherever an infected animal was found, the whole herd had to be destroyed.

When Hogg arrived in Luxembourg, looking woebegone in a scruffy mackintosh and battered hat, he offered the destruction of 30-month-old cattle as a confidence-building gesture. But his partners insisted on retrospective whole-herd slaughter. An estimated 147,000 animals had to be found and killed, but the necessary records had not been kept and Britain could not meet this demand. As argument raged through three days and a full night, agreement was impossible. The ministers did, as a gesture, agree to help finance the scheme for destroying 30-month-old cattle, and it was widely publicised that the EC would 'foot 70 percent of the bill'. However, this compensated only for the loss of the animals themselves, not the cost of destruction. Under the terms of the UK rebate, it emerged that British taxpayers must contribute 90 per cent of the cost of a policy that had done nothing to get the ban lifted.

On 15 April, agriculture commissioner Franz Fischler conceded that there were no public health grounds for the ban, later confirmed by Santer when he became installed as Commission president. Rather, it had been a measure intended to prevent the collapse of the European beef market. Some of Major's Cabinet demanded retaliation. Hogg said he would take

[72] *Daily Telegraph*, 26 March 1996.
[73] *Daily Telegraph*, 29 March 1996.
[74] *Independent*, 30 March 1996.

the ban to the ECJ. Major's private response was to dismiss the 'colleagues' as a 'bunch of shits'.[75]

When further compromise offers were rejected and the SVC again refused on 20 May to accept even a partial lifting of the ban, Major told MPs in an emergency statement that Britain would adopt a policy of 'non-cooperation' with the EU. In four weeks, Britain blocked more than 65 legislative proposals, in what the media dubbed the 'beef war', provoking intense resentment in Brussels.

The fieriest of the Commissioners, Emma Bonino, then took retaliatory action of her own, demanding a further 60 per cent cut in Britain's fishing fleet. Alleging that Britain had fallen short of decommissioning targets, she claimed that the UK fleet had 'doubled in size' since 1988. Yet Commission figures showed there had in fact been only a marginal increase, entirely attributable to foreign-owned 'flag boats' joining the UK register after the Factortame case. By contrast, EU taxpayers were now providing £739 million over seven years for the 'modernisation' of Spain's fishing fleet, and another £894 million to third-world governments, mainly in Africa, to buy fishing rights for Spain and Portugal. The contribution of UK taxpayers to these programmes was £228 million.[76]

On BSE, so critical had Britain's impasse with her partners become that a deal at the Florence Council on 21–22 June was imperative, but all Major got was a vague promise that the ban might be gradually relaxed, in return for agreeing to the measure previously ruled out: the 'selective cull' of 147,000 animals. Before he had left for Florence, Major told MPs that a start on lifting the ban could be made in the early autumn. When he could not say exactly when this would be, Blair suggested it was likely to be 'years, not months'. To loud Labour cheers, he asked Major whether he was now 'so desperate to extricate himself from this mess that he will settle for anything'. He added: 'There is humiliation in the deal. There is ignominy in the deal. In fact, it is not a deal at all: it is a rout.'[77]

A rout it was. As Commission officials freely admitted, the 'concessions' had been 'only a sop' to persuade Tory MPs that Major had not left the Council empty-handed. 'It has been very important to me that the Brits got nothing,' said Danish prime minister Poul Nyrup Rasmussen.[78] To Major, it was 'a vintage piece of back-stabbing'.[79]

---

[75] Daily Telegraph, 23 April 1996.
[76] Castle of Lies, pp. 86–87, based on parliamentary answers.
[77] HC Deb, 20 June 1996, Vol. 279, cc993-8.
[78] Daily Telegraph, 20 June 1996.
[79] Major, op. cit., p. 656.

The misery was not over. On 12 July, the ECJ rejected Britain's request to overturn the export ban.[80] By 16 September, armed with a scientific paper from *Nature* predicting that, even without the 'selective cull', BSE would be over by 2001, Hogg asked his fellow agriculture ministers for a reduction in the cull. There was no deal. Britain either kept to the Florence agreement or the ban would remain. Since Major faced certain defeat if he tried to put the necessary legislation before MPs, he abandoned the cull. Fischler responded: 'as long as they [the British] do not meet the pre-conditions ... an end to the export ban is simply not a possibility.'[81] Klaus Hänsch, president of the European Parliament, observed that, if Britain could not respect joint decisions, it would be better for her to quit the EU altogether.[82]

A CHANGE OF TUNE

Around this time there were signs of a distinct change of mood in the EU, as concern about unemployment intensified. This prompted Major to boast to the Commons that Britain had created 'more jobs over the past three years than Germany, France, Italy and Spain' added together.[83] The Germans, on the other hand, led by their foreign minister Klaus Kinkel, had effectively sabotaged the Commission's main initiative on unemployment by refusing to vote funds for Delors' grandiose Trans-European Network. 'The responsibility for tackling unemployment lies with national governments,' Kohl told a press conference.[84]

An effect of this change of mood was Germany's lessening enthusiasm for a 'big bang' solution at the IGC, and a wish to concentrate on the single currency. Top of its agenda, as the country with the strongest currency in the EU, was their idea that countries joining the single currency must sign up to a 'Stability and Growth Pact'. This was eventually agreed at the Amsterdam European Council the following year.[85] It committed the Council 'to impose sanctions if a participating Member State fails to take the necessary steps to bring the excessive deficit situation to an end and to apply rigorously the whole range of sanctions provided for'.

By September 1996, the Commission was complaining that, with the IGC due to end in less than a year, there was 'no trace of the excitement' for what was 'potentially another historic step on the road to European

[80] Agence Europe, 'Together in Europe' (Newsletter), No. 93, 15 July 1996.
[81] Reuters, 20 September 1996.
[82] *Independent*, 21 September 1996.
[83] *Hansard*, 24 June 1996, cols 22–23.
[84] Reuters, 23 June 1996.
[85] Resolution of the European Council on the Stability and Growth Pact (Amsterdam, 17 June 1997) (*Official Journal* C 236 of 2 August 1997).

unity'. Instead, it noted, the mood was morose. Failure to progress seemed 'largely structural'. There was no broad pro-European consensus, 'only fundamental divergences'.[86] But part of the strategy was a wish to avoid too much debate, until a new, more compliant government was elected in Britain, which seemed increasingly certain. Kohl and Chirac were also now anticipating the next enlargement. The idea was therefore emerging of a 'minimalist' treaty, focusing on institutional and procedural changes, as a prelude to the enlargement negotiations, with possibly a further treaty after that.[87]

Increasingly, however, there were serious problems with the preparations for the single currency. In September, a report from the IMF painted a bleak picture of a low-growth Europe 'plagued by sky-high unemployment and boxed in by its drive to launch the single currency'. If growth did not strengthen, European nations should temporarily increase their deficits in line with the weakness of their economies, rather than cut them to meet the 'tough Maastricht criteria'.[88] The Commission itself painted an equally gloomy picture.[89]

In Zurich to commemorate the fiftieth anniversary of Churchill's 1946 speech, Rifkind exploited the gloom. He warned that the relentless momentum towards EMU would split the European Union. 'We should not proceed down a path of integration faster or further than our people are prepared to go,' he warned.[90] Britain's Eurosceptics welcomed this as the most outspoken statement ever made by a foreign secretary, but it provoked the familiar claque of EU fellow travellers, including Brittan, Heath, Howe and Hurd, to protest that ruling out British membership of the euro 'would be to betray our national interest'.[91]

By now, there was anxiety over the way several keen euro-aspirants, including Spain and Italy, were running such huge budget deficits that they were unlikely to qualify. France was equally suspect. She was preparing to sell her state telephone company France Telecom for a sum equivalent to half a per cent of GDP, simply to achieve a one-off reduction in her deficit. Despite stern warnings from the Bundesbank about 'window dressing', another 'Euro-fudge' was in the making: the Commission signalled that the

[86] Agence Europe, 'Together in Europe' (Newsletter), No. 94, 15 September 1996.
[87] Ibid.
[88] Reuters Business Report, 25 September 1996.
[89] Reuters Business Report, 10 October 1996.
[90] Speech by Foreign Secretary, Malcolm Rifkind, at the Churchill Commemoration, University of Zurich, 18 September 1996, 'Europe Fifty Years On'.
[91] Letter to the *Independent*, 19 September 1996.

criteria could be 'flexibly interpreted' to allow as many countries as possible to join in the first wave.[92]

Still the IGC was drifting. On 5 October 1996 an 'Extraordinary' Council was held in Dublin. At the eve of Council press conference, Major again championed his notion of 'flexibility', only for Klaus Hänsch, president of the European Parliament, to complain about 14 governments having always 'to sacrifice their vision of Europe, and their principles, to keep on board a government which may jump ship in any case'.

It was Kohl who was the driving force though, pushing his colleagues into agreeing that the IGC should conclude at Amsterdam in June 1997. Only if that timetable was kept could enlargement negotiations start on time. Otherwise, they would be caught up in the euro launch. Kohl was already referring to the possibility of what he called 'Maastricht III' to follow 'Maastricht II'. Nevertheless, on behalf of the Parliament, Hänsch warned that, without institutional reforms, the Union would 'become a mere free trade area': 'institutional sacrifices for enlargement' were needed. Kohl spelt out what that meant: a major extension of qualified majority voting. 'Unanimity must go,' he said.[93]

Against this background, 'Europe' was in turmoil, as France, Germany, Spain and Italy introduced further harsh spending cuts to meet the 'criteria'. In Madrid, thousands of public sector workers, including policemen, chanted slogans outside the economics ministry and tipped a lorry-load of ice in the entrance. In France, tens of thousands of teachers stopped work in protest at job cuts. In Germany, thousands of IG Metall union members went on strike.[94] France and Germany then produced their joint proposals for the IGC, emphasising the need to include 'enhanced co-operation', allowing member states who wished to do so to move ahead in certain areas without being blocked by others. The 'ins' would become the 'vanguard' while the 'outs' would eventually be marginalised.[95] Major's 'flexibility' was getting left still further behind, with Britain looking more like the 'guard's van'.

On 13 December, Major was back in Dublin for yet another Council. This, according to the communiqué, 'achieved further decisive progress' on EMU and 'identified a broad range of measures to be implemented at national and Community level aimed at boosting employment'. With an agreement to add an 'employment chapter' to the new treaty, the Commission thought

[92] *Independent*, 20 September 1996.
[93] Agence Europe, 'Together in Europe' (Newsletter), No. 96, 15 October 1996.
[94] *Independent*, 1 October 1996.
[95] *Independent*, 19 October 1996.

the Council had been 'an undoubted success'.[96] Major told MPs he saw 'no purpose in an employment chapter. It will not create a single job.' He also saw no need for further qualified majority voting.[97] But he was going to get it anyway.

Ending the year as he started it, once again Major was on his own. Even his backbenchers were deserting him. The *Daily Telegraph* reported that 147 of them had decided to oppose the single currency in their election addresses, rejecting his policy that options must be kept open.

'TORY SPLITS', AGAIN

As 1997 began, acclaimed as 'European Year against Racism and Xenophobia', British opponents of the single currency were claiming it could not work without common taxation and a huge increase in 'regional transfers' around the Union (precisely as was suggested back in the 1970s and by Delors in the 1980s).[98] Furthermore, would-be euro members were still quite shamelessly fudging the entry criteria. Meanwhile, in Brussels, Santer was fighting off French attempts to create a 'stability council' to allow governments to control the proposed European Central Bank, when the whole point of the ECB was that it should be independent.

As Britain's general election approached, it was Labour's turn to set out its stall. Its notably Eurosceptic foreign affairs spokesman, Robin Cook, sought to tease out Tory divisions by hinting that a Labour government might join the euro in the next Parliament, 'on the basis of a hard-headed economic assessment'.[99] If his purpose was to re-ignite Tory passions, he was successful, ending up with the Tory 'big beasts' fighting among themselves. Blair exulted in this 'quite extraordinary situation'.[100] When 20 Conservative MPs decided to defy party policy by backing monetary union in their election addresses, a former minister observed: 'smells of death wish'.[101]

Rather more significant were events on the continent, not least the closure by car-maker Renault of its plant in Belgium, making 4,000 redundant. Santer called it a 'blow to the European spirit of trust'. But the decision was linked to the French government's earlier refusal to help pay for Renault and Peugeot to shed 40,000 workers through early retirement. France's finance minister explained that, with the need to meet the convergence criteria, 'the

---

[96] Agence Europe, 'Together in Europe' (Newsletter), No. 100, 15 December 1996.
[97] *Hansard*, 16 December 1996, col. 616.
[98] Redwood, John (1997), 'Jobless in Leipzig, taxed in Liverpool', in the *Independent*, 17 January.
[99] *The Economist*, 8 February 1997.
[100] *Independent*, 20 February 1997.
[101] *Independent*, 3 March 1997.

state can no longer afford this kind of subsidy'. With French elections due the following year, the pain had to be exported abroad.[102]

For Major, the time had come for his ordeal at the polls. On 17 March he asked for the dissolution of Parliament. With his party trailing by 22 points, even he realised it was unlikely he would be returning as prime minister after 1 May.[103]

GOODBYE XENOPHOBIA

The 1997 general election was unique. So great had been the recovery of Britain's economy since 1992 that it was now, by almost any measure, the most successful in the EU. Yet so great was the impact of the ERM debacle that the Tories' electoral standing had not recovered. Never before had the authors of such economic success gone into an election facing certain defeat.

Labour's slogan 'Britain will be better with New Labour' echoed the mood of a nation anxious to see the Conservatives gone. 'Europe' was a peripheral issue, despite the intervention of Goldsmith's Referendum Party. For New Labour's manifesto, hubris was on the menu. 'We will give Britain the leadership in Europe which Britain and Europe need', it said.[104] The Conservative manifesto echoed Major's familiar line of wanting not a federal European state but 'a partnership of nations', introducing a slogan that would remain an object of ridicule from Eurosceptics: 'we want to be in Europe but not run by Europe'.

Scenting a Labour victory, EU governments, led by the Dutch, planned a post-election 'mini-summit' with Blair, to sort out Britain's new position on what was to be the Amsterdam Treaty. Before that, on 25 March, a ceremony was held on the Capitoline Hill in Rome to mark the fortieth anniversary of the signing of the 1957 treaty, but it was a lacklustre affair. The Europhile *Economist* asked whether 'Europe' was suffering 'a mid-life crisis'. What it needed most, the magazine opined, was economic growth, 'which looked unlikely'.[105] Kohl sailed above it all. Architect of many of the economic miseries affecting Germany, he announced on 3 April that he would seek re-election the following year, 'to pursue his dream of a more unified Europe'.[106] Then Chirac, eight months early, also announced a general election, calling for a new mandate to address euro preparations.[107]

---

[102] *The European*, 6 March 1997.
[103] Major, op. cit., p. 707.
[104] www.psr.keele.ac.uk/area/uk/man/lab97.htm.
[105] *The Economist*, 29 March 1997.
[106] Associated Press (Newsday), 4 April 1997.
[107] *Independent*, 21 April 1997.

On 1 May Blair swept to his expected victory, but with an unexpectedly large majority, giving him an army of 418 Labour MPs. The Conservatives lost 178 seats while the Liberal Democrats doubled their representation to 46. The Referendum Party gained 810,000 votes, the highest tally by a fourth party in British history, but its contribution had already been made: the commitment of all three major parties that Britain would not join the euro without a referendum. Blair's new chancellor was Gordon Brown and his first act was to announce that the Bank of England would be made independent, free to set the basic national interest rate without reference to him.[108] The new foreign secretary, Robin Cook, was equally swift, delivering on a commitment stretching back to Maastricht days. On 4 May he announced that Britain would join the Social Chapter.

Blair's victory was greeted with relief by other EU leaders, though none was so triumphalist as Kohl, who described it as a rejection of Euroscepticism.[109] Later, the *Observer* greeted the result with the largest headline in its history: 'Goodbye Xenophobia'. The humiliation of the Tories had marked the moment when the British people turned their back on 'little Englander' nationalism forever. Under Blair, Britain would at last be enthusiastically involved with 'Europe' in every way. Everything would be different.

PLUS ÇA CHANGE

An early visitor to Downing Street was Wim Kok, inviting Blair to meet his new partners in the seaside town of Noordwijk on 21 May in order to discuss the rapidly approaching Amsterdam Summit.[110] What transpired during this 'informal Council' remains obscure: the communiqué was more than usually opaque.[111] On his return home, Blair chose not to make the customary statement to Parliament, provoking complaints that the House was being treated with 'contempt'.[112]

If Blair was riding high, not so Chirac. His gamble at the polls badly misfired, stripping more than two hundred seats from his centre-right coalition. Forced into a nightmare 'cohabitation', he appointed Socialist Lionel Jospin prime minister, with Communist and Green support. The French people had decisively rejected 'further and faster' reforms to prepare for the single currency, preferring measures to tackle unemployment. The

---

[108] The Maastricht Treaty required of all member states planning to join the euro to start the process leading to the independence of its central bank. Britain was exempted from this rule under its opt-out, but if she was to join at any time in the future this would be a pre-condition.

[109] *International Herald Tribune*, 3 May 1997.

[110] Ibid.

[111] Bulletin EU 5-1997, Intergovernmental Conference (1/2), point I.1.

[112] *Hansard*, 2 June 1997, col. 20.

fate of the Amsterdam Treaty was sealed. It was going to be the 'minimal solution'.

Meanwhile Giscard d'Estaing had marked the fiftieth anniversary of the Marshall Plan with a little-reported speech in Chicago on 14 April. Reviewing the history of post-war Europe, he noted that the 'institutions created by the Treaty of Rome went substantially beyond what was required to reach the economic objective'. It was the framework of a 'future European federal entity that was being established'. He asked: 'will there ever be the equivalent of the Philadelphia miracle for Europe [the 1787 Congress that succeeded in raising the pillars of the US Constitution]?', adding Delphically that miracles were 'always improbable' but 'never impossible'.[113] This would not be the last he had to say on this matter.

Seemingly oblivious to the political turmoil on the continent, Blair embarked on a tour of European capitals, preaching his new gospel of the 'third way', prompting the Dutch foreign minister to remark that some things never changed – another British leader was telling Europeans where they were going wrong.[114]

Blair moved on to Bonn on 6 June to give Kohl the benefit of his wisdom, but the German chancellor had other things on his mind. Having scorned France, Italy and others as he had struggled to meet the Maastricht criteria, finance minister Theo Waigel had discovered a DM19-billion ($11 billion) 'hole' in his 1997 budget. He was also out of options. With 4.3 million Germans unemployed, the Social Democrats, with a majority in the Bundesrat, were opposed to social security cuts. Reducing investment below the level of new government borrowing was forbidden by the constitution. Tax increases had been vetoed by Kohl's coalition partners, the Free Democrats.[115]

The hapless Waigel hit on the ingenious plan of revaluing the Bundesbank's gold and currency reserves and transferring the resulting 'surplus' to the Federal account. But Bundesbank president, Hans Tietmeyer, immediately objected to such a 'blatantly cynical move'.[116] Even Kohl had to back down. But this attempt to 'fiddle' the figures undermined Germany's credibility with just those countries it had accused of 'creative accounting' over EMU.[117]

Germany's deficit problem still had to be resolved, bringing pressure to delay the introduction of the euro. Adding fuel to the fire, Jospin called for a

[113] Giscard d'Estaing, Valéry (1997), 'The Seeds of European Union: Can 1997 Match Initiatives of 1947 and 1957?', in the *International Herald Tribune*, 28 May.
[114] Young, *Blessed Plot*, p. 491.
[115] *The Economist*, 7 June 1997.
[116] *International Herald Tribune*, 2 June 1997.
[117] *New Statesman*, 6 June 1997, p. 15.

more flexible interpretation of the deficit criteria, while his finance minister Dominique Strauss-Kahn rejected Germany's stability pact proposals. As the timing of the single currency looked shaky, Kohl stepped in to rescue it. He announced he would stake his 'political existence' on keeping to the timetable, even though 82 per cent of Germans wanted a delay if aspirant countries could not meet the entry criteria.[118]

Seemingly indifferent to these problems, Blair set out Britain's position for Amsterdam. As well as wanting 'legally binding rights' to keep frontier controls, he strongly opposed bringing defence under 'Community' control by integrating the WEU into the EU, and insisted that 'enhanced co-operation' should only be allowed if states agreed unanimously. He was also standing by a campaign pledge to Britain's fishermen that he would insist on a treaty change to curb the ability of foreign vessels to fish for British quotas.[119] When the EU leaders gathered in Amsterdam on 17 June, the steam had gone out of the process. As if to set the mood, demonstrators has already destroyed the 'summit logo', made from thousands of flowers, hurling the debris at the Royal Palace where the leaders were to dine.[120]

The outcome was the abolition of the veto in 16 more policy areas, including public health, measures to promote employment, the EU research programme and equality of treatment for men and women. There was a transfer of responsibilities to the 'Community framework', including the free movement of persons, the Schengen Agreement and measures relating to external border controls, asylum, immigration and police co-operation. For the time being, these would remain subject to unanimity. The Common Foreign and Security Policy was to be given 'a face', with the Council's appointment of a 'Mr CFSP', one day intended to become the EU's foreign minister. And, thanks to Britain, the Social Chapter could now be fully integrated into the treaty.

The verdict of one European official on the treaty was 'no leadership, no appetite'. Kohl was stoical: 'There were too many conflicting interests,' he said. German officials confirmed that Kohl was saving his political capital for the single currency. 'The rest can come later,' a German diplomat said.[121] Santer, on the other hand, seemed content. 'We are advancing step by step,' he observed.[122] The only one who seemed happy was Blair, who had been allowed by his colleagues to 'win' a photo-opportunity bicycle race and who

---

[118] Poll reported by the *International Herald Tribune*, 9 June 1997.
[119] *Independent*, 13 June 1997.
[120] Reuters, 18 June 1997.
[121] Ibid.
[122] www.eurunion.org/news/eurecom/1997/ecom0797.htm.

made much of an agreement struck with Bonino on 'quota hopping' – a supposed victory for British fishermen. Yet he had conceded on integration of the WEU into EU structures.

Simultaneously with the conclusion of the IGC, the leaders had been holding a European Council. At France's insistence, it issued a Resolution on Growth and Employment, keeping employment at the top of the EU's political agenda. It also affirmed that EMU would start in January 1999, and agreed Germany's proposals for Stability and Growth Pact regulations. Finally, it endorsed the designs for the euro currency to be issued in 2002. The notes showed architectural features and bridges loosely symbolising European history through the ages, but carefully intended not to represent any specific place or style too precisely.[123]

The central European countries were troubled by the implications of the treaty for enlargement. A Polish official wanted to see problems being 'solved, not just suspended'. But a senior EU official explained: 'with French unemployment and German economic stagnation, this is no time to throw open the doors to well-educated cheap labour'. 'If the Czechs, Poles and Hungarians haven't figured that out by now, there's something wrong with their figuring-out capacity'.[124]

Reporting back to MPs on 18 June, Blair singled out the 'real progress' made on the quota hoppers problem. There had to be an 'economic link between boats using our quotas and Britain', such as requiring 50 per cent of a boat's catch to be landed locally.[125] Major, now opposition leader, reminded Blair that, during the election, he had claimed the problem would need treaty changes – which he had made no effort to secure.[126] But the 'victory' was even more hollow than realised. Santer revealed that the conditions had been EU law since 1989.[127] Blair had gained nothing.

[123] Ibid.
[124] *International Herald Tribune*, 21 June 1997.
[125] *Hansard*, 18 June 1997, col. 315.
[126] Ibid., col. 318.
[127] *Sunday Telegraph*, 22 June 1997.

14

Towards 'Political Unity': 1997–1999

> What disturbs people in Britain and many elsewhere is that
> they see a constant transfer of power in one direction only.
> They see all the footprints leading into the cave and none
> coming out … where does it end?
>
> Malcolm Rifkind, 21 February 1997[1]

Forty years on from the Treaty of Rome, the 'project' had come a long way. It
had its own capital city, Brussels; its own citizens, flag, anthem and passport;
even its own driving licence. It had assumed powers to make laws over many
more areas of activity than most of its citizens were aware, from agriculture
and fisheries to trade, transport, energy and the environment. And it was
rapidly approaching the moment when it would have one of the defining
attributes of a state: its own currency. Its membership had already expanded
from 6 nations to 15, with up to 12 more expected.

What no one had ever properly explained, however, was where the
process of 'ever closer union' was heading. And yet, the template had been
defined in Paris in 1972 and further defined by Spinelli and others since. But
putting the final pieces of the jigsaw into place was going to prove the most
difficult phase of all, raising all sorts of contradictions. By the latter half of
1997, in the wake of the Amsterdam Treaty, many were still unresolved, but
there were essentially four issues that needed immediate attention.

First, and most importantly, was the question of where power should
ultimately lie. The central agenda remained what it had always been: to
complete the process whereby national governments handed over their
powers to a supranational authority required abolition of the national veto.

---

[1] Speech reported by Conservative Central Office, 21 February 1997.

This begged the question as to who was ultimately to control that authority. According to the Monnet orthodoxy, the 'Community method' insisted that power must ultimately reside in the Commission. Yet what had seemed comparatively easy when dealing with the Common Market began to look very different as it dwelt on issues such as taxation, foreign and defence policy, justice and criminal law, which lay at the heart of a nation's sense of identity.

The reluctance of the politicians to hand over more power to the Commission had already led to the clumsy 'pillar' structure set up by Maastricht. In these and other areas, 'intergovernmentalism' during the 1990s had developed a new lease of life, through the ever more prominent role of the European Council. This led to the re-emergence of tensions that had been at the heart of the 'project' since the days of de Gaulle, when national leaders had first begun to insist on playing a much greater role in managing Community affairs than Monnet intended.

A second stress point was 'enlargement'. The Union faced easily its greatest and most problematic expansion so far, not least because these impoverished, less developed newcomers would impose huge demands on the EU budget, competing for funds with existing members. Especially problematical would be agriculture. Poland alone had a million farmers, almost as many as the existing Union, provided a striking echo of France's situation in the 1960s. But, having manipulated the CAP to suit her own needs, France would not find it easy to accept reforms from which she would be a significant loser. Without radical action, though, enlargement would be impossible.

A third challenge was a growing realisation that the Community's existing policies were not working. The CAP, imposing a 'one-size-fits-all' policy from the Arctic Circle to the arid plains of Andalusia, was almost universally viewed as a disaster. The rigidities of the CFP were creating an ecological crisis. The 'internal market', far from having achieved its promised boost to trade, growth and jobs, was becoming the economic blackspot of the developed world. Furthermore, the ultimate 'one-size-fits-all' policy of EMU was giving rise to immense strains, as would-be members struggled to meet the Maastricht 'convergence criteria', even before this ambitious experiment was put to practical test.

The fourth problem was what was being described in Community jargon as the 'democratic deficit'. The 'citizens of the Union' were increasingly coming to see the EU as remote, bureaucratic, undemocratic and unaccountable. For decades, the idea of 'European co-operation' had inspired idealistic goodwill, but 'Europe' had seemed largely peripheral, except to those whose livelihoods it directly damaged and those who benefited from it financially.[2] But now, disillusionment was setting in, just when the need for popular support was becoming vital.

Such were the issues that would dominate the history of the 'project' over the next eight years, demanding more and more attention from EU leaders as they remained unresolved.

PREPARING FOR A STRAITJACKET

The most pressing of these issues was enlargement. Grasping the nettle, on 16 July 1997, Santer announced that accession negotiations should start with six countries: Poland, Hungary, the Czech Republic, Estonia, Slovenia and Cyprus. But, unless the rules were changed, the new entrants' claims on the CAP and structural funds would bankrupt the EU.

To resolve the problem, Santer came up with 'Agenda 2000'. This would cut subsidies, and then pay existing members 'compensation' for not receiving them. There would be a new 'rural development policy', partly funded from 'capping' payments to larger farmers – a device known as 'modulation' – and a sharp reduction in structural funds, which were taking £20 billion of the EU's £60 billion annual budget. These would now only be given to those regions with the highest unemployment. Finally, Santer proposed another IGC, to draw up a new treaty in 2000.

Responses were predictably hostile. Portugal, Greece and Ireland protested strongly at the threat to their structural payments. Spain, with the largest share, even threatened to veto enlargement altogether, unless her payments remained intact.[3] But the biggest loser on both counts would be Britain. Her larger farms would lose more to 'modulation', and her unemployment was much lower than the EU average.

As if that were not enough, euro preparations were also creating their own difficulties. France's new Socialist prime minister, Lionel Jospin, found he could not reconcile fulfilling the Maastricht criteria with meeting his election promises. Yet he decided to opt for the politically hazardous route of supporting the euro, postponing promised tax cuts and going ahead with the sale of France Telecom, thus breaking faith with the Communists. The Parisian air was thick with accusations of back-sliding and treachery.[4]

[2] The Commission's Eurobarometer polls consistently showed that the countries in which it was most popular, such as Luxembourg, Ireland and Greece, were those that financially were its largest net beneficiaries.
[3] *The European*, 25 September 1997.
[4] *The Economist*, 5 July 1997.

In Germany, its impasse on the budget deficit had reached crisis point. Finance minister Theo Waigel decided to meet the Maastricht criteria by increasing taxes, cutting state pensions and reducing Germany's payments to the EU budget. So serious was the resulting crisis that deputies had to be brought back from holiday for an emergency session of the Bundestag on 5 August. The parliament's president described Waigel's measures as 'the biggest challenge Germany has faced in fifty years'.[5] Britain's politicians were happily detached from all this. They were still debating whether Britain should join the euro. Blair thought UK entry was vital if he was to play a 'leading role in Europe'. But his chancellor was obviously less enthusiastic.[6]

For the Commission, its priority was the impending launch of the new currency. To no one's surprise, it announced that 14 of 15 member states met the Maastricht criteria (only Greece failing to qualify). But Santer still nurtured hopes of Britain joining. Staying outside the eurozone, he warned, would mean missing the benefits of being in 'a winning team'.[7] Gordon Brown's response was not 'helpful'. He announced that the economy must meet 'five tests' first. And, by reducing entry to an economic calculation, he had cannily retained the power to decide.[8] Despite Blair's ambitions, he was not in a hurry.

This left as the most active campaigners for British entry that familiar alliance of senior Conservatives, openly defying the cautiously Eurosceptic line taken by their party's new leader, William Hague. As well as the CBI and the TUC, they clearly had the support of the BBC, which continued to give disproportionate airtime to the likes of Clarke, Heseltine and Brittan, now Commission vice-president. As an example of what was to come, on 30 October Heseltine was given top spot of the day on the *Today* programme to declare, 'Let's be absolutely clear, there's going to be a single currency … the only issue is when Britain joins, because join we will.'

As Britain approached taking up the rotating presidency, December brought what was seen as a humiliation. When EU finance ministers proposed setting up a new committee, to co-ordinate economic policy in the eurozone, Brown was ostentatiously excluded. He protested that this could 'split Europe', but Germany's Waigel retorted: 'You cannot be both in

---

[5] *Daily Telegraph*, 29 July 1997.

[6] *The Times*, 18 October 1997, 'Brown rules out single currency for lifetime of this parliament'.

[7] *Independent*, 23 October 1997.

[8] *Independent*, 28 October 1997. Brown's 'five economic tests' were (i) whether there had been 'sustainable convergence' between the British economy and those of the eurozone; (ii) whether there was 'sufficient flexibility' to cope with economic change; (iii) the effect on overseas investment; (iv) the impact on the City of London; and (v) whether economic and monetary union would be good for employment.

and out.'[9] In a bid to restore his 'European credentials', on 5 December Blair staged a preview of Britain's presidency amid lavish hype, picking as his venue the London terminal of the Channel Tunnel rail service. As eminent continental guests emerged from the train, Blair assured them that Eurostar was 'a symbol of our unbreakable ties with the lands beyond the Channel'.[10] It was not considered wholly tactful to stage the occasion at a station named after an Anglo-German victory over the French at Waterloo.

Certainly, Blair failed to impress other EU leaders. At the Luxembourg Council, on 12–13 December, after five hours of bad-tempered argument, he obtained only a vague promise that Britain and the other 'outs' (or 'pre-ins' as they were now termed) could participate in discussions of 'common interest'. Kohl rebuked him for 'unnecessarily provoking the French delegation'.[11] Labour's honeymoon with the EU was over. Thus, an element of delusion was evident in Blair's report to the Commons on 15 December. 'The Luxembourg summit,' he proclaimed, 'showed again that the government are positively engaged in Europe as a leading and influential player.'[12]

Much of the devil was in the detail. The Council had dealt with the role of the newly named Ecofin Council. Comprising the finance ministers of all the member states, it was acknowledged that this was 'the only body empowered to formulate and adopt the broad economic policy guidelines' on economic issues. However, the European Council did allow that eurozone ministers 'may meet informally' to discuss single currency issues.[13] Originally called 'Euro-XI', after Greece joined in 2001 it was renamed the Eurogroup. Standing outside the treaty structure with no legal mandate, this shadowy body, in time, was to assume the character of a eurozone government, often working closely with the Commission, the ECB and the IMF in a structure frequently referred to as the 'troika'.

THE ISOLATED PRESIDENCY

Britain's six-month presidency between January and July 1998, under the slogan 'bringing Europe closer to the people', was an embarrassment. Inevitably, it provoked renewed calls from her partners to join the euro, including a warning from the monetary affairs commissioner, Yves-Thibault de Silguy, that, if Britain did not join immediately, she would face a range

---

[9] *Independent*, 2 December 1997.
[10] *Independent*, 5 December 1997.
[11] *Sunday Telegraph*, 14 December 1997.
[12] *Hansard*, 15 December 1997, col. 21.
[13] 'Presidency Conclusions', 12–13 December 1997, Luxembourg European Council.

of problems. Blair, he suggested, had no chance of 'leading' in Europe until Britain was inside the euro club.[14]

Constrained by Brown's 'five tests', Blair options were limited. He attempted to divert attention by highlighting 'reforms to tackle unemployment' – his presidency's theme.[15] Understandably, though, the 'colleagues' were focused on the euro. Germany's Hans Tietmeyer began the year by warning that it could not 'on its own' solve the problem of Europe's high unemployment.[16] Four German professors, later joined by more than a hundred and fifty others, vainly launched an action in Germany's constitutional court aimed at stopping the new currency. They feared it would collapse amid 'hatred and envy'.[17]

A bitter row developed over a French demand that the head of her central bank, Jean-Claude Trichet, must run the new European Central Bank. However, for the next eight years, a Dutchman, Wim Duisenberg, had already been agreed for this position. France eventually conceded on a 'job-share': Duisenberg could take the first four years and Trichet would complete the term.[18] The dispute spilled over into the first of the European Councils under Blair's chairmanship, held in Brussels, which turned into 'a day-long squabble'. But at least the Commission got the agreement that 11 European countries should join the single currency on 1 January 1999.

Much to Blair's chagrin, his 'partners' continued to press home the cost of Britain's self-exclusion from the euro. Again, the French made the running, deliberately engineering an incident centred on the Euro-XI committee. Since it fell to Gordon Brown to chair all Ecofin meetings under the UK presidency, the original plan was to spare his blushes by delaying the committee's inaugural meeting until after Britain had left the chair. Provocatively, the French moved the date forward.[19] When Brown took the chair, he was humiliatingly ordered to leave, to be replaced by Austria's finance minister Rudolf Edlinger.[20]

A more substantial challenge to Britain came from a Commission proposal for a 'tax on savings', the so-called 'withholding tax directive'. Member states would have to levy tax at a minimum of 20 per cent on the interest from all bonds and deposits held by nationals of other countries – in the name of preventing tax evasion. Many Germans, for instance,

[14] *Daily Telegraph*, 6 February 1998.
[15] *Financial Times*, 19 January 1998.
[16] *Daily Telegraph*, 1 January 1998.
[17] *Daily Telegraph*, 2 January 1998.
[18] *The Economist*, 17 January 1998.
[19] Ibid.
[20] *Financial Times*, 4 June 1998; *Daily Telegraph*, 5 June 1998.

could avoid tax by switching their funds to Luxembourg. For Britain, this would breach its fiercely guarded national sovereignty over taxation. More specifically, it would damage the City of London as the world's leading capital market. Billions of pounds' worth of business would be moved elsewhere, to jurisdictions such as Switzerland and Hong Kong where the tax did not apply.[21]

Britain was just as obviously isolated over foreign policy. A long-term problem was the continuing disagreement over Iraq. After the Gulf War, UN resolutions had called upon Saddam Hussein to disarm and UN inspectors had been appointed to monitor the process. When Saddam refused to co-operate and the inspectors withdrew, this precipitated a crisis. Britain sided with the United States in favouring a military solution. Chirac merely argued for more UN sanctions, although his own country had done more than any to undermine the existing sanctions regime. Nevertheless, it was Blair who was censured by the European Parliament for not trying to present a 'common European position'.[22]

Similar dissension arose over Milošević's Yugoslavia, when fighting flared up on the border between Albania and the Serbian province of Kosovo. The EU urged a weak policy towards the Serb leader.[23] Britain alone favoured the military intervention urged by the US, which would lead the following year to Milošević's overthrow.

Blair's more emollient approach to 'Europe' equally failed to reap dividends on the domestic front. His government had been unable to resolve the BSE export ban. Britain's farmers had been plunged into their worst crisis since before the Second World War, with farm incomes having dropped by 50 per cent in one year. This was due not least to the government's refusal to claim Community funding to compensate for the 'strong pound', because, under the 'Fontainebleau effect', most of this additional money would have then been deducted from the UK rebate. The result was that Britain's farmers had to contend with their much more highly subsidised EU competitors, who could afford to sell their produce in Britain at lower prices.[24]

There was also further evidence of the damage the CFP was inflicting on Britain's fishing industry. In just four years between 1993 and 1997, the number of fishing boats on the UK register had dropped by nearly a third,

---

[21] *Financial Times*, 18 May 1998. Britain had only become the centre of the world's international bond market after New York in the 1960s imposed its own version of such a tax. The market moved to London, where the tax did not apply.

[22] *Daily Telegraph*, 19 February 1998.

[23] Ibid.

[24] *Independent*, 27 May 1998.

from 11,108 to 7,809. The tonnage of Spanish and Dutch-owned 'flag boats' had actually risen, while 3,300 smaller British vessels and their crews were forced out of business.[25]

On 14 June came the crowning glory of Blair's presidency, the Cardiff European Council. Its slogan 'bringing Europe closer to the people' seemed peculiarly ironic, as the city was subjected to a ferocious security clampdown, designed to keep any potential protesters at least a mile from the conference hall. To create an illusion of popular support for the cameras, schoolchildren were bused in from across South Wales, issued with 'ring of stars' flags to wave at the leaders as they gathered round a specially built table, costing £50,000.

The Council was dismissed as little more than 'an exercise in stage management', its centrepiece a fleeting visit from Nelson Mandela. Blair continued to urge his 'reform' agenda, calling for 'a decentralised Europe', not 'some European federal superstate'.[26] But the main concern of his colleagues was whether Britain would join the euro. With Cook giving 'the strongest signal' that Britain would join 'probably in 2002', Santer proclaimed: 'It is no more a question of if Britain will join the euro, it is only a question of when.'[27]

When Blair himself ended the Council, he hailed the euro as a 'turning point' for Europe.[28] This provoked a dramatic response from Britain's top-selling tabloid, the *Sun*, hitherto an ardent Blair supporter. On 24 June its front page asked: 'Is this the most dangerous man in Britain?' The next day's front page claimed that a 'huge army of *Sun* readers' had 'rounded on Tony Blair for backing plans to ditch the Pound'.[29] On 30 June, he flew to Frankfurt to mark the end of the UK presidency. After music from a Dutch male voice choir, dancing from an Irish ensemble, and lunch in the opera house at three in the afternoon, the farce was over.[30] Down the road the same day, the European Central Bank opened for business.

'HIDDEN EUROPE': THE ELEPHANT IN THE ROOM

By now, the deliberately narrowed focus and trivial nature of the British debate on 'Europe' was becoming painfully obvious. Despite the fact that all three main political parties officially supported Britain's membership, their

---

[25] *Hansard*, written answer by Elliott Morley, 30 April 1998.
[26] AP Online, 15 June 1998.
[27] *Daily Telegraph*, 15 June 1998.
[28] *Daily Telegraph*, 16 June 1998.
[29] *Sun*, 25 June 1998.
[30] *Daily Telegraph*, 25 June 1998.

politicians were remarkably reluctant to defend or explain it in any detail. They confined themselves to uttering little more than well-worn mantras. Repeatedly, for instance, they would claim that the benefits of membership to Britain were 'self-evident': none more so than that she could now 'trade freely with the largest internal market in the world'.

What no politician ever mentioned was how unbalanced that 'trading advantage' had become. It was in the summer of 1998 that figures published by the OECD showed that the British economy was doing so well that it had now overhauled that of France to become the fourth largest in the world. But it also emerged that, in the 25 years since Britain joined the Common Market in 1973, she had run up a cumulative balance of payments deficit with her EU partners, through trade and net contributions to the Brussels budget, totalling £170 billion.[31]

Equally curious were the efforts made by ministers to conceal just how many areas of national policy were now being decided in Brussels, by pretending that these decisions were their own. One small instance was the new driver's licence, the design of which, according to a leaflet from the Driver and Vehicle Licensing Agency, had been 'decided by ministers'. Yet every detail of its format, including the EU 'ring of stars' logo, was based on the 'Community model driving licence' made mandatory by Directive 91/493/EEC. Similarly, there were the complications involved in carrying out simple banking transactions. Although customers were often baffled by new procedures they had to follow to prove their identity, it was never explained that these were dictated by a directive on 'money laundering', 91/308/EEC.

On an ever-widening range of controversial issues, ministers and officials had thus become accustomed to hiding away the extent to which British government policy was now being shaped by the need to comply with Community legislation. One of the most contentious, under the Major government, had been the decision at the time of railway denationalisation to separate the management of rail infrastructure from the operation of trains, as required by Directive 91/440. Another was the surrender of the power to legislate on genetically modified crops under Directive 90/220.

When John Prescott, as Secretary of State for the Environment, made a much-publicised announcement that he had ordered water companies to spend £8.5 billion on 'cleaning up Britain's water', this was presented as if it was entirely his own personal initiative. Nowhere was it explained that

---

[31] Figures compiled from relevant editions of the 'Pink Book' (*The United Kingdom Balance of Payments*), HMSO.

'his' decision derived solely from the need to comply with Brussels water directives.[32] In this respect, the influence of Brussels on British life had become like the proverbial 'elephant in the room': an object so huge and amorphous that it was not easy to see it was there.

There was no better example of this than another of Prescott's initiatives when, in his capacity as Secretary of State for the Regions, in 1997 and 1998 he put through six new Acts of Parliament. Four of these, hailed as 'devolution measures', were to set up elected assemblies for Scotland, Wales, Northern Ireland and London, based on the continental principle of proportional representation. A fifth set up 'regional development agencies' for eight 'regions' covering the remainder of England, with the intention that they too would eventually become part of elected regional governments. The sixth, for the purposes of future elections to the European Parliament, which would also be fought on the continental 'party list system', split the UK into 12 giant regional constituencies, based on the same boundaries.

Prescott presented all these new laws as if they had little or no connection with each other, aided by the fact that 'devolution' for Scotland and Wales had been an issue for years. The new Northern Irish Assembly was promoted as a way of returning the province to self-government as part of the 'peace process'. But the undeclared link was the grand design for a 'Europe of the Regions'.

The story of how regionalisation had come to play a central role in Europe's integration was complex. The original impetus, in the 1950s, had come from local government leaders in France and Germany, working through the Council of Europe and latterly through one of its subsidiary bodies, the Council of European Municipalities and Regions (CEMR), of which the president was Giscard d'Estaing. Then, in 1972–1973, Heath had pressed for a 'regional policy' to compensate Britain for the fact that she would lose so heavily from the CAP; and in 1975 the Tindemans Report had urged the need to develop a regional structure across the EEC as a precondition of monetary union, to give a means of redressing economic imbalances between richer and poorer regions.

The turning point had come in the late 1980s, when Delors had finally insisted on regionalisation becoming a central policy in the Single

[32] One former Conservative minister of state for agriculture privately expressed resentment at the constant pressure she had been put under by officials to conceal that almost all the policy initiatives she was given to propose had originated from Brussels (personal information). Another conspicuous example of such concealment was to be the EC legislation requiring an end to the monopoly on telephone directory enquiry services, and the introduction of competing services using '118' as a prefix. When this led in 2003 to widespread confusion and higher charges, the government went to absurd lengths to deny that this had any connection with Brussels.

European Act. He had then introduced the 1988 'framework' regulation 2052/88, allowing regional or local authorities to negotiate directly with the Commission for structural funds. It was this new system, requiring that regional authorities must be in place to receive Brussels funding, that in 1994 led John Gummer, as Secretary of State for the Environment, to set up a 'Government Office' in each of the English 'regions', thus calling them formally into existence.

This was the baton that Prescott picked up in 1995 when, in defiance of Labour Party policy (which favoured preserving the powers of local government), he set up his own 'Regional Policy Commission' under Bruce Millan, a former Brussels Commissioner for regional policy. It was Millan's recommendation that England should be given 'regional development agencies' that enabled Prescott to set up his embryonic regional governments, alongside the new 'regional parliaments' for Scotland, Wales, Northern Ireland and London.

Although Prescott and his colleagues were determined not to admit any link with European integration, the connection was openly acknowledged in Brussels, as in official maps showing the EU divided into 111 'Euro-regions', including the 12 in the UK. In May 1998, as the first senior UK politician to address the Committee of the Regions, Prescott said: 'Governments must be as close as possible to their citizens and a Europe of the regions is the best way of doing this. The UK has in the past lagged behind in this area, but the new government has been quick to start to put things right …'[33]

Curiously, the only politician to blow Prescott's cover was Heseltine. To a fringe meeting at the 1998 Conservative Party Conference, he announced that there were 'two European agendas'. In one, he said, he profoundly believed. But there was 'the agenda of the regions, which had Brussels disposing money directly to the regions and ultimately bypassing national parliaments'. 'I deplore that agenda,' he declared. Blair, he said, was 'playing into the hands of that agenda with his destruction of the United Kingdom'. If he was to continue this process of 'European federalism', it would 'weaken the UK and centralise power in a way I find totally unacceptable'.[34]

At the same conference, Heseltine was in another respect less in tune with delegates' views. Through the year, Conservatives had been embroiled in civil war over the euro. Not only had Heseltine and Clarke openly applauded

---

[33] The original record has not been kept. References to the website elicit the message: 'As the United Kingdom left the European Union, the European Commission Representation in the UK ceased all its activities as of 1 February 2020.'

[34] Speech given to Conservative Mainstream in Bournemouth, 6 October 1998 (transcribed by British Management Data Foundation).

Blair's stance on 'Europe', urging him to go further and faster; they had been joined by Hurd, Brittan and Patten, the former party chairman, in openly sniping at Hague's sceptical stance. In May, Hague infuriated the Europhiles still further, with a speech at Fontainebleau in which he warned that further European integration without democratic support could eventually lead to the kind of violent popular protest that had just broken out in Indonesia. Of the euro, which he predicted could herald a political union, he said: 'one could find oneself trapped in the economic equivalent of a burning building with no exits'. 'I fear the European Union is in danger,' he concluded, 'of accepting without debate a political destination agreed 40 years ago.'[35]

Over the summer, when Clarke, Heseltine and Brittan leaked plans to launch an all-out assault on his euro policy at the October party conference, Hague sought to outflank them by announcing a party ballot in the issue.[36] This was dismissed by Heseltine as a 'total irrelevance', followed by similar outbursts from Brittan and Heath.[37] But when the results came in, Hague was backed by 85 per cent of his party. His opponents simply announced that they would fight on, reinforcing the view that the Tories were hopelessly split.[38]

In another respect, however, that summer had seen a significant reverse for the pro-euro campaigners. In propaganda terms, for four years no organisation had played a more central role for their cause than the CBI, with its annual 'polls' purporting to show a sizeable majority of Britain's businessmen backing British entry. These had invariably been heavily publicised by the BBC, while it ignored a stream of polls by other business organisations, such as the Institute of Directors and the Federation of Small Businesses, showing overwhelming opposition to the euro.

In the summer of 1998, the CBI announced it was to stage its biggest membership 'poll' so far, supervised by Bob Worcester of Mori, famous for his role in the 1975 referendum. The previous surveys having been heavily rigged, Worcester was privately challenged that it would be 'unprofessional' to give his name to a further survey. He withdrew, forcing the CBI in some embarrassment to abandon its poll. The Europhiles' bluff had finally been called.[39] Senior CBI members then staged an internal counter-attack, setting up an organisation called 'Business for Sterling', to campaign against the euro. Within months, it had effectively neutralised the CBI's propaganda. Apart from the BBC, Heseltine, Clarke and Brittan had lost their most useful ally.

---

[35] *Financial Times*, 19 May 1998.
[36] *Daily Telegraph*, 8 September 1998.
[37] *Financial Times*, 14 September 1998.
[38] *Daily Telegraph*, 6 October 1998.
[39] Worcester's challenger was Brigadier Cowgill of the British Management Data Foundation.

A GERMAN EARTHQUAKE

On 30 September 1998, there was a political earthquake in Germany. The Christian Democrat Party under Chancellor Kohl suffered a decisive election defeat by a Social Democrat/Green alliance. After years of economic turmoil, what tipped the balance was a left-wing SDP and Green landslide in the former East Germany. Although it was not immediately apparent, for the first time the passing of Communism in eastern Europe was to have a very significant impact on the 'project's' future.

Before the election, the new chancellor, Gerhard Schröder, had projected a Eurosceptic line, even referring to the euro as a 'sickly premature infant, resulting from an over hasty monetary union'.[40] But after his victory, having been forced to appoint his left-wing party chairman Oskar Lafontaine as finance minister, and his Green coalition partner Joschka Fischer as foreign minister – both enthusiastic integrationists – Schröder's line appeared to change. At his inaugural address to the Federal parliament on 10 November, he spoke of the single currency as merely 'an important step on the way to European integration'. He then added: 'Only through the further development of a political union will we succeed in forming a Europe that is close to its citizens.' This must also include harmonisation of taxes.[41]

Twelve days later, in Brussels, 11 Socialist finance ministers, including Gordon Brown, gathered to consider a Socialist manifesto for Europe. With the euro approaching, this was a clarion call for EU tax harmonisation, to provide, as Austria's finance minister Edlinger put it, 'a common economic roof' for our 'common house of Europe'.[42] Although Brown signed the document, he immediately caused a storm by stating publicly that Britain would be prepared to use her veto to block any moves towards tax harmonisation.[43]

Over the next few days, 'Europe' dominated the British press as it had not done for years. First the temperature was raised by calls for tax harmonisation from three Commissioners, beginning with Santer himself. Mario Monti, the single market commissioner, then insisted that the Commission would proceed with plans to harmonise rates of VAT, energy taxes and excise duties.[44] Finally, de Silguy, the commissioner for monetary union, on a visit to London predicted that tax harmonisation would ultimately lead

[40] *Bild*, 25 March 1998.
[41] *Daily Telegraph*, 11 November 1998.
[42] *Daily Telegraph*, 23 November 1998.
[43] *Daily Telegraph*, 24 November 1998.
[44] *Daily Mail*, 26 November 1998.

to EU-wide rates of income tax.[45] This was reinforced by a promise from Oskar Lafontaine that tax harmonisation would be a top priority for the forthcoming German presidency. As a result, the *Sun*, on its front page of 25 November, dubbed him 'the most dangerous man in Europe'.

The temperature went up still further when Joschka Fischer promised that 'deeper integration' would be the priority of the German presidency in more than just tax matters. 'Just as we worked on the first real transfer of sovereignty in the field of currencies,' he said, 'we ought to work on a common constitution to turn the European Union into an entity under international law.' Asked whether he wanted a European army, he replied: 'if it is going to turn into a full union, then one day foreign and defence policy will also have to become Community tasks'.[46] Next day in Brussels, Schröder inspired frenzy in the Eurosceptic British press by reaffirming that the vision of an 'ever more integrated Europe' was an idea that 'unites all German politicians'.[47] However, Europe's front pages were about to focus on something rather different.

THE COMMISSION IN CRISIS

Over the next few months, the EU was dominated by an extraordinary crisis. This broke when, on 9 December 1998, Paul van Buitenen, a Dutch accountant employed by the Commission as an assistant auditor, sent MEPs a 34-page letter with 600 pages of supporting documents, detailing instances of corruption he had identified in his work. These included cases directly involving two Commissioners.[48]

His charges came as no great surprise. Reports and rumours of wholesale corruption, fraud and financial mismanagement in the Commission had been building up for a long time. In February 1998 the European Parliament's budgetary control committee had accused the Commission of giving misleading information and stalling inquiries into fraud among its officials, involving millions of pounds and dating back to 1989.[49] In August the Court of Auditors published a report criticising the Commission's anti-fraud measures as wholly inadequate, and its anti-fraud unit UCLAF as 'highly inefficient and unprofessional'.[50]

---

[45] *Daily Telegraph*, 27 November 1998.
[46] *Daily Telegraph*, 26 November 1998.
[47] *Financial Times*; *The Times*, 27 November 1998.
[48] Van Buitenen, Paul (2000), *Blowing the Whistle: One Man's Fight Against Fraud in the European Commission* (London: Politico's), p. vii.
[49] *Daily Telegraph*, 5 February 1998.
[50] *Financial Times*, 24 July 1998; *Daily Telegraph*, 29 July 1998.

Unlike in earlier times, however, the issue did not fade away. Next to hit the headlines was a scandal involving the European Community Humanitarian Office (ECHO), run by Commissioner Bonino, in which 500,000 ecu (£347,000) in humanitarian aid destined for Rwanda and Burundi had apparently been diverted by contractors to their own pockets, or passed back to the Commission.[51] The Commission's embarrassment was intensified when it was forced to cancel the results of all 30,000 candidates in its *Concours* entrance exams, after questions had been leaked and chaotic supervision led to widespread cheating.

The budget control committee then accused the director-general of administration, Stefan Schmidt, of conducting internal inquiries so close to a whitewash that his office had 'lost all credibility'. They demanded that he be fired, and Parliament threatened to delay discharge of the 1996 budget until the Commission released documents on the suspected fraud cases. When it appeared that £40 million had also gone missing from a programme designed to build relations between the EU and its Mediterranean neighbours, the committee complained that 'in 26 cases, the Commission's financial controllers have refused information or access to relevant documents or ... they have not been able to locate the partners associated with these projects'.

Most damaging of all was the case of Édith Cresson, former French prime minister turned Commissioner for research and education. Summoned by the Parliament to answer questions about her relations with René Berthelot, a 70-year-old dentist from her home town, who had been given lucrative Commission contracts for Aids-related research, she sent her public relations assistant, who refused to answer questions.[52]

In early October, more details emerged of the ECHO scandal, with the leaking of a secret audit report. This was so withering about the lack of reliable financial record-keeping that the Parliament's EPP group voted to freeze £250 million of the ECHO budget until the Commission came 'clean on its own inquiries' into fraud and financial mismanagement.[53] Under such pressure, Santer reluctantly agreed to set up an independent fraud investigation office. But, using tactics that were to become familiar, he then rejected MEPs' criticisms of a 'cover-up' as 'an intolerable insinuation'.[54] And while the Commission confirmed that the ECHO office had destroyed documents relating to 2,000 aid contracts worth £800 million, the two Commissioners at the heart of the row, Cresson and Bonino, threatened to

[51] *Financial Times*, 17 September 1998.
[52] *Guardian*, 24 September 1998.
[53] *Guardian*, 4 October 1998.
[54] *Financial Times*, 6 October 1998.

sue the *Financial Times* and *Libération* for defamation.[55] UCLAF officials were also accused of conducting a 'whispering campaign' against MEPs who had worked to uncover the scandals.

Undeterred, the media fought back. Belgium's *Le Soir* caught the mood with its headline 'The Commission turns into a den of vipers'.[56] So rapidly had the crisis developed that Santer, who had been anticipating a second term as president, looked doomed. A former Italian prime minister, Romano Prodi, was already being canvassed as a likely successor.[57] The next blow came in November, when the Court of Auditors report was published.[58] For the fifth year running, it had refused to 'sign off' the EU's accounts, because of the various types of 'recurrent irregularity'. This was followed by a claim by the Court's president Bernhard Friedmann, in an interview with *Stern*, that the scandal could destroy the EU.[59]

Yet more details emerged. The head of Air France, a friend of Cresson and former adviser to Mitterrand, had been employed by her in Brussels, but when he had returned to Paris, she kept him on the payroll. The regional Commissioner Monika Wulf-Mathies had appointed a close friend's husband to a £72,000-a-year post in charge of 'regional issues', but he now admitted he would never have passed the usual recruitment exams.[60] Nor had the Court of Auditors finished. It branded a £600 million nuclear safety project in eastern Europe a 'dismal failure', so badly run that, by the end of 1997, little more than a third of the money had been spent, much of it going to consultants and companies that had won their contracts without tendering.[61]

Further condemnation came from an unlikely source. Clare Short, Britain's International Development Secretary, attacked the EU's £2.7 billion overseas aid programme – to which Britain contributed over £530 million a year, a third of the UK's national aid budget – as 'dreadful', ill-conceived, poorly monitored and damaging to the environment. One EU-funded project to build roads in Cameroon had led to the part-felling of a rain forest designated a world heritage site, with mass destruction of wildlife and the bulldozing of a pygmy village. Short's department had refused to fund the project, but it was suspected that the Cameroon government had done a deal with French logging companies versed in exploiting EU aid funds.[62]

---

[55] *Daily Telegraph*, 7 October 1998.
[56] *Daily Telegraph*, 15 October 1998.
[57] *Daily Telegraph*, 26 October 1998.
[58] Court of Auditors, Annual Report concerning the financial year 1997.
[59] *Daily Telegraph*, 13 November 1998.
[60] *Scotsman*, 24 November 1998.
[61] *Daily Telegraph*, 18 November 1998.
[62] *Daily Telegraph*, 2 December 1998.

Only days after Short's outburst, on 9 December, van Buitenen had sent his incriminating dossier to an MEP. Rapidly circulated round the Parliament, it had caused a sensation. On 17 December the MEPs voted by 270 to 225 not to discharge the 1996 budget. Then Pauline Green, leader of the Socialists, the Parliament's largest group, tabled a censure motion seeking to dismiss the Commission.[63] But not all was what it seemed. To the jeers of her colleagues, she informed them that she would vote against her own motion, explaining that she merely wished to establish whether the Commission enjoyed parliament's confidence.[64]

BLAIR'S GREATEST GAMBLE

Although the fraud row dominated the headlines, the less dramatic but ultimately more important debate continued. In early October, to pave the way for Agenda 2000, the Commission had published a report entitled *Financing the European Union*.[65] Its strategy was to soften up the member states for a major redistribution of contributions, by showing which countries did well from the existing arrangements and which badly.[66]

Clearly evident was the way France and Ireland benefited disproportionately from the CAP. So was the relatively low proportion of national GDP paid by Britain, thanks to the rebate. Part of the report's purpose was to focus attention on this, as a prelude to calling for the rebate to be scrapped. Predictably, Britain protested that the key figure was net benefits, which showed her faring relatively poorly. However, others also reacted unfavourably. France refused to accept any change to the financing of the CAP. Germany was adamant that she wanted her £7.8 billion net contribution reduced. The Dutch, contributing more *per capita* than any other nation, threatened a first-ever use of their veto unless their payments were reduced. Spain dismissed the report, calling it 'this wretched document'.[67]

Underlining the need for 'reform', however, a Court of Auditors opinion noted the 'spectacular increase' in CAP spending implicit in the Agenda 2000 proposals. The package as a whole would exceed the budget by billions of pounds if subsidies were paid at full rate to the enlargement countries.[68]

---

[63] *Guardian*, 18 December 1998.

[64] *Financial Times*, 18 December 1998.

[65] Commission of the European Communities, Bulletin EU 12-1998, points 1.5.1–1.5.9.

[66] Earlier the budget Commissioner, Erkki Likaanen, had announced that the Commission was to discontinue publishing member states' budget contributions and receipts, on the grounds that 'budgetary flows do not capture all the benefits of membership' (*Sunday Telegraph*, 22 March 1998).

[67] *Financial Times*, 16 and 20 October 1998.

[68] Court of Auditors. Opinion No. 10/98 of the European Court of Auditors on certain proposals for regulations within the Agenda 2000 framework. *Official Journal*, 98/C 401/01, 22 December 1998, paras 6, 82 and 89.

Member states, therefore, agreed to conclude their negotiations no later than the Berlin Council planned for March 1999 under the German presidency.[69]

Another Commission report now surfaced, on *Corpus Juris*, a proposal to transform the EU into a 'common judicial area'. The justification claimed was that 'the more the borders of the single market are opened up, the more the persistence of "legal frontiers" proves disastrous'.[70] On the table was a powerful European public prosecutor's office, to which each country's own prosecution service would ultimately be answerable. Initially, it would investigate activities against 'the financial interests of the European Union', although it could later be extended to cover the whole of the EU's judicial system. As on other occasions, British ministers weakly tried to dismiss the initiative as merely 'a discussion paper', which could anyway not be adopted without unanimous agreement.[71]

From a quite different direction, however, Britain was herself about to launch an integrationist initiative that would eventually have the most far-reaching consequences. For some time, Blair and his advisers had noted that the UK's opt-out from the euro was hampering ambitions to be at 'the heart of Europe'. Blair needed a dramatic gesture to improve his 'Euro-credentials' and the answer was to barter Britain's highly regarded armed forces for a seat at the top table alongside France and Germany. Blair decided to offer these as a key part of a new 'European' defence force, capable of acting outside NATO.

On 3 December 1998, only four days after Chirac had met Schröder in Potsdam to reaffirm the strength of the Franco-German alliance, Blair arrived in St Malo for a 'summit' of his own with Chirac.[72] They afterwards issued a joint declaration that

> the Union (EU) must be given appropriate structures and a capacity for analysis of situations, sources of intelligence, and a capability for relevant strategic planning, without unnecessary duplication ... In this regard, the European Union will also need to have recourse to suitable military means.[73]

The communiqué underlined that the EU must be capable of asserting its new, autonomous military capability, if necessary, 'outside the Nato framework'. Although it was to be some years before the awesome implications of the

---

[69] *Daily Telegraph*, 16 November 1998.
[70] It had been published commercially in 1997. See Delmas-Marty, Mireille (ed.) (1997), *Corpus Juris: Introducing Penal Provisions for the Purpose of the Financial Interests of the European Union* (Paris: Direction Général du Contrôle Financier/Economica).
[71] *Daily Telegraph*, 30 November 1998.
[72] *Daily Telegraph*, 1 December 1998.
[73] Cited in www.cap.uni-muenchen.de/download/2004/2004_Venusberg_Report.pdf.

agreement fully emerged, it marked a historic watershed in the military relationships that had helped to preserve the peace of Europe throughout the post-war period. For more than twenty years, moves had been made behind the scenes towards closer integration of 'Europe's' defence efforts, mainly through the WEU. In 1996, under the Major government, Britain and France had set in train a series of bilateral agreements on closer naval and military co-operation between their two countries.[74] But now Blair was taking this process into a new dimension, with what he called 'an historic agreement'.[75]

But there was nothing to be had by way of a *quid pro quo*. Chirac equally insisted, following the calls from Lafontaine and Schröder for an end to national vetoes over taxation, that this was a 'reality' that Britain 'must also digest'.[76] Less than a week later, Chirac and Schröder reaffirmed the closeness of their alliance with a joint letter, ahead of the forthcoming Vienna Council, demanding more co-ordination of tax and employment policies at EU level, and reductions in national vetoes. In addition, the two leaders dropped dark hints about Britain's rebate, calling on 'all member states to make compromises and concessions'.[77] It looked as if the 'one plus two' were heading for a head-on clash.

The promised showdown failed to materialise. At Vienna, the main achievement was to reaffirm a 'determination to agree' their Agenda 2000 in Berlin, and to award Helmut Kohl 'for his outstanding contribution to the development of the European Union' the title 'Honorary Citizen of Europe'.[78] Everything else was on hold, pending the launch of the euro. With less than a week to go, de Silguy added fuel to the fire by claiming that Britain could not survive as a serious international power unless it joined the single currency. 'We can live without you,' he told the British people, 'but you can't live without us.'[79]

NO SUCH THING AS A FREE LAUNCH

On 1 January 1999, more than thirty thousand people joined a street party in front of the European Central Bank in Frankfurt to celebrate the launch of

[74] On 7/8 November 1996, as Britain's defence minister, Michael Portillo had signed an agreement in Bordeaux on Anglo-French naval co-operation, to be followed in 1997 and 1998 by similar agreements on army and air force co-operation. At a WEU meeting on 18/19 November 1996, he and his fellow defence ministers had also agreed to set up a Western European Armaments Organisation under the WEU, to work for closer co-operation on defence procurement. In due course this was to become part of the European Defence Agency.
[75] *Daily Telegraph*, 4 December 1998; *Financial Times*, 5 December 1998.
[76] *Financial Times*, 4 December 1998.
[77] *Daily Telegraph*, 9 December 1998.
[78] 'Presidency Conclusions', Vienna European Council 10–11 December 1998.
[79] *Sunday Telegraph*, 27 December 1998.

the euro and the first economic union in Europe since the Roman Empire. A band struck up a stirring tune to mark the historic day. Curiously, it was not Beethoven's 'EU Anthem' but 'Land of Hope and Glory'.[80] As the new currency immediately rose in value, EU finance ministers predicted that the euro would soon rank alongside the dollar as a world currency.[81] To mark Germany's new presidency, her Europe minister Günther Verheugen told the BBC: 'normally, a single currency is the final step in a process of political integration. This time the single currency isn't the final step but the beginning'.[82]

Yet, behind the euphoria was the approaching censure motion in the European Parliament. The Commission chose this moment to announce that it had suspended van Buitenen on half pay.[83] No one relished the idea of a leaderless Commission so soon after the launch of the euro, and Schröder offered a lifeline, suggesting that the charges should be investigated by an independent committee of inquiry. In a grovelling plea to the Parliament, Santer offered 'a zero-tolerance policy against fraud'. He was ready to bear his share of responsibility 'for the crisis of confidence that has come between us'.[84]

Just before the vote, however, he reverted to type. Following a tête-à-tête with Pauline Green in the Strasbourg Hilton, caught on film by a German television crew, he threatened that, if MEPs voted against any individual Commissioners, he would resign, taking his Commission with him. The gamble paid off. Reluctant to provoke such a crisis, Parliament backed away from its motion, settling instead for Schröder's suggestion of a 'Committee of Wise Men' to conduct an inquiry.[85]

With the situation stabilised for the moment, Fischer outlined to the Parliament Germany's plans for its presidency. Referring to the launch of the euro, he called it 'the first move towards their communitarisation in the EU', strengthening calls for a European constitution.[86] Elsewhere, there were more immediate crises. US-led NATO forces were preparing to intervene to save Kosovo from Serb ethnic-cleansing. Tension was also building over Iraq, as US and British aircraft bombed anti-aircraft installations in support of the designated 'no-fly' zones. Chirac chose this moment to express strong opposition to the Anglo-American axis.

Nearer home was the problem of CAP reform. As final negotiations took place between EU agriculture ministers, 30,000 angry farmers

[80] *Guardian*, 2 January 1999.
[81] *Financial Times*, 2 January 1999.
[82] *Daily Telegraph*, 2 January 1999.
[83] *Financial Times*, 5 January 1999.
[84] *Guardian*, 12 January 1999.
[85] *Independent*, 13 January 1999.
[86] Debates of the European Parliament, 12 January 1999.

converged on Brussels, challenging even Belgium's battle-hardened riot police. By the time the talks were over, with the French flatly rejecting cuts across the board, cuts in spending had turned into an increase of £1 billion.[87] Britain's minister Nick Brown declared it a 'good deal for taxpayers, farmers, consumers and the countryside'.[88] *The Times* declared it 'a mockery'.[89]

Then, on 15 March, came the publication of the parliamentary report of the 'wise men' on fraud and the Commission. It was a bombshell, essentially confirming all van Buitenen's allegations. Its most damning finding was its claim that, 'It is becoming difficult to find anyone who has even the slightest sense of responsibility'.[90] Rather than face the ignominy of a vote, on the morning of 16 March the entire College of Commissioners resigned. As the news flashed round Europe, it was hailed as the EU's 'biggest crisis in its 42-year history'.[91] But, after lunch, the same Commissioners resumed work as a 'caretaker Commission'. Their resignations were to prove little more than an extended lunch break.

Santer, however, had been fatally weakened. The Berlin European Council nine days later agreed to replace him with Romano Prodi. Despite being dogged at home by persistent suspicions of corruption, for which he had twice been investigated by local prosecutors, Prodi was universally acclaimed by the Council, not least by Blair, who described him, somewhat oddly, as 'a high-quality person'.[92]

With German farmers driving 400 tractors through Berlin's streets, and 2,000 journalists in the press tent blacked out by a power cut, the Council then got down to Agenda 2000. Spanish prime minister José María Aznar held out for additional funding, so agreement, of a sort, was not reached until five in the morning, after a brutal 20 hours of negotiation. The Commission's original 'reform' proposals, already watered down by the Agriculture Council, had been diluted still further, making the result a travesty. Intended to cut spending, not only had it been increased, but the settlement had been locked

[87] *Daily Telegraph*, 12 March 1999.
[88] *Sun*, 12 March 1999.
[89] 12 March 1999 (leader).
[90] Committee of Independent Experts, *First Report on Allegations regarding Fraud, Mismanagement and Nepotism in the European Commission* (15 March 1999), http://aei.pitt.edu/4579/1/4579.pdf.
[91] *Daily Telegraph*, 16 March 1999.
[92] Various allegations had been made against Prodi, of which the most serious was that in the 1980s, while prime minister, he had attempted to sell off the state-owned food conglomerate SME to a political crony at half the price it was worth. Italy's most successful businessman, Silvio Berlusconi, had stepped in with a much higher rival bid, and had apparently bribed a judge to stop the Prodi deal. This had created a lasting feud between the two men.

in until 2006, with a 'mid-term review' in 2002. Any idea of early enlargement seemed to have been ruled out. But at least Blair had kept his rebate.

EUROPE'S 'MR CLEAN'

Media attention now turned to the economics professor who was about to take centre-stage as the new head of the Commission. Despite his somewhat chequered past, Prodi was widely welcomed as 'Europe's Mr Clean'. What soon became rather more obvious was that he was as outspoken an advocate for integration as Delors. With war raging in Kosovo, he called for the EU to take control as soon as hostilities were over. He predicted that Britain would not be able to stay out of the euro. And he suggested to the *Financial Times* that, if Blair had hoped his St Malo defence initiative might be accepted as 'a substitute for euro membership', he was mistaken.[93]

To the European Parliament on 13 April, Prodi set out his own 'vision' of Europe. 'The Single Market,' he proclaimed, 'was the theme of the 80s; the single currency was the theme of the 90s; we must now face the difficult task of moving towards a single economy and political unity.'[94] But as he was to confirm in a series of interviews, he had no doubt as to who should lead Europe towards that 'unity'. Europe, he said, needed a 'strong government' to take 'strong decisions', and 'let's be clear', he added, 'the Commissioners have a political responsibility. They will be the government.'[95]

Where there did seem to be agreement was on the prospect of a European army. Prodi acknowledged that, for the common defence policy, this was a 'logical next step'. One day it would be 'inevitable' that the soldiers of participating states should be called to fight by a European commander, under a European flag. Countries that failed to join would be 'marginalised in the new world history'.[96]

The day after this interview appeared, EU defence ministers in Marseilles took a further step towards a 'European Defence Identity'. They agreed, on a German initiative, that efforts to co-ordinate their military forces should make 'concrete progress' within 18 months.[97] They also agreed that the operational functions of the WEU should be formally absorbed into the EU.[98] Only two days earlier, Blair had called for 'greater integration in the defence industry and procurement', and, referring to the war still raging in the Balkans,

---

[93] *Financial Times*, 6 April 1999.
[94] European Parliament, verbatim record, 13 April 1999.
[95] *On the Record*, BBC, 9 May 1999.
[96] *Financial Times*, 10 May 1999.
[97] *Financial Times*, 11 May 1999.
[98] *Guardian*, 12 May 1999.

suggested that 'if we were in any doubts about this before, Kosovo should have removed them'. His comments, made in Aachen where he was receiving the Charlemagne prize for his 'outstanding contribution to European unification', came during what was billed as 'probably the most pro-European speech by a British premier since Sir Edward Heath in the 1970s'.[99]

This theme was taken forward by Schröder and Chirac in Toulouse on 28–29 May. To Blair's dismay, they accepted the need for a separate European force – the 'Eurocorps' – suitable for rapid deployment in crisis areas or for peacekeeping missions. This Franco-German hijack of what he had intended to be an Anglo-French initiative largely negated his efforts in St Malo.[100] Blair was again being marginalised. The best way to proceed would be to set up another small group of 'wise men', to explore what institutional reforms were necessary for enlargement.[101]

After the meeting, Schröder and Chirac were in obvious good humour. They told a selected group of journalists that their renewal of Franco-German co-operation would be 'particularly useful when, during the next European summit in Cologne, it will be a question of advancing yet further European integration'. Schröder continued, in a further sideswipe at the British: 'it will be necessary to encourage those member states in this direction who perhaps have not yet gone as far, or do not wish to go so far on the subject of integration'.[102]

REALITY GAP

The Cologne European Council on 4–5 June 1999 provided a vivid picture of the growing gulf between theory and practice. Not least, it hailed the introduction of the euro as a 'success' when at that very moment it was facing its first real crisis, triggered by Italy's breach of the budget deficit limit. When Italy was allowed to increase the deficit, the markets feared that the strict disciplines set for managing the new currency would be undermined.[103] As a result, the euro had fallen 11 per cent in five months. Yet the Council proclaimed that 'a stable euro will increase Europe's ability to promote growth and employment'.[104] Faced with recession and unemployment, it could only respond with platitudes.[105]

What the Cologne Council also marked, though, was a major advance on the St Malo agreement. Resolving that, under the 'Common Foreign and

[99] *Financial Times*, 14 May 1999.
[100] AFX (UK), 30 May 1999.
[101] Ibid.
[102] Transcript of press conference: BMDF translation, 6 July 1999.
[103] *Financial Times*, 26 May 1999.
[104] *Daily Telegraph*, 5 June 1999.
[105] 'Presidency Conclusions', European Council Cologne, 4–5 June 1999, point 6.

Security Policy', the EU must 'play its full role on the international stage', the 15 leaders first nominated Javier Solana, the Spanish director-general of NATO, as its 'High Representative': in effect the EU's first foreign minister. They, alongside the president of the Commission, then agreed that the Council must have:

> the ability to take decisions on the full range of conflict prevention and crisis management tasks defined in the Treaty on European Union, the 'Petersberg Tasks'. To this end, the Union must have the capacity for autonomous action, backed up by credible military forces, the means to decide to use them and a readiness to do so, in order to respond to international crises without prejudice to actions by Nato. The EU will thereby increase its ability to contribute to international peace and security in accordance with the principles of the UN Charter.

So was born the ESDP, the European Security and Defence Policy. But this would be no more than empty bravado unless the Council also had the necessary military means to back its ambitious new posture on the world stage.[106] Nothing had more cruelly exposed these inadequacies than the war in Kosovo, now nearing its climax. The EU combined defence spending was £120 billion, close to 60 per cent of America's, supporting more than two million troops under arms compared with the USA's 1.4 million. Yet the 'out of theatre' capacity was less than 10 per cent of America's. Thus, over the preceding weeks, it had been US bombers, with British help, that pounded Milošević to the peace table, under the aegis of NATO. The 'Europeans' merely bickered over what should happen next.

At last, however, the new ESDP planned to remedy the glaring deficiency in military capacity and political will. Such was the far-reaching significance for the whole European integration process of what had been agreed at Cologne.[107] The only other issue on which the Council could show itself as decisive was the timetable for a new treaty. Without irony, it resolved that, to ensure EU institutions could 'continue to work efficiently after enlargement', the IGC should begin and end in 2000. It would deal with just three main issues, described as 'the Amsterdam leftovers': the size and composition

---

[106] 'Presidency Conclusions', Annex III.

[107] The first public acknowledgement of this came from Solana himself at a conference organised by the Commission in Berlin on 17 December 1999, on 'The Development of a Common European Defence and Security Policy: The Integration Project of the Next Decade', when he said 'the development of an effective ESDP ... will be a sign that the European integration dreamed of by Europe's founding fathers has come of age' (press release issued by the European Political Institute on www.fas.org/news/europe/991217-eu-fp.htm).

of the Commission; adjustment of Council voting to give added weight to larger states; and a 'possible extension of QMV', reducing still further the number of vetoes.

DEMOCRATIC DEFICIT

A week after Cologne came the European Parliament elections. In the UK these were the first fought under new proportional representation rules, with a 'party list' in each of the UK's 12 'Euro-regions'.

Hoping to capitalise on what they saw as the public's Eurosceptic mood, the Conservatives kept their slogan of 'in Europe but not run by Europe'.[108] But Hague was careful not to get involved in admitting just how much Britain already was 'run by Europe', concentrating his appeal on opposition to the euro. On polling day, 10 June, the Conservatives more than doubled their representation, from 17 to 36. The UK Independence Party, committed to Britain's withdrawal from the EU, won three seats. But the overall turnout of 23 per cent was by far the lowest ever recorded in a British national election, and easily the lowest in the EU (although most countries also recorded their lowest ever poll). Joining the new Parliament were two members of the disgraced former Commission, Bonino and Santer. Its first business was to approve the 20 members of the new Commission, whom Prodi presented to the MEPs on 21 July 1999 as 'Europe's government'.[109]

Ten days earlier, just after he had revealed their names, the *Sunday Telegraph* reported from Brussels that Prodi was 'planning the biggest centralisation of power in the history of Brussels politics'.[110] He had decided 'to model his administration on a national government', giving himself 'an unprecedented prime ministerial role at the heart of Europe'. Brussels was 'to rival London, Paris and Berlin'. The new Commission president had 'abandoned the collegiate idea' and aimed 'to create a European government … set to become an aggressive promoter of causes such as tax harmonisation and a European army'. The report did, however, suggest that his ambitions might conflict with those of France and Germany. Few could have realised just how prescient this was.

---

[108] *Daily Telegraph*, 10 May 1999.
[109] Prodi speech, 21 July 1999. Verbatim record.
[110] 11 July 1999.

15

Hearts and Minds: 1999–2001

The present generation should lay the final brick in the edifice
of Europe. That is our task and we ought to get down to it.
Joschka Fischer, 6 July 2000[1]

Europe, yes, but what sort of Europe?
Tony Blair, 6 October 2000[2]

It is said of Rome that most of its great buildings were completed long after
the power of the Empire had reached its zenith. No such thought troubled
EU leaders when, on 15 September 1999 a vast, futuristic building on the
edge of Strasbourg was the scene of an unprecedented ceremony. This
£300 million complex was one of two newly built venues for the European
Parliament (the other, even larger, had just been completed at a cost of £750
million in Brussels). And in the gleaming new building, politicians, officials
and journalists gathered from all over Europe to see the Commission's
new president, flanked by the 19 members of what he liked to call 'my
government', appearing before MEPs to be confirmed by acclamation.

Just six months after the former Commissioners had resigned in disgrace
(although five had now returned), all the pressing structural problems
affecting 'le projet' remained. Yet Prodi's 'coronation' was marked by a
strange air of triumphalism. Speaker after speaker enthused over how the
EU was about to take over most of Europe, its sacred mission being to bring
peace to trouble spots across the globe. As one observer put it, there was
an unmistakable sense of 'today Europe, tomorrow the world'.[3] But still

---

[1] Speech at Humboldt University, translated by BMDF.
[2] Speech at Warsaw Stock Exchange, reported by the *Financial Times*, 7 October 2000.
[3] *Sunday Telegraph*, 19 September 1999.

there was the looming problem of enlargement. That alone was enough to occupy Prodi's entire presidency, requiring strengthened institutions, ready to rule effectively over a 'Union' of as many as 30 nations.[4] Already, two weeks earlier, he had acted on a Franco-German proposal by appointing three 'eminent persons' to produce an urgent report on the 'institutional implications of enlargement'.[5]

But Prodi also had something else in mind, the so-called 'democratic deficit' – most evident in the way 'increasingly disillusioned citizens' had in June so conspicuously stayed away from the polls. The new president thought he had the answers. What the people of Europe 'persist in demanding', he declared in his acceptance speech, were 'clear answers to the important problems in their everyday lives'.[6] In a determined effort to win 'hearts and minds', he argued that the EU should capitalise on issues of popular concern such as 'the safety of the food we eat', a point that had not appeared in the preview copies of his speech. One of his top priorities was to be the restoration of 'consumer confidence'.

His excuse for singling out food safety was the Belgian 'dioxin scandal', which had been making headlines as Europe's biggest food scare since BSE. Having cost Belgium's food industry £1 billion and brought down the government of Jean-Luc Dehaene, this – on top of the turmoil caused by BSE – seemed a perfect example of the type of 'beneficial crisis' the Commission could exploit to make itself more relevant to the 'citizens' of Europe.[7]

Nevertheless, enlargement remained Prodi's immediate priority. After his hubristic speech in Strasbourg, his next call was Poland where support for EU entry was rapidly declining, down 15 points from the 85 per cent seen five years earlier.[8] Similar messages were coming from the Czech Republic and Hungary.[9] Among their concerns were the difficulty of passing into law the 80,000 pages of the *acquis communautaire*, the financial and social costs of entry, and, having only lately escaped from Communism, the prospect of taking on the deadweight of another draconian regulatory system.

[4] Prodi speech, 21 July 1999, op. cit.
[5] Dehaene, the defeated Belgian prime minister; Richard von Weiszacker, a former German president; and Lord Simon of Highbury, ex-chairman of British Petroleum and, subsequently, Blair's junior trade minister.
[6] Prodi speech, 21 July 1999, European Parliament.
[7] What Prodi was not aware of, because it had not yet come fully to light, was that the Belgian 'dioxin scandal' turned out to be a classic example of a groundless food scare. It arose when it was discovered that vegetable oil used in poultry feed had become contaminated by industrial oil, but this had posed no risk whatsoever to human health (*Sunday Telegraph*, 11 June 2000).
[8] *Financial Times*, 9 September 1999. See also 25 August 1999.
[9] *Der Spiegel*, 30 August 1999; MTI news agency, Budapest, 9 September 1999.

Conscious that if enlargement was left too long, it might never happen, Prodi decided to take the huge gamble of speeding up the whole process.[10] On 22 September, he proposed to go for a 'grand slam', pulling all the candidate countries together. Malta, Latvia, Lithuania, Slovakia, Romania and Bulgaria should also be invited into active negotiation, expanding the candidates to 12.[11] Not least of the advantages, the 'big bang' approach would increase pressure for the institutional reforms he wanted.

Prodi's three *eminenti* presented their report on 18 October.[12] Echoing the Santer Commission's views, they proposed splitting the existing treaties into two parts: the first a 'basic treaty' setting out the Union's institutional framework, amounting to a constitution.[13] Inevitably, more vetoes would go, and the two intergovernmental 'pillars' were to be brought into the Community framework, subject to QMV. Another key recommendation was 'closer co-operation' between states wishing to move towards integration 'further or faster than others'.

Meanwhile the European Council had been launching its own initiative. In Tampere, Finland, on 15–16 October 1999, EU leaders defined an 'area of freedom, security and justice', with the aim of turning the Union into 'a single judicial space'. They also agreed on a 'Charter of Fundamental Rights' to be drafted by a 62-strong 'Convention', drawn from the Commission, the European Parliament and national parliaments, deliberately modelled on the 1787 Philadelphia constitutional convention.[14]

LITTLE ENGLAND

None of this grandiose thinking seemed to be impacting on the political debate in England (for the EU was largely an English preoccupation). Blair was still obsessed with the lost opportunity of the euro, but he had realised that, to get his way, he had to sell the whole concept of 'Europe' to an increasingly sceptical public. Thus, on 14 October, Blair had appeared on the stage of a London cinema, alongside Brown, Clarke, Heseltine and Charles Kennedy, leader of the Lib-Dems. Their aim was to launch a new propaganda campaign, sponsored by Britain in Europe, to educate the British people on the 'benefits of being in Europe'.

---

[10] *Der Spiegel*, 30 August 1999.
[11] *Financial Times*, 22 September 1999.
[12] Commission of the European Communities, 'Reinforcing Political Union and Preparing for Enlargement', Brussels, 28 February 1996, COM(96) 90 Final.
[13] The University Institute at Florence was then asked to produce a draft treaty along these lines, published on 15 May 2000.
[14] 'Presidency Conclusions', Tampere European Council, 15–16 October 1999.

As Blair called for 'honest, clear debate', the media were sent a leaflet headed 'Twenty things you didn't know about Britain and Europe'. Most were only too familiar, but what was notable was the lack of any soaring rhetoric or appeal to higher values, such as 'peace in Europe'. Instead, the focus was on detail, such as the EU's 'generosity' in funding 'improved fencing' on Northern Irish farms, failing to mention that for every pound received in regional grants, UK taxpayers had to give two pounds to Community funds and then another pound in match funding.

Although no one could know it then, the lacklustre 'pitch' was to mirror the 'remain' campaign in the 2016 referendum, with the suggestion that another 'benefit' was the 'freedom of movement' that supposedly allowed British people to take more holidays in Europe than anywhere else in the world.[15] Interviewed on BBC Radio, John Major went one better by suggesting that another benefit was that the British could enjoy the music of 'Bellini, Wagner and Mozart'.

BLAIR 'OUT IN THE COLD'

Across the Channel, Prodi was concerned with higher things, to which Britain actually presented the main obstacle. One was the abolition of national vetoes; the other taxation. Speaking in Karlsruhe on 12 November, he noted the 'extreme reluctance' of some member states to surrender their veto over taxation – an oblique reference to Britain's refusal to accept the 'withholding tax'. How 'much more easily' such matters could be resolved, Prodi suggested, if such a tax 'could be adopted under a QMV arrangement'.[16]

Three weeks later, addressing the European Parliament, Prodi returned to the charge. 'The European tax package,' he admitted, 'is now in great difficulty.' Not only was it 'an important initiative to combat harmful tax competition, but [it was] also an essential piece of our employment strategy.' So impatient was he at being 'handicapped by the unanimity requirement' that he compared Europe to 'a soldier trying to march with a ball and chain round one leg'.[17] Even as he spoke, the value of the euro was plummeting. On 3 December it broke through the psychological barrier of parity with the dollar. The ECB's Duisenburg laid the blame squarely on Schröder and his failure to address the need for 'market reforms'. Schröder sought to shift the blame onto Blair for blocking the withholding tax.[18]

---

[15] *Sunday Telegraph*, 17 October 1999.
[16] Prodi speech, 21st Forum on Financial Policy and Taxation, Karlsruhe, 12 November 1999.
[17] Prodi speech, 1 December 1999.
[18] *Daily Telegraph*, 4 December 1999.

On the eve of the Helsinki European Council, this issue was now regarded as the 'acid test' of Blair's commitment to European integration.[19] But the UK press was concerned only with the beef export ban, finally lifted by the Commission on 1 August. Yet both Germany and France had refused to accept British exports. On the eve of the Council, Jospin reaffirmed the French ban. Only five years earlier, Hurd had proclaimed as one of the benefits of EU membership that 'the French cannot block our lamb, or the Germans our beef'. Small wonder, at the pre-Council dinner, that Jospin and Blair were barely on speaking terms.

Scarcely noticed at the time was another step towards a European Army. The EU leaders lodged what was henceforth to be known as the 'Helsinki Agenda', setting as a target for 2003 the development of 'new political and military bodies and structures', within the Council. The aim was, eventually, to deploy independently of NATO 'military forces of up to 50,000–60,000 persons', the so-called 'European Rapid Reaction Force' (ERRF). In working towards this, the Council agreed on a 'Headline Goal' that defined all the necessary force requirements and equipment needed, to which each member state had to contribute.[20] Such ambitious plans required an autonomous airlift capability, for which 'national' – i.e., European – pride demanded European aircraft. Blair struck a sour note by refusing to order the proposed aircraft, not yet off the drawing board, in preference to well-tried and more capable US equivalents.[21]

On the tax issue, the Council communiqué made impatient reference to continuing failure to make progress. To resolve the problem, a 'High Level Working Group' was to be set up to investigate Britain's proposal that, as an alternative to the 'withholding tax', member states should make full disclosure of banking details to other countries' tax authorities. When Blair was then obliged to sign a 'Millennium Declaration' extolling the benefits of monetary union, *The Times* reported that it had been for him 'a bad summit in anyone's language'.[22] To the *Observer*, Blair was 'left out in the cold'.[23]

At least on some issues there had been agreement, such as Prodi's call for six more countries to be added to the accession negotiations. And it was agreed that the IGC should begin the following February. But on that rocky

[19] *Daily Telegraph*, 9 December 1999.
[20] 'Presidency Conclusions', Helsinki European Council, 10–11 December 1999.
[21] In terms of its specification, the A-400M, to be built by the European Airbus consortium, would provide an unhappy compromise between the familiar US-built C-130 (Hercules) and the larger C-17s, both of which were long-established mainstays of the RAF.
[22] 11 December 1999.
[23] 12 December 1999.

road, due to end in Nice in December 2000, Blair was already trudging a solitary path.

PRODI SETS THE PACE

On 1 January 2000, there were world-wide celebrations for the dawn of a new Millennium. Then, on 18 March, the last significant phase of compulsory metrication was completed in the UK, when the Price Marking Order 1999 came into force, implementing two EC directives. The effect of the order was to require the compulsory use of metric weights and measures for goods sold 'loose from bulk'. For a British market trader to sell 'a pound' of apples or tomatoes was now a criminal offence.

Meanwhile, on 12 January at a press conference in London an Oxford biologist, Sir John Krebs, was introduced as the first head of Britain's new Food Standards Agency, long promised by the Labour Party as the 'wholly independent' body that would exercise control over all aspects of food safety law. Almost simultaneously in Brussels, following up Prodi's pledge in Strasbourg, the Commissioner for consumer protection, David Byrne, announced that the EU was to take 'competence' over all aspects of food safety law throughout the Union. It would launch 84 'initiatives', including a sheaf of new hygiene laws, overseen by its own European Food Safety Authority, of which the supposedly independent Food Standards Agency would be a branch office.[24] Yet, so ingrained was the deceit that pervaded the British government, that there was no acknowledgement of this new reality.

On 26 January, the Prodi Commission put forward its proposals for the IGC. Under the title 'Adapting the institutions to make a success of enlargement', it predictably urged that 'qualified majority voting should be the rule'.[25] To keep the Commission to a manageable size after enlargement, it should either be limited to 20 members or be split into 'two tiers'. This would inevitably mean 'a stronger President', with an inner cabinet of senior Commissioners to 'co-ordinate' the work of their lesser colleagues. Finally, the Commission took on a suggestion by Delors' that *avant-garde* nations could engage in 'enhanced co-operation', as long as it was supported by eight member states.[26]

When Hague suggested in a speech in Poland that the Commission now seemed hell-bent on producing 'the blueprint for a single European state', with 'its own government, its own army, its own taxes, its own foreign policy,

[24] *Financial Times*, 13 January 2000; *Sunday Telegraph*, 16 January 2000.
[25] https://ec.europa.eu/commission/presscorner/detail/en/IP_00_79.
[26] European Commission, *General Report on the Activities of the European Union 2000*, Brussels, Luxembourg, 2001, pp. 7–8.

its own criminal justice system, its own constitution and its own citizenship, as well as its own currency', Prodi seemed eager to confirm his worst fears.[27]

Interviewed by the *Independent*, he claimed that unless the EU's larger states were prepared to join in a political union with its own army, they would 'disappear from the history books'. He emphasised that it was now the Commission that was behaving like a 'growing government' for Europe, although what caught notice was his sardonic insistence that the EU must have its own army: 'I was not joking ... If you don't want to call it a European army, don't call it a European army. You can call it "Margaret", you can call it "Mary-Ann", you can find any name ...'[28]

Prodi went on to issue a paper setting out his Commission's 'strategic objectives' for the next five years. 'What we are aiming at is a new kind of global governance,' he explained. 'Europe's model of integration, working successfully on a continental scale, is a quarry from which ideas for global governance can and should be drawn.' And in all this, he wished to emphasise, the 'pivotal role' would be played by the Commission, which 'has always been the driving force for European integration'.[29]

BRITAIN DEBATES 'EUROPE'

On 14 February, as the IGC opened in Brussels, the British government gave its own views in a 'White Paper', although this glossy full-colour brochure looked more like an advertising promotion.[30] Not until nearly half-way through its 38 pages did it set out the government's position. This consisted not so much of positive proposals of what it wished to see included in the treaty, as merely a defensive list of items it was not prepared to give away. Britain would fight to retain the national veto over five areas: taxation, social security, defence, border controls and the budget contribution. So remote was all this from the debate now raging on the continent that one Lib-Dem MEP observed, 'no wonder our European partners sometimes think we are on another planet'.[31]

As if to confirm the unreality of Britain's 'debate', a curious row blew up over a campaign launched by Britain in Europe, entitled 'Out of Europe, Out of Work'. On Friday 18 February, in advance of the launch, headline coverage by the BBC and Europhile newspapers claimed that, according to a

[27] *Financial Times*, 29 January 2000.
[28] *Independent*, 4 February 2000.
[29] Commission of the European Communities, 'Strategic Objectives 2000–2005: Shaping the New Europe', COM(2000) 154 final, Brussels, 9 February 2000.
[30] Foreign and Commonwealth Office, IGC, 'Reform for Enlargement: The British Approach to the EU Intergovernmental Conference', Cmd 4595, 14 February 2000.
[31] Nick Clegg MEP, *Independent*, 15 February 2000.

new study by the National Institute for Economic and Social Research, up to eight million jobs could be lost if Britain left the EU.[32] Almost immediately NIESR's director, Dr Martin Weale, angrily disowned the campaign, calling its claims 'absurd'. His institute's report had found no long-term impact on employment. 'It's pure Goebbels,' he complained: 'I cannot recall such a wilful distortion of the facts.'[33]

On Monday 21 February, BiE's campaign was launched by the trade secretary, Stephen Byers, supported by yet another letter to *The Times* from Heseltine, Clarke and Patten. But the initiative was in total disarray. Hastily, BiE published another survey from South Bank University claiming that 3.4 million jobs were related to trade with the EU, and the BBC faithfully reported Byers claiming that 'millions of British jobs depend on Europe'. Next day the BBC tried to resuscitate the drive by inviting Gordon Brown onto the *Today* programme, claiming that '750,000 British companies export from Britain to Europe'. When government figures disclosed that the number was only 18,000, the campaign fizzled out. But Blair and his colleagues would continue to recycle the discredited claim that 'three million jobs depend on Britain's membership of the EU' for years to come.

Tony Blair had no better grasp of reality when speaking in Ghent in late February. He asserted that it was 'Britain's destiny' to be a leading partner in Europe, playing her 'full part'. Replaying a version of history that the Europhiles had so assiduously cultivated over 50 years, he claimed that hesitation over Europe had been one of Britain's greatest post-war mistakes:

We opted out of the European Coal and Steel Community. We opted out of the European Economic Community. We opted out of the social chapter. We played little part in the debate over the single currency. When we finally decided to join many of these institutions, we found – unsurprisingly – that they did not reflect British interests or experience.[34]

Just how Britain could now play that leading role in shaping a Europe that did 'reflect British interests', Blair was unable to explain. But behind the scenes his government was now secretly preparing to commit itself to an integrationist initiative so far-reaching in its implications that it would in its own way be as significant for Britain's future as joining the euro.

Another telling symptom of the self-deception that now pervaded every aspect of the British government's approach to 'Europe' was the spin

[32] E.g: 'Eight Million Jobs Could Be Lost If Britain Quits EU', *Independent*, 18 February 2000.
[33] *Sunday Business*, 20 February 2000.
[34] Blair speech: 'To withdraw is not patriotic', 23 February 2000.

given by Blair and his ministers to the Lisbon European Council of 23–24 March. Portentously entitled 'Employment, Economic Reform and Social Cohesion', this, they claimed, would show they were 'winning the economic argument in Europe'.[35] They were persuading their partners, Blair claimed, to move away from 'heavy-handed intervention and regulation' towards a new agenda of 'jobs, competitiveness, economic change and dynamism'.[36]

THE CONTINENTAL DEBATE

It was hard to see any of Blair's agenda reflected in an even more than usually turgid Council communiqué, promising that by 2010 the EU would be transformed into the 'most competitive, dynamic and knowledge-based economy in the world'. Sounding more like human resource managers than politicians, the leaders resolved that 'the combat against illiteracy must be reinforced', and that a 'European framework' should be established to 'define the new basic skills to be provided through lifelong learning, IT skills, foreign languages, technological culture, entrepreneurship and social skills'.[37]

What Lisbon also highlighted was the rivalry now emerging between Council and Commission as to which was the true 'government of Europe'. Portugal's prime minister António Guterres crowed that the European Council was 'taking the lead'. Prodi was seen to be losing ground.[38] After an unprecedented secret meeting with his fellow Commissioners, from which even interpreters were excluded, it took a 'confirmation of unity' from Prodi's colleagues to quell rumours of his departure.[39] Prodi now hit back, calling on the leaders of France and Germany, as custodians of the 'project', to do their duty. The Franco-German 'motor' was idling. Prodi told *Die Zeit* 'the Germans must remember their European responsibilities', adding that 'progress is only possible when it is driven by a Franco-German initiative'.[40]

Contrasting with the trivial approach to the issue in Britain, over the summer months of 2000, a series of 'heavy hitters' laid out their views of where 'Europe' should be heading. The first contribution came in a speech from Jospin on 9 May, marking the fiftieth anniversary of the Schuman Declaration, when he called for the newly drafted Charter of Fundamental Rights to be included in the new treaty, interpreted and enforced by the ECJ.

[35] 'Presidency Conclusions', Lisbon European Council, 23–24 March 2000.
[36] *The Economist*, 19 February 2000.
[37] Lisbon European Council, op. cit.
[38] *Diario de Noticias*, 24 March; *Financial Times*, 27 March 2000.
[39] *Daily Telegraph*, 6 April 2000.
[40] *Daily Telegraph*, 8 April 2000.

This was a direct challenge to the long-established Court of Human Rights in Strasbourg.[41]

Next off the mark was Germany's foreign minister Joschka Fischer, who at Berlin's Humboldt University on 12 May gave his 'Thoughts on the Finality of Europe'.[42] He again argued for a European constitution', with precisely defined new powers for the parliament and government. This idea marked a decisive break with the 'Monnet method'. The Commission should no longer be able to indulge in the creeping acquisition of powers, exemplified in the open-ended process of *engrenage*. However, within weeks, Michel Barnier, the Commissioner responsible for the IGC, responded with a paper entitled 'Europe's Future: Two Steps and Three Paths'.[43] He recommended that 'the keystone' of EU government should be a strengthened Commission, under an elected president.

Barnier made no mention of a constitution, but the Commission's European University Institute in Florence had just delivered a draft in response to the recommendation of Prodi's 'wise men' the previous year.[44] This split the existing treaties into two parts, a 'Basic Treaty', would set out the EU's institutional framework and objectives, as a constitution, a second part setting out the rules governing specific policies, such as the CAP and the internal market. The latter could be amended without requiring the unanimity of an IGC. With that, it seemed a 'constitution' of some kind was now on almost everyone's agenda. As these views emerged, it seemed timely that the EU acquired its own motto: *Unité dans la diversité*, 'unity in diversity'. This supposedly resulted from a two-year-long competition involving schoolchildren all over Europe; but it bore a distinct similarity to the motto of the USA: *E pluribus unum*, 'out of many, the one'.[45]

With drawing up the agenda for the new treaty the immediate priority, the EU leaders met in Santa Maria da Feira on 19–20 June, the final Council of the Portuguese presidency. They agreed to focus on the three 'Amsterdam leftovers', although majority voting now covered an unprecedented new 39 policy areas, some highly sensitive. There was also a fourth issue: 'flexible

[41] Speech to French National Assembly, 9 May 2000 (BMDF translation, 9 June 2000).
[42] Fischer, Joschka, Speech: 'From Confederacy to Federation: Thoughts on the Finality of European Integration', Humboldt University, Berlin, 12 May 2000. Reproduced in Joerges, C., Mény, Y. and Weller, J. H. H. (2000), *What Kind of Constitution for What Kind of Polity?* (Florence: Robert Schuman Centre for Advanced Studies), pp. 19–30.
[43] Barnier, Michel, 'Europe's Future: Two Steps and Three Paths, a Personal Note' (European Commission), 8 June 2000.
[44] European University Institute, *A Basic Treaty for the European Union: A Study of the Reorganisation of the Treaties*, Report submitted on 15 May 2000 to Mr Romano Prodi, President of the European Commission.
[45] *Guardian*, 16 May 2000.

co-operation'. And the Council agreed to 'allow' the Charter of Fundamental Rights to be considered for inclusion in the treaty.[46]

No sooner was Feira concluded than Schröder proposed that Nice must be followed by another IGC, to be completed no later than 2004, to tackle the 'big issues'. Echoing Fischer, he said that these must include drawing up a new EU constitution, to replace the existing treaties.[47] It was now clear that Nice would be only a sideshow. With France's presidency due to start on 1 July, Chirac entered the debate.[48] On 27 June he was in Berlin as the first foreign leader to address the Bundestag in the new Reichstag building. Once Nice had been got out of the way, he declared, there should begin 'what I call the great transition period', its chief theme being 'the initiative of those countries' who 'wish to go further or faster'. France and Germany would lead a 'pioneer group' of member states, served by its own 'secretariat', in addressing 'the other institutional issues facing Europe', ranging from reorganising the treaties to clarifying the 'nature of the Charter of Fundamental Rights'. Then the governments and peoples of Europe would be called on to establish the first 'European Constitution'.[49] He concluded with the words:

> what Germany and France have lived through and suffered in the course of History is unlike anything else. They, better than any other nation, grasp the fundamental meaning of peace and the European project. In Europe, only they, by forcing the pace, were able to give the signal for a rallying of forces. Together, at the pace dictated by the renewal of their relations and the determination of their peoples, they have ensured the progress of the idea of Europe. Only they can take the action which will carry Europe further.[50]

The speech, far more aggressive than Fischer's a month earlier, attracted considerable media attention.[51] Particularly glaring was the way Chirac brushed aside not only the Commission but also all the other member states, in assuming that Europe's future should be reshaped essentially by a Franco-German alliance. Other states could tag along, but only so far as they accepted French and German leadership.

---

[46] 'Presidency Conclusions', Santa Maria da Feira European Council, 19–20 June 2000.
[47] *Guardian*, 23 June 2000.
[48] *Financial Times*, 27 June 2000.
[49] Luxembourg University archive.
[50] Ibid.
[51] http://news.bbc.co.uk/1/hi/world/monitoring/media_reports/808337.stm.

The first response from a member of the Commission came from Mario Monti. Writing in *Corriere della Sera*, he warned that Chirac's approach posed a 'more serious and far-reaching' risk than the decision to create the single currency in the 1990s. Italy, he said, should support further European integration only as long as this involved strengthening institutions such as the Commission, the parliament and the ECJ. Chirac's 'concert of nations' would not be 'based on community rules', policed by the Commission and the ECJ, which ensured that all states, large and small, were treated equally. The interests of countries such as Italy could thus be overridden, in a way that might do them 'grave damage'.[52]

When Chirac came to Strasbourg on 4 July to address MEPs on the plans for the French presidency, Prodi lost no time in launching a counter-attack. 'The whole point of what we are aiming for at Nice and beyond,' he said, is that 'with 27 or 28 more member states, the Union will need stronger institutions, not weaker ones':

> it is therefore an illusion to believe that the 'Monnet method' is a thing of the past, something that could more effectively be replaced by *ad hoc* arrangements. The European Parliament, the Council, the Commission and the Court are our institutions. They provide the guarantees, the checks and balances, without which nothing lasting will be built ... this is the task to which we are all committed at Nice.[53]

Two days later, on 6 July, Fischer came to Strasbourg to deliver a German response to Chirac's proposals. He backed the idea of a 'pioneer group' and suggested that its 'obvious core' would be the 11 members of the eurozone. Directly challenging the British government's line that joining the euro was purely an economic issue without constitutional implications, Fischer pointed out that the Maastricht Treaty, creating the single currency, had been a 'quantum leap' towards federalism. 'Let us be clear,' he said,

> the 11 countries in the euro have already given up part of their sovereignty. They have transferred it to the EU. Adopting the euro was a step towards a certain objective. We try to avoid the word federation, but how else can it be described? It is a democratic federation. We have a federation already.

[52] *Financial Times*, 2 July 2000.
[53] Speech by Romano Prodi, President of the European Commission, 'Handing over the Torch', to the European Parliament and the Council President at the start of the French presidency, Strasbourg, 4 July 2000. Emphasis in the original.

Of course, the best solution, he added, would be 'for all 15 states to do their historical homework and rise to the challenge together'. But if they could not do that, the 'countries that want to proceed will march on'. He then pointedly told MEPs: 'you can't tie progress in the Union to the slowest ship in the convoy'. There could be little doubt which country Fischer had in mind.[54]

A FRACTIOUS AUTUMN

With just three months to go before Nice, it was clear that not all was well in the European Union. The euro plumbed new lows against the dollar, having lost more than 27 per cent of its original value. As world oil prices hit their highest level for a decade, there were widespread popular protests against record levels of tax on petrol and diesel, notably in France and Britain, scarcely helped when it emerged that EU finance ministers had agreed in Versailles on 9 September not to lower fuel taxes for 'environmental' reasons.

On 28 September all this was overshadowed by Denmark's referendum on the single currency. On an 85 per cent turnout, the Danes snubbed their political, big business and media establishment in rejecting the euro by 53 to 47 per cent. In Italy, *La Stampa* called it a tragedy that 'a few thousand Hamlets', voting 'irresponsibly and foolishly', for reasons that were 'both irrational and foolish', had been able to weaken the onward march of integration. With Denmark consigned to the 'naughty step', it was time for the main players to resume their battle. In Dresden, at a ceremony to mark ten years of German reunification, Chirac renewed his call for a Franco-German alliance to lead a core of countries towards deeper integration after the EU had enlarged. Schröder agreed it would be the 'joint efforts' of France and Germany that would ensure agreement on essential EU reforms.[55]

Prodi, back in Strasbourg, warned MEPs that moves to strengthen direct co-operation between member states at the expense of the Commission 'undermined the democratic nature of the whole EU structure'. He suggested that the Commission should take over control of EU economic policy from the ECB, and also, from the Council of Ministers, the role played by Solana as spokesman for EU foreign policy.[56]

It was finally Blair's turn to re-enter the debate, with a much-trailed speech in Warsaw on 6 October 2000.[57] Predictably, he called for an early decision on enlargement, reflecting Britain's wish to see the new member

---

[54] *Daily Telegraph*, 7 July 2000, 'German minister backs fast track to federal Europe'.
[55] BBC News, 3 October 2000, 'Germans mark decade of unity'.
[56] *Financial Times*, 4 October 2000.
[57] www.number-10.gov.uk/news.asp?NewsId=1341&SectionId=32.

states participating in the next post-Nice IGC. Turning to EU reform, he asked: 'Europe, yes, but what sort of Europe?' Cautiously, he tried to pick his way between the three main contending arguments without coming down too firmly for or against any of them. He could not see any profit in 'pitting the European institutions against intergovernmental co-operation'. Europe was and must 'remain a unique combination of the intergovernmental and the supranational'.

Certainly, there was a need for a strong, independent Commission, as this protected smaller states and allowed Europe to overcome purely sectional interests. But equally important was the European Council, whose purpose, he oddly asserted, had been 'formally' laid down in the Treaty of Rome as being to set 'Europe's' agenda (originating only in 1974, the Council was of course not referred to in that treaty). Blair now wanted the Council to set out an 'annual agenda for Europe' in a 'far more organised and structured way', thus effectively displacing the Commission's traditional 'work programme'.

So far Blair had tried to appease both Prodi and Chirac. But he then rejected calls for a constitution, suggesting instead a mere 'statement of principles', setting out what was best done at 'European' level and what should be retained at national level. He echoed Fischer's suggestion that the European Parliament should have a second chamber, but only to monitor the application of his 'statement of principles', and the EU's common foreign and security policy. On 'enhanced co-operation' he said he had 'no problem', but then contradicted the very reason why this was so constantly under discussion, by insisting that it 'must not lead to a hard core; a Europe in which some member states create their own ... policies and institutions from which others are in practice excluded'. The EU was, Blair concluded, 'building a Europe of equal partners served by institutions which need to be independent but responsive and accountable'. It should aspire to be a 'superpower, but not a superstate'.

This incoherent mish-mash, plagiarised from little bits of everyone else's proposals, stuck together with a few wistful platitudes, perfectly reflected how, for decades, Britain's politicians had tried to contribute to a game they did not understand. Since it offered nothing new, Blair's contribution was ignored. A few days later, the Commission suggested that the Charter of Fundamental Rights would be turned into a legally binding document, as the quintessential component of an EU constitution. Responding to the ensuing furore, Blair's minister for Europe, Keith Vaz, dismissed the Charter as having no more legal significance than a copy of the *Beano* or the *Sun*.[58]

---

[58] *Daily Telegraph*, 14 October 2000. 'European summit Charter on rights "no more binding than the Beano"'.

'NIGHTMARE IN NICE'

As the deadline for Nice approached, pre-summit manoeuvring reached a frenzy, with an informal European Council amid the faded Edwardian grandeur of Biarritz on 13–14 October to settle the final agenda. Although both Chirac and Jospin were under fire at home over corruption scandals, the government most under pressure was Britain's. Blair seemed at odds on a whole tranche of issues, from the surrender of national vetoes to tax harmonisation, from the constitution to inclusion in the treaty of the Charter of Fundamental Rights.[59] Under continuous sniping from the Conservatives, he pledged to veto any attempt to include the Charter in the treaty, asserting that it was only a 'declaration', with no legal status.

Britain was also at odds with France for her undermining of sanctions on Iraq. A Foreign Office minister, Peter Hain, described French conduct in sending flights to Baghdad without UN approval as 'contemptible'.[60] There was another spat about the withholding tax and a row about the EU's 'Rapid Reaction Force' replacing NATO. France. at the last moment, tried to spring a 'social agenda' on the IGC. Then, with weary consistency, the British government began to signal the ground it was prepared to surrender. By the end of November, it was reported that Blair was ready to give up 17 vetoes in 12 areas of EU decision-making. There were only six areas on which he remained immovable: tax, social security, borders, treaty change, raising EU revenue and defence.[61]

Even now, Prodi was not satisfied. His 'shopping list' included abolition of the veto on taxation, social security, border controls, external trade and the EU budget. And Britain was not the only problem. Most member states were fighting to hold on to their veto in one area or another. France was blocking moves to QMV on foreign trade, fearing that French culture would be swamped by Hollywood films. Spain was holding out on regional aid, fearing it would lose billions in subsidies. The Germans were worried about asylum and immigration. Prodi was gloomily forecasting a 50–50 chance of breakdown at the summit.[62]

In a bid to stave off humiliation, Chirac embarked on a 15,000-mile odyssey across Europe, to meet every head of government in ten days.[63] Last on the list was Schröder. Under pressure from the *Länder* to insist on a constitution to define the division of power between the EU and the regions,

[59] *Financial Times*, 12 October 2000.
[60] *Financial Times*, 8 November 2000.
[61] *Daily Telegraph*, 30 November 2000.
[62] *Daily Telegraph*, 1 December 2000.
[63] *Financial Times*, 1 December 2000.

his central objective was an IGC before enlargement. He was also holding out for greater voting power than France in the Council of Ministers, to reflect Germany's larger population. This was Chirac's nightmare. If he conceded, it would be politically disastrous at home. When the two leaders failed to agree, Chirac commented, 'A solution will come, or not come. But it can only come at the last minute, in Nice.'[64]

So, on Thursday 7 December 2000, began a summit scheduled to last three days. It was the culmination of a process begun in February, taking 330 hours of negotiation, involving hundreds of ministers and thousands of officials, watched by a similar number of journalists, many of them now present in the resort of Nice. For all this, the 15 member states had not yet reached agreement on any of the main agenda items.

In what was now almost a tradition, thousands of demonstrators gave the local riot police an opportunity to practise their tear gas skills. Blair might have wished for some of it inside the conference room, where, right at the start, his colleagues insisted on proclaiming the new Charter of Fundamental Rights. But it was not to be in the treaty – not yet – and, although Blair refused to sign the declaration that accompanied it, this was not the last of it.[65] He gained another early success, of sorts, when his colleagues agreed that NATO should remain the cornerstone of Europe's defence. And they agreed that some of the candidate states could become members by mid-2004. But before the leaders got down to the main agenda, 'institutional reform', there was still the date of the next IGC.

Despite Blair's Warsaw speech, opposing an EU constitution, he was one of the first to agree to the German demand for a new treaty by 2004, on the basis that by then the first new entrants would have been admitted. Putting the best gloss he could on his climbdown, he told waiting journalists, 'I don't think we've got anything to fear from that. There is much for us to gain from a conference that sets out clearly where it is that the Brussels Commission operates and where it doesn't.' Hungary's foreign minister was not the only one to voice concern: 'We wouldn't want to see a date set for the next IGC ... we want to be involved fully, having equal rights.'[66]

For Blair, however, things were to get worse. Having spent months building alliances so that he would not become 'isolated in Europe' like his predecessors, he suddenly became just that. Ally after ally deserted him. Denmark, Britain's leading supporter in stopping harmonisation of social security, backed down after being offered a compromise. Germany,

---

[64] *Financial Times*, 3 December 2000.
[65] *Guardian*, 8 December 2000.
[66] *Financial Times*, 8 December 2000.

meanwhile, appeared ready to drop its veto on asylum policy. Sweden edged away from its support on taxation. A senior EU official said the 'moment of truth' had arrived for Blair and other leaders if they were not to block the treaty.[67]

As the summit entered an unprecedented fourth day, a Sunday, tempers were fraying and failure was predicted. One blockage was over reallocation of voting rights, and the first attempt by France had triggered a mutiny among the smaller countries. They believed they were being disadvantaged against Germany, France, Italy and Spain. Furthermore, there was dissatisfaction among the accession countries, particularly Poland, which had the same population as Spain yet was to get fewer votes. Nor had Germany got a bigger share of votes than other large countries.[68]

News then trickled out of a 'furious confrontation' between Blair and Chirac. The French president, in a move that had 'infuriated and shocked the British delegation', had produced a revised treaty draft that included abandoning the veto on tax and social security. The British responded with a strongly worded warning that Blair would wield his veto unless the proposals were abandoned. For once, Blair was not alone. Portugal's Guterres joined him and Ireland's Bertie Ahern was described as going 'ballistic'.

Others were equally unhappy about the voting system. Britain, Spain, Germany, Italy and France had all increased their share of voting power in the Council, but small and medium-sized member states had suffered painful reductions. The Portuguese foreign minister protested: 'our votes are being confiscated'. Negotiations were described by one delegate as 'hand-to-hand fighting', with a coalition of smaller states seeking to recalculate their shares. Other stories filtered out about Chirac's 'high-handed behaviour', most notably when he shouted that one of Prodi's aides should not have been allowed to enter the room. When Chirac ordered him out, Prodi was reported to have rejoined, 'I see my civil servants wherever I want and whenever I want.'[69]

The summit was deteriorating into bad-tempered chaos, at times verging on farce, as when Chirac put forward proposals that were then promptly vetoed by his own government. 'If this is what a Europe run by the so-called big member states, rather than the Commission and the EU institutions, looks like, we want no part of it,' a senior Finnish diplomat observed.[70] Eventually, agreement of a sort was reached. The final draft maintained

[67] *Daily Telegraph*, 9 December 2000.
[68] *Financial Times*, 10 December 2000.
[69] *Sunday Telegraph*; *Sunday Mirror*; *Observer*, 10 December 2000.
[70] *Observer*, 10 December 2000.

voting parity between France and Germany, giving them each 29 votes (14 per cent of the total), along with Britain and Italy. Thanks to their determined lobbying, Spain and Poland (after enlargement) would both get 27, considerably more than their population size justified. Chirac got his 'enhanced co-operation' and British officials claimed a victory when QMV on tax and social security was dropped. Schröder, despite describing the proceedings as 'utter chaos', got his commitment for an IGC in 2004.

Embodied in a declaration attached to the treaty, there would be four points on the agenda for the next IGC, to be discussed at the Laeken Council in Belgium in December 2001: 'a more precise delimitation of powers between the European Union and Member States, reflecting the principle of subsidiarity'; the legal status of the Charter of Rights; simplification of the treaties to make them 'clearer and better understood'; and 'the role of national parliaments in the European architecture'.[71] But all this was for the future. The consensus was that the French had made a mess of it. Journalists from across the EU dubbed it 'nightmare in Nice'.[72]

Despite that, it was a confident Tony Blair who reported back to the Commons, defending his decision to surrender Britain's veto in 23 more areas. The new treaty, he claimed, would produce a 'more rational way of decision making'. Already, however, attention was turning to the next IGC. Through this, Blair promised, some of the powers currently exercised at a European level could be repatriated to member states.[73] This was responding to an opinion poll commissioned by the French foreign ministry, published in *Le Figaro*, showing that 53 per cent of voters in France, 56 per cent in Germany and 67 per cent in the UK believed national sovereignty should be maintained, even if this meant limiting EU powers. In Sweden, five years after she had joined the EU, voters opposed to EU membership now outnumbered those in favour, by 43 to 37 per cent. Nice had done nothing to resolve the underlying tension between member states. Apart from the voting changes, real decisions had been postponed.[74] All Blair would admit was 'we cannot do business like this in future'.[75]

HANGOVER

For some time into the new year, an air of exhaustion fell over those responsible for guiding the 'project'. After the trauma of Nice, they were

[71] 'Presidency Conclusions', Nice European Council, 7, 8 and 9 December 2000.
[72] *Daily Telegraph*, 11 December 2000.
[73] HC Deb, 11 December 2000, Vol. 359, cc349-69.
[74] Ibid.
[75] *Financial Times*, 12 December 2000.

aware that just over the horizon was that much more important IGC which by 2005 would give 'Europe' a constitution. They were equally aware that hanging over them was that Damoclean sword of enlargement. Unless by then the constitution was agreed, the new members would take part in its drafting, with veto power. Much of 2001 would thus be taken up with the main players simply restating the positions they had laid out in 2000.

In late January, Schröder looked forward to a Europe where decisions on tax, defence, health and a plethora of other key policies would be 'defined by the EU and not national governments'. Meanwhile, as Germany's economy continued to decline, despite being aided by the weakness of the euro, the days of her 'economic miracle' seemed a distant memory. However, the first country seriously to collide with the system now governing the euro-zone economies was Ireland. On 24 January Pedro Solbes, the Spanish commissioner for economic and monetary affairs, reprimanded Dublin for making inflationary tax cuts and threatened sanctions unless steps were taken to curb public spending.[76]

In February, Barnier announced that the December European Council planned for Laeken, near Brussels, would be the moment when the EU must decide whether to adopt a constitution.[77] Prodi urged 'a frank and fundamental appraisal' of the EU's ultimate purpose, asking MEPs: 'are we all clear that we want to build something that can aspire to be a world power ... not just a trading bloc but a political entity?'[78] Visiting London, he met Blair and lunched with journalists in the House of Commons, to press home his message that Britain's economy could not remain successful outside the euro. As for Blair's pretensions to be at the heart of Europe, he said, 'if you stay out, that's your choice, but you can't then pretend to be in'.[79]

Prodi then took command in a way that was to have huge impact on subsequent events, although his action was scarcely reported. Touring central Europe, he told the Czechs that a 'very probable' date for enlargement was 2004.[80] This would effectively bring forward accession by a year. Unless the timing of the IGC itself was brought forward, the new members would have to be included in the negotiations, with veto power over the constitution. And the fractious issues of CAP reform and regional funding still remained unsettled.

[76] Irish Times, 8 February 2001.
[77] Financial Times, 7 February 2001.
[78] Financial Times, 14 February 2001.
[79] Guardian, 16 February 2001.
[80] AFX Europe, 5 April 2001.

THE DANCE CONTINUES

On 8 May 2001, at a conference of Europe's left-wing parties in Berlin, the German SPD came up with what was known as the Schröder Plan. This called for a constitution to restructure EU institutions, turning the Commission into a strong executive, but controlled by a Council of Ministers transformed into a 'chamber of European states'. Some responsibilities, including those for agriculture, should be repatriated. This 'hyperactivity', commented the *Financial Times*, reflected the pressure from the leaders of the *Länder*, such as Bavaria's Edmund Stoiber, to prevent the EU gradually extending its power at their expense.[81]

Belgium's prime minister Guy Verhofstadt, on the other hand, feared that the EU might be dominated by a *Directoire* of larger states.[82] No one reacted more sharply to the Schröder Plan, however, than the French, as chief champions of both the *Directoire* model and the existing CAP.[83] The response from Chirac, now faced at home with a threat of impeachment for alleged corruption when he was mayor of Paris, was to repeat his call for a constitution reconstituting the EU as 'a federation of nation states'. Giscard d'Estaing suggested that the EU should regroup around its six original members, or the countries of the eurozone, with a looser structure to accommodate the others.[84] Pressure from the applicant countries was mounting, as when Poland's prime minister, in Brussels on 22 May, announced that his country's target-date for entry was 2003.[85] But the EU-wide polls were now showing little enthusiasm for enlargement, with only 34 per cent in favour.[86]

Back in Britain, Blair was preoccupied by his election campaign, with polling due on 7 June. Labour's manifesto made no mention of a European constitution or further integration. Hague's Conservatives were equally silent, the party preferring to focus on 'saving the pound', a tactic that failed to strike a chord with the voters. On polling day, voters gave Blair a second overwhelming victory, prompting Hague's resignation as Conservative leader. He was replaced by Iain Duncan Smith. Politicians and officials across Europe welcomed Blair's triumph as a sign that Britain had rejected Euroscepticism. Blair hinted at an early referendum on entry to the euro.[87]

[81] 1 May 2001.
[82] Ibid.
[83] *Guardian*, 7 May 2001.
[84] *Financial Times*, 10 May 2001.
[85] TV Polonia, Warsaw, 22 May 2001.
[86] *Scotsman*, 10 May 2001.
[87] *Financial Times*, 9 June 2001.

Any euphoria in the 'European' camp, however, was diluted by the news, a day later, that Ireland had rejected the Nice treaty by 53.9 per cent, albeit on a mere 32 per cent turnout. Although the Irish had been the most enthusiastic 'pro-Europeans' of them all, they were now fearful of the EU's growing power over their lives, not least through the euro. Prodi merely saw the vote as underlining the need 'for greater efforts from all of us to explain Europe to our citizens'.[88] There was no question of renegotiating the treaty.[89] Ireland's prime minister Ahern immediately announced plans for another referendum. Having delivered the wrong result, the Irish must now try again.

So it came to 15 June when EU leaders, in sombre mood, met at Göteborg, for the concluding European Council of a lacklustre Swedish presidency. A leading Dutch politician admitted privately that his country would also have rejected Nice had it held a referendum.[90] The Council agreed that enlargement was 'irreversible', but achieved little else.[91] Outside, 15,000 protesters ran amok, with 43 injured and one killed by the police.[92] Immediately afterwards, Ireland began to receive a stream of high-level visitations from EU dignitaries and MEPs, leading the *Irish Times* to comment, 'they tour EU capitals much as our Cabinet tours the provinces'.[93] When Prodi himself, on a four-day 'listening tour', met leaders of the 'No' campaign, they were not impressed. 'For a listening exercise, he did quite a lot of talking,' said one campaigner.[94]

It was now Belgium's turn to assume the EU presidency, and its fervently integrationist prime minister, Verhofstadt, declared that its most important achievement would be the 'Laeken Declaration' on the constitution at the end of the year. But another Eurobarometer poll showed that only 45 per cent of the EU's population now believed that they benefited from EU membership.[95]

LOSING THE BATTLE

Prodi was not indulging in empty rhetoric when he proclaimed during his acceptance speech in September 1999 that the 'hearts and minds' of 'European citizens' would be high up on his list of priorities. But it took

---

[88] *Herald*, 9 June 2001.
[89] *Guardian*, 9 June 2001.
[90] *Irish Independent*, 18 June 2001.
[91] 'Presidency Conclusions', Göteborg European Council, 15–16 June, Bulletin 18.06.2001.
[92] *Financial Times*, 18 June 2001.
[93] 16 June 2001.
[94] Ibid.
[95] *De Standaard*, 18 July 2001.

nearly a year for him to come up with plans on how to deal with what could, in the longer term, prove an existential threat.

The template for the fight-back appeared in the form of a 'White Paper on European Governance', published on 25 July 2000.[96] It represented input not just from the Commission's own staff but from hundreds of academics part-funded by Brussels in universities across Europe. Its purpose was to set out a strategy whereby Europe's 'government' could use its existing powers under the *acquis* to reach its hundreds of millions of citizens.

Dealing with the 'democratic deficit', the Commission acknowledged that, unless the people were engaged more fully, they might eventually rebel. And the problem, it was argued, was that there was no genuine European 'demos' – no sense of a collective identity. The answer was to recruit support from all those representative bodies making up what the Commission called 'organised civil society'.[97] Its components included anything from regional and local authorities to trade unions and trade associations, to churches and women's groups. The aim was to foster Europe-wide 'networks' linking such organisations, thus building the necessary 'European identity', a 'transnational political space', free of national loyalties. Then, the traditional 'representative democracy' based on nation states would give way to an EU-wide 'consultative democracy', as EU institutions bypassed national governments and spoke directly to these groups.

Influence would also be exerted through its own network of agencies, such as the European Food Standards Authority and the Medicines Evaluation Agency, the European Aviation Safety Agency and, eventually, even a European Space Agency, all of which would add visibility to 'Europe' and make it more relevant to its citizens' lives. Key players drafted into this battle were the Europe-wide network of academics whose background role in the work of the Commission was one of the least widely recognised features of how it operated.[98] Central to this was the 'Jean Monnet Project', co-financing 2,319 university teaching schemes across Europe to 'promote European integration'.[99] Not only did these and similar schemes provide the Commission with a vast pool of 'experts', but again Brussels was able to get their services on the cheap, as posts were 'match funded' by member states.

---

[96] COM(2001) 428, Brussels.

[97] Prodi speech: European Parliament, Strasbourg, 4 September 2001.

[98] Much of the background work was carried out by the Commission's own 'think-tank', the Forward Studies Unit, headed by two academics.

[99] https://ec.europa.eu/programmes/erasmus-plus/programme-guide/part-b/three-key-actions/jean-monnet-activities/projects_en.

Unfortunately for the Commission, in England at least, the battle was already being joined, as EU powers reached into the lives of ordinary people. For instance, on 4 July 2000, in a Sunderland market, council officials supported by two policemen converged on a fruit and vegetable stall owned by Steve Thoburn, to seize his scales. The offence for which he faced criminal prosecution was to sell his wares by the 'pound', as his customers preferred, rather than in the kilograms that since 1 January had become compulsory.

This was the first time the EU's new metrication law had been put to the test, the culmination of the process of compulsory metrication that had been imposed on Britain without Parliament ever being consulted. With Thoburn in the national headlines, and through the efforts of his fellow marketeer-turned-publicist, Neil Herron, the legend of the 'metric martyrs' was born. It attracted massive nationwide and international publicity for the anti-EU cause.

When a case taken by Sunderland Council against Thoburn reached the High Court, its decision in 2002 reaffirmed the supremacy of EU law.[100] Metrication thus became a *cause célèbre* in the growing Eurosceptic community, more so when in 2004 Thoburn died prematurely at the age of 39.[101] His funeral and the subsequent wake at the Stadium of Light, home of Sunderland Football Club, was attended by many devoted followers. Thus the 'metric martyrs' acquired cult status. Their efforts did much to shift political sentiment in the north-east of England against the EU.

THE FOOT AND MOUTH CRISIS

Another defining moment came on 19 February 2001 when a new strain of Foot and Mouth Disease (FMD), Pan-Asian O, had been identified in pigs in Essex. Within ten days, the virus had spread through sheep, cattle and pigs, right down the west side of England, from Cumbria via the Welsh borders to Devon. It was already clear that Britain's farmers faced the worst epidemic of the disease on record. The timing could not have been worse. Almost every sector of British farming was struggling to compete with the much more highly subsidised farmers of countries such as France and Ireland. And, as the disease spread, it soon became clear that the government was not remotely prepared. As ministry officials began to order huge pyres of dead animals and to designate '3 kilometre protection zones' and '10 kilometre surveillance zones', baffled vets wondered why they seemed to be ignoring every recommendation of a report drawn up after Britain's previous epidemic in 1967–1968.

---

[100] https://oup-arc.com/static/5c0e79ef50eddf00160f35ad/casebook_119.htm.
[101] *Northern Echo*, 17 March 2004.

What only gradually emerged, because politicians of all parties were at pains not to advertise the fact, was that during the 1980s, handling of FMD had become a Community competence.[102] The innovations that puzzled local vets, such as the need to ask the ministry for permission to slaughter and the ban on burying animals on-farm, all derived from EU legislation.

By mid-March, the Ministry had lost control: outbreaks topped 300 and were doubling every ten days. The panic response was to order wholesale slaughter: a 'pre-emptive cull', destroying millions of healthy sheep, cattle and pigs simply to prevent the disease spreading. Although this was of dubious legality under British law (the 1981 Animal Health Act only allowed the killing of infected animals or those directly exposed to infection), it was 'recommended' by inspectors of the EU's Food and Veterinary Office in Dublin, on a visit to Britain between 12 and 16 March.[103]

By now the world's leading veterinary scientists, including Professor Fred Brown, an Englishman working for the US government, and Dr Simon Barteling from Holland, were asking why Britain had not launched an emergency vaccination programme, which could bring the epidemic to a halt within weeks, making the mass-slaughter unnecessary. Until 1990, routine use of vaccination on the continent had eliminated foot and mouth. But general use of vaccines was then prohibited by Directive 90/423/EEC.

Nevertheless, the Directive also stated that, when FMD had been confirmed and threatened 'to become extensive', emergency vaccination was permitted. However, despite the Community requirement in 1991 for member states to submit contingency plans, that submitted by Britain had been inadequate, planning for no more than 150 outbreaks.[104] It had been approved by the Commission without proper examination, but now its inadequacies were exposed. The ministry did not have the means to carry out a mass vaccination programme. This was despite the fact that, in 1998, the EU itself had used emergency vaccination in the Balkans to prevent the new Pan-Asian O strain crossing its borders, whence the Commission had advised member states to take additional measures 'to prevent a local

---

[102] Council Directive 85/511/EC introducing Community measures for the control of foot-and-mouth disease.

[103] The precise recommendation was to 'consider preventative slaughter in certain circumstances in an attempt to "get ahead" of the disease, and to reduce the weight of infection to which the animals are being exposed'. European Commission, Heath and Consumer Protection Directorate, DG (SANCO)/3318/2001-MR final, point 9.1.

[104] Based on the assessment of threat determined by the Commission. See Commission working documents VI/5211/95 – 'Contingency plans for epidemic diseases' – and VI/6319/98 – 'Guidelines for FMD contingency plans in non-vaccinating countries' (redesignated XXIV/2655/1999). The working basis was confirmed by the Commission in its written response to the European Parliament Temporary Committee of Inquiry, Document: SANCO/10018/2002 – Rev.2., Section C, Q3, p. 18.

outbreak becoming a disaster'.[105] Furthermore, in 1999 the Commission had warned that the risks of 'a very large outbreak' in the EU were now 'extraordinarily high' and laid down ten criteria to guide member states as to when to use emergency vaccination.

Within days of the epidemic breaking out in the UK, Barteling was convinced that at least seven of these had been met. On 3 April 2001, Commissioner Byrne in Strasbourg rehearsed the issues on vaccination, promising a thorough review into the circumstances of the epidemic.[106] Change was not long in coming, when it was acknowledged that too much importance had been attached to the trade-policy aspects of the disease, with the result that protective vaccination had not been carried out even when it had been authorised. Too late, a new law was framed.[107]

What, therefore, the FMD outbreak had illustrated was a failure of both London and Brussels, with a devastating lack of co-ordination, and a confusion of responsibility. It had cost Britain and the EU at least £8 billion, devastating Britain's rural economy and, incidentally, forcing Blair to postpone a long-planned election campaign. A trivial national media barely covered the EU aspects, but as Cumbria – the epicentre of the epidemic – became a vast killing field under undeclared martial law, and as the world woke to the obscenity of the disused airfield at Great Orton near Carlisle being used to bury the carcases of millions of slaughtered animals, the lessons were not lost on the residents of the county. Just as Thoburn's metrication battle had 'radicalised' the North-East, sleepy rural villages in Cumbria took against the EU.

Added to the slaughterhouse crisis – where livestock farmers were having to send animals hundreds of miles for slaughter because so many facilities had been closed down – and coupled with the near crippling burden of bureaucracy to maintain inadequate CAP subsidies that were driving hill farmers into penury, this was another brick in the wall. In response, all Prodi could offer was European knitting circles, and subsidies for academics to churn out unreadable and over-priced tomes on the theory of neo-functional integration. His battle was being lost and he did not have the first idea as to why. Although no one could have known it at the time, the campaign for the UK's 2016 referendum had already begun.

[105] European Commission, *Strategy for Emergency Vaccination against Foot and Mouth Disease (FMD)*, Report of the Scientific Committee on Animal Health and Animal Welfare, adopted 10 March 1999.
[106] Statement of Commissioner David Byrne to the European Parliament on the latest developments on foot-and-mouth disease (FMD), 3 April 2001.
[107] Council Directive 2003/85/EC of 29 September 2003 on Community measures for the control of foot-and-mouth disease.

9/11: ANOTHER BENEFICIAL CRISIS

On 11 September 2001, New York's World Trade Center was destroyed by the most dramatic terrorist atrocity in history. In an unprecedented demonstration of solidarity, *Le Monde* proclaimed '*Nous sommes tous Américains*.'[108] The US, on the other hand, declared war on the 'Axis of Evil' and prepared to launch military action against Afghanistan. Blair set out on a tour of world capitals, building support for an American-led alliance against terrorism. Prodi flew to meet the presidents of the USA and Russia, calling for 'international solidarity'. Ostensibly, Europe stood with America.[109]

The reality was different. Before '9/11', the EU had been starting to shape a distinct 'European' voice on foreign policy, not least on the Balkans. But this fragile accord was now unravelling. Power had gone back to capitals; a Commission official complained, 'We have lost the diplomatic initiative.' When Prodi was blamed for failing to take the lead, he simply called for more integration, arguing for a 'convention' to prepare for EU reform.[110] To reinforce his message, Delors and 12 former European Council members – including Kohl and Dehaene – pressed for a new political project to 're-float the EU'. A manifesto entitled 'Let us shake Europe awake' was handed over in front of the cameras to Prodi.[111]

Despite this plea, centrifugal forces were pulling against the integrationists. An informal European Council had been called for 19 October, in Ghent, but to the consternation of Prodi and the fury of the smaller member states, it was upstaged by the 'big three', Blair, Chirac and Schröder, holding their own 'mini-summit'. Theirs were the three nations asked by America to contribute militarily to the fight against terrorism. EU officials were 'disturbed' by this development. Prodi remarked pointedly, 'Where the Commission has a presence, that is where Europe is.'[112]

Attempting to paper over the cracks, the Council unanimously pledged its 'full support' for action in Afghanistan, calling for the al-Q'aeda terrorist network to be eliminated.[113] Although rancour at having to watch from the sidelines was palpable, the crisis did provide the excuse for more integration. The Council dusted down its two-year-old 'Tampere programme' for an EU-wide system of internal security and justice. As an EU 'action plan' against terrorism, it spawned no fewer than 79 initiatives, including several

[108] 13 September 2001.
[109] *Guardian*, 8 October 2001.
[110] *Financial Times*, 12/15 October 2001; *Guardian*, 18 October 2001.
[111] *De Standaard*, 16 October 2001.
[112] *Independent*, 19 October 2001.
[113] *Independent*, 20 October 2001.

controversial proposals such as the European arrest warrant.[114] The 9/11 outrage was proving to be the most useful 'beneficial crisis' of them all.

PRELUDE TO LAEKEN

With the Laeken Council approaching, the next two months were dominated by the jockeying of the main players, each pushing their own agendas. On the sidelines of the Ghent Council, a curious spat had taken place between Verhofstadt and Prodi, reminiscent of the *froideur* between Thatcher and Delors in 1988. During the Council press conferences, Prodi complained of Verhofstadt 'hogging' the limelight, to such an extent that Prodi had absented himself from the final conference in protest.[115] Commentators saw this as a reflection of the Commission's waning influence.[116] Prodi issued a statement threatening to boycott Laeken unless it was resolved.[117]

For a while, it was 'open season' on Prodi, but he was soon back on the attack, demanding that 'Europe' 'speak with one voice' if it wanted to be a leading player on the international stage. That 'voice' had to be the Commission.[118] Prodi also took it upon himself to announce that a convention to draw up a constitution would start 'early next year'. National governments would have to agree this prior to the entry to the EU of its new members, 'scheduled for spring 2004'.[119] Despite Laeken still being two months away, it seemed that both the decision to hold a constitutional convention and the accession date of the new members had already been fixed.

None of this was noted by the British media, which were more interested in a belated attempt by Blair to re-establish his 'leading role' in Europe. He had summoned a 'council of war' in Downing Street, in anticipation of a ground offensive in Afghanistan. This impromptu 'summit' on 4 November was attended by Chirac and Jospin, Schröder, Verhofstadt, Aznar and Berlusconi. Solana and the Dutch prime minister, Wim Kok, also asked to attend.[120] Prodi was not invited.[121] He explained that this was because he had earlier told Blair on the telephone not to bother as he would not accept.[122]

Prodi was further embarrassed when the International Securities Market Association revealed that, during his time as prime minister,

[114] *Financial Times*, 22 October 2001.
[115] *De Standaard*, 22 October 2001.
[116] For instance, see the *Financial Times*, 25 October 2001.
[117] *De Standaard*, 23 October 2001.
[118] *Corriere della Sera*, 27 October 2001.
[119] Ibid.
[120] *Guardian*, 5 November 2001.
[121] *Independent*, 3 November 2001.
[122] RDP Antena 1 radio, Lisbon, 15 November 2001.

Italy had 'juggled the books' in order to qualify for the euro.[123] By a secret arrangement with an unnamed bank, the Italian government had been able to defer payments on its debt in 1996 and 1997, to create the illusion that it had met the 3 per cent deficit target set by Maastricht.[124]

On 12 November, in Bruges, Prodi was again claiming that the 9/11 crisis called for an EU-wide police force and tighter border controls, under Commission control. In what was to become a constant refrain, he spoke of the 'Community method' being crucial to 'our security, our well-being and the peace of our continent'.[125] He also wanted the Commission to tighten its grip over tax and spending policies. The Stability and Growth Pact alone did not go far enough to safeguard the euro, he said, proposing that 'a model budget policy' for member states was a crucial next step towards economic union.[126]

However, just when Prodi was calling for greater central control over the budgets of member states, the Court of Auditors yet again reported 'an unacceptable incidence of error'.[127] Unabashed, Prodi pressed for the speeding up of economic reforms needed 'to ensure that the EU fulfils its promise' of having the world's most competitive economy by 2010'. The 'Lisbon agenda' had so far achieved nothing. He urged that a 'priority reform package' should be agreed by the Barcelona Council, scheduled for March 2002, to show the EU 'delivering promises'.[128]

Finally, Germany and France, despite earlier disagreements, joined in supporting a constitutional convention, even offering a draft 'Laeken Declaration', declaring that it was 'an essential step in the historic process of European integration'.[129] Blair, opposed to a constitution, was left stranded. It would go ahead, and there was no doubting its objective. All that remained was the crucial choice of the convention's president. But when Schröder moved to back France's choice of Giscard, the result was a foregone conclusion. Europe's central 'motor of integration' was working as smoothly as ever.

LAEKEN, AS ARRANGED

On 14 December, to the ritual accompaniment of shouting demonstrators, the motor cavalcades of the EU leaders swept into the former Royal Palace

[123] ANSA news agency, Rome, 5 November 2001.
[124] *Guardian*, 6 November 2001.
[125] *Guardian*, 13 November 2001.
[126] *Daily Telegraph*, 13 November 2001.
[127] European Court of Auditors' Annual Report 2000, Luxembourg, 13 November 2001.
[128] *Financial Times*, 13 November 2001.
[129] *Daily Telegraph*, 24 November 2001.

at Laeken. Perhaps as a testament to the skill of the Belgian police, only 40 demonstrators were arrested there.[130]

After the sham of negotiation, the 'EU leaders' issued their pre-prepared Laeken Declaration, subtitled 'The Future of the European Union'.[131] The EU, it proclaimed, 'is a success story', having developed from 'an economic and technical collaboration' towards 'the construction of a political union'. But it was now at a 'crossroads', facing 'the democratic challenge'. European institutions had to be brought closer to their citizens, while playing a leading role in 'a new world order'. The EU would intervene in world trouble spots, to take action on such issues as climate change and food safety. But citizens did not want the Union to become 'too bureaucratic' or be a 'superstate'. It needed to 'become more democratic, more transparent and more efficient', finding ways to bring 'citizens, and primarily the young, closer to the European design'.

Ways must be found to extend the Union's powers, as well as restore some power to member states. 'The creeping expansion of the competence of the Union' must be halted, so long as this did not also halt 'the European dynamic'. In particular, the Laeken Declaration asked, should the treaties be reorganised? Should the Union even be working 'towards a Constitution'? And to consider all these issues, there was to be a convention. Giscard would be its president, with the former prime ministers of Italy and Belgium, Amato and Dehaene, his vice-chairmen. The aim would be to draw up 'a final document' that would be the starting point for the IGC in 2003, paving the way for a new treaty.

With Laeken concluded, thoughts turned to the euro, with the introduction of notes and coins due in less than two weeks. This led a German paper to ask Prodi whether, philosophically, 'could it be said that the euro is a way of buying the European soul?' Prodi's response was revealing: 'Money is not only substance, it is also identity.'[132] At midnight on 31 December 2001, the euro 'became tangible'. After three years as a virtual currency, it had finally arrived. More than 15 billion banknotes and 51 billion coins were soon to be the only legal tender for 306 million people in 12 countries. Prodi declared that this would now make 'common rules' for the running of Europe's economies 'inevitable'.[133] The greatest step so far in the march of integration was now irreversible. The 1972 Paris agenda had finally come of age, but the 'hearts and minds' were still trailing far behind.

[130] *Guardian*, 14 December 2001.
[131] https://www.consilium.europa.eu/media/20950/68827.pdf.
[132] *Welt am Sonntag*, Hamburg, 16 December 2001.
[133] AFX Europe, 31 December 2001.

16

The Crowning Dream: 2002–2004

Their crowning dream is a constituent assembly ... which ...
must decide on the constitution they want ...
Altiero Spinelli, Ventotene Manifesto, 1941

Reflecting the will of the citizens and States of Europe ...
Opening words of the 'Constitution for Europe'

On the morning of 28 February 2002, a crowd of politicians, officials and journalists streamed into the European Parliament complex in Brussels, heading for the hemicycle, the main parliamentary chamber. They were there for the opening of the Convention that was to draft a 'Constitution for Europe'.

Dominating the occasion was the Convention's 76-year-old president, Giscard d'Estaing. He told the packed 'hemicycle' that his task was 'to seek consensus' on a single proposal for 'a constitutional treaty'.[1] The next speaker was Prodi, who lost no time in telling delegates that he wanted a 'European democracy' based on the peoples and states of Europe rather than just on 'the laws of the few largest, strongest or most senior members'. Nor, he went on, as if speaking for the shade of Monnet, should there be a 'new League of Nations reduced to impotence by selfishness and the right of veto'.[2] His message was clear. It was to be the 'Community method' or nothing.

In terms of organisation, there was no doubt that Giscard was running the show, aided by his two vice-presidents and a secretariat, headed by Sir John Kerr, a former head of the UK's permanent representation in Brussels.

---

[1] http://european-convention.europa.eu/docs/speeches/1.pdf.
[2] http://european-convention.europa.eu/docs/speeches/181.pdf.

In theory, the agenda would be set by a 13-member 'Praesidium'.[3] Chosen by Giscard himself, this included two Commissioners, Michel Barnier of France and António Vitorino of Portugal, but most smaller countries and the ten new entrants were not represented. There would be no vote on the final draft. It would be up to Giscard himself to decide where that 'consensus' lay.[4]

It quickly became clear to German-born Labour MP Gisela Stuart – one of the 13 members of the Praesidium – that the proceedings were rigged. She later wrote:

> there was an unspoken assumption that the *acquis communautaire* ... was untouchable. The debates focused solely on where we could do more at European Union level. Any representative who took issue with the fundamental goal of deeper integration was sidelined. Government representatives were accused of being obstructive because they protected national interests. And yet the concerted efforts by the Commission and the European Parliament to enhance their influence were not seen as power grabbing, but as being good Europeans.[5]

After the grand launch, the sense of occasion quickly dissipated. Meetings became a humdrum routine, ignored even by the insiders in the parliament that was hosting the proceedings. Public events were thinly attended and largely ignored. The Convention website only recorded an average of 47,000 visitors per month – around 1,500 a day.[6] And in Britain, even the Convention's launch had been given little publicity, apart from cursory reporting of the appointment of the three UK delegates, led by the Foreign Office's Europe minister Peter Hain.[7]

The Convention itself was organised in three sections: a 'listening phase' that would last until the summer; a 'discussion phase' through the autumn, with delegates split into working groups to deal with specific issues; and

---

[3] In the convention itself, there were 105 delegates, made up of one from each of 28 governments (including 13 candidate countries), 2 from each national parliament, 16 MEPs and 2 representing the Commission. Each delegate had an 'alternate' entitled to take part in meetings, bringing the total participants to 207. Kerr's secretariat was mainly made up of officials from the Council of Ministers, with some from the Commission and the Parliament.

[4] *Daily Telegraph*; *Irish Times*; *Financial Times*, 1 March 2002.

[5] See reference below: Stuart, p. 16.

[6] http://european-convention.europa.eu/docs/Treaty/cv00851.en03.pdf.

[7] The two others were Gisela Stuart, who was also the only woman on the Praesidium, and Conservative MP David Heathcoat-Amory. They were later to publish pamphlets on their experiences: Stuart, Gisela (2003), *The Making of Europe's Constitution* (London: Fabian Society); Heathcoat-Amory, David (2004), *The European Constitution and What it Means for Britain* (London: Centre for Policy Studies).

at the end of the year, a 'drafting phase', to complete the text that would be handed over to heads of government.

The so-called 'listening phase' – described as an 'empty charade' – finished in July. Heathcoat-Amory, the other Westminster MP attending, recalled how two days had been set aside to listen to 'representatives of civil society'. These mostly turned out to be familiar Brussels lobby groups, dependent on EU funding for their existence. This was followed by the 'discussion phase', centred on six (later to become 11) 'working groups'.[8] A Youth Convention was also organised, with the same number of representatives as the Convention itself, and the same rules of debate.[9] Some of the more independent youth members signed a petition criticising the way the conclusions had been organised in advance by the main political groups and then orchestrated by the secretariat without proper debate.[10]

At the beginning of August, in a theatrical gesture, Giscard invited Kerr to his home near Tours, supposedly to discuss what general form the constitution should take.[11] Whatever discussions did take place, they were resolved by the end of October when Giscard unveiled a 'skeleton' draft. This had three sections, beginning with a 'basic constitution', incorporating the Charter of Fundamental Rights and 'collapsing' the three Maastricht 'pillars' into one single structure. But since the 'working groups' had not yet come up with their recommendations (indeed some had not yet started), it was already clear that proceedings were being directed from above.

Just precisely who drafted the skeleton, and when, was 'unclear' to Gisela Stuart.[12] In fact, it bore an uncanny resemblance to the 'Basic Treaty for the European Union', produced by the European University Institute at Florence for Prodi on 15 May 2000. In what was called 'a study of the reorganisation of the treaties', the three-section structure was the key feature. With the incorporation of the Fundamental Rights Charter, the authors took the view that their document 'would have a symbolic and identity-creating value that could bring the European integration process close to civil society'.[13]

A clue as to what was really happening came on Friday 13 June 2003 when Giscard chose to unveil the product of his labours to the European Parliament. Although parts were not yet ready, he held up the incomplete

[8] Heathcoat-Amory, op. cit., p. 10.
[9] http://european-convention.europa.eu/docs/youthconv/484.pdf.
[10] Ibid.
[11] Ibid., p. 20.
[12] Stuart, op. cit., p. 20.
[13] European University Institute, op. cit.

text and, in a theatrical display of emotion, 'divined' a consensus. Thus spoke 'the people of Europe'.[14]

The second clue came a week later, when Giscard handed over a blue leather-bound copy of the draft treaty to the European Council in Porto Carras in northern Greece. At that point, he told the EU leaders that it represented 'an important step forward in the construction of Europe'.[15] In an unscripted comment, he warned them 'not to unravel it'.[16] On 3 July, the president of the European Parliament, Pat Cox, repeated the sentiment to the Reform Club in London. The draft constitution, he said, 'should not be lightly discarded or unbundled. Those who seek to unravel the broad consensus which was created would bear the responsibility of a result which would be the lowest common denominator, precisely the result which the Convention wished to avoid.'[17]

To put these events into context, one must go back to the Amsterdam and then the Nice Treaty IGCs. Both were failures. Particularly after the fractious Nice experience, there were those who were asking whether member states could ever again agree a treaty on the scale of the original Treaty of Rome, or Maastricht. With a little help from his friends, what Giscard was effectively trying to do was to 'bounce' the member states into an agreement without detailed negotiations. The draft treaty, emblazoned with the legend 'Adopted by consensus by the European Convention on 13 June and 10 July 2003', and opening with the words: 'Reflecting the will of the citizens and States of Europe', was being presented as a done deal.[18] 'The draft is a success because it is a finished product, with no loose ends to be tied up, no options left open,' Giscard told Berlusconi at the final handover.[19]

To Jack Straw, who had nursed the treaty through its procedural steps on behalf of the British government, Giscard's text finally gave the lie to Eurosceptic 'myths and hysteria'. It 'confirms the EU as a union of nations, not a superstate,' he proclaimed.[20] *The Economist* also dismissed the idea of an emerging superstate. Its front cover had a picture of a large wastebasket, filled with paper, with the question: 'Where to file Europe's new constitution?' The Convention had produced a lamentable piece of work that in many

[14] *Financial Times*, 14 June 2003.
[15] http://european-convention.europa.eu/docs/speeches/9604.pdf.
[16] Giscard was to repeat his emotional warning when the Convention was recalled for its final session in Brussels on 10 July (EU Observer, 10 July 2003) and again at the final handover. See also BBC News, 18 July 2003, 'EU receives draft constitution'.
[17] https://www.europarl.europa.eu/former_ep_presidents/president-cox/speeches/en/sp0064.htm.
[18] Draft Treaty Establishing a Constitution for Europe.
[19] Luxembourg University archive.
[20] *Guardian*, 17 June 2003.

ways made the Union's constitutional architecture 'harder to understand', it wrote: 'an incredible feat'.[21] The criticism was deserved. None of the main issues had been resolved.

In a way, both Straw and *The Economist* were right. The soaring aspirations of generations of 'Europeans', not least Spinelli, had been left unfulfilled. This was no constitution in the manner conceived by the founding fathers of the United States. Rather, it was another leaden European treaty, packed with minutiae and institutional detail.

Giscard had served his masters well. His work would end the clumsy 'three-pillar' structure set up by Maastricht. There would no longer be a distinction between the 'European Community', giving supranational pre-eminence to the Commission, and the 'European Union', run by the member states intergovernmentally, covering foreign and defence policy and 'justice and home affairs'. Everything would now be united under one umbrella, to include all the powers, policies and concerns of the all-embracing 'Union'. This, for the first time, would be given 'legal personality', enabling it to conduct almost all the normal activities of a state, including signing international treaties. For the first time also, it would be made explicit in a treaty that the laws of the Union enjoyed primacy over the laws of its members. Although since 1964 this principle had been declared and upheld by the ECJ, it had never before been formally enacted in a treaty.

In support of these innovations, the treaty formally established the European Council as a Union institution, with a president elected by the heads of government for a term of up to five years. There would, however, still be a rotating chair for the Council of Ministers, which was to be renamed the Council of the European Union. That Union would have two full-time 'super-presidents', each serving for up to five years: the presidents of the European Commission and the European Council. Giscard had ducked the question of direct elections but he did propose that the Council should appoint a single 'Union Minister of Foreign Affairs'. The post-holder would serve as a vice-president of the Commission to co-ordinate and act as chief spokesman for the Union's foreign and defence policies (supported by the Union's own 'foreign ministry' and diplomatic representation across the world).

To complicate matters still further, Giscard wanted to reduce the Commission to 15, thus ending the rule that every country should have at least one Commissioner. This would reinforce its supranational character, since at any given time ten member states would have to submit to laws imposed by a body on which they were not represented.

[21] 19 June 2003.

The draft proposed significant extension of the Union's powers, to include a wide range of new objectives and competences. These would include setting up a European Defence Agency (EDA) to co-ordinate defence policy, drawing up a Union space programme and developing a common energy policy.[22] There would be much closer co-ordination of the policies of member states, most notably in how they ran their economies. Inevitably, it was proposed that there should be a further significant reduction in national vetoes, bringing to exactly 100 the areas of policy where, over the decades, the QMV had been adopted. The old QMV threshold requiring a 73 per cent majority, according to the votes given to each country at Nice, so long as these came from countries representing 62 per cent of the population, would be replaced by a new formula. In future, half the member states could carry a vote, but their vote would only be valid if, collectively, they represented 60 per cent of the Community's population.

Then there was the new status accorded to the European Charter of Fundamental Rights. In less than four years this had graduated from being a mere statement of principles to a central ingredient in the treaty, ultimately enforceable by the ECJ. All this added up to a prescription for by far the most ambitious state of integration the 'project' had yet aspired to. But the entity that would emerge from Giscard's proposals would retain an essential ambiguity. It would have many of the attributes of a fully-fledged state, but could still deny that it was a 'superstate'. More subtly, it would be a 'super-government': unique in form and exercising much of its power through member state institutions. In this respect, the 'constitution' would not really provide anything like a full picture of how this government worked, any more than previous treaties had done. This was because so much of its power and influence was exercised behind the scenes.

Not the least striking feature of Giscard's proposals was how signally they ignored several of the chief proclaimed intentions of the Laeken Declaration, reiterated in a preface to the draft constitution itself. As eight Convention members pointed out in a minority report, the draft offered nothing to make the Union more transparent or less bureaucratic, and did nothing of substance to bring the 'European' institutions 'closer to the citizens' or to give a greater role to national parliaments.

Despite its opening boast that it was 'reflecting the will of the citizens and States of Europe', there was nothing that indicated any desire to involve

---

[22] The Council made a pre-emptive move on the EDA. It instructed the General Affairs Council to set up the agency, 'to support the Council and Member States'. This meant it would remain firmly under the Council's control, rather than under the Commission. See Council Decision (CFSP) 2015/1835 of 12 October 2015 defining the statute, seat and operational rules of the European Defence Agency.

citizens more closely, by way of making the institutions more accountable to the democratic will; and no proposal to allow the peoples of Europe to dismiss or replace the governing power. As for the claim that the constitution would give greater powers to national parliaments, Giscard offered nothing of substance. They would simply enjoy slightly greater opportunities to examine proposed Union legislation. The only new 'right' they acquired came if enough of them were in agreement, whence they could send legislative proposals back to Brussels to be reviewed, without any guarantee that the slightest notice would be taken of their views.

Nor, for all the talk of the finality of this proposed constitution, was there any indication that it would mark the end of the road. On the contrary, the inclusion of the *passerelle* or escalator clause, allowing further erosions of the national veto without the need for another treaty, and the inclusion of further clauses to allow 'enhanced co-operation', showed that the constitution was merely another landmark on the same familiar path of continuous integration towards that distant, still undefined goal.

There was, however, one concession to 'people power'. It scarcely registered at the time but was to trigger the final fracture between the United Kingdom and the rest of the EU member states. This was Article 59 (which became Article 50 in the final treaty), headed 'Voluntary withdrawal from the Union', declaring that, 'Any Member State may decide to withdraw from the European Union in accordance with its own constitutional requirements.'[23] There were some 47 amendments to this Article, many suggesting that it was unnecessary because leaving was already provided for in the Vienna Convention on the Law of Treaties.[24] But none were so bold as Joschka Fischer, who wrote: 'The article should be deleted ... there is no requirement to leave the Union.'[25] In just over a decade, millions would disagree.

For the moment, though, the focus was on the core articles of the draft constitution. They represented the maximum that Giscard thought at this stage it was possible to achieve. It was now up to the IGC to see whether they could agree.

LIFE GOES ON

While the world's attention had not been focused on the European convention, life continued in what passed for normal. In France, for instance, Chirac had been accused of multiple misdemeanours, ranging from paying party activists from public funds to 'skimming' public

[23] http://european-convention.europa.eu/docs/Treaty/cv00850.en03.pdf.
[24] Article 59: 'Voluntary withdrawal from the Union: Amendments'.
[25] http://european-convention.europa.eu/docs/Treaty/pdf/46/Art46fischerDE.pdf.

contracts and forging invoices. Enjoying presidential immunity, he was safe from conviction, enabling him to fight a hotly contested presidential election against right-wing nationalist, Jean-Marie Le Pen. Forced to choose between 'the Fascist' and 'the Crook', the French held their noses, giving '*l'escroc*' an unprecedented victory, with an 81.7 per cent vote.[26]

In Brussels, the Commission weathered a tremendous storm over fisheries when it tried to delay giving the Spanish fleet 'equal access' to Community waters. Through April, Spain tried to sabotage the Commission's plans. Under wholly improper pressure from a Spanish Commissioner (the rules were clear that Commissioners must not act in a national interest), the top Brussels fisheries official, Stefan Schmidt, a Dane, was forced from his post. Schmidt himself was already accused of favouring Denmark's destructive 'industrial' fishing fleet, which had somehow been exempted from the 'cod ban' under which 40,000 square miles of the North Sea were closed to all other fishing, further accelerating the decline of the British fleet.

On 6 May, attention switched to Holland, with the murder of Pym Fortuyn, the charismatic leader of a far-right nationalist party. Campaigning on an anti-Islam, anti-immigration ticket, his party had been expected to hold the balance of power in the country's forthcoming general election. This prompted much heart-searching on the rise of right-wing parties in the EU, with suggestions that the European project was going too far, too fast. But Prodi disagreed. There was not enough 'Europe'.[27] The day after Fortuyn died, he unveiled plans to set up a 'European Corps of Border Guards', to police the EU's frontiers against illegal immigrants.[28]

Having weathered the fishing crisis, the Commission became embroiled in the 'Andreasen affair', which brought back echoes of Connolly and van Buitenen. Marta Andreasen was a Spanish accountant who, in January 2002, had been appointed by the budget and anti-fraud commissioner, Michaele Schreyer, to clean up the Commission's accounts. She quickly found what she called 'serious and glaring' shortcomings. Like those before her, she was dismissed. When Dougal Watt, a whistleblower within the Court of Auditors, supported her charges, he too was 'let go'.

Such matters were of little concern, however, to the final Council of the Spanish presidency in Seville on 21–22 June. The main item, once again, was enlargement, focused on fears that existing members might be swamped by job-seekers from the new members. There were also fears for the EU budget,

---

[26] *Daily Telegraph*, 22 April 2002; AFX (UK), 5 May 2002.
[27] AFX (UK), 7 May 2002.
[28] Brussels, 7 May 2002, COM(2002) 233 final, Towards Integrated Management of External Borders of the Member States of the European Union.

unless the newcomers' access to the CAP was delayed.[29] Commissioner Fischler launched a 'mid-term review', declaring that 'our agricultural policy is doomed to fail'.[30] He proposed cuts in subsidies to larger farms, through 'dynamic modulation'. The changes posed such a threat to East Germany's large former collective farms that Schröder immediately opposed them. He faced an election in September, and farming was where his SPD drew much of its support. He wanted an additional £3 billion a year for agriculture, more than the EU could afford. Britain, Germany, Holland and Sweden, all net contributors, refused to pay more. The CAP was now poisoning enlargement.

Another row was brewing over public spending in France, Italy and Germany, which was out of control. The row intensified when Chirac's new premier, Jean-Pierre Raffarin, put tax cuts above the Maastricht criteria, stating that they were 'not written in stone'. Portugal, whose budget deficit was set to smash through the ceiling within the year, was also causing concern. Budgetary discipline, at the core of the euro project, was disintegrating.[31] But with France, Germany and Italy facing alarming budget deficits, the Commission caved in to pressure, giving the defaulters until 2006 to balance their budgets. Smaller member states, especially Portugal, were furious when they found that French public spending plans made a mockery of the rules.[32] France's finance minister was unapologetic. His government had won the election on spending pledges. The EU would have to wait.[33] Even *Le Monde* regretted France's 'national selfishness'.[34]

Back in July, when the Danes took over the presidency from Spain, enlargement had been the top priority. If the accession talks were not concluded by October, the 2004 deadline would be missed.[35] By then, the new entrants were realising that the EU was offering them the worst of all worlds. On one hand, there were the costs of complying with the 100,000-plus-page *accquis*, and the requirement to open frontiers to goods from the rest of the EU.[36] On the other hand, the deal shaping up would exclude their citizens from the Western jobs market for seven years, while

---

[29] 'Presidency Conclusions', Seville European Council, 21–22 June 2002.
[30] European Commission Press Release, 12 July 2002, 'Winning back the trust of consumers, Fischler says on the mid-term review'.
[31] *Daily Telegraph*, 20 June 2002.
[32] *Financial Times*, 26 September 2002.
[33] *Independent*, 9 October 2002.
[34] 8 October 2002.
[35] AFX Europe, 27 June 2002.
[36] 'By the end of 2002, the body of binding secondary legislation adopted by the European institutions amounted to 97,000 pages of the Official Journal' (Commission press release, 11 February 2003). This refers only to regulations ('secondary legislation'). Adding in tens of thousands of pages of directives, the total quantity of laws to be complied with would by now have been very much greater.

their farmers would only get a quarter of the subsidies enjoyed by their established counterparts. To add insult to injury, they would become net contributors to the EU budget.[37] Amid angry protests, France also rejected Fischler's plans for CAP reform, sticking to the Berlin agreement that blocked any significant changes until 2006. This was echoed by Stoiber, due to be the right-wing standard-bearer in Germany's forthcoming elections. Enlargement looked to be in serious disarray.[38]

Adding to the misery, in August 2002, torrential rain swamped the Rhine and Danube basins, submerging towns and cities in Austria, Germany, Hungary, the Czech Republic and Slovakia. For Schröder, however, trailing in the polls against Stoiber, it was a godsend. He toured the affected areas, meeting the heads of governments of the countries affected and co-ordinating aid, so capturing the headlines. Prodi was right behind him, offering €1 billion from the EU coffers.[39] Stoiber was wrong-footed. On holiday when the 'flood of a century' struck, his occasional clumsy appearances on waterlogged dykes lacked conviction. The chancellor also benefited from the growing international tension over Iraq, which helped divert attention from Germany's dire domestic problems. Schröder began to pull back.[40]

By now, Iraq and its 'weapons of mass destruction' were dominating the international agenda. US vice-president Dick Cheney warned that if the world waited until the Iraqis had developed a nuclear bomb, it would be too late. Prodi told Washington to obtain UN support: 'otherwise I fear that the greatest achievement of all will be destroyed, the keystone of US diplomacy after 11 September, which is the global anti-terrorist alliance'.[41] Nevertheless, 'decisive action' by the US was only a matter of time. At least for Schröder, his 'anti-war' policy contributed to his re-election, albeit on a reduced share of the vote.[42]

With Germany on one side, Italy supported the US. Prodi conceded the obvious: 'there are no elements for a common European Union position'.[43] On 9 October, though – 13 years after the Berlin Wall came down – a note of optimism was allowed when EU foreign ministers agreed to a 'big bang' enlargement, admitting ten applicants to the Union. Final details on financing had still to be agreed, but Prodi ecstatically proclaimed, 'we have

[37] Daily Telegraph, 2 July 2002.
[38] Daily Telegraph, 11 July 2002; Financial Times, 15 July 2002.
[39] Financial Times, 17 August 2002.
[40] Independent, 17 August 2002.
[41] Independent, 11 September 2002.
[42] Independent, 23 September 2002.
[43] Corriere della Sera, 24 September 2002.

rediscovered a historic unity between all our peoples. Our common destiny is to build our future together'.[44]

What won more headlines was his intervention on 17 October, when he branded the Stability and Growth Pact 'stupid'. His point, however, was that the Commission lacked the power to enforce the rules. He was supported by Schröder, Chirac and Gordon Brown. A month later he was proposing a revised pact, to give the Commission more powers.[45] This came just as Ireland was preparing for its second referendum on the Nice Treaty. Pouring vast sums of money into the campaign, the Irish government and its Brussels allies pulled out all the stops. The law requiring equal airtime for both sides had been scrapped. The question had been rigged, so that the Irish could not reject the treaty unless they also voted for Ireland to abandon its traditional neutrality by supporting the EU army. On 19 October, the Irish voted 'Yes' to Nice, by 63 to 37 per cent, on a turnout of 48 per cent.[46]

The crucial link between enlargement and CAP spending was finally reaching crisis point. At an extraordinary Council in Brussels on 24 October, Germany was adamant that CAP costs must drop after the end of the 2006 budget period. Chirac, predictably, refused to agree, demanding instead a cut in Britain's rebate.[47] Blair countered with ideas for reform that Chirac opposed. Impasse loomed until, to Blair's fury, Chirac and Schröder secretly agreed to freeze farm spending for six years.[48] Tempers flared and Chirac cancelled a planned Franco-British summit, telling Blair, 'You have been very rude and I have never been spoken to like this before.'[49]

Then there was the enlargement problem to resolve. The EU had imposed ever tougher conditions on its prospective members. Their citizens could not move to find new jobs in the west for seven years. CAP subsidies would start at only 25 per cent, to be phased in over the same period; by which time hundreds of thousands of eastern European farmers, unable to compete with their much more highly subsidised western counterparts, might have been driven off the land. The only consolation prize on offer was a €1.3 billion (£830m) lump sum payment, to tide the new entrants over their first year of accession.

A day before the Copenhagen Council, Poland's prime minister, Leszek Miller, pressed for an extra €2 billion. But all he and his colleagues got was

[44] Independent, 10 October 2002.
[45] Financial Times, 17 October 2002; Daily Mail, 8 November 2002; Independent, 28 November 2002.
[46] Financial Times; Sunday Telegraph, 20 October 2002.
[47] Financial Times, 24 October 2002.
[48] Daily Telegraph, 26 October 2002.
[49] The Times, 29 October, 2002.

permission to transfer the €1 billion already promised from the regional aid fund direct to government coffers. There would be no extra money.[50] With that, ten more countries were on their way into the EU, with 1 May 2004 set as 'the day of accession'.[51]

SADDAM THE 'DISINTEGRATOR'

The year 2003 did not start well for the 'Union'. Early in January, as Schröder and Chirac met for dinner in Paris to mark the fortieth anniversary of the Élysée Treaty, they did not have much to celebrate. Business conditions in the eurozone were deteriorating, and Germany faced censure for breaching the deficit criteria. Faced by public spending cuts, 2.8 million public sector workers threatened to strike. Schröder's domestic polls were plummeting.[52]

By the end of January, it was evident that the US invasion of Iraq, with full British support, was imminent, strongly opposed by most EU members. Chirac was particularly resentful, since no country had done more than France to breach UN sanctions, not least in becoming Iraq's leading supplier of illicit arms. But Solana spoke for the rest in declaring that the UN Security Council would need proof of weapons of mass destruction before authorising a war. Dominique de Villepin called on other European governments to oppose American plans.[53] When Bush declared that UN weapons inspections, demanded by the French, would not work, the Germans and Putin's Russia lined up with Chirac to refuse backing for a UN resolution.[54]

US Secretary of State Donald Rumsfeld had previously dismissed the Franco-German alliance as 'old Europe' and Bush had already indicated that the US would go to war, even without UN authorisation.[55] Rumsfeld's comments seemed to signal that 'Europe' was no longer seen as a homogeneous entity, but as separate blocs. If Nasser had been the great 'federator', another Middle East leader, Saddam, now promised to be its 'disintegrator'. Blair did his best to bring the EU together, but when Chirac invited Zimbabwe leader Robert Mugabe to a summit in Paris, in breach of the EU's own travel ban and ignoring Blair's objections, relations hit an all-time low.[56]

---

[50] *Financial Times*, 10 and 13 December 2002.
[51] 'Presidency Conclusions', Copenhagen European Council, 12–13 December 2002.
[52] *Independent*, 9 January 2003.
[53] *Independent*, 22 January 2003.
[54] *Guardian*, 5 March 2003.
[55] *Daily Telegraph*, 24 January 2003.
[56] *Guardian; Financial Times*, 5 February 2003.

As headlines were increasingly dominated by the impending war, mass anti-war demonstrations took place across Europe. EU leaders met at a special Council in Brussels on 17 February, where they all agreed that UN weapons inspectors should be given more time to find and destroy Iraq's weapons of mass destruction. War against Saddam should be a 'last resort'.[57] But this fragile unity was quickly shattered when Chirac condemned the candidate countries for supporting America. Within hours, Blair had exploited this outburst by writing to the objects of Chirac's ire in a bid to present himself as their closest ally in Europe.[58]

In a brief break from the tension, EU leaders took heart from the first of the planned referendums on entry in the ten applicant countries. It was worked out that the £4 million spent by the EU on a massive propaganda blitz in the tiny island of Malta, with its population of only 370,000, equated to more money per voter than the combined total spent by political parties in every election campaign in British history. Such lavish investment was rewarded: a 53.5 per cent 'Yes' vote, which was subsequently confirmed in a general election.[59]

Blair's main attention was now concentrated on whether the UN would authorise the 'coalition of the willing' to invade Iraq. By 14 March, with France set to use its veto on the Security Council, the US had withdrawn its UN motion and Blair, defying 'old Europe', threw in his lot with Bush. On 17 March, Bush issued an ultimatum to Saddam. On 20 March the invasion began. Three weeks later, on 9 April, US Marines were helping jubilant Iraqis tear down a statue of Saddam Hussein in the centre of Baghdad. The *Daily Mail* summed up the event with one word: 'Toppled'.

Given these events, the atmosphere at the spring European Council was frigid. Blair and Chirac studiously avoided each other. But Blair had not abandoned his strategy of 'constructive engagement'. After post-war talks with Bush, he made a special point of briefing European colleagues on the outcome, offering honeyed words about the UN having a central role in the reconstruction of Iraq.[60] Solana had meanwhile told *Die Welt* that the lesson of the war was that the EU should in future have only one representative on the UN Security Council: 'imagine what influence Europe could have had if it had spoken with only one voice,' he said.[61]

---

[57] *Washington Post*, 17 February 2003.
[58] *Financial Times*, 19 February 2003.
[59] *Financial Times*, 10 March; *Sunday Telegraph*, 16 March 2003.
[60] *Financial Times*, 1 April 2003.
[61] *Sunday Telegraph*, 30 March 2003.

On 16 April 2003 everything stopped for a grand ceremony at the Parthenon in Athens, when leaders of 'old' and 'new' Europe joined to sign the accession treaties for the new members. The 2,500-page document, with multiple cross-references to the *acquis*, was unreadable. Not for the first time, leaders of Europe's ancient nations were signing something they had not read. Subject to ratification, however, the Europe of 15 was now 25.

In May 2003, there was an awful sense of *dèja vu* as yet another fraud scandal broke cover. Olaf and French prosecutors were investigating 'a vast enterprise of looting' of EU funds after £640,000 had gone missing from the accounts of Eurostat, the EU's statistical agency. No one had been suspended and the Commission was still considering whether to take disciplinary action.[62] After a month of frenzied inactivity, the Commission would be forced to concede that the allegations were 'far more significant' than had been admitted. Schreyer, the budget control and anti-fraud commissioner, admitted her department had received a report in February 2000 warning of possible fraud.[63] In an uncertain world, there was comfort in the knowledge that some things never changed.

As one crisis started, another drew to its close – the row over Jean-Claude Trichet's claim to become president of the ECB. In January he had gone on trial, charged with having covered up a scandal at the formerly state-owned Credit Lyonnais bank, involving losses of $20 billion.[64] Few believed he was entirely innocent. Five months later, however, he was acquitted of all charges. The European Council confirmed that Duisenberg would step down, to allow Trichet to take over.[65]

By then Blair had been to Kuwait and thence to Warsaw for a speech celebrating the accession of Poland to the EU.[66] From there, it was to St Petersburg to meet world leaders for the city's 300th birthday, followed by a flying visit to Evian for a G8 Summit. There, Bush, who had also come via Poland and Russia, reminded Chirac that all was not forgotten, let alone forgiven. In a deliberate snub, he left early to attend to business in the Middle East. Back at the Convention, last-minute negotiations were going on before submitting the constitution to the European Council at Thessalonika on 20 June. But they were largely for show. Giscard alone would decide whether consensus had been reached.

---

[62] *Independent; Irish Times*, 17 May 2003.
[63] *Financial Times*, 17 June 2003.
[64] Bloomberg, 6 January 2003.
[65] *EurActiv*, 23 June 2003.
[66] Full text: *Guardian*, 30 May 2003.

The following week, enough Poles gritted their teeth to edge the turnout just over the 50 per cent needed to validate their referendum, bringing an 82 per cent victory for the 'Yes' camp. Millions of despondent or bewildered Poles simply stayed at home. For the Commission, it was 'a turning point in European history', adding to Lithuania, Hungary, Slovenia and Slovakia, all of which had now voted 'Yes'.[67] The Czech Republic was to follow. Within weeks, its government would be launching an austerity package aimed at cutting the deficit, preparatory to joining the euro. *Lidove Noviny* ran a headline, 'Welcome to the EU and back to reality'.[68]

For Britain, there was an earlier deadline – 9 June 2003. That was when the two years expired on the promise to Parliament on an assessment of Brown's 'five tests' for the euro. In January, Blair had already ruled out calling a referendum in 2003 on the basis that public hostility was so deep that he could not win it.[69] Now, it was decision day of a different sort. After years of work by the Treasury, producing 18 studies totalling some 1.5 million words filling over 2,000 pages, Brown's answer – to little surprise – was 'maybe'. The chancellor offered another review in the autumn, leaving open the remote chance of a referendum in 2004, but he made it clear there was no change in policy.[70] For the time being, Blair's euro-ambitions were dead.

By then, the action had moved to Luxembourg, where Fischler had offered yet another CAP 'reform' package, seeking to shift yet more funds from direct support to 'rural development' to reduce the overall cost. He was fighting for the Community's survival, for otherwise the EU would be bankrupt. There was also the 'Doha Round' of the GATT talks, where a deal on cutting export subsidies was desperately needed to reduce dumping surpluses on world markets.[71]

Yet again, France and Germany struck a deal: to the *Financial Times*, 'a contemptible deal'. Germany would help France emasculate Fischler's plan, to protect French farmers, in return for French support in opposing the Commission's plans for a takeover directive that would undermine the powers of the *Länder*. With awesome symmetry, the Franco-German alliance had gone back to its roots. Faced with outrage from other member states, Chirac calmly threatened to invoke the Luxembourg Compromise. Nor did it end there. The expected deficit on the Community budget still had to be met, and an obvious source was the British rebate. To its horror, the Foreign

---

[67] *Daily Telegraph*, 9 June 2003.
[68] *Boston Globe*, 22 June 2003.
[69] *Independent*, 20 January 2003.
[70] *Daily Telegraph*, 19 June 2003.
[71] *Financial Times*, 13 June 2003.

Office had discovered in the 'escalator clause' a backdoor mechanism whereby Britain could be robbed of her most coveted concession.[72] From de Gaulle to Chirac, history had gone full circle.

Elsewhere, asymmetry was manifest. Unlike the French back in the 1960s, the Poles were not to get a cushion for their peasantry. They were to be exposed to highly subsidised EU produce, transported down the Trans-European Network to Warsaw at a speed and cost with which many local farmers could not hope to compete. The only result could be an accelerated drift to the cities. Yet the EU had also forced the 'rationalisation' of Poland's core industries, such as steel, intensifying already serious unemployment and wiping out any potential jobs for the dispossessed farmers. Emigration would be the only option, something foreseen by the existing member states, most of which had refused to allow rights of establishment for seven years. Not so Britain. Following Ireland's lead, she would welcome eastern Europeans from day one of their accession. The Home Office believed that only 5,000 to 13,000 would come, but Migration Watch UK, a specialist think-tank, warned that the UK could be facing 2.1 million immigrants by the year 2021.[73]

A NEW ROAD TO ROME

The closing of the Convention marked only the end of Act One in what was to be a three-act drama. Act Two, just beginning, would centre on the 'Constitutional Treaty', to be negotiated by the member state governments. This would come to a climax with their agreement in June 2004 and its formal signing in October 2004.

Act Three would then centre on the process whereby the treaty was ratified. Only here would a new and quite different player be called onto the stage, those anonymous millions described by the treaty as 'the citizens of Europe'. This would be the moment of which Altiero Spinelli had dreamed six decades before, when the peoples of Europe would finally see what had been done in their name, to hail it with acclamation. In reality, the outcome was to be rather different.

With Italy taking over the six-monthly presidency at the start of July, the baton now passed to Berlusconi, who immediately upset German MEP Martin Schulz by comparing him with a concentration camp guard, after his criticism of Italian immigration policy.[74] It was then left to the Italian prime minister to host the start of Act Two. Giscard's complete text was

---

[72] *Daily Telegraph*, 17 June 2003.
[73] *Sunday Times*, 20 July 2003.
[74] BBC News, 2 July 2003, 'Berlusconi in EU "Nazi" slur'.

only handed over at a European Council in Rome on 18 July (after several weeks of frenzied work hastily cobbling together Part III). The plan was that, after a three-month pause, a brief IGC beginning in October should spend a few weeks reaching all-but-final agreement on Giscard's proposals. In December the heads of government would then assemble in Brussels to agree the definitive text, before proceeding to the Italian capital to sign it, thus making it a new 'Treaty of Rome'.

While the 25 governments withdrew to consider their formal responses to Giscard's draft, two of Europe's *eminenti* were quick to criticise it from polarically opposing viewpoints. To Prodi, keeping national vetoes on foreign policy, defence and taxation 'destroyed the harmony between the "big" and "little" states'. It marked a lurch back to 'the intergovernmental method'.[75] To President Václav Klaus of the Czech Republic, now emerging as the most outspoken Eurosceptic from the prospective member states, the draft represented 'a visible move in only one direction ... from intergovernmentalism to supranationalism' and this 'should be explained to the people of Europe'.[76]

The Commission was again under the shadow of a fraud scandal. In June the economic affairs commissioner Pedro Solbes had admitted that 'financial irregularities' in the running of Eurostat were worse than feared. The head of Eurostat and his deputy were relieved of their posts, and it was claimed that three other Commissioners, including Kinnock, as administration commissioner tasked with eliminating fraud, had known 'more than they have so far admitted'.[77] In July, Kinnock and Solbes admitted that the offices of Eurostat had been raided and its files secured. Proceedings would be taken against three Commission officials. Various Eurostat managers had been moved to 'advisory functions'. A 20-strong inquiry team had been set up to investigate further.

A rather more far-reaching financial issue was about to re-emerge when, on 14 July, eurozone finance ministers met in Brussels under growing political pressure to review the Stability and Growth Pact. With France in serious breach of the rules, Chirac was pushing for them to be relaxed to allow increased government spending in face of anaemic growth. Germany, wracked by strikes in favour of a cut in the working week from 38 hours to 35, supported France. Other smaller countries were appalled to see the governments in charge of the eurozone's two largest economies showing

---

[75] Prodi, Romano, speech on Europe and the Constitution: 'Letting the People Have Their Say', Bologna, 5 July 2003.
[76] AFP, 4 July 2003.
[77] *Scotsman*, 18 June 2003.

such contempt for rules that Germany had insisted on. Particularly angry was Portugal, whose prime minister José Manuel Barroso had imposed a series of highly unpopular measures, including a rise in the sales tax, specifically to ensure that his economy kept within the limit of 3 per cent of GDP.

Meanwhile news was emerging of a report by 'a team of top economists appointed by the Commission' calling for 'a massive and urgent change' in economic policy to head off long-term decline in Europe.[78] Headed by a Belgian economist, André Sapir, the group had written to Prodi, warning him that the EU had seen 'a steady decline of the average growth rate decade after decade' compared with the United States. It was now stagnating with a *per capita* GDP at 70 per cent of US levels. At fault was the EU's reliance on an outdated model that discouraged innovation and had failed to adapt. The growing crisis had reached the point where it threatened 'the very process of European integration', and could ultimately lead to the breakdown of the social contract underpinning Europe's welfare societies.

It was against this background that, through the late summer of 2003, the 25 governments meditated on their response to Giscard's draft. In Holland, polls showed 80 per cent support for a referendum. Reflecting his country's growing disenchantment with the EU, the president of the Dutch central bank, Nout Wellink, was among the most forthright in calling for the Stability and Growth Pact to be properly enforced. 'Penalties are part of the system we've all signed up to,' he said.[79]

In September, as a further portent of Europe's shifting mood, came Sweden's referendum on the euro. On the eve of the vote, the country was stunned when the pro-euro foreign minister Anna Lindh was murdered by a lone assassin. Although active campaigning stopped, this did not affect the outcome. On an abnormally high turnout of 81 per cent, the Swedes rejected the euro by 56 per cent to 42 per cent.

As if on cue, the eurozone's economic performance came under unprecedented attack from the IMF. Kenneth Rogoff, the Fund's chief economist, pointed to revised forecasts cutting the eurozone's growth in 2003 from 1.1 per cent to just 0.5, with Germany showing no growth. He contrasted this with the US, where the economy was enjoying 'the best recovery money can buy'. Europeans wanting to see an economic recovery, Rogoff said, 'will have to watch it on TV'.[80] Britain's Gordon Brown then pitched in, accusing EU leaders of planning a 'federal state' with harmonised

---

[78] *Daily Telegraph*, 16 July 2003.
[79] AFP, 10 September 2003.
[80] *The Times*, 19 September 2003.

taxes that would be a recipe for economic failure. 'The credibility of Europe is at stake', he wrote in an article for the *Wall Street Journal Europe*, insisting that, if the EU economy was not to fall further behind that of the United States, economic reform was an 'urgent necessity'.

The joint response from Chirac and Schröder was a massive public works programme. A ten-point list of headline projects ranged from high-speed railway tracks and the EU's ambitious Galileo satellite navigation programme to the provision of digital television and broadband internet links. But this would not count against their government deficits. Spending would be financed by huge loans from the European Investment Bank and other EU agencies.

On 25 September, following a damning report over the Eurostat scandal, Prodi appeared before the Parliament to answer calls for the resignation of three of his Commissioners: Kinnock, Solbes and Schreyer. He refused to accept them.[81] At least there was good news for the 'project' from Latvia, the last entrant country to vote on joining. Another overwhelming 'Yes' vote of 68.5 per cent meant that all ten were now safely in the bag.[82]

THE ROAD TO ROME GETS ROCKIER

On 4 October, the heads of state and government gathered in Rome, at Mussolini's grandiose Palazzo dei Congressi, to launch the IGC. The plan was to hold two more 'summits' in mid-October and December before the constitution was agreed, with a 'conclave' of foreign ministers in late November. Meanwhile, eight groups of diplomats and ministers would be at work behind closed doors in Brussels, thrashing out unresolved issues.

One head of state who refused to attend was the Czech president Klaus, who criticised Giscard's draft as the blueprint for a European superstate, run by 'a remote federal government in Brussels'. 'This is crossing the Rubicon,' he warned, 'after which there will be no more sovereign states in Europe with fully fledged governments and parliaments which represent legitimate interests of their citizens.'

The most obviously intractable issue was the strong objection of Spain and Poland to Giscard's 'double majority' proposal for QMV, which reduced the effect of the generous voting weights they had won with such difficulty at Nice. Opposing them was Germany, demanding that her own voting power should be increased to reflect her pre-eminent population size. But, as was to become clear over the coming weeks, most countries had

[81] *The Times*, 26 September 2003.
[82] *Daily Telegraph*, 5 October 2003.

strong objections to one or another of Giscard's proposals. Those planning referendums before ratifying the final text had already grown to five, with others likely to follow.

Blair, preparing for a battle over his 'red line' issues such as the erosion of the veto on taxation, social security and foreign policy, was looking for concessions as a trade-off. The most significant of these, which only came to light through a document leaked to *Der Spiegel* on the eve of the 'summit', was his offer of support to a Franco-German plan for autonomous defence operations outside the NATO command structure, commissioning a new operational headquarters with a staff of 40 or 50 officers. The train of events started at St Malo in 1998 was now taking on tangible form.[83]

For weeks, negotiations proceeded in the granite fortress of the Justus Lipsius building in Brussels, headquarters of the Council of Ministers. As the end of November approached, with foreign ministers scheduled to meet in Naples to discuss an Italian revised draft, it was clear that divisions on many key proposals were threatening impasse.

The Spaniards and Poles were still adamant in defending their voting rights, backed by Britain in return for their support on tax. Britain and Ireland were among several countries hostile to the idea of harmonising their criminal law procedures with the general continental model. Britain was belatedly trying to weaken the proposed common energy policy, for fear of losing control of her North Sea oil and gas reserves and her ability to make bilateral deals with third countries such as Norway to secure her future energy supplies. Britain's Treasury was allied with a bevy of finance ministers in wanting to limit the European Parliament's planned powers over the EU budget. Britain was again allied with other countries in strongly opposing Giscard's proposal for an 'EU foreign minister'. With only days to go before Naples, the Foreign Office judiciously let it be known that the new treaty was 'highly desirable but not absolutely essential'.[84]

Just at this moment, another contentious issue exploded into the headlines when, after a ten-hour session in Brussels lasting until dawn, France and Germany bludgeoned their fellow eurozone finance ministers into ditching the budget deficit rules. Despite the Commission's insistence that the two big countries must be penalised, the meeting finally conceded that they should be allowed to continue breaking the rules, under a formula that rendered them all but meaningless.

[83] *Daily Telegraph*, 22 September 2003.
[84] *Financial Times*, 24 November 2003.

THE GREAT DECEPTION

This example of Franco-German bullying left a sense of bitterness and betrayal in all directions. Theo Waigel, the former German finance minister who drew up the pact, declared, 'I wasn't disappointed, I was outraged – that Germany, which was responsible with other countries for getting the pact through, should disregard it in this way.'[85] After a separate session in Brussels the same day, when one of Poland's leading 'pro-Europeans' complained about 'double standards', the German commissioner Günther Verheugen, who had been responsible for negotiating enlargement, lashed out, 'if this is the way Poland begins its membership in the EU, I regret my efforts for Poland'.

The previous day, at a full meeting of all the EU finance ministers, Gordon Brown had attacked Commission proposals for harmonisation of company taxation, angrily insisting that this would be devastating for Europe's competitiveness. Backed by Ireland, France and the Netherlands, he told the Commission it would do much better to put the need to reduce harmful regulation at the top of its agenda.[86]

As furious recriminations continued over the breakdown of budgetary discipline, the EU's foreign ministers were preparing to head for their Naples 'conclave' when the Italians stunned their fellow governments by producing their revised version of Giscard's text. It contained many more changes than expected, not least an amendment allowing the new 'EU foreign minister' to decide foreign policy by majority voting. This would make it all but impossible for member states to conduct independent foreign policy initiatives. A British government spokesman witheringly commented: 'we are surprised to see this proposal, which is totally unacceptable to us in any shape or form'. It was simply 'loony'.[87]

Britain was also unhappy with other amendments, challenging Blair's 'red lines' on tax, social security and the budget rebate. Matters were further complicated when the foreign ministers arrived in Naples.

The Dutch Europe minister Atzo Nicolaï argued that it was illogical that they should be debating new rules when two leading member states, France and Germany, had just trampled over the EU's deficit criteria. 'We can't just go on with business as usual', he said. 'The impression has been given that there is one law for the big countries and another for the rest.' The Commission, humiliated by the rejection of its attempts to sanction France and Germany, claimed this only showed it must be given stronger powers.

[85] *Scotsman*, 28 November 2003.
[86] *The Times*, 25 November 2003.
[87] *The Times*, 27 November 2003.

416

The sole supporter of the Franco-German coup was Straw, tartly observing: 'if you have a set of rules which conflict with reality, reality usually wins'.[88]

The two-day meeting brought a long succession of objections to the amended text from almost every minister present, not least over the Italians' inclusion in the preamble of a reference to Europe's 'Christian heritage'. The Catholic countries led by Poland and Spain were strongly in favour, more secular countries led by France equally strongly against. For once, Britain remained out of it. But as the 'conclave' broke up, prospects for final agreement in Brussels two weeks later looked slim. Several ministers, including Straw, were now asking whether the constitution was actually necessary, claiming that 'life will go on' under the existing treaties.[89]

DEBACLE IN BRUSSELS

For two weeks, the chancelleries of Europe were abuzz as ministers and officials worked on their final positions for the two-day Brussels meeting starting on 11 December. Among the issues in contention were voting rights, the retention of Commissioners, the 'mutual defence' clause and the Stability and Growth Pact.[90] As evidence piled up to suggest that agreement would be impossible, a Eurobarometer poll showed that, for the first time ever, popular support for the EU across Europe had dropped below 50 per cent. In Britain it was only 28 per cent. Prodi blamed the decline on squabbling between national governments and the EU's institutions.[91]

By day two of the meeting, Berlusconi had given up any hope of a settlement. There had been only one and a half hours of formal negotiations. He allowed the gathering to spend several more hours discussing routine business, including an hour-long speech from himself on economic reform, before announcing that the IGC was adjourned. It was the first time in history that an IGC had failed to reach its conclusion by the appointed date. While Europe's journalists were busy setting up banner headlines such as 'EU Summit Talks Collapse', few heeded the two-minute discussion that immediately followed, when the heads of government formally nodded through approval for the siting of 11 new EU agencies.

The first tranche comprised 'regulatory agencies'. These included the European Aviation Safety Agency, with huge powers over Europe's aviation industry. It was to be sited in Cologne. National agencies, such as Britain's Civil Aviation Authority, would now act as its local branch

---

[88] *The Times*, 29 November 2003.
[89] *Daily Telegraph*, 29 November 2003.
[90] *Independent*, 12 December 2003.
[91] *Guardian*, 10 December 2003.

offices. The European Maritime Safety Agency, with similar powers over the shipping industry, was to be in Lisbon. The European Railways Agency would be in Valenciennes, headquarters of France's giant rail engineering company Alstom. The European Food Safety Agency would be in Parma, headquarters of Italy's giant food empire Parmalat. Finland was to get the European Chemicals Agency, responsible for directing enforcement of the immensely costly and cumbersome 'REACH' system. And the headquarters of the European Fisheries Control Agency, set up to direct enforcement of the CFP, was to be in Vigo, Spain, termed by one journalist as 'the world capital of illegal fishing'.[92]

On the non-regulatory agencies, one was the new European Human Rights Agency (formerly the European Monitoring Centre on Racism and Xenophobia), headquartered in Vienna. Britain was to get the European Police College, at Bramshill, Hampshire, to train senior policemen from across the EU in a common approach to police procedures. Eurojust, in Holland, would lead the EU-wide harmonisation of judicial procedures. Greece would get the European Network and Information Security Agency, to co-ordinate EU policy on data protection and information technology. Sweden would have the European Centre for Disease Prevention and Control, duplicating work carried out by the World Health Organization.

The creation of these agencies in its own way represented as much of an extension of supranational power as the proposed constitution, yet was barely reported. As for the constitution itself, responsibility for taking it forward now passed to the Irish presidency, due to start work on 1 January 2004. Premier Bertie Ahern announced he would wait until March before reconvening the IGC. 'This is a huge project,' he said, 'a fundamental change for the whole of Europe. It's not unusual on such a big project that people have to reflect on it.'[93]

THE LUCK OF THE IRISH

As the 'ring of stars' flag was raised over Dublin Castle in January 2004, prospects for the IGC seemed bleak. Ahern bravely insisted he was 'confident that we will have a constitution', but could not predict when that might be.[94] After admitting to 'a couple of weeks of personal depression' after Brussels, Prodi defiantly claimed that he was now ready to begin 'fighting to salvage

[92] Clover, Charles (2004), *The End of the Line: How Over-fishing is Changing the World* (London: Ebury Press).
[93] *Sunday Times*, 14 December 2003.
[94] AFP, 1 January 2004.

and restart the work of the European Convention'.[95] He suggested that the priority should now be simply to return to the Convention's text and approve it.[96]

For several weeks Ahern busied himself with seeing everyone who mattered: Prodi, Chirac, Verhofstadt, above all the leaders locked in dispute over their voting rights, Schröder, Aznar and Poland's Miller.[97] As for Blair, who had been insisting that Britain's position was now accepted by everyone, he was reminded by Ireland's Europe minister, Dick Roche, that: 'in negotiations nothing is agreed until everything is agreed'.[98] To strengthen his position, Blair pledged that he would get Britain into the single currency by 2007. He had also asked to join Chirac and Schröder in Berlin on 18 February for the first of what he hoped would be regular meetings of the EU's 'big three'.[99]

The mood was momentarily lightened when a leading member of Spain's Socialist opposition, José Bono, irritated by Blair's friendship with Aznar, broke through the miasma of diplomatic niceties to express his true opinion of the British prime minister. He was inadvertently recorded in a television studio calling Blair 'a complete dickhead (un gilipollas integral) … an imbecile'.[100]

January also brought two rather more serious developments. First, the Commission's lawyers decided that the eurozone finance ministers had acted illegally in suspending the deficit rules the previous October. Pedro Solbes, the Commissioner for economic and monetary affairs, now intended to go to the ECJ. Then Javier Solana, the EU's foreign policy spokesman, announced that Nick Witney, a senior British Ministry of Defence official, was to set up a European Defence Agency, its purpose to co-ordinate defence planning and procurement.

In February, while positions on the constitution still seemed deadlocked, the focus shifted to the Franco-German-British 'summit' in Berlin. Spokesmen for the three claimed that the talks were aimed at transforming the European economy. It was a 'brainstorming' session to exchange ideas and draw up joint proposals for the next European Council in March.[101] The meeting nevertheless draw a barrage of criticism from the countries left out. Frattini returned to the charge by insisting, 'We want a Europe which

---

[95] Reuters, 15 January 2004.
[96] AFP, 2 January 2004.
[97] Deutsche Welle, 3 January 2004; AFP, 10 January 2004.
[98] 10 January 2004, 'Blair barges in on EU's Gang of Two'.
[99] AFP, 23 January 2004.
[100] Daily Telegraph, 16 January 2004.
[101] AFP, 18 February 2004.

grows with the agreement of all, not with triumvirates which damage the construction of Europe.'[102]

While Straw attempted to defend the 'trilateral summit' by arguing that 'if the three of us agree, Europe is likely to be more united', a French diplomat then rather spoiled it by claiming that the triumvirate was 'very powerful' and 'could perhaps even make Washington think twice, which is a very attractive idea for all three leaders'. Berlusconi declared the summit 'a botch', asserting that this was an opinion shared by 'almost all' member states.[103]

Nevertheless, in the first days of March, the general air of drift continued. Ahern was now telling everyone that work on the constitution was unlikely to resume after the European Council due later in the month.[104] Blair meanwhile was in Rome, still trying to reassure Berlusconi that the 'tripartite meeting' had no sinister undertones.[105] At this point, the presidents of Italy and Germany chose to intervene. Carlo Ciampi and Johannes Rau issued a statement saying: 'time is running out. The constitution cannot fail. National interests cannot oppose common interests for a European future in peace and justice.'[106] Meanwhile, the Vatican was being lobbied to confirm the claims to beatification of Robert Schuman, the 'Father of Europe', as a candidate for full sainthood.[107]

With only two weeks to go before Ahern was due to advise the European Council on whether there was any point to restarting the IGC, Germany offered a modest concession on voting rights, but to no avail. Spain rejected the idea out of hand.[108] On 10 March, a gloomy Ahern launched consultations to salvage a deal, proposing to meet the Danish prime minister and Blair in Dublin before going on to meet Poland's prime minister Miller. Ahern himself was leaning towards support for Germany and France in backing Giscard's original 'double majority' formula.[109] Then, out of the blue, came the shocking event that was to transform the story.

In the morning rush hour on 11 March, a series of bombs ripped through crowded commuter trains in Madrid. Nearly two hundred people were killed, over one thousand four hundred injured. Despite suspicions of Basque terrorist involvement, evidence soon pointed to an al-Q'aeda

[102] AFP, 17 February 2004.
[103] AFP, 18 February 2004.
[104] AFP, 3 March 2004.
[105] AFP, 4 March 2004.
[106] AFP, 5 March 2004.
[107] IHT/Irish Independent, 6 March 2004.
[108] Financial Times, 10 March 2004.
[109] AFP, 12 March 2004.

cell taking vengeance for Aznar's support for the Iraqi invasion. In a fevered eve-of-poll atmosphere, accusations of inefficiency, cover-up and even conspiracy abounded. Three days later, on 14 March, an angry and confused electorate took its own revenge on Aznar. Blair's closest EU ally, was unexpectedly deposed.

His replacement was José Luis Rodríguez Zapatero, one of whose closest Socialist colleagues was the man who weeks before had called Blair 'un gilipollas'. Spain's new prime minister immediately announced a dramatic switch of national policy. Not only would he pull Spanish troops out of Iraq; he also wanted an 'accelerated' adoption of the constitution. 'I believe we will rapidly reach an agreement,' he told *Cadena Ser* radio.[110] Half of the greatest single obstacle to that agreement, on which the Brussels IGC had foundered, had been removed. Poland was now on her own.

The EU's immediate response to the Madrid bombing was 'emergency terror talks' between the EU's 'justice and home affairs' ministers, designed to give 'new momentum to Europe's combined anti-terror measures'. These included stepping up cross-border co-operation on security and intelligence.[111] With Prodi calling for 'joint action' that went further than anything agreed after 9/11, the integrationists had been quick to recognise yet another 'beneficial crisis'.[112]

But the real impact of the events in Spain was the transformation they had wrought on prospects for the constitution. 'Now Poland has been abandoned by Spain,' wrote a leading Warsaw analyst, 'the Polish government is looking for a face-saving option.'[113] Within days it was being reported that Miller and Schröder were discussing a compromise on voting rights, then that Ahern was planning to restart the IGC and looking forward to final agreement on 17–18 June.[114]

For the 'big three', as the European Council approached, all was not going well at home. In local elections in Hamburg, Schröder's Social Democrats had just suffered a humiliating defeat by the CDU. Chirac's party then suffered a similar reverse in France's regional elections, leading to calls for him to replace his prime minister, Jean-Pierre Raffarin, with the more popular Nicolas Sarkozy, then interior minister. For both leaders it was to mark the start of a long electoral decline. Meanwhile in Britain, reports that Blair was offering to abandon yet another of his 'red lines', removing the

[110] AFP, 15 March 2004.
[111] *Scotsman*, 15 March 2004.
[112] AFP, 15 March 2004.
[113] Alexsandr Smolar, quoted in the *Guardian*, 17 March 2004.
[114] *Financial Times*, 23 March 2004.

veto from key areas of judicial co-operation, prompted a wave of scornful press comment, led by banner headlines in the *Sun* such as 'PM will sell out laws to EU' and '12 weeks to stop Euro Superstate'.

As EU leaders gathered in Brussels on 26 March, they accepted Ahern's proposal that the IGC should soon resume, with every prospect it could be agreed in June. The only cloud on the horizon was an admission by Prodi that the Lisbon dream of catching up the US economy by 2010 had become 'a chimera'.[115] At this point, with Poland joining the lengthening list of nations considering a popular vote, the EU's leaders prepared for the moment when, on 1 May 2004, the ten newcomers would finally be received into the fold. It was an historic moment.

THE FINAL SLOG

At the stroke of midnight on 1 May 2004, fireworks exploded over Dublin, Malta and Prague, and orchestras from Brussels to Nicosia and Warsaw sawed out versions of Beethoven's 'Ode to Joy', as the European Union celebrated the biggest enlargement in its history. Its population had reached 450 million, its territories stretching across three time zones, with 20 working languages adding €800 million a year to translation costs. The next day, Poland celebrated by dumping its unpopular prime minister. It replaced him in June with Marek Belka, a former finance minister who had returned to Warsaw after a year running economic policy in Iraq for the US-led coalition.[116]

The chorus of warnings as to what would happen to countries that rejected the constitution continued. The French trade commissioner Pascal Lamy said they would find themselves in the position of Switzerland, which prompted the *Daily Telegraph* to observe that 'if the worst Eurocrats can threaten us with is being like Switzerland, the richest and most democratic state in Europe, then roll on the referendum'.[117] Lamy's warning was echoed by his fellow commissioner Patten, now being touted as a possible Commission president in succession to Prodi, due soon to retire back to Italian politics.

On 4 May, talks on the constitution resumed in Dublin. With just six weeks to go before the final summit, the presidency produced the first of what was to become a torrent of documents proposing amendments to Giscard's text. Also on the agenda was a grand tour by Ahern, planning to visit all 25 capitals of the enlarged Union in a bid to resolve the remaining

---

[115] *Daily Telegraph*, 25 March 2004.
[116] UPI, 1 June 2004. https://www.upi.com/Top_News/2004/06/01/Polands-Belka-to-be-appointed-premier/98681086084220/?ur3=1.
[117] 3 May 2004.

disagreements.[118] He cannot have been pleased to hear Spain's new foreign minister offering a formula on voting rights in which a majority of states representing 66 per cent of the population must be in favour of a measure, thus allowing states with 34 per cent of the population to block decisions. The Poles also still wanted percentages closer to those agreed at Nice. Thus, the great European vision degenerated to haggling over percentage points.

On 9 May, 'Europe Day', Blair appeared on television with Chirac in Paris, reassuring French viewers that the majority in Britain supported 'the idea of a constitutional treaty which is appropriate for Europe'.[119] Chirac himself was now under pressure to hold a referendum from senior members of his government.[120] But three days later, when Chirac and Schröder met in Paris, the only possibility they could contemplate was a failure to ratify by Britain, which might even lead to her expulsion from the EU. Otherwise, the two men were confident that treaty would go through.[121]

The EU's foreign ministers were due to meet in Brussels on 17–18 May. Even before they gathered, Ireland had come up with yet more amendments. To the relief of Downing Street, the proposal on energy policy, threatening Britain's rights to North Sea oil, had been dropped. Also diluted were articles that would have given the EU huge new powers over justice. A compromise on the size of the Commission proposed that it should be reduced to 18 members, which still meant there would be times when each country had no commissioner.[122]

By the time the foreign ministers met, several countries had come up with yet more proposals.[123] Brian Cowen, then Irish foreign minister, responded by arranging a further 'emergency meeting' to focus on 'the most sensitive institutional questions', notably voting rights. This left the Poles still not happy, but at least they conceded that chances of agreement looked better.[124] Then came another hiccup, when the Polish leader, Belka, his party facing a corruption scandal, tried to placate his parliament by upping the ante on voting rights yet again, demanding a population split of 80–20.[125] With this unexpected setback, the Irish president of the European Parliament, Pat

[118] AFP, 4 May 2004.
[119] Reuters, 9 May 2004.
[120] *Financial Times*, 9 May 2004.
[121] AFP, 13 May 2004.
[122] Reuters, 13 May 2004.
[123] http://european-convention.europa.eu/docs/Treaty/cv00850.en03.pdf.
[124] *Financial Times*, 24 May 2004.
[125] *Frankfurter Allgemeine Sonntagszeitung*, 31 May 2004.

Cox, gloomily joined Ahern in predicting that the chances for success at the IGC had now dropped back again to only 50–50.[126]

THE TREATY IS AGREED (WITH NOISES OFF)

It was curiously timely that the final run-in to the summit should coincide with the elections to the European Parliament. On one hand, Europe's political elite was preoccupied with their last-minute manoeuvrings over the constitution. On the other, the peoples of Europe were being given the collective chance to vote, if only for candidates of whom most had never heard, to sit in an institution of which they knew little.

Between Thursday 10 June and the following Sunday, 25 nations elected their MEPs, in what was the lowest turnout on record. It dropped below 50 per cent, most conspicuously in the former Communist countries, where Slovakia recorded only 16.7 per cent, with Poland not far behind on 20.4. Even western Europe plumbed new lows. One of the few countries to report an increase was Britain, up from its 1999 low of 24 per cent to 39. Undoubtedly, that reflected the success of UKIP, whose 2,660,278 votes put it into third place, giving it 12 MEPs, by far the highest vote ever achieved by a fourth party in a UK election (a record previously held by Goldsmith's Referendum Party in 1997).[127] This was the culmination of a campaign that had seen the party attract a number of celebrity supporters, including the television personality and former Labour MP, Robert Kilroy-Silk who pledged to 'wreck' the European Parliament when he took his seat.[128]

The response of the Conservative leader, now Michael Howard, far from being to harden his party's highly ambivalent 'European' policy, was to order his MPs to keep quiet about it. 'I am not interested in presiding over a debating society,' he told them at a private meeting; 'frankly nobody is interested in hearing your views.'[129] And although ruling parties throughout the EU had been damaged, there was no hint of contrition from Anne Anderson, the Irish ambassador to the EU. To her, the abstainers and people who voted for Eurosceptic parties were saying: 'Europe cannot afford a failure because of the depressing message that such a failure would send.' She was speaking on behalf of the presidency.[130]

---

[126] Reuters; AFP, 31 May 2004.
[127] BBC News, European Election: United Kingdom Result, 14 June 2004.
[128] BBC News, 14 June 2004, 'Kilroy: We'll wreck EU Parliament'. Under the impression that he had been offered the party leadership, Kilroy-Silk quickly fell out with UKIP and left to form his own party, which he called Veritas. After none of 65 candidates made an impression in the 2005 general election, he resigned his leadership on 29 July of the same year.
[129] *Daily Telegraph*, 15 June 2004.
[130] *Irish Times*, 17 June 2004.

Meanwhile, the foreign ministers had met in Brussels on 14 June, prompting more lengthy papers from the Irish, in preparation for the morning of Thursday 17 June 2004 when the heads of government met in Brussels for the fateful summit. Day one was largely uneventful until dinner in the evening, which saw a blazing row over the next Commission president, a decision that had to be taken before the end of the month. Schröder and Chirac wanted their ally Verhofstadt. Blair (echoing Major's veto of another Belgian, Dehaene) was strongly opposed, and with the backing of Berlusconi had put forward Patten as a blocking candidate.[131]

Focused on the constitution, the Irish produced yet another document, clarifying the complex voting formula. On Friday, a two-hour discussion was followed by six hours of private 'confessionals', with Ahern desperately seeking to tie up the last loose ends. Just after 5 p.m. an excited BBC correspondent announced: 'It's all over – it's done!' But it was not until just before 10 p.m. that there was a final text to agree. Then, by 10.30, it *was* over.

Blair, pale and bleary-eyed, came out to claim that the constitution was a 'success for Britain and a success for Europe'. His words were echoed by many others, including Giscard, who pronounced '*c'est un bon texte pour l'Europe, c'est un bon texte pour les Européens*'.[132] Graham Watson, now leader of the European Liberal Democrat group of MEPs, declared: 'the governments who have approved this Constitution now have a duty to go home and sell it to their people'. At that moment, amid the sound of popping champagne corks, and 27 wearisome months after Giscard's Convention first met, it must have seemed to most of those involved that this would now be little more than a formality. For the UK, however, the writing was already on the wall.

THE BATTLE FOR THE REFERENDUM – ROUND ONE

That 'writing', of course, was the prospect of a referendum, a distant dream when Giscard stood up to launch the Convention, but one that increasingly gained momentum. Going back slightly in the timeline, if there was a specific moment when the battle started, it can be placed in May 2003. It was then, after more than a year when the Convention had been almost entirely ignored by Britain's media, that its 'right-wing' press finally woke up to what was going on. First off the stocks was the *Daily Mail*, which denounced the constitution as 'a blueprint for tyranny'. Next day it blasted 'Non!' in huge capitals across its front page. The *Daily Telegraph* followed

---

[131] Wall, Stephen (2020), *Reluctant European* (Oxford University Press), pp. 249–250.
[132] *EurActiv*, 25 June 2004.

with a leader proclaiming: 'This is it: the moment that we have repeatedly been told would never come about. The EU is about to transform itself, *de jure* and *de facto*, into a single state.'[133] The cat was out of the bag.

Breaking his party's long self-imposed near-silence on 'Europe', Iain Duncan Smith, in his last days as Conservative leader, challenged Blair to hold a referendum. Hain countered that there had been no referendums on the Single European Act or Maastricht. 'Those were big constitutional treaties,' he said; 'this is more of a tidying-up exercise.'[134] The words were to haunt him. On 15 May the *Sun* yelled, 'The biggest betrayal in our history', as its political editor Trevor Kavanagh reported that Blair was 'about to sign away 1,000 years of British sovereignty'. A *Sun* poll had 60 per cent against 'surrendering more power to Brussels', 'a whopping 84 per cent' wanted a referendum, and 61 per cent thought Britain should consider leaving the EU to avoid ceding more power.[135]

In the Commons, Blair claimed referendums were held only when 'exceptional changes in the system of government' were involved. Duncan Smith was ready for him: 'Since you came to power there have been 34 referendums on issues as momentous as Hartlepool having a mayor ... But the European constitution will decide how every citizen of this country will be governed. Why won't you simply let the British people have their say?'[136] In a poll next day, 83 per cent believed that the British people should decide, rather than the British government.[137] Hain's reaction was merely to turn on the 'Eurosceptic press', accusing it of publishing 'lurid fantasy'.[138] Those campaigning for a vote 'might as well put away their placards and stop wasting their money because we are not going to do it,' he said.[139] Never one to take no for an answer, the *Daily Mail* on 16 May offered its own vote. Of the 1.7 million people who voted, 89.8 per cent wanted a referendum. In a parallel ICM poll – the 'biggest ever' – 88 per cent of respondents agreed with them. 'Now will you listen Mr Blair?' the *Mail* demanded.

Blair's response came on 30 May during his Warsaw visit. He explained his refusal by comparing Britain with Poland. 'I note,' he said, 'that though you here in Poland are having a referendum on membership of the EU, you

---

[133] 12 May 2003.

[134] *Financial Times*, 13 May 2003.

[135] A trigger for this explosion was a briefing at the Centre for Policy Studies, addressed by Heathcoat-Amory. It was attended by a gaggle of Eurosceptic peers including Conrad Black, proprietor of the *Daily Telegraph*, and senior journalists from *The Times*, the *Sun* and the *Daily Mail*, all the papers which within days were launching their anti-constitution crusade.

[136] HC Deb 14, May 2003, Vol. 405, cc304-10.

[137] *Daily Telegraph*, 15 May 2003.

[138] *Daily Telegraph*, 16 May 2003.

[139] *Daily Telegraph*, 19 May 2003.

are not having one on the Convention.' Developing this theme, he added: 'Likewise, for us, if we recommend entry to the euro it would be a step of such economic and constitutional significance that a referendum would be sensible and right.' Incredibly, after years of denial, Blair was now arguing that the euro was 'constitutionally significant'. But the constitution was not.

This did not stop the Conservatives, on 11 June, using a debate to call for the new treaty to be ratified by Parliament only after it had 'received the consent of the British people, democratically given in a referendum'. Straw countered that, since there was no fundamental change in the relationship between the EU and its member states, there was no case for a referendum.[140] Although the Tory motion was heavily defeated, from then on, the issue never really went away. Support even came from 30 Labour MPs on all wings of the party, including ex-ministers, and trade unions. Rejecting their calls, Hain himself admitted concern over the proposal for an EU 'Foreign Minister', but insisted that otherwise Britain had got 99 per cent of what she wanted.[141]

In September, Blair was questioned about a referendum in PMQs. It was raised in a full-blown debate on the constitution on 14 October, and then again when Blair returned from the European Council on 15 December.[142] In March 2004, the press renewed the clamour.[143] Then, in April, amid rumours that Blair was to call a poll in the autumn, the Conservatives again piled on the pressure.[144] Blair's initial response was scorn. All these Eurosceptic objections, he said, were just 'dumb'.[145] If a treaty was agreed by June, he told Parliament, his government would quickly introduce a Bill to ratify it. Tory objections, he said, were merely part of the party's 'secret agenda' to take Britain out of Europe.

Only two months away, however, were the elections for the European Parliament, and Blair did not want his stance on the referendum to become the focal point of the campaign. Furthermore, for the first time, the Euro-elections had been timed to coincide with local and regional elections. At stake were a quarter of England's 20,000 council seats, all those in Wales, and in London the mayoralty and the assembly. By putting all these elections together, the intention was that both public interest and turnout would be increased.

---

[140] HC Deb, 11 June 2003, Vol. 406, cc705-57.
[141] *Daily Mail*, 16 July 2003.
[142] HC Deb, 10 September 2003, Vol. 410, cc323-30; HC Deb, 14 October 2003, Vol. 411, cc12-5; HC Deb, 15 December 2003, Vol. 415, cc1319-36.
[143] 28 March 2004.
[144] BBC News, 6 April 2004, 'Tories renew EU referendum call'.
[145] *Independent*, 27 March 2004.

Tory Leader Michael Howard turned the screw by embarking on a nationwide campaign to convert June's Euro-elections into a 'referendum on a referendum'. On 8 April, Charles Kennedy, for the Liberal Democrats, joined in, arguing that any measure involving significant transfers of power away from Westminster 'must be approved by the British people'.[146] Even ministers in Blair's own Cabinet, led by Straw and Brown, urged him to drop his opposition to a referendum. He did. Despite a *Sun*/YouGov poll showing that only 16 per cent of Britons would vote 'Yes', and 53 per cent 'No', on 20 April he told Parliament:

> It is time to resolve once and for all whether this country, Britain, wants to be at the centre and heart of European decision-making or not; time to decide whether our destiny lies as a leading partner and ally of Europe or on its margins. Let the Eurosceptics whose true agenda we will expose, make their case. Let those of us who believe in Britain in Europe ... make ours. Let the issue be put. Let the battle be joined.[147]

He had not used the word 'referendum', but everyone knew what he meant. He was taking one of the greatest gambles of his career: that he could somehow turn a referendum on the constitution into a vote for staying in 'Europe'. It was what his staff called the 'nuclear option': the one vote they thought they could win.[148] It would be 12 years before they were proved wrong.

---

[146] *Daily Telegraph*, 9 April 2004.
[147] *Hansard*, 20 April 2003.
[148] BBC News, 20 April 2004, 'Campaigns gear up for poll fight'.

17

Downfall: 2004–2005

If it's a Yes we will say 'on we go', and if it's a No we will say 'we continue'.

Jean-Claude Juncker, President of the
European Council, 25 May 2005

European integration is fortunately a train moving too fast for anyone to stop it

Václav Havel, Prague Daily Monitor, 8 July 2005

Although on 18 June 2004 the EU's leaders had supposedly agreed their 'Treaty Establishing a Constitution for Europe', not one of them could have read it. The complete text, 844 pages in typescript, would not be available until November. In all but points of detail, the contents were substantially the same as those of the Convention's draft. Giscard himself took pride in observing that, of 14,800 words in his original document, 13,500 or 90 per cent had been kept, with the original 465 articles cut to 448. But it also included 36 Protocols, 30 Declarations, 20 Declarations on the Protocols and two Annexes.[1] The architecture remained that which had been proposed by Giscard, which in turn had been framed by the European University Institute back in May 2000.

OVERTURE TO THE FINAL ACT

All that now remained was for the treaty to be ceremonially signed, then for each country to ratify it. Once ratification was complete, with a target set for November 2006, the constitution would come into force, replacing the

---

[1] Norman, op. cit., pp. 283f.

existing treaties. If any countries 'encountered difficulties with ratification', the matter would be 'referred to the European Council'.

As different governments announced their plans, Spain announced she would hold a referendum 'as quickly as possible'. The three Benelux countries and Portugal would follow. Poland and the Czech Republic were 'probable' referendum candidates, with France, Denmark and Ireland still undecided. On the other side, Germany, Italy, Malta the Baltic states and Greece would ratify through their parliaments, with the Greeks declaring that this was 'no less democratic' than a referendum. In the meantime, the Commission discreetly announced that the new members would receive a 'pay-off' for agreeing the constitution. Between 2004 and 2006 the accession countries would receive a special grant of €24 billion (approximately £16 billion) in 'economic and social development aid', of which the largest share, €8.2 billion, would go to Poland.

Time was now fast running out for choosing a new Commission president. With Chirac rejecting Patten, at the last minute, on 26 June, Bertie Ahern announced a compromise candidate: Portugal's centre-right prime minister, José Manuel Durão Barroso.[2] Holland took over the rotating Council presidency on 1 July 2004 and, on 14 July during a television broadcast commemorating the French Revolution, Chirac finally agreed to France holding a referendum on the constitution. Barroso was approved by the European Parliament by 21 July, whence he plunged into the urgent task of allocating 24 portfolios in the newly enlarged College of Commissioners to the member states' nominees.

At the beginning of September, the existing Commissioners returned to work until their successors were approved. Following news that Germany's public deficit had soared to 4 per cent of GDP, taking the country dangerously close to breaching the deficit rules for the third year running, the Commission published its proposals on how enforcement might be tightened. These were so vague that the Bundesbank angrily commented: 'the proposed changes will not strengthen but weaken the Pact'.[3] On 6 October the Commission recommended that, 45 years after Turkey had first applied for membership of the Community, accession talks could begin in the autumn of 2005. If these were successful, her fast-growing, predominantly Muslim population of 68 million would make her easily the largest member state (and, of course, largely outside Europe).

---

[2] *Guardian*, 26 June 2004, 'Portuguese PM chosen to succeed Prodi'.
[3] AFP, 7 September 2004.

Leaving it less than a week before he was due to fly to Rome to sign the constitution, on 24 October, Blair announced he would hold a referendum in mid-March 2006, ten weeks after Britain ended its six-month EU presidency. Straw told colleagues: 'We can't do it while we are holding the presidency. But we need to strike while the iron is hot.' Meanwhile, an ICM poll had found that 59 per cent opposed the treaty.[4]

The following Friday, Blair joined the other EU leaders in putting his signature to the constitution (the complete text of which had still not been published), declaring that it represented a 'solemn obligation' for the British government. The lavish ceremony was staged in the Sala Degli Orazi e Curiazi, the same spectacular Renaissance hall where in 1957 the leaders of the original Six had signed the first Treaty of Rome. So was fired the starting gun on the ratification process.[5] As soon as the ceremony was over, Blair headed for home, choosing not to attend the banquet that followed.

The Conservatives, meanwhile, were having their own problems. On 30 September, there had been a by-election in Hartlepool, occasioned by its MP, Peter Mandelson, moving to Brussels as trade commissioner. Deep in the Labour heartland, the Conservatives were never going to do well, but their humiliation was complete when their candidate, Jeremy Middleton, was shunted into fourth place by UKIP.[6] Ruminating on the defeat, Michael Howard observed that every vote for UKIP made it more likely that, after the election, Labour would still be in power, 'It is very simple. If you want another Blair government, vote Ukip or Liberal Democrat,' he warned. If the Conservatives won power at the next election, he then promised, they would hold a referendum on the constitution by October 2005 – in the middle of the British presidency of the EU. 'I will campaign for a No vote,' he said. 'I am confident we will get a No vote. I will then go to the EU with a double mandate – a general election mandate and a referendum mandate. I would say we are against the constitution. The constitution is dead.'[7]

On 2 November the people of Holland, with its fast-growing population of Muslim immigrants, were shaken by the murder of Theo van Gogh, a film-maker who had recently made a critical documentary about the Islamic suppression of women. A North African Muslim was charged with the crime. On 3 November, President George W. Bush was re-elected for a second term. The next day, the north-east of England rejected the proposed elected regional assembly by a margin of four to one. This was a crushing

[4] *Daily Telegraph*, 24 October 2004.
[5] *Independent*, 29 October 2004, 'Blair signs new EU Constitution'.
[6] *The Times*, 2 October 2004, 'Hartlepool makes monkeys of Tories'.
[7] *Daily Telegraph*, 2 October 2004.

rebuff for Prescott's hopes of completing his long-cherished plans to align Britain with much of continental Europe by giving England eight regional assemblies.

As to the constitution, Lithuania, on 11 November, became the first to ratify it. Prodi bowed out as Commission president two months later, claiming in his final interview on Belgian television that to have introduced the single currency without a single economic policy to protect it was 'a great risk'. As for his successor, Barroso had been able to announce his new team within three weeks of his confirmation by the European Parliament, but it was not until 18 November, after an embarrassing false start, that it was approved. It was a far cry from the triumphalism that had attended Prodi's 'coronation' only five years previously. Just before Christmas, Hungary became the second country to ratify the constitution, with a parliamentary vote of 322 to 12.

On the morning after Christmas, 26 December, just before 8 a.m. local time, a massive undersea earthquake in the Indian Ocean off the north-west coast of Sumatra set off a tsunami that was to kill nearly three hundred thousand people. Immediately, the US government offered $35 million in aid and, within a matter of hours, ordered a powerful task force, led by the 90,000-ton US aircraft carrier *Abraham Lincoln*, to steam from Hong Kong to the disaster zone at top speed. By contrast, having offered by 5 January long-term aid worth €100 million, the best the new Luxembourg presidency could manage, of behalf of the EU, was to organise a 'three-minute silence' in memory of the victims, before announcing a 'donors' conference' to discuss the next moves. As *Frankfurter Allgemeine Zeitung* put it, 'Europe is not painting a very convincing picture of itself.' Even Prodi had to agree that the EU had been caught out by events.[8]

While US service members were busy dropping supplies over Indonesia and Australian doctors were treating people in improvised clinics, MEPs spent £262,000 of taxpayers' money on a party in Strasbourg to toast the constitution. Twenty-five thousand pounds went on inviting two *grands penseurs* (thinkers) and 20 *grandes plumes* (columnists) from states holding referendums. Other expenditure included £87,000 on redecorations.[9] As 'pro-constitution' MEPs assembled for a photo-opportunity, demonstrators gathered behind them, waving 'not in my name' placards. Two female assistants were manhandled and kicked to the ground by security officers. When asked why his men had been so violent,

[8] BBC Radio 4, *Today* programme, 4 January 2005.
[9] *Sunday Times*, 9 January 2005.

a senior security officer replied: 'we cannot have politics in the European Parliament'.[10]

Sunday 20 February brought the result of the first referendum to be held on the constitution. The outcome was never in doubt. Since 1986 Spain had received €86 billion from Brussels in aid, more than any other country.[11] The 'Yes' camp won by 79 per cent to 16. Although this was hailed as an 'overwhelming victory', the turnout was only 41 per cent, 4 per cent less than that for June's Euro-elections. The constitution had been endorsed by fewer than a third of Spain's citizens.[12]

FRANCE PREPARES A POLITICAL EARTHQUAKE

Despite the Spanish result, prospects for the constitution suddenly began to look somewhat shaky in France. Chirac's referendum was now expected as early as May, but the country's largest trade union, the General Labour Confederation (CGT), until recently linked to the Communist Party, had defied its leadership to recommend a 'No' vote. It feared the constitution would entrench 'free-market economics' at the expense of 'social priorities'.[13]

Chirac's government took another knock when scandal erupted over his finance minister and personal *protégé*, Hervé Gaymard, who was presiding over an unpopular austerity programme designed to cut France's budget deficit. Pleading poverty, he had been given a £9,700-a-month Paris flat at the taxpayers' expense. But it was then found he had been renting out his own flat in the city, as well as enjoying two homes in the country. From Chirac's admitted use of state cash for his family holidays, to the lodgings and limousines enjoyed by hundreds of provincial officials, the regal habits of the Gallic governing elite were beginning to provoke a mutinous backlash. As *The Times* remarked: this 'let them eat cake' attitude could yet cost Europe its constitution.[14]

In March, the drama moved to centre-stage. As the month began, Chirac announced that the referendum would be on 29 May. The polls still showed the 'Yes' camp in the lead, by 58 per cent to 42 per cent. But left-wing posters were on the streets of Paris proclaiming 'Vote No to the Constitution and to Chirac'.

Elsewhere, tension was growing over the Commission's proposed EU multi-annual financial framework for 2007–2013. In the months to come

[10] Personal communication from eyewitness.
[11] *The Times*, 11 February 2005.
[12] BBC News, 20 February 2005, 'Spain voters approve EU charter'.
[13] AFP, 4 February 2005.
[14] 26 February 2005.

this was to explode into the headlines, as one country after another faced funding cutbacks. The Spanish finance minister Miguel Ordóñez described as 'absolutely intolerable' Brussels's plan to cut Spain's net receipts from €8.7 billion in 2003 to €1.9 billion in 2007, reducing to zero by 2010.[15] Increasingly loud mutterings were heard about the UK's rebate. Yet another meeting of finance ministers broke up without agreement. Austria's Karl-Heinz Grasser observed: 'I think it is progress ... but largely in the wrong direction.'[16]

In France the referendum campaign was now so deeply dividing the left that a former Socialist minister claimed his party's mood was 'terrible, dramatic, the worst I've known in 20 years'.[17] Anti-constitution Socialists booed François Hollande, the leader of the Socialist 'Yes' camp, pelting him with snowballs. The party's former secretary general, Henri Emmanuelli, said that any Socialist voting 'Yes' would be making a mistake as serious as the support given to Pétain in 1940. At huge demonstrations in French cities, it became clear that left-wing opposition to the constitution was made up in equal parts of hostility to Chirac, distrust of an 'Anglo-Saxon' takeover of 'Europe' undermining the French 'social model', and fear of enlargement, particularly the admission of Turkey.

On 17 March, a poll in *Le Parisien* for the first time recorded a narrow lead for the 'No' campaign.[18] On the eve of the spring European Council, Barroso sought belatedly to inject some life into the failed Lisbon process by reviving the Services Directive originally proposed by former commissioner Frits Bolkestein. The proposal provoked uproar from trade unions across western Europe. Fifty thousand demonstrators assembled in Brussels to chant 'stop Bolkestein'. In France both 'No' and 'Yes' campaign leaders joined the protest, with Chirac demanding that the directive be rewritten. Foreign minister Barnier dismissed it as 'social dumping'. Phillipe de Villiers, a 'sovereignist' MEP and leading member of the 'No' camp, railed that it 'would permit a Polish plumber to work in France with the salary and employment protection of his own country'.[19] This fear of the 'Polish plumber' was to become a dominant theme of the campaign.

Nothing was going right for Chirac. On 20 March, 47 people, including some of his closest former political associates, appeared in court on charges relating to a huge corruption racket that had flourished during the 18 years

[15] *El País*, 4 March 2005.
[16] *Deutsche Welle*, 8 March 2005.
[17] *Independent*, 14 March 2005.
[18] *The Times*, 18 March 2005.
[19] AFP, Reuters, AFX, 20 March 2005.

before 1996 when Chirac had been mayor of Paris. Officials of his party were alleged to have siphoned off £60 million in bribes from construction companies, in exchange for school contracts worth £2.8 billion. Among those accused were four former ministers, twenty-four businessmen and several senior party officials. Most admitted that they knew of the scam, and faced up to ten years in jail. Chirac himself remained immune from prosecution or even questioning, as long as he remained president, but his position was not helped when Michel Roussin, his chief of staff for more than a decade, was accused of 'complicity in and receipt of the proceeds of corruption'.

A party treasurer, Louise Casetta, had testified that it was Roussin's responsibility to inform Chirac of all corporate 'gifts' to the party. In a videotaped confession before his death of cancer in 1999, another senior party official, Jean-Claude Méry, had directly accused Chirac of setting up the covert fundraising system, describing how he had once handed over a suitcase containing £500,000 to Roussin in Chirac's presence. Méry said that payments to the party reached £3.5–£4 million every year for more than seven years, and that 'we worked only on orders from M. Chirac'.

Unsurprisingly, given the circumstances, a second poll, in *Le Figaro*, put 'No' support at 52 per cent. Delors warned of a 'political cataclysm', opening up 'a very serious crisis which will slow down European construction, at the expense of French interests'.[20] At the March European Council, Barroso rounded on France's political elite, condemning their 'failure to explain the constitution' to voters.[21] Chirac responded by persuading his fellow heads of government to reject the Services Directive.[22] After consulting Barroso, Juncker issued a presidency statement that 'the directive will not be withdrawn. Only the Commission could do this. The European Council does not have the right to pass injunctions of this type to the European Commission.'

The following day, headlines in Britain were reserved for Blair's anger when, after he had supported Chirac over the directive, the French president had immediately launched a new attack on '*le cheque Britannique*', the UK rebate.[23] This was to become Chirac's favourite strategy for diverting attention from his difficulties over the constitution: whipping up hostility to Britain. The rebate might have had some justification when it was secured by 'Monsieur Thatcher', he said, but it could 'no longer be justified. It is from

---

[20] AFP and Agencies, 21–22 March 2005.
[21] *Daily Telegraph*, 22 March 2005.
[22] *Guardian, The Times, Independent*, Wednesday 23 March 2005.
[23] *Daily Telegraph*, 24 March 2005.

the past.' But playing to his domestic audience did not work. A third poll showed 55 per cent of voters opposed to the constitution.[24]

WHITE WATER
In April, the constitution document become a surprise best-seller in France, with 200,000 copies bought in four months.[25] Despite, or because of this, polls continued to show a majority for the 'No' camp. Europe's political elite began contemplating the possibility of a disaster that weeks earlier would have seemed unthinkable. However, Barroso remained confident that the 'great French tradition' would be upheld, since France was 'essential to this whole major European project'. Portugal's foreign minister Diogo Freitas do Amaral insisted that a 'No' vote would not mean the end. 'There is no need to make a big drama,' he said. 'There will be other ways to move forward.'[26] France's former EU trade commissioner, Pascal Lamy, blamed the rising 'No' support on 'uncertainty, ignorance of the issues and confusion'.[27]

On 6 April, Barroso's Commission adopted a package of detailed proposals related to the Financial Framework for 2007–2013. It called for the total expenditure to rise to €1,025 billion, representing 1.26 per cent of the 25 member states' Gross National Income (GNI). Spending on research and development, transport and education was to be tripled, 'in an effort to create jobs and revitalise the EU's struggling economy'. 'Europe,' said Barroso, 'must have the means to match its ambitions.'[28]

Italy became the first of the founder members to ratify the constitution, by a Senate vote of 217 votes to 16, bringing to four the number of national parliaments that had ratified. But in those countries that had opted for a referendum, including Holland, Denmark, the Czech Republic and Britain, the polls showed 'No' support continuing to strengthen. Meanwhile, the Commission announced that an Italian astronaut, Roberto Vittori, would be carrying a copy of the constitution into space, courtesy of a Russian Soyuz rocket. Günther Verheugen, a Commission vice president, lyrically declared that 'in orbit, the Constitution will not only encompass Europe, but the whole world'.[29]

In France, as an eleventh consecutive poll put the 'No' camp in the lead, Chirac planned his counter-attack. On 13 April, in a two-hour televised

[24] Reuters, 30 March 2005.
[25] BBC News website, 3 April 2005.
[26] AFP, 1 April 2005.
[27] Le Figaro, 3 April 2005.
[28] European Commission, Brussels, 6 April, 'New proposals for growth and jobs under the next Financial Framework 2007–13 (IP/05/389)', and 'Questions and Answers' (Memo 05/109).
[29] Reuters, 14 April 2005.

'debate' with 80 hand-picked 'young people', he asserted that, if France voted 'No', 'European construction would stop'. It would make France the 'black sheep' of the EU. 'France would cease to exist politically'. Rejection of the constitution would lead 'to the kind of Europe which is driven by the ultra-liberal current, an Anglo-Saxon, Atlanticist kind of Europe. This is not the kind of Europe we want'.

His ramblings prompted a hail of criticism, not least from Jacques Séguéla, chief 'image adviser' to the late President Mitterrand, who said that Chirac had blundered by turning the constitution into entertainment. 'More than 86 percent of the French have not read the Constitution and will not read it,' he said. 'They want to be told seriously and sincerely what is in it, not served-up show business'. One poll reported that only 22 per cent of his audience had found Chirac's arguments convincing.[30]

Responses among 'Europe's' political elites to the growing likelihood of a 'No' victory was now falling into two camps. Some insisted that, if the French people rejected the constitution, the ratification process must continue regardless. 'Just because the French have said "non"', said a spokesman for the Luxembourg presidency, 'does that mean that they decide for the whole of Europe? That would be undemocratic'.[31] Barroso's chief spokesman claimed that the Council could only gauge the true depth of EU support for the constitution if voting continued.[32] Delors insisted that ratification must continue and, if everyone else voted 'Yes', the French people could be invited to vote again.[33]

Others took a bleaker view. Prodi, for instance, warned that if the French voted '*Non*', 'we will pass through a long period of crisis. The problem will not only be a catastrophe for France, but the fall of Europe'.[34] With the growing prospect of a Dutch '*Nee*' to add to their woes, the new trade commissioner, Peter Mandelson, visited Holland to warn that this would give the rest of the world the impression that Europe was falling apart.[35] At least on 19 April, Greece became the fifth country to ratify, by a parliamentary vote of 268 to 17. Given that Greece had for 24 years been the second-highest beneficiary *per capita* of Brussels funding, this was hardly surprising.

In May the increasingly alarmed 'pro-Europeans' raised the ante. A poster campaign in France showed sinister-looking pictures of five supposedly

---

[30] Press Association, 18 April 2005.
[31] *Financial Times*, 22 April 2005.
[32] *Daily Telegraph*, 23 April 2005.
[33] BBC Radio 4, *Today* programme, 29 April 2005.
[34] *Financial Times*, 25 April 2005.
[35] Reuters, 14 April 2005.

typical '*Non*' supporters, identifiable as representing the far right and far left. The caption proclaimed: 'When I see this lot I vote "Yes"'.[36] On 9 May, 'Europe Day', in a speech made at the former Nazi concentration camp of Theresienstadt, Commission vice-president Margot Wallström, in charge of 'communication', was reported as accusing Eurosceptics of risking a return to the horrors of the Second World War by clinging to 'nationalistic pride'.[37] This provoked such a furore that the Commission hurriedly sanitised the comments to read: 'Yet there are those today who want to scrap the supranational idea. They want the European Union to go back to the old purely intergovernmental way of doing things'.[38]

In Holland, similar uproar greeted the news that four Dutch MEPs had fronted a series of short campaign videos, extolling a vote for the constitution against a background of Jewish prisoners, set to the sound of marching feet and machine-gun fire. Along with pictures of the Srebrenica massacre and the Madrid bombings, the clear implication was that a '*Nee*' vote would result in a return to such atrocities. Amid outrage, the commercials were withdrawn, but when they were featured on news broadcasts and anti-constitution websites, they boosted the '*Nee*' majority still further.[39] It also did not help when the director of the Dutch National Bank revealed that, at the time of the introduction of the euro, the Dutch guilder had been deliberately undervalued by 5–10 per cent. The Dutch had thus been robbed of up to a tenth of their incomes, pensions and savings.[40]

In France, Chirac decided to make another television appearance, allowing himself to be questioned by two tame journalists. He denied that the constitution would destroy the French social model and replace it with an Anglo-Saxon-style economy. On the contrary, he said, the treaty was 'essentially of French inspiration'. It was 'the best possible' choice for France. He called the text the 'daughter of 1989', the year the Berlin Wall fell, and 'especially the daughter of 1789', referring to the French Revolution. 'It would only increase French and German influence in Europe, ensuring that the two founding nations had a decisive say in the new, enlarged EU of 25.'[41]

The Eurosceptic campaigner Philippe de Villiers MEP complained at the 'outpouring of state propaganda, funded with public money and supported by almost every branch of the mainstream French media'. 'On the radio, in

---

[36] 2 May 2005.
[37] *Daily Telegraph*, 9 May 2005, 'Vote for EU constitution or risk new Holocaust, says Brussels'.
[38] The exchanges were part of a 'comment' sequence, part of Margot Wallström's 'blog'.
[39] For instance, www.vrijspreker.nl/blog/?itemid=2286.
[40] *Het Parool*, 30 April 2005.
[41] BBC News website, 4 May 2005.

the newspapers, on all television channels, there is just one single editorial voice: for the "Yes", he told an audience in Caen, claiming the tactics of the campaign were 'worthy of Fidel Castro'.[42]

One country where discussion of the EU had for a while been conspicuously absent was Britain. On 5 May, the nation went to the polls in a general election. Commentators noted how determined all the major parties had been to keep 'Europe' out of view, not least in their reluctance to discuss any of the main policy areas in which 'competence' had been surrendered to Brussels. The campaign was obsessively focused on those few policy areas in which Britain retained the right to govern herself, such as 'schools 'n' hospitals'. When the Tories, under Michael Howard, attempted to make an election issue of immigration and asylum, they carefully omitted to mention the extent of Brussels involvement.

After an unreal, trivialising campaign, Blair was returned to power for a third term, albeit on a reduced majority of 65. The turnout of 61 per cent was only just above the record low of 2001 (in 1992 it had been 78 per cent), reflecting an alienation from politics. The only influence 'Europe' had on the result was the so-called 'UKIP effect'. In 26 constituencies, the Conservatives lost by a margin smaller than the votes won by their UKIP and Veritas opponents. Had most of those Eurosceptic votes gone to Conservative candidates, the Tories might have gained 26 more seats, cutting the Lib-Dem gains from 11 to just 2, and Blair's majority to 32. Howard resigned as Tory leader, opening the way for a leadership contest between David Davis and David Cameron.

The day before the election, almost unnoticed by the British media, 17 smaller member states met in Lisbon to discuss the vexed issue of the 2007–2013 Financial Framework, in which they had demanded an end to the UK rebate. Calling themselves 'the friends of cohesion', all were net beneficiaries.[43] As the majority, they thus served notice on the net contributor states – Germany, Britain, France, Austria, Sweden and the Netherlands – that a real battle now lay ahead. It did not escape Chirac's notice that, if he were to support the 17 in calling for an end to the UK rebate, he might find a popular means of diverting attention from the repercussions of any French failure to ratify the constitution.[44]

Those countries that had rejected referendums continued to ratify. On 11 May the Slovak parliament endorsed the constitution by 116 to 27. The

---

[42] *Daily Telegraph*, 4 May 2005.
[43] The 17 were Belgium, Cyprus, the Czech Republic, Estonia, Finland, Greece, Hungary, Ireland, Italy, Latvia, Lithuania, Malta, Poland, Portugal, Slovakia, Slovenia and Spain.
[44] AFX, 5 May 2005.

following day, Germany's Bundestag overwhelmingly followed suit, with a vote of 569 to 23. The lower house of the Belgian Parliament emulated its Senate's endorsement by 118 to 18. Meanwhile, in the Netherlands, with the referendum due on 2 June, four days after France, polls were now consistently putting the 'No' camp far in the lead.

From Brussels, the *Financial Times* reported that the Commission was working on damage limitation in the event of 'No' votes. Any sense of crisis should be downplayed, and decisions left to the next European Council, scheduled for 16–17 June. In the meantime, the political leaders had been advised to avoid alarmist rhetoric. By then, it was hoped that a common position would have been crafted, reflecting the line already being offered by Juncker and Barroso: that all other member states should have their say on the constitution. The Commission's line was that: 'the procedures have been completed in nine countries representing over 220 million citizens; that is almost 49 percent of the EU population'. On this basis, the ratification process should continue. This meant the referendums in Luxembourg, Denmark, Poland, Ireland, Britain and the Czech Republic should go ahead as planned. Only when the process was concluded by November 2006 would there be a special 'summit' to discuss what to do about those countries that had failed to ratify.

Carefully choreographed for the eve of France's referendum was completing the ratification by Germany's federal parliament, with its upper house, the Bundesrat, due to vote on 27 May. So unpopular now was Schröder that, in a *Land* election, his Social Democrats lost one of their strongholds, North Rhine-Westphalia. One consequence was to bring forward the general election from 2006 to autumn 2005. But an even more immediate effect was that Schröder now controlled only five of the 16 seats in the Bundesrat, against the 11 his party had held in 1999. Despite this, the constitution was passed by all but one of the 16 *Länder*. Giscard had been allowed to address the deputies before the vote, saying, 'the day after tomorrow, the French will – I hope with all my heart – ratify the constitution by means of a referendum', and adding, 'the double ratification by Germany and France would mark a historic passage for the future of the constitution and for Europe'.[45]

So arrived the fateful Sunday, 29 May 2005. Early indications were that, despite 'massive abstentions' in the overseas departments, the turnout in France itself exceeded the Maastricht referendum count. Before the polls closed, it was reported that a tattered European Union flag had been lowered

45 AP, 27 May 2005.

to half-mast in the heart of the 'European quarter' in Brussels. On the stroke of ten, an exit poll revealed that the constitution had been rejected by 55 per cent to 45. Chirac appeared on television shortly afterwards, looking subdued. 'France,' he said, 'has expressed its democratic choice ... It is your sovereign decision, and I take note.' However, France, as a founder member of the Union, was 'naturally' to stay in the Union. 'But let us make no mistake,' he added; 'France's decision inevitably creates a difficult context for the defence of our interests in Europe.'[46]

At a press conference in Brussels, Juncker could not quite believe what had happened. He told incredulous journalists: 'many of those who voted "no" were voting for more Europe. If some of their votes are added to the "yes" vote, we have won.'[47] Both Juncker and Barroso insisted the ratification process must continue. The following day it was confirmed that almost all the member states agreed.

The French people having spoken, a scapegoat had to be found. The unpopular Raffarin 'resigned', his place as prime minister taken by Dominique de Villepin, the intellectual ex-diplomat who was such a quintessential representative of France's *fonctionnaire* elite that he had never held an elected office in his life. It was left to a Dublin correspondent to the letters page of the *Daily Telegraph*, Jonathan Wilson, to sum up the likely outcome of these events. 'The French "non" will not stop the EU or even make it think again', he wrote.

> The hallmark of the EU is its contempt for democracy and the will of the people ... The EU will push ahead regardless. When we in Ireland previously voted 'no', we were, in effect, sent to bed without any supper and told to vote the correct way the next time, which, to our shame, we did.

THE EARTHQUAKE CONTINUES

Now it was the turn of the Dutch people. On 2 June, despite the fact that their government, the opposition, the media, the trade unions and big business had all been unanimously in favour of a 'Yes' vote, 63 per cent of them turned out to deliver a stunning rejection of the constitution – an even greater margin than in France: 61.6–38.4 per cent. The Dutch *Volkskrant* daily called the outcome 'the reckoning of the common man', adding: 'The Dutch were always at the forefront of European Union, but now the good kid in the class is the scene of an anti-European rebellion.'[48]

[46] www.forbes.com/work/feeds/afx/2005/05/29/afx2063320.html.
[47] Personal communication, eyewitness report.
[48] *Guardian*, 2 June 2005.

The immediate response of 'Europe's' political elite was again one of denial. Sir John (now Lord) Kerr, who had assisted Giscard in drafting the constitution, told the BBC that the Dutch people had not voted against the constitution *per se*. They were merely unhappy with the EU as it was now, and had not realised that the constitution was intended to remedy all those shortcomings which worried them.[49] Commissioner Wallström insisted that, despite any specific doubts the 'No' voters might have had about the constitution, many of them 'believe in the European project' and 'want European integration to continue'.[50]

No government wished to be the one that first broke ranks in admitting that their creation was effectively dead. Dutch prime minister, Jan Peter Balkenende, half an hour after the exit poll result had been declared, called for all other member states to continue with the ratification process. This was endorsed by Barroso, who told BBC's *Newsnight* that every member state had a right to give its opinion on the treaty. All the 25 leaders had signed up to a process. He wanted them to 'respect the procedure'. The rest, led by Chirac and Schröder, were quick to follow, until Blair was in a minority of one. But he would only allow Straw to say that, since the constitution was 'owned' by the member states, it was for the European Council, due to meet on 16 June, to decide whether ratification should continue.

Thus began a strange little dance. Portugal and Denmark indicated that they would suspend their referendums if Britain led the way, while Britain wanted France and the Netherlands to say whether they thought the constitution had any future. After staging a private emergency 'summit', Chirac and Schröder urged that ratification should continue. Barroso agreed, calling on Europe's leaders to 'turn a crisis into an opportunity'.[51] But Sweden's prime minister Göran Persson condemned the 'thinking among European leaders' that the referendum results should be ignored.[52] In Germany, 390,694 readers of the tabloid *Bild* rang in to record their own verdict on the constitution, with 96.9 per cent voting '*Nein*'. By contrast, 95 per cent of the Bundestag had voted '*Ja*'.

On 5 June, a newspaper claimed that Blair 'has given up on Europe as an issue worth fighting for'. He was tired of the squabbling, and had switched his attention to poverty in Africa.[53] Straw told the Commons that there was

---

[49] BBC, *The World Tonight*, 2 June 2005.
[50] Wallström blog.
[51] BBC News website, 5 June 2005.
[52] Swedish news agency TT, 3 June 2005.
[53] *Sunday Telegraph*, 5 June 2005.

'no point' in proceeding.[54] Juncker, though, was quick to emphasise that Britain had not actually refused to hold a referendum; she was just waiting for the European Council to see what other EU states thought.[55] Chirac and Schröder called on Poland, their partner in the so-called 'Weimar Triangle', to dilute the impact of the British announcement. The Polish foreign minister Adam Rotfeld complied, telling a Warsaw press conference: 'the position taken by the British does not change anything.'[56] However, on 21 June, President Aleksander Kwaśniewski announced that his country was to delay 'indefinitely' the referendum scheduled for October. The original date was 'not realistic', he said.[57]

CHIRAC VERSUS BLAIR: THE GREAT BUDGET DIVERSION

Now onto centre-stage moved the great row over the budget and the UK rebate. For two players, this served as a diversionary tactic to obscure their own failures. The first was Chirac, hoping to distract attention from the constitution. The other was Juncker, wanting to salvage something from his presidency. There was no urgent necessity to settle the EU's budget for 2007–2013. It did not have to be finalised for another year. But Juncker, believing a quick decision could demonstrate that 'Europe' could still act, chose to play for high stakes. A failure to agree the budget now, he warned, would turn 'political difficulties into a big European crisis'. But crisis there was, and it was largely manufactured.

Politically, Blair was in a difficult position. He later wrote that the budget 'had assumed a mythical, almost cult status'. To question it was akin to betrayal. The Spanish Inquisition would have afforded more leeway to an apostate. As big a problem was his chancellor, Gordon Brown. He was 'taking a very hard line', demanding linkage between any reductions and reform of the CAP.[58]

Trying to force the pace, one of Juncker's aides said: 'the British rebate is the key to everything ... a psychological key. If it stays where it is, there are quite a few new member states from eastern Europe who would be financing the rebate, and to many eyes that is not quite decent.'[59] The Dutch finance minister, Gerrit Zalm, added to the pressure by saying it was 'unacceptable' that the UK alone should enjoy a rebate. Chirac was even more aggressive,

---

[54] *Hansard*, 6 June 2005, col. 991.
[55] AFX, 6 June 2005.
[56] AFX, 7 June 2005.
[57] BBC News, 21 June 2005, 'Poland puts EU referendum on hold'.
[58] Blair, Tony (2010), *A Journey* (London: Hutchinson), p. 535, *et seq.*
[59] Reuters, 8 June 2005.

demanding that Britain gave it up as a 'gesture of solidarity for Europe'. Predictably, Blair reacted angrily, saying he was not prepared to take 'lectures' from France, which did so much better out of the EU than Britain. Without the rebate Britain would be paying a 'quite unfair proportion' of the budget. Even with the rebate, he said, 'we have been making a contribution into Europe two and a half times that of France. Without the rebate, it would have been 15 times as much. That is our gesture.'[60]

As the European Council neared, the argument intensified. Blair now demanded a 'fundamental overhaul' of the budget, in particular a drastic cut in farm spending, from which France was the main beneficiary. And British officials, waking up to what was happening, accused Chirac and Schröder of using diversionary tactics to make Britain the 'bad boy' of the impending summit rather than face the facts. Brown took an even firmer line, stating that the rebate was 'simply not up for negotiation'.

Chirac remained implacable. 'I am not disposed to compromise on the unanimous accord reached in 2002 on the CAP,' he said, adding: 'our British friends must be aware of how things are changing'. Greater fairness in the burden carried by each member was necessary.[61] On Sunday, 12 June, the foreign ministers met in a bid to resolve the growing crisis. Straw flew to Luxembourg to meet his counterparts, but not to make peace. Instead, he launched a 'withering assault' on Chirac and his allies, saying they were 'deluded' if they thought the rebate was the real problem facing Europe. He told them that plans to increase overall EU spending, while leaving French farm subsidies untouched, were 'unfair', and 'wasteful'.[62]

However, the budget was not the only subject discussed. High on the agenda was the constitution. Although France and Germany were still adamant that ratification should continue, their view failed to prevail. Instead, the ministers decided on a fudge. Effectively, at the European Council, the constitution was to be 'ditched'. Without any formal announcement, it would be allowed to slip quietly into oblivion. 'The whole thing is being kicked into some very long grass indeed,' said one EU official, adding: 'You could say it is effectively dead.'[63]

Undoubtedly a factor influencing this 'non-decision' had been two opinion polls. In the Czech Republic where, prior to the referendums, 65 per cent had been in favour of the constitution and only 20 per cent against,

[60] *Daily Telegraph*, 10 June 2005.
[61] *The Times*, 11 June 2005.
[62] *Daily Telegraph*, 13 June 2005.
[63] Press Association, 13 June 2005.

a poll now showed the almost complete reverse, with 54–19.[64] Another showed that the 'No' camp was ahead in Ireland.[65] The evidence suggested further referendums would simply endorse the French and Dutch decisions. The game was up.

But the rebate continued to dominate the headlines. France's new foreign minister, Philippe Douste-Blazy, had accused Britain of refusing to pay the bill for enlargement, expecting the new states to pay for her rebate. He was now joined by Britain's own trade commissioner, Peter Mandelson, who branded the rebate 'unfair', saying it was 'wrong to ask the new, poorer member states to contribute towards it'.[66] He wanted Britain to hand over €440m of her rebate. Schröder joined in to declare that 'Germany has a good habit of sticking to the agreements it concludes and the contracts it signs', forgetting that the rebate itself was a contract to which Germany had agreed.[67]

Just before the Council, on his way back from Moscow, Blair met Chirac in Paris. After 81 minutes, the French president retreated behind the barriers of the Élysée Palace, leaving his spokesman to utter a terse 'No comment!' when asked for a statement. Blair, on his own, held forth at the British embassy, saying 'obviously there is sharp disagreement ... I think it is difficult to see these differences being bridged.'[68]

Interviewed by the *Suddeutsche Zeitung*, Commission vice-president Günter Verheugen admitted he was worried by how widespread disillusionment with the EU had become. 'The mood has changed everywhere,' he said. 'Something really fundamental has happened. A feeling of discontent that has been building up for a long time has spilled over. This crisis touches on something quite fundamental.' He concluded gloomily: 'We have to see leadership. At the moment, I have the feeling that the ground is shaking beneath our feet.'

'NOT A CRISIS, A DEEP CRISIS'

So, on Thursday 16 June, came the European Council in Brussels. A huge throng of the world's media had assembled in anticipation of mortal combat, matched by a fleet of satellite vans and hundreds of camera teams. A temporary stage had been built overlooking the Rue de la Loi, a six-lane

---

[64] *Financial Times Deutschland*, 13 June 2005.
[65] *Irish Times*, 14 June 2005.
[66] Ibid.
[67] *Daily Telegraph*, 15 June 2005.
[68] BBC News 24 programme, authors' verbatim notes, 14 June 2005.

highway running alongside the Justus Lipsius building where the drama was to unfold.

Few participants were prepared to say anything in the early stages, but Straw confidently addressed the media scrum, forecasting that, by 7.30 in the evening, he would be able to announce that the constitution was officially dead. The assassin, he indicated, would be the Dutch premier Balkenende, who had adamantly refused, under any circumstances, to resubmit the constitution to a referendum in his country. Without a commitment to a second referendum, the treaty could not be ratified.

Straw's confidence was not justified. About 10.30 that evening, the word came down that the EU leaders were merely declaring a 'pause for reflection'. They were keeping the priest at bay and denying the poor creature its last rites. By all accounts it had been an ill-tempered meeting, with Blair demanding an unequivocal declaration that the constitution was indeed dead.[69] But this had been resisted by Chirac, who attacked both Britain and Denmark for shelving their referendums. 'It is your duty to Europe,' he said, 'to go ahead with the referendums irrespective of the result.'

Shortly after that, Juncker and Barroso faced the media. Juncker confirmed that the Council believed the ratification process should continue, but that there should be a pause, given the French and Dutch rejections. There would be no renegotiation. 'We believe the constitutional treaty has the answers to many questions that Europeans are asking,' he added. 'In all the countries, those who have ratified and those still to ratify there should be a period of reflection.' Those committed to a referendum, he said, simply needed a little more time to have a dialogue with their citizens. Then came Barroso. 'Europe is not going to stop,' he declared. 'We're going on acting ... we're going to debate.' To emphasise his determination, he repeated: 'we're not going to stop ... we have a plan'. Defiantly, he concluded: 'we affirmed that there is no alternative to this Constitution'.[70]

Strangely, after all the high drama, media comment on the 'death' of the constitution was relatively superficial. The main event had become the budget, with the emphasis on the British rebate. As Friday morning dwindled away, there was nothing to keep the press corps active until, just after midday, there was much excitement as news broke of a major row between Chirac and Blair. Chirac had 'helpfully' released his speaking notes, provoking a headline from the *London Evening Standard*: 'Europe – Now it is war with France'. But not everyone was impressed. Sweden's prime

69 BBC News, 14 June 2005, Blair urges constitution 'pause'.
70 Verbatim notes taken from BBC News 24 broadcast.

minister Persson seemed genuinely annoyed by the coverage, regretting the focus on personalities. There was a great deal more going on, he said, claiming that there was no real crisis: 'it had all been got up by the media'.[71]

Even at 10.30 that evening, Juncker was still trying to broker a deal, getting into such a state that his officials feared that he would lose his composure completely. 'Basically, they had to take him off into a small room and hose him down,' said a British source. But, despite a last-minute offer by the accession countries to forgo some of their funds in order to facilitate a deal, the finalé was pre-ordained. Just after midnight on Friday, the main players in the drama appeared in different briefing rooms, each to present the media with his side of the story.

It was Juncker who set the tone. 'People will tell you that Europe is not in crisis,' he said. 'It is in deep crisis.' This was echoed by Schröder, who declared that the EU was in 'one of the worst political crises Europe has ever seen'. As to who was to blame, Juncker had no doubts: Mr Blair. He accused him of lacking the 'political will' to reach a deal. Asked how he felt about handing on the presidency two weeks later to Blair, Juncker replied bitterly: 'No comment, no opinion, and no advice, because people are obviously not interested in my advice.'

Blair had already arrived grim-faced in the British briefing room in the Council building. Fifteen minutes later, Jacques Chirac marched into the French suite, separated from its British counterpart merely by a wall and a door, which was firmly closed. Chirac was at one with Juncker, blaming Blair's 'stubborn refusal to compromise', which he described as 'pathetic'. He deplored the fact that the UK had 'refused to take on board a reasonable share of the enlargement costs ... It is a bad result for Europe.' He went on to declare – raising eyebrows among even the most ardent Europhiles – that the much-criticised CAP was a 'modern and dynamic policy that conformed to the interests of Europe'.

Amid growing incredulity among the British delegation, watching his performance on closed-circuit television, he went on to proclaim: 'To say today that the CAP is not a modern policy is to show evidence of a profound ignorance. There is no link between the British cheque and agriculture and nobody was asking for this besides the UK, because it was not legitimate or justified.'

Blair, on what was now the 190th anniversary of the Battle of Waterloo, described Chirac's defence of the CAP as 'bizarre'. He declared: 'let's not try to characterise this as a debate about who's most in favour of Europe.

[71] AFX, 17 June 2005.

447

That's not what the issue's about, and I'm not having anyone call me out on that basis. I'm not prepared to have someone tell me there is only one view of what Europe is, and that is the view expressed by certain people at certain points in time. Europe isn't owned by anybody; Europe is owned by all of us.'

In actuality, Britain was far from isolated, despite Juncker's attempts to make it seem so.[72] Five countries had rejected the budget deal: Britain, the Netherlands, Sweden, Spain and Finland. But the fact remained that the Council had ended in a shambles for which there was no historical precedent. Juncker's summing up in the presidency communiqué was simply to restate his faith that 'the constitutional treaty gives the right answers to the many questions that European citizens pose. We therefore consider that the process of ratification must continue.'[73] Instead of a 'Plan B' he suggested a 'Plan D', for dialogue and debate. But it seemed this could only be a dialogue of the deaf.

LE PROJET EST MORTE ...

On the face of it, the debacle of the summer of 2005 had plunged '*le projet*' into by far the most profound crisis it had ever known. For the first time in 50 years its onward advance had been seriously checked. The constitution, regarded as the symbolic culmination of decades of integration, had apparently been poleaxed. Most of 'Europe's' political leaders seemed in complete disarray.

The exception, who seemed to have emerged with his status enhanced from the Council, was Blair. Even the French press accorded him extravagant praise. 'It was supposed to have been he who made the summit fail, but he comes out as the reformer,' said *Libération*. *Le Monde* noted that 'Mr Blair appears to be the new strong man of Europe.'[74] On 1 July he was due to take over the presidency, his position further enhanced by the fact that he would be simultaneously taking over the chair of G8, representing eight of the world's leading economies.

In the closing days of June, this new would-be 'reformer of Europe' was almost daily winning new headlines for the initiatives he was about to launch, to save not just 'Europe' but the world. The twin themes of his G8

---

[72] See, for instance, the *Independent*, 18 June 2005, which reported: 'European budget talks collapsed in disarray last night, after an isolated Tony Blair rejected a last-ditch compromise plan designed to avert a new political crisis.'
[73] Presidency communiqué: www.eu2005.lu/en/actualites/communiques/2005/06/16jcljratif/index.html.
[74] *Financial Times*, 22 June 2005; http://news.bbc.co.uk/1/hi/uk_politics/4122288.stm.

presidency were to be to 'make poverty history' in Africa, and to redouble the world's efforts to fight global warming. On 1 July, as the UK took over the Council presidency, he announced 'a full-scale review of whether Europe's welfare system is fit for the modern world'.[75] The following week he would be in Singapore to lobby for London to be picked to host the 2012 Olympic Games, then flying back to the Gleneagles Hotel in Scotland to join world leaders headed by Bush for the inaugural meeting of his G8 presidency.

Meanwhile, on 'Europe', the new global statesman built on the position he had begun to develop at the time of the European Council, setting out how he believed the EU should respond to the awesome challenges it now faced. 'The people,' he told MEPs in Brussels on 23 June, 'are blowing the trumpets around the city walls.' The crisis confronting the EU, he said, was not 'a crisis of institutions' but 'a crisis of leadership'.[76]

As rhetoric, Blair's speech was widely hailed as a *tour de force*. But those who paused to analyse it were struck by its complete absence of any specific proposals. His vision was not based on any disciplined understanding of what the European project was actually about, or how his vague but high-sounding goals might be achieved. This was subsequently underlined by his call for a reduction in the avalanche of Brussels 'red tape', and on 30 June by a startling offer that the UK might be prepared to negotiate over the rebate in return for outright abolition of the CAP (one that was not to be repeated).

THE BRITISH PRESIDENCY

As Blair's presidency began, the sense of melodrama only heightened, when the explosion of media euphoria that surrounded Live 8 concerts, organised in support of Blair's Africa agenda, and the success of London's bid to host the 2102 Olympics were quickly followed by the horror of the four terrorist bombs that halted London's transport system on the morning of 7 July. Again, Blair took centre-stage, flying down to London from Gleneagles, leaving Bush, Chirac, Schröder, Putin and the other leaders to play only a supporting role in the shadows. His acting of the part of leader in a time of crisis could scarcely be faulted.

When, three days later, tiny Luxembourg voted by 55–42 per cent for the constitution, the thirteenth country to ratify, this again brought home the extent to which Blair had offered not a single specific proposal as to how the crisis might be resolved. Although he was still prepared to say, without conviction, that he supported the constitution (the one he had never wanted

[75] BBC News, 1 July 2005, 'Blair urges debate on EU's future'.
[76] Speech text: BBC News, 23 June 2005.

in the first place), he was only too happy to preserve an impasse that let him off the hook of a referendum he knew he would lose. He had no plans to get the ratification process back on the agenda. It is perhaps ironic that, as his beloved 'Europe' appeared to be sinking into disarray, the news came in during the day on 17 July 2005 that Edward Heath was 'nearing end of life'. That evening, he died peacefully in his bed, just a week after he had celebrated his eighty-ninth birthday. The now ennobled Lord Hurd described him as 'a man of integrity and determination'.

Keeping the flame of integration burning now fell to Prodi, heading a centre-left coalition in Italy and preparing for the next presidential elections. Of the constitution, he had to say: 'It is difficult to think that it will be approved, but it is important to go ahead with the ratification process to show that the position expressed by the majority of the French and Dutch is not prevalent.' He added: 'Integration remains the only strategy for growth in Europe. Europe can only participate effectively in the global system when it speaks with one voice – in other words when there is a political Europe.'[77]

As the torpor of the continental summer took hold, Austrian chancellor Wolfgang Schüssel took advantage of reduced media activity to tell the *Frankfurter Allgemeine Zeitung* that the EU should take two years to reflect on why French and Dutch voters had rejected the constitution. Only then should there be a fresh attempt to ratify it. 'People are worried about the EU becoming over-stretched if it takes in Turkey, Ukraine and other countries,' he said. 'If a cautious approach is taken then we can say to the French and Dutch: "So you see we have understood and acted".'[78] Schüssel's German neighbours, however, had more pressing concerns. The Federal budget deficit had again breached the 3 per cent limit, standing at 3.6 per cent of GDP in the first half of the year. There was some comfort, though: it was a slight improvement on the previous year.[79]

But bigger changes were afoot in the Federal Republic. On 18 September, a motion of confidence in Schröder had triggered a general election. The lead challenger was 51-year-old Angela Merkel, who had grown up in Communist East Germany and had been a protégé of Helmut Kohl. Although her own Christian Democrat Party (CDU) failed to win an absolute majority, by 22 November she had 'painstakingly' crafted a 'left–right grand coalition' sufficient for her to be sworn in as chancellor – the ninth since the war and

---

[77] Reuters, 22 July 2005.
[78] 16 August 2005.
[79] *Deutsche Welle*, 23 August 2005, 'Germany may flout EU budget rules again'.

the first female to hold the post.[80] With Tony Blair and Nicolas Sarkozy, who was tipped to succeed Chirac, the balance of power in Europe was shifting.[81]

Shortly after the German election, Barroso admitted that the EU would not have a constitution for 'at least two or three years'. Despite being in a 'period of reflection', he also conceded: 'There hasn't been much reflection so far', adding that it was important to convince citizens of the relevance of the EU by creating jobs, improving security and protecting the environment.[82] In something of a confessional mood, the following day in Lisbon he spoke of 'Europe' needing reform. 'The double "no" to the European Constitution and failure to agree on new financial perspectives have shaken people's faith in the European project,' he said. 'The rising tide of Euroscepticism, even in traditionally supportive Member States, means that a growing number of our citizens now see the European Union as part of the problem, not part of the solution.'[83]

Despite the forthcoming change of leadership in Germany, the Commission was not giving the Republic any breaks. For once, it was Germany rather than the UK in the frame as Joaquín Almunia, the Commissioner for economic and monetary affairs, raised the spectre of punishment. Eurostat, the EU's statistics office, believed the deficit would be closer to 4 per cent, as it did not accept the sale of former state-run enterprises Deutsche Telekom and Deutsche Post as deficit-reducing measures.[84]

Somehow, after the heady days earlier in the year, the steam seemed to have gone out of *le projet*. In an attempt to restore some dynamism, in early October, Blair flew once more to Paris, again to see Chirac. This was their first face-to-face meeting since the June Council. The pair spent 90 minutes together – twice as long as expected – discussing the EU's future and planning for the informal Council at Hampton Court later that month. Said Chirac: 'For the Europe of tomorrow, we are both determined to be … not a force of division, but a force of harmony.'[85] Yet the *Independent* commented: 'Friendly talks fail to hide deep rift between Chirac and Blair.'[86]

In what was being described as 'an almost invisible presidency', Blair was said to be 'rather embarrassed' by the chorus of people asking what was being done about the constitution, about the budget, and about economic

[80] *Deutsche Welle*, 22 November 2005, 'Angela Merkel sworn in as German chancellor'.
[81] *Euractiv*, 16 September 2005, 'Europe's new triumvirate'.
[82] BBC News, 21 September 2005, 'EU admits constitution is on ice'.
[83] European Commission, 22 September 2005, President Prodi speech, European Ideas Network, Lisbon.
[84] *Deutche Welle*, 26 September 2005, 'EU Ready to Punish Germany Over Deficit'.
[85] *Daily Telegraph*, 7 October 2007, 'Blair and Chirac seek "new vision" for Europe'.
[86] 8 October 2005.

reform. Hampton Court, famous for its hedge maze, commissioned around 1700 by William III, was seen as an appropriate venue for the informal Council. 'It's a maze in which the presidency is in the middle, wondering how to get out, rather than one where visitors are outside trying to get in,' one observer noted.[87] The Commission was doing its own bit, though, publishing on 13 October its contribution to the period of reflection and beyond: 'Plan-D for Democracy, Dialogue and Debate'.[88] The 29-page document was the predictable mix of aspiration designed to 'restore public confidence' in 'Europe', the immediate objective being to 'stimulate a wider debate between the European Union's democratic institutions and citizens'.

On the day of the Council, 27 October 2005, Blair got plenty of help from Barroso in conveying the feeling of a successful event, delivering this summary: 'What people really believe is this, that Europe sometimes needs to do more and sometimes needs to do less, but in each case needs to do it better.'[89] Despite that, nothing substantive was achieved – unsurprising in the view of the *Independent*. 'Europe' had hardly featured on Blair's agenda at all, it complained. He had spent such little time among European representatives that an Austrian MEP had circulated a mock missing person's notice featuring him, in the European Parliament building.[90]

At the time, Blair's Cabinet was said to be 'riven with disputes' over a smoking ban, with ministers 'briefing against each other and making public discussions which should be kept private'.[91] Chirac, on the other hand, was struggling to overcome what was being described as one of France's gravest post-war crises. Every major city in the country faced the threat of fierce rioting that seemed to have spun out of control.[92] His Cabinet had met in emergency session to declare a state of emergency. It may have seemed a minor matter compared with this, but France had lost control of several key posts at the European Commission in Brussels, handed to Britain and Ireland, bastions of the 'Anglo-Saxon free market'. The reshuffle had been masterminded by Barroso. Chirac was not amused.[93]

THE BUDGET DANCE

For Blair, 'Europe' presented a different order of problems. The seven-year, multi-annual budget now dominated his presidency and he was

[87] BBC News, 14 October 2005, 'UK trims Hampton Court summit plan'.
[88] European Commission, Brussels, 13 October 2005, COM(2005) 494 final.
[89] *Euractiv*, 28 October 2005, 'Feelgood summit fails to make real progress'.
[90] 27 October 2005.
[91] *Daily Telegraph*, 28 October 2005, 'Blair urged to get a grip of feuding, leaking ministers'.
[92] *Daily Telegraph*, 8 November 2005, 'Leaders fiddle as France burns'.
[93] *Daily Telegraph*, 10 November 2005, 'France is snubbed in EU jobs shake-up'.

contemplating a climbdown on the British rebate in order to avoid a repetition of the June debacle. To pave the way, Straw met his counterparts in Brussels, making it clear that there would be no repeat of Britain's earlier hard-line stance. Britain had accepted that it would have to increase its contributions. Nevertheless, Whitehall 'sources' said there would not be 'a deal at any cost'.[94]

For his next move, Straw had a 'cunning plan'. Britain would not publish 'comprehensive proposals' on the financial package until early December, depriving the 'colleagues' of anything specific to fight about. Then, in the run-up to the Brussels Council on 15–16 December, he would present a 'take it or leave it' offer on reducing the rebate, leaving less than two weeks for squabbling.[95] The plan did not go down well. In a 'bad-tempered meeting' in Brussels on 21 November, Straw had to face down his European 'colleagues' and suffer homilies from a sanctimonious Philippe Douste-Blazy, the French foreign minister: 'Why should Britain be exempted from paying its share of enlargement?' he asked, when there were 'ethical, moral, and political' issues at stake. Press reports spoke ominously of Blair 'isolated in Europe', yet if he caved in, the bill could be £17 billion extra over the budget period.[96]

From over the hill, though, came the thunder of hooves as the cavalry galloped to the rescue in the form of newly elected Angela Merkel. She counselled Blair to 'look at all the issues'. 'We can't reduce it to one point,' she said.[97] By now, Blair was planning an even more radical move. He decided to slash £120 billion from the Commission's original proposal, reducing all member state contributions. Although this would hurt the most recent members, the winners would outnumber the losers. It was a high-risk strategy, made 'in hope of success, not in fear of failure'.[98]

The biggest obstacle, of course, was Chirac, and prospects cannot have been helped by a French opinion poll. It found 72 per cent of those polled regarded the influence of their president over what happened in France as 'weak'. Two-thirds said his clout on the world stage was feeble, while only 36 per cent thought he held any significant sway over European politics.[99] Sure enough, Chirac launched a scathing attack on Blair, saying he was too 'isolated' in Europe to be able to broker a budget deal.[100] Almost as if to

[94] Daily Telegraph, 8 November 2005, 'Britain softens line over EU rebate'.
[95] Financial Times, 16 November 2005, 'Britain plans to compress EU budget talks'.
[96] Daily Telegraph, 22 November 2005, 'Blair is all alone in Britain's EU rebate row'.
[97] Euractiv, 24 November 2005, 'Merkel sets agenda on European trip'.
[98] Daily Telegraph, 28 November 2005, 'Blair targets new EU states with £118bn budget cut'.
[99] Daily Telegraph, 28 November 2005, 'Chirac's influence sinks to new low'.
[100] Daily Telegraph, 29 November 2005, 'Blair too weak to win deal, says Chirac'.

prove Chirac wrong, another 'cunning plan' was emerging from Whitehall, this one aiming to split the rebate into parts that could be defended as 'fair' – including the claw-back from the CAP – and others that were less easy to justify, including spending on enlargement.[101] Merkel, meanwhile, had given her first speech to parliament as German chancellor, pledging to find a compromise, but warning that Germany's 'frightening' debt levels meant the economy would not be able to tolerate new budget obligations.[102]

It was time for the Commission to intervene. Responding to Blair's idea for an across-the-board cut, Barroso's spokesman, Johannes Laitenberger, quipped that the British presidency was like the Sheriff of Nottingham, 'taking from the poor to give to the rich'. Straw retorted: 'Mr Barroso is a great man but I dare say his spokesman knows less about what happened in Sherwood Forest than some of us.' EU diplomats thought Britain was losing the war of words.[103]

That seemed to be the case. In Tallinn, the Estonian capital, and then in Budapest for tense meetings with leaders of seven ex-Communist nations, Blair found his gamble had backfired. The new member states would not back him. Then, speaking at an EU–Ukraine summit in Kiev, he suggested that, if the EU could not reach a 'big deal', reforming both the rebate and the CAP, then an alternative might be an 'intelligent' short-term compromise, backed by a 'mid-term review'. In the coffee shops of Budapest's old town, however, observers said it was 'too late'. Blair had badly eroded the goodwill earned by Britain as a champion of enlargement, having failed to confront Chirac on the CAP. From Oszkár Füzes, the political analyst for *Népszabadság*, Hungary's biggest newspaper, came a caustic verdict on Blair: 'Because he wants to keep his own money, and because he's afraid of taking on the big guys like France, he's taking on the small guys like us.'[104]

After failing to please the ex-Communist nations, Blair also found he was getting no plaudits at home. In the latest twist of the soap opera, he announced that he was abandoning hopes of major reform of the EU budget and would unilaterally cut Britain's rebate if it proved necessary to forge a compromise deal. He immediately faced accusations of 'surrender'.[105] But some thought it 'a dramatic move' to isolate France, attempting to paint Chirac as a brake on reform and the only leader unwilling to give ground.[106]

---

[101] *Daily Telegraph*, 30 November 2005, 'Blair ready to surrender EU rebate with no payback'.
[102] *Deutsche Welle*, 30 November 2005, 'Merkel urges recovery and resolve in first speech'.
[103] *Daily Telegraph*, 1 December 2005, 'Tony Blair cast as EU's Sheriff of Nottingham in budget row'.
[104] *Daily Telegraph*, 2 December 2005, 'Blair loses EU allies in budget rebate row'.
[105] *Guardian*, 2 December 2005, 'Blair accused of sellout over EU rebate deal'.
[106] *Daily Telegraph*, 3 December 2005, 'Blair and Brown hatch plan to make France the EU villain'.

Before the next soap opera instalment, the real world intruded briefly when ten British skippers and two trawler owners in Whitby, North Yorkshire, were fined for exceeding EU fish quotas in 2003. Their defence was that they were in 'dire straits' caused by a reduction in quotas, unfair subsidies and a decommissioning scheme that would force some of the men into debt. They did not glibly take the view that they were going to breach EU rules. The offences were not motivated by greed. They were viewed as a commercial necessity.[107]

It was Germany that made the next play. Finance minister Peer Steinbrück wanted to cut its net EU contribution, so that it could better respect the Stability and Growth Pact. 'Our net payments must fall,' he told *Welt am Sonntag*. It was not possible 'one day to urge Germany to respect the Maastricht criteria' while 'already the next day it is not being ruled out in Europe that Germany should strengthen its position as a net contributor'.[108]

With there being no possibility of anyone being able to appreciate the full significance of the development, on 3 December another piece was about to fall into place that would lead to the UK's eventual departure from the EU. David Cameron, the man who would give the UK a referendum on 'Europe', was forecast to become leader of the Conservative Party, by a vote of two-to-one of its members.[109] When, days later, his appointment was confirmed, he became by far the least experienced leader of the Opposition for about 80 years.[110]

In quick order, the budget soap opera resumed. Blair was to unveil a proposal aimed at resolving the dispute, sacrificing part of Britain's rebate while cutting the overall budget. The newest and poorest member states would lose about one-tenth of the billions they were expecting in EU regional and social cash aid. There was no further attempt to wring concessions from the French over cutting the size of the CAP.[111] There was nothing new here, but Barroso shot it down anyway, calling it 'simply not realistic'.[112] A senior French official accused Blair of trying to 'shatter the spirit of balance' between national interests and the EU's noble ideal of 'solidarity' between rich states and poor regions.[113]

Procedure now required the General Affairs Council – comprising the foreign ministers of the member states – to take over, preparing the brief for the European Council. As they were due to meet, Commission vice-president Günter Verheugen warned that the credibility and negotiating

---

[107] *Daily Telegraph*, 2 December 2005, 'Skippers fined for fish quota breaches'.
[108] *Deutsche Welle*, 3 December 2005, 'Steinbrück: Germany wants to cut EU budget contributions'.
[109] *Daily Telegraph*, 'Tories have voted for Cameron as leader'.
[110] *Daily Telegraph*, 7 December 2005, 'Opposition has its least experienced leader for 80 years'.
[111] *Daily Telegraph*, 5 December 2005, 'Blair plans last attempt at EU budget deal'.
[112] *Deutsche Welle*, 5 December 2005, 'British EU budget proposal shot down'.
[113] *Daily Telegraph*, 6 December 2005, Spending row may end Blair's EU dreams'.

competency of the EU was at stake.[114] Blair was being told, 'You can't do Europe on the cheap.' Britain had been one of the most enthusiastic advocates of enlargement. Now there was a price to pay.[115]

To add to the gaiety of life, Chirac insisted that Britain double its rebate cut from the proposed £800 million a year. He also rejected the idea of a mid-term review of the budget and rebate.[116] Come the Council meeting, Philippe Douste-Blazy declared: 'Britain is isolated, they have to propose another offer.' Straw tartly remarked: 'The French are always happy to negotiate with our money.'[117] Portuguese prime minister José Sócrates summed up: Blair wanted a larger budget, a smaller rebate and more funds for poor regions.' On all three counts, Britain was at odds with the rest of the EU. After a bruising, four-hour meeting at which foreign ministers queued up to denounce the British proposal, Straw mused that the chances of reaching agreement were 'very finely balanced'.[118]

At least his 'cunning plan' was working. Three days before the European Council, EU diplomats were still waiting for formal proposals from the UK. Foreign ministers, who were making preparations for the Council, had something of an empty agenda. And it was not only the budget. The British presidency had also neglected the constitution. In general, they had to 'be pushed to engage' with any important topics.[119] At the meeting itself, even the modicum of hope brought by those expecting new proposals died quickly as Straw announced there would be nothing to discuss.[120]

SHOWDOWN IN BRUSSELS

As the EU leaders gathered in Brussels, hopes of a settlement had not improved. But in the Council chamber – in what Blair called a 'wretched meeting in that boring and soulless room' – they got down to business. As to the outcome, Blair wrote:

> We got a deal which actually left Britain paying roughly the same as France for the first time. The UK media called it a betrayal, but frankly they would have done that even if I had led Jacques Chirac in chains through the streets of London. And by then I was past caring.[121]

[114] *Deutsche Welle*, 7 December 2005, 'European Foreign Ministers to meet over EU budget'.
[115] *The Times*, 7 December 2005, 'You can't do Europe on the cheap, Blair is told'.
[116] *Daily Telegraph*, 7 December 2005, 'Chirac tells Blair to give up even more cash in EU row'.
[117] *Financial Times*, 7 December 2005.
[118] *Daily Telegraph*, 8 December 2005, 'France calls for £10bn back from Britain's EU rebate'.
[119] *Deutsche Welle*, 12 December 2005, 'Moaning tops agenda at EU wrap-up'.
[120] *Deutsche Welle*, 12 December 2005, 'Britain tells EU to expect no surprises as budget crisis looms'.
[121] Blair, op. cit.

Possibly one of the most generous media reports came from the *Guardian*, which headlined: 'Blair clinches deal with offer of big rebate cut'. Britain had given up £7 billion of the rebate negotiated by Margaret Thatcher, committing to contributions over the seven-year period 2007–2013 of £40 billion – a 63 per cent net increase. Overall, the EU-25 had agreed an €862 billion spending package. But Chirac seemed to differ in his understanding of what had transpired. He had 'immediately hailed the deal after the British withdrew a call for a review of EU spending before the end of the budget period'.

The paper predicted that Britain's vocal Eurosceptics would be unappeased by a 116 per cent increase in France's contributions in the same period, bringing them almost to the same level as Britain's, a long-sought-after goal.[122] But contrary to the *Guardian* report, Blair had got his review. It was a 'complementary and inseparable' part of the agreement, with the Commission to report in 2008/9.[123] It was not wrong about the Eurosceptic reaction though. The *Daily Telegraph* stormed: 'Blair set to give up £7bn in rebate fiasco', bitterly complaining of a 'climbdown' and 'surrender'. The *Daily Mail* spat, 'Blair's surrender'. In return for the 'gigantic cash handover' of 'more than £1billion', Tony Blair had 'got virtually nothing'.[124] Even the relatively neutral *Times* reported: 'Blair surrenders chunk of rebate'. The *Sunday Express* was incandescent. It headed a double-page spread with the single word: 'Loser'.[125] The *Sunday Times* was not that much better, claiming that the Brussels deal made 'every family £445 poorer'.

Largely lost in the 'noise' had been the role of Angela Merkel, at her very first European Council. She had brought Blair and Chirac together, and added €4 billion to the budget. That had made it easier for Blair to 'buy off' the Netherlands, Sweden and Ireland. To square Poland, Merkel offered €100 million of EU aid earmarked for East Germany. Polish prime minister Kazimierz Marcinkiewicz described it as 'the most beautiful and wonderful gesture of solidarity'. Rather less starry-eyed British officials said the offer had been 'pre-cooked' in case he had 'kicked up rough'.[126] Merkel's intervention was seen to hint at a possible shift in power in 'Europe'.[127] But it had come at a price. Germany was having to pay another €2 billion a year into the budget.[128]

[122] Both 17 December 2005.
[123] Council of the European Union, Brussels, 19 December 2005, *Financial Perspective 2007–2013*.
[124] 17 December 2005.
[125] 18 December 2005.
[126] *Financial Times*, 18 December 2005, 'Early morning deal ends year of horsetrading'.
[127] *Deutsche Welle*, 19 December 2005, 'Budget deal hints at changing power structure in Europe'.
[128] *Deutsche Welle*, 23 December 2005, 'EU budget deal costs Germany more than expected'.

As to the constitution, the European Council decided it would 'return to the issue in the first half of 2006 under the Austrian presidency'.[129] When he returned to the Commons, Blair faced the new leader of the Opposition, David Cameron. After Blair's 1996 jibe to Major on his BSE 'rout', Cameron neatly turned the tables. 'On the budget,' he said, 'does the Prime Minister remember having three clear objectives: first, to limit its size, when almost every country in Europe is taxing and borrowing too much; second, to ensure fundamental reform of the CAP; and, third, to keep the British rebate unless such reform occurs? Is it not now clear that he failed in every single one?'[130]

In the dying days of the British presidency, Ursula Plassnik, the Austrian foreign minister, flew to Brussels to hail the constitution as holding the answers to key questions about Europe. Austria would re-launch the debate on the future of Europe at the June Council, Plassnik said.[131] She added: 'As far as the constitution is concerned, I don't think that we can succeed with cosmetic changes only. That would not do justice to the great importance of this topic.'[132] But there was no disguising that 2005 was the year the European Union would rather forget. For Blair, the kindest verdict of his presidency was that it had failed to impress.[133]

---

[129] 'Presidency Conclusions', Brussels European Council, 17 December 2005.
[130] HC Deb, 19 December 2005, Vol. 454, col. 1566.
[131] *Daily Telegraph*, 20 December 2005, 'Time is ripe' for reviving constitution, say Britain's EU partners'.
[132] *Deutsche Welle*, 29 December 2005, 'Austria preps for challenging EU presidency'.
[133] *Deutsche Welle*, 27 December 2005, 'British EU presidency tenure fails to impress'.

18

The Road to Lisbon: 2006–2009

We will put it – the EU Constitution – to the British people in a referendum and campaign whole-heartedly for a 'Yes' vote.
Labour Party manifesto, May 2005

We will have a referendum on the constitution in any event – and that is a Government promise.
Tony Blair, Sun, 13 May 2005

Well, if it were necessary to hold a referendum, of course [we wouldn't hesitate]. I suspect that the best deal for Britain will be won, where we will get what we want, at this summit.
Gordon Brown, GMTV, 19 June 2007

We would not agree to a deal that crossed the red lines, therefore, we did not believe a referendum would be necessary.
Later that day, Downing Street website

The manifesto is what we put to the public. We've got to honour that manifesto.
Gordon Brown, BBC 1, The Politics Show, 24 June 2007

After a terrible year for the EU, the Austrian chancellor Wolfgang Schüssel started his tenure as Council president in harmony, attending the famous New Year's concert in Vienna in company with Angela Merkel. As well as traditional Strauss waltzes, the programme featured pieces by Mozart, whose 250th birthday was to be celebrated later in the year. As to the presidency,

Austria wanted 'to bring Europe closer to its citizens and increase confidence in the European project'. Schüssel also wanted to see 'radical changes' in the way the EU was funded. On the constitution, he hinted that there was 'another way of proceeding', without going into detail.[1]

In Britain, not one in a thousand might have recognised Schüssel's name, but the listeners of the BBC Radio 4 *Today* programme had no problem with José Manuel Barroso. In a 'Who Runs Britain?' poll, held over the Christmas period, they had voted him the most powerful person in Britain.[2]

Less than two weeks into the new year and the entire 25-member European Commission was on its way to meet the Austrian government in Vienna, where Ursula Plassnik was calling for a period of 'confidence building', to improve the prospects of salvaging all or part of the constitutional treaty. 'The Constitution is covered in snow and it's waiting for spring,' she said. 'We need a climate change, to a certain extent.'[3] Even within the Austrian government, though, there were tensions: Hubert Gorbach, the vice-chancellor, suggested redrafting the text 'from the beginning', with new emphasis on the powers of member states.[4]

A new face at the Commission was Javier Solana, responsible for foreign policy, and potentially the EU's first 'foreign minister', if the constitution was ever ratified. And, in the period of reflection – or 'deep sleep', as some would have it – his idea for breaking the impasse was to cherry-pick 'some elements' that could be agreed by member states. Those would include, as coincidence would have it, provision for an EU foreign minister.

Solana was backed by transport commissioner, Frenchman Jacques Barrot, who thought it would be a good idea to push ahead with sections that 'reformed' EU institutions. These would include the creation of a separate 'President of the European Union', elected by national governments – and abolishing more vetoes. But this was to breach a major Brussels taboo. The treaty was supposed to be 'deeply frozen', treated as indivisible despite having been rejected by the French and the Dutch.[5] Barroso was not enthusiastic about reviving the constitution – not immediately. The year 2006 'can and should be the year of a new drive for Europe', focused on 'what matters to people', he said. A fresh bout of institutional navel-gazing would only expose deep divisions within Europe.[6]

---

[1] *Deutsche Welle*, 1 January 2006, 'New EU president Austria wants "momentum" for Europe'.
[2] *Daily Telegraph*, 2 January 2006, 'Euro chief Barroso "is man who really runs Britain"'.
[3] *Financial Times*, 8 January 2006, 'Austria aims to bring EU constitution in from the cold'.
[4] *Independent*, 9 January, 2006, 'Austria aims to revive EU constitution'.
[5] *Daily Telegraph*, 9 January 2006, 'Pressure to salvage parts of wrecked EU constitution'.
[6] *Daily Telegraph*, 10 January 2006, 'Barroso cautions against EU treaty talk'.

Schüssel seemed not to be listening. 'The Constitution is not dead, but it is not in force,' he declared at a news conference with Barroso. It was 'still in the midst of a ratification process'. Austria planned to present proposals on the future of Europe at the end of the presidency. 'We must give Europe new momentum this year,' he said. 'We cannot do it with just rhetoric; we must support it with concrete action.'[7]

Chirac was not getting much mileage from his proposals. Saving the constitution by splitting it up into single chapters and integrating those into the existing EU framework was being widely condemned as keeping the EU 'in a state of inertia and paralysis'.[8] The man slated to replace him in the 2007 election, Nicolas Sarkozy, suggested a slimmed-down version, for approval by the French parliament. Member states, he said, might then try to claim the new treaty was a relatively modest affair, side-stepping the need for referendums.[9]

From Holland came an altogether different view. When Ursula Plassnik flew to The Hague to sound out the Dutch, foreign minister Bernard Bot was unequivocal: the treaty was 'dead'.[10] The UK's Jack Straw was of like mind: 'the treaty is in limbo', he had said. 'That is somewhere between heaven and hell. It is difficult to argue, that it's not dead.' But Gordon Brown was more concerned with his 'embarrassing reprimand'. The Commission had told him to cut the 'excessive' budget deficit over the next year to below 3 per cent, from the current 3.3 per cent.[11]

Meanwhile, David Cameron was putting together his broader policy on 'Europe'. His party, he thought – perhaps naïvely – would be 'genuinely Eurosceptic', not seeking to leave the EU altogether but arguing consistently and cogently for reform. Integration had gone too far. Brussels was too bureaucratic and Britain needed greater protections. And far from rejecting referendums on future treaties, he felt 'the public should have its say'. From that, it 'followed logically', that Conservatives could not continue to sit as part of the 'federalist' European People's Party (EPP) group in the European Parliament.[12] Tory MEPs, after the next European elections, had to pull out of the EPP.[13]

---

[7] *Deutsche Welle*, 10 January 2006, 'Austria set to revive EU constitution'; BBC News, 9 January 2005, 'Austria sees hope for EU treaty'.

[8] *Euractiv*, 12 January 2006, 'Germany rejects Chirac Constitution proposal'.

[9] *Financial Times*, 12 January 2006, 'Sarkozy proposes slimmer version of EU treaty'.

[10] *Daily Telegraph*, 12 January 2006, 'EU constitution is dead, says Dutch minister'.

[11] *Independent*, 12 January 2006, 'EU tells Brown to cut "excessive" budget deficit to below 3 percent'.

[12] Cameron, David (2019), *For the Record* (London: William Collins), p. 84.

[13] *Daily Telegraph*, 13 January 2006, 'Cameron threat to sack pro-Euro Tory MEPs'.

Towards the end of the month, the Austrian presidency launched a two-day 'Sound of Europe' conference in Salzburg, to 'motivate and stimulate' a debate that could lead to resurrecting parts of the constitution. The public were excluded, because of 'shortage of space'.[14] This did not stop Finland announcing that it was delaying formal ratification, seen as a particular blow because the Finns were due to take over the Council presidency in July. Prime Minister Matti Vanhanen said the constitution might have to be changed if it was ever to come into force.[15]

In early February, Blair was in a reflective mood, speaking to an invited audience at St Antony's College, Oxford. But it was not the sort of 'reflection' that Barroso might have wanted. Of the constitution, he said:

> We spent two or three years in an intense institutional debate. Giscard, with characteristic brilliance, negotiated a solution. There was only one drawback. Apart from better rules of internal governance, no-one in Europe knew what it was meant to solve. As the problems of the citizen grew ever more pressing, instead of bold policy reform and decisive change, we locked ourselves in a room at the top of the tower and debated things no ordinary citizen could understand. And yet I remind you the Constitution was launched under the title of 'Bringing Europe closer to its citizens'.[16]

This was the document that, less than 18 months previously, Blair had proclaimed represented a 'solemn obligation' for the British government.[17] That he was criticising it, only months after endorsing it in the Labour election manifesto, did not go unnoticed.[18] When the Tories had argued that the constitution was bad for democracy and jobs, Blair had called Michael Howard, then leader, 'gutless' and accused him of pandering to UKIP.[19] At least Blair finally had something in common with French politicians. They too were slowly waking up to how little they knew about EU affairs.[20]

---

[14] *Financial Times*, 26 January 2006, 'Salzburg meeting to examine future of the EU'.
[15] *Financial Times*, 29 January 2006, 'Finns dash hopes for EU treaty'.
[16] Tony Blair, 2 February 2006, Annual European Studies Centre Lecture.
[17] *Independent*, 29 October 2004, op. cit.
[18] The 2005 manifesto had said: 'The new Constitutional Treaty ensures the new Europe can work effectively, and that Britain keeps control of key national interests like foreign policy, taxation, social security and defence. The Treaty sets out what the EU can do and what it cannot. It strengthens the voice of national parliaments and governments in EU affairs. It is a good treaty for Britain and for the new Europe. We will put it to the British people in a referendum and campaign wholeheartedly for a "Yes" vote to keep Britain a leading nation in Europe' (pp. 83–84).
[19] *Daily Telegraph*, 3 February 2006, 'Euro constitution did not address needs of citizens, Blair admits'.
[20] *Euractiv*, 3 February 2006, 'French politicians try to catch up with "Brussels"'.

If the British prime minister was having second thoughts, Barroso was fulfilling his role as keeper of the flame. Speaking in Pittsburgh, USA, he acknowledged that the previous year had not been 'a highlight in Europe's half-century history of integration'. A 'lot of energy' had been spent discussing why voters had rejected the constitution, and how it could be salvaged. And, with that, he was 'convinced that by taking effective action in the areas that matter to Europe's citizens, we will generate the support and consensus we need to solve the institutional issues later'.[21]

In the UK, hardly any 'action' was reported. Apart from the occasional 'Euro-silly' or 'daft' EU regulation story in the press, publicity on 'Europe' was almost completely absent. Any sense of a 'national debate' was entirely missing. The only issue of any significance to emerge, and then briefly, came towards the end of April. Then, the nation learned that, since the 'big bang' enlargement, 3.5 million eastern and central Europeans had visited Britain. By far the largest number – 1.7 million – had come from Poland. With the forthcoming accessions, 41,000 Romanians and 15,000 Bulgarians might arrive in the first year.[22] Later, the number was put at 300,000, by the end of 2008.[23] To the chagrin of anti-EU groups, such migrant workers were filling jobs that indigenous Brits would not do, and for much lower wages.[24]

Only Britain, Ireland and Sweden had opened their labour markets to the new entrants. Other EU members had wanted to see reduced the huge differences in standards of living, such as between Austria and Slovakia. France, Germany and Austria were keeping barriers intact. But Finland, Spain and Portugal were relaxing theirs, as would Greece. Italy had increased its quota for foreign workers, while the Netherlands had postponed a decision until the end of 2006.[25]

Coming up in May was another issue that had British Eurosceptics on high alert for what they saw as a classic example of the UK's own version of *engrenage*: having opted out of the 'sensitive' issue of cross-border police and judicial co-operation in Europe, Blair was now mooting relinquishing veto rights in that area.[26]

---

[21] José Manuel Barroso, President of the European Commission 'From Pittsburgh to Lisbon: reform in times of change', University of Pittsburgh, 10 February 2006.
[22] *Independent*, 24 April 2006, 'Britain opens its doors to 3.5 million visitors from eastern Europe'.
[23] *Daily Telegraph*, 15 May 2006, 'Bigger EU "may bring 300,000 workers to Britain"'.
[24] *Independent*, 30 April 2006, 'Employers prefer workers from new EU states to "lazy" Britons'.
[25] BBC News, 1 May 2006, 'EU split over easing job access'.
[26] *Daily Telegraph*, 6 May 2006, 'Britain may give up EU veto on justice matters'.

DELIVERING RESULTS FOR EUROPE

By now, the official 'period of reflection' was about to draw to a close. Seven months had passed since the publication of the Commission's 'Plan-D'. That occasioned a speech by Barroso, when he asserted that people were asking for 'more Europe' in order to combat terrorism and organised crime. For this reason, he wanted the European Council to 'exploit to the full the headroom available to them under the present Treaties'. It should take over a large number of the decisions in the fields of justice, freedom and security. These, Barroso said, could be dealt with more effectively at European level than at national level.[27]

As for 'Plan-D', the Commission had concluded that 'delivery failures' were the main cause of the EU's 'legitimacy crisis'.[28] Its response was a Communication entitled: 'A Citizens' Agenda – Delivering Results for Europe'. Citizens' expectations of the EU had grown over 50 years ... the Constitutional Treaty was intended to help bridge the gap, but citizens wanted the EU to function effectively, now. The debates held under Plan-D had shown a strong wish by Europe's citizens for more EU action in many areas: 'creating jobs, managing globalisation, fighting terrorism and organised crime, promoting sustainable development and solidarity'.[29]

For opponents of the constitution, the BBC reported, 'this will set alarm bells ringing. They are on the alert for any sign of "cherry-picking": evidence that the Commission is trying to implement parts of the draft constitution by the back door'.[30] But, for the moment, there was only that back door. The prevailing view in Brussels was that no serious decisions on the constitution could be taken until after Dutch and French elections in the spring. Barroso's challenge was to prove the EU was not paralysed in the meantime.[31] In another speech, this one in Brussels, his refrain was once again 'more Europe'. People knew that the 'efficient answer' to the challenges they faced was 'the European answer'.[32]

Now it was Merkel's turn. 'We have to realise that Europe is not very popular among Europeans,' she told the Bundestag. But her idea of putting 'the citizens first' was to ignore their rejection of the constitution and work to promote it. She also made an allusion to negotiations with Turkey, pointing

[27] José Manuel Barroso, *Strengthening a Citizen's Europe*, 9 May Celebrations Bélem Cultural Centre, 8 May 2006.
[28] *Euractiv*, 10 May 2006, '"Citizens" agenda" to move EU from reflection to delivery'.
[29] European Commission, Brussels, 10 May 2006, COM(2006) 211 final.
[30] BBC News, 8 May 2006, 'Euro-constitution makes a comeback'.
[31] *Financial Times*, 10 May 2006, 'Barroso calls for less talk and more action'.
[32] José Manuel Barroso, 'A Citizen's Agenda: Delivering Results for Europe', Press Conference, Brussels, 10 May 2006.

to battles to come. Expansion could not be a 'one-way street'. Alternatives to full membership were needed. Before taking over as chancellor, she had advocated a 'privileged partnership' status for Ankara, warning that full membership for the largely Muslim country could prove too heavy a burden for the Union.[33]

Finnish MPs gave the 'colleagues' a brief glow when they voted in favour of the constitution.[34] And ideas of what to do were firming up. First, the member state foreign ministers decided that there was little immediate hope of a re-launch.[35] Then, almost as if by osmosis, the idea emerged that, rather than being scrapped, it should be rebranded. Erkki Tuomioja, the Finnish foreign minister, warming up to take over the rotating presidency in July, said: 'Everybody agrees it was a mistake to call it a constitution, so that would be a very sensible change.'[36]

In crucial areas, though, the EU was going ahead as if the constitution had never hit the buffers. A proposal for an EU diplomatic service was secreted onto the agenda of the June European Council.[37] A pre-Council bilateral between Merkel and Chirac brought an agreement on fresh solutions to the crisis, and a European Parliament resolution set its position. This warned against 'any attempts to unravel the global compromise achieved' and opposed 'the piecemeal implementation of parts of the constitutional package deal'.[38] The scene was thus set for the Council meeting.

By contrast to the heady days of the previous December, this was a muted affair. The leaders were allowed to air their views: Britain wanted the smallest possible treaty, in the hope that it would be so innocuous that it did not have to be put to a referendum; the Netherlands was 'allergic to a Constitution'; and France's preference was for something that 'wasn't called a constitution'. A UK official agreed. 'We don't like the "C" word,' he said. On the other hand, the 16 countries that had already ratified the treaty wanted to save as much of it as possible.

Romano Prodi, newly elected as Italian prime minister, had become a vocal supporter of the original text. But the immediate future was pre-ordained, as he explained: 'The real discussions on the Constitution can only start under the German presidency and after French elections.' In the

---

[33] *Deutsche Welle*, 11 May 2006, 'Merkel makes case for EU constitution'.
[34] CNN International, 12 May 2006, 'Finn MPs approve EU constitution'.
[35] BBC News, 27 May 2006, 'EU charter "won't be revived yet"'.
[36] *Guardian*, 29 May 2006, 'Rebranding plan for failed EU constitution'.
[37] *Daily Telegraph*, 2 June 2006, 'EU consular service back on agenda'. See also Council of the European Union, General Affairs Council, Luxembourg 2006.
[38] *Deutsche Welle*, 6 June 2006, 'Germany, France vow new push for EU constitution and European Parliament', 12 June 2006, Resolution: B6-0327/2006 – Rapporteur: Jo Leinen.

interim, 'Europe' would move forward with a series of projects.[39] One of those would be the implementation of 'action plans' under the EU's Counter Terrorism Strategy.[40] This was quickly condemned as 'cherry-picking' from the moribund constitution.[41]

When Blair returned home to tell his MPs that there was 'no consensus on how to proceed', a triumphant Cameron demanded that the 'constitution should be declared null and void'. Although the prime minister had repeatedly stressed that the constitution was essential to make enlargement work, *Die Welt* had said that 'the last 12 months have shown that Europe can live without a constitution', he pointed out.[42]

EUROPE OFF THE AGENDA

With that, except for the occasional cameo appearance, 'Europe' was off the agenda in the UK, out of sight and mind. This was hardly surprising. Unlike other member states, the UK was heavily engaged in a vicious insurgency in southern Iraq, and had recently committed forces to Afghanistan. Troops were badly equipped for both theatres and, by the early summer, more than a quarter of the 84 British soldiers killed in action in Iraq had died patrolling in poorly protected 'Snatch' Land Rovers.[43]

In terms of land warfare equipment procurement, there was a suspicion – borne out by observation – that the MoD was committed to a 'Europe first' policy, buying expensive, European-made equipment specifically geared to the demands of the European Rapid Reaction Force, all within the context of the Helsinki goals. But, when the army – grudgingly – was forced to re-equip with protected patrol vehicles and other kit more suitable for counter-insurgency, much of it American-made, the doctrine, structure and the equipment of the British Army began substantially to diverge from European norms. The ghost of Saddam, together with the very real presence of the Taliban, were proving to be the new disintegrators.[44]

Although by the standards of past wars, casualties were relatively low, new procedures required fallen soldiers' bodies to be repatriated and their deaths to be investigated by Coroner's Courts. In publicity terms, this meant that every soldier, in effect, died three times: the actual incident;

[39] *Financial Times*, 15 June 2006, 'EU's divisive treaty put on hold'; *Deutsche Welle*, 16 June 2006, 'EU seeks extra time to keep constitution in play'; *Euractiv*, 16 June 2006, 'EU leaders agree to keep on reflecting'; and others.
[40] 'Presidency Conclusions', 15–16 June 2006, Brussels European Council.
[41] *Daily Telegraph*, 18 June 2006, 'EU ignores constitution vote to launch anti-terror squad'.
[42] HC Deb, 19 June 2006, Vol. 447, cc1067 and 1069.
[43] *Sunday Telegraph*, 25 June 2006, 'Christopher Booker's Notebook'.
[44] Richard North (2009), *Ministry of Defeat* (London: Continuum UK).

the repatriation ceremony; and the inquest. Combined with the steady drumbeat of stories about 'inadequate kit', and the deteriorating military position, this consigned 'Europe' to invisibility.

As for Barroso's 'more Europe', when Directive 2002/95/EC 'on the restriction of the use of certain hazardous substances in electrical and electronic equipment' came into force in 1 July in the UK, banning or restricting the use of low-melting-point solder, there were many who would have welcomed considerably less. The law was said to be causing chaos and could hike consumer prices by 5 per cent.[45] Such sentiment could only intensify when a leaked Home Office report disclosed that the rising number of immigrants from eastern Europe posed 'huge problems for public services and community relations', to such an extent that every government department had been told to draw up contingency plans to deal with them.[46]

When France only managed to contribute 200 troops to a UN peacekeeping force for south Lebanon, 'new Europe' seemed something of a busted flush.[47] Few in Britain were taking notice of the future president, Nicolas Sarkozy, who in his run-up campaign for the French presidency demanded a 'mini-treaty' designed to 'burst the lock' on more efficient institutions.[48] There was far more interest in the Conservative's youthful new leader, who, at the party conference in Bournemouth, warned that the party was alienating voters by 'banging on about Europe'.[49] Henceforth, such talk was not encouraged.

Merkel seemed more interested in what 'Europe' shouldn't be doing. She made this clear by declaring that the EU did not intend to admit new members 'in the foreseeable future'. No one was in any doubt that she was referring to Turkey.[50] And one thing the EU was definitely not doing was fining Germany for exceeding the deficit criteria. Its deficit was projected to be 2.6 per cent of GDP or lower in the year and the Commission had decided officially to suspend disciplinary proceedings.[51]

In October, Merkel met Barroso to plan for the EU presidency, telling him she was 'firmly convinced' of the need for a constitution and rejecting Dutch calls for a stripped-down text. 'We'll need the treaty before the next

[45] *Daily Telegraph*, 1 July 2006, 'EU ruling on poison metals to raise cost of electrical goods'.
[46] *Daily Telegraph*, 31 July 2006, 'Whitehall alert at EU migrant influx'.
[47] *Daily Telegraph*, 21 August 2006, 'France calls EU summit on troops for UN'.
[48] *Guardian*, 9 September 2006, 'French frontrunner rocks Europe's boat'.
[49] BBC News, 1 October 2006, 'Cameron places focus on optimism'.
[50] *Deutsche Welle*, 7 October 2006, 'Merkel: EU's door closing for near future'.
[51] *Deutsche Welle*, 10 October 2006, 'EU rules out fines against Germany for deficit'.

European elections,' she said. 'And we'll get down to it ambitiously.'[52] Days later, Barroso was arguing that the use of the word 'constitution' had set it up as a hostage to fortune. 'Let us be clear about the label which should be attached to further institutional reform,' he said. 'What Europe needs is a capacity to act.'[53] In May, Jack Straw had been replaced as foreign secretary by Margaret Beckett, the first woman to hold the post. Responding to Barroso, she dismissed the 'grandiose project' of the constitution as a failure.[54] But neither he nor Merkel were listening. In fact, plans had already been settled.

Wilhelm Schönfelder – Germany's ambassador to the EU – spelt them out. Attempts to revive the text, he said, had to work: 'Everyone knows if we don't succeed this time, this thing will be dead.' But there would not be another convention. Instead, negotiations would be handled only by national capitals. 'This can only be solved at the highest political level,' he warned. There would be a 'very short' intergovernmental conference under the Portuguese presidency in the second half of 2007, leaving a year for the new text to be ratified in time for the European Parliament elections.[55]

That was for the future. For Merkel, the end of a lacklustre year brought a small compensation. The EU froze Turkish entry talks, punishment for Ankara's failure to open up ports and airports to trade with Cyprus, while the European Council tightened up the accession criteria for new members.[56]

ANOTHER YEAR, ANOTHER BATTLE

For the European Union, 2007 was always going to be different. It was the fiftieth anniversary of the Treaty of Rome, and the scriptures would need to be honoured. Already, according to the German government, a review of the past 50 years revealed 'an unprecedented success story'.[57]

Before the honours, there were the battles. Now holding the rotating presidency, Merkel lost little time setting out her stall with a 35-page presidency programme entitled 'Europe – succeeding together'. In this, the ratification process had only 'faltered' and the presidency was set to explore 'how to continue the EU reform process'.[58] Slowly, carefully, the constitution was being transformed into a 'reform' treaty. Addressing the European

[52] *Deutsche Welle*, 11 October 2006, 'Germany wants a clear roadmap for EU constitution'.
[53] *Guardian*, 16 October 2006, 'Barroso calls for EU to move beyond constitution debacle'.
[54] *Guardian*, Wednesday 18 October 2006, 'EU constitution a grandiose project that failed, says Beckett'.
[55] *Politico*, 12 December 2006, 'Top German diplomat sees deal on treaty by end 2007'.
[56] 'Presidency Conclusions', Brussels European Council, 14–15 December.
[57] Federal Government of Germany, 'Europe – succeeding together', Presidency Programme, 1 January to 30 June 2007.
[58] Ibid.

Parliament in Strasbourg on 17 January, the German chancellor told MEPs: 'The period of reflection is over. Until June, we now have to come to new decisions.'[59] *The Times* thought she had 'boldly linked her own reputation as a European stateswoman to a successful resuscitation of the controversial EU constitution', with a declaration: 'failure would be an historic let-down'.[60]

Inevitably, that put Britain 'on a collision course with Germany'. British negotiators were said to be ready to insist that any future EU treaty was light enough to avoid triggering a referendum.[61] Thus, Blair and Gordon Brown both – the latter in six months' time to take up the mantle as prime minister – were determined to block new treaty changes unless they got a commitment that there would be no revival of the constitution. They were anxious to avoid it dominating British politics in the run-up to the next election.[62]

Poland was another potential trouble-maker. It had categorically refused to adopt the current constitution on the grounds that the revised voting system would undermine its influence in the EU. Foreign minister Anna Fotyga suggested that the best solution was to draft a new treaty altogether.[63] Shaping up for a stiff fight were the so-called 'Friends of the Constitution' – the 18 member states that had already ratified it. They wanted to see the current text kept. One of their number, Spanish foreign minister Miguel Ángel Moratinos, said: 'It is preferable to come at the present crisis in the Union with a daring proposal rather than a minimal one.'[64]

Spring brought with it the first European Council of the year, on 8–9 March, the presidential conclusions of which enigmatically refrained from mentioning the constitution. The main focus of the Council was climate change, the EU making 'a firm independent commitment to achieve at least a 20 per cent reduction of greenhouse gas emissions by 2020 compared to 1990'.[65] But the 'not-the-constitution' was discussed at the pre-Council dinner. Up to now, the German presidency had been keeping its consultations behind closed doors. Now Merkel wanted to 'reach out' to citizens with a 'Berlin Declaration', to coincide with the Community's fiftieth birthday celebrations on 25 March. The statement, the leaders were told, was likely

[59] *Euractiv*, 18 January 2007, 'Merkel wants EU Constitution deal by 2009'.
[60] 17 January 2007.
[61] *Daily Telegraph*, 18 January 2007, 'Merkel faces clash on EU constitution'.
[62] *The Times*, 1 February 2007, 'Forget constitution or we veto all plans, Britain tells the EU'.
[63] *Euractiv*, 19 January 2007, 'Merkel's EU Constitution plans face opposition'.
[64] *Euractiv*, 29 January 2007, 'Friends of the Constitution' want "maxi-EU Treaty"'.
[65] 'Presidency Conclusions', 8–9 March 2007, Brussels European Council.

to refer to the need for an 'institutional settlement'.[66] Following that, the German presidency wanted a new treaty agreed by February 2008.[67]

Come the day, there was no mention of the 'institutional settlement'. All the two-page document could manage was the somewhat tendentious assertion, signed by Merkel, Barroso and European Parliament president, Hans-Gert Pöttering, that: 'we are united in our aim of placing the European Union on a renewed common basis before the European Parliament elections in 2009'. The trio signed off with the slogan: 'For we know, Europe is our Common Future.'[68] This was the only text to which all the member states could agree, the very same who were shortly expected to agree a lengthy treaty.[69]

Their immediate duty done, the leaders consoled themselves with an 'Organic-Teutonic' banquet, comprising braised ox, beer and cake, in brilliant sunshine in Berlin. German-born Pope Benedict XVI, angry that the declaration had made no reference to the continent's Christian roots, damned them for bringing about in the EU 'a singular form of apostasy, not so much from God as from itself'.[70] Out on the streets, anti-globalisation protesters celebrated by setting fire to a 'Europe Information' caravan.[71]

In April, Blair and Dutch prime minister Jan Peter Balkenende joined forces in a press conference in London to reject the idea of a new constitution and demand a slimmed-down treaty confined to institutional changes. Blair insisted this was not just about dropping the 'constitutional' label. 'It is important we go back to the idea of a conventional treaty where the idea is to make Europe more effective,' he said. Balkenende added: 'If we do not have the characteristics of a constitution, that is also relevant to the question of do you have a referendum or not.'[72]

Meanwhile, Germany was holding more 'closed-door' talks, where the real decisions were being made. Piece by piece, a new treaty was being assembled. Dropping the 'constitution' label had been agreed, although the institutional changes proposed were to be preserved, including the enlargement criteria. The treaty would also underline the EU's social dimension and refer to specific policies such as energy and climate change.[73]

[66] *Daily Telegraph*, 9 March 2007, 'Merkel's push for EU constitution'.
[67] *Euractiv*, 13 March 2007, 'Merkel drops "Constitution" label at EU summit'.
[68] Declaration on the occasion of the 50th anniversary of the signature of the Treaties of Rome.
[69] *Irish Times*, 23 March 2007, 'No explicit reference to constitution in Berlin Declaration'.
[70] *Guardian*, 26 March 2007, 'As the EU turns 50, Pope says it's on path to oblivion'.
[71] *Daily Telegraph*, 25 March 2007, 'Smiles but EU's party can't hide divisions'.
[72] *Euractiv*, 17 April 2007, 'UK and Netherlands back slimmed-down EU Treaty'.
[73] *Euractiv*, 26 April 2007, 'Barroso backs down on informal EU Treaty "Summit"'.

A leaked letter from Merkel to member states clarified her strategy. Work was confined to making 'presentational changes'; 'different terminology' was being used without changing 'the legal substance'. 'Every effort will have to be made to restrict changes to what is absolutely necessary to reach an overall agreement and ensure ratification', she wrote.[74] Blair argued that, 'If it's not a constitutional treaty, so that it alters the basic relationship between Europe and the member states, then there isn't the same case for a referendum.'[75]

The turn of the month saw Sarkozy win the presidential election, soon to take over as French leader.[76] Chirac was to exit to a 21-gun salute on 16 May. Before that, on 10 May, Blair resigned as leader of the Labour Party, standing down as prime minister on 27 June. Work on the treaty went on. The influential MEP Jo Leinen proposed splitting it, producing a Fundamental Treaty, consisting of 70 articles, based on part I of the Constitutional Treaty, and a Treaty on the EU's policies, based on part III of the EU constitution. He would then add protocols on climate change and Social Europe.[77] This would be the treaty's final shape.

A POISONED CHALICE

It was now evident that the new treaty was being handled at two levels. The public was given the theatre but, behind the scenes, the real work was going on. To ensure continuity beyond the German presidency, Merkel adopted the 'troika' structure used by the Community in Yugoslavia, comprising the presidency-trio of herself, Portugal's prime minister José Sócrates and Slovenia's Janez Janša, as well as Hans-Gert Pöttering and Barroso. Styled as a 'mini-summit', it published neither agendas nor formal conclusions, meeting in Sintra, Portugal, on 12–13 May.[78]

'New broom' Sarkozy made his contribution to the theatre, flying to Germany just hours after being sworn in as the new president, where he announced he was going to end the EU's 'paralysis'.[79] By stark contrast, the soon-to-be-departed Tony Blair seemed set on creating a paralysis of his very own, albeit initially confined to British politics. He believed that, instead of attempting to revive the original wide-ranging constitution, member states should simply agree on a series of amendments. Then, no referendum would be necessary.[80]

---

[74] *Daily Mail*, 20 April 2007, 'Blair "showing his contempt for voters" over new EU treaty'.
[75] *Guardian*, 20 April 2007, 'Blair rules out referendum on new EU treaty'.
[76] *Euractiv*, 7 May 2007, 'European leaders react to Sarkozy's election'.
[77] *Euractiv*, 11 May 2007, 'Steinmeier: June summit will be "solidarity test"'.
[78] *Deutsche Welle*, 12 May 2007, 'Merkel calls for EU constitution push at mini summit'.
[79] *Daily Telegraph*, 17 May 2007, 'I will fight EU paralysis and domestic inertia'.
[80] *Euractiv*, 8 June 2007, 'Brown, Blair and the Constitutional Treaty'.

THE GREAT DECEPTION

Although it was increasingly obvious that the majority of member states had something far more ambitious in mind, Blair was convinced that the new work could be passed off as an amending treaty. Worse still, he had been secretly conducting talks on the margins of the G8 summit in Germany, where he had met Sarkozy. Having agreed the framework for the new treaty, he was now presenting his successor, Gordon Brown, with a poisoned chalice. David Cameron pointed to things to come: 'Any treaty that is about the transfer of powers to the EU must be put to the country in a referendum,' he declared.[81]

COUNTDOWN TO 'REFORM'

By now, the countdown to the European Council had started, scheduled for Brussels on 21–22 June. Even the BBC had become aware that Merkel's plan was to rename the constitution and repackage it. It had seen a report by German officials warning that this 'major concession' would only be made if the 'substance' of the original constitution was preserved.[82] But, with an IGC due to follow shortly after the Council, the starting gun had been fired for diverse member states to run their own agendas for domestic consumption. First in the queue was Polish president Lech Kaczyński, who was promoting his version of the Council voting system as 'worth dying for'. After a meeting with the president and his twin brother, Prime Minister Jarosław Kaczyński, Angela Merkel did not rush to disagree.[83]

Next in line to demonstrate his credentials was Blair, setting out his 'red lines' amid the fiction that he was dealing with a simple amending treaty. Conservative MEP Timothy Kirkhope had the measure of the man: 'Tony Blair says he won't sign up to anything in Brussels this week that would necessitate a referendum' he said, then adding: 'On past form, he cannot be trusted to defend the national interest and the British people must therefore be the final judge if the EU acquires new competences.'[84] But that was the very last thing Blair intended to allow: no sooner had he set out his 'red lines' than reports came in that he was ready to give them up – not least Britain's right of veto over 52 areas of EU policy.[85]

As expected, the European Council convened an IGC, calling for it to open before the end of July. It was asked to:

[81] *Sunday Telegraph*, 10 June 2007, 'Dilemma for Brown as Blair plans EU deal'.
[82] BBC News, 14 June 2007, 'EU constitution "can be simple"'.
[83] BBC News, 16 June 2007, 'Merkel urges EU treaty compromise'.
[84] *Euractiv*, 19 June 2007, 'UK hardens stance on Treaty negotiations'.
[85] *Daily Telegraph*, 21 June 2007, 'Blair to surrender British vetoes at EU summit'.

draw up a Treaty (hereinafter called the 'Reform Treaty') amending the existing Treaties with a view to enhancing the efficiency and democratic legitimacy of the enlarged Union, as well as the coherence of its external action. The constitutional concept, which consisted in repealing all existing Treaties and replacing them by a single text called 'Constitution', is abandoned.[86]

The 32-page mandate, attached to the presidential conclusions, was to provide the 'exclusive basis' for the new treaty. Its scope effectively meant that the normal negotiation process had been almost wholly concluded before the IGC opened on 23 July 2007, under the Portuguese presidency. On that same day, the presidency published the first draft of the treaty. The process was a done deal, over before it had even started. That much was evident in the European Council, where EU leaders 'expressed measured approval of a draft treaty to reform EU systems'. For an EU institution to agree its own treaty was akin to pulling oneself up by one's shoelaces – a travesty of international treaty law. But that did not stop the BBC reporting that the treaty was to be 'finalised later this year' and to 'come into force in mid-2009'.[87] At the conclusion of the Council, Barroso paid tribute to Angela Merkel, as well he might, and handed her a bunch of flowers.

In the following days, Blair sought to confuse the issue by talking of 'red lines' and the legal status of the Charter of Fundamental Rights, which was to be included in the treaty.[88] In the House of Commons, though, Cameron quoted Blair himself, saying of the constitution, 'What you can't do is have a situation where you get a rejection of the treaty and then you just bring it back with a few amendments and say we will have another go.' Yet, Cameron asserted: 'Is that not exactly what he has done? That was a promise clearly made and a promise clearly broken.'[89] Blair could only perpetuate the deceit embedded in the presidency conclusions: 'The constitutional concept ... is abandoned.'

Cameron, conscious that Blair only had two days left in office, addressed himself to his replacement, 'one who has promised, unlike his predecessor, to be humble, to be a servant of the people and to listen'. If he 'really believes in power to the people', Cameron argued, 'he must hold a referendum and let the people decide'.[90] On 27 June 2007, Blair stood down after ten years

---

[86] Presidential Conclusions, 21–22 June 2007, Brussels European Council.
[87] BBC News, 23 June 2007, 'EU chiefs "satisfied" with treaty'.
[88] *Daily Telegraph*, 26 June 2007, 'Blair's EU safeguards "may not be watertight"'.
[89] HC Debates, 25 June 2007, Vol. 462, col. 23.
[90] Op. cit., col. 25.

in the only job in government he had ever had. He also resigned as an MP, ready to take up a new role as an international envoy to the Middle East. Gordon Brown, after a decade in the shadows, took over, bequeathed a poisoned chalice in the name of another European treaty.

Even as Blair had been addressing MPs, European Parliament president, Hans-Gert Pöttering – who had been working with Merkel's 'troika' on the new treaty – told the Council of Europe that while a proposed anthem and flag had been dropped, 'the substance of the constitution has been retained'.[91] He was later to claim that the treaty had been designed to 'keep the advances' of the old constitution 'that we would not have dared present directly'.[92] Barroso, meanwhile, added fuel to the fire by proclaiming: 'We have the dimensions of an empire.'[93]

Before the treaty draft had even been published, Jean-Claude Juncker, Luxembourg's premier, spoke to the Belgian edition of Le Soir, supporting public debate on the treaty – except in Britain. 'I am astonished at those who are afraid of the people: one can always explain that what is in the interest of Europe is in the interests of our countries,' he said, adding: 'Britain is different. Of course, there will be transfers of sovereignty. But would I be intelligent to draw the attention of public opinion to this fact?'[94]

Nevertheless, it was former Italian prime minister, Giuliano Amato, who really gave the game away. Of the new treaty, he said, 'EU leaders had decided that the document should be "unreadable". Thus, the UK prime minister could go to the Commons and say, 'Look, you see, it's absolutely unreadable, it's the typical Brussels treaty, nothing new, no need for a referendum,' On the other hand, he said, 'Should you succeed in understanding it there might be some reason for a referendum, because it would mean that there is something new.'[95]

What was described by some as a 'playful observation' spoke to a greater truth,[96] even more so when the full 287-page version of the treaty was finally published on 3 December, by which time it was known as the Treaty of Lisbon.[97] It was indeed 'unreadable', comprising thousands of amendments rather than a finished document. Once the current treaties had been

---

[91] Daily Telegraph, op. cit.

[92] Daily Telegraph, 28 July 2007, 'Brown's EU fraud exposed by letter'.

[93] Daily Telegraph, 11 July 2007, 'Barroso hails the European "empire"'.

[94] Daily Telegraph, 3 July 2007, 'Don't tell British about the EU treaty'.

[95] Daily Telegraph, 17 July 2007, 'EU banks on "unreadable" treaty'.

[96] Described by Hugo Brady, a research fellow at the Centre for European Reform, 'Of Mice, men and the language of EU reform', 18 July 2007.

[97] Treaty of Lisbon amending the Treaty on European Union and the Treaty establishing the European Community.

amended by this text, there was no doubt that the end product was very little different from the original constitution.

So said the House of Commons European scrutiny committee, which described it as 'substantially equivalent'.[98] But the most powerful figure to attest to the similarity was Valéry Giscard d'Estaing, architect of the original. The difference is one of approach, rather than content, he said. 'In terms of content, the proposed institutional reforms – the only ones which mattered to the drafting Convention – are all to be found in the Treaty of Lisbon. They have merely been ordered differently and split up between previous treaties.'[99]

The day after the treaty draft had been first published, William Hague, then shadow foreign secretary, delivered a long speech conveying his party's belief that the treaty should not be ratified without a referendum.[100] He was joined by Labour MP Gisela Stuart, the former Praesidium member. 'One of Tony Blair's last acts was to renege on a promise and it is almost unbelievable that one of Gordon Brown's first has been to do the same', she wrote in a national newspaper. 'There is still time for Gordon Brown to put this right.' Up to forty rebel Labour MPs were of like mind.[101] Two major trade unions, the GMB and RMT, also demanded a referendum, but Brown was unmoved. 'The proper way to discuss this is through detailed discussion in the House of Commons and the House of Lords,' he asserted, adding that he was confident Parliament would pass the treaty.[102]

A CAST-IRON GUARANTEE

Europe-wide, politicians were closing ranks. In Holland, the cabinet refused to hold a referendum, after reports indicated the public would vote against the new treaty. Prime Minister Balkenende, so staunch the first time around, argued that there were no constitutional changes. 'This is a normal change of treaty and only needs a normal procedure to approve it,' he said.[103] Sarkozy held the line, as did Barroso. He told Brown during a meeting in Downing Street, just a week prior to final summit agreeing the treaty: 'It's not a constitution. I have been a constitution lawyer teaching in Geneva and Washington.'[104]

---

[98] BBC News, 9 October 2007, 'EU treaty "same as Constitution"'.
[99] *Independent*, 30 October 2007, 'Valéry Giscard d'Estaing: the EU Treaty is the same as the Constitution'.
[100] William Hague, 'The new EU treaty: the case for a referendum', *Policy Exchange*, 24 July 2007.
[101] *Sunday Telegraph*, 27 July 2007, 'Keep EU referendum promise, MPs tell Brown'.
[102] BBC News, 23 August 2007, 'Brown rejects union EU vote call'.
[103] BBC News, 21 September 2007, 'Dutch cabinet rules out EU vote'.
[104] *Guardian*, 11 October 2007, 'Barroso backs Brown over EU treaty'.

The *Sun*, on 24 September, produced a graphic showing a smirking Gordon Brown in Churchillian garb delivering an 'old-fashioned' two-finger salute. The text read: 'Europe. Never have so few decided so much for so many.' Its '*Sun* says' piece declared: 'Gordon Brown is about to sign an EU Constitution that would change for ever the way we are governed', the 'Greatest threat since WW2'. Two days later, in the same newspaper, David Cameron – referring to the 'two-finger salute' – wrote in unequivocal terms: 'Today, I will give this cast-iron guarantee: If I become PM, a Conservative government will hold a referendum on any EU treaty that emerges from these negotiations.'

There was strong public support for this stance. The *Sun* had run a poll showing that a 'massive 81 per cent' wanted a referendum and two-thirds – 64 per cent – believed Brown was going back on earlier promises. Later, a YouGov poll recorded 69 per cent in favour. But Brown, a man who had come to the highest office without the benefit of a general election, was not to be deflected by mere public opinion. Before leaving for Lisbon to attend the final IGC summit, he wrote to Portuguese leader José Sócrates, drawing a line under the discussion. 'The Reform Treaty sets the framework to ensure that an enlarged EU can function well', he wrote. 'This is the right time to bring to an end this prolonged period of inward-looking institutional debate.' Hague complained: 'He has absolutely no democratic mandate to agree to this treaty.'[105]

This, of course, had no immediate impact. Gathered in Lisbon on 19 October, EU leaders agreed the final draft, putting it to bed after midnight once last-minute objections from Italy and Poland had been overcome.[106] There were smiles all around, back-slapping and even kisses.[107]

Just under a month later, the leaders attended a formal signing ceremony at the ornate Jeronimos Monastery, to the background music of Dulce Pontes, one of Portugal's most renowned singers. It was supposed to be a celebration of togetherness, but Brown turned up three hours late, claiming a 'diary clash'.[108] Hague claimed that the prime minister was 'ashamed' to sign the treaty.[109] His solo appearance was rewarded by a *Daily Express* front page with: 'Mr Bean signs away our freedom'. It was, the paper said, a 'cynical betrayal of Britain to Europe'. On a slightly more uplifting note, Portuguese premier José Sócrates declared: 'History will remember this day

[105] *Daily Telegraph*, 18 October 2007, 'Gordon Brown rules out EU treaty referendum'.
[106] BBC News, 19 October 2007, 'EU leaders agree new treaty deal'.
[107] *Der Spiegel*, 19 October 2007, 'The Lisbon coup'.
[108] *Deutsche Welle*, 13 December 2007, 'Leaders commit to EU's future by signing the Lisbon Treaty'.
[109] *The Times*, 11 December 2007, 'Gordon Brown "ashamed" to sign Lisbon Treaty, say Tories'.

as a day when new paths of hope were opened to the European ideal.' Hans-Gert Pöttering added, 'Remember, it is our solidarity that unites us.'[110]

The end of year saw the appointment of a reflection group of 'wise' people to help shape the Union's long-term future, triggering a clash between the UK and France over the possible accession of Turkey.[111] But nothing could dent the ebullience of Communications Commissioner Margot Wallström. Reviewing the year, she thought the Lisbon Treaty 'a wonderful birthday gift for the EU'. As a result, she said, 'There's more trust in its institutions. It's encouraging for those of us who work for the EU.'[112]

THE BATTLE FOR RATIFICATION

The European Council in December had called for a swift completion of national ratification processes with a view to allowing entry into force of the Lisbon Treaty on 1 January 2009.[113] Most countries were keen to comply, but the 'unknown, unknown' was the Irish Republic. It was obliged by its constitution to hold a referendum. In a slow start to the political year, the British media entertained speculation on whether Tony Blair was to take up the newly created post of president of the European Council.[114] Despite the column inches given to it, this was never going to happen.

The UK parliamentary battle for the treaty took off with a report from the Foreign Affairs select committee concluding that there was no material difference between the provisions on foreign policy in the Constitutional Treaty, which the government had made subject to approval in a referendum, and those in the Lisbon Treaty, on which a referendum was being denied. The government, it said, risked underestimating, and certainly was downplaying in public, 'the importance and potential of the new foreign policy institutions established by the Lisbon Treaty, namely the new High Representative and the European External Action Service'.[115]

This was but a warm-up to the second reading debate in the Commons on the ratification Bill, which opened on 21 January. It was the start of a five-week marathon, with Gordon Brown attracting a 'barrage of criticism' for being out of the country, receiving an honorary doctorate from the University of Delhi in India.[116] In pole position was David Miliband, the

[110] *Deutsche Welle*, op. cit.
[111] *Euractiv*, 17 December 2007, 'UK, France clash on future EU vision'.
[112] *Deutsche Welle*, 25 December 2007, 'Landmark Treaty deal EU's biggest success in 2007'.
[113] 'Presidency Conclusions', 14 December 2007, Brussels European Council.
[114] *Daily Telegraph*, 13 January 2008, 'Tony Blair fuels speculation over EU presidency'.
[115] *Daily Telegraph*, 20 January 2008, 'Tell truth on EU treaty, say MPs'.
[116] *Daily Telegraph*, 21 January 2008, 'Brown skips key EU treaty Commons debate'.

foreign secretary, whose sole justification for denying a referendum was that the new treaty did not constitute 'fundamental constitutional change'.[117]

Miliband was challenged by Malcolm Rifkind, who pointed out that when Blair had announced a referendum in 2004, 'at no time did he cite as the basis for his decision the fact that what was before us was a constitution'. From this emerged the remarkable claim from Miliband that, indeed, 'the constitution did not constitute fundamental constitutional change'.[118] Thus, although Blair had agreed a referendum despite the constitution not constituting 'fundamental constitutional change', there was to be no referendum on the Lisbon Treaty because it did not constitute fundamental constitutional change.

Parliamentarians, therefore, were confronting the reality that the government had made up its mind, without even troubling to offer a credible defence of its action. And, under the present system, there was no way anyone could force it to change. At the end of a rowdy five-hour debate, the motion to approve the Bill in principle was won by 362 votes to 224, the BBC reporting: 'Commons EU battle will continue'.[119] But, for all the sound and fury, Brussels was not going to be troubled by Westminster.

Nick Clegg, the Lib-Dem leader, argued for a referendum, saying it was time to give the country its first chance in 33 years to decide if it wanted to be in or out of the EU. 'Nobody in this country under the age of 51 has ever been asked that simple question. That includes half of all MPs,' he said.[120] Nevertheless, a motion for a referendum was defeated on 5 March, despite a rebellion by Labour MPs, after pro-EU Liberal Democrats had abstained.[121] The Times called it 'a shameful, squalid moment'.[122]

The British public and MPs were not, of course, alone in being ignored. The French parliament was doing this to perfection with its own people. On 4 February, the National Assembly voted 336 for the treaty with 52 against, the Senate by 265 to 42. All it needed was the formal assent of President Sarkozy, who had refused a referendum as being 'too risky'.[123] The formalities were completed by the 14th. Hungary, in December, had been the first to ratify. Slovenia and Malta had followed in January and Romania left it until February. Slovakia's parliament was due to follow, which made

[117] HC Debates, 21 January 2008, Vol. 470, col. 1241.
[118] Ibid., col. 1243.
[119] BBC News, 22 January 2008.
[120] Guardian, 25 February 2008, 'Clegg calls for EU referendum to end "crazy" debate'.
[121] Reuters, 5 March 2008, 'Brown defeats drive for EU treaty vote'.
[122] 7 March 2008.
[123] Deutsche Welle, 8 February 2008, 'Ignoring the public, French Parliament approves EU Treaty'.

France the fifth country to approve the treaty. Said Sarkozy: 'France is back in Europe'.[124]

Also 'in Europe' was the perennial corruption associated with the European Parliament. Late February disclosed the presence of a 'secret European Parliament report' that had uncovered 'extensive, widespread and criminal abuse' by MEPs of staff allowances worth almost £100 million a year. Few of the readers expected anything to change.[125]

March was a thin month for ratifications: only Bulgaria stepped up to the plate. Poland completed the process in early April, barring the president's signature. Late in the month, Germany's Bundestag approved the treaty by considerably more than the required two-thirds majority.[126] But there were more hurdles to come. Austria, however, managed to complete on 28 April, the treaty gaining presidential assent. A few days later, Denmark joined the club, following Royal Assent. Ireland took its first, tentative step, with its lower house, the Dáil Éireann, approving a referendum Bill. May saw the Senate approve the Bill. Portugal and Slovakia also ratified, alongside Lithuania. By then, both houses of the Czech Parliament had done the deed. The Republic now awaited a reluctant President Václav Klaus. The Irish Senate approved the referendum Bill.

THE IRISH REFERENDUM

Then, on 12 June, the Irish people rejected the treaty in their referendum by a margin of 53.4 to 46.6 per cent. The turnout was 53.1 per cent – higher than the two Nice Treaty referendums. All but ten constituencies voted 'No', with a total of 862,415 votes; 752,451 voted 'Yes'.[127]

The result should not have come as a surprise. The more committed 'No' voters had dominated the debate, while the 'Yes' campaign had difficulty mobilising the potentially large but lukewarm segment of the pro-EU electorate.[128] The week before the vote, an *Irish Times* poll had given the 'No' campaigners a lead of 35–30 per cent. Yet one thing thought to be in favour of the 'Yes' campaign was that no one knew exactly what was in the treaty. Ireland's Commissioner Charlie McCreevy estimated that, at best, 250 of Ireland's 4.2 million citizens had read the complete text.[129] Not only did he admit that he had not read the treaty, making do with a summary, but he

---

[124] BBC News, 14 February 2008, 'France ratifies EU reform treaty'.
[125] *Daily Telegraph*, 21 February 2008, '"Criminal abuse" of expenses by Euro-MPs'.
[126] *Deutsche Welle*, 24 April 2008, 'Germany's Bundestag ratifies the Treaty of Lisbon'.
[127] *Irish Times*, 13 June 2008, 'Lisbon Treaty rejected by Irish electorate'.
[128] *Irish Times*, 9 February 2008, 'Lisbon referendum debate needs more passion'.
[129] *Der Spiegel*, 10 June 2008, 'Fate of the European Union lies with Ireland'.

also said that 'no sane, sensible person' would read it either. To him, it was a 'tidying up exercise'.[130] This was a claim that was to be repeated many times, by all manner of EU apologists.

Barroso said he believed the treaty was still 'alive', but was immediately contradicted by Luxembourg's prime minister, Jean-Claude Juncker – the longest-serving leader in the EU – who said the result meant it could not enter into force in January 2009 as planned. The Irish prime minister, now Brian Cowen, admitted the vote had been a 'potential setback' for Europe. But he refused to answer questions. 'We have to absorb what happened. There is no quick fix but the government will respect the wishes of the Irish people,' he said.[131] After the immediate shock reactions, the default response did not take long to emerge. 'The Irish will have to vote again,' Sarkozy declared.[132] There were ritual protests and 'quiet fury', but that was the 'European' way. Less than 1 per cent of the EU's 490 million people would not be allowed to interfere with the dream.

Part of the ritual would be to demonstrate that the 'Noes' did not understand what they had voted for, against the presumption that 'Yes' voters had perfect knowledge. The 'ignorance' was duly established in early September via an opinion poll conducted for the Irish government. A total of 42 per cent of 'No' voters obligingly cited a lack of knowledge or understanding of what they were voting on. Some 33 per cent thought European army conscription was part of the treaty, while 34 per cent believed they would lose control over the country's abortion policy.[133] An earlier European Commission poll indicated that almost three-quarters of people had mistakenly believed the treaty could be easily renegotiated.[134]

As the way was being cleared for a re-run, the media pointed to a not-so-secret EU plan to force Ireland to vote again. French officials were said to have penned an 'explosive document' entitled 'Solution to the Irish Problem'; a timetable for a second referendum was being set for the following year. In return, the Irish would be promised concessions that would make their retreat more palatable.[135]

However, ripples from the Irish vote had been spreading. Veteran campaigner, MP Bill Cash, sought a judicial review of the ratification process, arguing that it would be unlawful for the UK government to

---

[130] *Irish Times*, 24 May 2008, 'No "sane" person would read full treaty – McCreevy'.
[131] *Guardian*, 13 June 2008, 'Irish voters reject EU treaty'.
[132] *Irish Times*, 16 July 2008, Ireland will have to vote again on Lisbon, says Sarkozy'.
[133] *Irish Times*, 10 September 2008, 'Lack of understanding main reason for Lisbon No vote'.
[134] *Independent*, 17 June 2008, 'Revealed: Why we voted "No" to Lisbon'.
[135] *Daily Mail*, 12 September 2008, 'EU begins secret drive to force Ireland to vote again on rejected Lisbon Treaty'.

continue with it. Mr Justice Collins ruled on this. It was not helpful. 'It will be for Parliament, not the court, to decide whether the Bill should be passed,' he said. Ratification was 'a matter of political not judicial decision'. Cash's case was 'totally without merit since it is an attempt to pursue a political agenda through the court'.[136] On 19 June, after a last-ditch Tory bid to delay the ratification process for four months was defeated by a margin of 93, and peers had given the Bill a third reading, Royal Assent followed and papers were deposited in Rome on 16 July.[137]

Two weeks before that, Polish president Lech Kaczyński had said he would not sign the treaty, as ratified by his parliament. 'For the moment, the question of the treaty is pointless,' he said.[138] Nor was this the only hiccup. Despite the completion of parliamentary ratification, Germany's Left Party had announced on 27 June that it intended to apply to the constitutional court to have the treaty declared unconstitutional.[139] Three days later, President Köhler's office announced that ratification had been put on hold, pending a ruling.[140] Even its best friends were prepared to admit that the ratification process was looking a bit ragged. But events on the other side of the Atlantic were about to claim attention, so serious that even the ratification crisis was swept aside, albeit temporarily.

A GREAT OPPORTUNITY FOR EUROPE

On 15 September 2008, Lehmann Brothers, the fourth-largest investment bank in the United States, filed for bankruptcy protection. It triggered a one-day drop in the Dow Jones of 4.5 per cent, at the time the largest decline since 9/11, heralding what is generally taken to be the start of a global financial crisis. Confidence collapsed, investors massively liquidated their positions and stock markets went into a tailspin. From then onwards, the EU economy entered the steepest downturn on record since the 1930s.[141] And it was to get far worse.

For all its pretensions, the EU was now a bystander in a crisis of global proportions. By early October 2008, the world's financial system was on the brink of systemic collapse and, in spite of multi-million pound bailouts, major British banks were headed the same way. Treasury officials and ministers, led by Gordon Brown, worked out a rescue package, co-ordinated

[136] BBC News, 19 June 2008, 'Court rejects EU treaty block bid'.
[137] BBC News, 17 July 2008, 'UK ratifies the EU Lisbon Treaty'.
[138] Irish Times, 1 July 2008, 'Polish president refuses to ratify Lisbon Treaty'.
[139] Deutsche Welle, 27 June 2008, 'Germany's left party takes Lisbon Treaty to Constitutional Court'.
[140] Deutsche Welle, 30 June 2008, German president suspends ratification of EU Lisbon Treaty.
[141] European Commission, 'Economic Crisis in Europe: Causes, Consequences and Responses', The European Economy, series 7, 2009.

at an international level. The government took stakes in HBOS, Lloyds TSB and RBS in return for a £37 billion injection of capital, while Barclays was recapitalised from private sources. The state was now the majority shareholder of RBS and would own 40 per cent of the new bank created by merging HBOS and Lloyds.

Most people never knew how close Britain had come to tumbling into the abyss. Whatever else the rescue of that long weekend ultimately failed to do, it successfully set an example to the world and saved the country from a total banking collapse.[142] This dramatic rescue, the details of which were only to emerge slowly, had been achieved without the direct intervention of EU officials. Nevertheless, by the time the final European Council of the year met, on 11–12 December, the world was looking a very different place from when the sun had dawned on the new year. The main business of the Council, therefore, had been to approve a 'European Economic Recovery Plan', introduced by the Commission in an attempt to stave off the recession that was set to follow the crisis. It was equivalent to about 1.5 per cent of the EU's GDP (amounting to around €200 billion) – an unthinkable intervention even months previously.[143]

The Council also reached an agreement on a comprehensive energy/climate change package, ready for the end-of-year summit at Copenhagen. And it was prepared to give guarantees to the Irish people that the new treaty did not affect taxation powers, that it did not 'prejudice the security and defence policy of Member States, including Ireland's traditional policy of neutrality', and that the Irish Constitution in relation to the right to life was not affected.[144] As for the financial crisis, Barroso was upbeat: 'This is a great opportunity for Europe', he wrote.[145]

A DOMINANT CRISIS

In January 2009, the City of London's 'Square Mile' was being described as a paranoid, shell-shocked place. Tens of thousands of jobs had gone and even the most experienced grandees had no clue about the shape of things to come.[146] There was not much less gloom in the Berlaymont either. The Commission forecast a 'deep and protracted' recession. The 16-nation eurozone would see their economies shrink by 1.9 per cent, while the

---

[142] This narrative taken from the *Observer*, 21 February 2020, 'The weekend Gordon Brown saved the banks from the abyss'.
[143] 'Presidency Conclusions', 11–12 December 2008, Brussels European Council. See also COM(2008) 800 final, 26 November 2008, *A European Economic Recovery Plan*.
[144] Ibid.
[145] Ibid.
[146] Nick Mathiason, *Observer*, 11 January 2009, 'From Big Bang to whimper: welcome to the new City'.

EU-wide contraction would be almost as bad, at 1.8 per cent. The labour market could see 3.5 million jobs disappearing.[147] German employment was particularly badly affected, with jobless totals having jumped more than expected to 8.3 per cent in January.[148]

And not only was prosperity under threat: 'peace' was looking distinctly fragile. From Riga in Latvia, Vilnius in Lithuania, Nikea in Greece and Sofia in Bulgaria, to Reykjavik in Iceland, Paris and other cities in France, as well as London and Edinburgh, demonstrators were out and about as the financial crisis fuelled civil unrest.[149] But it was in Iceland, outside the EU but in the EEA, where the first government fell as a direct result of the global economic crisis.[150]

Yet life went on. On 10 February, the German constitutional court considered the case on the Lisbon Treaty, looking at whether the treaty prejudiced the basic principles of representative democracy by undermining the power of national parliaments. Peter Gauweiler, a member of the Bundestag and one of the complainants, offered the example of a German environment minister trying to get a certain type of lightbulb banned by the Bundestag. If he failed, the minister could bring the same initiative to the EU, which could create a lightbulb ban of its own, forcing it to be incorporated into German law, despite it having been rejected by the national parliament.[151]

Having been centre-stage for so long, the Lisbon Treaty had nevertheless dropped down the agenda. The financial crisis dominated and would continue to do so for some time. As its grip had tightened back in October, the European Commission had appointed a 'high-level group' under the chairmanship of Jacques de Larosière to give advice on the future of European financial regulation and supervision. Its 86-page report was delivered on 25 February.[152] For once, this was not an across-the-board call for 'more Europe'. Instead, it looked at two alternatives: the first were '*chacun pour soi*' beggar-thy-neighbour solutions; and the second was enhanced, pragmatic, sensible European co-operation for the benefit of all to preserve an open world economy. The group favoured the latter.

Asked why he had not opted for a single pan-EU super-regulator, de Larosière, a former managing director of the IMF, admitted: 'We might

---

[147] *Deutsche Welle*, 19 January 2009, 'Brussels paints dark picture of EU economy in 2009'.
[148] *Deutsche Welle*, 29 January 2009, 'German unemployment soars as economic crisis deepens'.
[149] *Guardian*, 31 January 2009, 'Credit-crunch protests in Europe'.
[150] Reuters, 26 January 2009, 'Iceland's government collapses over financial crisis'.
[151] *Deutsche Welle*, 10 February 2009, 'EU's Lisbon Treaty hangs on German court ruling'.
[152] The High-Level Group on Financial Supervision in the EU, chaired by Jacques de Larosière, Report, Brussels, 25 February 2009.

have been accused of being unrealistic.'[153] Barroso described the report as 'balanced and rich', suggesting that it could shape EU thinking ahead of the G20 summit in April. The reference to the G20 was significant. It was a tacit recognition of the march of globalisation, in which not only trade but financial regulation had gone global. The EU in the financial sector – as with others – was no longer the primary regulator.[154]

Although de Larosière argued that Europe needed new bodies to monitor systemic risk and co-ordinate oversight of financial institutions, the G20 got there first. When it met at the beginning of April, it took one of its obscure forums and reinvented it as the Financial Stability Board (FSB).[155] Based in Basel, sharing the same facilities as the Basel Committee in the offices of the Bank of International Settlements (BIS), it worked in close collaboration with the OECD and the World Bank, to become a powerful financial policy driver and de facto global regulator.[156]

To an extent, the EU would co-ordinate its activities with these bodies, but differences created yet another source of friction. However, when a special European Council convened on 19–20 March, the leaders were talking of the need to 'reshape macroeconomic global management and the regulatory framework for financial markets'. To that effect, the Council urged the FSF (the predecessor to the FSB, soon to be replaced), the Basel Committee and Commission to 'accelerate their work and to swiftly submit appropriate recommendations'. It was to be international action first, 'complemented with a strong EU initiative'.[157]

Other stresses within the Union boiled over into a spat between Czech prime minister Mirek Topolánek, who was holding the EU chair, and the French government, which was complaining about the drift of car production to the Czech Republic. Sarkozy wanted special protection

[153] *Financial Times*, 26 February 2009, 'EU taskforce proposes tougher regulation'.
[154] Some aspects of financial regulation were already managed by the Committee on Banking Regulations and Supervisory Practices – known as the Basel Committee. It had been established by the central bank Governors of the Group of Ten countries at the end of 1974 in the aftermath of serious disturbances in international currency and banking markets. See History of the Basel Committee (website), https://www.bis.org/bcbs/history.htm.
[155] *Financial Times*, 2 April 2009, 'Financial forum emerges from shadows'.
[156] 'History of the FSB' (website), https://www.fsb.org/history-of-the-fsb/. The organisation was considerably strengthened in 2012 (see Report to the G20 Los Cabos Summit on *Strengthening FSB Capacity, Resources and Governance*, 18–19 June 2012) and on 28 January 2013, the FSB established itself as a not-for-profit association under Swiss law with its seat in Basel, Switzerland. Between 2011 and 2018, its chair was Mark Carney, Governor of the Bank of England.
[157] 'Presidency Conclusions', 19–20 March, Brussels European Council. The international action was, of course, to include the United States. There, President Barack Obama had been inaugurated on 20 January 2009, when Barack Obama, a Democrat from Illinois, was inaugurated as the 44th president – another unknown factor in an already volatile mix.

for his car producers.[158] The threat of a rift between 'old Europe' and the east European economies was real enough for the Council hastily to issue a statement of unity.[159] Behind Sarkozy's agitation lay the ever-present spectre of street violence in France. As he spoke to Brussels, riot police were out in force as a general strike was set to paralyse the country. As so often, the Community was being forced to pay lip-service to the needs of public order in the Fifth Republic.[160] But against a background of eurozone unemployment that had unexpectedly jumped to 8.5 per cent, all the leaders had cause to be nervous.[161]

Competition pressure between member states was also evident in what was regarded as a 'blatant attack' on hedge funds and private equity firms, to the disadvantage of London's financial services. António Borges, chairman of the Hedge Fund Standards Board, saw continental countries, which had neither a tradition of alternative investments nor a proper understanding of them, seeking to bring down UK and US financial systems. 'With the European elections coming up, this is clearly political,' he said.[162] Whatever the merits or otherwise of Commission proposals, London-based hedge fund money was now beginning to drift into the Eurosceptic camp. The City was open to being convinced that the EU was a threat.

Ever-present to an extent not yet seen in the UK was the underlying street violence. May Day saw clashes in Berlin between police and what were described as groups of far-right and left-wing militants, the worst violence the city had experienced in four years. In central Athens, more than four thousand police officers had been deployed in an attempt to prevent a repetition of the December riots. The worst violence, however, was seen in Turkey, where security forces fired tear gas and water cannon in Istanbul and Ankara.[163]

The Czech Republic, meanwhile, was sending mixed messages to Brussels. In mid-tenure of its EU presidency, the government had fallen, leaving the 'chair' unintentionally vacant (no replication of de Gaulle's strategy here), but not before the Czech upper house had endorsed the Lisbon Treaty by a comfortable majority. All it needed was a signature from President Václav Klaus.[164] This was not going to happen sometime soon. Strongly Eurosceptic, Klaus was working in loose alliance with Cameron

---

[158] *Deutsche Welle*, 28 February 2009, 'Unity at stake as EU summit begins under protectionism cloud'.
[159] *Deutsche Welle*, 2 March 2009, 'EU papers over cracks amid fears of economic iron curtain'.
[160] *Daily Telegraph*, 19 March 2009, 'France braced for riots on day of protests against Nicolas Sarkozy'.
[161] *Deutsche Welle*, 2 April 2009, 'European jobless rates surged in February'.
[162] *Guardian*, 21 April 2009, 'EU deadlocked on financial regulation crackdown'; *Daily Telegraph*, 30 April 2009, 'UK and Europe heading for rift over regulation'.
[163] *Deutsche Welle*, 3 May 2009, 'A look at May Day protests around Europe'.
[164] *Guardian*, 6 May 2009, 'Czech parliament puts doubts aside to ratify Lisbon treaty'.

and other British Eurosceptics, seeking to buy time for a referendum.[165] Across the border in Poland, President Lech Kaczyński was also refusing to sign the treaty, claiming its fate was unclear until the Irish vote.[166]

THE EUROPEAN ELECTIONS

It was, by now, too late to get the treaty in place for the European elections. And with only a day to go before the UK poll, Cameron was getting into trouble on the BBC Radio 4 *Today* programme, trying to explain how he would fulfil his promise to renegotiate the Lisbon Treaty if it had been ratified by all EU members by the time he won an election. A Conservative government would use forthcoming negotiations about the EU's budget as an opportunity to demand the return of powers to the UK, he said. This recognised that, by the time the Tories got into office, there was a strong possibility that the treaty would have come into force. All he could offer was the enigmatic promise that, in such circumstances, he would 'not let matters rest'.[167]

When the poll was carried out on 4 June, the Conservatives were rewarded with 26 seats out of the 72 available, only one less than they had gained in 2004. UKIP had come second in percentage terms, on 16 per cent of the vote, gaining 13 seats, one more than in the previous elections. That put it, on seat terms, level with Labour, which had lost over 6 percentage points and five seats. But UKIP's vote was only marginally up on 2004. Significantly, given their interest in immigration, the BNP won two seats. UK turnout was 34.5 per cent, against the EU-wide figure of 43 per cent.[168]

The election did nothing to interrupt the Commission's legislative programme, which continued apace. Newly elected MEPs picked up where their predecessors had left off. And high up in the Commission's priorities were the regulations governing hedge funds and private equity firms. The UK concern was that individual institutions should stay under national supervisors. Adair Turner, chairman of the Financial Services Authority, said, 'If one was absolutely confident that European supervision was going to be completely politics-free, in a neutral, technocratic fashion, we would be more relaxed about it.'[169]

Here, the measure had significant international dimensions, with US involvement via the G8 group of nations. The new Obama administration

---

[165] In 2006, through the good offices of President Klaus, this book was translated and published in the Czech Republic.
[166] Ibid.
[167] 2 June 2009.
[168] House of Commons Library, *European Parliament Elections 2009*.
[169] *Guardian*, 14 June 2009, 'UK resists EU plans for stricter financial regulation'.

was also pushing for legislation and the French were talking happily of a 'pincer movement on Britain'. In the Single Market, EU law would be decided by QMV and there was real concern that the City would come under direct EU supervision.[170]

In the midst of the deepest global recession since the Second World War, the European Council met on 18 June, whence their first task was to restore the Lisbon Treaty to its pre-eminent position. 'Convinced' that it would 'provide a better framework for action by the Union in a large number of fields', the first order of business had been to agree on 'legal' guarantees designed to respond to concerns raised by the Irish people. Only then came 'a number of decisions' directed at creating a new financial supervisory architecture. This aimed to protect the European financial system from future risks, 'ensuring that the mistakes of the past can never be repeated'. Almost as an aside, the Council unanimously approved the nomination of Barroso for another five-year term as Commission president.[171]

After the Council, leaders of Britain's financial community were giving a 'cautious welcome' to the latest iteration of the Commission proposals on financial regulation. It appeared that a compromise solution was in the air, with the EU adopting a 'European System of Financial Supervisors', and the European Banking Authority (EBA) becoming 'a supervisor of supervisors'. That the City was prepared to accept this drew a jibe from Sarkozy: 'Mr Brown has assumed his responsibilities. This is a sea-change in Anglo-Saxon strategy.'[172]

LISBON: THE FINAL STRAIGHT

As mid-year approached, there were only four hold-outs on the Lisbon Treaty: Germany, Ireland, Poland and the Czech Republic. At the end of June, full ratification crept a step closer when the German constitutional court ruled that the treaty was compatible with the basic law. But it withheld approval for immediate ratification, pending changes to domestic law to strengthen parliament's right to participation.[173] They were soon made and ratification papers were deposited on 25 September.

This was the first of the remaining dominos to fall. On 3 October, Irish voters had obediently given the treaty a resounding 67 per cent 'Yes' in their second referendum. Turnout was 58 per cent. Many saw the financial

[170] *Daily Telegraph*, 17 June 2009, 'UK "powerless" to stop EU regulation'.
[171] 'Presidency Conclusions', 18–19 June 2009, Brussels European Council.
[172] *Daily Telegraph*, 19 June 2009, 'UK wins concessions on EU rules'.
[173] *Deutsche Welle*, 29 June 2009, 'Germany's top court gives green light for Lisbon Treaty but delays ratification'.

crisis as a primary reason for the turnaround. Predictably, Barroso said it was a 'great day for Europe'.[174] Less than a week later, Polish president Lech Kaczyński was to sign the treaty. That left Václav Klaus, who said he would not sign until his country's constitutional court had pronounced on it.[175] He was also seeking last-minute amendments, in the hope that negotiations would have to be reopened, possibly allowing time for Cameron to win his election and hold a referendum.[176]

On 30 October, the EU granted a largely meaningless concession to the Czech Republic, stating that the Charter of Fundamental Rights would not apply directly to the country.[177] It had long been established that it would only apply to EU legislation in the formulation stage, but the move closed off the renegotiation ploy. Four days later, the Czech constitutional court ruled that the treaty was in line with the constitution.[178] With all his options exhausted, Klaus signed the treaty. 'The road has been a marathon of hurdles but the last hurdle is now removed,' Barroso said, with palpable relief.[179] The treaty came into force on 1 December, nearly a year later than planned, ending an eight-year battle to create the European Constitution – for that is what the Lisbon Treaty was.

After the Irish result, a correspondent had written a letter to the *Daily Telegraph*, which had been published under the heading: 'Our political class has failed us by not holding a referendum.' 'If the Lisbon Treaty comes into force, it will be a Pyrrhic victory. So much dirt clings to the project now that support for it will continue to fall rapidly. No political structure can survive complete lack of support', Dr Helen Szamuely wrote. She was not wrong.[180]

The person most politically exposed by the 'success' of the treaty was David Cameron. Tory Eurosceptics wanted him to hold a referendum if he became prime minister, even after the treaty has been ratified. He had sat on the fence. Even immediately after the Irish result, he had refused to come down for or against.[181]

Once Klaus had thrown in the towel, though, Cameron had nowhere to go. On 4 November, he explained that the treaty was being incorporated into EU law. 'We cannot hold a referendum and magically the treaty disappears, any

---

[174] BBC News, 3 October 2009, 'Ireland backs EU's Lisbon Treaty'; *Der Spiegel*, 3 October 2009, 'Ireland overturns its "No" to EU reform'.
[175] *Daily Telegraph*, 10 October 2009, 'President of Poland signs Lisbon Treaty'.
[176] *The Times*, 12 October 2009, 'Czech Cabinet in emergency session to force President Klaus to sign Lisbon treaty'.
[177] *Guardian*, 30 October 2009, 'EU grants Czech Republic Lisbon treaty concession'.
[178] BBC News, 3 November 2009, 'Czech court clears Lisbon Treaty'.
[179] *Guardian*, 3 November 2009, 'Václav Klaus sets seal on Lisbon treaty ratification'.
[180] 4 October 2009.
[181] *Guardian*, 4 October 2009, 'David Cameron accused of "dithering" over EU referendum question'.

more than we could hold a referendum to stop the sun rising in the morning,' he said.[182] Logical though the argument might have been, supporters and detractors alike characterised it as reneging on the 'cast-iron guarantee'.[183] By way of compensation, Cameron promised that a Conservative government would guarantee a referendum if there were any further attempts to transfer powers from Britain to the EU, and he pledged a renegotiation aimed at repatriating some powers.[184] Neither was enough.[185]

A GREEK TRAGEDY – PART 1

If the gods had allowed the 'colleagues' their victory on the treaty, from their vantage point of Mount Olympus, they were about to extract their price. In Greece, home of democracy, a long-running saga was about to commence. A convenient starting point can be taken as the election in October 2009 of the Greek Socialists, led by George Papandreou, ousting the governing conservatives of Premier Kostas Karamanlis. His victory was in no small measure due to his promise of a three-billion-euro stimulus package on a platform of taxing the rich and helping the poor. The incumbent had called for two years of austerity.[186]

Within a fortnight, the European Commission was sharply criticising a budget deficit set to reach 12.7 per cent – four times the permitted level.[187] Papandreou was forced to take a humiliating public dressing-down from Jean-Claude Juncker, the chairman of the Eurogroup. Looking at the figures offered by the Greek government – which at the start of the decade had falsified data on its national debt in order to qualify for the eurozone – Juncker declared: 'The game is over. We need serious statistics.'[188]

No improvement was seen at the end of November, with Papandreou admitting that the economy was 'in intensive care'. The national debt – the

---

[182] BBC News, 4 November 2009, 'Full text: Cameron speech on EU'.
[183] For instance, The New Statesman, 4 November 2009, 'Cameron to set out harsh new EU policy of Lisbon Treaty referendum'.
[184] BBC, op. cit.
[185] On 28 September 2008, William Hague had told the Sunday Times that a new Conservative government could still hold a referendum, even if the Lisbon Treaty had already been fully ratified. The idea was to hold a special ballot to give him the authority to renegotiate Britain's relationship with the EU. At the time it was resisted by some Tory strategists, who feared the party would get bogged down in a prolonged debate on the minutiae of EU procedures. This time, there was no repetition of the idea.
[186] Deutsche Welle, 5 October 2009, 'Socialist George Papandreou claims victory in Greek elections'.
[187] Deutsche Welle, 20 October 2009, 'EU reprimands Greece for out-of-control budget'.
[188] Deutsche Welle, 22 October 2009, 'Greece faces a ballooning budget deficit'. Juncker, some years earlier, in respect of economic reform in the under-performing eurozone countries, was said to have declared, 'We all know what to do, we just don't know how to get re-elected after we've done it.' This was attributed by The Economist, 17 March 2007, 'The quest for prosperity'. There seems to be no direct record of him having made this statement, but it certainly could have applied to Papandreou.

highest in the EU and projected to rise to 135.4 per cent in 2011 – had made the outlook grimmer still. After years of posting 4 per cent growth rates, the economy was expected to contract 1.2 per cent, with unemployment topping 9 per cent.[189] And the news kept getting worse. The Fitch rating agency cut Greece's long-term debt to BBB+ from A minus, the first time in ten years that the country's rating had dropped below an A grade.[190] The immediate effect was to increase the government's cost of borrowing. In desperation, Papandreou tore up his election manifesto and announced sweeping changes, acknowledging the 'reasonable concerns' of his EU partners.[191] As the financial turmoil intensified, thousands of workers backed by militant trade unions did their 'European' thing and went on strike, marching on parliament shouting: 'Don't forget your promises George.' Unsurprisingly, international confidence plummeted.[192]

THE PRICE OF POWER

As the year drew to a close, in Copenhagen EU and member state representatives were attempting to forge a deal on climate change. When, finally, the parties stitched together something, environment activists immediately branded it 'toothless and a failure'.[193] But at least one group was happy. Despite earlier accusations of criminal corruption, MEPs were to receive an increase to their staff allowances that would see them climb to £220,000 a year. This was to help them implement the Lisbon Treaty, once described as a 'tidying up exercise'. 'With more power comes more work,' explained a parliament official.[194]

[189] *Guardian*, 30 November 2009, 'The new Iceland? Greece fights to rein in debt'.
[190] *Guardian*, 8 December 2009, 'Financial markets tumble after Fitch downgrades Greece's credit rating'.
[191] *Guardian*, 14 December 2009, 'Papandreou unveils radical reforms to salvage Greece's public finances'.
[192] *Guardian*, 17 December 2009, 'Strikes hit Greece as debt crisis grows'.
[193] *Daily Telegraph*, 19 December 2009, 'Climate summit ends in chaos and "toothless" deal'.
[194] *Daily Telegraph*, 17 December 2009, 'MEPs to receive extra £32,000 a year on top of pay rise'.

19

The Euro Crisis: 2010–2012

If the euro collapses, then Europe and the idea of European union will fail.

Angela Merkel, 13 May 2010

We don't need economists negotiating for Ireland, we need liquidators.

David McWilliams, *Guardian*, 20 November 2010

I have the impression that there have been scenes where France and Germany created problems ahead of an EU summit and then came to Brussels and showed theatrically: 'We have solved the problem and brought Europe forward.'

Jean Asselborn, Luxembourg foreign minister, *Der Spiegel*, 15 December 2010

It felt like we were flying a plane while we were still building the engine.

Kalin Anev Janse, ESM/EFSF Secretary General[1]

After eight years of struggle getting the not-the-constitution in place, the pinnacle of this endeavour was to bring the post of High Representative, aka 'foreign minister', fully into the Community maw. To celebrate this milestone, the person chosen to preside over a budget of £5.8 billion and a staff of seven thousand was the cause of much bewilderment. It

---

[1] *Safeguarding the Euro in Times of Crisis: The Inside Story of the ESM* (Luxembourg: Publications Office of the European Union), 2019. p. 105.

was to be Catherine Margaret Ashton, Baroness Ashton of Upholland, a former official in the Campaign for Nuclear Disarmament (CND) who had never held elected political office and was completely without foreign policy experience. Herman Van Rompuy, former prime minister of Belgium, took another of the new posts, becoming president of the European Council. A Whitehall source dismissed the appointments as a 'complete disgrace'. 'They are no more than garden gnomes,' he said.[2] But, to the more sanguine voices, Baroness Ashton's appointment appeared to signal that the Union *per se* would not be setting any agendas or taking any initiatives on the world stage. The member states would be staying firmly in charge.[3]

A BENEFICIAL CRISIS

With or without Catherine Ashton, foreign and security policy was not to dominate Union affairs. Instead, the year was to be swamped by successive crises affecting the single currency.

In many respects, this is the way it had to be. The euro was akin to an aircraft without wings or engines, built that way because the makers had rightly judged that the 'shareholders' would not fund a complete aeroplane. So they built what they could, filled it with passengers, gave it a piggy-back ride to the upper atmosphere and cast it loose. The hope was that, as it hurtled to the ground, the shareholders would see disaster looming and shell out for the missing parts – so making the aircraft whole and flyable. That is the beneficial crisis. As applied to the Community, former *Telegraph* Brussels correspondent, Ambrose Evans Pritchard, thought it was a Monnet concept that lots of people in Brussels talked about – mostly behind closed doors. The idea had certainly been promoted by Monnet's associate, Robert Marjolin, back in 1975. But the concept pre-dates Monnet: *Una Crisi Benefica* is found in nineteenth-century literature.[4]

While it clearly goes way back, it is a very continental phenomenon, only recently finding a home in the UK. Ambrose's first reference to it seems to be in May 2005, when he wrote that 'EMU's architects always expected trouble, but counted on a "beneficial crisis" that would help push Europe further towards full economic federalism.' 'The euro', wrote Ambrose, 'was to be the midwife of the federal state.' Since then, only a few other British

[2] *Guardian*, 20 November 2009, 'Lady Ashton: principled, charming … or just plain lucky'.
[3] Howarth, Jolyon (2014), 'Catherine Ashton's Five-year Term: A Difficult Assessment', *Les Cahiers européens de Sciences Po* – no. 03/2014.
[4] *Nuova Antologia (di Scienze, Lettere ed Arti)*, Roma, 1888.

journalists have used the term.[5] But in the opening decade of the twenty-first century, it dominated the European stage and threatened the entire global economy. And all because the 'colleagues' thought they could build a currency without 'wings' and glue them on later.[6]

GREEKS REFUSING GIFTS

Throughout this 'beneficial crisis', Greece was to feature prominently. And with barely a pause for Christmas and the New Year, the country was back in the headlines, setting what became something of a pattern. This started with denial. As officials flew in from Brussels to scrutinise the government's tax and spending plans, finance minister George Papaconstantinou declared: 'We don't expect to be bailed out by anybody, as I think it's perfectly clear we're doing what needs to be done to bring the deficit down and control the public debt.'[7]

The word of a Greek politician, though, was a wasting asset. In a damning report, Commission officials noted that the recent (upwards) revisions to the deficit were 'an illustration of the lack of quality of the Greek fiscal statistics'. The intense scrutiny by Eurostat since 2004 had 'not sufficed to bring the quality of Greek fiscal data to the level reached by other EU Member States'.[8] This, the officials averred, was a 'country-specific problem', lamenting that it could not 'prevent deliberate misreporting of data'.[9]

Greece's handicap, though, was its eurozone membership. Unlike other countries with massive budget deficits – the UK, for example – it could not print money or devalue its currency.[10] The conventional alternative was 'internal devaluation': shrinking the public sector, and cutting wages and pensions, together with widespread tax increases and tougher enforcement.[11] The resultant 'austerity' was rarely popular.

Even knowing that the financial data were based on foundations of (statistical) sand, the newly re-elected president of the Eurogroup, Jean-Claude Juncker, still exuded confidence. In the run-up to the January Ecofin meeting, he chirped that Greece would emerge from its crisis 'in reasonable

---

[5] Although used by one of us (CB), *Sunday Telegraph*, 2 June 2012, 'The EU's "beneficial crisis" has spun out of control'.
[6] Taken from the EU Referendum blog, 29 May 2012, 'Eurocrash: *una crisi salutare* – a currency without wings'.
[7] *Financial Times*, 6 January 2010, 'Greece rejects speculation of bail-out'.
[8] European Commission, Brussels, 8 January 2010, COM(2010) 1 final: *Report on Greek Government Deficit and Debt Statistics.*
[9] Ibid.
[10] *Financial Times*, 19 January 2010, 'The Greek tragedy deserves a global audience'.
[11] Received wisdom is highly controversial. See Petroulakis, Filippos (2017), 'Internal devaluation in currency unions: the role of trade costs and taxes', ECB Working Paper Series No. 2049.

time', although the Greek population would have to prepare for significant cuts.[12] Prime Minister Papandreou pondered whether his real problem was a 'credibility' rather than financial deficit. Few investors believed what he had to say.[13] At this point, Papandreou was continuing to deny a bailout was needed. Signals suggested otherwise. But help, it was mooted, would involve eurozone governments and the Commission, rather than the traditional lender of last resort, the IMF. EU officials were worried about contagion, with the Portuguese economy showing signs of stress.[14]

Nevertheless, there were mixed feelings about eurozone involvement. Some thought the Greeks had been living beyond their means and were to blame for the mess. It was conceded, though, that other eurozone nations and the European Central Bank had not been 'attentive enough' when Greece had joined the eurozone with falsified statistics, or when they continued their lax economic management, still faking the statistics. Eurozone aid would be sending the wrong signal; the IMF was 'the right address to aid the Greeks'.[15]

Even without aid, the EU was demanding a stringent regime of budget cuts and financial reforms.[16] These were set out by the Council in mid-February.[17] Given the lack of trust, the EU also reserved the right to monitor Greece's progress, and demand more drastic measures if need be. The Greek parliament and government were virtually stripped of power, and finance minister Giorgos Papakonstantinou was required to report every four weeks on progress made in budget restructuring.[18] Journalist Dennis Telefakotos thought there was an element of scapegoating. Greece, he suggested, was 'the perfect victim', a way for Brussels to send a warning signal to other indebted member states.[19]

What did not help was emerging details of the tricks employed by the Greek government to mask the true extent of its deficit. One particularly brazen ploy had involved so-called cross-currency swaps, arranged by US investment bank Goldman Sachs. These had been based on fictional exchange rates that enabled a $1 billion loan to be concealed.[20] Also particularly damning was the extensive corruption, at all levels of society,

[12] *Deutsche Welle*, 19 January 2010, 'EU gives backing to Greek debt crisis plan'.
[13] *Financial Times*, 28 January 2010, 'Greece suffers from "credibility deficit"'.
[14] *Financial Times*, 29 January 2010, 'EU signals last-resort backing for Greece'.
[15] *Deutsche Welle*, 1 February 2010, 'Opinion: bailing out Greece would "send the wrong signal"'.
[16] *Sunday Times*, 31 January 2010, 'EU sets tough targets for Greece rescue'.
[17] Council Decision 2010/182/EU of 16 February 2010 giving notice to Greece to take measures for the deficit reduction judged necessary in order to remedy the situation of excessive deficit.
[18] *Deutsche Welle*, 3 February 2010, 'EU to monitor money-saving efforts by cash-strapped Greece'.
[19] Ibid.
[20] *Der Spiegel*, 8 February 2010, 'How Goldman Sachs helped Greece to mask its true debt'.

and especially in trade with Germany: there had been multiple episodes of bribes from major German companies to secure business. Transparency International rated Greece as one of the most corrupt countries in Europe.[21]

Nevertheless, it did not pass unnoticed that, back in 2004 when Greece had first admitted 'faking it', the country had not been bounced out of the eurozone. Nor had other sanctions been imposed. But then, Barroso's conservative allies had been in power. Not until the Socialists had been elected, who had then revealed the true state of the country's finances, had Brussels acted.[22]

As February progressed, the situation was spiralling out of control. Fevered speculation forced Angela Merkel to deny that Germany was preparing to lead a bailout, while Greek public sector workers, caught in the squeeze between Brussels and Athens, began a series of nationwide strikes.[23] The drama had become a daily soap opera, fuelled by multiple meetings in Brussels, all-night sessions, dramatic announcements and much to-ing and fro-ing between capitals. Papandreou, in what had become the eurozone's first big test, likened Greece to 'a laboratory animal in the battle between Europe and the markets'.[24]

And yet, for all the huge expenditure of energy and the arc-light media focus, it was not until 25 March that Eurogroup members committed to taking determined and co-ordinated action, 'if needed'.[25] Then, at last, the Greek government asked for talks with the European Commission, the ECB and IMF. On 23 April, it finally requested assistance. By 2 May, the parties announced an agreement on a bailout.[26] This was a €80 billion package, called the Greek Loan Facility (GLF), a cumbersome grouping of 15 separate bilateral loans from Eurogroup members pooled by the European Commission, to be paid between May 2010 and June 2013. The amount was subsequently cut by €2.7 billion when Slovakia dropped out, and Ireland and Portugal stepped down. It was topped up by €30 billion from the IMF.[27] The GLF's first €14.5 billion instalment was disbursed on 18 May.[28]

---

[21] *Der Spiegel*, 11 May 2010, 'How German companies bribed their way to Greek deals'.
[22] *Der Spiegel*, 9 February 2010, 'How Brussels is trying to prevent a collapse of the euro'.
[23] *The Times*, 10 February 2010, 'Storm over bailout of Greece, EU's most ailing economy'; *Deutsche Welle*, 10 February 2010, 'Greek unions strike over spending cuts'.
[24] *Financial Times*, 12 February 2010, 'Greece turns on EU critics'.
[25] 'Statement by the Heads of State and Government of the Euro Area', Brussels, 25 March 2010.
[26] A detailed timeline can be found in Occasional Papers 61, May 2010: 'The Economic Adjustment Programme for Greece', European Commission, Directorate-General for Economic and Financial Affairs.
[27] European Commission: 'Financial assistance to Greece' (website).
[28] Occasional Papers 61, op. cit.

Terms were deliberately harsh, Merkel arguing that this was the only way to save the single currency. 'These countries can see that the path taken by Greece with the IMF is not an easy one. As a result, they will do all they can to avoid this themselves,' she said. Papaconstantinou ruminated that Greece had been called on to make a 'basic choice between collapse or salvation'.[29] This was by no means to be the last time. As a European Commissioner was later ruefully to observe: 'Marathon is a Greek word'.[30] So too was austerity, he might have noted, ultimately derived from *austērós*, meaning 'harsh, rough, bitter'.

THE EYJAFJALLAJÖKULL EFFECT

To add to the sense of crisis pervading European capitals, on 14 May the Icelandic volcano Eyjafjallajökull erupted, spewing a plume of ash that spread across northern Europe.[31] The only jet aircraft equipped to sample the atmosphere at high altitude, and test whether it was safe to fly, was a converted BAE 146 airliner operated by the British Met Office. As luck would have it, the aircraft had been stripped of its gear in preparation for repainting, despite warnings that it might be needed.[32]

Without actual data on ash concentration, and evidently struggling with the concept of dilution effect, European flight safety authorities relied on computer modelling undertaken by the London-based Volcanic Ash Advisory Centre (VAAC), partly funded by Eurocontrol. Using their theoretical data, the authorities closed commercial airspace over 20 countries, causing disruption to millions of travellers. By the time an alternative aircraft had been pressed into service, a less-capable Dornier 228, ash concentrations in the order of 100 micrograms per cubic metre of air were measured – well below the 2,000-microgram level set as a safety threshold for modern jet engines. The flying ban was lifted, but not before airlines had lost around £2 billion in revenue.[33]

After the event, the EU – whose Eurocontrol had co-ordinated the ban – denied responsibility for the shambles, asserting that decisions to close airspace had been made by national authorities.[34] But those actions had been based on the International Civil Aviation Organisation's contingency

---

[29] BBC News, 2 May 2010, 'Eurozone approves massive Greece bail-out'.
[30] Olli Rehn, European Commissioner responsible for Economic and Monetary Affairs. Cited in the *Guardian* live blog, 21 February 2012.
[31] *Guardian*, 16 April 2010, 'Ash cloud over Europe causes worst travel chaos since 9/11'.
[32] *Mail on Sunday*, 'As the cloud thickens, some pilots are asking … Why can't we just fly beneath it?'; *Der Spiegel*, 'Airline bosses attack volcano flight ban'. Both 19 April 2010.
[33] Ibid.
[34] EU Business, 20 April 2010, *The Volcanic Ash Crisis and the EU – briefing*.

plan, recently agreed by the EU, its member state governments and their safety agencies.[35] According to International Air Transport Association director-general Giovanni Bisignani, there had been 'no risk assessment, no consultation, no organisation and no leadership'.[36]

In early May, to the sound of stable doors slamming shut, EU transport ministers met to discuss how to respond more swiftly to future aviation crises.[37] The outcome was the revision of the ICAO contingency plan, and the establishment of a European Aviation Crisis Coordination Cell.[38]

GENERAL ELECTION 2010

In the United Kingdom on 6 May, a dying, unpopular government led by Gordon Brown – bogged down by failed military campaigns in southern Iraq and Afghanistan – went to the polls. It faced a challenge from a youthful David Cameron, who had famously sneered that Blair 'was the future once'.[39]

When the polls closed, Cameron learned that his future was not just yet – at least, not in the way he had hoped: the exit poll forecast a hung parliament, with Conservatives the largest party.[40] The final results gave the Tories 307 seats and Labour 258. The resurgent Liberal Democrats – the only party to offer an in/out referendum in its manifesto – gained 57. In a parliament of 650, Cameron was 18 shy of an absolute majority.[41] He had achieved a swing on a par with Margaret Thatcher in 1979, but – as he wrote in his memoirs – 'we didn't clinch it'. He claims to be 'fairly sure' why his party did not win outright: 'There was too much "and" to our campaign – the Big Society *and* austerity; cutting some public services *and* increasing others; continuing to modernise *and* hammering Brown and Labour.'[42] Completely missing from his analysis was any estimate of the effect of his reneging on his 'cast-iron' referendum guarantee. This was despite his admitting in the April that: 'people feel rather cheated that they did not have a referendum on the European constitution'.[43]

---

[35] ICAO, *Volcanic Ash Contingency Plan: EUR Region* (2nd edn), September 2009.
[36] *Mail on Sunday*, 25 April 2010, 'The ash cloud that never was: how volcanic plume over UK was only a twentieth of safe-flying limit and blunders led to ban'.
[37] *Deutsche Welle*, 4 May 2010, 'EU makes plans to avoid a repeat of ash cloud chaos'.
[38] Commission Regulation (EU) No. 677/2011.
[39] HC Debates, 7 December 2005, Vol. 440, col. 861.
[40] Cameron, op. cit., pp. 130–131.
[41] BBC Election 2010 website.
[42] Cameron, op. cit., pp. 132–133.
[43] *Daily Telegraph*, 13 April 2010, 'David Cameron says voters were "cheated" of vote on Lisbon treaty'.

Outside the London bubble, UKIP and the British National Party (BNP) had polled nearly 1.5 million votes. More significantly, in 42 seats, either UKIP, or the combined UKIP/BNP vote, exceeded the majority of the Labour or Liberal Democrat winners' margin over the Conservatives. UKIP alone affected 23 seats.[44] Potentially, the 'UKIP effect', evident in 2005, had grown in strength to cost Cameron his victory. The price of failure was a coalition with Nick Clegg's Lib-Dems, which took five days to negotiate. When he walked into Downing Street as prime minister on 11 May, Cameron told the nation that one of his tasks was 'about being honest about what government can achieve'.[45]

THE EURO FIGHTS BACK

Across the Channel, the euro crisis continued unabated. All 27 EU finance ministers – which included Labour's about-to-be deposed Alistair Darling – were summoned to Brussels on the Sunday after the election to approve a bailout instrument called the European Financial Stabilisation Mechanism (EFSM).[46] The need was long-standing, but the urgency was dictated by the anticipated market reaction to riots in Athens – the worst since 2008. Three people had been killed, one a pregnant woman.[47] Member states wanted a fund in place to defend the euro. 'This is a full-scale mobilisation,' Sarkozy said.[48]

In the UK, some reports had Sarkozy and Merkel devising the scheme behind closed doors and attempting to push it through when there was no clear government in Britain. The Brussels perspective was somewhat different: this was a race to create a 'firewall' to protect the euro, before Monday-morning trading began in Asia.[49] It invoked Article 122 (TFEU), intended to aid member states threatened with 'severe difficulties caused by natural disasters or exceptional occurrences beyond its control'. Not specifically intended to defend the euro, the Article had the merit of requiring only qualified majority approval.[50]

After frenetic late-night talks, the mechanism was approved on 11 May.[51] It could, however, only raise €60 billion, as it used the EU budget as collateral.

[44] Analysis taken from EU Referendum blog, 8 May 2010, 'UKIP effect 2010 – the full list (revised)', compiled by one of us (RN).
[45] *Guardian*, 11 May 2010, 'David Cameron's speech in full'.
[46] *Daily Telegraph*, 8 May 2010, 'British taxpayers ordered to bail out euro'.
[47] Reuters, 5 May 2010, 'Greek anti-austerity march erupts in violence, 3 dead'.
[48] *Daily Telegraph*, op. cit.
[49] A detailed account of events can be read in *Safeguarding the Euro in Times of Crisis: The Inside Story of the ESM* (Luxembourg: Publications Office of the European Union, 2019).
[50] Ibid.
[51] Council Regulation (EU) No. 407/2010 of 11 May 2010 establishing a European financial stabilisation mechanism.

More was needed to calm the markets, so the finance ministers created the European Financial Stability Facility (EFSF), a Special Purpose Vehicle to raise funds guaranteed on a *pro rata* basis by participating member states. The Facility could borrow up to €440 billion, with a mandate set to expire after three years.[52] Collectively, the EU now had a fighting fund worth €500 billion, with the possibility of an even 'bigger bazooka' when €250 billion from the IMF was added. It was just in time. In Aachen later in the week, Merkel warned: 'If the euro collapses, then Europe and the idea of European union will fail.'[53]

TRENCH WARFARE

Cameron had his own problems, one of which threatened to ruin any chance of his forming a coalition with the Lib-Dems: a secret memorandum written by soon-to-become foreign secretary William Hague, leaked to the *Observer* newspaper. It set out a 'hardline' position on the EU, including a commitment 'to returning powers from the European level to the UK in three key areas – the Charter of Fundamental Rights, criminal justice, and social and employment legislation'.[54]

'Nick and Dave' were, of course, soon to make up, Clegg becoming the deputy prime minister, fortified with a promise of a referendum on alternative voting – which in the fullness of time was to be held and the proposition defeated. The new Chancellor of the Exchequer was George Osborne, who was soon battling with the EU over hedge fund regulation. Ominously, *The Times* predicted defeat.[55] That was not to happen until June 2011.[56] In the interim, the ongoing squabble was another source of irritation and friction.

Despite this, in a triumph of hope over experience, Cameron decided on a 'constructive approach' to 'Europe', treading a path littered with the shattered hopes of his predecessors. On his agenda were visits to Sarkozy and Merkel.[57] There was nothing he could do, though, to stop the inexorable spread of what was being called the 'debt crisis' as it ripped through the eurozone. The latest casualty was Italy, with its 5.3 per cent deficit and a national debt standing at 115.8 per cent of GDP. To avoid a

---

[52] Council of the European Union, Press Release 9596/10 (presse 108), Extraordinary Council meeting, Economic and Financial Affairs, Brussels, 9/10 May 2010.

[53] *Der Spiegel*, 13 May 2010, 'If Euro fails, so will the idea of European Union'.

[54] *Observer*, 9 May 2010, 'Tory–Lib Dem coalition threatened by secret hardline memo on Europe'.

[55] *The Times*, 14 May 2010, 'Osborne faces EU defeat on hedge funds'.

[56] *Deutsche Welle*, 19 May 2010, 'Europe tightens the screws on hedge funds'.

[57] *Guardian*, 19 May 2010, 'David Cameron signals new approach on Europe with visits to Paris and Berlin'.

Greek-style crisis, Prime Minister Silvio Berlusconi launched a €24 billion austerity package.[58]

Cameron turned to immigration – the subject of earnest pre-election promises. But, with either remarkable naivety or a complete lack of joined-up thinking, he announced a 'cap' on skilled non-EU immigrants. Then, on a visit to Ankara, he promised to fight for Turkey's EU membership, thereby opening up the prospect of yet more immigration.[59] This was not the brightest of moves.

BUDGET SHENANIGANS

There were some uncomfortable moments for the British prime minister in September when Janusz Lewandowski, the EU budget commissioner, told German business newspaper *Handelsblatt* that 'the British rebate has lost its original justification'. However, Lewandowski was only warming up for the next round of multi-annual financial framework talks, covering the period 2014–2020.[60] The time had not yet come for a major battle. Of more immediate concern was the approval of the annual budget for 2011. The original Commission proposals, lodged in April, had been opposed by the European Parliament – exercising the one major power it had at its disposal. On 20 October 2010, it called for a 6 per cent increase compared to the current budget, amounting to €143.1 billion. Unable to agree, the Commission set about presenting a new draft.[61]

With an egregious lack of political acumen, Cameron chose to make this increase his 'Canute moment', when he held back the tide of rising expenditure. On 20 October, he told the Commons: 'We have called for a cash freeze in the size of the EU budget for 2011 and we are working hard to make this case across Europe.'[62] Three days later, he announced in the *Mail on Sunday* 'Britain's revolt against a "completely unacceptable" demand by the European Union for a 6 percent budget increase'. He would, he said, use the 'summit' – i.e., European Council – of 29 October 'to say "No" to the EU's plan to increase funding'.[63]

Possibly unaware that the annual budget approval did not involve the European Council, he was left to discuss it on the margins with other EU

[58] *Deutsche Welle*, 25 May 2010, 'Italy becomes latest to release austerity measures'.
[59] *Deutsche Welle*, 28 June 2010, 'Britain takes first step in cutting non-EU immigration'; BBC News, 27 July 2010, 'Cameron "anger" at slow pace of Turkish EU negotiations'.
[60] *Financial Times*, 6 September 2010, 'Cameron faces fresh EU rebate struggle'.
[61] European Commission, EU Budget 2011, Financial Report.
[62] HC Debates, 20 October 2010, Vol. 516, col. 938.
[63] *Mail on Sunday*, 23 October 2010, 'Stop spending so much, furious Cameron tells EU as it demands 6 per cent budget increase'.

leaders. But all he got was an increase of 2.9 per cent, exactly the amount in the new draft budget presented by the Commission. Despite this, Cameron unwisely told reporters, 'We have succeeded quite spectacularly. I hit the phones yesterday before coming to the summit and stopped that [budget] juggernaut in its tracks.'[64] He had achieved absolutely nothing, and certainly not the 'cash freeze' he had set out to achieve.

The final budget proposal went through unchanged, but not before Ed Miliband, the current UK Opposition leader, had exploited Cameron's discomfort. Jubilantly, he told the Commons, 'As far as we can gather, it was sleeves rolled up, full steam ahead and when it came to 2.9 percent, it was "fight them on the beaches". Now the Prime Minister has said that he changed his position ... [and] ... has agreed to 2.9 percent ... If that is his view of spectacular success,' he crowed, 'I would hate to see what happens when things go wrong in his negotiations in Brussels.'[65]

While Cameron had been grandstanding, the grown-ups were looking at the EFSF, incorporated since 7 June under Luxembourg law as a *société anonyme*.[66] Given its limited term and slender legal base, they needed a permanent mechanism. This, would require 'a limited treaty change.'[67] That idea was not universally popular, but Merkel was adamant: 'We need a new, robust framework. It must be legally watertight and this will happen only with a change of the European treaties,' she insisted.[68] Domestic matters continued to preoccupy the British prime minister. In early November, he introduced his promised EU Referendum Bill into the Commons, in what was called an 'attempt to reassert his Eurosceptic credentials'. But the move was never going to placate his hard-core Eurosceptic MPs. They condemned it as a 'cosmetic gesture.'[69]

At the October European Council, a task force on the governance of the euro, which had been set up the March, reported to the EU leaders.[70] It proposed increased budgetary surveillance and a wider range of sanctions when eurozone members failed to meet financial criteria. But elsewhere, events were already crowding in. The euro crisis had entered a new and ominous phase, with economists and bond market investors questioning the ability of 'peripheral' European economies to survive without their

[64] BBC News, 29 October 2010, 'David Cameron claims EU budget success'.
[65] HC Debates, 1 November 2010, Vol. 517, col. 617.
[66] EFSF Framework Agreement, Consolidated version.
[67] 'Presidency Conclusions', 28–29 October 2010, Brussels European Council.
[68] *Deutsche Welle*, 28 October 2010, 'Merkel defends German–French call for changes to EU treaty'.
[69] *Daily Telegraph*, 6 November 2010, 'David Cameron's EU Bill "too little too late", say MPs'.
[70] *Strengthening Economic Governance in the EU: Report of the Task Force to the European Council*, Brussels, 21 October 2010.

own rescue packages. Not only Greece, but Ireland, Portugal and Spain were at risk.[71]

Of the three, Ireland was the first to crumble, following a familiar pattern – starting with denying the need for a bailout.[72] But, in what was to be the first test of the EFSF, the eurozone was better prepared. When, on 21 November, the Irish government asked for help, an €85 billion package was arranged, financed partly by the EFSF, with bilateral loans from Denmark, Sweden and the UK, plus a contribution from the IMF. An agreement was concluded on 6–7 December at the EU finance ministers meeting.[73] When the first €3.6 billion tranche of the loan was paid on 1 February 2011, the eurozone had passed a major test. Gradually, the euro was acquiring its missing 'wings'.

The crisis, of course, was far from over. With some pundits predicting the imminent demise of the euro, ECB president Jean-Claude Trichet waded into the argument to assert:

> We have got a monetary federation. We need quasi-budget federation as well. Yes, we could achieve that if there is strong monitoring and supervision of what there is. Because what exists doesn't correspond with the actual situation that we are facing. It is a situation where we need quasi-federation of the budget.[74]

To the background of yet another general strike in Greece, EU leaders arrived at the final European Council of a tumultuous year. High up in their deliberations was the EFSF replacement. Here, the Lisbon Treaty came to the rescue. It had given them a 'simplified revision procedure' that allowed them to make treaty amendments without an IGC.[75] The procedures were set in motion. And, as the year closed, the eurozone leaders were at last given something of a break. For a few weeks, there had been a relative lull in financial market pressure, attributed to investors and traders closing their books ahead of the end of the year. Nevertheless, analysts expected pressure to resume in 2011. They were not to be disappointed.

---

[71] *Financial Times*, 9 November 2010, 'Doubts grow over "peripheral" eurozone nations'.
[72] *Guardian*, 12 November 2010, 'Ireland denies reports of EU bailout amid rumours of rescue talks'.
[73] Council of the European Union, Press Release 17447/10 (presse 333), 3054th Council meeting, Economic and Financial Affairs, Brussels, 7 December 2010.
[74] *Guardian*, 30 November 2010, 'European Central Bank boss calls for even greater euro harmonisation'.
[75] 'Presidency Conclusions', 16–17 December 2010, Brussels European Council (Annex I).

SOMETHING OLD, SOMETHING NEW

For the EU, the new year started on a positive note. Estonia joined the eurozone, bringing its numbers to 17. But, as before, the debt crisis was to preoccupy EU leaders, although even these problems could not shut out the rest of the world. Waiting for them was another major crisis: the 'Arab Spring'.

There had been plenty of warning, but not until 17 December 2010, when Mohamed Bouazizi, a Tunisian trader living in Sidi Bouzid, set himself on fire after police had seized the vegetable cart from which he earned his living, did a wave of revolt kick off through the Arab world. In time, it led to the overthrow of governments in Tunisia and Egypt, civil war in Libya, a prolonged war in Syria, and bloody conflict in Yemen.[76]

Events moved quickly. The second week of January saw Tunisian president Ben Ali leaving the country amid severe civil unrest, after having imposed a state of emergency across the country and a night-time curfew.[77] A week later saw continuing protests in Algeria and Yemen.[78] By February, the unrest had spread to Libya, with the eventual overthrow of Gaddafi, but not before NATO intervention in a widespread bombing campaign.[79] And on 15 March, a bitter civil war was to break out in Syria, with the emergence of the Islamic State faction and Russian military support for the Syrian government.[80]

The immediate impact on member states was a surge of migration from Tunisia. Starting in mid-January, by early February Italian authorities had to deal with 5,200 migrants who had landed on the tiny Mediterranean island of Lampedusa, 105 miles south-west of Sicily. Rome had declared a 'humanitarian emergency'.[81] By May, some 25,000 migrants – most of them Tunisians – had arrived. As they were brought to mainland Italy, many left to join relatives and friends in France. The Commission was forced to consider whether to allow member states to restore some border controls that had disappeared under the Schengen Treaty.[82] This wave of migration, which was later reinforced by a massive diaspora from Syria, was another crisis

---

[76] Lin Noueihed and Alex Warren (2013), *The Battle for the Arab Spring: Revolution, Counter-revolution and the Making of a New Era* (New Haven and London: Yale University Press).

[77] *Deutsche Welle*, 14 January 2011, 'Tunisian president leaves country after imposing state of emergency'.

[78] *Deutsche Welle*, 22 January 2011, 'Renewed protests in Algeria and Tunisia as Arab unrest spreads'.

[79] *Deutsche Welle*, 22 August 2011, 'Libya: chronology of a revolt against a dictator'.

[80] *Deutsche Welle*, 14 August 2017, 'Syria civil war timeline: a summary of critical events'.

[81] *Deutsche Welle*, 10 February 2011, 'EU grants Italy emergency funds to deal with migrant influx'.

[82] *Deutsche Welle*, 1 May 2011, 'EU executive may allow members to reinstate border checks'.

for which the EU was entirely unprepared. It led to claims that European refugee policy had failed.[83]

By June 2012, the situation had deteriorated to such an extent that European interior ministers, representing Schengen members, collectively agreed that they should be allowed to close their borders when they felt it necessary. This was in defiance of Brussels, directly contravening freedom of movement rules. But, with refugees from the fighting in Syria making their way through Turkey to the Greek border, and thence onwards into other EU countries, there was little alternative.[84]

A lacklustre response in the field also reopened old wounds, summoning up the ghosts from the 1990s, redolent in some critics' views of the 'division, appeasement, and impotence when the EU failed to halt the fighting in former Yugoslavia'. There were weaknesses evident in EU foreign policy and in the performance of Catherine Ashton. And although there was some measure of accord over Libya between France and the UK, the crisis as a whole intensified still further stresses between the UK and the rest of the EU – and especially with Germany.[85]

THE CALL OF THE EURO

Notwithstanding the Arab Spring, the EU still had its own existential – if partly self-inflicted – euro crisis. Upon its successful resolution rested the survival of the economies of the 17 members of the eurozone, and possibly even the global financial system. But with the crisis now entering its second year, the auguries were not good. Not least, the complexities presented what might be termed 'bandwith' problems for the EU leaders. The demands were so onerous that there was little spare capacity to focus on anything else for any length of time.

In addition to Greece, Portugal and Spain were now in the firing line. Of the two, Portugal was particularly fragile. It had declared a budget deficit of 9.3 per cent and was expected to introduce measures in the coming year to reduce it by 2 per cent. Although it needed to borrow €20 billion to finance immediate debts, the market was pulling away. To add to its travails, the country was expected to fall back into recession.[86]

The eurozone, of course, still suffered the 'wings and engines' problem, lacking the essential currency management tools of a sovereign state. One of those was the ability to take on debt on its own account, issuing so-called

[83] *Deutsche Welle*, 15 February 2011, 'Opinion: European refugee policy has failed'.
[84] *Deutsche Welle*, 7 June 2012, 'EU interior ministers agree new emergency border rules'.
[85] See, for instance, *Guardian*, 11 March 2011, 'Libya no-fly zone plan rejected by EU leaders'.
[86] BBC News, 7 January 2011, 'Timetable of the euro-showdown'.

Eurobonds. To do so indiscriminately was contrary to the ECB's mandate, and it was not allowed to interfere directly in the economic governance of member states. That was a territory guarded by the most powerful nation in the eurozone and by the ever-vigilant Bundesbank.

With these constraints in mind, eurozone leaders came to the European Council of 11 March determined to secure two objectives. The first was an agreement on the so-called 'Euro Plus Pact'. This was aimed at strengthening economic co-ordination between members, and introduced a more sophisticated monitoring system, letting the Commission pick up 'financial imbalances' in individual EU countries. EU fiscal rules were to be translated into national legislation, the stability of the financial sector was to be enhanced, and there was to be 'pragmatic coordination of tax policies'.[87]

The second task was to make further progress on the EFSF replacement. It would have a lending capacity of €500 billion and be charged with running the eurozone's bailout programme. Until it was established, the EFSF would continue in place, with a lending capacity of €440 billion.[88] As to the 'Euro Plus Pact', it sat outside the treaty framework. Lacking 'teeth', it was to be monitored politically by the heads of state or government of the euro area and participating countries, employing what was known as the 'open method of coordination'. Only 23 of the 27 member states signed up.[89]

It was left to the next Council, on 24–25 March, to agree the treaty amendment that paved the way for the EFSF replacement. It was to be called the 'European Stability Mechanism' (ESM), and would start work on 1 January 2013.[90] Crucially, to qualify for its loans, borrowers would have to agree to reforms – known as 'strict conditionality'.[91] This, although no one could know it yet, was to be the hinge on which the eventual survival of the euro turned. Helpfully, Cameron supported the treaty change, but he was aware that some of his backbenchers might be asking, 'If *they* can change treaties to sort out the Eurozone, why can't we change treaties to get out of the Social Chapter, get rid of "ever closer union", or get some of our national vetoes back.'[92]

---

[87] 'Presidency Conclusions', 11–12 March 2011, European Council, Brussels.
[88] Ibid.
[89] *Conclusions of the Heads of State of Government of the Euro Area of 11 March 2011*. See also Europarl website page: 'Communautarisation of the Euro Plus Pact on Competitiveness'.
[90] 'Presidency Conclusions', 24–25 March 2011, European Council, Brussels.
[91] European Council Decision 2011/1999/EU of 25 March 2011, amending Article 136 of the Treaty on the Functioning of the European Union with regard to a stability mechanism for member states whose currency is the euro.
[92] Cameron, op. cit., p. 324.

While the treaty amendment gave the ESM a sound legal base, it also meant it was a hybrid, set up outside the EU framework. Vitor Gaspar, shortly to become the Portuguese finance minister, observed that the intergovernmental route had expedited the set-up.[93] Germany's finance minister Wolfgang Schäuble said that financial aid could now go ahead without violating the no-bailout clause, 'as a last resort to ensure the stability of the currency union and only under strict conditions'.[94]

Outside the specialist financial journals and business columns, this development scarcely registered. But gradually, inexorably, the eurozone was slipping the leash of the Community method, as new institutions and procedures were created to respond to the pressures of the financial markets. Any scintilla of democratic legitimacy was being left behind as small groups of politicians and officials battled to save the single currency. Furthermore, the 'two-tier' Europe had arrived with a vengeance.

PORTUGAL FAILS

Rather as expected, Portugal's economy was the next to crumble. The trigger was a vote in the parliament on 23 March against the government's austerity measures.[95] Prime Minister José Sócrates promised he would resign if his plans were defeated, and that was not long in coming. The loss of the vote 'has taken away from the government all conditions to govern,' he complained. 'It brings the country closer to needing a bailout.' Five-year bond yields, representing the cost of government borrowing, hit a euro lifetime high of 8.2 per cent. This was unsustainable.[96]

Thus, on 7 April 2011, Portugal asked for help, the third country to do so.[97] A programme was formally adopted on 17 May, at the Eurogroup/ Ecofin meeting in Brussels, covering the period 2011 to mid-2014. The joint financing package of €78 billion included €26 billion from the EFSM, €26 billion from the EFSF and about €26 billion provided by the IMF.[98]

Meanwhile, as eurozone politicians struggled over sums in their billions, they were brought down to earth by David Cameron's now annual ritual of complaining about the UK's annual budget contribution for the forthcoming year. Brussels had demanded £682 million extra from the British and was to ignore pleas from Cameron, Merkel and Sarkozy for reduced overall

[93] *Safeguards*, op. cit., p. 137.
[94] Ibid.
[95] Reuters, 23 March 2011, 'Portugal parliament rejects govt austerity plan'.
[96] *Guardian*, 23 March 2011, 'Portugal in crisis after prime minister resigns over austerity measures'.
[97] *Euractiv*, 11 April 2011, 'Portugal seeks bailout amid political crisis'.
[98] European Commission, 'Financial assistance to Portugal' (website).

expenditure. Instead of a freeze, or a cut, the Commission asked for an extra 4.9 per cent.[99] Janusz Lewandowski claimed the money was needed to meet the cost of previous EU decisions, made earlier in the seven-year budget cycle. And, he said, 'despite the climate of austerity, we have to grow'.[100]

GREECE RESURGENT

The very same day that Portugal had asked for help, *The Economist* magazine published a long article declaring that 'the international plan to rescue Greece is instead starting to paralyse it'.[101] Rescue was never going to be easy, the magazine wrote, and some important reforms had certainly been made. But the short-term price had been intolerable. A forecast that GDP would shrink by 4 per cent in 2010 and 2.5 per cent in 2011 had been bad enough, but the actual rate for 2010 had been 4.5 per cent, with 3.2 per cent expected for 2011. Unemployment for 2011 was forecast at 15.5 per cent.

Problems were so deeply entrenched that, at every level, the economy was underperforming, and progress in cutting the deficit in 2010 had been slower than envisaged. Provisional estimates put it at an oppressively high 10.6 per cent of GDP rather than the original target of 8.1 per cent. Debt was close to 145 per cent of GDP. Ten-year government bond yields had climbed to almost 13 per cent and the credit-rating agencies had recently downgraded sovereign debt 'from junk to junkier'. Under the original bailout plan, Greece had been scheduled to raise about half its finance in 2012 from the markets. Since that was now looking infeasible, it was obvious that the country would need a second bailout.[102]

Unsurprisingly, a month later, sentiment had not improved. A report was circulating that Papandreou's government was thinking of dumping the euro and bringing back the drachma.[103] This was quickly denied, although it had been taken seriously enough to trigger a crisis meeting in Luxembourg for the EU to consider its next moves.[104]

Come 9 May, there were no banquets in sunlit Berlin on this Europe Day, the 'Europe is our Common Future' slogan of five years' previously looking distinctly threadbare. There were many who questioned whether 'Europe' even had a future. *Die Presse* in Vienna suggested that if Greece gave up the single currency, Portugal, Ireland, Spain and maybe Italy might follow.

[99] *Daily Telegraph*, 20 April 2011, 'British taxpayers face £600m bill as EU defies Cameron's calls for austerity'.
[100] *Guardian*, 21 April 2011, 'David Cameron vows to fight proposed EU budget rise'.
[101] *The Economist*, 7 April 2011, 'The labours of austerity'.
[102] Ibid.
[103] *Der Spiegel*, 6 May 2011, 'Greece considers exit from euro zone'.
[104] *Deutsche Welle*, 7 May 2011, 'Greek exit from euro out of the question, says eurozone head'.

'Then', it warned, 'the euro, and with it the European Union, is dead.'[105] Never in the entire history of *le projet* had so much been at stake.

Nor was the fate of Greece merely a European affair. News of 30,000 protesters marching outside the parliament building in Athens, 'jeering lawmakers and calling them "thieves" and "robbers"' made the west coast of the United States.[106] And, given the circumstances, it could only get worse. Towards the end of the month, as thousands again gathered in front of the parliament to protest against the latest austerity package, the IMF was mooting withholding its next tranche of funding, due in June.[107]

Less than a month later, *Der Spiegel* was arguing that the euro was becoming 'an ever-greater threat to Europe's common future'. The currency union, it said, 'chains together economies that are simply incompatible'. Politicians, it complained, 'approve one bailout package after the other and, in doing so, have set down a dangerous path that could burden Europeans for generations to come and set the EU back by decades'. The magazine also cited American economist Milton Friedman, who had predicted that the euro would not survive its first major crisis, later, in 2002, adding: 'Euroland will collapse in five to 15 years.'[108]

UK input throughout the period had remained limited, but unhelpful. Charles Grant, the biographer of Jacques Delors – and guru on all things European – opined that Greece should leave the euro, claiming that the prime minister of an unspecified eurozone country had told him that 'it would not contribute to any more bailouts and that Greece should quit the euro'. Much of the current mess, he asserted, 'stems from poor leadership'.[109]

The same day, in the Westminster parliament, now former foreign secretary Jack Straw warned that the euro 'cannot last'. British exposure to Greek debt, he said, was about €13 billion. 'It is the responsibility of the British Government to be open with the British people now about the alternative prospects,' he said, then asking: 'Since the euro in its current form is going to collapse, is it not better that that happens quickly rather than it dying a slow death?'[110] Next day, the BBC had Neil MacKinnon, chief economist at VTB Capital, saying a Greek default was 'now probable'. An

---

[105] *Deutsche Welle*, 9 May 2011, 'European press review: the EU is running out of options'.
[106] *Los Angeles Times*, 11 May 2011, 'Greek general strike protests austerity measures'. The interest was perhaps unsurprising as the world's largest investor in government bonds, the Pacific Investment Company (PIMCO) – an autonomous subsidiary of Allianz – has its headquarters in Newport Beach, California, about an hour's drive south of Los Angeles.
[107] Reuters, 26 May 2011, 'IMF threat to withhold Greek aid spooks markets'.
[108] *Der Spiegel*, 20 June 2011, 'How the euro became Europe's greatest threat'.
[109] *The Times*, 20 June 2011, 'Greece doesn't belong in the euro. It must go'.
[110] HC Deb, 20 June 2011, Vol. 530, col. 26.

exit from monetary union could not be ruled out, he said.[111] David Cameron added his voice to the debate later that day, flatly stating that Britain should not fund the Greek bailout.[112] Meanwhile Eurogroup ministers decided to define 'by early July' the main parameters of 'a clear financing strategy' for Greece.[113]

At the June G7 meeting, a few days later, Cameron decided to offer some entirely gratuitous advice to the EU leaders, telling then to 'agree a plan and to stick to it'. This supposedly reflected concerns of non-euro G7 members about EU 'dithering' on a second Greek bailout. They saw a risk of a 'spill over' effect into a global economy already weakened by recession.[114] Still playing to a domestic audience, Cameron used the European Council on 24 June to demand that the 'European Financial Stability Mechanism' would not be used for the next Greek bailout.[115] He need not have worried. There was no intention to use the 'Stabilisation' mechanism, as it was more correctly known.[116] The more powerful EFSF was in play.[117] It, with the IMF, would deliver the aid package.[118] Thus, when Cameron got his assurance, it was about as useful as a promise not to feed the elephants in Lambeth High Street – even if it gave him some raw meat to feed to his Eurosceptic backbenchers. A signal of the determination of EU leaders to resolve the crisis came towards the end of the month when Van Rompuy and Barroso addressed the European Parliament. Barroso insisted there was no alternative to 'painful reforms'. 'There is no Plan B to avoid default,' he said.[119]

Things certainly seemed to be looking up when, despite a two-day general strike in Greece, Papandreou – with a mere five-vote parliamentary majority – pushed through the EU's package. To the pungent aroma of tear gas, all 154 of the Socialists plus one conservative voted for the measures, with 136 votes against. However, some had doubts about what had been achieved. 'I am not sure at all that the government really

---

[111] BBC *Today* programme, 21 June 2011, 'Greek debt default 'now probable''.
[112] *Daily Telegraph*, 21 June 2011, 'David Cameron: we won't bail out Greece'.
[113] European Commission, Memo/11/426, Brussels, 20 June 2011, statement by the Eurogroup on Greece.
[114] *Daily Telegraph*, 23 June 2011, 'David Cameron calls for unity over EU strategy on Greece'.
[115] *Daily Telegraph*, 24 June 2011, 'David Cameron: Europe has promised Britain won't need to bail out Greece'.
[116] Cameron repeats the error in his memoirs, possibly confusing it with the European Financial Stability Facility, Cameron, op. cit., p. 325.
[117] 'Presidency Conclusions', 23–24 June 2011, Brussels European Council.
[118] Use of the EFSM was proposed in 2015 to provide short-term bridge loans to Greece. See European Commission: 'European Financial Stabilisation Mechanism' (website).
[119] BBC News, 28 June 2011, 'EU leaders "have no Plan B" to deal with Greek crisis'.

intends to move forward with the actual implementation of the plan, or if it's counting on the forthcoming readjustment of the Greek debt plan, effectively buying time so as to move on to elections,' said Professor Elias Nikolakopoulos.[120] Despite the misgivings, on the last day of June, the Van Rompuy and Barroso duo gave their go-ahead for the next loan tranche of €12 billion.[121] This was followed by a formal approval from the IMF to release €3.2 billion.[122]

On 11 July, the treaty setting up the ESM was ready. It was signed by Eurogroup ministers, but complications over the next Greek bailout meant that the text was never ratified. Instead, the Eurogroup, when it met on 21 July, decided to adapt and strengthen the ESM's powers.[123] Thus, the final version of the treaty was not ready for signature until 2 February 2012.[124] As to the new Greek bailout, this launched a new package worth €109 billion. For the first time, private lenders, including banks, were involved, contributing €37 billion.[125]

Conscious that the EU – and in particular the eurozone – was now involved in a process of developing the 'institutional architecture' to manage the euro, a thoroughly confused David Cameron sought to remove the UK from the ESM 'bailout' fund, evidently failing to realise that Britain was not part of it.[126] Addressing his backbench 1922 Committee, he had told them that as the eurozone moved 'towards much more single economic government', Britain should use the negotiations to win concessions. 'There will be opportunities for Britain to maximise what we want in terms of our engagement with Europe,' he said, going on to claim: 'I got us out of the [euro] bailout mechanism', apparently as an illustration of what could be done.[127] But not only was this opening a rift with his coalition partner, Nick Clegg; he was also setting himself up for a major confrontation with the EU, which was to come to a head in December.

---

[120] *New York Times*, 28 June 2011, 'Two-day strike in Greece ahead of austerity vote'; 30 June 2011, 'Greek Parliament approves implementation of austerity plan'.

[121] European Commission, 30 June 2011, joint statement by President Barroso and President Van Rompuy following the vote in the Greek Parliament on the implementing measures for the revised economic programme.

[122] IMF Press Release 11/273, 8 July 2011, 'Press Release: IMF Executive Board Completes Fourth Review Under Stand-By Arrangement for Greece and Approves €3.2 Billion Disbursement'.

[123] Council of the European Union, Brussels, 21 July 2011, 'Statement by the Heads of State or Government of the Euro Area and EU Institutions'. See also *Safeguarding*, op. cit., p. 140.

[124] 'Treaty Establishing the European Stability Mechanism'. The recitals provide a useful timeline.

[125] BBC News, 21 July 2011, 'Eurozone agrees new 109bn euros Greek bailout'.

[126] Cameron, op. cit., pp. 328–330. The term 'institutional architecture' was used by Rafael Behr in his column in the *New Statesman*, 22 July 2011, 'Greek bailout sets Europe on collision course with Tories'.

[127] *Guardian*, 21 July 2011, 'Nick Clegg opens rift with David Cameron over eurozone crisis'.

The holiday season brought no respite for the beleaguered euro. Only days into August, Barroso was warning that the 'debt crisis' was spreading beyond the periphery of the eurozone.[128] With the markets reacting badly, in less than a week the ECB was promising to buy government bonds from Italy and Spain through what it called its 'Securities Markets Programme'.[129] However, Nomura's Robert Law said that the markets were looking for a 'permanent solution' to the eurozone rather than just purchases of bonds.[130] They were not alone in doubting the effect of this limited intervention.

With September, though, came a welcome piece of good news. Germany's participation in the bailouts for Greece, Ireland and Portugal has been questioned in the constitutional court, and an adverse ruling could have prevented its participation in the ESM. But the court allowed Germany a role, as long as the government first gained the approval of the parliament. The court ruled that it must not be allowed to degenerate into one of simple implementation. Instead, it had to remain the body that 'autonomously decides on revenues and expenditures, including those related to international and European obligations'.[131]

A LITTLE LOCAL DIFFICULTY

Cameron's news was less good. The secretary of his troublesome 1922 Committee, Mark Pritchard – representing a like-minded group of 120 Conservative MPs – was telling him that he must call a referendum on 'Europe' or face a rebellion from his own party. The 'unquestioning support' of backbenchers was no longer guaranteed, he said.[132] And bad news for the euro continued to mount. Italy had its debt rating cut by Standard & Poor's to A from A+. Berlusconi dismissed the move, saying it had been influenced by 'political considerations'.[133] To add to the gloom, the IMF warned of 'slowing growth and rising risks', asserting that the global economy was 'now in a dangerous new phase'.[134] The eurozone's private sector had shrunk for the first time in two years.

Emerging now were discussions on the possibility of another treaty change – this one to protect the euro from future crises. Merkel and Sarkozy had discussed it, and a draft position paper on European policy for the party congress of Merkel's conservative Christian Democrats in November argued

[128] BBC News, 4 August 2011, 'Barroso warns debt crisis is spreading'.
[129] European Central Bank, 7 August 2011, Statement by the President of the ECB.
[130] *Guardian*, 8 August 2011, 'Europe's bank acts to ease debt crisis and calm markets'.
[131] *Deutsche Welle*, 8 September 2011, 'German court ruling complicates future European bailouts'.
[132] *Daily Telegraph*, 18 September 2011, 'Tory MPs demand referendum on Europe'.
[133] BBC News, 20 September 2011, 'Italy's sovereign debt rating cut by S&P on growth fear'.
[134] IMF World Economic Outlook, 20 September 2011, 'Slowing Growth, Rising Risks'.

for change. 'There is no way around it,' foreign minister Guido Westerwelle declared. 'A change to the treaties is necessary for there to be an effective change in the stability rules.'[135] The effect of this would be to give 'teeth' to the Euro Plus Pact.

If this registered with Cameron, he gave no immediate sign of it. But he did urge eurozone countries to act swiftly and tackle their levels of debt, prompting a rejoinder from Ed Miliband that the prime minister had 'woken up to the crisis' but had not come up with a plan to tackle it. He was 'quite good at lecturing other people on getting their problems sorted out', but was not taking action himself.[136] Miliband was soon joined by Sarkozy, who, at the European Council on 23 October, snapped at the British prime minister, 'We're sick of you criticising us and telling us what to do. You say you hate the euro, you didn't want to join and now you want to interfere in our meetings.'[137]

The Council itself had noted the significant progress made in acquiring what it described as 'more powerful tools to enhance its economic governance and to ensure that the required measures are taken to pull Europe out of the crisis'. In addition to the Euro Plus Pact, and some highly technical changes to the way business was managed and co-ordinated, this included a 'package of six legislative acts on economic governance', which allowed 'a much higher degree of surveillance and coordination, necessary to ensure sustainable public finances and avoid the accumulation of excessive imbalances'.[138]

The so-called 'six-pack', which was to come into force on 12 December, itself included an amended Stability and Growth Pact (tightening still further the additional rules agreed in 2005), and a new way of applying sanctions to defaulters. This used 'reverse qualified majority voting', which meant fines would be applied automatically, unless the majority disapplied them.[139] Further measures were pursued at a Euro Summit on 26 October, where there was a consensus on the need for a specific 'banking package', dealing with recapitalisation and much else.[140] This cleared the way for an announcement the following day that private investors had agreed to take a notional 50 per cent cut in their holdings of Greek debt, gleefully described by the media as a 'haircut'.[141]

---

[135] *Der Spiegel*, 14 October 2011, 'German politicians call for changes to EU treaties'.
[136] BBC News, 23 September 2011, 'Eurozone debt: Cameron demands swift action'.
[137] *Daily Telegraph*, 23 October 2011, 'Nicolas Sarkozy tells David Cameron: "We're sick of you telling us what to do"'.
[138] 'Presidency Conclusions', 23 October 2011, Brussels European Council.
[139] European Commission, Memo/11.898, Brussels, 12 December 2011, 'EU Economic Governance "Six-Pack" enters into force'.
[140] Euro Summit Statement, Brussels, 26 October 2011.
[141] *Guardian*, 27 October 2011, 'Eurozone crisis: banks agree 50% reduction on Greece's debt'.

Lost in the noise was the amount of 'aerospace engineering' that had been undertaken. Slowly, almost imperceptibly, on a scale scarcely recognised or understood by the media and the majority of British politicians, the 'wings and engines' were being fashioned for the euro 'airliner', ready to arrest its fall to earth.

To further this 'engineering', embedded in both the Eurogroup statement and the presidency conclusions had been a 'ticking time bomb'. The Eurogroup had formally asked for the exploration of 'the possibility of limited Treaty changes', with a view to strengthening economic convergence within the euro area, improving fiscal discipline and deepening economic union. The European Council pledged to return to the issue in December, noting that any treaty change must be agreed by the 27 member states.[142] An 'interim report' was to be presented by Van Rompuy to the December meeting so as 'to agree on first orientations'. This had Cameron at his press conference after the Council suggesting that this was the time to look to repatriating powers back to Britain. 'Obviously the idea of some limited treaty change in the future might give us that opportunity,' he said.[143]

There was no immediate opportunity for Cameron to dwell on this issue. In September, a petition calling for an EU referendum, organised by former UKIP and now independent MEP Nikki Sinclaire, had exceeded 100,000 signatories, triggering a Commons debate.[144] A motion tabled by Tory 'rebel' Bill Cash calling for a referendum came to a vote on 24 October. As demonstrators led by Nigel Farage paraded outside Parliament to show their support, it was pointed out that the UKIP leader had hitherto refused to sign the petition. Only with a TV camera pointing at him and a petition sheet thrust into his hands did he hastily scrawl his name on it.[145]

Cameron instructed his MPs to vote against the motion, but 79 disobeyed him, 2 abstained and 12 did not vote. The motion was defeated, 483 votes to 111, only because Labour and Liberal Democrat MPs opposed it. But it was the biggest Conservative rebellion on 'Europe' since Maastricht.[146] Cameron acknowledged that 'it showed the extent to which the ground was moving under us'.[147] On the Sunday after the vote, the prospect of a forthcoming

---

[142] Conclusions and Statement, op. cit.

[143] *Daily Telegraph*, 24 October 2011, 'David Cameron: closer European integration could marginalise Britain'.

[144] BBC News, 8 September 2011, '100,000 sign petition calling for EU referendum'.

[145] Sinclaire, Nikki (2013), *Never Give Up* (Birmingham: Junius Press), p. 188. Augmented by discussions with the author.

[146] *Daily Telegraph*, 24 October 2011, 'EU referendum: David Cameron hit by biggest Conservative rebellion'.

[147] Cameron, op. cit., p. 332.

treaty change resurfaced when Cameron was interviewed on *The Andrew Marr Show*. Challenged on whether he would repatriate powers from the EU, he suggested that the Germans and others were going to be looking for treaty change for the eurozone. 'If they do that,' he said, 'there may well be opportunities for Britain to further our national interest.'[148]

Before the events of the previous weeks could settle, Papandreou shocked the entire European establishment with plans to put the EU bailout to his own referendum, in the hope that it would unite his fractious coalition.[149] Summoned to the G20 summit in Cannes, held on 3–4 November, he was accused by an incandescent Sarkozy of betrayal. When he was prevailed upon to turn it into an 'in/out' referendum on euro membership, this triggered an angry intervention from his own finance minister, Evangelos Venizelos. Papandreou was forced to call off the poll.[150] Within a week, he had resigned, to be replaced by Lucas Papademos – an alumnus of Goldman Sachs and former vice-president of the ECB. Almost simultaneously, after Italian government borrowing costs had spiked, Berlusconi was forced to resign, to be replaced by ex-EU Commissioner Mario Monti, another alumnus of Goldman Sachs.[151] French television complained of an 'inside job', but equilibrium had been restored – for the time being.[152]

By now, though, the idea of treaty change had been firmly lodged in the public domain, with Cameron being warned not to go too far in demanding repatriation of powers; otherwise he risked creating an unstoppable momentum behind a 'two-speed Europe'.[153] He seemed to need little persuasion. On 14 November, in a speech to the Lord Mayor's Banquet in the City of London's ornate Guildhall, he spoke at length on foreign policy, declaring: 'Leaving the EU is not in our national interest.' Referring to a theme to which he was to resort increasingly in future years, he then pronounced:

> Outside, we would end up like Norway, subject to every rule for the Single Market made in Brussels but unable to shape those rules. And believe me: if we weren't in there helping write the rules, they would be written without us – the biggest supporter of open markets and free trade – and we wouldn't like the outcome.[154]

---

[148] BBC News, *The Andrew Marr Show*, Interview: David Cameron, 30 October 2011.
[149] *France24*, 3 November 2011, 'Greek PM gambles with referendum on EU bailout'.
[150] *New York Times*, 3 November 2011, 'Greek leader calls off referendum on bailout plan'.
[151] BBC News, 13 November 2011, 'Italy crisis: Mario Monti appointed new PM-designate'.
[152] *France24*, 16 November 2011, 'Goldman Sachs and Europe's "inside job"'.
[153] *Guardian*, 17 November 2011, 'Cameron warned his eurozone stance risks forcing two-speed Europe'.
[154] Gov.uk, 14 November 2011, 'Prime Minister's speech at the Lord Mayor's Banquet: Foreign Policy in the National Interest'.

One person who responded was Nigel Farage. He recorded his views on a YouTube clip, stating:

> There is absolutely nothing to fear in terms of trade from leaving the European Union because, on D-plus one, we'll find ourselves part of the European Economic Area and with a free trade deal. And we should use our membership of the EEA as a holding position from which we can negotiate, as the European Union's biggest export market in the world.[155]

Two days before the December European Council, Cameron was taunted by Ed Miliband, who demanded to know: 'what powers will he be arguing to repatriate?'[156] The day earlier, Van Rompuy's 'interim report' had been leaked. Headed 'Towards a stronger economic union', it set out two options: limited changes to one of the Protocols in the consolidated treaty, requiring a unanimous decision of the Council; use of the simplified revision procedure that had been used for the ESM treaty, also requiring unanimous agreement. There was another option also being mooted by Merkel and Sarkozy: a separate, intergovernmental treaty agreed only between the eurozone members.[157]

What was very clear was that there was no treaty text for the EU leaders to consider, much less sign. The European Council would only 'decide whether the new treaty will be signed by all 27 EU members, as most states and the European Commission would like, or only by the 17 eurozone countries, which France and Germany are proposing if they cannot win EU-wide support'. Already, though, Cameron was talking about using his veto.[158] Come the day, when the discussion focused on the options for change, Cameron demanded adoption of his own agenda as a condition for his support of an EU treaty. Van Rompuy closed the meeting, saying the UK could not be accommodated.[159] There was no vote. Outside, holding his own press conference, Cameron told the media that he had vetoed 'an EU treaty'.[160] But there had been no treaty to veto.

[155] https://www.youtube.com/watch?v=VtNr4z3YrYo&ab_channel=FullEnglishBrexit.
[156] HC Deb, 7 December 2011, Vol. 537, col. 293.
[157] *Financial Times*, 6 December 2011, 'Fast-track "fiscal compact" drawn up'.
[158] *Daily Telegraph*, 7 December 2011, 'Eurozone debt crisis: safeguard the City or I'll veto new EU treaty, warns David Cameron'.
[159] *Financial Times*, 16 December 2011, 'False assumptions underpinned British strategy'. Although reference is made to Cameron's 'financial protocol', which he presented (in whole or part of the Council), nothing of this has been published, before or since.
[160] Cameron, op. cit., pp. 337–338.

Although lionised by his Eurosceptic backbenchers and sympathetic media, Cameron had achieved nothing. Days later, Van Rompuy was addressing the European Parliament, telling MEPs that the intergovernmental route had been chosen.[161] It would be 'negotiated as a matter of urgency' in order to be ready for March. This was to become the Treaty on Stability, Coordination and Governance in the Economic and Monetary Union.[162] Cameron's main contribution had been to confirm the reality of a two-speed Europe and widen an already substantial gulf into an irreconcilable split.[163] Looking back in his memoirs, he thought his 'veto' was a very important moment and choice.[164] In retrospect, it was another milestone on the road to Brexit.

As for 2011, academic Henning Meyer wrote: 'it is fair to say that this year has been one of the most disastrous for the European Union in its history'. Unless EU leaders completely changed course and overcame political and legal obstacles to installing the European Central Bank as a lender of last resort, drew up plans for a real fiscal union, introduced eurobonds, devised a strategy for new growth, pursued necessary structural reforms in surplus as well as deficit countries and finally reformed the financial sector, he wrote, there was little hope that the current malaise could be overcome.[165]

THAT SINKING FEELING

As the eurozone plunged into its third year of crisis, even its most fervent enthusiasts could hardly claim that the EU had retained its original air of adventure. Not two weeks into 2012 and the credit-rating agency Standard & Poor's downgraded France and eight other eurozone countries, claiming that 'policy initiatives that have been taken by European policy-makers in recent weeks may be insufficient to fully address ongoing systemic stresses in the eurozone'.[166]

That same day, the real world intruded again. The Italian cruise ship *Costa Concordia* ran aground and capsized rapidly after striking an underwater rock off Isola del Giglio, Tuscany, with 32 deaths. What gave it a European

---

[161] European Parliament, Debates, Tuesday 13 December 2011 – Strasbourg, Conclusions of the European Council meeting (8–9 December 2011).
[162] Also referred to as the TSCG, the Fiscal Stability Treaty and sometimes, confusingly, the 'Stability Compact', it was effectively a stricter version of the Stability and Growth Pact. The treaty was signed in March 2012 by all EU members with the exception of the Czech Republic and the United Kingdom, and entered into force on 1 January 2013.
[163] *Der Spiegel*, 9 December 2011, 'The birth of a two-speed Europe'.
[164] Cameron, op. cit., p. 338.
[165] *Guardian*, 19 December 2011, 'Europe, prepare for a riotous 2012'.
[166] Business Insider, 13 January 2012, 'It's official: S&P announces mass downgrade of eurozone countries'.

dimension was that passenger ship safety was an EU competence, governed by a 2009 Directive, with the Commission also implementing International Maritime Organisation (IMO) standards.[167] What was immediately striking about the EU law and the IMO standards was their relative age, the core IMO standard going back to 1993. And even the date of the EU's 2009 Directive was misleading. It was basically a recast of a 1998 directive.

Significantly, the EU had funded considerable research into the effect of collision damage, carried out in Glasgow and Strathclyde Universities nearly a decade before the latest legislation had been passed. Scientists had tested three cruise ship designs – all complied with then current regulations. In the research, 33 damage scenarios had been tested, and in 16 cases the vessels had capsized within two hours. In particular, a newly discovered phenomenon had been tested, known as the multiple free surface (MFS) effect, where traditional calculation and testing could not adequately describe the behaviour of a damaged ship.

A later report noted that 'the current measure of survivability of a damaged ship in a seaway has been shown to be inaccurate and inadequate practically from the moment of its introduction'.[168] Nothing in the regulatory standards at the time, therefore, reflected the work on multiple free surface effect, or transient flooding, either of which could have been responsible for the *Costa Concordia*'s rapid capsize, also explaining why the ship listed away from the damaged side. The EU, so keen to exercise its power, was once again proving less adept at producing legislation that actually worked.

In a sense, the ship could almost have been a metaphor for the euro, although the UK media scarcely, if at all, mentioned the EU link. This characterised a significant phenomenon, where EU involvement was often unacknowledged, becoming not so much an elephant in the room as a rampant herd.[169] A good example of this came when Cameron responded to a question in the Commons on the safety of cruise ships. If any changes to regulations or other things needed to be made, he said, 'of course we will

[167] Directive 2009/45/EC of 6 May 2009 on safety rules and standards for passenger ships.
[168] Jakub Cichowicz, Nikolaos Tsakalakis, Dracos Vassalos and Andrzej Jasionowski, 'Damage Survivability of Passenger Ships: Re-Engineering the Safety Factor', *Safety*, 19 February 2016.
[169] One exception was the Booker column in the *Sunday Telegraph* of 21 January 2012, headed: 'The EU ignored years of expert warnings on cruise ship safety'. This provoked a complaint from Transport Commissioner Siim Kallas, who demanded a rebuttal. Booker published a rebuttal to the rebuttal on 4 February 2012, headed: 'The EU, "mega-ships" and a paper trail of warnings that still remains'. He wrote that Professor Dracos Vassalos – arguably Europe's leading expert on ship safety, who had carried out research funded by the Commission for 17 years – had warned of precisely the disaster that befell the *Costa Concordia*, arguing in 2007 that 'the regulatory system is stretched to breaking point'.

make them'.[170] Not one MP then or later remarked that the prime minister had no power to make changes in an area that was an EU competence.

But another reason for the EU's extraordinary failure was that regulation was also handled by the IMO. This moved at an even more glacial pace than Brussels. However, the Commission was reluctant to take unilateral action because it had been told by European shipping interests that this could lead to the industry escaping from the EU to countries not under its jurisdiction.[171] Here, almost entirely unremarked, was a graphic example of the reach of globalisation. Once supreme, even Brussels was no longer master in its own house.

HIGH NOON IN THE EUROZONE

If Greece had been a cruise ship, it would have been listing heavily as its government tried to negotiate a debt write-off. In publicity terms, though, it could not compete with the Tuscany drama. Nor could it be denied that the economic situation generally was deteriorating. Eurozone unemployment had hit a new record, with Greece recording 18.8 per cent, while Spain had the highest in Europe at 22.9 per cent.[172] At least on 2 February, the final text of the ESM Treaty had been signed, but there was little other cheer in that bleak month. The progress of economic reforms in Greece was still glacial. Commission spokesman Amadeu Altafaj declared that Greece's troubles 'were not caused by the troika', implying that the Greeks had no one to blame but themselves. The crisis only 'worsened chronic problems that had existed in the Greek economy for many years,' he said.[173] More generally, on 23 February, the European Commission confirmed that the eurozone was in 'mild recession'.[174]

The bad news was as relentless as it was depressing, relieved briefly on 13 March when the eurozone finally backed a second Greek bailout of €130 billion, despite the country not having met the conditions set for the first.[175] IMF backing was also required and later given.[176] The following month, despite Monti's appointment, Italian government borrowing costs continued to rise.[177] Even then attention was shifting to Spain, where the

[170] HC Deb, 18 January 2012, Vol. 538, col. 742.
[171] Booker. See previous footnote.
[172] *Guardian*, 6 January 2012, 'Eurozone unemployment hits new record'.
[173] *Deutsche Welle*, 7 February 2012, 'EU Commission losing patience with Greece'.
[174] European Commission, Press release 23 February 2012, 'Interim forecast: euro area in mild recession with signs of stabilisation'.
[175] BBC News, 13 March 2012, 'Eurozone group backs second Greek bailout'.
[176] IMF Press Release No. 12/85: 15 March 2012, IMF Executive Board Approves €28 Billion Arrangement Under Extended Fund Facility for Greece.
[177] BBC News, 12 April 2012, 'Italy's borrowing costs rise in bond auction'.

familiar pattern of increasing borrowing costs and declining share values was being seen, made worse when S&P's cut its credit rating to BBB+ in late April.[178]

On 6 May, the Greeks delivered another shock to the system when, in a general election, the main 'pro-bailout' parties, the Socialists and the New Democracy Party, took a drubbing while the radical leftist Syriza gained ground – as did the neo-Nazi Golden Dawn. When the pro-bailout factions failed to form a coalition, new elections were announced for 17 June. Second time round, New Democracy gained the lead, enough 'to bring Greece back on a path of sustainable growth'.[179] The immediate crisis was over.

In the interim, while France had been electing a new president, deposing the incumbent Nicolas Sarkozy and installing François Hollande with a slender 51.64 per cent of the vote, contagion had brought Spain's fourth largest bank, Bankia, to the brink of collapse. The bank called on the government for €19 billion in aid.[180] On 9 June, after first denying the need for a bailout, it fell to economy minister Luis de Guindos to request up to €100 billion from the eurozone, in order to recapitalise Spain's banking system.[181]

On 13 June, Barroso was in Strasbourg addressing the European Parliament. In a detailed, technical speech, he laid out what was needed to achieve financial stability. That included a regulation-based 'banking union', refining the ESM 'to strengthen our potential to intervene', a serious discussion of 'the joint issuance and mutualisation of national debt in the form of stability bonds', more co-ordination in taxation policy and a much stronger European approach to budgetary matters. Acknowledging that 'deeper fiscal integration' would need treaty change, he told MEPs that a roadmap and a timetable would have to be worked out, taking into account 'the need to build the necessary political and democratic momentum'.[182]

Conservative MEP Martin Callanan was not impressed. 'You are creating ever more centralisation with the increasingly desperate attempt to control a crisis in which you have failed,' he complained.[183] He had a point. No matter how desirable the 'Community method' might have been to Barroso, there was hardly enough time for the full treaty change process. Within a fortnight of Barroso's speech, Cyprus became the fifth eurozone country to

[178] Reuters, 3 May 2012, 'Spanish borrowing costs to jump at auction, bank buying eyed'.
[179] New York Times, 17 June 2012, 'Supporters of Bailout Claim Victory in Greek Election'.
[180] Reuters, 26 May 2012, 'Spain's Bankia eyes stake sales after record bailout'.
[181] Financial Times, 10 June 2012, 'Spain seeks eurozone bailout'.
[182] European Commission, 13 June 2012, José Manuel Durão Barroso President of the European Commission Joint European Parliament Debate on the forthcoming European Council meeting.
[183] Deutsche Welle, 14 June 2012, 'Barroso warns EU parliament of eurozone breakup'.

request a bailout.[184] Something had to be done to relieve the pressure, and it had to be soon.

THE ECB TO THE RESCUE

The European Council's response was a ponderous debate on a report presented by Van Rompuy with the grandiose heading: 'Towards a genuine Economic and Monetary Union'.[185] Prepared 'in close cooperation with the Presidents of the Commission, the Eurogroup and the European Central Bank', this marked the beginning of closer co-operation between the institutions. In setting out a 'vision for the future', though, it did not capture the enormity of the crisis. As it stood, EMU would be lucky to have a future.

Relief came in the form of Mario Draghi, president of the ECB. In a speech in London on 26 July, he surprised his audience by telling them that, within its mandate, the ECB was ready to do whatever it took to preserve the euro. 'And believe me, it will be enough,' he declared.[186] The speech galvanised the financial markets. On Wall Street, US stocks rose and the Dow Jones was up 1.5 per cent.[187] They might have been less bullish, however, had they realised that Draghi had come to the fight with an empty holster. The ECB was still prohibited by its mandate from direct intervention. As yet, it had not worked out a mechanism that would survive the dual scrutiny of the German constitutional court and the ECJ, much less the opposition of the Bundesbank.

What then transpired is the subject of conflicting reports. But it is a matter of record that ECB staff spent 'a furious summer' constructing a system that could be used to support the ailing euro, within the ECB's mandate.[188] The result was 'Outright Monetary Transactions' (OMTs), unveiled on 6 September.[189] Described as Draghi's 'bazooka', it was restricted to the secondary bond markets, preventing troubled government issuing bonds in the expectation that the ECB would buy them. The necessary condition was 'strict and effective conditionality' via country-specific EFSF/ESM programmes. The wings had been glued on to the euro and the engines were stuttering into life.

---

[184] *Deutsche Welle*, 26 June 2012, 'Cyprus becomes fifth country to seek bailout'.

[185] European Council, The President, Brussels, 26 June 2012, EUCO 120/12, *Remarks by President of the European Council Herman Van Rompuy*.

[186] Speech by Mario Draghi, President of the European Central Bank at the Global Investment Conference in London, 26 July 2012, European Central Bank (website).

[187] BBC News, 26 July 2012, 'ECB will act to save euro, says Mario Draghi'.

[188] One of many detailed analyses was produced by the *Financial Times*. On 15 May 2014, it published the third article in a series entitled: 'If the euro falls, Europe falls', setting out its version of events.

[189] ECB press release, 6 September 2012, 'Technical features of Outright Monetary Transactions'.

Without political support, the scheme would have been dead in the water. It took weeks of deft lobbying by Draghi and his allies before Merkel came onside and Bundesbank opposition had been marginalised. The turnkey had been the understanding that 'conditionality' would be thorough and legally binding, which, through the EFSF/ESM programme, it was. Draghi's reward was to have Merkel openly defend the new system, the day after it had been announced.[190] The day she spoke, Italian ten-year bonds yields closed below 5.1 per cent for the first time in five months and Spain's fell below 6 per cent.

But the final piece of the jigsaw had to wait until 8 October when the ESM opened for business, an event made possible by the German constitutional court clearing the way for ratification of the treaty.[191] *Handelsblatt* wondered whether Draghi had made the ESM superfluous.[192] Christoph Weil, an economist at Commerzbank, answered: 'Of course not', he said: 'The ESM is the key programme for the national crises.' It was a necessary condition as the ECB would only buy government bonds from the crisis countries if they were under the protection of the aid programme. 'It cannot be otherwise. Because the ESM can finance states in an emergency, but the ECB is prohibited from doing this,' he explained. 'The ESM rescue package hides the shortcomings of the ECB's announcement.'

With that, the worst of Europe's debt crisis was over. The price, apart from the pain of 'austerity' spreading throughout Europe, was a substantial loss of power within the eurozone countries and, as a bastard form of intergovernmentalism emerged, France and especially Germany had gained in strength.

CAMERON'S PRIVATE WAR

While EU leaders had earned some respite, David Cameron had his own battles to fight. Under pressure from his MPs to repatriate powers from the EU, he bought time by having William Hague commission a comprehensive review of 'the balance of competences' between the UK and the EU. Launched on 12 July 2012 and not due for completion until 2014, this could provide a solid evidence on which to base the forthcoming negotiations.[193]

This move was essential to Cameron's plans. A YouGov poll emphasised how important it was: given an immediate referendum, 48 per cent supported

[190] Reuters, 7 September 2012, 'Merkel defends ECB after German outcry'.
[191] Reuters, 12 September 2012, 'German court removes hurdle to euro zone bailout fund'.
[192] 8 October 2012.
[193] Command Paper 8415, Review of the Balance of Competences between the United Kingdom and the European Union, July 2012.

'leave' while 31 per cent opted to remain. Given successful renegotiations, though, 42 per cent switched to favouring 'remain' as opposed to 34 per cent voting to leave. This compared with Wilson's experience in January 1975, when a simple majority had been in favour of leaving but, if offered 'new terms', 71 per cent preferred to stay in.[194] Extremely conscious of this effect was Andrea Leadsom, leader of the 'Fresh Start Project', which she and two other Tory backbenchers, Chris Heaton-Harris and George Eustice, had launched in September 2011. Committed to reform rather than withdrawal, it had produced in June a lengthy report setting out options in 11 sectors where changes might be secured.[195]

If he was aware of the report, Cameron did not use it.[196] Instead, he complained that his party 'was becoming increasingly ungovernable' on 'Europe'. He also wrote that 'Britain's current status in Europe was becoming increasingly unsustainable, as the whole project continued to mutate into something so different from what we signed up to all those years ago.'[197] There, writ large, was the Tory 'foundation myth' on the EU. Unable to reconcile the fact that a Conservative leader, Edward Heath, had taken the country into an EEC dedicated to political integration, successive generations of Tory politicians had fostered the myth that we had joined a trading bloc – the 'Common Market' – only for the fiendish continentals to go off the rails and attempt to turn it into a 'federal superstate'.[198] Behind that grew the conviction that all that was needed was 'reform from within', whence the continentals could be gently advised of the error of their ways and led down the true path of free trade.

As this threadbare argument increasingly failed to convince the Tory backbenchers, battle was rejoined in parliament when, on 31 October, the EU's multi-annual financial framework came to the Commons for a vote. Intended to approve Cameron's negotiating mandate at the forthcoming European Council, it became the occasion of a 'humiliating defeat' when the Labour Party joined 53 Eurosceptic Tory rebels to demand a reduction 'in real terms' to the budget.[199] Despite a commitment from the government to

---

[194] YouGov, 11 July 2012, Peter Kellner: 'Europe: Cameron as wily as Wilson?'
[195] Fresh Start Project, 'Options for Change' Green Paper: Renegotiating the UK's relationship with the EU.
[196] Nor, indeed, does he seem to have mentioned the Review of the Balance of Competences. Thus, he ignored two potentially powerful tools which could have assisted in the renegotiations.
[197] Cameron, op. cit., p. 339.
[198] The myth was extraordinarily pervasive, and not confined to politicians. For instance, in an 'explainer' piece on 1 April 2019, ITV political correspondent Paul Brand wrote: 'The Common Market was the precursor to the European Union – originally just an economic project, which later evolved to become a political one too.'
[199] Reuters, 31 October 2012, 'UK's Cameron rocked by defeat in Europe budget vote'.

'veto' any proposal that did not cut or at least freeze this, the rebels' motion was carried by 307 votes to 294, a majority of 13.[200]

Unsurprisingly, the European Council of 22–23 November failed to reach an agreement, with Van Rompuy refusing to cut the Commission's original proposal of €1.025 trillion – the first trillion-euro framework in the EU's history.[201] A terse communiqué noted that there was 'a sufficient degree of potential convergence to make an agreement possible in the beginning of next year'.[202] The showdown was thus deferred.

Before the EU leaders met again for the final European Council of the year, on 13–14 December, they were fortified by two events. The first was the ECJ ruling that the treaty amendment that had brought about the ESM was valid – thus supporting the earlier Karlsruhe judgement.[203] The second was an award to the EU of the 2012 Nobel Peace Prize, in recognition of its role in 'stabilising' Europe and transforming it 'from a continent of war to a continent of peace'.[204] At the Council, with the budget decision deferred, the leaders continued with the theme broached by Van Rompuy in June on the future of EMU. Barroso, for instance, delivered in September his State of the Union speech, when he promised a 'blueprint' that would identify treaty changes the Commission felt necessary. 'A deep and genuine economic and monetary union, a political union, with a coherent foreign and defence policy, means ultimately that the present European Union must evolve', and this 'federation of nation states' would require treaty change, he intoned. 'This is our political horizon.'[205]

Now the Council had the promised 'blueprint', aimed at starting the 'European Debate'.[206] This noted that EMU had been 'overhauled', but the work was not yet complete. It complained, among other things, about the lack of strong, integrated EU-level institutions, which had 'effectively resulted in the reversal of integration and caused damage to the level playing field'. With this very much in mind, the Council agreed on a roadmap for the completion of EMU, based on 'deeper integration and reinforced solidarity'.[207] The groundwork was being laid for the next EU treaty.

Leaving it to a few days before Christmas, Mario Monti resigned as Italian prime minister, paving the way for elections in February.[208]

[200] HC Deb, 31 October 2012, Vol. 552, cols 296 and 341.
[201] BBC News, 23 November 2012.
[202] The European Council in 2012, Annual Report, p. 64.
[203] Court of Justice of the European Union, 27 November 2012 – Case C-370/12 Pringle.
[204] Deutsche Welle, 10 December 2012, 'EU receives Nobel Peace Prize at Oslo ceremony'.
[205] European Council, 12 September 2012, José Manuel Durão Barroso, President of the European Commission, State of the Union 2012 Address. Plenary session of the European Parliament/Strasbourg.
[206] European Commission, Brussels, 30 November 2012, COM(2012) 777 final/2.
[207] 'Presidency Conclusions', 14 December 2012, Brussels European Council.
[208] Daily Telegraph, 21 December 2012, 'Mario Monti resigns as Italian prime minister'.

With that, *Deutsche Welle* reported, the EU 'happily closes the books on a tumultuous 2012'.[209] The debt crisis had been 2012's dominant force, relegating everything else to a sideshow: the civil war in Syria, the sharpening of the Middle East conflict, the upheavals in Egypt. But, for all the turmoil, it ended on an optimistic note. For many, it said, 'a sense of a shared European destiny has strengthened'. Others in Britain would disagree and, within the next four years, would convert that disagreement into something more tangible.

[209] 26 December 2012.

20

Countdown to Referendum: 2012–2013

I was bringing forward something that would have happened regardless. When the inevitable treaty came, the lock would have kicked in and meant we'd have to hold a referendum – and the pressure for an in/out one would be huge.

David Cameron[1]

There's little chance of Britain leaving the EU.

Peter Kellner, YouGov[2]

The year 2013 was the twentieth anniversary of the establishment of European Union Citizenship under the Maastricht Treaty, in celebration of which the Commission designated it the 'European Year of Citizens'. For British Eurosceptics, however, it was a year of anticipation: a speech from David Cameron on the 'future of Europe' was expected, in which he was to announce an in/out referendum. He had been seriously mulling over the possibility since January 2012, while UKIP had still been a small force. The party's role in the formulation of his referendum pledge, he thought, 'tends to be overstated'.[3] His resolve had been strengthened at the European Council on 28–29 June 2012 when there had been an attempt to create a banking union and Britain had been pressured to join in. No. 10 branded this as one of the prime minister's greatest negotiating triumphs.[4]

---

[1] Cameron, op. cit., p. 405.
[2] *Guardian*, 7 May 2013.
[3] Ibid., p. 406.
[4] Cameron states that, at his behest, this decision was passed to the Eurogroup. See Euro Area Summit Statement, 29 June 2012. The provision allowed for ECB supervision of the banks in the euro area, which could then be recapitalised directly by the ESM, if need be. With the involvement of the ESM – of which the UK was not part – it is not clear how the UK could have joined the banking union.

At his press conference afterwards, he said that 'Europe was changing rapidly, that this would bring opportunities for us, and that we needed to think how to make the most of that – with the backing of our people.'[5] However, he added, the newspapers missed the hint completely and had him ruling out a referendum.[6] The following day, therefore, he typed out an article for the *Sunday Telegraph*, affirming his support for a referendum, when 'the time is right'.[7]

Liam Fox, a former defence secretary and avowed Eurosceptic, was quick on the uptake, using a speech in London to argue for withdrawal unless there was a 'rebalancing' of the relationship.[8] Cameron's response was to repeat his Sunday message in the Commons when he reported on the European Council. To a noisy chamber, he declared it would be 'wrong to rule out any type of referendum for the future'. In so doing, he placed an in/out referendum firmly on the political agenda.[9] When the likely, if not inevitable, 'fundamental treaty change' went ahead, he would piggy-back the negotiations 'to find a settlement for the UK' and confirm it through a popular vote. 'Far from ruling out a referendum for the future, as a fresh deal in Europe becomes clear, we should consider how best to get the fresh consent of the British people,' he told MPs.[10]

Elaborating on this point, he later explained to officials, 'I was bringing forward something that would have happened regardless.' When the inevitable treaty came, this would have forced a referendum. The pressure for an in/out one 'would be huge', he said.[11] And if he had needed any convincing about the path to take, the intervention by backbencher John Baron at the end of June might have helped him focus. This MP had orchestrated a letter signed by a hundred of his colleagues calling for legislation committing the UK to a referendum after the forthcoming election. A law would 'address the lack of public trust' that meant promises to hold such a vote 'hold little sway', Baron said.[12] For all that, he was pushing at an open door. Cameron was waiting to get the autumn European Councils out of the way first, having pencilled in his speech for 2013.[13]

[5] Cameron, op. cit., p. 410.
[6] *Daily Telegraph*, 29 June 2012, 'David Cameron rules out EU referendum'.
[7] *Sunday Telegraph*, 1 July 2012, 'David Cameron: We need to be clear about the best way of getting what is best for Britain'.
[8] BBC News, 2 July 2012, 'Liam Fox urges government to issue "quit EU" ultimatum'.
[9] HC Debates, 2 July 2012, Vol. 547, col. 586.
[10] Ibid., col. 587.
[11] Cameron, op. cit., p. 405.
[12] BBC News, 28 June 2012, 'EU referendum: 100 Tory MPs back call for vote'.
[13] Cameron, op. cit., pp. 410–411.

Nevertheless, the media pressure continued to mount. In September, when he was in Brazil on a trade mission, journalists quizzed the prime minister on the referendum. The BBC's political editor, Nick Robinson, confidently predicted the speech would come before December's EU leaders 'summit'.[14] The *Daily Mail* focused on the idea that Cameron was to 'claw back 100 powers' from the EU – a reference to the 'balance of competences' – but it, too, went for a 'pre-summit' timing.[15] At the height of the party conference in Birmingham, when 'rock star' Boris Johnson, still London mayor, was making a determined pitch to be anointed as the next party leader, fringe meetings were full of referendum talk. Cameron spoke to the *Today* programme, once again backing a referendum as the 'cleanest, neatest and simplest way' of giving the public a say on Britain's position in Europe.[16] However, there was frustration at his refusal to name the day.[17]

In October, Cameron invited Boris Johnson and his family to Chequers for lunch, to discuss the prospect of a referendum. Johnson, he wrote later, was a Eurosceptic but had never argued for leaving the EU. 'He seemed to have done almost no thinking about what sort of referendum, when it should be held, or what the government's view should be.' Nevertheless, Cameron mused, as a popular figure 'his support for a referendum – however inchoate – was a potentially dangerous development if we decided against holding one'. And his apparent support, however muddled, for an immediate vote was an 'irritation'.[18]

On 5 December, topping a front-page lead story, *The Times* ran the headline: 'Cameron set to offer "in or out" vote on Europe'. 'In this gamble', he 'would urge the public to support a looser relationship with Brussels', which he hoped to negotiate over the coming years. But, the report continued, 'he is ready to give the country a chance to say "no" to such a deal, a result that would effectively be seen as a vote to quit the EU, at least on the proposed terms'. Also quoted was Johnson, arguing for a relationship akin to Norway's and Switzerland's and confined to the 'Single Market'.

KILLING 'NORWAY'

By December, it was too late in the year for his referendum, but this did not stop Cameron extolling the virtues of the Single Market to the

[14] BBC News, 27 September 2012, 'David Cameron considers a referendum on Europe'.
[15] *Daily Mail*, 28 September 2012, 'Cameron prepares series of moves to claw back 100 powers from EU'.
[16] For instance: *Guardian*, 9 October 2012, 'David Cameron backs referendum on Europe'.
[17] *Daily Mail*, 9 October 2012, 'I'd back a public vote on Europe, says David Cameron (but he won't say when it will be)'.
[18] Cameron, op. cit., p. 409.

Parliamentary Press Gallery in Westminster. And, in what appeared to be a recognition of the threat posed by the 'inchoate' Johnson offering Norway and Switzerland as alternatives to the EU – and more so, the EFTA/EEA 'Norway' option, which was a favourite among Eurosceptics – he went into high gear in an attempt to demolish the idea, building on his Guildhall speech of November 2011. 'I think it is worth understanding what leaving would involve,' he said:

> there is the Norway option. You can be like Norway – and you can have full access to the single market but you have absolutely no say over the rules of that market. In Norway they sometimes call it 'Government by fax' because you are simply taking the instructions about every rule in the single market from Brussels without any say on what those rules are.[19]

His comments were quickly reinforced by Norwegian foreign minister, Espen Eide, telling the BBC's *The World This Weekend* two days before Christmas that Oslo had 'limited scope for influence'. 'We are not at the table when decisions are made,' he said.[20]

On 6 January, Cameron appeared on BBC television's *Andrew Marr Show*, to preview his speech. He returned to 'Norway', declaring that, within the Single Market, the UK 'had a seat at the table' and helped write the rules. 'If we were outside the EU altogether,' he asserted, 'we'd still be trading with all these European countries ... but we'd have no say over the rules of the market into which we sell.'[21] He was at it again on 15 January, speaking to the *Today* programme: Britain needed access to the Single Market, he said. 'More than that, we need a say in the rules of that market.' The day previously, the House of Commons Library had published a report on Norway and the EU. With dreary predictability, it intoned:

> Norway has adopted three quarters of the EU's rules and legislation. But Norway has little say in any of this. Although it can attend and talk at various meetings, it does not generally have the right to make or amend proposals which affect it, or to vote on them. This democratic deficit is seen as the biggest problem with Norway's position.[22]

[19] *Daily Telegraph*, 10 December 2012, 'We will be governed "by fax" from Brussels if UK quits EU, David Cameron says'.
[20] BBC News, 23 December 2012, 'Norwegian minister Espen Eide urges UK caution on quitting EU'.
[21] *The Andrew Marr Show*, Interview: David Cameron MP, prime minister, 6 January 2013.
[22] House of Commons Library, 14 January 2013, 'Norway's relationship with the EU'.

The claims being made were at best misleading and, at worst, false. Norway paid nothing into the EU budget and, while it had no vote on Single Market measures, it did have a right to be consulted through the so-called 'two-pillar structure'.[23] That Norway had adopted three-quarters of the EU's 'rules and legislation', was certainly false. Yet it was to be repeated many times, by Cameron, the BBC and Norwegian politicians. In fact, they were citing a mistake in the introduction of a 2012 official Norwegian government report.[24] The true figure, in the body of the report, was about 28 per cent.[25]

Nevertheless, even the correct figure did not do justice to the actual situation. With globalisation, most trade regulation and many related matters came within the purview of regional and global standards-setting bodies, from which the EU took direction. As Norway was a member of most of these bodies in its own right, and was adept in exercising its influence in them, it was often able to shape the rules before they reached the EU. By contrast, the UK was often represented by the EU, and had to abide by the 'common position', even when it went against the national interest. In certain respects, therefore, Norway often had more influence than the UK in the framing of regulation.

Such nuances, however, were not for the prime minister, nor for Andrew Marr or others. Theirs was a gilded circle of ignorance where they endlessly recycled each other's errors.[26] But then, the Norway 'EFTA/EEA' option' was potentially an attractive alternative to EU membership, which made it a key target for EU-enthusiasts. Anti-'Norway option' propaganda was thus to become a consistent part of the narrative.[27]

As to the much-anticipated speech, it was finally delivered on Wednesday 23 January at the London headquarters of the Bloomberg group. It had been trailed so often and previewed so many times that there were no surprises. But the nation now had a firm promise of an in/out referendum. Legislation was to be drafted before the election and if a Conservative government

---

[23] EEA (website): 'The two-pillar structure of the EEA Agreement – incorporation of new EU acts'.
[24] Official Norwegian Reports NOU 2012: 'Outside and Inside', Norway's Agreements with the European Union, Report by the EEA Review Committee, appointed on 7 January 2010. Submitted to the Ministry of Foreign Affairs on 17 January 2012.
[25] Evaluated on the EUReferendum blog: 'EU Referendum: the EEA acquis', 31 October 2015.
[26] The lament of Charles Louis Etienne (1796): 'Personne n'est corrigé; personne n'a su ni rien oublier ni rien apprendre'. Some things never change.
[27] Another of the claims made by Cameron was that Norway was the passive recipient of EU law, which it received 'by fax' and simply adopted it. This was not true. EFTA/EEA states did not adopt EU law – they first assessed whether it was appropriate to the treaty and then converted it into EEA law – with the option to refuse adoption, the so-called right of reservation. Some of this was addressed by Booker in Sunday Telegraph, 19 January 2013. 'Norway's "fax democracy" is nothing for Britain to fear'. It had no impact on Cameron, who continued to repeat the canard.

was elected, enabling legislation would be introduced immediately and passed by the end of that year. Negotiations would be completed and the referendum held within the first half of the next parliament – effectively before the end of 2017.[28]

Predictably, in his speech, Cameron complained about 'excessive regulation'. This, he argued, 'is not some external plague that's been visited on our businesses'. People, he said, 'resent the interference in our national life by what they see as unnecessary rules and regulation'. Already in train, though, was another of those occasional crises that stemmed in part from such 'interference'. Yet, by the time the crisis was over, few would be any the wiser as to why it had happened.

THE GREAT HORSEMEAT SCANDAL

In the nature of things, as it stemmed from criminal enterprise, no one can be sure when exactly the sequence leading to the 'great horsemeat scandal' actually started. The adulteration of (mainly) processed beef products with cheaper horsemeat may have been, and most probably had been going on for some time, albeit on a relatively small scale.

On 15 January 2013, however, the Food Safety Authority of Ireland announced that its testing programme had detected equine DNA in 37 per cent of products examined, mainly frozen beefburgers. One sample was approximately 29 per cent horsemeat. Products were being supplied to supermarkets by Silvercrest Foods in Ireland, and Dalepak, in Hambleton in Yorkshire, all subsidiaries of the Irish-based ABP Food Group.[29] The story remained relatively low-key until early February, by which time there had been multiple reports of adulteration involving many household brands, escalating the issue into a full-blown food scare – even though (despite attempts to show otherwise) there were few health implications.

What characterised this 'scare' in the early stages was the inability of the media to recognise or understand that food safety regulation – arising from Prodi's intervention in 1999 – was an exclusive EU competence, coupled with a profound ignorance of how the regulatory system worked. Comprehension was not assisted by the intervention of Mary Creagh, for the Labour opposition, blaming the government and retailers for 'rolling

---

[28] There are two versions of the speech on the record. One, on the gov.uk website, has had the 'political' content removed, which essentially neuters what was a political speech. The full text is available on multiple non-governmental sites.

[29] For instance, see *Daily Telegraph*, 15 January 2013, 'Tesco beef burgers found to contain 29pc horse meat'.

back regulation that protects our food', and demanding to know why the problem had not been detected by British food authorities.[30]

Creagh was to return to the 'deregulation' charge at the Labour Party Conference in September, telling delegates what she had 'learned' from the horsemeat scandal. 'David Cameron's drive to deregulate the food industry', she asserted, 'coupled with his cost of living crisis created the perfect conditions for the horsemeat scandal.' Warming to her theme, she declared: 'Deregulation, fewer trading standards officers and the end of food sampling meant it was open season. Horse meat was dripped into our food for 2 or 3 years by criminals who knew their chances of getting caught here were small. Deregulation gave us horse meat in our burgers.' Thus, she proclaimed: 'I think it's time we had a bit more regulation of our food.'[31]

Back in February, some of the horsemeat had been traced to abattoirs in Romania. But there, it had been correctly labelled before being sent to a Cyprus-registered company, Draap Trading Ltd, a company with a Dutch director, run from Antwerp and owned by an offshore vehicle based in the British Virgin Islands. The meat was then delivered to the French company Spanghero, which, in turn, had supplied other French companies, and a firm called Comigel with a plant in Luxembourg.[32] Some minor players were also picked up. Through DNA testing, the source of the meat sold to the APB Group was tracked to Poland.[33] But those responsible for the fraud were never found, the adulterated meat having 'criss-crossed international frontiers', before arriving at its destinations.[34] In 2017, however, 66 people were arrested in a co-ordinated operation organised by Europol.[35] Two years later, a Paris court found four men guilty of falsely labelling horsemeat as beef.[36] Other prosecutions were also mounted elsewhere.

Throughout the whole affair, though, there seemed to be a remarkable lack of curiosity as to why the system had become so vulnerable to fraud. The European Commission, just as it had with the volcanic ash debacle, denied responsibility.[37] Commissioner Tonio Borg, in charge of food safety, dumped the blame on 'food business operators', then declaring that

---

[30] Archive site: https://labour-speeches.sayit.mysociety.org/speech/596314.
[31] Website: https://press-archive.labour.org.uk/post/61966631139/mary-creaghs-speech-to-labour-party-annual.
[32] *Guardian*, 13 February 2013, 'Horsemeat scandal: Dutch meat trader could be central figure'.
[33] *Guardian*, 27 January 2013, 'Horsemeat in burgers traced to Polish suppliers'.
[34] *Guardian*, 23 October 2013, 'Horsemeat: the mystery 'Polish beef trimmings' at the heart of a scandal'.
[35] *Deutsche Welle*, 16 July 2017, 'Europol makes 66 arrests in horsemeat scandal'.
[36] *Deutsche Welle*, 16 April 2019, 'Paris court hands down convictions over 2013 horsemeat scandal'.
[37] *Independent*, 13 February 2013, 'Don't blame us for horsemeat scandal, says EU consumer chief'.

states were responsible for enforcement.[38] In comments to the media, he warned: 'Let no one use this incident in order to undermine one of the greatest achievements of the European Union, the free movement of goods, including meat products throughout the European Union.' The *Irish Times* was not buying it. 'The impression was of an institution more concerned with protecting the single market than getting to the bottom of what now appears to be widespread fraud in the European food chain', it wrote.[39]

Thus, it would have been quite reasonable to ask why major firms, many of them highly reputable such as Findus, Nestlé and Tesco, had been so easily caught out, risking massive reputational damage, costly product recalls and prosecution. After all, as a Romanian meat trade spokesman had told the French media when his country's abattoirs had been implicated, it should have been obvious that it was horsemeat. 'It looks different and it smells different. If you are in the trade, you have to know the difference.'[40]

The clue came in a French newspaper report, retailing the defence offered by Comigel, explaining why it had not detected horsemeat in beef supplied by Spanghero. The meat had been delivered frozen, making it impossible 'to detect deception' by its colour or its smell. And it bore 'the French health stamp affixed by Spanghero'.[41] The reference to the frozen state is crucial and more than adequate evidence exists that the bulk (if not all) of the horsemeat supplied came in frozen blocks. In that state, it would be impossible to tell whether it was beef or horsemeat. And in normal practice, these blocks were added to bulk chilled meats during processing products such as burgers and pie fillings, in order to keep the mixes cool. As they fed frozen blocks into the machines, operators would have next to no chance of detecting the substitution.[42]

Nevertheless, the fraud could have been picked up by a simple 'boiling test', to bring up the characteristic smell. However, such procedures had been dropped in favour of paper audits using a system known as Hazard Analysis and Critical Control Points (HACCP), written into EU law.[43] Thus, it had become entirely normal to base controls on paper records, as did Comigel in its reference to 'the French health stamp affixed by Spanghero'.

---

[38] European Commission, 13 February 2013, 'Commissioner Borg proposes Member States a coordinated control plan on horsemeat'.
[39] 14 February 2013, 'European Commission abdicates responsibility for horse meat scandal'.
[40] *Independent on Sunday*, op. cit.
[41] *L'Express*, 14 February 2013, 'Horse meat: Comigel assures that it was impossible "to detect deception"'.
[42] Personal observation (RN), The process is explained in the EUReferendum blog: 'Horsemeat fraud: let them eat horse', 8 February 2013, and 'Horsemeat fraud: a crashing EU failure', 15 February 2013.
[43] Regulation (EC) No. 852/2004 of 29 April 2004 on the hygiene of foodstuffs.

As the Secretary of State for the Environment, Owen Paterson, had put it in a Commons debate, 'the system is very much paper-based and too much is taken on trust'.[44] Under the regime as it then stood, the likes of Comigel were entitled to rely on the policing of health stamps by national officials who, in turn, had their systems evaluated by the Commission's own inspectors from its Food and Veterinary Office (FVO).

However, there had been a double-whammy. First, the Single Market, with its abolition of border controls, had not only freed up trade but also opened up massive opportunities for cross-border crime. Then, the replacement of traditional food controls by a document-based system had created a perfect storm. There was no 'deregulation', nor was the regulation 'excessive', in the sense that Cameron meant. Simply, it was the wrong tool for a task that had not been properly anticipated. But few understood the lesson they had been given. In many cases, they did not even appreciate that there was a lesson to learn, calling instead – as did Mary Creagh – for more regulation.

Creagh was not alone. In a stern editorial, the *Observer* intoned that: 'If the horsemeat scandal tells us anything it is that we need more government regulation, not less.' It's all well and good, it said, 'to tell the supermarkets that they have "ultimate responsibility". But if they will not voluntarily police themselves with genuine rigour, then the state will have to do the job for them.'[45] Tellingly, the paper offered this diagnosis without knowing the background to the scandal, much less acknowledging that food law was an EU competence.

MATTERS OF LIFE AND DEATH

Neither Cameron's speech nor the horsemeat scandal could be allowed to interfere with the routine business of the Union. As planned, when the first European Council of the year met in Brussels on 8 February, talks continued on the multi-annual financial framework. After 20 hours of rancorous discussion, a deal was done, setting a top limit to financial commitments for the seven-year period of 2014–2020 of €960 billion, with spending capped at €908.4 billion. For the first time in its history, the leaders had agreed a reduction on the previous period, representing a 3 per cent cut.[46]

This was not the end of it. European Parliament approval was needed and Martin Schulz, EP president, threatened a veto.[47] Nor was the annual budget saga at an end. In March, the Commission calculated that it would run

---

[44] HC Debates, 12 February 2013, Vol. 558, col. 740.
[45] 10 February 2013, 'Horsemeat scandal: more food regulation, not less, is the answer'.
[46] European Council Conclusions (Multiannual Financial Framework), 8 February 2013.
[47] *Daily Telegraph*, 8 February 2013, 'EU budget is cut for first time but Britain could pay more'.

out of money before the end of the year and issued an 'amending budget' demanding an extra €11.2 billion from member states, of which the UK would have to find €1.2 billion. This was not received in Downing Street with wild enthusiasm. In his defence, Budget Commissioner Lewandowski said that in recent years EU budgets had been 'increasingly below the real needs', creating 'a snowballing effect of unpaid claims transferred onto the following year'.[48]

Back in the UK, the strongly Europhile Lib-Dem MP, Chris Huhne, resigned his seat in Eastleigh in Hampshire, on the eve of a court hearing about a speeding offence. This precipitated a by-election in which UKIP's Diane James came within touching distance of winning, with 11,571 votes as against the Lib-Dem victor's tally of 13,342. The Conservatives languished in third place.[49]

The contest was significant in many ways. Since the coalition agreement had been signed on 20 May 2010, the Lib-Dems had suffered badly as junior partners. Barely one month in, the party's poll rating had fallen by 8 per cent. Three months on, it had more than halved to 11 per cent and by the seven-month anniversary of the coalition agreement, a YouGov poll had them languishing at 8 per cent. The Eastleigh result fuelled hope, false as it turned out, that the party could still win elections.[50] As the fall was sustained through to the 2015 election, it was to have a profound – although largely unrecognised – effect on the progress of David Cameron's referendum.

A more immediate effect of UKIP's performance was to goad Cameron into publishing plans to arrest the flood of migrants.[51] Prevented by EU law from imposing direct controls, he was forced to work at the margins, tackling 'benefit tourism'. He thus promised to strip jobseekers' allowance from new migrants after six months unless they could prove they had been actively looking for a job and stood a 'genuine chance' of finding one.

The 'range and depth' of questions in the habitual residence test, determining whether migrants met residence requirements for housing and income-related benefits, would also be increased. The maximum fine for

[48] BBC News, 27 March 2013, 'UK challenges new EU demand for 2013 budget cash'.
[49] Daily Telegraph, 1 March 2013, 'Eastleigh by-election: Ukip inflicts major setback on David Cameron'.
[50] Cutts, D. and Russell, A. (2015), From Coalition to Catastrophe: The Electoral Meltdown of the Liberal Democrats, Britain Votes (2015), published by Oxford University Press on behalf of the Hansard Society.
[51] Gov.UK (website), 25 March 2013, 'David Cameron's immigration speech'. The issue was to crop up again at the end of the year, when Cameron announced he was 'accelerating' the start of the restrictions in a bid to 'make the UK a less attractive place for EU migrants – prior to Romanians and Bulgarians gaining full rights of establishment and freedom of movement on 1 January'. (Daily Telegraph, 18 December 2013, 'We will block benefits to new EU migrants, says Cameron'.)

companies using illegal workers doubled to £20,000 and 'health tourism' was also targeted, with non-EU nationals having to prove they held health insurance before they received NHS care. There was little doubt in media circles that the real objective was to stem the migration of Conservative voters to UKIP, especially with the European Elections coming up in 2014.[52]

Away from the cauldron of daily politics, a sad moment for many marked the end of an era. On 8 April 2013, Margaret Thatcher died, aged 87. She was to receive a state funeral. But life went on. Pursuing their current leader's promise, in mid-May the Conservatives published a draft Bill setting out the referendum terms, just prior to the Queen's speech. The question proposed was: 'Do you think the United Kingdom should remain a member of the European Union?' But, with no support from the Lib-Dems as coalition partners, it could not proceed as a government measure.[53] In the Queen's speech debate, on 15 May, an attempt was made to introduce an amendment to the motion approving the speech, 'regretting' that a referendum had not been included in the legislative programme. It was defeated by 277 votes to 130, after six hours of fierce debate.[54]

Happier days beckoned for the EU leaders. Barroso announced a tentative deal between the Commission, the European Parliament leadership and Ireland, which currently held the rotating EU presidency, on the multi-annual financial framework.[55] And the European Council on 28 June warmly welcomed Croatia as a member of the EU as of 1 July 2013, bringing the members to 28. They also congratulated Latvia on adopting the euro as of 1 January 2014.[56] Then, Serbia had started accession talks and Kosovo had expanded its ties with the Union. For once, a sense of optimism prevailed.[57]

Although the referendum was many years away, intense skirmishing had already begun. The two sides – which would soon be known 'leavers' and 'remainers' – were attempting to capture the high ground. In the early stages, the focus had been very much on the 'Norway option', with the remainers keen to neutralise the attractions of this alternative. This was to continue. On 18 April, the LSE – a hotbed of Europhilia – invited Norwegian Conservative Party leader Erna Solberg to address its European Institute.

Prominently reported by the BBC, Solberg dismissed the 'Norway model'. It 'would not work for the UK', she declared.[58] Claiming that

[52] Channel 4 News, 25 March 2013, 'Cameron unveils immigrant benefits crackdown'.
[53] BBC News, 14 May 2013, 'Conservatives publish EU referendum bill'.
[54] BBC News, 15 May 2013, 'Attempt to amend Queen's Speech over EU referendum fails'.
[55] Deutsche Welle, 27 June 2013, 'Breakthrough deal on EU budget for 2014–2020'.
[56] Conclusions, 27/28 June 2013, Brussels European Council.
[57] Deutsche Welle, 28 June 2013, 'EU politicians call Brussels summit a success'.
[58] BBC News, 18 April 2013, 'Norway's EU deal "not right for UK"'.

Norway's total financial contribution linked to the EEA agreement was 'roughly around €340 million per year' – more than many EU member states paid – she developed Cameron's theme, complaining about the 'democratic deficit'. 'We have no formal political representation in Brussels or Strasbourg, and no voting rights on the legislation that eventually will become national laws,' she said, also repeating the error made by the Commons Library – that Norway had 'implemented three-quarters of all of the EU's legislative acts'.[59]

By now, it was becoming evident that the debate would be sternly guarded by media 'gatekeepers' and their political handmaidens.[60] Errors were rarely acknowledged and even less often corrected. Media discourse was effectively restricted to 'permitted participants', defined as much by prestige as knowledge. One of those was former chancellor Nigel (now Lord) Lawson, who grandly dismissed Cameron's renegotiation plan as 'likely to fail'. The British people, he said, were not 'going to be taken in by Wilsonian make-believe'.[61] That set the bar, highlighting suspicions that Cameron was travelling the same road as Harold Wilson. Others suggested that the newly introduced Article 50, defining the procedures for withdrawal, was the only way the EU could be forced to negotiate a new relationship.[62]

Later, William Hague – in written evidence to the Commons Foreign Affairs Committee – argued that the Article was not *intended* for such a purpose.[63] The same Committee also took evidence on the positions of Norway and Switzerland. But it seemed keen only to hear witnesses who asserted that both were 'obliged to adopt EU legislation over which they have had no effective say'.[64] Their report concluded:

> We agree with the Government that the current arrangements for relations with the EU which are maintained by Norway, as a member of the European Economic Area, or Switzerland, would not be appropriate

[59] LSE blog (undated), 'The "Norwegian model" would be a poor alternative to EU membership for the UK'.

[60] This was a thesis advanced by Stephen D. Cooper, associate professor of communication at Marshall University, Huntington, West Virginia, in his book, *Watching the Watchdog* (2006) (Spokane, Washington: Marquette Books). The function of the media was no longer to inform, *per se*, but one of 'agenda-setting', defining the topics for public discussion.

[61] *Financial Times*, 31 January 2013, 'EU renegotiation set to fail, says Lawson'.

[62] *Sunday Telegraph*, 24 November 2012, Booker column: 'Politicians of all stripes talk about "renegotiation", but none can countenance talk of quitting'.

[63] House of Commons Foreign Affairs Committee, *The Future of the EU: UK Government Policy*, First Report of Session 2013–14, Volume II, Ev.83, published 21 May 2013.

[64] Ibid., Volume I, p. 75.

for the UK if it were to leave the EU. In both cases, the non-EU country is obliged to adopt some or all of the body of EU Single Market law with no effective power to shape it.[65]

When the CBI Director General joined the fray, he trotted out a similar line: Norway's EEA status meant it 'still pays the bills and follows the rules but has much lower influence on EU decision-making than if it had a seat at the table'.[66]

On 10 June, Cameron offered his 'Plan for Britain's success'.[67] Talking of his 'desire to shape the world', he argued that a key part of his international ambitions for the UK was 'our place at the top table. At the UN. The Commonwealth. NATO. The WTO. The G8. The G20 and yes – the EU'. The fact is, he said, 'that it is international institutions, and in them, that many of the rules of the game are set: on trade, on tax, on regulation. And when a country like ours is affected profoundly by those rules, I want us to have a say on them.' No one told him that, on most 'top tables', the UK was obliged slavishly to follow the EU's 'common position', whereas Norway was its own master.

The end of the month then saw the new CBI president, Mike Rake, preaching that continued membership of the EU was 'overwhelmingly' in the UK's economic interests. 'As a global trading nation, we want the rest of the world to play by an open and enforceable set of rules,' he said. 'Britain could call for that alone then watch as others made the decisions. Or, as the EU's third-largest member, Britain can push the world's largest economic bloc in a liberal direction.' If Britain were to adopt a similar association, businesses would be left 'operating under market rules over which they would have little or no influence'.

In a prescient comment, Katja Hall, CBI chief policy director, said:

The test for those arguing that the UK must remain in the EU and for those pressing for our departure is to come up with a clear vision of our future, inside or out. Whether we are in or out of membership we will still need a relationship with the EU. But Norway and Switzerland simply don't appear to have set-ups the UK should aspire to. They are half-way houses on the margins of Europe with no influence over the market rules under which they operate.

[65] Ibid., p. 9.
[66] *Guardian*, 17 May 2013, 'CBI chief issues warning over European Union exit'.
[67] BBC News, 10 June 2013, 'David Cameron: UK must be at EU top table'.

She added: 'Norway still pays the bills and has as much of a say on the single market as Liechtenstein, which is not my idea of greater sovereignty.'[68]

This was followed up by CBI Director-General John Cridland, previewing his organisation's report on 'lessons from Norway and Switzerland', where he too echoed the call for those on each side of the divide to 'come up with a clear, evidence-based vision for the future'. Cridland's idea of 'evidence', however, was to assert that Norway and Switzerland paid the costs of membership with no say over EU law, and then to argue that 'a half-way house isn't the answer'.[69] With that, he had introduced another distortion into the narrative. The EFTA countries had joined EEA as an alternative to the EU, not as a step towards membership.

Waiting in the wings was the 'pro-European group', Business for New Europe, founded in 2006, of which Rake was a member. Having earlier organised a letter from 20 FTSE 100 chief executives, it mirrored the CBI, claiming: 'The benefit of European Union membership outweighs the cost.' To suggest otherwise, the executives had said, 'is putting politics before economics'.[70] The campaign proper had not yet started and it was beginning to look like a re-run of 1975.

UNHEARD VOICES

What was not being heard were the voices of people such as Norwegian veterinarian Bjørn Knudtsen, who gave an example of how the 'top table' really worked. Knudtsen was Chairman of the Fish and Fisheries Product Committee of the UN *Codex Alimentarius* Commission (CAC). His committee had 170 representatives from the fifty to sixty countries most interested in seafood, and made the global rules for the sector.[71] Thus, most of the laws covering fish and fisheries products did not originate in Brussels. Rather, they came from the *Codex* committee, in which Norway was fully involved. Knudtsen's government paid approximately £250,000 a year to host the committee, giving it an early and complete insight into what was going through the system.

[68] *This is Money*, 5 July 2013, 'British business warns Europe exit will leave them 'on the margins' with no influence ahead of Commons vote.'
[69] *The Times*, 4 July 2013, 'In or out, Britain has to play by Europe's rules'.
[70] *Independent*, 19 May 2013, 'Letters: the benefit of European Union membership outweighs the cost'.
[71] Codex standards have no direct legal force. They are a reference for international trade and are implemented voluntarily. The EU joined Codex in 2004 and was engaged in a systematic process of adopting Codex and other global rules through its REFIT programme. It actively fosters International Regulatory Cooperation (IRC), working with the UN, the OECD and the World Bank. See Commission website: 'Better regulation: why and how'.

At no stage, therefore, was Norway the passive receiver of rules from Brussels. The idea of 'fax democracy' was absurd. His country, Knudtsen said, was involved at every step of the process from inception to the final formulation of the rules. Brussels then added the EEA 'packaging', before passing them on, but the substantive issues had been agreed long before standards formally reached the EU.[72] By contrast, the UK was represented on the *Codex* committee by the EU, the 'common position' determined in advance by 'consensus', which, as Margaret Thatcher had found to her cost, meant majority rule. When Norway sat at the 'top table', it was its own master.

As to Eide's comments to the BBC in December, these were taken up in August by Anne Tvinnereim. At the time, she was state secretary for the Norwegian Ministry of Local Government and Regional Development and a member of the Centre Party, which had consistently opposed EU membership. Eide, she said, was a member of the Conservative Party, which had always supported EU membership. His views, and the many like them from EU supporters, did not represent the majority position. But when the BBC wanted a comment from Norwegian politicians, they always went to the parties that supported membership, she complained.

Tvinnereim disputed the claim that Norway had no influence over EU law. 'It is true that we are not there when they vote,' she conceded, 'but we do get to influence the position.' Most of the politics was done long before a new law gets to the voting stage, she said. Far from lacking influence, she had found that Sweden, which as a member of the EU had to vote with the common position at the UN, on some issues had informally asked Norway to represent a different position because it no longer had a voice.

People like Eide, who supported the EU, Tvinnereim added, had not given up, despite two rejections. There was, maybe, no chance of Norway joining in the near future, but they were looking ahead, perhaps to 20 years, when they hoped the situation would change. Not only did they want the EU to succeed, they needed the UK to continue its membership. If it left, it would weaken Norwegian support for the EU and vastly strengthen the 'No' campaign, especially if Britain joined EFTA. They were protecting their own positions.[73]

Such sentiments, and the insight of Knudtsen, were never to break into the mainstream debate. When the BBC's 'Europe' correspondent, Matthew Price, went to Norway, supposedly on a fact-finding mission, he trotted out

---

[72] Interview (RN), 25 June 2013. See EUReferendum.com (blog), 'Codex is the top table'.
[73] Interview (RN), 1 August 2013. See EUReferendum.com (blog): 'Norway: "We do not need Brussels to tell us what to do"'.

the received wisdom: 'Norway has to obey the trading rules of the European Union,' he intoned. 'And yet, unlike the 28 member countries that make up the EU, it has no say in what those rules actually are. They are, literally, imposed by Brussels.'[74] For his political input, he turned to Erna Solberg.

The 'anti-Norway' rhetoric did not abate. At the CBI's annual conference in November, John Cridland once again endorsed EU membership, claiming it was worth between £62 billion and 78 billion to the UK, renewing his attack on the 'Norwegian or Swiss model', saying it 'would leave UK businesses operating under market rules over which [they have] little or no influence'.[75] However, the CBI's members did want to see a moratorium on legislation that could be made at national level.

BALANCE OF COMPETENCES

In nothing else, the CBI's call for some legislation to be made nationally was a sign of the way things existed in their own detached bubbles. Months previously, on 22 July, the government had published the first six reports from its balance of competences review – covering the Single Market, taxation, animal health and welfare and food safety, health, development co-operation and humanitarian aid, and foreign policy. These reports were the place to find details of laws that could be repatriated or a moratorium applied. But despite government hopes, the findings were not helpful.

In the report on the Single Market, it was concluded that it was 'not possible to establish a clear division between Member State and EU competence in the Single Market area'. On the whole, businesses valued the additional access to EU markets that the Single Market brought, and recognised that this would bring a regulatory burden. Views on the nature of that burden focused mainly on standards of enforcement and whether the UK 'gold plated' EU legislation.[76]

What was missing from the reports was perhaps as significant as the content. The food safety report, for instance, might have evaluated the role of the EU in the horsemeat scandal, where the EU had made a fundamental error. It had taken the HACCP system, which had been devised as a food safety management tool, and turned it into a statutory requirement, diverting enforcement officials into checking procedures, rather than outcomes. Yet there was no attempt at an evaluation, even though the report

[74] BBC News, 3 September 2013. 'Would Norway's special EU arrangement work for Britain?'
[75] *Euractiv*, 4 November 2013. 'EU membership "significantly outweighs costs", says UK's leading business group'.
[76] HM Government, *Review of the Balance of Competences between the United Kingdom and the European Union: The Single Market*, July 2013.

acknowledged that the horsemeat incident had reduced confidence in the EU. But then, an online survey carried out by the Food Standards Agency had found that only 20 per cent of consumers knew that food law was made by the EU – meaning that 80 per cent did not.[77]

Cameron, in looking for opportunities to repatriate EU law, was to be frustrated by relationships now so complex that this exercise simply skimmed the surface. The BBC thus observed: broadly, the report (sic) 'found the balance of power between the member states and the EU appropriate'. In the trade-off between cost and benefit, 'most of those consulted answered positively and that was supported by the evidence'.[78]

BACK ON THE TREADMILL

The break from party politics that would usually have prevailed during the holiday period was rudely interrupted on 21 August when President Assad of Syria mounted a chemical attack near Damascus with hundreds of deaths.[79] When Cameron mooted joining the United States in direct military action, parliament rejected a motion paving the way for intervention by 285 votes to 213.[80] Some argued that this represented a 'devastating blow' to the authority of the prime minister, but in other respects it reignited the debate on how far the electoral mandate of the government ran, familiar even from the 1940s when it had been ventured that 'we have long outlived the idea that at an electoral contest we confer unlimited authority on the member we elect'.[81] The idea of a referendum emerged stronger.

Through the summer, there were warning signs of troubles to come as Ukrainian companies accused Russian customs officials of discriminating against their exports. The measures were seen as the onset of a bilateral trade war aimed at discouraging Ukraine from signing a trade agreement with the EU in the autumn, pressuring it instead to join a Moscow-led customs union with other former Soviet republics.[82] This was to erupt later in the year in a spectacular fashion.

Meanwhile, the autumn saw a return of low-key campaigning around the yet-to-be-declared referendum, with the London *Evening Standard* hosting a debate on Britain's future in the EU. Previewing the debate was

---

[77] HM Government, *Animal Health and Welfare and Food Safety Report*, July 2013.
[78] BBC News, 22 July 2013, 'UK begins great European Union debate'.
[79] BBC News, 24 September 2013, 'Syria chemical attack: What we know'.
[80] *Guardian*, 29 August 2013, 'Cameron forced to rule out British attack on Syria after MPs reject motion'.
[81] *Reynolds News*, 21 July 1940, 'Let public opinion have its say', Professor Arthur Berriedale Keith (a well-known constitutional lawyer of his time).
[82] *Financial Times*, 15 August 2013, 'Russia accused of triggering trade war with Ukraine'.

Lord Wolfson, chief executive of the clothing retailer Next, who was to become a prominent figure in the 'remain' campaign. Those who argued for EU withdrawal, regardless of economic consequences, he argued, were 'needlessly reckless'.[83] Tony Blair joined in, warning that it would be 'economic suicide' for Britain to leave.[84] The stage had not been reached where this type of input was labelled 'project fear', but when it came to the debate, the potential for it to backfire was evident. Tory backbencher, Jesse Norman, joked that if the former prime minister was against exit, 'no sane person can be anything other than for it'.[85]

Almost lost in the 'noise' was the European Commission president's state of the union address on 12 September, but dedicated 'Europe watchers' were quick to notice the repeated call for a 'deep and genuine Economic and Monetary Union'. The Commission would continue to work for the implementation of its blueprint, step by step, one phase after the other, ready to report before the European elections in 2014 'further ideas on the future of our Union and how best to consolidate and deepen the community method and community approach in the longer term'. The spectre of a new treaty had not receded.

Had Cameron been better focused, he might have been especially interested in the Commission initiative on 19 September, when it announced that an estimated €193 billion had been lost as a result of non-compliance or non-collection of VAT in 2011.[86] This had been a running sore, so extensive that it had a measurable impact on the GDPs of member states and even on trade figures.[87] Despite continuous and continuing efforts at reform, each time changes were made, criminals found new opportunities. But the Commission fought shy of admitting the obvious – that the vulnerabilities were inherent in the system and the only long-term solution was to replace it with something more robust. Despite the obvious potential reform, though, Cameron was never to mention it.

Fortunately for the prime minister, with the polls showing consistent support for a referendum and a steady majority in favour of leaving the EU – now beginning to be known by the title of Brexit – Labour decided it

---

[83] *Evening Standard*, 5 September 2013, 'Simon Wolfson: we must radically reform the EU – or prepare to leave it'.

[84] *Evening Standard*, 9 September 2013, 'Tony Blair: for Britain to leave the EU would be economic suicide'.

[85] *Evening Standard*, 10 September 2013, 'Stay in EU or quit: our panel trade blows over effect on Square Mile'.

[86] European Commission, press release 19 September 2013, 'Fight against fraud: new study confirms billions lost in VAT gap'.

[87] Eucrim, 26 April 2020, 'Kiel Study: EU's Trade Self-Surplus Goes Back to VAT Fraud'.

would not match the Tory offer. Having forgotten the lessons of 1997, when all the parties had neutralised the Referendum Party by agreeing to a vote, Labour's Europe spokeswoman Emma Reynolds told the party conference: '[We] are very, very committed to the position we have,' adding: 'If we were to change, it would look incredibly cynical at this stage. It would look weak because it would look like we were being pushed into it.'[88]

It was thus the Conservative Party, rather than Labour, that stood to benefit politically from yet another EU cash demand. Not content with its €7.3 billion top-up earlier in the year – on which the UK had been out-voted – the Commission wanted another €3.9 billion. Once again, enthusiasm was notably lacking in Whitehall when a Treasury spokesperson remarked: 'When citizens across Europe are seeing their family budgets under pressure, it is unjustifiable that the European budget should be going up in this way.'[89]

On the regulation front, the end of September saw a rash of newspaper articles describing airline pilots falling asleep in their cockpits.[90] These reports presaged the Commission setting revised flight time limits for crews of EU registered airlines. They were strongly contested by the British Air Line Pilots Association (BALPA), as a retrograde step for UK operators who were already bound by higher standards.[91] But they were still introduced. The Commission was as much concerned with creating a 'level playing field' as it was with crew safety, complaining that 'the current patchwork of national provisions' made it 'difficult to achieve legal certainty'.[92] There could be few better examples of how the EU's pursuit of 'one-size-fits-all' standards actually reduced UK safety standards, but there was no formal complaint from Cameron's administration.[93]

But if Cameron's attempt at building a practical case for repatriating powers was not making much headway, neither at a European level was it gaining any traction. A scornful Barroso dismissed his initiative as 'theological' and 'unreasonable', arguing that the only way to reform the EU was to review the *acquis*, estimated to comprise of over 150,000 pages of regulations, on a case-by-case basis. This, he claimed was being done: the

---

[88] Reuters, 25 September 2013, 'Britain's Labour rules out EU membership vote for now'.
[89] BBC News, 26 September 2013, 'UK opposes extra EU budget funds for 2013'.
[90] For instance: Press Association, 26 September 2013, 'Airbus pilots fell asleep at same time, says incident report'.
[91] *Flight Global*, 20 October 2011, 'EU fatigue rules would endanger public: BALPA'.
[92] European Commission, Memo: 4 October 2013, 'Pilot and crew fatigue: frequently asked questions'.
[93] This was despite BALPA's call for a 'ministerial review' of what it called 'a botched process by the EC from start to finish'. Press Association, 9 October 2013, 'UK pilots lose fight against new European rules on pilots' flying hours'. Six years later, this headline was seen: 'Pilots in Europe suffering fatigue despite new rules: ECA' (Air Traffic Management, 5 March 2019).

Commission had reduced the regulatory burden for businesses by 26 per cent between 2007 and 2012, with annual savings of £27 billion. In his view, a fundamental discussion about the competences of the EU was 'doomed to failure'.[94]

No fewer than 210 MEPs, however, were determined that a new EU treaty should be a success. As members of the Spinelli Group, they collaborated with the German Bertelsmann Stiftung to produce a 'Fundamental Law of the European Union', offering a 'comprehensive revision of the Lisbon Treaty'.[95] One particularly notable aspect of the draft was that, in pushing for a more federal union, it also proposed a new category of 'associate membership' for any member state that chose not to join in.[96]

It was fractious MPs who were troubling David Cameron though. He was faced with another rebellion by his own backbenchers, this one led by Adam Afriyie, who claimed that people did not trust him to hold a referendum in 2017. Back in July, backbencher James Wharton had introduced a private member's Bill, taking forward the draft Bill lodged by the Conservative Party to enshrine into law an in/out referendum before the end of 2017 – something Cameron, hampered by coalition politics, could not do. The Bill had sailed through its second reading with 304 votes, after Labour and Lib-Dem abstentions. No one voted against. But then Afriyie tabled an amendment aimed at bringing a referendum forward to October 2014.[97] Most of the Tory Eurosceptics pleaded for 'unity'.[98] The amendment was defeated by 290 votes to 0.[99]

Nevertheless, a Survation poll had 61 per cent in favour of a 2014 referendum, with 46 per cent in favour of leaving the EU and 38 per cent wanting to 'remain'. Once again, the position reversed if the EU 'made concessions', with 47 per cent opting to stay in while only 30 per cent favoured 'leave'.[100] Cameron had everything to play for, especially as a separate poll had 85 per cent of 200 major manufacturers choosing to stay

---

[94] *Daily Telegraph*, 2 October 2013, 'José Manuel Barroso: David Cameron's plan to claw back powers from the EU is "doomed to failure"'.

[95] *Euractiv*, 4 October 2013, 'Federalists table "Treaty of Bozar"'.

[96] The Spinelli Group, Bertelsmann Stiftung, *A Fundamental Law of the European Union*, 2013.

[97] *Mail on Sunday*, 5 October 2013, 'PM panics as Tories bid to quit EU next year: MPs hijack Commons vote to get 2014 referendum three years early'.

[98] *Guardian*, 6 October 2013, 'Rebel Tory plot for early EU referendum backfires'.

[99] HC Debates, 8 November 2013, Vol. 570, col. 533. Wharton's Bill competed its passage through the Commons but was blocked in the Lords in January 2014.

[100] *Mail on Sunday*, 13 October 2013, 'Most voters want 2014 poll on quitting EU: survey reveals backing for Tory rebel's controversial referendum call'.

in the EU, with three-fifths wanting reform of Europe as a whole rather than special treatment for Britain.[101]

Meanwhile, his idea of tackling EU 'red tape' was to appoint a 'Business Taskforce' comprising six of the 'great and the good' – CEOs from well-known companies – to help 'sweep away barriers to growth' with 'a set of recommendations for reform for the British and European governments as well as the EU institutions'. With 'input from hundreds of firms, individuals and business associations across Europe', they developed 30 'priority recommendations to address five kinds of barriers'. These were summed up in an acronym 'COMPETE', setting out supposedly 'common sense filters' to be applied by the EU before bringing forward legislation.[102]

Among those was a 'one-in, one-out' principle for European legislation, offsetting any new burdens on business by reducing burdens of an equivalent value elsewhere.[103] Needless to say, a media rooted in prestige gloried in the idea of 'top business executives' presenting proposals for 'slashing the burden of European red tape'.[104] Not one newspaper had the wit to perform a forensic analysis, to illustrate the intrinsically superficial approach to an issue on which Cameron was staking his entire premiership. Justifying his stance in front of the annual CBI conference, he explained that the problem with the European debate was that:

> until I came up with this, I think very bold and correct strategy of saying, 'let us renegotiate and then let's have an 'in–out' referendum so we settle this issue properly in Britain', 'til that time, I think the trouble is the debate was just slipping away and, as I put it, consent for our membership of the EU was getting wafer thin.[105]

Emphasising the need for reform, he was setting himself a task that had eluded all his predecessors. But he was also aligning himself with the CBI,

---

[101] Reuters, 14 October 2013, 'Most British manufacturers want to stay in EU – poll'.

[102] Report from the Business Taskforce: *Cut EU Red Tape*, October 2013.

[103] The fatuity of this approach was readily illustrated by the Commission's own REFIT programme, which was steadily going through the *acquis* consolidating legislation and thereby reducing the number of individual instruments. Thus, for example, a dozen or so regulations might be replaced by a single, consolidated version, although, with various additions, the overall length might be increased. There were many other devices by which regulation numbers could be decreased, not least by adopting multiple international regulations in one instrument, replacing many single EU regulations.

[104] For instance: *Sunday Times*, 13 October 2013; *Sunday Telegraph*, 13 October 2013, 'Cut EU red tape to save billions, business chiefs tell Cameron'.

[105] Video transcript: BBC News, 4 November 2013. The BBC offered the headline: 'UK support for staying in EU is wafer thin, says Cameron', with other media offering similar renditions. This, however, is not what Cameron said. Effectively, he was saying that *consent* was getting wafer thin until he intervened.

which remained unequivocal in its support for membership, claiming it benefited each household by £3,000 a year. Director-General Cridland offered what would become the hallmark 'project fear' statement: 'Being outside the world's largest trading bloc would leave the UK isolated and without influence.'[106] Gradually, the 'set' was being dressed for an epic fight that was still years away, with popular sentiment clearly at odds with the elites. An Opinium poll in mid-November had 56 per cent in favour of 'leave', with 'remain' at 30 per cent.[107]

POKING THE BEAR

In an extraordinary episode during a trip to Kazakhstan that summer, Cameron found himself discussing EU enlargement, expressing the hope that it would go beyond the three Baltic states of Latvia, Lithuania and Estonia – the only former members of the USSR so far to join the EU. Talking to students at the Nazarbayev University in the Kazakh capital, he went on to say, 'Britain has always supported the widening of the EU. Our vision of the EU is that it should be a large trading and co-operating organisation that effectively stretches, as it were, from the Atlantic to the Urals.'[108] Cameron was, of course, speaking in former Soviet territory, with Putin having already shown a willingness to intervene in his neighbour's affairs in his 2008 South Ossetia adventure – a leader of a nation prone to fears of *okruzhenie* (encirclement).[109]

Cameron was not alone in his lack of caution, the EU having concluded in 1994 a Partnership and Cooperation Agreement with the former Soviet Republic of Ukraine. For the end of 2014, it had been negotiating an ambitious 2,000-page Association Agreement. Few had any illusions that this was a precursor to EU membership. But enthusiasm for the agreement – especially after the Russian reaction earlier in the year – was waning.[110] Nevertheless, in September, the Ukrainian government approved the draft, with Prime Minister Mykola Azarow promising 'a path towards European standards of living'.[111] A week before it was due to be signed, though, Kiev

---

[106] *Observer*, 3 November 2017, 'Britain must stay in EU, says business lobby group'.
[107] *Guardian*, 19 November 2012, 'Britain "sleepwalking towards EU exit" under Cameron, says Labour'.
[108] *Guardian*, 1 July 2013, 'EU should extend further into former Soviet Union, says David Cameron'.
[109] The concept is explored in multiple papers, such as this: Vagts, Alfred (1956), 'Capitalist Encirclement: A Russian Obsession – Genuine or Feigned?', *Journal of Politics*, Vol. 18, No. 3 (August 1956), pp. 499–519. Whether real or imagined, this was a factor in Russian domestic and foreign policy that could not be ignored.
[110] *Deutsche Welle*, 29 October 2013, 'Ukrainian support for EU association agreement declines'.
[111] *Deutsche Welle*, 18 September 2013, 'Ukraine commits to EU association deal'.

decided to put it on hold, preferring links with 'Russia and other countries from the Community of Independent States'.[112]

Public protests erupted in Maidan Nezalezhnosti (Independence Square) in the capital, Kiev, demanding the resignation of Viktor Yanukovich, the country's president. As the protests – peaceful at first – intensified, they adopted the title *Euromaidan*, fortified by cash pouring in from the EU, a seemingly endless supply of pristine EU flags and a visit by Catherine Ashton.[113] To follow was the secession of parts of the eastern Donetsk and Luhansk oblasts by Russian sympathisers and a messy, miserable 'sitting war', which, after thousands of casualties and seven years later, had still to be resolved.

After armed intervention by its special forces, Russia also annexed the Crimea, whence a disputed referendum had the overwhelming majority voting to re-join Russia. However, after Yanukovich had been deposed, the EU got its treaty with the now broken Ukraine.[114] This was not before the European Council had solemnly emphasised 'the right of all sovereign States to make their own foreign policy decisions without undue external pressure'.[115]

THINGS CAN ONLY GET BETTER?

With havoc about to break out on its eastern borders, at least the EU could congratulate itself on bringing Turkey a little closer to the fold. Accession negotiations were to resume on 5 November, having started formally in October 2005. Of the 35 'chapters' to be negotiated, the fourteenth was now on the table.[116] And, at last, the European Parliament approved the multi-annual budget, agreeing the cut to €960 billion.[117]

Back in Germany, elections had been held on 22 September, giving Merkel her third term. In her first speech to the Bundestag after her election, she urged her European partners to cede control over economic policy and make politically sensitive treaty changes.[118] The regular recommendations for reform by the EU Commission to member states have been accepted 'more or less in a friendly way', but they have not led to binding agreement, she complained, promising that, 'We are going to speak to the European

---

[112] *Euractiv*, 21 November 2013, 'Ukraine stuns EU by putting association deal on ice'.
[113] *Sunday Telegraph*, 9 August 2014, Booker column: 'Fresh evidence of how the West lured Ukraine into its orbit'.
[114] European Commission (website), Trade Policy: Ukraine.
[115] Conclusions, 19/20 December 2013, Brussels, European Council.
[116] *Deutsche Welle*, 22 October 2013, 'EU ministers set date for Turkey accession talks'.
[117] *Deutsche Welle*, 19 November 2013, 'EU parliament approves bloc's seven-year budget plan'.
[118] Reuters, 18 December 2013, 'Merkel urges EU treaty change in first speech of new term'.

Council about [implementing] such contractual agreements.' We have a situation in Europe, she said, 'where everyone says, "we can develop everything but we can't change the treaties."' 'I don't think that we can build a truly functioning Europe that way,' she added.[119]

At the end of the year, therefore, Cameron's strategy appeared to be assured. The German chancellor seemingly pushing for treaty change would allow him to press his demands when the other eurozone members sought to rewrite the treaty to include a fully-fledged banking union.

Alex Barker of the *Financial Times* was not sure. Despite Merkel's comments, she was in no rush, he argued. Germany would happily solve problems through pacts outside the EU treaties, just to avoid giving the UK a veto. He cited a senior EU official saying, 'Nobody wants to give the keys to the UK.'[120] In fact, Merkel had been talking about changes to the eurozone 'ultimately' requiring a reform of the EU treaties.[121] Her first priority was 'contractual agreements' between the states and the EU Commission. Only secondarily did she favour 'further developing the European Treaties.'[122] And Cameron had been instrumental in settling Merkel's policy. His 'bust-up' over the phantom veto in 2011 had shown Berlin that there was a workable alternative to treaty change. Through his own action, it seemed, he was not going to get his treaty. But the countdown for his referendum had already started.

---

[119] *Deutsche Welle*, 18 December 2013, 'Merkel gives first address to Bundestag, calls for EU reform'.
[120] *Financial Times*, 18 December 2013, 'The Brits and banking union: bad omens for Cameron's referendum'.
[121] *FAZ*, 18 December 2013, 'Merkel back in everyday European life'.
[122] Bundeskanzlerin.de – Government declaration by Chancellor Merkel on the European Council on 19/20 December, 18 December 2013.

21

The Impossible Dream: 2014–2016

A new deal of permanent particular roads is wishful thinking.
It is unacceptable for a lot of the other countries.
> Martin Schulz, president of the European Parliament[1]

We were no longer in the realms of bending or stretching the
truth, but ditching it altogether. Leave was lying.
> David Cameron[2]

In pursuing treaty change – and then committing to a referendum by the
end of 2017 – Cameron had sealed his own fate. He could have one or
the other, but not both. Ironically, he was up against the Lisbon Treaty,
which had altered the procedures for amending EU treaties. Under the
'ordinary revision procedure', the simplicity of an IGC – voted on by the
European Council – was gone. Instead, proposals had to be submitted to
the European Council by the Council and national parliaments had to be
notified.

Also gone was the 'consensus' that had so flummoxed Thatcher in Milan.
Now, the European Council had to consult the European Parliament and
the Commission, and then had to decide, by a simple majority, whether
the proposed amendments should be examined. If yes, the president of the
European Council was required to convene 'a Convention composed of
representatives of the national Parliaments, Heads of State or Government

---

[1] *Guardian*, 6 January 2014, 'Cameron's plan to rewrite EU treaties is wishful thinking, says Martin
Schulz'.
[2] Op. cit., p. 669.

of the Member States, the European Parliament and the Commission'.[3] This would then examine the proposals and 'adopt by consensus' a recommendation to a conference of representatives of the governments of the member states – the IGC.

In terms of timing, from the Laeken Declaration in December 2001 to the signing of the constitution in October 2004, nearly three years had elapsed. In the expectation that serious negotiations would not start until after the 2015 general election, the chances of securing a full-blown treaty by 2017 were remote. In addition, Cameron would have to pass a referendum Bill through parliament and allow time for a campaign. Time pressures apart, one of the first hurdles would be the newly empowered European Parliament, and here there was a distinct lack of good news. In the very first week of January 2014, its president, Martin Schulz, demolished any hopes of an easy passage. 'A new deal of permanent particular roads is wishful thinking. It is unacceptable for a lot of the other countries,' he declared.[4]

Furthermore, with Merkel already having put treaty change on hold, Cameron's troubles continued to multiply. During a visit to the UK at the end of the month, President Hollande unhelpfully remarked that revising the treaties was 'not a priority'. In his own defence, Cameron pointed to the two treaties agreed during his premiership. Perhaps recognising something of the magnitude of his task, he talked of his 'renegotiation' merely involving 'elements' of treaty change. This might have been a reference to the simplified revision procedure, but it was not explicitly mentioned. Nevertheless, he insisted that a referendum would be held before the end of 2017, 'come what may'.[5]

At the end of February, Merkel was to come to London. Contrasting with the French president's visit, she was to be given the 'red carpet' treatment, with private discussions in No. 10, an address to both Houses of Parliament and tea with the Queen. As the date approached, some media commentators had convinced themselves that she might ease the way for Cameron's treaty change.[6] There was even an idea floated of an alliance of 'like-minded countries' willing to reform the rules on free movement of people.[7]

Since her address to the Bundestag in December, though, nothing had changed. Nor, after a visit to Paris to see Hollande, was the Franco-German

[3] There was a provision for bypassing a Convention if the European Council (with the permission of the European Parliament) decided (by a simple majority) that a Convention was not justified by the extent of the proposed amendments (Article 48(3) TEU).
[4] *Guardian*, 6 January 2014, op. cit.
[5] *The Times*, 31 January 2014, 'Hollande blunts Cameron EU treaty plan "it's not a priority"'.
[6] *The Spectator*, 22 February 2014, 'Only Angela Merkel can save David Cameron now'.
[7] *Daily Telegraph*, 23 February 2013, 'Cameron aims to get close to Merkel with immigration talks'.

motor going to deliver conflicting signals. Come the day, however, Downing Street briefed that she was 'sympathetic' to treaty change. In her address to Parliament, therefore, she abruptly dismissed the idea, telling the hopefuls that they were 'in for a disappointment'.[8] 'The Chancellor sent an unmistakable message to London,' said an EU diplomat. 'We hear you and we're with you, tinkering and tailoring yes, but upending and overhauling the European treaties, no way'.[9]

Yet, even without a practical route to a treaty change, at least there seemed to be an electoral dividend in Cameron's strategy. Ed Miliband told a London audience that it was 'unlikely' that Labour would offer a referendum if it won the general election.[10] That opened the way for Cameron to make the referendum a central plank of his campaign and a counter to UKIP.[11] Exploiting his advantage, he used the Sunday press to set out seven 'specific changes' for his renegotiation. There would be new controls to stop 'vast migrations' when new countries joined the EU; tighter immigration rules to ensure that migrants came to Britain to work, not as tourists planning to cash in on 'free benefits'; and a new power for groups of national parliaments to work together to block unwanted European legislation.

In his brave new 'reformed' EU, businesses would be freed from red tape and 'excessive interference' from Brussels, and given access to new markets through 'turbo charging' free trade deals with America and Asia; British police and courts would be liberated from 'unnecessary interference' from the European Court of Human Rights (even though this was not an EU body); and there would be more power 'flowing away' from Brussels to Britain and other member states. Finally, the principle of 'ever closer union' would be abolished. This, Cameron said, was 'not right for Britain'.[12] Rounding on his critics as 'defeatists', he declared that the British people had a very clear choice: If you want a referendum, only the Conservative Party will guarantee one.[13]

EMPTY VESSELS

Whether or not in response to the comment by the CBI's Katja Hall, the previous July, on the need for a 'clear vision' of a post-Brexit future, one organisation at least did wake up to that need: The Institute of Economic

[8] Speech by Federal Chancellor Angela Merkel in London – Thursday 27 February 2014.
[9] Reuters, 27 February 2014, 'Germany's Merkel to Cameron: I can't satisfy all Britain's EU wishes'.
[10] BBC News, 12 March 2014, 'EU referendum "unlikely" under Labour, says Ed Miliband'.
[11] *Daily Telegraph*, 12 March 2014, 'EU referendum: Tories will be the only party to let you choose, says Cameron'.
[12] *Sunday Telegraph*, 15 March 2014, 'David Cameron: my seven targets for a new EU'.
[13] *Sunday Telegraph*, 15 March 2013, 'David Cameron: the EU is not working and we will change it'.

Affairs, one of Margaret Thatcher's favourite think-tanks. In July 2013, it had announced a €100,000-prize competition to find 'the best blueprint for the UK after the EU'. The panel of judges was to be chaired by Lord Lawson, who called for the coming referendum to be 'preceded by a well-informed debate', adding that the winning entries would be 'an important contribution to that process'.[14]

In 8 April 2014, after several rule changes and the disqualification of one of the judges, not one but six 'winners' were announced. In an embarrassingly gauche celebration, an attaché case full of euros was presented to the first-prize winner, Iain Mansfield, a junior civil servant based in the FCO's Manila office, who managed to produce an essay that did not even meet the IEA's rather flexible approach to its own rules.[15] All entries advocating the 'Norway option' had been excluded. The six winners offered the same, rather unusual option based on a 'free trade' relationship with the EU, via EFTA.[16]

The winner's text was panned by John McDermott in the *Financial Times* – one of the few newspapers to review it – not least because it underestimated the strength of the ties between the EU and the UK, and therefore the costs of exit.[17] Mansfield's muddled paper argued that, while the UK might lose £9.3 billion a year in trade by leaving the Single Market, it could make £2.1 billion by increasing trade with the rest of the world and save £2.5 billion by repealing various regulations, ending up £1.3 billion better off. The *Sunday Telegraph* dismissed the effort as 'a gift to Europhiles'.[18]

So distant were the six finalists' papers from any mainstream Eurosceptic thinking that none played any part in the ongoing debate. An important opportunity had been lost – and not for the first time. Through 2002–2003, some members of UKIP had called on the party to set up its own think-tank, partially funded by its own MEPs and using Brussels facilities, to work on what was called an 'exit and survival plan' for a post-exit Britain. The idea was blocked by Nigel Farage, who insisted on devoting resources to his 'Westminster strategy'.[19] He wanted to contest Westminster elections

---

[14] BBC News, 16 July 2013, '"Brexit": IEA offers prize for UK exit plan from EU'.

[15] 'A Blueprint for Britain: Openness not Isolation' by Iain Mansfield.

[16] EUReferendum.com, 15 April 2014, 'Brexit: interesting coincidences'. One of us (RN) submitted an essay, based on a variation of the Norway option (Flexcit), which was included in the original shortlist but not in the six finalists.

[17] *Financial Times*, 9 April 2014, 'If this is the case for Brexit, I worry for Eurosceptics'.

[18] Booker column, 12 April 2014, 'Dismal "Brexit" prize is a gift to Europhiles'.

[19] Personal observations/witness accounts. One of us (RN) was employed in the European Parliament at the time, for the EDD Group, of which UKIP was part. The lack of a plan became a running sore in the party, but with no enthusiasm within the party hierarchy to define an intellectual base for Brexit, UKIP was to go into the 2016 referendum campaign with no coherent (or any) exit plan.

in order to build a cadre of UKIP MPs big enough to hold the balance of power. He reasoned that the Conservatives would then split, whence the Eurosceptic wing would join him to form a government that would take the country out of the EU.[20]

UNHELPFUL TIMES

Central to the credibility of Cameron's renegotiation strategy was his impossible dream of securing treaty amendments, thus avoiding accusations of a 'Wilsonian fudge'. It was not at all helpful, therefore, for the *Financial Times* to recruit Jean-Claude Piris, former legal counsel of the European Council and the Council of Ministers, to evaluate his seven key changes. He concluded that the demands could be met with some deft legal drafting, provided there was political will and a mood for compromise on both sides. In some, this prompted suspicions that Cameron's demands were too timid and open to a political fudge.[21] For many others, it simply confirmed that he was merely going through the motions. One of those was Lord Taverne, a founder of the Liberal Democrats. To meet the 2017 deadline, he said, there was simply not enough time to get a treaty change. Cameron's timetable was 'impossible'. A Conservatives victory in the next election, therefore, was 'likely to lead to Britain's exit from the EU'.[22]

The gaping holes in Cameron's strategy were further exposed by Barroso, speaking to the Humboldt University of Berlin, just before he stepped down from eight years as Commission president. The UK, he said, was a 'special' member of the EU but, 'precisely because of this', it would be a mistake to transform an exception into a rule. 'We can, and should,' he added, 'find ways to cater to the UK's specificity, inasmuch as this does not threaten the Union's overall coherence.' But even if in some issues, the specificity was shared by several governments, this should not be confounded with an overall situation of the Union.[23] In a few words in a speech of almost Soviet-style length and opacity, he had ruled out the idea of general changes, condemning Cameron to negotiate nothing more than a few country-specific changes.

That message was beginning to get through. 'We are not going to get full-blown treaty change by 2017,' said MP Tim Loughton, co-chairman of the

---

[20] Discussions with the author (RN), who shared an office in Strasbourg with Farage between 1999 and 2003. Committed to his own strategy, Farage never seriously pursued the idea of a referendum, which he considered an unnecessary distraction.

[21] *Financial Times*, 5 May 2014, 'Legal loopholes for David Cameron on EU treaty, says top lawyer'.

[22] *Guardian*, 2 May 2014, 'David Cameron's EU referendum pledge will be a disaster for him'.

[23] European Commission, Speech: 'On Europe Considerations on the present and the future of the European Union', 8 May 2014, José Manuel Durão Barroso, President of the European Commission.

Fresh Start Project, who argued that there were 'a whole load of things that do not require treaty change'.[24] However, as the European elections loomed and the Conservatives faced a drubbing from UKIP, Loughton took a sterner line, calling on Cameron to threaten withdrawal from the EU if significant treaty changes were not secured before 2017. 'By just saying he would want to stay in the EU, whatever, plays to Euroscepticism,' he said. 'If he says he can envisage a situation where he reluctantly says Britain would have to go it alone, then that adds credibility [to negotiations for some powers to be repatriated to the UK].'[25]

At this stage, Cameron was not even sure he could win a general election. But he had to tell Andrew Marr on his show that 'I'm hoping and believing I can win an overall majority', to which he added: 'people should be in no doubt I will not become prime minister unless I can guarantee that we will hold that referendum'. Unhelpfully, Marr had asked whether this was a 'cast iron' guarantee, a phrase with unfortunate connotations.[26] It provoked a predictable response from UKIP's leader, Nigel Farage: voters would struggle to believe Cameron's promise was 'worth a row of beans'.[27]

With only days to go before the European elections, Cameron's unreal aspirations were further challenged when Günther Krichbaum, head of the German government's committee on EU affairs – and one of Merkel's closest political allies – firmly rejected one of the central planks of his 'renegotiation': the removal of the UK from the commitment to 'ever closer union'. This, said Krichbaum, was simply a 'desperate attempt to appease Ukip'.[28]

Come the elections, the worst fears were realised. UKIP ended up with 24 MEPs, against Labour's 20 and 19 for the Conservatives. It was the first time a minor political party had won the popular vote in a British election since 1906. Significantly, Cameron's Lib-Dem partners crashed to one seat, down from 11 in 2009, their vote halved to 7 per cent.[29] Turnout in the UK was 34.19 per cent, compared with 42.54 per cent Europe-wide, the lowest figure since 1979, when elections were first held.[30] Commentators dubbed the result a 'political earthquake', as Farage looked to the fruition of his 'Westminster strategy'. 'It is now not beyond the bounds of possibility that we hold the balance of power in another hung parliament,' he gloated.[31]

---

[24] *New York Times*, 9 May 2014, 'UK finds way out of impasse on ties to EU'.

[25] *Independent on Sunday*, 11 May 2014, 'European elections 2014: looming disaster rattles Tories'.

[26] *The Andrew Marr Show*, Interview: David Cameron MP, Leader, Conservative Party, 11 May 2014.

[27] *Guardian*, 11 May 2014, 'David Cameron: in–out referendum on EU by 2017 is cast-iron pledge'.

[28] *Observer*, 18 May 2014, 'David Cameron is trying to "appease Ukip", say Germans'.

[29] BBC News, *Vote 2014: UK European Election Results*.

[30] *Euractiv*, 7 August 2014, 'It's official: last EU election had lowest-ever turnout'.

[31] *Guardian*, 26 May 2014, 'Ukip wins European elections with ease to set off political earthquake'.

There was nevertheless some comfort for Cameron in an Opinium poll published in June. Although it had 48 per cent in favour of leaving the EU, as opposed to 37 remaining, once again the 'renegotiation' dynamic was evident. Should he secure 'favourable terms', the split became 42–36 per cent in favour of 'remain'. However, there was a sting in the tail: only 18 per cent (including 34 per cent of Conservatives) thought he could secure the necessary concessions.[32]

Meanwhile, a tense squabble had developed over who was to be the new Commission president. The selection process was fraught at the best of times, but the European Parliament had insisted that the lead candidate or *Spitzenkandidaten* should be chosen from the parliamentary grouping that had gained the most votes in the recent elections. The favourite was former Luxembourg prime minister Jean-Claude Juncker, supported by Merkel but opposed by Cameron. Despite a 'mini-summit' in Sweden in early June, where the prime minister took to a rowing boat with Merkel and the Swedish and Dutch prime ministers, Juncker was to be nominated by the European Council on 26 June, with twenty-six votes for and only two against. This was seen as another 'humiliating defeat' for Cameron.[33]

Nevertheless, the situation was not a total loss. Van Rompuy was to be succeeded as European Council president by former Polish prime minister Donald Tusk. He was to inherit a council that had formally acknowledged the UK's concerns 'related to the future development of the EU', accepting that they 'will need to be addressed'. The Council noted that 'the concept of ever closer union allows for different paths of integration for different countries, allowing those that want to deepen integration to move ahead, while respecting the wish of those who do not'.[34] A British official grudgingly admitted, 'It is a start. We have got that marker down now.'[35]

JOHNSON INTERVENES

Somebody else in the 'marker' business was then London mayor Boris Johnson, desperate to get back into mainstream politics in pursuit of his ambition to lead the Conservative Party. Mounting a direct challenge to Cameron, he sought to carve out a unique position on the EU, arguing that the UK should 'not be frightened' of quitting the EU if the negotiations failed. His 'big idea' was that EU leaders would be more willing to deal if the UK threatened to leave.[36]

---

[32] *Observer*, 21 June 2014, 'British people favour leaving the European Union, according to poll'.
[33] *Guardian*, 27 June 2014, 'David Cameron loses Jean-Claude Juncker vote'.
[34] Conclusions, 26/27 June 2014, Brussels, European Council.
[35] Reuters, 27 June 2014, 'EU leaders make concessions to Britain after Juncker vote'.
[36] *Sunday Times*, 3 August 2014, 'Boris warns PM: be ready to leave EU'.

This was a preview of a speech he delivered later in the week, provocatively in the same Bloomberg office from which Cameron had given his referendum promise. Ostensibly, it was to launch a report from his economics adviser, Dr Gerard Lyons, which offered a bundle of EU 'reforms', including the abolition of the CAP.[37] Another idea was to use a 'No' vote in a referendum, and the threat of invoking Article 50, as leverage to secure talks on a new free trade agreement. Johnson denied that his ideas would be impossible to deliver, even asserting that the 2017 timetable was feasible. 'I'm not so pessimistic,' he said. 'I think you could easily.' All you needed to do, he declared, was 'go in hard and low'.[38] The *Daily Express* rewarded him with a front-page banner headline: 'Boris Johnson tells Cameron: EU shake-up is simple – we just need to get TOUGH'.[39]

Almost at the same time Johnson was speaking, Dr Nigel Wilson, chief executive of the insurers Legal & General, observed that: 'Leaving the EU would not be as disastrous a scenario as some people have painted it as.' He added: 'If we get a terrible deal we should stay out. I see the world as a huge opportunity for the UK but we are underachieving by concentrating on Europe, which is growing too slowly. This will not lead to economic growth in the UK.' The significance of this was that Wilson was the first head of a FTSE 100 company publicly to suggest leaving the EU.[40] The cumulative pressure, quite evidently, had an effect on Cameron. By the end of August, he was hinting that he would seek an exit should the EU 'reject a large overhaul of its rules'. Nevertheless, his aides 'remained confident' that significant powers would be returned to Britain.[41]

DEFECTIONS AND ELECTIONS

Before this message could gain any momentum, Cameron and his party were shocked by a development that had profound electoral implications. The sitting Tory MP for Clacton, Douglas Carswell, resigned his seat and announced he was defecting to UKIP. He said he had realised that the prime minister's advisers were 'looking to cut a deal that gives them just enough to persuade enough voters to vote to stay in'. Following that, he said, 'my position in the Conservative Party became untenable'.[42] This was the same

---

[37] Mayor of London, 'The Europe Report: A win-win situation', August 2014.
[38] *Evening Standard*, 7 August 2014, 'Reforming EU is easy, says Boris in challenge to David Cameron'.
[39] 8 August 2014.
[40] *Daily Mail*, 7 August 2014, 'Let's quit EU unless we get a better deal: Legal & General boss delivers Brussels blast'.
[41] *The Times*, 25 August 2014, 'Cameron to threaten EU with British exit'; *Daily Mail*, 25 August 2014, 'Cameron set to threaten Brussels that he is prepared to leave the EU if Britain does not get its way'.
[42] BBC News, 28 August 2014, 'Tory MP Douglas Carswell defects to UKIP and forces by-election'.

Douglas Carswell who, on 12 March 2014, had used his Twitter account to declare: 'Only the Conservatives will guarantee and deliver an In/Out referendum. It will only happen if Cameron is Prime Minister.'[43]

On 18 September, there was another, rather different referendum – on Scottish independence. The 'No' campaign won with 55 per cent of the vote on a turnout of 85 per cent. Although the Scottish government had produced a comprehensive, 670-page 'exit plan' in the form of a White Paper, it had been described by Scottish Secretary Alistair Carmichael as 'more of a black mark than a blueprint', with 12 major faults identified.[44] Alistair Darling, leader of the 'No' campaign, branded the document a 'work of fiction, full of meaningless assertions'.[45] With the status quo effect working in the government's favour, the implications for Brexit were obvious. The absence of a credible exit plan could be a vulnerability for any 'leave' campaign.

By now, Cameron was gearing up for his final party conference before the general election and, on 27 September, when he was on his way to the conference hall in Birmingham, the news of another UKIP defector came in – Mark Reckless, MP for Rochester and Strood. Rumours abounded throughout the conference that there would be more, but the line held. These were to be the only two.

Carswell was the first to the polls, with his by-election held on 9 October. He knocked his former party into second place, taking for UKIP a majority of 12,404, a slight increase on his general election count.[46] Also being contested was the Greater Manchester seat of Heywood and Middleton, vacant following the death of the incumbent. As expected, Labour won the seat with 11,633 votes, but UKIP challenger John Bickley came a close second with 11,016 votes. He cleared 38.7 per cent of the vote, shunting the Conservatives into third place. Although no one could know it at the time, Bickley's result was the high-water mark for Farage's 'Westminster strategy'. Never again would a UKIP candidate – rather than a defector – come so close to taking a seat. Having failed to deliver, and doomed to repeat that failure, Farage was now reliant on Cameron's re-election for a referendum – something he would do his very best to frustrate.

Confronted with a seemingly unstoppable UKIP surge, Cameron did exactly what he had done in the aftermath of the Eastleigh by-election.

---

[43] Carswell subsequently deleted the tweet.
[44] Scottish Government, November 2013, 'Scotland's Future: Your Guide to an Independent Scotland'; Office of the Secretary of State for Scotland, 27 January 2014. Twelve of the faults in the Scottish government's independence White Paper.
[45] BBC News, 26 November 2013, 'Scottish independence: Referendum White Paper unveiled'.
[46] BBC News, 10 October 2014, 'UKIP gains first elected MP with Clacton win'.

He turned to immigration. In less than a week, the media was flooded with stories heralding a new initiative – an 'emergency brake' on the number of European job-seekers, put forward as a counter to a Farage-inspired offering of an 'Australian-style points system' for controlling immigration. It would give ministers the power to block new arrivals if numbers increased above a set level, on the grounds that further influxes would put unacceptable strains on public services and social cohesion.[47]

This seems to have been the first time the 'emergency brake' concept broke cover, but it was to become a prominent part of the narrative, even though Professor Damian Chalmers from the LSE argued that it would 'clearly violate the EU treaty'.[48] Perceptively, the *FT* noted: 'it is not clear exactly what Mr Cameron is seeking'. Unfortunately, but in an entirely different field, the EU was very clear what it was seeking. On 23 October, Cameron had been 'ambushed' with a demand for an extra £1.7 billion in contributions, due on 1 December, 'because Britain's economy has performed better than other economies in Europe since 1995'. Downing Street was not happy. 'It's not acceptable to just change the fees for previous years and demand them back at a moment's notice,' its spokesman huffed.[49] A 'visibly furious' prime minister then denounced the 'appalling' way Britain had been treated. 'I'm not paying that bill on 1 December. It is not going to happen,' he declared.[50]

However, it then transpired that the UK, with other member states, had been warned the previous January.[51] This followed adoption of new methodologies for calculating GNPs, mandated by the UN Statistical Commission in 2003, and introduced by an EU law proposed in December 2010.[52] The proposal had been agreed by William Hague on 22 April 2013, and passed into law on 21 May, comprising a mere 727 pages.[53] The implications nevertheless were missed by the Treasury.[54] When Cameron tried to raise the issue at the European Council, he got

[47] *The Times*, 16 October 2014, 'No 10 seeks emergency brake on immigration'. See also Channel 4 News, 16 October 2014, 'Can Cameron put the brakes on immigration?'; *Financial Times*, 16 October 2014, 'David Cameron floats "emergency brake" on EU immigration'.
[48] Channel 4 News report, op. cit.
[49] *Daily Telegraph*, 23 October 2014, 'EU makes Britain pay for recovery'.
[50] *Daily Telegraph*, 24 October 2014, 'David Cameron: Britain will not pay extra £1.7bn for EU budget'.
[51] *Sunday Telegraph*, 26 October 2014, 'George Osborne under pressure over EU budget row'.
[52] European Commission, Brussels, 20 December 2010, COM(2010) 774 final, Proposal for a Regulation ... on the European system of national and regional accounts in the European Union.
[53] Regulation (EU) No. 549/2013 of 21 May 2013.
[54] See Technical Press Briefing, Brussels, 16 January 2014: 'Why a New ESA?'; and *Monthly Bulletin*, August 2014, 'New International Standards in Statistics: Enhancements to Methodology and Data Availability'.

short shrift from Merkel, who remarked that the demand 'should have been expected'.[55] Despite a claim by Chancellor George Osborne that the bill had been halved, the UK ended up paying the demand in full, the only concession being that it was deferred until September 2015, after the general election.[56] Predictably, the episode did little to enhance the reputation of the Cameron administration, or the love of the British people for the European Union.

The timing could not have been worse for Rochester and Strood, where Mark Reckless was standing for re-election on 20 November. Even a spirited Conservative campaign, with Cameron visiting the constituency five times, could not recover the position. Reckless retook his old seat, although his majority was reduced to 2,920 from his general election showing of 9,953. His share of the vote also dropped. Victory this was for UKIP, but the Tories held second place, ahead of Labour. Once again, though, the Lib-Dem vote collapsed, dropping from 16.3 per cent to just 0.9 per cent of the vote – their lowest ever tally in a by-election.[57]

In the wake of the by-election, former environment secretary Owen Paterson delivered a speech to the 'Business for Britain' campaign group in London, offering 'an optimistic vision of a post-EU United Kingdom'. He argued that Cameron should take his mandate from the general election and invoke Article 50 straight away, without a referendum. An exit settlement should be based on the 'Norway option', involving joining EFTA and adopting the EEA agreement. Influence would be regained by restoring the UK's standing in international organisations. There would be no 'fax democracy' as such. The UK would be sending laws down to Brussels – not the other way around.

The fact of the speech was widely reported, but little of the detail was conveyed. *The Times* reported it as a challenge to the prime minister, its headline declaring: 'Tory right turns up heat on Cameron over Europe'. The BBC report devoted most of the space to immigration issues, unrelated to the speech. There and elsewhere, the EEA/Norway option was not mentioned.[58] Thus, the speech became a salutary illustration of how little the national media was interested in the details of an EU exit. During the Rochester and Strood by-election, the most widely reported exchanges between the Tories

[55] *Daily Telegraph*, 24 October 2014, 'George Osborne failed to tell David Cameron about EU bill'.
[56] *Guardian*, 7 November 2014, 'UK to pay £1.7bn EU bill in full despite Osborne's claim to have halved it'.
[57] *Daily Telegraph*, 21 November 2014, 'Mark Reckless wins Rochester by-election for Ukip with 2,900 majority'.
[58] BBC News, 24 November 2014, 'Ex-Conservative minister Owen Paterson urges UK's EU exit'.

and UKIP had been on immigration.[59] It was immigration, more than anything, that attracted the headlines, so if the politicians wanted publicity, they talked about immigration.

DROPPING THE BALL

The week after the by-election found Cameron at the JCB headquarters in Rocester, Staffordshire, speaking on immigration. But there was no sign of his much-touted 'emergency brake'.[60] Instead, there were weak substitutes: EU migrants would need job offers before they came to the UK and benefits would be withheld for four years. These, Cameron tried to pass off as 'radical changes' that he was 'confident' would 'reduce significantly EU migration to the UK'. He would negotiate them for the whole EU or, if that was not possible, for the UK only. To add weight to what were modest proposals, he asserted that they would 'require some treaty change', although he was not clear exactly which bits of the treaty needed changing. That rather gave the game away that treaty change would most likely not be required.[61]

Questioned about the missing 'emergency brake', Cameron's line was that it would not be effective, 'because there are countries in Europe with very high levels of immigration that don't want the sort of controls that I want to put in place'.[62] Yet he still hoped his speech would end the argument.[63] Some of his backbenchers, however, thought that he had 'written his own death warrant'. If he failed to win the election as a result, he was finished as leader.[64] As to European reaction, the Commission was 'unimpressed'.[65] Elmar Brok, chair of the European Parliament's foreign affairs committee, thought Cameron was digging himself into a pit. 'I regard it as inconceivable that all 28 states would agree to the principle of free movement of workers being *de facto* eroded or juristically undermined,' he said.[66]

---

[59] *Guardian*, 19 November 2014, 'Mark Reckless sparks immigration row on eve of Rochester byelection'.

[60] Cameron had been listening to Mats Persson, then director of the think-tank, Open Europe, and soon to become his special adviser on EU issues. Persson had advised against the 'emergency brake' idea. The arguments against were set out in the Open Europe blog, 27 November 2014, 'Why Cameron should stay clear of an "emergency brake" on EU free movement'. History may record, therefore, that Persson was partially responsible for Cameron losing the 2016 referendum.

[61] Gov.uk website, 'JCB Staffordshire: Prime Minister's speech', 28 November 2014.

[62] Ibid.

[63] *Mail on Sunday*, 30 November 2014, 'James Forsyth: silence ... it's Dave's biggest immigration gamble yet'.

[64] *Sunday Times*, 30 November 2014, 'Failure on migrants may sink Cameron'.

[65] *Euractiv*, 7 December 2014, 'Commission unimpressed by Cameron's immigration rhetoric'.

[66] *Deutsche Welle*, 29 November 2014, Cameron's migration demands are "extortion," says EU's Brok'.

Cameron's fortunes did not improve. One of the problems was that, in 2017, both Hollande and Merkel went to the polls. Neither would want the complication of treaty negotiations while they were campaigning for re-election. A solution was thus mooted, where a 'sweet spot' could be exploited in the summer of 2017 – 'the tantalising gap between French and German elections'. With victory anticipated for Sarkozy in May of that year, it was supposed that he and Merkel could be induced to give Cameron what he wanted.[67]

Nevertheless, there was a more immediate opportunity in the last European Council of the year, on 18 December. But the signs were not looking good. With pressure from his own right wing on immigration and other matters, Hollande was not prepared to concede a treaty change that might trigger a referendum in France.[68] Instead, he accused Cameron of being 'obsessed with his own problems', rejecting Britain's wish for special rights within the EU. For these, 'it is unacceptable to revise founding European commitments,' he said.[69]

DOGGED PERSISTENCE

Despite all this, Cameron continued to argue for 'full-on treaty change', telling Andrew Marr that we needed 'these very big changes' that he was putting forward. And, if he did not get what he wanted, he held out the prospect of campaigning to leave the EU.[70]

He was able to put his case personally to Merkel when she made London her first trip abroad for the year, although the visit was marred by the terrorist attack on the Paris office of the *Charlie Hebdo* satirical magazine, killing ten staff. An optimistic Cameron was 'convinced' he could 'fix the problems' in the UK's relationship, still insisting that his proposals needed treaty change. Subtly shifting his stance, he put to the chancellor that he fully supported freedom of movement and was merely focused on abuse of the system. Merkel could hardly disagree, but her solution gave no solace to Cameron – 'a very close look at the social security systems of individual Member States'. These, after all, were 'not part of communal law'.[71]

A rather less emollient approach was taken by Jean-Claude Juncker. In Paris, speaking to French officials, he compared British membership of the

[67] *Financial Times*, 14 December 2014, 'Cameron aims for 2017 "sweet spot" for EU deal'.
[68] *Daily Telegraph*, 18 December 2014, 'France to block David Cameron's treaty change plan'.
[69] *Deutsche Welle*, 18 December 2014, 'UK PM David Cameron pleads with EU leaders in Brussels over reforms'.
[70] BBC News, *The Andrew Marr Show*, 4 January 2015.
[71] Gov.uk (website), 8 January 2015, 'David Cameron and Angela Merkel press conference'.

EU to a doomed romance. He would not get down on his knees to beg Britain to stay, and dismissed Cameron's treaty change aspiration. 'When one mentions the end of the free circulation of workers, there can be no debate, dialogue or compromise. We can fight against abuses but the EU won't change the treaties to satisfy the whim of certain politicians,' he said.[72]

AN ELECTION YEAR

With the election year upon him and less than four months to go to the polls, Cameron was determined not to let 'UKIP issues' dominate his agenda.[73] Farage, on the other hand, after the successes of Carswell and Reckless, felt his party was on a roll, having earlier predicted that his party could 'snatch' up to 40 seats.[74]

Matthew Goodwin, an associate professor of politics at Nottingham University and 'one of the most widely respected experts on the rise of Ukip', argued that UKIP was likely to win six seats. 'They have pretty much got three or four seats now in the bag unless there is a monumental mistake and a car crash before 7 May,' he forecast two months before the polls.[75] Farage thus speculated on 'the likelihood of Britain waking up to something that resembled a loose three-party coalition'. He could see the Tories, UKIP and the Democratic Ulster Unionist Party 'doing some kind of deal'.[76] This was his 'Westminster strategy' writ large. His MPs would hold Cameron's 'feet to the fire', making him keep his promise on the referendum.

April was manifesto time for the Conservatives, their chosen theme, 'Strong leadership, a clear economic plan [and] a brighter, more secure future.'[77] As to the EU, the promise of an in/out referendum by the end of 2017 was repeated. For the rest, Cameron committed to keeping the pound and staying out of the eurozone – something not on the table – to reforming the workings of the EU, 'which is too big, too bossy and too bureaucratic'; reclaiming power from Brussels and safeguarding British interests in the Single Market; and backing businesses 'to create jobs in Britain by completing ambitious trade deals and reducing red tape'. The only commitment to reducing EU immigration was expressed in terms

---

[72] *Daily Telegraph*, 18 January 2015, 'Jean-Claude Juncker compares British membership of EU to doomed romance'.

[73] *Daily Telegraph*, 12 January 2015, 'David Cameron has stopped trying to wrestle the Ukip pig'.

[74] *Daily Express*, 22 November 2014, 'Nigel Farage: Ukip to snatch 40 seats at General Election as more MPs swap blue for purple'.

[75] *Daily Telegraph*, 4 March 2015, 'Ukip already has four seats "in the bag", says leading expert Matthew Goodwin'.

[76] Farage, Nigel (2015), *The Purple Revolution* (London: Biteback Publishing), pp. 292–293.

[77] *Guardian*, 14 April 2015, 'Conservatives election manifesto 2015: the key points'.

of 'reforming welfare rules'. Compared with the February 1974 Labour manifesto, which also promised a referendum, there were fewer items and the language was vaguer. A common element was the absence of any mention of treaty change. A Wilsonian fudge was in the making.

RED TAPE FOLLY

The commitment to 'reducing red tape' was as unconvincing as it was vague. At the end of the previous month, the Lords' European Union Committee had accused ministers of trying to bury the results of the 'balance of competences' review. Far from supporting Cameron's call for repatriation of powers, of the 32 reports into different areas of the EU's operation, none demonstrated that 'too much power resided in Brussels'.[78] Yet days earlier, on *Jeremy Paxman*, Cameron had asserted that Europe 'isn't working properly', adding: 'The EU is trying to become too much of a state. It's got too much power. We want to be in Europe for trade. We don't want to be a part of an ever-closer union'.[79] But he was getting no help in making a case in detail.

Had Cameron been looking for a good place to start, he could well have used the experience of the previous winter, when part of the Somerset Levels had suffered catastrophic flooding, defying immediate attempts at relief. Although ostensibly a weather-related incident, in historical terms the rain had not been particularly severe. What had made the difference had been a toxic combination of EU legislation, UK law and local interests. At the heart of the problem had been the EU's Birds and Habitats Directives, combined with the Water Framework Directive, applied through the EU's Natura 2000 programme, augmented by the so-called 'Floods Directive'. These laid the foundation for a policy of 'restoration' – i.e., flooding – of drained wetlands as a specific EU policy objective, to be executed throughout Europe.

With few available sites in England, the Somerset Levels had been chosen to meet mandatory EU quotas. When the long-term weather forecast had indicated that the winter would be drier than usual, this cleared the way for the deliberate flooding of Southlake Moor, part of the Levels. The localised flooding then had the unfortunate effect of creating a 'hydraulic block' preventing the escape of water running off the Malvern Hills, when the rain turned out to be heavier than expected. The situation was subsequently made worse by EU-mandated restrictions on dredging, which slowed down

---

[78] *Observer*, 28 March 2015, 'Lords accuse Tories of "burying" review that cleared EU of interference'.
[79] Sky News, 26 March 2015, 'The Prime Minister says "Europe is Not Working Properly"'.

the evacuation of water from the flood plain. The resultant disaster had been entirely man-made.[80]

Yet, so complex had been the interaction between EU and national legislation, policy initiatives, guidelines and other actions, that the hand of the EU was near-invisible – easily disputed by those who wished to see other factors at work. Much the same had applied to the horsemeat scandal, the Icelandic volcano response, Foot & Mouth Disease and much, much more. When Lord Denning had observed in 1974 that European law was 'now like a tidal wave bringing down our sea walls and flowing inland over our fields and houses', he never meant his words to be taken literally. But so disguised were the impacts that no 'balance of competences' exercise was ever going to identify them. Politicians seeking to claw back powers from Brussels did not have the first idea of where to look.

THE PEOPLE SPEAK

In an overheated election campaign, the media had fixated on the possibility of a hung parliament, with much speculation about a Conservative–UKIP coalition. The terms, Farage airily laid out, would be very precise and simple: 'I want a full and fair referendum to be held in 2015 to allow Britain to vote on being in or out of the European Union.' 'There would be no wiggle room for "renegotiation" somewhere down the line,' he added.[81]

For all the hype, opinion polls had been signalling a steadily decline in support for UKIP, down from 17 per cent in January to just over 13 in April, and falling – the classic two-party squeeze that typified the 'first past the post' system. On the night, the exit poll put the Conservatives ahead with 316 seats; Labour on 239; the Scottish National Party on 58 and the Lib-Dems trailing on 10. UKIP was to get a mere two seats. 'It's fair to say no one was expecting that,' said Jonathan Freedland in the *Guardian*; 'not the political parties, not the punditocracy and – least of all – the pollsters.'[82]

In the event, Cameron walked away with 330 seats and a clear majority against Labour with 232 seats, the latter's vote heavily eroded in its Scottish heartland by the SNP, which took 56 seats. UKIP's Carswell kept his seat while Reckless lost his, leaving the party with one seat, despite 3.8 million

---

[80] Multiple reports, including: *Daily Mail*, 21 February 2014, 'Could Met Office have been more wrong? Just before floods, report told councils: Winter will be "drier than normal" – including the West Country!'; *Sunday Telegraph* (Booker Column), 22 February 2014, 'The flooding of the Somerset Levels was deliberately engineered'; and North, Richard, *A Very European Disaster: The Somerset Levels Flooding – Political Aspects of the Flooding, Winter 2013–14* (7 March 2014).

[81] Farage, op. cit., p. 301.

[82] Details recorded contemporaneously. There are multiple confirmatory sources.

votes, as against the SNP, which polled a mere 1.5 million. Farage – having lost in the Thanet South constituency to Craig Mackinlay, a former UKIP party secretary now standing for the Conservatives – promptly resigned as party leader.[83]

However, the story of the night was the collapse of the Lib-Dems. Although this had been clearly signalled in opinion polls and by-elections, the decline of the party – heavily damaged by a broken promise on tuition fees – had barely registered. From a heady 57 seats in 2010, it had plummeted to a mere 8. As to its significance, in the 2010 election, the combined UKIP/BNP vote had deprived Cameron of potentially 43 seats, costing him his victory. In this election, the UKIP vote had increased by 9.5 per cent, enough to deprive Cameron of his winning margin once again. But its gains had been more than offset by the Lib-Dem losses.

Had the Lib-Dems maintained their vote, the outcome of the 2015 general election could have been a Labour/Lib-Dem coalition, with UKIP having kept the Tories out of power. There would have been no referendum. By a perverse twist of fate, the Lib-Dem collapse had brought Cameron victory, neutralising the best efforts of Farage. With that, an EU referendum was assured – by the very party that least wanted one. If Farage eventually embraced a referendum, it was the Lib-Dems, albeit unwittingly, who made it happen. Like Farage, Nick Clegg fell on his sword, resigning as Lib-Dem leader, followed by Ed Miliband. Unlike Clegg and Miliband, Farage – the man who said it would no longer be credible for him to lead the party – resumed its leadership a few days later.[84]

RENEGOTIATION

Quick off the mark, Jean-Claude Juncker promised to help Cameron 'to strike a fair deal for the United Kingdom', although the president's spokesman was later to add that 'EU rights like free movement are not negotiable'.[85] On his own account, Cameron told the media that negotiations had started, he having 'already made calls' to other European leaders. But he also hinted that he was considering bringing the referendum forward to 2016 – following a quick renegotiation.[86]

The hint of an earlier referendum was quickly reinforced, with suggestions that he was intent on avoiding a politically dangerous clash with the French

[83] He was convinced he would win the seat. See: Farage, op. cit., p. 298.
[84] *Daily Telegraph*, 11 May 2015, 'By bringing back Nigel Farage, Ukip condemns itself to life as a one-man band'.
[85] *Daily Telegraph*, 9 May 2015, 'Jean-Claude Juncker pledge to help David Cameron win acceptable EU deal for Britain'.
[86] *Daily Telegraph*, 10 May 2015, 'David Cameron: I've already started EU negotiations'.

and German elections in 2017.[87] In his memoirs, Cameron acknowledged that the renegotiation would not be based on the wider-scale treaty change 'that many had forecast' (especially himself). Change would be brought about 'unilaterally', he wrote, adding: 'I planned to start a fight in a room all by myself.'[88] But he was planning to take a water pistol to a tank battle – in a torrential downpour. Even though he wrote that, 'the absence of a general treaty negotiation and Europe-wide reform wasn't necessarily a disaster', he was massively reducing his chances of coming home with anything more than a Wilsonian fudge.[89] Effectively, the game was over before it had even started.

Had there been any doubt about prospects of a treaty change, on 22 June the Commission unveiled its 'Five Presidents Report', entitled *Completing Europe's Economic and Monetary Union*. Compiled by Juncker 'in close cooperation' with the presidents of the European Council, the Eurogroup, the ECB and the European Parliament, the effect of this was to kick the ball down the road, setting the timetable to 2025, outside Cameron's self-imposed time frame.[90]

The period between May 2015 and February 2016 when negotiations were concluded, Cameron recalls, felt as if it had been spent 'largely on board a series of ageing RAF planes ... travelling from capital to capital, conference to conference and summit to summit', to 'become the biggest diplomatic tour in recent history'.[91] It was to no avail. By January 2016, Cameron had conceded so much ground since his Bloomberg speech that all that remained were four modest proposals. He was left with no recourse but to talk them up as 'key reforms', even though they would leave the EU untouched.[92]

Nor was Cameron's position improved by the Electoral Commission ruling that a referendum question to which the answer was either 'Yes' or 'No' would advantage 'remain'. The Commission's preferred question was: 'Should the United Kingdom remain a member of the European Union or leave the European Union?' Voters could mark: 'Remain a member of the European Union' or: 'Leave the European Union'. Cameron accepted this version.[93]

[87] *Guardian*, 11 May 2015, 'David Cameron may bring EU referendum forward to 2016'.
[88] Cameron, op. cit., p. 627.
[89] Ibid.
[90] *Euractiv*, 25 June 2015, 'The eurozone's Five Presidents' report, and what it means for Britain'.
[91] Cameron, op. cit., p. 637.
[92] *Deutsche Welle*, 26 January 2016, 'Merkel, Cameron pledge progress on EU reform deal'.
[93] *Guardian*, 1 September 2015, 'EU referendum: Cameron accepts advice to change wording of question'.

Thus disarmed, he approached the European Council on 18 February, cap in hand, for the concessions the other leaders were prepared to give him. The outcome was an intergovernmental agreement, outside the framework of the EU treaties, between the 28 EU leaders, meeting within the European Council but not acting as the council. While Cameron was quick to claim this to be legally binding, others thought differently.[94] A crucial part of the 'settlement' was a recognition that the UK was not committed to further political integration into the EU, where the EU leaders had promised to incorporate this sentiment 'into the Treaties at the time of their next revision in accordance with the relevant provisions of the Treaties and the respective constitutional requirements of the Member States, so as to make it clear that the references to ever closer union do not apply to the United Kingdom'.

The current leaders, however, were making a promise they could not keep, nor could they bind their successors.[95] When it came to fulfilling the promise, the leaders could have been replaced, not least the German and French chancellor and president.[96] Cameron's claim was further undermined when a leaked diplomatic report revealed that Merkel had told her fellow EU leaders not to be overly concerned about treaty changes because, 'we do not know if we ever will have to change them'.[97]

On immigration, the Commission agreed to provide a 'safeguard mechanism' to address UK concerns about the exceptional inflow of workers from elsewhere in the EU, with legislation that would authorise a member state to restrict 'access of union workers newly entering its labour market to in-work benefits for a total of up to four years from the commencement of employment'. The other, grudging, technical concessions, made for a tedious litany of small print – a long way from the clear victory that Cameron needed.

There was no new power for national parliaments to block unwanted EU legislation and the powers of the Commission had been left untouched. There were no new trade deals, no controls on the European Court of Human Rights and no attempt to get power flowing back from Brussels to Britain and other member states. As to the abolition of the principle of 'ever closer union', the only thing on offer was a legalistic fudge. Responding

---

[94] *Guardian*, 24 February 2016, 'European court could challenge Cameron's deal, says Michael Gove'.
[95] The dictum *res inter alios acta vel iudicata, aliis nec nocet nec prodocet* applied (two or more people cannot agree among each other to establish an obligation for a third party who was not involved in the agreement).
[96] House of Commons European Scrutiny Committee, *UK Government's Renegotiation of EU Membership: Parliamentary Sovereignty and Scrutiny*, Fourteenth Report of Session 2015–2016, published 15 December 2015.
[97] *Independent on Sunday*, 20 February 2016, 'EU referendum: Michael Gove attacks David Cameron's claim Brexit would damage national security'.

to the draft of the agreement issued two weeks previously, a snap poll conducted by Sky News had 69 per cent thinking the deal 'bad for Britain', while only 31 per cent thought it 'good'.[98] There was nothing in the final version to change that view.

With the renegotiation concluded, however, Cameron was true to his word. From a temporary lectern in Downing Street, he announced the date of the referendum. It was to be 23 June – a mere four months to prepare the British public for 'one of the biggest decisions this country will face in our lifetimes. Whether to remain in a reformed European Union – or to leave.' 'You will decide,' he declared. 'And whatever your decision, I will do my best to deliver it.'[99] The first statement was true. The second was not.

THE TWO BATTLES

In many respects, the campaign to leave had never stopped since the failure of the 'No' campaign in 1975. Now, 41 years later, while history appeared to be repeating itself, the situation was very different. In 1975, the then EEC had been a relatively immature organisation, recently enlarged to a mere nine member states. The EU of 2016 was a very different proposition. Furthermore, the United Kingdom of 2016 was a very different nation, heavily integrated, having delegated many of its powers and responsibilities to EU institutions. It would emerge into a very different world, irrevocably altered by the transport and communications revolutions and decades of globalisation.

When David Cameron announced the date of his referendum, he may have been kick-starting a new campaign, but there was already that other campaign in place. Ostensibly, the new one was a continuation of the old, but the reality – barely, if at all perceived by the commentariat – was that the new battle was directed not so much at leaving the EU, but at winning the referendum. The distinction was far from subtle. Leaving would be a very complex, multi-level process and, having left, the UK would have to forge an entirely new relationship with the EU. But the new campaign was not preparing for these eventualities.

Attempts to define that relationship, initially through UKIP and then via the IEA 'Brexit prize', had already failed. But there was a third try, when Dominic Cummings – soon to become a key member of the Leave campaign – toyed with the problem. 'Creating an exit plan that makes sense and which all reasonable people could unite around seems an almost insuperable task,' he observed. However, he noted that 'Eurosceptic groups

[98] *Independent*, 3 February 2016, 'People overwhelmingly think David Cameron's EU deal is "bad for Britain", poll finds'.
[99] Gov.uk (website), 'PM statement following Cabinet meeting on EU settlement, 20 February 2016'.

have been divided for years about many of the basic policy and political questions'. Thus, he rejected the idea, arguing that the sheer complexity of leaving would involve endless questions of detail that could not be answered in such a plan 'even were it to be 20,000 pages long'. He concluded: 'There is much to be gained by swerving the whole issue'.[100]

With that, 'Vote Leave' was to go into the fray with no settled (or any) exit plan. At times, both Cummings and Boris Johnson, who was later to join the campaign, advanced the idea of using the referendum result to broker further negotiations with the EU, followed by yet another referendum.[101] To Cameron, this was 'for the birds'. The Article 50 process, he scorned, 'is not an invitation to re-join; it is a process for leaving'. To pursue the second referendum, he averred, 'cannot be described as anything other than risk, uncertainty and a leap in the dark'.[102] Nevertheless, 'Vote Leave' kept the option on its website.[103]

Thus, when it sought and successfully gained the designation from the Electoral Commission as lead campaigner, on 13 April – headed by Matthew Elliott as chief executive and Cummings as campaign director – 'Vote Leave' was essentially structured to fight the referendum, with barely any thought of what would follow. Ranged against it, representing 'Remain', was 'Britain Stronger in Europe' – known as 'Stronger In' – headed by Will Straw, son of Jack Straw, acting as Chief Executive and Campaign Director. Each campaign was to receive £600,000 of public funds. Unlike the 1975 referendum, there was no great disparity in spending. Overall, 'Remain' was to spend £19,309,588 and 'Leave', £13,332,569.[104]

Although Straw nominally ran the 'Remain' campaign, the real leader was Cameron, who was handicapped by the preponderance of Conservative figures working for 'Leave'. He needed to avoid 'blue on blue' attacks that might cause long-term damage to the Conservative Party. For similar reasons, 'Vote Leave' failed to exploit what was potentially its strongest weapon: Cameron's failure to deliver a credible renegotiation package. Instead, it relied on a synthesis of research conducted by Cummings in May 2014, for Business for Britain, when the views of six focus groups were explored, comprising swing voters in three marginal seats, Warwickshire North, Thurrock and Hendon.[105]

[100] Dominic Cummings blog, 'On the Referendum #6: Exit plans and a second referendum', 23 June 2015. He refers to this author's (RN) Flexcit plan.
[101] *Daily Telegraph*, 22 February 2016, 'Fragile Tory truce over EU referendum shattered as David Cameron savages Boris Johnson'. See also Dominic Cummings blog, op. cit.
[102] HC Debates, 22 February 2016, Vol. 606, cols 24–25.
[103] 'What happens when we vote leave?' Summary. Undated.
[104] Electoral Commission website, Campaign spending at the EU referendum.
[105] Report by North Wood for Business for Britain on research into attitudes towards the possible renegotiation of our EU membership and a possible IN/OUT referendum, June 2014.

From this work, Cummings concluded that the two things his groups most wanted were control of immigration and 'paying in less money' to the EU. The attraction of 'the Australian points system' for controlling immigration was the best reason for leaving. The next strongest argument was that 'we stop sending all the money over to Brussels and we could spend that money on the NHS or tax cuts or whatever we want'.[106] It was on this slender foundation that Cummings was to base his campaign, deploying the slogan: 'We send the EU £350 million a week. Let's fund our NHS instead', which was emblazoned on the side of the bright red battle bus.

The £350 million figure was a lie – and deliberately so, designed to provoke controversy. It represented the gross payment, from which the rebate was deducted, and allowance had to be made for receipts, such as agricultural subsidies. But, recalled Cameron, if the bus was 'disingenuous', the claims on immigration went much further. Michael Gove, giving the political lead to the 'Leave' campaign, asserted that EU immigration could mean 'five million extra people coming to Britain' by 2030 – particularly with the accession of Turkey.[107]

Somewhat hoist by his own petard, having been a supporter of Turkish accession talks, Cameron was left to complain that 'there was no prospect of Turkey joining the EU for decades'.[108] But what raised the issue to another level was Penny Mordaunt, armed forces minister – supporting the 'Leave' campaign. She went on *The Andrew Marr Show* to deny that the UK could veto Turkey's accession. When challenged, she later repeated the lie. Cameron protested: 'We were no longer in the realms of bending or stretching the truth, but ditching it altogether. Leave was lying.'[109] Such lies undoubtedly tarnished the campaign, so much so that many seasoned anti-EU campaigners refused to have anything to do with 'Vote Leave'. Some publicly disowned the campaign. Even Farage – who ran his own campaign alongside businessman Arron Banks – later conceded that the '£350 million pledge' had been 'a mistake'.[110]

REGULATORY CONFUSION

It was not only the lies and the dissimulation that dragged the campaign down. There was also the triviality of the debate. With only just over a month to go to the polls, for instance, Johnson descended from his 'Boris

---

[106] Ibid.
[107] Cameron, op. cit., p. 668.
[108] Ibid.
[109] Cameron, op. cit., p. 669.
[110] *Daily Telegraph*, 24 June 2016, 'Nigel Farage: £350 million pledge to fund the NHS was "a mistake"'.

bus' in Stafford to tell an enthusiastic audience that 'you cannot sell bananas in bunches of more than two or three bananas' or with 'abnormal curvature of the fingers'. 'Why should they [the EU] tell us?' he demanded. 'This is not a matter for an international supranational body to dictate to the British people.'[111]

Johnson was, of course, wrong in his claims, but when his aides rushed out a correction, neither they nor most of the journalists realised that the standard only applied to bananas when they first arrived in the country. From there on, 'national rules' applied.[112] Furthermore, the standard was not an EU rule, *per se*, but a global *Codex* standard adopted by the EU. Far from being 'pointless', as Johnson had asserted, conformity brought important benefits to growers, giving them access to the lucrative European and US markets. Losses were reduced on transport, as the quality standard helped ensure the product could withstand the rigours of long-distance distribution and still be marketable. But above all else, conformity ensured that the product could not be refused access to the market on technical grounds.

The untold background to this affair illustrated how little understanding there was of the regulatory environment and the reasons why, in so many cases, industry saw regulation as beneficial. But if there had been awards for ignorance, a leading contender must have been celebrity journalist Jeremy Paxman. On 19 May – only days after Johnson's outburst – he opened a BBC documentary entitled *Who Really Rules Us?*. Declaring that: 'Everywhere you look, the European Union is telling us what to do', he chose to illustrate his point by brandishing a cucumber and regaling his viewers with details of Commission Regulation (EEC) No. 1677/88, laying down quality standards for cucumbers.

Having made his point, Paxman noted that this 'notorious curved cucumbers rule has now been repealed, along with the one about bendy bananas'. Yet he failed to reveal that the regulation had been replaced by a new three-tier system of control.[113] The lower tier was a new EU regulation – applicable to a wide range of fruits and vegetables, including cucumbers, which required each type to meet a 'General Marketing Standard'. However, these standards were no longer defined by the EU but by UNECE. In turn,

---

[111] ITN News, 17 May 2016, 'Boris Johnson slips up over "absurd" EU rules on bananas'; *Daily Telegraph*, 17 May 2016, 'Boris Johnson accused of "making it up as he goes along" after claiming EU prevents bananas being sold in more than threes'.

[112] Commission Implementing Regulation (EU) No. 1333/2011 of 19 December 2011 laying down marketing standards for bananas, rules on the verification of compliance with those marketing standards and requirements for notifications in the banana sector.

[113] In the case of cucumbers, UNECE standard FFV-15, now in its 2017 edition.

they were based on the relevant *Codex* standards. The EU had outsourced much of its vegetable and fruit marketing regulation, bumping it up to the regional level and, via *Codex*, to global level.

When it came to who 'ruled' us, therefore, Paxman had no idea. Later in June, UNECE's executive secretary, Christian Friis Bach, 'confessed' to his organisation's part in cucumber regulation. 'Do not blame the EU. Credit the UN', he wrote.[114] Yet his 'confession' had no impact whatsoever on the debate, the whole episode demonstrating that there was no longer any serious media capability to discuss how Britain was governed.

THE FINAL RESULT

While Cameron was to rail against 'disingenuous' claims, as well as outright lying, he was no stranger to bending the truth. Right through the campaign, he had freely propagandised on the demerits of the 'Norway option', repeating canards such as Oslo having to accept 'about three-quarters of EU rules', long after the figure had been discredited.[115] But the referendum campaign had not been about the truth. It became an intellectual desert, with the media treating it as a personality contest, highlighting the 'star' players such as Johnson and Farage – and David Cameron – on a level of palace gossip.

After the votes had been cast, no exit polls were published. However, the final YouGov poll had given Remain a 52–48 lead. Cameron had been briefed on how the results needed to fall, for him to win. Newcastle would declare first and it needed to vote strongly in his favour. But when the result came in, just after midnight, it had only voted to remain by 51–49 per cent, way below expectations. Shortly afterwards, Sunderland not only voted to leave, but by a larger margin than expected: 61–39 per cent. The game was over. The ghost of Steve Thoburn, metric martyr, must have smiled.

The nation had to wait until twenty minutes to five in the morning of 24 June before David Dimbleby, on BBC television, ponderously announced: 'We can now say the decision taken in 1975 by this country to join the Common Market has been reversed by this referendum to leave the EU.' Thus was a historic moment marred by an egregious error, 1975 being the year in which the country decided to *stay* in the Common Market, not join it. Nothing, though, could change the fact that, when the overall result was finally declared, the UK had voted to leave the EU by 52–48 per cent – 17,410,742 votes to 16,141,241 on a turnout of 77 per cent. It was a narrow margin, but it was enough.

[114] Huffpost blog, 21 June 2016, 'Cucumbers? Blame the UN'.
[115] *Guardian*, 28 October 2015, 'Cameron tells anti-EU campaigners: "Norway option" won't work for Britain'.

572

Later, Cameron reflected on criticism that the government had not planned for the medium- to long-term fallout of the 'Leave' vote. But, he wrote in his memoirs, 'we had set out the basic alternatives to remaining a close partnership with the EU, like Norway; a Canada-style trade deal; or falling back on WTO trade rules'. Despite having consistently trashed all three, he argued that the 'subsequent difficulties' were due in large part 'to failing to choose speedily between them'.[116] Maybe there had not been so much to be gained by swerving the whole issue, contrary to Dominic Cummings' earlier assertion.[117] The man who was to be hailed as the 'genius' who won the referendum had declined to engage in the second, more important battle, for which the country was now completely unprepared.

[116] Cameron, op. cit., p. 685.
[117] Cummings blog, op. cit.

22

End Game: 2016–2020

We have proven the doubters wrong and are making progress towards a successful exit from the EU.

Theresa May, 16 December 2017

Parliament's now rejected that deal three times and right now, as things stand, I can't see them accepting it.

Theresa May, 7 April 2019

I have done my best.

Theresa May, 24 May 2019

It is absolutely vital that we prepare for a no-deal Brexit if we are going to get a deal. But I don't think that is where we are going to end up – I think it is a million-to-one against – but it is vital that we prepare.

Boris Johnson, 26 June 2019

At 8.15 a.m. on 24 June 2016, Cameron resigned as prime minister, although he was to stay on as 'caretaker' until a replacement was found. Within hours, his heir apparent, Boris Johnson, gave a 'victory' speech from the 'Vote Leave' headquarters. Employing somewhat wonky arithmetic, he thanked Cameron for giving the country 'the first referendum on the European Union for 43 years'.[1] Juncker acidly observed: 'I thought that if you wanted to leave, you had a plan. They don't have it.'[2]

---

[1] *Daily Telegraph*, 24 June 2016, Boris Johnson speech in full.
[2] *Guardian*, 29 June 2016, 'Brexit: EU leaders say UK cannot have "à la carte" single market'.

In the absence of a plan, the EU-27 leaders took the initiative. Meeting in Brussels, they decided that there would be no negotiations until the UK had triggered Article 50.[3] Hollande demanded speed. 'As soon as Britain's new government is formed, it must file its notification and open the two-year negotiating period laid down in the treaty,' he declared, 'so we expect this to happen in early September.' Donald Tusk, after his baptism of fire during Cameron's 'renegotiation', added that access to the Single Market 'requires acceptance of all four EU freedoms – including freedom of movement'. There could be, 'no single market *à la carte*'.[4]

It was this issue that was to set the tone of the negotiations for the next four years and beyond, exposing the huge gulf in the understanding of what the nation was confronting. Many Tory politicians were convinced that the treaty relationship with the EU could be converted into a free trade agreement, giving unencumbered access to the Single Market. They were about to find out the hard way that it could not.

MAY AT 10

At first, it seemed as if Boris Johnson would replace Cameron, but after a 'betrayal' by his close colleague Michael Gove, he pulled out of the leadership race.[5] This left former Home Secretary Theresa May as the front runner. Riding on 'Brexit means Brexit' as her campaign slogan, she outdistanced her opposition and moved into Downing Street, inauspiciously on 13 July. For her foreign secretary, she appointed Boris Johnson. Liam Fox took on international trade. To deal with Brexit, a new department was created, headed by David Davis, who was to be the UK's chief negotiator. In between, on 4 July, Nigel Farage resigned as UKIP leader for the third and final time.

Soon to dominate the media was a challenge over which body had the power to invoke Article 50. On 19 July, the High Court was told that the right belonged to parliament rather than the prime minister relying on Crown prerogative.[6] While the UK media and body politic were thus engrossed in the soap opera, the EU was quietly preparing for the negotiations to come. On 27 July, Juncker appointed veteran ex-Commissioner and former French minister, Michel Barnier, to head a Brexit 'taskforce'.[7] In time, he was to lead the EU's negotiating team.

[3] European Council, 'Informal meeting at 27 Brussels – 29 June 2016 – Statement'.
[4] *Guardian*, 29 June 2016, 'Brexit: EU leaders say UK cannot have "à la carte" single market'.
[5] *Guardian*, 30 June 2016, 'Boris Johnson rules himself out of Tory leadership race'.
[6] *Guardian*, 19 July 2016, 'Theresa May does not intend to trigger article 50 this year, court told'.
[7] European Commission, Brussels, 27 July 2016, 'President Juncker appoints Michel Barnier as Chief Negotiator in charge of the Preparation and Conduct of the Negotiations with the United Kingdom under Article 50 of the TEU'.

In the run-up to the Conservative Party Conference, on 30 September, Liam Fox and Boris Johnson joined forces to support breaking from the customs union and the Single Market. Brexit was a 'massive opportunity' that liberated the UK 'to champion free trade round the world'. Johnson also insisted that the UK would get immigration controls back, as well as continuing open trade with the EU. 'Our policy is having our cake and eating it. We are Pro-secco but by no means anti-pasto,' he declared.[8]

At the conference, May held firm on Article 50, invoking it was the right of 'the government alone'. Those who argued otherwise, she said, are 'trying to kill it by delaying it'.[9] As to her exit strategy, rather than a 'Norway' or 'Switzerland' model, she wanted an agreement between an independent, sovereign UK and the EU, giving British companies 'the maximum freedom to trade with and operate in the Single Market' and letting European businesses 'do the same here'. But, she added: 'We are not leaving the European Union only to give up control of immigration again. And we are not leaving only to return to the jurisdiction of the European Court of Justice.'

Her view of the Article 50 legal challenge was shared by many, with suspicions that a largely Europhile parliament would attempt to block Brexit. But when in mid-January the Supreme Court ruled in parliament's favour, MPs obediently voted by a massive 498 votes to 114 in favour of a Bill, hastily laid before the House, to give the government the authority to invoke Article 50.[10]

Long before this had come to pass, Michel Barnier had set out his stall for the forthcoming negotiations, for which, he said, there would be less than 18 months. He would be guided by four main principles: unity and the interest of the EU-27; third countries could never have the same rights and benefits as EU member states, since they were not subject to the same obligations; negotiations would not start before notification; and the Single Market and its four freedoms were indivisible. Cherry-picking was not an option.[11] In early October, Merkel had warned that any exception to Single Market rules would represent 'a systemic challenge' for the entire

---

[8] *Sun*, 30 September 2016, '"WE'LL HAVE OUR CAKE AND EAT IT": Boris Johnson joins forces with Liam Fox and declares support for "hard" Brexit which will "liberate" Britain to champion free trade'.
[9] BBC News, 2 October 2016, 'Theresa May's Conservative conference speech: Key quotes'.
[10] BBC News, 1 February 2017, 'Brexit: MPs overwhelmingly back Article 50 bill'. The Bill was passed by Parliament on 13 March and received Royal Assent on 16 March.
[11] European Commission, Brussels, *Task Force for Relations with the United Kingdom: Introductory comments by Michel Barnier*, 6 December 2016.

EU.[12] François Hollande added that it was 'absolutely necessary' to deter other countries from leaving 'in order to have the supposed benefits and no downsides or rules'.[13]

In mid-December, Sir Ivan Rogers, the UK's permanent representative to Brussels – and a key member of Cameron's renegotiation team – warned that a trade deal might take ten years to finalise and could still fail when some of the EU-27 members refused to ratify it. This directly contradicted the optimistic insistence from Downing Street that a deal could be done in the two years after Article 50 had been triggered.[14] Three days into the New Year, Rogers resigned, complaining of 'muddled thinking' and urging remaining staff to 'speak truth to power'. He observed that 'serious multilateral negotiating experience is in short supply in Whitehall'.[15]

For an example of 'muddled thinking', Rogers needed only to look at Boris Johnson's latest comments on the settlement he wanted from the EU. 'What we need to do is something new and ambitious, which allows zero tariffs and frictionless trade but still gives us that important freedom to decide our own regulatory framework, our own laws and do things in a distinctive way in the future.'[16] 'Cakeism' was alive and well.

THE LANCASTER HOUSE SPEECH

On 17 January, in a heavily trailed speech delivered in the historic setting of Lancaster House, Mrs May set out her own negotiating position, unequivocally ruling out continued membership of the Single Market. To stay in, she said, 'would mean complying with the EU's rules and regulations', without having a vote on them, and accepting ECJ jurisdiction. To all intents and purposes, 'that would mean not leaving the EU at all'. Memorably, she then delivered another catchphrase, which was to become famous. 'No deal for Britain,' she said, 'is better than a bad deal for Britain.'[17]

The speech was followed by a White Paper confirming that the UK would pursue a new strategic partnership with the EU, including 'an ambitious and comprehensive Free Trade Agreement and a new customs agreement'. In the preface, David Davis wrote:

[12] *Guardian*, 5 October 2016, 'Angela Merkel urges German firms to back tough stance in Brexit talk'.
[13] *Guardian*, 7 October 2016, 'UK must pay price for Brexit, says François Hollande'.
[14] BBC News, 15 December 2016, 'Brexit trade deal could take 10 years, says UK's ambassador'.
[15] *Independent*, 3 January 2017, 'Sir Ivan Rogers quits: Britain's EU ambassador attacks "muddled" Brexit thinking in scathing resignation letter'.
[16] *Sunday Times*, 17 December 2017, 'Boris Johnson exclusive interview: Russia, Yemen, Brexit … beavers – leave it all to me'.
[17] Gov.uk (website), 'The government's negotiating objectives for exiting the EU: PM speech'.

We approach these negotiations from a unique position. As things stand, we have the exact same rules, regulations and standards as the rest of the EU. Unlike most negotiations, these talks will not be about bringing together two divergent systems but about managing the continued cooperation of the UK and the EU. The focus will not be about removing existing barriers or questioning certain protections but about ensuring new barriers do not arise.[18]

Jacques Audibert, diplomatic adviser to Hollande, responded. Britain could not expect to get a better deal outside the EU than it enjoyed inside, he said. This triggered a comment from Johnson, who was in Delhi at the time on foreign office business. 'If Monsieur Hollande wants to administer punishment beatings to anyone who chooses to escape, rather in the manner of some World War Two movie, then I don't think that's the way forward,' he said.[19]

Then came the key step in the drama. On 29 March, May signed the formal Article 50 notification letter, starting the countdown to Brexit. Without extensions, the UK would leave the EU in two years' time.[20] In her letter, though, Mrs May was unwittingly setting herself up for a fall, calling for a 'deep and special partnership' that was to be of 'greater scope and ambition than any such agreement before', covering sectors such as financial services and network industries. Furthermore, she wanted them agreed 'alongside those of our withdrawal from the European Union'.[21]

Highlighting the unreality of that position, on 27 April, Angela Merkel addressed the Bundestag, repeating that the UK, as a third country, 'cannot and will not enjoy the same rights or possibly be better off than a member of the European Union'. Unfortunately, she added, 'I have a feeling that some in the UK are still delusional about this.'[22] Merkel touched on the money issue. As well as budget contributions of around £20.4 billion in 2019–2020, the UK would have to pay its share of the so-called *reste à liquider* (RAL) representing commitments carried over into future budget periods. For 2014–2020, the total was estimated at some €326 billion.[23] The UK's proportion, plus pensions and special funds, brought the overall 'Brexit bill'

[18] HM Government, CM 9417, 'The United Kingdom's exit from and new partnership with the European Union'.
[19] RTE News, 18 January 2017, 'Johnson triggers row over "punishment beating" comment'.
[20] *Guardian*, 27 March 2017, 'Sir Tim Barrow to hand-deliver article 50 letter to Donald Tusk'.
[21] Prime Minister, Letter to President Tusk, 29 March 2017.
[22] *Die Bundeskanzlerin*, government statement by Chancellor Merkel, 27 April 2017.
[23] European Parliament, 25 May 2012, Working Document on outstanding commitments (RAL) and the payments issue.

to around £50 billion. Before anything else, Britain had to agree on how and when payments would be made.[24]

Soon after Merkel had addressed her own parliament, May, together with Davis, met Commission president Jean-Claude Juncker and Barnier in Downing Street for a working dinner. May insisted that before the UK agreed to pay anything to Brussels, a 'detailed outline' of a future free trade deal had to be in place. This, an EU diplomat dismissed as 'a rather incredible demand'. 'It seemed as if it came from a parallel reality,' he said. Another felt it bordered on the delusional.

A month after Mrs May's Article 50 letter had been delivered to Brussels, the European Council agreed its own negotiating guidelines.[25] Once again, the same message was sent. Preserving the integrity of the Single Market excluded participation based on a sector-by sector approach. A non-member of the Union that did not live up to the same obligations as a member could not have the same rights and enjoy the same benefits as a member. The four freedoms of the Single Market were indivisible and there could be no 'cherry-picking'. Crucially, the guidelines also noted that the agreement on a future relationship could only be finalised once the United Kingdom became a third country.

This refusal to negotiate a trade deal was to be a running sore, as the UK wanted one agreed before leaving the EU. Thus, half-way into the month of May, a combative David Davis tried to link the cash settlement with the conclusion of a trade deal. There was also the Irish land border, which both sides were committed to keeping free of checks, maintaining cross-border co-operation within the spirit of the Good Friday Agreement (GFA). Davis also wanted these issues linked with a trade deal. Then there were the concerns of UK nationals living in EU member states, and EU residents in the UK. Famously, Davis declared that the dispute over their treatment would be 'the row of the summer'.[26]

MAY'S GENERAL ELECTION

Negotiations, though, had to wait. On 18 May, Mrs May, seduced by a series of flattering opinion polls, announced her intention to call for a snap general election, ostensibly to secure a stronger Brexit mandate.[27] When the Commons approved her request, necessary under the fixed term

[24] *Guardian*, 29 April 2017, 'EU leaders to insist UK pays its Brexit bills as precursor to trade talks'.
[25] European Council, *Guidelines Following the United Kingdom's Notification Under Article 50 TEU*, Brussels, 29 April 2017.
[26] *Financial Times*, 14 May 2017, 'Davis warns Brexit timetable will be "row of the summer"'.
[27] *Guardian*, 19 April 2017, 'Theresa May calls for general election to secure Brexit mandate'.

arrangements, it triggered the usual orgy of personality-based politics, focused on a limited range of domestic issues, in which social care featured strongly. Meanwhile, on 22 May, the EU finalised its negotiating directives, the final stage in its preparations.[28]

The election, for which Mrs May had campaigned with the slogan 'strong and stable', was held on 8 June. It was a 'strategic disaster', as she lost her overall majority.[29] She now had to rely on a 'confidence and supply' agreement with the Democratic Unionist Party, putting her in thrall to a sectarian Northern Irish party, when Irish politics were to play a pivotal role in the talks. It was thus a politically weakened Mrs May who, on 19 June 2017, sent David Davis to Brussels for the formal opening of talks. He had with him Olly Robbins, the Permanent Secretary for the Department for Exiting the EU.[30] By then, the scene had been set. Despite Davis's bluster, his 'summer row' had not materialised. The EU plan for 'sequencing' the talks was to prevail. First on the agenda was the 'divorce bill', with no trade talks in sight.[31]

On *The Andrew Marr Show*, the Sunday following the opening of the talks, Davis was reminded of a speech he had given just before the referendum, when he had boasted that he would bypass Brussels and go straight to Berlin, seeking absolute access for German cars and industrial goods in exchange for 'a sensible deal on everything else'.[32]

The second round of talks in mid-July brought little clarity and some concerns that the UK team was 'woefully underprepared'.[33] In fact, the British were distracted by an effective state of war in the Conservative Party over the form Brexit should take.[34] A debate, absent before the referendum, was now polarising between the so-called 'soft' and 'hard' approaches. There were those who wanted to stay in the Single Market and/or the customs union, with free movement of people – often described as Brexit in Name Only (BRINO). Others insisted on a 'clean break', paving the way for a free trade agreement on the lines of the EU–Canada deal.

[28] European Council, *Directives for the Negotiation of an Agreement with the United Kingdom of Great Britain and Northern Ireland Setting Out the Arrangements for its Withdrawal from the European Union.*
[29] *Financial Times*, 9 June 2017, 'How Theresa May's election move led to strategic disaster'.
[30] *Guardian*, 13 June 2017, 'Theresa May confirms start date for Brexit talks after pressure from EU'.
[31] *Business Insider*, 20 June 2017, 'David Davis caves in to EU negotiation demands on first day of Brexit talks'.
[32] BBC News, *The Andrew Marr Show*, 25 June 2017, David Davis MP, Secretary of State for Exiting the EU.
[33] *Guardian*, 17 July 2017, 'Day two of Brexit talks – and the UK looks as underprepared as ever'.
[34] *Guardian*, 17 July 2017, 'Theresa May to tell ministers: stop leaking details of cabinet rifts'.

After what was termed a summer of 'bitter Cabinet infighting', the warring tribes forged an uneasy truce when Chancellor of the Exchequer Philip Hammond, favouring a 'soft' Brexit, and Liam Fox, champion of the 'hard' option, jointly wrote a newspaper article pledging that the UK would completely leave the Single Market and customs union. Sentiment had tilted towards a hard exit.

Late summer brought the third round of talks, which ran from 28 to 31 August, preceded by the publication of three UK position papers, four 'future partnership papers' and four technical notes. One partnership paper suggested staying close to the EU's customs union for a while after leaving, as a solution to the Irish border problem. Guy Verhofstadt, the European Parliament's Brexit co-ordinator, called this a 'fantasy'.[35] A senior EU official accused the UK of 'magical thinking'.[36] Barnier's response was to urge the UK to start 'negotiating seriously', but the third round brought no success.[37] Like Davis, May thus started thinking of going straight to Macron and Merkel, over the heads of the EU negotiating team.[38] But the European Council had already ruled out separate negotiations. Nor was Davis making any progress on the cash issue. It was clear that there was not going to be an early resolution to the talks.[39]

THE FLORENCE SPEECH

The time was ripe for Mrs May to intervene directly, choosing to go to Florence on 22 September to give a speech. She also made a £20 billion cash offer. Crucially, she then dismissed a Canada-style deal. It would, she said, 'represent such a restriction on our mutual market access that it would benefit neither of our economies'.[40] Although her speech was short on detail, she had done just enough to unblock the talks. But she had left a dangerous ambiguity in the UK's ideas for a 'future relationship', which was to fester over the years, never properly to be resolved. She did, however, lodge the idea of a 'status quo' transition period, where for up to two years after leaving, Britain could stay in the Single Market as long as she kept to

---

[35] *Guardian*, 15 August 2017, 'UK will "mirror" much of EU customs system for Brexit, plans reveal'.
[36] *Daily Telegraph*, 25 August 2017, 'EU accuses Britain of "magical thinking" over Brexit'.
[37] *The Times*, 29 August 2017, 'Time to get serious about Brexit talks, EU tells Britain'.
[38] See the *Sun*, 30 August 2017, 'Breaking the deadlock: with Michel Barnier and Jean-Claude Juncker refusing to budge the PM is looking to deal directly with Paris and Berlin'; and *Daily Mail*, 30 August 2017, 'Macron and Merkel could kick-start Brexit trade deal: Theresa May believes she can broker an agreement by going direct to the EU leaders'.
[39] HC Debates, 5 September 2017, Vol. 628, cols 42–46.
[40] Gov.uk (website), 22 September 2017, 'PM's Florence speech: a new era of cooperation and partnership between the UK and the EU'.

EU rules and stayed under the jurisdiction of the ECJ, while a trade deal was negotiated.[41]

Delayed a week by May's intervention, the fourth round of the 'divorce' talks started on 25 September. The following day, Tusk visited May in Downing Street. Greeted in the street on the way in, he was left to do a solo press statement afterwards.[42] The meeting had not been a success. And at the end of four days in Brussels, any hopes of moving on were dashed. Not only had the financial question yet to be settled, but moving up the agenda was the Irish border, for which Barnier stressed that the parties needed to find 'a unique solution'.[43]

By now, the focus was on the October European Council, when a decision would be made on whether the talks could move on to the second phase, concerned with 'future relations'. With that in mind, May went to the informal European Council in Tallinn at the end of the month, intending to lobby the EU-27 leaders. But she was upstaged by Juncker, who sneered at her hopes of sufficient progress by October, 'unless miracles would happen'.[44]

On *The Andrew Marr Show* the following Sunday, prior to the Conservative Party Conference in Manchester, one thing that particularly stood out was May's continued reference to the transition period as an 'implementation period'. She was still convinced she could get a trade deal before the UK left the EU. This was not an auspicious lead into conference, but things were to get worse when her keynote speech degenerated into what was later described as a 'calamity', plagued by the combination of a prank, a hacking cough and a letter on the set behind her falling off.[45]

On 9 October, the fifth round of Brexit talks began, but, three days later, Barnier ruled out talks on the future relationship.[46] Despite that, David Davis urged EU leaders to instruct Barnier to start the talks anyway.[47] Come the European Council on 20 October, though, EU leaders decided to defer the decision until December.[48] On 9 November, negotiators met again for

[41] *Guardian*, 22 September 2017, 'Theresa May's Florence speech: key points'.
[42] European Council, 26 September 2017, 'Remarks by President Donald Tusk after his meeting with Prime Minister of the United Kingdom Theresa May'.
[43] European Commission, 28 September 2017, Press statement by Michel Barnier following the fourth round of Article 50 negotiations with the United Kingdom.
[44] *Daily Telegraph*, 29 September 2017, 'Theresa May vows "unconditional" support for European defence after Brexit'.
[45] *Guardian*, 4 October 2017, 'The cough, the P45, the falling F: Theresa May's speech calamity'.
[46] European Commission, 12 October 2017, 'Press statement by Michel Barnier following the fifth round of Article 50 negotiations with the United Kingdom'.
[47] BBC News, 12 October 2017.
[48] European Council (Art. 50) meeting (20 October 2017) – Conclusions.

the sixth round of talks, but only for two days. At the close, a tight-lipped Barnier told reporters not to expect any announcements or decisions.[49]

IRISH BORDER PROBLEMS

It was now left to Theresa May once again to intervene, this time at the informal European Council in Gothenburg on 17 November. There, Irish Premier Leo Varadkar, backed by Tusk, demanded a formal promise there would be no hard border in Ireland.[50] From Gothenburg to Brussels a week later and again Mrs May was meeting Donald Tusk. She came away with a deadline of ten days to improve her cash offer. And there was still trouble brewing in Northern Ireland.

Essentially, there was a near-intractable problem as, with Brexit, the internal Irish border became the external border of the EU. Normally, this would require physical barriers and rigorous controls, but all parties had committed to maintaining the status quo. This left two broad solutions: either the whole of the UK had to stay in the customs union and the Single Market, or Northern Ireland would have to do so, leaving a regulatory border in the Irish Sea – the so-called 'wet' border – with customs and other checks at Northern Irish ports. The latter solution was rejected outright by Arlene Foster, DUP leader. During her party's annual conference on 25 November, she assured delegates that May's government would not agree to any special status for Northern Ireland. 'We joined the then-European Community as one nation, will leave as one United Kingdom,' Foster told delegates.[51]

The chancellor was also making his own contribution to the debate. Tucked into his budget speech on 22 November was an additional £1.5 billion in each of the next two financial years for Brexit preparations, plus £2.1 billion more on the civil service. Having already committed £700 million, Hammond also assured MPs that he was ready to spend more if needed.[52] More generally, the mood was not helped when an aide was spotted by a sharp-eyed photographer in Downing Street, coming from a meeting on Brexit. She was bearing handwritten notes with the legend, 'Have cake and eat it?'[53]

Racking up air miles, May was back in Brussels on 4 December, only ten days before the vital Council meeting, this time planning to meet

---

[49] European Commission, 10 November 2017, Speech by Michel Barnier following the sixth round of Article 50 negotiations with the United Kingdom.
[50] *Guardian*, 17 November 2017, 'Ireland will block progress of Brexit talks without border guarantee'.
[51] *Guardian*, 25 November 2017, 'Arlene Foster says DUP will prevent "internal barriers" after Brexit'.
[52] *Financial Times*, 22 November 2017, 'Budget 2017: Hammond ramps up spending on Brexit preparations'.
[53] BBC News, 29 November 2016, '"Have cake and eat it": Brexit notes played down by government'.

Juncker and Barnier to agree the 'choreography' of a deal.[54] As she arrived, a leaked text suggested that a deal had been struck on the border issue, with a celebratory press conference being planned. However, after a fraught telephone conversation with Mrs May while she was in Brussels, Foster – who had not been consulted on the content – disowned the deal, fearing that, after all, Northern Ireland was to be subject to a special arrangement. Foster warned: 'We have been very clear. Northern Ireland must leave the EU on the same terms as the rest of the United Kingdom.' The deal collapsed and the press conference was cancelled. Yet, for all that, Tusk stated that a December agreement was still possible.[55]

Within three days, that turned out to be the case. After tense discussions with May, Foster announced that there would be 'no red line down the Irish Sea'.[56] A deal, of sorts, could go ahead, which was duly set out in a Joint Report on 8 December, accompanied by a communication from the Commission.[57] Donald Tusk, and then the European Council of 15 December, both accepted that sufficient progress had been made. There could be discussions on the transition period and an exploration of 'the British vision of its future relationship with the EU'.[58] Reflecting on these events in an authored newspaper column in mid-December, Mrs May confidently wrote: 'We have proven the doubters wrong and are making progress towards a successful exit from the EU.'[59]

RAISING BARRIERS

Although Theresa May had revelled in her declaration that 'no deal is better than a bad deal', neither she nor her Cabinet colleagues, nor even the media, took the trouble to spell out the consequences of a no-deal scenario. This was not the case in the EU, where the European Commission, from November 2017 onwards, published a series of 'Notices to Stakeholders', setting out in brutal detail – sector by sector – what might be expected. These notices

---

[54] Reuters, 23 November 2017, 'May to meet EU's Juncker, Barnier December 4, EU confirms'.

[55] *Daily Telegraph*, 4 December 2017, 'How a phone-call from Arlene Foster in the middle of lunch ended Theresa May's hopes of an Irish border deal'; *Guardian*, 5 December 2017, 'May's weakness exposed as DUP derails Brexit progress'.

[56] BBC News, 8 December 2017, 'DUP leader Arlene Foster welcomes Brexit deal'; ITV News, 8 December 2017, 'Arlene Foster "substantial progress" made in Brexit deal but says more work needed on managing Irish border'.

[57] European Commission, Brussels, 8 December 2017, COM(2017) 784 final on the state of progress of the negotiations with the United Kingdom under Article 50 of the Treaty on European Union.

[58] European Council, 8 December 2017, 'Statement by President Donald Tusk on the draft guidelines for the second phase of the Brexit negotiations'; European Council (Art. 50), 15 December 2017.

[59] *Sunday Telegraph*, 16 December 2017, 'We are getting on with the job of Brexit, and we will not be derailed'.

were eventually to exceed a hundred in number. Though these were largely ignored by the UK media and seldom mentioned by British politicians, in the second week of the New Year, the *Financial Times* reported a response from David Davis, in the form of a letter sent to the prime minister. He complained that the Notices could jeopardise existing UK contracts or force British companies to decamp to the continent in the event of a no-deal.[60]

Chancellor Philip Hammond was also in accusatory mode, fulminating that EU governments were failing to specify their ideas for a future relationship with Britain.[61] His views were amplified in an article in *Frankfurter Allgemeine Zeitung*, jointly authored with David Davis, in which they wrote: 'As two of Europe's biggest economies, it makes no sense to either Germany or Britain to put in place unnecessary barriers to trade in goods and services that would only damage businesses and economic growth on both sides of the Channel.'[62]

In these two episodes were embodied the fundamentally flawed approach of the British government, building on the misconceptions expressed by David Davis in the 2017 White Paper, where he was concerned that new barriers did not arise as a result of Brexit. In fact, Single Market membership was like a medieval walled city, inside which the traders did business in the market square. But when a trader decided to move outside the walls, he interposed a barrier between himself and his customers. So it was that the Single Market 'walls' already existed, in the form of so-called non-tariff barriers (NTBs). When the UK voluntarily moved outside, it automatically exposed itself to them. There was no need – and no intent – on the part of the EU to create new ones.

And while it was indeed the case that the UK (prior to Brexit) had adopted EU standards, once it became a 'third country', the EU would no longer have the means by which it could ensure that they were being fully implemented. As with other third countries, therefore, it would check conformity at the points of entry into EU member states. Yet, May, her chancellor and the UK's chief negotiator – and many others – seemed to have considerable difficulty understanding that conformity with EU regulations alone was not going to buy the UK a free pass into the Single Market.

This was but one of the issues that defined the increasingly strident debate, with 'leaver' sentiment splintering. There were the 'hard' Brexiteers

[60] 9 January 2018, 'Brussels warns UK companies of shutout in event of no-deal Brexit'.
[61] *Guardian*, 10 January 2018, 'Philip Hammond tells EU "it takes two to tango" over future relationship'.
[62] Gov.uk (website), 'Joint article: a deep and special partnership': a joint article by Philip Hammond and David Davis that originally appeared in *Frankfurter Allgemeine Zeitung* on 10 January 2018.

who wanted a complete break, reverting to WTO rules. Others wanted a Canada-style free trade agreement, and 'soft' leavers sought something akin to Norway's EFTA/EEA membership, with its participation in the Single Market. It was not the case, though, that these had suddenly fallen in love with the Single Market. Rather, they were building on the very ideas Farage himself had offered in November 2011, in response to David Cameron's Guildhall speech, advocating this option as an interim solution, acknowledging that the hazards for business were uncertainty and rapid change. The aim was a measured, cautious transition that minimised disruption, spreading the costs of leaving the EU.

Then there was Mrs May, trapped by her ambitions for a 'deep and special partnership' that went further than the Canada-style deal, seeking the advantages of the Single Market, without the obligations – something that an exasperated EU was adamant was not on offer. As a compromise measure, others wanted a new customs union with the EU, a route preferred by Carolyn Fairbairn, Director-General of the CBI, who argued that this solution would deliver a good measure of both access and control.[63] That left the 'remainers', equally split, with the 'irreconcilables' still disputing the result of the referendum, some calling for a 'second' referendum, organising themselves as a noisy lobby group called the 'Peoples' Vote'.[64]

Above the fray, the EU was finalising the details for the transition period, settling on a period ending 31 December 2020, during which time the whole of the EU *acquis* would continue to apply to the UK as if it were a member state. Early February then brought the seventh round of negotiations, the first to deal with the second phase of the talks. Then 28 February saw a landmark of sorts, with the publication of the first draft of the Withdrawal Agreement, based on December's Joint Statement but produced entirely by the Commission. It was in this that the concept of the 'backstop' emerged in relation to the Irish border. Undesirable though it was to the British, a 'Common Regulatory Area' for the entire island of Ireland would apply, unless other solutions could be found. Other options suggested by the UK, yet to be tested, were the creation of a 'virtual border' where goods would be checked electronically, and the possibility of a trade deal, which obviated the need for checks.

AN ULTIMATUM FROM TUSK

Speaking in Parliament the same day, Mrs May rejected the Commission's proposal. Potentially, it undermined the UK common market and threatened

---

[63] CBI press release, 21 January 2018, 'Evidence not ideology: why a customs union is best for Britain – CBI'.

[64] Taking into account the 1975 referendum, it would, of course, have been the third vote.

the constitutional integrity of the UK by creating a customs and regulatory border down the Irish Sea. 'No UK Prime Minister could ever agree to it,' she declared.[65] In a speech at the Mansion House two days later, she then argued: 'If we want good access to each other's markets, it has to be on fair terms', although she did accept the need for 'binding commitments' such as regulation on state aid and competition. The UK, she said, might have to remain 'in step' with the EU. On the Irish border question, she conceded that the UK had 'a responsibility to help find a solution', but she had no alternative to the Commission proposal.[66]

By now, Tusk was losing patience. On a visit to Dublin to confer with Leo Varadkar, he effectively threw down an ultimatum to Mrs May. 'We know today that the UK government rejects a customs and regulatory border down the Irish Sea; the EU Single Market and the customs union,' he said, adding:

> While we must respect this position, we also expect the UK to propose a specific and realistic solution to avoid a hard border. As long as the UK doesn't present such a solution, it is very difficult to imagine substantive progress in Brexit negotiations. If in London someone assumes that the negotiations will deal with other issues first, before moving to the Irish issue, my response would be: Ireland first.[67]

On 19 March, after a further round of talks, Barnier unveiled with great fanfare a revised version of the Withdrawal Agreement, colour-coded with the agreed areas marked in green. Although three-quarters of the text was green-tinted, the Irish border question had still not been settled. But what attracted the ire of Jacob Rees-Mogg and his 60-strong European Research Group of MPs were the transition arrangements. These were seen as an 'abject betrayal' of Britain's fishermen, because the CFP would stay in place until the end of 2020, along with the rest of the EU *acquis*.[68]

Days later, on 23 March, the European Council adopted a framework for a future relationship, covering trade and economic co-operation, security and defence, among other areas. But the EU-27 leaders noted that the UK's

---

[65] HC Debates, 28 February 2018, Vol. 636, col. 823.
[66] Gov.uk (website), 2 March 2018, 'PM speech on our future economic partnership with the European Union'.
[67] European Council, 8 March 2018, 'Remarks by President Donald Tusk after his meeting with Taoiseach Leo Varadkar'.
[68] *Daily Telegraph*, 20 March 2018, 'Tory MPs to fling fish from trawler on Thames in protest for fishermen "betrayed" by Brexit deal'.

current positions 'limited its depth'.[69] It was then nearly a month before the next round of talks, which took place from 16 to 18 April, and were marked by the EU side rejecting British proposals on the Irish border. In what was described as a 'detailed and forensic rebuttal', it was made clear that none of the UK's customs options would work.[70]

To add to its woes, the government suffered two big defeats in the Lords, when peers backed an amendment to the European Union (Withdrawal) Bill that called on the government to explore a customs union, and a separate amendment limiting the power of ministers to slash red tape without the approval of parliament.[71] There was, though, a confusion over the terms 'customs union' and 'Single Market'.[72] In their pursuit of 'frictionless trade', some of the peers – like the CBI – seemed unaware that it could not be delivered by a customs union.

A week later, the lacuna was repeated in the Commons by Yvette Cooper. She led a debate on 'Customs and Borders' on behalf of 12 select committee chairs, calling for the government to establish 'an effective customs union' between the EU and the UK. Although this meant 'no tariffs on the goods we buy and sell with the European Union', she also thought it meant 'no customs checks at the border'.[73]

Early May brought yet another round of talks. With the focus on the June European Council, the two sides on 19 June – after frantic, cross-Channel diplomacy – published another joint statement. This set out the areas that had been agreed and those outstanding. On the Irish border question, a Protocol to the Withdrawal Agreement was being worked up, with both parties accepting that the 'backstop' would need 'customs and regulatory alignment'.[74] With no substantial progress made, though, all the European Council on 29 June could do was 'insist' on 'intensified efforts'.[75] It had spent no more than 15 minutes discussing Brexit.

Trapped between the 'rock' of the EU and the 'hard place' of her own Cabinet dissenters, Mrs May had almost no room to manoeuvre. She tried to break the impasse by crafting a new White Paper, to 'include detailed,

[69] European Council (Art. 50) guidelines on the framework for the future EU–UK relationship, 23 March 2018.
[70] *Daily Telegraph*, 20 April 2018, 'Exclusive: EU rejects Theresa May's Brexit Irish border solution as doubts grow over whether UK can leave customs union'.
[71] *Guardian*, 18 April 2018, 'Brexit bill: May under pressure after two big defeats in Lords'.
[72] HL Debates, 18 April 2018, Vol. 790.
[73] HC Debates, 26 April 2018, Vol. 639, cols 1053–1054.
[74] Joint statement from the negotiators of the European Union and the United Kingdom Government on progress of negotiations under Article 50 TEU on the United Kingdom's orderly withdrawal from the European Union. 19 June 2018.
[75] European Council, 29 June 2018, Art. 50 meeting – Conclusions.

ambitious and precise explanations' of the UK positions, setting out 'what will change and what will feel different outside the EU', due for publication in June.[76] But senior EU officials, responding to early drafts, warned that the proposals would never be accepted. 'We read the white paper and we read "cake"', one EU official said.[77]

Mrs May's more immediate problem was her own Cabinet. Without its agreement, publication had to be delayed and, by early July, all pretence of unity had been abandoned. Cabinet minister James Brokenshire conceded on *The Andrew Marr Show* that there were 'strong views on either side'.[78] No minister, in public, had expressed them more strongly than Boris Johnson, who, when challenged about dismay from Airbus and BMW over the threat to jobs and investment from Brexit, had retorted: 'Fuck business.'[79]

SHOWDOWN AT CHEQUERS

In an attempt to reconcile the warring factions, May summoned her Cabinet to an 'away day' at Chequers on Friday 6 July. There, she offered a rehash of an old plan, a 'New Customs Partnership', in an attempt to resolve the Irish border problem. It involved the UK collecting tariffs on behalf of the EU, and the adoption of a 'common regulatory framework' – essentially the UK continuing to adopt EU law. Davis championed a scheme called 'maximum facilitation', or 'max fac' for short, using as yet unspecified technology in a buffer zone on the border. Critics described it as combining a lack of feasibility with a complete ignorance of the history of the region – both dangerous and impractical.[80]

In the event, Johnson again made the running, calling May's plan a 'big turd'.[81] Despite that, the meeting concluded with an apparent display of unity, allowing May to publish a statement on her 'Chequers plan'.[82] But this proved too much for Davis. He resigned on the Sunday, along with his second in command, Steve Baker. Johnson followed on the Monday.[83]

---

[76] *Financial Times*, 15 May 2018, 'Theresa May to publish Brexit white paper ahead of June summit'; *Independent*, 15 May 2018, 'Brexit: Theresa May pledges to publish white paper with "precise explanations" on key aspects of Britain's post-EU vision'.
[77] *Guardian*, 2 July 2018, 'UK's latest Brexit proposal is unrealistic, say EU officials'.
[78] BBC News, *The Andrew Marr Show*, 1 July 2018, James Brokenshire.
[79] *Financial Times*, 25 June 2018, 'Boris Johnson's Brexit explosion ruins Tory business credentials'.
[80] *Independent*, 1 June 2018, 'Brexit: David Davis mocked for "fantastical" plans for Northern Ireland "buffer zone"'.
[81] *Sunday Times*, 8 July 2018, 'Chequers mate: Theresa May ambush routs cabinet Brexiteers'.
[82] Statement from HM Government, Chequers, 6 July 2018.
[83] BBC News, 9 July 2018, 'Brexit Secretary David Davis resigns'; *Guardian*, 9 July 2018, 'Brexit secretary David Davis resigns plunging government into crisis' and 'May's plan "sticks in the throat", says Boris Johnson as he resigns over Brexit'.

In a hasty reshuffle, Dominic Raab took the Brexit portfolio and Jeremy Hunt moved from health to become foreign secretary.[84] But the new Cabinet could not conceal the fact that Mrs May's political authority was ebbing away.

On 12 July, the long-awaited White Paper was published, running to 104 pages.[85] The media, though, was distracted by the state visit of President Trump and the publication in the *Sun* of a personal interview with him, bearing the banner headline, 'May has wrecked Brexit – US deal is off'. Trump, objecting to May's 'soft' Brexit blueprint, was warning that it would 'kill' any future trade deal with the US – the cornerstone of the UK's 'Global Britain' strategy. He also asserted that Johnson would make 'a great prime minister', hardly an endorsement May would have wished to hear.

Perhaps it was just as well that the media was pursuing the Trump visit. With the devil in the highly technical detail, it was no more capable of analysing the contents of the White Paper than Mrs May and her team were of writing something that could be acceptable to the EU. For instance, the paper pursued the idea of mutual recognition of Vehicle Type Approvals, with the 'common rulebook' allowing the UK and the EU to continue recognising the activities of one another's regulatory authorities.[86] Yet the concept of mutual recognition of standards lay at the heart of the EU's Single Market doctrine, and no third country, anywhere in the world, was permitted this option.[87]

Furthermore, May wanted continued participation in EU agencies, covering key sectors such as aviation, chemicals and medicines – privileges afforded to no countries outside the EEA. And her White Paper also proposed that the EU should waive border checks on products of animal and plant origin – the so-called Sanitary and Phytosanitary (SPS) checks – even though these, again, were fundamental to the Single Market.

The proposals were so staggeringly unrealistic that it was barely conceivable that the EU response could have been positive. Yet media coverage was muted and uninformative, with some commentators believing

[84] BBC News, 10 July 2018, 'Theresa May's new-look cabinet meets amid Brexit turmoil'.
[85] Cm 9593, July 2018, *The Future Relationship Between The United Kingdom and the European Union*.
[86] Ibid., p. 21.
[87] Standards for vehicle parts were in fact set not by the EU but by UNECE, but the 'Whole Vehicle Type Approval' was reserved as an EU competence. See Regulation (EU) 2018/858 of 30 May 2018 on the approval and market surveillance of motor vehicles and their trailers, and of systems, components and separate technical units intended for such vehicles.

May would be given an easy ride.[88] Rejection came at the 'informal summit' in Salzburg, under the Austrian presidency on 20 September. There, Donald Tusk noted the 'positive elements', then dismissed May's initiative because it risked 'undermining the Single Market'.[89] The 27 EU leaders declared that there would be no Withdrawal Agreement 'without a solid, operational and legally binding Irish backstop'.[90] So detached from reality was Mrs May, though, that she felt she had been 'ambushed'. She reacted angrily to what could only have been an expected outcome, warning that she was prepared to walk away from the talks.[91]

Already, Johnson had been on the case, writing: 'We have wrapped a suicide vest around our constitution and handed the detonator to Brussels' – a comment that was not universally applauded.[92] But he was back on 27 September, after Salzburg, offering his own 'plan for a better Brexit'. Calling for a 'SuperCanada' deal, he showed no better grasp of the realities than Mrs May, proposing 'Mutual Recognition Agreements covering UK and EU regulations', while also arguing for 'regulatory divergence'. To him, this was 'one of the key attractions of Brexit'. For Northern Ireland, he rejected the 'backstop' and any form of physical controls, asserting that any 'extra procedures' could be carried out 'away from the border'.

Common to competing post-Brexit visions, therefore, were areas that could never be acceptable to Brussels. They rendered the UK debate utterly sterile, carried out in a London-centric bubble that had no links to the real world. In particular, in the grip of globalisation, where nations throughout the world were steadily harmonising their trade laws (and much else), 'Little Englander' Johnson wanted freedom to diverge, while still expecting the EU to recognise UK standards. This was delusion on steroids.

May now had a three-corner fight on her hands: the EU; her own Cabinet; and Parliament. What might satisfy the EU could well come unstuck in

---

[88] For instance, BBC News, 12 July 2018 ('Reality Check'), 'Brexit: What does the government White Paper reveal?' and *Daily Telegraph*, 12 July 2018, 'The danger is that Europe might accept our Brexit White Paper'. Not least of the optimistic notes was from the BBC's Katya Adler, who believed that the action plan for EU leaders coming to Salzburg – briefed over and again in advance of the summit in off-the-record conversations with European diplomats – had been to spout words of support for Theresa May to help her secure an EU/UK Brexit divorce deal not just with Brussels, but with political opponents back home. See BBC News, 20 September 2018, 'What just happened in Salzburg? The EU view'.

[89] European Council, 20 September 2018, 'Remarks by President Donald Tusk after the Salzburg informal summit'.

[90] European Council, 'Informal meeting of heads of state or government, 19–20 September 2018'.

[91] *Politico*, 20 December 2018, 'EU's Brexit hard line angers Theresa May'.

[92] *Mail Online*, 9 September 2018, '"Suicide bomber murdered many in front of me and they died in horrific pain": Boris Johnson's claim that PM is wrapping a "suicide vest" around Britain disgusts senior Tory who saw real bombing in Afghanistan'.

Cabinet, and even if she managed to keep her ministers onside (those who did not resign), MPs could well reject her efforts. In the event, this was precisely the shape of things to come. Faced with an unyielding EU – which could not and would not compromise on the fundamentals – Mrs May opted to seek the best fit she could with the EU, and then battle it out with her domestic adversaries.

After briefly wowing her party conference on 3 October, when she danced onto the stage to Abba's 'Dancing Queen', there followed a terse European Council on 17 October, where Mrs May was allowed to address the leaders. Nevertheless, they decided that not enough progress had been made and instructed Barnier to 'continue his efforts'.[93] Days later, a crowd estimated at seven hundred thousand under the campaign banner 'People's Vote' marched in London to demand a second referendum. Lib-Dem leader, Vince Cable, said the march showed that British people were realising that politicians could not deliver a successful Brexit.[94]

NEMESIS

On 14 November, a breakthrough came, in the form of a draft Withdrawal Agreement running to 585 pages and an eight-page outline political declaration setting out the framework for the future relationship. The publication coincided with a Cabinet meeting, held back until 2 p.m. to allow ministers to read the documents. After a 'long, detailed and impassioned debate', Mrs May delivered a short statement in front of No. 10, declaring that the 'collective decision' had been to agree the drafts. It was 'the best that could be negotiated', she said.[95] The following day, four ministers resigned, including Brexit Secretary, Dominic Raab. To that date, 19 ministers had resigned over Brexit.[96]

On the EU side, the draft Withdrawal Agreement was endorsed by a special meeting of the European Council on 25 November, together with a completed political declaration, 36 pages long. But now the Westminster parliament would block progress, rejecting three times Mrs May's attempts to get the Agreement accepted.[97] The first was on 15 January, when she

[93] European Council (Art. 50), 17 October 2018.
[94] *Guardian*, 20 October 2018, 'Almost 700,000 march to demand "people's vote" on Brexit deal'.
[95] Gov.uk, 14 November 2018, 'PM's statement on Brexit'.
[96] *Evening Standard*, 15 November 2018, 'Brexit resignations in full: the list of ministers to quit Theresa May's Cabinet'.
[97] The saga is set out in the book by Anthony Seldon (2020, updated edition), *May at 10: The Verdict* (London: Biteback Publishing). This dedicates 715 pages to a soap opera version of the May premiership, although it scarcely touches on the technical aspects of the negotiations and subsequent agreements. Given that the Withdrawal Agreement alone ran to 585 pages (and was to go through several iterations), a full appraisal would probably be longer than this entire book – unreadable and, most likely, unread.

lost by a resounding 230 votes, the worst government defeat in modern history.[98] She also had to survive a leadership challenge, which she beat off by 200 votes to 117, and a Labour motion of no-confidence, which she won by the slender margin of 325 to 306.[99], [100]

A day before the first attempt, May had enlisted the help of both Juncker and Donald Tusk, to whom she wrote, conveying her MPs' concerns about the 'backstop'. She wanted re-affirmation that it was a temporary expedient pending arrival of something better and more durable. The response was speedy and evidently orchestrated, but it had no impact on the outcome of the vote. Tusk made his displeasure known. After a visit to Dublin to confer with Varadkar, he declared that there was a 'special place in hell' for 'those who promoted Brexit without even a sketch of a plan of how to carry it out safely'. Brussels was quick to clarify the remarks, stressing that the special place in hell would be for when they are dead and 'not right now'.[101]

Nevertheless, the exchange of letters paved the way for May to make a last-minute dash to Strasbourg on 11 March where she secured a 'legally binding' declaration on the 'backstop', committing the EU to early talks on an alternative. The 'backstop', the parties agreed, 'would represent a suboptimal trading arrangement for both sides'.[102] Despite this, she lost the second 'meaningful' vote on 12 March, in what was called a 'humiliating defeat', by a 'crushing majority of 149'.[103]

Two days later, an unexpected vote turned a government motion on whether to leave without a deal into a categorical rejection of the no-deal option, by four votes.[104] The delay on approving the Agreement then required an extension to the Article 50 timing, the first of several.[105] In between, Parliament awarded itself the opportunity to decide on its own preference for Brexit, on 27 March casting 'indicative votes' for eight separate options. All failed to achieve a majority.[106] Another round was held on 1 April, this

[98] *Guardian*, 16 January 2019, 'May suffers heaviest parliamentary defeat of a British PM in the democratic era'.

[99] BBC News, 12 December 2018, 'Theresa May survives confidence vote of Tory MPs'.

[100] BBC News, 16 January 2019, 'May's government survives no-confidence vote'.

[101] BBC News, 6 February 2019, 'Donald Tusk: Special place in hell for Brexiteers without a plan'.

[102] Council of the European Union, Brussels, 20 March 2019, *Instrument relating to the agreement on the withdrawal of the United Kingdom of Great Britain and Northern Ireland from the European Union and the European Atomic Energy Community*, XT 21014/19.

[103] *Guardian*, 12 March 2019, 'MPs ignore May's pleas and defeat her Brexit deal by 149 votes'.

[104] BBC News, 14 March 2019, 'Brexit: MPs vote to reject no-deal Brexit'.

[105] European Council Decision taken in agreement with the United Kingdom, extending the period under Article 50(3)TEU, 22 March 2019, EUCO XT 20006/19.

[106] *Daily Telegraph*, 27 March 2019, 'MPs reject all eight Brexit options in indicative votes as backbench bid to seize control ends in deadlock'.

time with four propositions, and again none could command a majority.[107] As an institution, this was Parliament at its worst. Unable or unwilling to give leadership to the country, the only time it could unite was to express what it did not want.

After losing the third 'meaningful' vote on 29 March by 344 votes to 286, Mrs May briefly toyed with the idea of another general election, ruling out a fourth vote in the Commons. Wistfully, she remarked that 'Parliament's now rejected that deal three times and right now, as things stand, I can't see them accepting it.'[108] Instead, she reached out to Jeremy Corbyn's Labour, hoping he would help her, securing another Article 50 extension to give time for joint talks.[109] Pinning her hopes on a deal, in early May she had reversed her stance and was promising to bring the Withdrawal Agreement back to the Commons for yet another vote, even as the talks were on the edge of collapse.[110]

By 24 May, it was all over. Unable to make any progress, she announced that she would step down on 7 June, leaving time for her successor to be appointed. 'It will always remain a matter of deep regret for me that I have not been able to deliver Brexit,' she said from a podium outside Number 10, adding: 'I have done my best.' Self-evidently, her best had not been good enough and, as she tearfully conceded, 'It is now clear to me that it is in the best interest of the UK for a new PM to lead that effort.'[111] Another prime minister had been broken on the wheel of 'Europe'.

THE RISE OF BORIS JOHNSON

Johnson's accession to Downing Street had the air of inevitability. May's second extension to the Article 50 period, to 31 October, became Johnson's 'do or die' target for leaving. Before that, he intended to seek a completely new Withdrawal Agreement.[112] In his own success, he had complete faith, declaring that the chances of a no-deal were 'a million-to-one against'.[113] However, it was part of Johnson's *amour propre* that he had to keep the

---

[107] *Daily Telegraph*, 1 April 2019, 'Brexit vote results: Theresa May hints at long delay after MPs fail to agree on indicative votes'.

[108] *Daily Telegraph*, 7 April 2019, 'Theresa May rules out fourth meaningful vote and no-deal Brexit as she prepares for customs union climbdown'.

[109] *Daily Telegraph*, 29 March 2019, 'Theresa May's deal defeated again by 58 votes – PM hints at general election to break deadlock'; *Guardian*, 2 April 2019, 'May to ask for short Brexit extension and reaches out to Labour'.

[110] *Financial Times*, 8 May 2019, 'May promises new vote on Brexit deal in next two weeks'.

[111] BBC News, 24 May 2019, 'Theresa May resigns over Brexit'.

[112] *Guardian*, 25 June 2019, 'Brexit: Johnson says Britain will leave EU on 31 October "do or die"'.

[113] *Guardian*, 27 June 2019, 'Boris Johnson: odds of no-deal Brexit are "a million-to-one against"'.

threat of a no-deal alive as leverage, reducing complex EU negotiations to the level of bargaining in a souk.

A defining moment of the leadership campaign came during the final hustings, when Johnson produced a kipper, saying he had been contacted by an Isle of Man kipper smoker who had complained of rocketing costs because the EU insisted every fish had to be posted along with 'a plastic icepillow'. This, he said, was a perfect example of what Britain would soon be free from.[114] However, even the sympathetic *Telegraph*, after consulting with a European Commission spokeswoman in Brussels, concluded he was wrong. 'The sale of products from the food business operator to the final consumer is not covered by EU legislation on food hygiene,' the spokeswoman had said. 'The case described by Mr Johnson falls thus purely under UK national competence.'[115]

The Commission spokeswoman was wrong. This was mail order, which came under different provisions. She had also neglected the all-important fact that the producer was based on the Isle of Man, an island that did not participate in the Single Market. The Tynwald, however, had adopted EU food law in its entirety, augmenting it with a recent code of practice from a Brussels-based trade association, endorsed by a European Commission Standing Committee, which had recommended the cooling of fish products (such as kippers) in transit. Such conformity, approved and verified by the EU, was essential for Isle of Man businesses, without which they would not be allowed to sell mail order foodstuffs into the Single Market without border inspections. This 'pointless, expensive, environmentally damaging, "elf and safety"', as Johnson put it, actually enabled the trade with the UK.[116]

The media, having lapped up uncritically the Commission errors, had missed the point.[117] The EU legal regime (or parts of it) had now become so complicated that even its officials did not understand it, much less the soon-to-be prime minister of the UK, who had failed to appreciate that the Isle of Man had already decided to re-enact EU law, via its European Union and Trade Act 2019, after Brexit. Liberating IoM kippers from their 'ice-pillows'

[114] *Daily Telegraph*, 17 July 2019, 'Tory leadership – final hustings: Boris Johnson promises "comeback" for party as Jeremy Hunt asks members to "vote with your heads and your hearts"'.
[115] *Daily Telegraph*, 18 July 2019, 'Boris Johnson's claim that EU forces kippers to be packed with "ice pillows" exposed as false'.
[116] Details are set out on the EU Referendum blog, 27 July 2019, 'Brexit: kippergate revisited', with links to previous posts on the subject.
[117] As did Tom Bower, 'Britain's top investigative author', in his book *Boris Johnson: The Gambler* (London: W. H. Allen, 2020). He wrote of Johnson's claim: 'That was untrue. British rules had introduced the measure', p. 387.

lay outside Johnson's jurisdiction. Yet this was the man who had ambitions of reforming the system.

NUMBER 10

Confirmed as party leader on 23 July, the next day he delivered his first speech as prime minister, again promising to leave the EU on 31 October.[118] To assist him, he recruited Dominic Cummings – the man without a plan – as his chief adviser.[119] In Brussels, it was all change as well, with the nomination of Ursula von der Leyen, formerly the German minister of defence, as the new Commission president. She formally took office in November and, on 1 December, she was joined by Charles Michel, former Belgian prime minister, as the new president of the European Council.

The immediate response of Brussels to Johnson's call for a renegotiation was to insist on ratification of the agreement as it stood. Barnier pointedly stated that negotiations on a trade deal could only start once that had happened. Therefore, he said, 'the UK has now come to a moment of truth and it must decide if it leaves the EU with or without an agreement. If it chooses the latter, it means that there will be no transition period and no so-called "mini-deals", as the EU will only act to protect its own interests.'[120]

Still relying on the threat of a no-deal bludgeon, it was not long before Johnson had alienated large numbers of his backbenchers, not least over the unlawful prorogation of parliament and his refusal to extend the Article 50 period. By September, he had converted a working majority of one into a minority of 43. No fewer than 21 Conservative MPs had the whip removed.[121] Despite that, he defiantly declared, in front of a backdrop of police recruits in West Yorkshire, wilting in the afternoon sun, that he would 'rather be dead in a ditch' than ask Brussels for a delay to Brexit.[122]

On 10 October, he managed to 'kick-start' the negotiations by meeting Leo Varadkar at Thornton Manor in the Wirral, a location described as a 'luxury' wedding venue.[123] Seven days later – at breakneck speed – revised versions of the Withdrawal Agreement and the Political Declaration were

---

[118] Gov.uk, 'Boris Johnson's first speech as Prime Minister: 24 July 2019'.

[119] *Guardian*, 24 July 2019, 'Dominic Cummings of Vote Leave named key Johnson adviser'.

[120] *Daily Telegraph*, 31 August 2019, 'We will only start work on alternative arrangements if the current deal is ratified'.

[121] *Evening Standard*, 4 September 2019, 'Tory whip removed: the 21 Conservative MPs who voted against Boris Johnson's government'.

[122] *Guardian*, 5 September 2019, 'Boris Johnson: I'd rather be dead in ditch than agree Brexit extension'.

[123] Sky News, 10 October 2019, 'Boris Johnson arrives for meeting with Irish PM Leo Varadkar in race for Brexit deal'.

agreed by negotiators, with the formalities completed by 17 October.[124] The main change was in the Irish Protocol, where the 'backstop' had become a 'frontstop'. Northern Ireland was to remain aligned with a set of Single Market regulations. Goods from the rest of the UK destined for the EU would be subject to border checks. The 'wet' border was back with a vengeance, a 'permanent' solution, subject only to a consent mechanism whereby the Northern Ireland Assembly would be required to vote on the continued application of the Protocol every four years. In essence, this was the very solution that May had rejected.

An unhappy Arlene Foster threatened to withhold her party's ten votes from the Tories.[125] As the implications sunk in, her rhetoric hardened and she accused Johnson of 'betrayal'.[126] But he no longer cared. Having got his deal, all he wanted was parliamentary ratification. For that, a special Saturday sitting was arranged, but rebellious MPs withheld approval until legislation implementing the deal had been passed, and instructed the government to request a delay to Brexit until 31 January 2020.[127]

In a fit of pique, Johnson sent an unsigned photocopy of a specimen request letter drawn up by MPs, describing it as 'Parliament's letter'. He sent his own note to Donald Tusk, complaining that any additional delay to Brexit would be 'deeply corrosive'.[128] Nevertheless, an extension was granted by the European Council on 29 October. With that, Corbyn agreed to a general election, endorsed in the Commons by 438 votes to 20.[129] As he launched his campaign on the slogan 'Get Brexit Done', Johnson now promised to leave the EU by January, boasting that, 'We have an oven-ready deal', ready to put in the microwave.[130] This, he later asserted was 'a great deal'.[131]

The poll was held on 12 December, the first winter election since 1923, when Johnson emerging with an overall majority of 80. A now-compliant backbench quickly passed the EU (Withdrawal Agreement) Bill. It received

[124] European Council, Brussels, 17 October 2019, Special meeting (Art. 50) – Conclusions.
[125] *Guardian*, 26 October 2019, 'DUP says Johnson's Brexit deal would take Northern Ireland in "wrong direction"'.
[126] *Independent*, 9 December 2019, 'Arlene Foster turns on Boris Johnson, saying she will never take him at his word again: "Once bitten, twice shy"'.
[127] *Guardian*, 19 October 2019, 'MPs put brakes on Boris Johnson's Brexit deal with rebel amendment'.
[128] *Daily Telegraph*, 19 October 2019, 'Boris Johnson refuses to sign Brexit extension request and instead sends photocopy, saying: "This is not my letter, it's Parliament's"'.
[129] *Guardian*, 29 October 2019, 'General election: Labour says it will back pre-Christmas poll'.
[130] *Sun*, 31 October 2019, 'DO OR PIE. Boris Johnson vows Brexit deal is "oven ready" and he'll get Britain out by January as he launches election campaign'.
[131] *Daily Telegraph*, 5 November 2019, 'A deal is oven-ready. Let's get Brexit done and take this country forward'.

its Royal Assent on 23 January 2020. The very next day, Johnson signed the Withdrawal Agreement, describing it as a 'fantastic moment' for the country.[132] The deal was sealed by the EU on the 31st.[133]

For all the decades of expectation, celebrations were relatively modest. There was a gathering in Parliament Square amid a forest of Union Jacks, and, with Big Ben under repair, a countdown clock was projected onto the wall of 10 Downing Street.[134] In the final minutes to midnight, Johnson addressed the nation, asserting that, 'whatever the bumps in the road', the nation would succeed. It was time, he said, to 'unleash the full potential of this brilliant country'.[135]

THE START OF TRANSITION

With Brexit over, the transition period started, set to expire on 31 December 2020. The period could be extended, but only once, for one to two years. Any decision had to be taken before 1 July. An agreement on the future EU–UK relationship had to be fully concluded before the end of the period, to allow time for the European Parliament to approve it. If a deal covered competences that the EU shared with member states, each of the EU-27 member states would also need to ratify it.[136]

Within days of the UK leaving, the European Commission had published its proposals for the 'future relationship' negotiations. Referring to its guidelines of 23 March 2018, it reiterated the parameters for 'as close as possible a partnership with the United Kingdom'.[137] Johnson was in Greenwich, outlining his own choices for a relationship with the EU. They lay between 'the Norway model, or a free trade agreement ... like the Canada deal'. He preferred the latter.[138] When von der Leyen met him in London on 8 January, however, she warned that it would be 'basically impossible' to negotiate as close a relationship by the end of the year. The two sides would have to 'prioritise' objectives.[139]

On 25 February, the EU formally adopted its negotiating mandate and, two days later, the British government published a White Paper setting out

[132] *Guardian*, 24 January 2020, '"Fantastic moment": Boris Johnson signs Brexit withdrawal deal'.
[133] European Parliament, 29 January 2020, 'Press Release: Brexit deal approved'.
[134] *Daily Telegraph*, 31 January 2020, 'UK exits European Union with parties across the country'.
[135] Gov.uk, 31 January 2019, 'PM address to the nation'.
[136] European Parliament, 29 January 2020, op. cit.
[137] European Commission, Brussels, 3 February 2020, COM(2020) 35 final, *Recommendation for a Council Decision Authorising the Opening of Negotiations for a New Partnership with the United Kingdom of Great Britain and Northern Ireland*.
[138] Gov.uk, 'PM speech in Greenwich: 3 February 2020'.
[139] *Daily Telegraph*, 8 January 2020, 'Boris Johnson says he is ready to negotiate Canada-style Free Trade Agreement with the EU'.

its own approach.[140] On 2 March, the first round of talks was underway, with Barnier in the hot seat once more. Across the table was David Frost, Johnson's chief Europe adviser.[141] The round lasted until 5 March, during which 11 topics were discussed, including trade in goods and, separately, services, transport, energy and fisheries. High up on the list was: 'Level playing field for open and fair competition', and the list finished off with 'Horizontal arrangements and governance'.[142] With fisheries, these two items were to be the main sticking points.

THE COVID-19 PANDEMIC

Before the talks could become established as a routine, another, even greater event was emerging – a new disease was ripping through the country, about to bring normal life (and economic activity) to a halt. Covid-19, caused by the coronavirus SARS-Cov-2, unleashed a global pandemic. And although its control lay within the realms of national authorities, there was still a significant EU dimension; one that had contributed to leaving the country dangerously unprepared for the challenge.

SARS (standing for severe acute respiratory syndrome) had been recognised as a pandemic disease since 2003, after an outbreak in Guangdong Province, China. So distinct and threatening was this new disease that the World Health Organization, in 2005, rewrote its international regulations, requiring its members to prepare for SARS, alongside but separate from pandemic influenza.[143] It was then that the UK, in common with other countries in Europe, made a serious mistake, grouping SARS with pandemic influenza, despite the diseases being very different, each requiring their own, unique control strategies. From the very beginning, therefore, the British government made no preparations for this separate disease.[144]

When the WHO failed to notice the mistake, the EU could have provided the longstop, having acquired powers in 1998 to set up a network for the epidemiological surveillance and control of communicable diseases.[145]

---

[140] Gov.uk, CP211.

[141] *Guardian*, 27 January 2020, 'Brexit adviser David Frost to lead UK trade negotiations with EU'.

[142] European Commission, 'Negotiation rounds on the future partnership between the European Union and the United Kingdom'.

[143] WHO, *International Health Regulations*, 2005.

[144] For a full analysis, see Booker, Christopher and North, Richard (2020), *Scared to Death* (London: Bloomsbury, 2nd edn), pp. 453–467. Belatedly, on 12 November 2020, five months after this edition had been completed, the *Daily Telegraph* published an 'exclusive' report headlined: 'UK prepared for wrong sort of pandemic, says former chief medical officer', with the sub-heading: 'Dame Sally Davies says scientific advice to focus on influenza threat meant UK never put plans in place to tackle major coronavirus'.

[145] Decision No. 2119/98/EC of 24 September 1998, setting up a network for the epidemiological surveillance and control of communicable diseases in the Community.

In November 2001, all members states had been asked to 'complete and to implement national plans'.[146] Then, in 2004, along with a raft of other agencies, the EU had established the European Centre for Disease Prevention and Control (ECDC), based in Solna, Sweden, aimed at 'strengthening Europe's defences against infectious diseases'.[147] But it too failed to pick up the planning error.

Instead, when the agency started assessing member states' disease control preparedness, it suffered the same myopia, producing in January 2007 an evaluation on pandemic influenza.[148] In that year, it claimed Europe was 'the best prepared region in the world for the next pandemic', without making a single reference to SARS.[149] In June 2009, it produced a guide to dealing with pandemic influenza, but never produced separate guidance on SARS before the 2020 pandemic.[150] Thus, while the EU characterised its own objective as adding 'value to the protection and improvement of human health', its actual role was to reinforce the mistakes made, not just by the UK but by most of its member states.

Yet, as always, poor historic performance was merely a prelude to 'more Europe'. On 11 November 2020, the Commission was to propose of new regulation on 'serious cross-border threats to health', setting out 'a comprehensive legislative framework to govern action at Union level on preparedness, surveillance, risk assessment, and early warning and responses'.[151] What had previously been a matter of co-operation was now to become mandatory – a typical application of Monnet's community method. Shortly then to be outside the regulatory orbit of the EU, the UK was unaffected by this development, free to make its own mess, which it had been doing with uncommon verve.

THE INVISIBLE TALKS

Back in the spring, one effect of the pandemic was to drive news and speculation about the 'future relationship' talks off the front pages. But what also assisted that process was the tedious sameness of the reports, when it quickly emerged that the talks had stalled over the same issues: fishing,

---

[146] European Commission, Health & Consumer Protection DG, *Pandemic Preparedness in the Community: Influenza and other Health Threats*, Conference, Brussels, 27 November 2001.

[147] ECDC website: https://www.ecdc.europa.eu/en/about-ecdc.

[148] ECDC, January 2007, *Technical Report: Pandemic Influenza Preparedness in the EU*.

[149] ECDC, Report for Policymakers, *Pandemic Preparedness in the European Union*, autumn 2007.

[150] ECDC, *Guide to Public Health Measures to Reduce the Impact of Influenza Pandemics in Europe: 'The ECDC Menu'*.

[151] European Commission, Brussels, 11 November 2020, COM(2020) 727 final.

the level playing field provisions, and governance. For most people, the negotiations were as invisible as they were unsuccessful.

In an attempt to break the growing impasse, Frost tabled a draft Comprehensive Free Trade Agreement, together with annexes and agreements on fisheries, air transport, energy and other matters.[152] The draft, he claimed, 'approximates very closely those the EU has agreed with Canada or Japan.'[153] However, in important respects, the UK had offered substantially less than had been conceded by Canada, while demanding more.[154] Barnier himself commented that the UK was 'looking to go much further' than other free trade agreements, making the proposals 'unacceptable'. The UK, he said, was still trying to keep as many Single Market benefits as it could, but it had ceased to apply 'our common ecosystem of rules, supervision and enforcement mechanisms.'[155]

These comments had followed a 'high-level' video conference on 15 June between Johnson, von der Leyen, Charles Michel and the newly appointed president of the European Parliament, David Sassoli. Johnson had recovered from a bout of Covid-19, which had him hospitalised in April, and despite four rounds of talks having been completed, with the negotiators struggling even to reach an understanding on basic principles, he had confirmed that there would be no extension of the transition period. It would end on 31 December 2020. After Johnson called on the three presidents to 'put a tiger in the tank' and conclude an agreement in June, they agreed that the talks should be 'intensified.'[156]

This brought no progress, leaving Barnier on 2 July to restate the EU's position. There would be no economic partnership, he said, without 'robust guarantees' for a level playing field – including on state aid – a 'balanced, sustainable and long-term solution' on fishing, and 'an overarching institutional framework and effective dispute settlement mechanisms.'[157] Yet round six brought Barnier to the podium on 23 July, complaining that the UK was not engaging or showing any readiness to find solutions; 'the time

---

[152] Gov.uk policy paper, 'Our approach to the Future Relationship with the EU' (updated 19 May 2020).

[153] Gov.uk, 'Letter: David Frost to Michel Barnier, 19 May 2020: UK Draft legal texts'.

[154] For instance, while the UK had yet to table any formal proposals on competition policy, Canada and the EU had in 1999 concluded a 12-page formal agreement 'regarding the application of their competition laws', which complemented the provisions set out in Chapters 17 & 18 of CETA.

[155] European Commission, 30 June 2020, Eurofi General Assembly, *Remarks by Michel Barnier*.

[156] Gov.uk, press release, 'EU–UK Statement following the High-Level Meeting on 15 June'; *Daily Telegraph*, 15 June 2020, 'Boris Johnson calls on EU to put "a tiger in the tank" of Brexit talks, as deal hopes rise'.

[157] European Commission, 2 July 2020, *Statement by Michel Barnier following the restricted round of negotiations for a new partnership between the European Union and the United Kingdom*.

for answers is quickly running out, he warned'.[158] Johnson's optimism in June had been completely unfounded.

When the seventh round ended on 21 August, the outcome was no better. Barnier was 'disappointed and concerned', warning that a deal seemed 'unlikely'.[159] The German government, holding the EU's rotating presidency, called off plans to discuss the talks at a meeting of EU ambassadors on 2 September. Brussels lamented a 'completely wasted summer' and EU officials were said to be convinced that the UK government was prepared to risk a no-deal, pinning the blame on Brussels if the talks failed.[160] But the day before round eight, due to be held in London between 8 and 10 September, Johnson imposed another deadline, this time for 15 October when the next European Council was due. If there was no agreement by then, he said, we should 'move on'.[161]

Even as he was speaking, a new hurdle was being erected in the form of the UK Internal Market Bill.[162] To a stunned Commons, on 8 September, Northern Ireland secretary Brandon Lewis admitted that the Bill broke international law in a 'very specific and limited way', negating certain provisions of the Irish Protocol.[163] The action triggered formal infringement proceedings and a threat from the European Parliament that it would refuse to ratify the future relationship treaty if the Bill passed into law unchanged.[164] At the end of round eight, Barnier was still complaining that the UK had not properly engaged.[165] When the ninth round came and went, alongside a special European Council on 1–2 October, followed by a meeting on 3 October between Johnson and von der Leyen, 'significant gaps' remained' between the two sides.[166] They did, however, agree to another 11 days of 'intensified' talks.[167]

---

[158] European Commission, 23 July 2020, *Press statement by Michel Barnier following Round 6 of the negotiations for a new partnership between the European Union and the United Kingdom.*
[159] European Commission, 21 August, *Remarks by Michel Barnier following the seventh round of negotiations on a future partnership between the European Union and the United Kingdom.*
[160] *Guardian*, 25 August 2020, 'Germany scraps plans for Brexit talks at EU Ambassadors summit'.
[161] Gov.uk, 'Prime Minister's words on EU negotiations: 7 September 2020'.
[162] *Financial Times*, 6 September 2020, 'UK plan to undermine withdrawal treaty puts Brexit talks at risk'.
[163] *Independent*, 8 September 2020, 'Minister admits Boris Johnson's Brexit plans break international law'.
[164] European Commission, 10 September 2020, 'Statement by the European Commission following the extraordinary meeting of the EU–UK Joint Committee'; European Parliament, press release 11 September 2020, *Statement of the UK Coordination Group and the leaders of the political groups of the EP.*
[165] European Commission, 10 September 2020, *Statement by Michel Barnier following Round 8 of negotiations for a new partnership between the European Union and the United Kingdom.*
[166] Gov.uk, 'Joint Statement by the Prime Minister and the President of the European Commission: 3 October 2020'.
[167] *Sunday Times*, 4 October 2020, '11 days for a Brexit deal – Boris Johnson sets deadline'.

THE FINAL STRETCH

As Johnson's deadline approached, Barnier insisted that the negotiations would continue.[168] But, when the Council reported, it called on the UK 'to make the necessary moves to make an agreement possible'.[169] This phrasing, added to the original draft, drew a sharp response from Johnson. He charged that the EU had refused to negotiate seriously for much of the last few months, and a Canada-style deal appeared explicitly to have been ruled out. The UK, he concluded, should get ready for 1 January with arrangements more like Australia's. 'With high hearts and complete confidence, we will prepare to embrace the alternative,' he said.[170]

With Barnier told not to come to London the following week, this was seen as a necessary moment of 'crisis' before both sides finally made concessions to reach a deal.[171] As to Johnson's 'Australian' arrangement, this had become a synonym for 'no-deal', even though Australia had 86 trade-related agreements to which the EU was party, of which 20 were bilateral, including a vital mutual recognition agreement on conformity assessment.[172] Canberra's relationship with the EU was a long way from a no-deal scenario.

In the event, there was hardly a pause in the negotiations, which, by 22 October, had been 'rebooted'.[173] At this point, the EU was suggesting the first week in November as a deadline, while Barnier cautioned that leakage of sensitive information could derail the talks.[174] He need not have worried. The media was absorbed by the US presidential elections, and the battle between Donald Trump and Joe Biden. The combination of Covid-19 – cases of which were increasing again – and the elections served to 'bury' news of the negotiations.

The elections, however, were not without relevance. It was thought that Johnson was hedging his bets. If Trump prevailed, it would open the way to strike a quick and substantial US–UK trade deal. If Biden won, no-deal was 'too risky'.[175] It was well into November by the time the media had sated their interest in the elections, with the European Council of 19 November being mooted as the new deadline – no sooner considered than abandoned.

[168] *Daily Telegraph*, 9 October 2020, 'Brexit negotiations will continue beyond Boris Johnson's October 15 deadline, Michel Barnier tells EU ambassadors'.

[169] *European Council conclusions on EU–UK relations, 15 October 2020*.

[170] Gov.uk, 'PM statement on negotiations with the EU: 16 October 2020'.

[171] *Financial Times*, 16 October 2020, 'Boris Johnson throws down "no deal" gauntlet to EU'.

[172] Treaties Office Database of the European External Action Service.

[173] European Commission, 21 October 2020, *Organising principles for further negotiations*.

[174] *Daily Telegraph*, 22 October 2020, 'Brexit: Michel Barnier says UK and EU have "huge common responsibility" to avoid no deal'.

[175] *Observer*, 24 October 2020, 'Johnson will wait for US election result before no-deal Brexit decision'.

By that date a 'final push' was being talked about, while 'gloomy diplomatic sources' were saying there was 'no reason for optimism'.[176]

Before this new deadline arrived, the nation was briefly entertained by pictures of Dominic Cummings departing from No. 10 Downing Street clutching a cardboard box of his possessions, having resigned his post over a spat concerning a new chief for staff for Johnson.[177] In the coming days, several of Cummings' allies were also to depart, signifying a change of the guard in No. 10, but no fundamental change in the negotiation policy.[178] And with no movement, the European Parliament was telling Barnier that the very latest time for a deal was 10 December, the date of the final European Council of the year.[179]

Despite the gloom, there was a glimmer of optimism, as the Irish premier claimed he could see 'landing zones' for agreement.[180] Meanwhile, the Department for Education was telling schools to stock up on long-life products in case of a 'no-deal' outcome.[181] Nevertheless, a false dawn sustained the optimism, as there was more talk of a 'final push', with expectations of a deal by 20 November.[182] But the heady sense of an imminent resolution came crashing to earth that very day when face-to-face talks were suspended after a member of Barnier's personal team tested positive for the coronavirus.[183] As to when it would finally end, all the *Financial Times* could do was observe: 'I don't think the PM knows.'[184]

It was now being suggested that Johnson himself should intervene.[185] But, before this could happen, on 25 November, Barnier was telling his counterpart, David Frost, that further talks would be 'pointless' without 'a major negotiating shift by Downing Street'.[186] Von der Leyen, meanwhile, was explaining to MEPs in Brussels what she expected of the talks. In the context of the UK government's attempt to bypass the Withdrawal

[176] *Sun*, 18 November 2020, 'FINAL PUSH: Brussels leaders ramp up emergency No Deal Brexit plans as Macron vows to defy UK over fish fight'.

[177] ITV News, 13 November 2020, 'Dominic Cummings resigns from No 10 role with immediate effect'.

[178] *Observer*, 15 November 2020, 'No-deal fears rise as Boris Johnson "least willing to budge on Brexit"'.

[179] *Daily Telegraph*, 13 November 2020, 'Brexit trade deal could be done in "10 days" claims senior MEP'.

[180] *Financial Times*, 17 November 2020, 'Hopes grow for post-Brexit trade deal next week'.

[181] *Guardian*, 17 November 2020, 'DfE tells schools to stock up on long-life products in case of no-deal Brexit'.

[182] *Daily Telegraph*, 18 November 2020, 'Brexit talks in "final push" as EU capitals call for launch of no deal plans'.

[183] *The Times*, 20 November 2020, 'Brexit talks halted after Covid-19 hits Barnier's team'.

[184] 20 November 2020.

[185] *Daily Telegraph*, 22 November 2020, 'Boris Johnson prepares significant Brexit intervention as negotiators begin the "final push"'.

[186] *Guardian*, 25 November 2020. 'EU threatens to pull out of Brexit talks if UK refuses to compromise'.

Agreement, she emphasised that 'trust is good, but law is better'. It was essential, she said, 'to ensure that what has been agreed is actually done'.[187]

With rumours swirling – all on the basis of anonymous briefings – by the end of the week the *Daily Telegraph* had settled on a breakthrough on fishing being 'close'.[188] Notwithstanding the diplomatic niceties, though, work in hand to provide lorry parks in Kent, to deal with delayed traffic – all equipped with multiple toilets – had wags rechristening the county, 'The Toilet of England'.[189]

No sooner had the thought of a breakthrough been lodged, than Downing Street was warning that Britain could be just seven days away from ending the talks.[190] The *Sunday Times*, just to ring the changes, had Brussels putting 'pressure' on Barnier to conclude a deal, with von der Leyen being 'quite helpful'.[191] As talks drifted into the Sunday, reporters seeking comment from a terse Barnier were greeted with one word: '*poisson*'.[192] The following day, William Hague was writing that 'no-deal' was 'far more likely than anyone is prepared to admit'.[193]

Into December, nearly two months after the original deadline, Barnier was again reported to be under pressure from member states to settle. But the UK government added insult to injury with a new taxation bill, set to add to the Internal Market Bill in weakening the Irish Protocol. EU officials warned that this risked destabilising the talks.[194] With that, President Macron started emerging as a serious factor in the talks, demanding a specific settlement for French fishermen, as well as state aid provisions favourable to Paris.[195] The irony of the situation was not lost: having made it so difficult for Britain to join the Communities, the French were now making it difficult for her to leave.

After another week of intense negotiations, Barnier and Frost agreed to 'pause the talks' as a prelude to von der Leyen and Johnson engaging

[187] European Commission, Brussels, 25 November 2020, 'Speech by President von der Leyen at the European Parliament Plenary on the preparation of the European Council meeting of 10–11 December'.
[188] 27 November 2020, 'Brexit fishing breakthrough close, with EU set to recognise British sovereignty over UK waters'.
[189] *Guardian*, 27 November 2020, 'Kent rebranded "toilet of England" by anti-Brexit protesters'.
[190] *Daily Telegraph*, 28 November 2020, 'No-deal Brexit is "underpriced", No 10 warns'.
[191] 29 November 2020, 'Brussels puts pressure on Barnier for a Brexit deal'.
[192] ITV News, 30 November 2020, 'Trade talks in "last chance saloon" with fish and state aid still sticking points, minister says'.
[193] *Daily Telegraph*, 30 November 2020.
[194] *Financial Times*, 1 December 2020, 'Barnier faces pressure from national capitals over Brexit compromises'.
[195] *Financial Times*, 3 December 2020, 'Tough Macron stance leaves Brexit deal hanging in balance'.

in direct dialogue.[196] In a telephone conversation lasting an hour, the pair agreed that talks could resume with yet another deadline set. This was the Monday before the European Council, when they were to confer again.[197] As the talks resumed, the media continued to offer a diverse fare, ranging from 'breakthrough' to 'significant progress'.[198] *The Times* chipped in with a 'downbeat' assessment from Barnier, predicting that there was 'little chance' of a deal in the coming days.[199]

After the next phone call between von der Leyen and Johnson, when 'no progress at all' was reported in the talks, it was agreed that the pair should meet in Brussels for dinner. The one bright spot was that the government agreed to abandon the controversial clauses in the Internal Market and Finance Bills, which would have breached the Irish Protocol.[200] Despite this, the meeting was not a success. The only level of agreement reached was that talks would continue until the Sunday, whence a 'firm decision' should be taken about their future.[201] The 10 December European Council deadline had been abandoned, with the showdown reset for the 13th. The European Council, meantime, asked the Commission to publish its contingency plans for a no-deal outcome.[202]

In what had become a weary ritual, this deadline came and went and, as talks continued into the following week, Barnier reported that the pathway to agreement remained 'very narrow'. The talks on fishing had 'gone backwards', raising the risk that they could run deep into December.[203] As they ground on, the European Parliament decided on another intervention, setting a new deadline, initially for 18 December, after which it would not ratify any agreement before the end of the year. When Barnier successfully pleaded for an extension to the Sunday, telling the leaders of the political groups that a deal was 'difficult but possible', that immediately raised speculation that a finale was in the offing.[204]

[196] Michel Barnier, 4 December 2020, Twitter.
[197] Ursula von der Leyen, 5 December, Twitter.
[198] *Guardian*, 6 December 2020, 'Breakthrough on fishing rights as Brexit talks hang in the balance'; Sky News, 7 December 2020, '"Significant progress" in talks over fishing rights during trade negotiations: EU sources'.
[199] 6 December 2020, 'Outlook gloomy as Brexit talks reach "endgame"'.
[200] *Guardian*, 8 December 2020, 'UK drops plans to break international law as Northern Ireland deal is reached'.
[201] *Guardian*, 9 December 2020, 'Boris Johnson sets out red lines at last-ditch Brexit dinner'.
[202] European Commission, Brussels, 10 December 2020, COM(2020) 831 final, Communication on targeted contingency measures in the absence of an agreement with the United Kingdom on a future partnership.
[203] *Guardian*, 14 December 2020, 'Brexit trade deal possible within days after Johnson concession, says EU'.
[204] *Daily Telegraph*, 17 December 2020, 'Hopes for Brexit deal rise after European Parliament sets Sunday deadline'.

Events were then to intrude in the form of a 'new variant' coronavirus, believed to be responsible for a sudden surge in cases, especially in the south-east of England. This led Johnson to cancel a promised relaxation in restrictions over the Christmas period, causing chaos throughout the country, as it was reduced to one day, on Christmas Day itself. As yet another deadline for the talks expired – the 'narrow path' dwindling to a goat track – an entirely new drama gripped the country. Holland and other countries, followed by France and many others, totalling over forty, closed their borders to the UK in an attempt to contain the spread of the virus.[205] While talks continued past the weekend, queues of lorries unable to cross the Channel built up outside Dover and other ports, a foretaste of a no-deal end to the transition period. However, calls for an extension to the transition period went unheeded.[206]

On the Wednesday, with Johnson and von der Leyen in constant touch by phone, a media frenzy erupted as rumours spread of an imminent deal, some newspapers certain that it had been done. The claims were premature. It was not until 1.14 p.m. the following day, Christmas Eve – after last-minute haggling on fish quotas – that exhausted negotiators finally put the deal to bed. 'That's the good news from Brussels – now for the sprouts,' Johnson concluded in his speech that evening, having falsely claimed that 'there will be no non-tariff barriers to trade'.[207] After snow fell in parts of the country overnight, the Met Office officially declared a white Christmas. While EU ambassadors convened in Brussels to examine the treaty, at least one wearing 'a Father Christmas bobble hat', thousands of lorry drivers, stranded in Kent, spent the day with their vehicles.[208]

The logjam was not cleared until Boxing Day, coinciding with the publication of the treaty, a 1,246-page volume entitled the 'EU–UK Trade and Cooperation Agreement' (TCA). It came with 26 pages of declarations, and separate agreements for co-operation on the safe and peaceful use of nuclear energy and on Security Procedures for Exchanging and Protecting Classified Information. They were formally signed by the Council on 29 December and approved for 'provisional application' pending ratification by the European Parliament in the new year. This body had refused to

[205] BBC News, 21 December 2020, 'Covid-19: More than 40 countries ban UK arrivals'.

[206] *Evening Standard*, 21 December 2020, 'There will "absolutely not" be a Brexit extension despite border chaos, insist ministers'.

[207] Gov.uk, 24 December 2020, 'Prime Minister's statement on EU negotiations'.

[208] *Guardian*, 25 December 2020, 'Brexit trade deal to be approved by EU27 "within days"'; *Daily Mirror*, 25 December 2020, 'Army called in to help stranded lorry drivers in Dover spending Xmas day in their cabs'.

rush its procedures, arguing that the late completion meant that there was insufficient time for scrutiny in the days left before the end of the year.

The Westminster Parliament had no such scruples. It was recalled on 30 December to pass the EU (future relationship) Bill, implementing the agreements, in a single day. Addressing the House of Commons at the start of proceedings on the day, Johnson declared:

> The central purpose of this Bill is to accomplish something which the British people always knew in their hearts could be done, but which we were told was impossible – namely that we could trade and cooperate with our European neighbours on the closest terms of friendship and goodwill, whilst retaining sovereign control of our laws and our national destiny.

The MPs approved the Bill at its crucial second reading by 521 votes to 73 – a majority of 448, the time limits preventing more than 59 from speaking. Because of the continuing (and, in fact, intensifying) Covid epidemic, most of those did so remotely, from the comfort of their own homes. Nevertheless, MPs were awarded an extra week's holiday as a reward for their efforts.[209] And even as they were speaking, signed copy of the treaties were winging their way over from Brussels in an RAF transport for Johnson to sign, thus enabling the completion of all the procedural steps required for the treaties to take effect at 11 p.m. GMT on 31 December.

Come the day, with snow still on the ground in some parts of the country, it was not the freezing conditions that kept the crowds away, but the resurgent Covid epidemic. Big Ben had been switched on in time to mark Britain's departure from the European Union's Single Market and customs union, and, as the last 'bong' faded in a near-deserted Parliament Square, it was over – the last traces of 47 years of membership had been excised. Dover was 'eerily quiet'.

---

[209] Only then to be recalled the following Wednesday to deal with the deteriorating Covid situation.

CONCLUSION

End and a Beginning

That such an unnecessary and irrational project as building a European superstate was ever embarked on will seem in future years to be perhaps the greatest folly of the modern era. And that Britain, with traditional strengths and global destiny, should ever have become part of it will appear a political error of the first magnitude.

Margaret Thatcher[1]

... it is likely that the UK would have implemented the vast bulk of the financial sector regulatory framework had it acted unilaterally, not least because it was closely engaged in the development of the international standards from which much EU legislation derives.

House of Lords European Union Committee[2]

Through the years that this book has been published, we have encountered some who have argued that our title, *The Great Deception*, is overblown. But it is the case that the 'project' was built on a foundation of deception. Nevertheless, there are two concessions I would make to our critics. The first is that there are many deceptions, which make up the whole, that have accumulated over time, like barnacles on a seagoing vessel. The second reflects precisely the point we rehearsed in the first and subsequent editions: that, all too often, we have not only been seeing deception, *per se*, but self-deception, sometimes verging on delusion.

[1] *Statecraft: Strategies for a Changing World* (London: HarperCollins, 2003), p. 410.
[2] HoL European Union Committee, 5th Report of Session 2014–15, *The Post-crisis EU Financial Regulatory Framework: Do the Pieces Fit?* 2 February 2015, HL Paper 103, p. 13.

Many of these deceptions have morphed into foundation myths, shaped by an army of sympathetic historians, journalists, politicians and the Commission, which have been superbly successful in reinventing the past. This is why, when one returns to the documentary record, as we have tried to do in this book, there is almost no episode of the European Union's history that does not emerge looking radically different from the version that has been generally presented.

Some of these myths are now better known for what they are than when this book was first published in 2003. But they are just as potent and insidious as they have ever been. Collectively, they form part of the European Union's *amour propre*, a collection of myths that sustain and seemingly justifies its existence. In so doing, it provides supporters with ready-made arguments to help conceal its true purpose, which has remained unchanged since Jean Monnet's first tentative steps in 1950: the establishment of a 'United States of Europe'.

THE ROOTS OF DECEPTION

The story we have told could not have unfolded in the way it has without the remarkable gifts of Monnet, His unique achievement was not that he inspired the nations of Europe to an unprecedented degree of peaceful co-operation. Both in the 1920s and again in the late 1940s, many others more prominent than him were gripped by the same vision. What marked out Monnet – and his colleague Arthur Salter – when they first conceived their own version of this dream was their conviction that it could only be brought about by giving Europe a government that was supranational.

Thus, it was not nationalism that they regarded as their greatest enemy. Rather, it was that rival form of internationalism through voluntary co-operation between sovereign governments, under the general banner of 'intergovernmentalism'. Monnet, in particular, regarded its ineffectuality as having destroyed the League of Nations. No language of condemnation was strong enough to convey his hatred of it. He regarded it as a 'poison', 'pollution', the ultimate delusion.

Part of Monnet's genius lay in his extraordinary ability, operating behind the scenes, to manipulate other people. But the other part was his realisation that he was never going to win acceptance for what he wanted if he went for it directly and all at once. There were heady moments when he was tempted to burst out into the open: most notably in the early 1950s when, carried away by his coup in setting up the Coal and Steel Community, he spoke of it as 'the first government of Europe', and then, two years later, launched his plan for a 'European Political Community'. But, with Spaak's aid, he soon learned from these mistakes. Thus emerged what was perhaps his most influential bequest to the 'European project', that strategy which came to be known as *engrenage* or 'the Monnet method'.

There would never be any single, clear definition of these terms. But every insider would know what was meant by *engrenage*, or 'gearing'. It provided a blanket word to describe all those various techniques whereby the 'project' could apply a steady, relentless pressure to extend the Commission's supranational powers. Each new advance it made would merely be regarded as a means of gearing up for the next. Each new addition might begin with a small, innocuous-seeming proposal to which nobody could object: until the principle was conceded and those powers could then be steadily enlarged. Each new problem or setback could be used as a 'beneficial crisis' to justify further extending the Commission's reach.

Thus, brick by brick, would the great supranational structure be assembled. Above all, it would be vital never to define too clearly the ultimate goal, for fear this would arouse countervailing forces. In this sense, an intention to obscure and to deceive was implicit in the nature of the 'project' from the moment it was launched. This habit of concealment was to become a defining characteristic. Despite that, there are those who argue that, if there was deception, it was easily penetrated. The intentions of the founding fathers of the EEC, and their successors, were either openly declared or otherwise accessible to anyone who took the trouble to seek them out.

This claim probably had its greatest force when applied to the outcome of the 1975 referendum, but the arguments tend to ignore the very different political and social environments of the time. In that pre-internet age, information was not always easily accessible. During the campaign, this current author (RN) sought to obtain a copy of the Treaty of Rome. It could only be bought from a very limited number of HMSO shops, necessitating a visit to High Holborn in central London to obtain one.[3] But it could be bought and, reading for myself that the parties were 'determined to lay the foundations of an ever closer union among the peoples of Europe', I voted 'No' in the referendum.

For sure, the treaty was to hand, but, for most people, obtaining it would not have been easy. One is reminded of the opening scene in *The Hitchhiker's Guide to the Galaxy*, where Prostetnic Vogon Jeltz of the Galactic Hyperspace Planning Council dismisses protests against the imminent demolition of the planet Earth, declaring:

---

[3] For the princely sum of £1.20, equivalent to about £25 at current prices.

There's no point acting all surprised about it. All the planning charts and demolition orders have been on display in your local planning department in Alpha Centauri for fifty of your Earth years, so you've had plenty of time to lodge any formal complaint and it's far too late to start making a fuss about it now.

Clearly, the fact that information is available, somewhere, does not mean that it has been seen, or that the implications have been understood. In the 1975 referendum, with 'Common Market' on the ballot paper, most people were content to accept the prevailing narrative, that we were joining a trading bloc. Booker voted 'Yes'. Then the Vogon destructor fleet arrived.

Nevertheless, it is true that, when it came to political unity and a European monetary system, during the early 1970s, Edward Heath went into print openly and often, hailing these as the ultimate objectives of the EEC. He can be found, for instance, on the front page of *The Times* on 18 September 1971 asserting – among other things – that there was a need for a new monetary system. The front page of the lowly *Daily Express* of 20 October 1972 has him stating that a 'regional policy was an essential feature of the Community's economic and monetary union' – a clear enough indication that EMU was on the agenda.

This brings to mind another classic, the scenario depicted in the comic genius series *Yes, Prime Minister*, where vital information about a planned invasion was concealed from Hacker by referring to it only in one paragraph on page 107 of a 138-page report in the bottom of his 'red box'.[4] When it comes to the population at large, publishing a piece in the 'top people's paper', or burying a reference half-way down a dense report in the *Express*, has much the same effect. It is disingenuous to assert that, because some evidence was available at the time, this refutes the 'deception' thesis.

Even if such material was read, much of what was said about the future of the EEC was opinion or aspiration. Others had different opinions and the public was often confronted with radically opposed positions. As we know, when he reported to the Cabinet on Wilson's renegotiations in 1974, Callaghan told his colleagues that the agreement at the 1972 Paris Summit to establish a 'European Union' by 1980 'turns out on investigation to have been completely without content'. 'European Union by 1980,' he said, 'is a slogan or a banner to which many Europeans attach great importance

---

[4] BBC, *Yes, Prime Minister*, Season 1, 'Episode 6: A Victory for Democracy'.

and which the German and other Governments need for internal political reasons to hold out to their people as a long-term aim.'[5]

To that extent, much of what was being said by Heath, and others, was simply background 'noise', a concept familiar to advertisers. Dominating commercial television at the time were advertisements for competing laundry detergents. One product, Daz, assured prospective buyers, that it 'boils whitest of all'. Its competitor, Persil, sought to convince that it 'washes whiter'. Where Heath preached political unity and monetary union, Wilson spoke dismissively of 'theology'. Given the choice between what appeared to be high-flown rhetoric about some indeterminate future, and the down-to-earth present, the majority accepted the latter. They wanted to 'wash whiter' without the boil. To have convinced 'buyers' of the merits of the competing rhetoric would have required penetrating the 'noise', which is something Heath and the 'Europeanists' never sought to do.

To have ensured that the message of 'ever closer union' was fully understood to be the declared policy of the government, with all that that entailed, an extensive advertising campaign would have been required, simply to overcome the 'noise'.

KEEPING THE PEACE

Perhaps the most pervasive deception of them all, though – and certainly one assiduously fostered by the European Commission and many others – is that the genesis of the EU lies in the post-Second World War period, with Churchill's Zurich speech in 1946 often used as the starting point. But, as we have established in these pages, Monnet and Salter conceived their ideas in the 1920s, based on their experiences during the First World War and of the pre-war failure of the League of Nations. Thus, the EU is a post-war child, but its intellectual base lies not in the aftermath of the second war, but the first. Yet, the misplaced timing facilitates the more pernicious myth that, because Monnet (through Schuman) sold his plans as a means of preventing another European war, that – necessarily – the EEC and then the EU have been successful in keeping the peace in Europe, notwithstanding the tragedy of the Balkans.

However, when Monnet devised his theory – and before him Loucheur and Mayrisch – in the aftermath of the 1914–18 war, the type of warfare that the world had witnessed was one that relied on massed guns and expenditure of millions of shells, typified by the slaughter at Verdun and on the Somme. Control of coal and steel, limiting the capability of adversaries

---

[5] National Archives, CAB 129/177, op. cit.

to make war on the same scale, made absolute sense. But, in 1945, the world had changed beyond all recognition. Germany was an occupied country, split between two nuclear superpowers that, in time, would acquire enough weapons of sufficient power to destroy the planet. The idea that controlling the production of coal and steel in France and Germany, and four other countries, would prevent Germany from once more invading France, or vice versa, in a continent on the brink of nuclear Armageddon was and is beyond absurd.

By a quirk of history, the 100th anniversary of the battles of the Somme and Verdun coincided with the year of the EU referendum. The importance of Verdun evoked a stern lecture from the *Guardian* during the referendum campaign. 'It is all too easy, after 70 years of European peace and 100 years after Europeans slaughtered one another on the western front, to ignore what has been achieved by Europe's common institutions in providing a stability in Europe that did not exist there before', the paper intoned. 'We in Britain have a responsibility to do our part to ensure that this stability and unity do not unravel. We should all remember Verdun.'[6]

Some 13 years previously – in this book – Verdun was indeed remembered. But the lessons drawn were entirely different. That the French and Germans (particularly) needed a formal reconciliation was indisputable. But then to argue that measures to limit the capability to embark on the obsolete form of warfare that so marked Verdun were subsequently to lay the foundations of peace in Europe is not intellectually sustainable.

THE MISSED OPPORTUNITIES

There is no more glaring example of the European mythology, and the way history has been rewritten, than the assertion by a long procession of the project's sympathisers up to Tony Blair, who have followed Dean Acheson in calling Britain's 'worst mistake of the post-war period', its 'failure' to join the project at its inception, after the launch of the Schuman Plan. Others cite the failure to join the 'Common Market' in 1957 by signing the Treaty of Rome.

Yet, as we record, at the behest of Monnet, when the French government formally invited the UK to the talks on the Coal and Steel Community, it insisted that all participating governments should commit themselves in advance to accepting the principle of the scheme before it was discussed in detail. As Attlee later explained to the House of Commons, governments had to accept at the outset the principles of the pooling of resources and of a

---

[6] *Guardian*, 29 May 2016, 'The *Guardian* view on the centenary of Verdun: lessons for us all'.

high authority whose decisions would be binding, and the next step should be the conclusion of a treaty in which these principles would be embodied. Monnet had, therefore, 'Britain-proofed' the Plan by making joining the talks conditional on accepting the supranational principle, something no British government, at that time, could have accepted.

All this was, of course, to be repeated even more dramatically a few years later when Monnet, now head of his Action Committee for a United States of Europe, began discussing with Spaak the next leap forward. It was Spaak who more than anyone was responsible for guiding the project towards its greatest breakthrough of all: the Treaty of Rome. And it was Spaak who steered Monnet into accepting what was to become the central deception of the whole story, when he urged that all mentions of political or 'federal' union should be suppressed and that the project should be sold to the world as no more than a 'common market', designed to promote peaceful economic co-operation, trade and general prosperity.

Again, the 'myth', as developed by British publicists such as Young and Denman, has presented this as the second occasion when Britain 'missed a historic opportunity' to become involved and thus to shape the project in ways that, to quote Blair, might have 'reflected British interests'. But again, this is to stand the facts of history on their head. Britain's post-war record in promoting European co-operation on an intergovernmental basis was second to none, from the OEEC and the Council of Europe to NATO and the WEU. This was precisely why Monnet and Spaak were again determined to keep Britain out of their project at all costs: not least by making membership of the EEC conditional on joining Euratom, on terms they knew would make it impossible for the British to accept.

When Britain then persisted in trying to promote intergovernmental co-operation through free trade, the OEEC, the FTA and EFTA, Monnet used his influence, not least through the USA, to sabotage those efforts. Only when he became seriously alarmed that his old ally de Gaulle was trying to subvert the project from within, by dragging it back towards intergovernmentalism, did Monnet go through that U-turn that led him to want Britain in.

POST-REFERENDUM LESSONS
For all that, the controversies attendant on Britain joining the institutions that were to become the European Union are old history. But to assume that they have no relevance to today would be a mistake. What motivated the British government initially to reject Monnet's dreams more than anything was its post-war commitment to intergovernmentalism. Its change of heart around

1960 stemmed largely from the post-Suez loss of national self-confidence and from the onset of that collective inferiority complex that resulted from comparing the performance of its own faltering, obsolescent economy with the new-found 'dynamism' of its Common Market neighbours.

It was this loss of nerve that led London almost overnight to abandon all its old inhibitions about subordinating Britain's affairs to a supranational form of government. From the Cabinet papers of the time, it is clear that Macmillan and his ministers were fully aware of the wider political implications of what they were doing: that the real purpose of the European project was to work towards ultimate political union. But despite the open-ended commitment to surrendering power from Westminster to Brussels, this was regarded as an acceptable price to pay for participation in the European project.

The extent to which the public was deceived as to the true nature of the project will never be agreed between its supporters and those who oppose it. But it is certainly the case that, after the failure of Monnet's grand experiment in creating the EDC, references to the 'supranational' nature of the ECSC were suppressed.

As we record, by 1965, when the 'Merger Treaty' was agreed between the Six, any reference to the 'supranational character' of the Commission's duties was omitted. In debates about 'Europe' in the Commons during the early 1960s, it was not at all unusual to find the merits, or otherwise, of supranationalism being discussed. But, as the debate progressed, the word slipped from the parliamentary lexicon, and in contemporary debates it is relatively rare to see any reference made to the supranational nature of the EU.

This became highly relevant when Britain's post-Brexit future had to be addressed, as there was no real debate about the core of the dispute, the relative merits of supranationalism *versus* intergovernmentalism. When 'Vote Leave' failed to formulate a coherent (or any) exit plan, compounded by Parliament in 2019, which failed to identify, through a series of 'indicative votes', its own preferred option, this rendered the exit debate sterile. It became dominated by the ultimate delusion that the alternative to membership of the European Union was no membership, leaving the same policy vacuum that, in the aftermath of the 1958 Suez crisis, had impelled the political classes to join the European communities in the first place. More than sixty years on, their successors had no better idea of how to define the post-colonial future.

Without it being clearly stated, therefore, leaving the EU has reopened that pre-Suez debate about how to organise our relations with 'Europe' and the rest of the world, given that the UK has once again rejected Monnet's supranationalism. For the foreseeable future, though, this will be an arduous path, and there is a general consensus that the UK, in reorientating its affairs, will suffer a short- to medium-term loss of GDP. As post-Brexit difficulties multiply – not helped by the economic 'hit' the economy has suffered as a result of the Covid-19 pandemic – siren voices calling for our re-entry to the EU, in some form or other, will undoubtedly intensify, even if, in the immediate future, it is unlikely that the present 27 member states would be keen to re-admit the UK. But, as Cameron rightly surmised in all but the timing, the EU is overdue for another treaty. At that point, one might expect the creation of a new form of associate membership, as was foreseen in 2013, in the Bertelsmann/Spinelli Group draft treaty setting out a 'Fundamental Law of the European Union'.

Through our difficulties to come, therefore, the important fact to remember is that we are dealing with far more than the simple membership of a 'club' – as an associate or otherwise. Our relations with the EU depend on us resolving that age-old dispute that, even to this day, has not been properly addressed.

This is of crucial importance when one bears in mind that, although the other 27 member states have been our partners in a collective experiment, not all of them have been our friends. For instance, we have accumulated powerful evidence that, throughout the 1960s, France was acting in its own national interest to shape the CAP as a tool to finance its burgeoning agricultural subsidies that it could no longer afford, but dare not reduce. Only in 1969, when she had finally locked in place the financial mechanism to ensure a flow of funds, did the French then actively embrace British entry. Its disproportionately high budget payments could then be used to finance the CAP, the shape of which Britain had not been allowed to influence.

That France should assert its national interest, however, is possibly less remarkable than the fact that British politicians failed to protect British interests. There is little evidence that they or their civil servants understood just how profoundly they had been stitched up twice over by the French CAP arrangements, even though these would eventually lead to the battle over Britain's disproportionate contribution to the EC budget. And what were presented as 'negotiations' were no more than a prolonged act of surrender, on everything from the Commonwealth to the CAP, summed up by Con O'Neill as 'swallow it whole and swallow it now'.

The point is that, when it comes to membership of the EU, its supranational nature has made it very difficult for British governments to protect the unique interests of the British people. For reasons that have been more than adequately set out in this book, the British simply have not taken to the milieu. And what holds good for the past doubtless will apply to the future. To re-join would simply open up the same old wounds.

THE SINGLE MARKET DILEMMA
Centre-stage during the Brexit talks were discussions on both sides about the extent to which the UK could remain in, or retain access to, the EU's Single Market, making it one of the most highly contested issues of the period – and one where deception morphed into self-deception and even delusion, in which it has been believed that the supposed merits of 'free trade' somehow compensate for being shackled to a supranational construct.

The abolition of borders was a key part of the original Treaty of Rome, but during the doldrums that affected the EEC after its birth and continued for some decades, the necessary process of harmonisation of product standards and customs procedures had stalled. As we have seen, though, by 1984, France and Germany were already taking action to improve border flows, with the Saarbrücken Agreement – a bilateral treaty completely outside the framework of the Treaty of Rome and its customs union, which was followed by the Schengen Treaty, also outside the framework of the Community.

Thus, as we record in this book, when the Commission White Paper on the completion of the internal market was published, on the same day as the Schengen Agreement, its proposal to secure the complete abolition of frontiers was nothing new. Not by any means can it be said with any accuracy that Mrs Thatcher 'invented' the Single Market, even if her support for the Single European Act did assist Delors in his efforts to bring border controls back into the Community maw.

However, as Booker and I were writing in the early 1990s, when preparations were under way to 'complete' the Single Market, something very odd was happening to British public life. It was then that hundreds of thousands of businesses, directly affected by the preparations, could judge whether all those grandiose claims made for the advantages the Single Market would bring were true or not. Very soon, the verdict of countless businesses was that it had been so much hype. They had been faced with an unprecedented avalanche of time-consuming and costly new regulations and bureaucracy. But the benefits promised as their reward seemed in most cases to be non-existent.

That was the case at the time. But much of the cost and disruption was caused by the speed and extent of the changes, and by the fact that many of the new laws – in the rush to finalise them against an unrealistic timetable

– were ill-considered and poorly framed. The problems were intensified by the UK civil service's habit of 'gold-plating', adding to Community provisions with requirements of their own. When this was combined with over-zealous enforcement and a propensity in some sectors to implement guidelines as if they were law, it created a perfect storm of regulatory overload, the like of which had not been since the Second Word War.

Although this was to shape the thinking and experiences of a generation of Conservative MPs, many of whom were to play an active part in the referendum campaign and the post-referendum debate, over the thirty years or so of the workings of the Single Market, things did settle down. Businesses that had been forced to close, of course, no longer had a voice. The rest adapted, paying whatever costs were incurred as the price of doing business. And, as the years passed, some of the claimed benefits did materialise, transforming – for instance – car manufacturing, where plants could draw components from all over Europe, via complex 'just-in-time' supply chains. Services, and especially financial services, blossomed, inwards investment improved, taking advantage of the free movement of capital. Many enterprises, including the NHS and care services, farming and the hospitality sector, benefited from cheap, well-educated immigrant labour. For better or worse, the Single Market became the new normal.

With the advent of Brexit, however, all this was to change, once more putting businesses through the trauma of having to adjust at great speed to a new trading environment – with far less warning and minimal information. Most businesses would remain adaptable, but speed of change and ventures into the unknown were always going to be problematical.

It was here that the businesses of Britain were caught by a new delusion, reinforced by the Conservative 'foundation myth', that the European Union was essentially a trading agreement that had gone 'off the rails'. The thrust of both May's and Johnson's approach to the negotiations was an attempt to 'restore' some form of trading arrangement with the Union, without the 'level playing field' provisions and other perceived encumbrances that the Brussels negotiators were demanding. There was thus an almost child-like simplicity to the British position, based on the mantra of 'free trade', the like of which existed only in the imaginations of our leaders and their negotiating teams, belying the complexities of the real world.

THE MARCH OF GLOBALISATION

The most significant of these complexities is the degree to which, in the years since the early 1990s, the regulatory environment had been transformed by globalisation. Increasingly, the EU's *acquis* was defined not by its own initiatives but by the activities of regional bodies such as UNECE and the OECD, and global bodies such as the International Maritime Organization (IMO), the International Civil Aviation Organization (ICAO) and the International Labour Organization (ILO), and many, many more, especially those under the umbrella of the United Nations.

Given Boris Johnson's enthusiasm for Australian-style arrangements, it is appropriate to note that Australia – along with most other trading nations – has also been exposed to this transformation. Of this, an Australian academic wrote:

> In the world system, Australia is substantially a law-taker rather than a law-maker. This process of globalisation of regulatory law has been accelerated by the General Agreement on Tariffs and Trade (GATT). Thanks to GATT, our food standards will now, effectively, be set in Rome rather than Canberra or Sydney. The impact of the GATT is no more than an accelerant of what has been going on a long time.
>
> For years, some of our air safety standards have been written by the Boeing Corporation in Seattle, or if not by them, by the US Federal Aviation Administration in Washington. Our ship safety standards have been written by the International Maritime Organisation in London. Our motor vehicle safety standards have been written by Working Party 29 of the Economic Commission for Europe. Our telecommunications standards have been substantially set in Geneva by the International Telecommunications Union.[7]

With EU institutions and agencies, however, this can be a two-way process, as they also strongly influence standards-setting bodies. This interaction was so prevalent that special terminology had been invented to cover it. The EU was variously said to 'upload' rules to, or 'download' them from, international bodies. 'Downloading' was defined as the incorporation of international 'soft' rules (standards, principles, guidelines) into EU legislation. 'Uploading' was the incorporation of EU legislation (or parts of it) into international regulation.[8]

---

[7] Braithwaite, John, 'Sovereignty and Globalisation of Business Regulation', in Alston and Chiam (eds) (1995), *Treaty-Making in Australia: Globalisation versus Sovereignty* (Annadale, NSW: The Federation Press).

[8] See Quaglia, Lucia (2012), *The European Union and Global Financial Harmonisation* (Florence: European University Institute, Department of Political and Social Sciences).

Nevertheless, as more and more issues were addressed at regional and global level, the EU gradually outsourced its regulatory agenda.[9] More than 80 per cent of the EEA *acquis* (and therefore the EU's Single Market legislation) fell within the ambit of existing international organisations and agreements, and was thus potentially amenable to this process.[10] In terms of detail, over 33 per cent of the *acquis* comprised 'technical regulations, standards, testing and certification'. Much of this is implemented through standards bodies which will eventually emerge as ISO standards. Another 28 per cent of the *acquis* came into a category defined as 'veterinary and phytosanitary matters'. This included compositional standards for food and food safety.

It is there that the hidden hand of globalisation is extremely powerful, not least because these standards build on the Agreement on the Application of Sanitary and Phytosanitary Measures (known as the 'SPS Agreement'), which entered into force with the establishment of the World Trade Organization on 1 January 1995. Although this allows countries to set their own standards, it encourages members to use international standards, guidelines and recommendations where they exist.[11] It came into force alongside the WTO's Agreement of Technical Barriers to Trade (the 'TBT Agreement'), which has a similar effect with non-food products, the measures between them providing a powerful incentive for trading nations (and trading blocs) to work within the framework of international standards.

THE 'HIDDEN HAND'
One of the reasons why this 'hidden hand' has largely escaped recognition is due to the lack of transparency by Brussels in declaring the origins of their standards. A typical example occurred in September 2013, when a Commission programme to rationalise food labelling was interpreted by the media as an 'EU plan' to prohibit the use of the Union flag on retail packs of meat.[12] But the programme did not originate in Brussels. It was implementing a standard produced by the international organisation, *Codex Alimentarius*.[13] Portions of the exact text had been copied into the

[9] For a detailed treatment of this argument, see North, Richard A. E., *The Norway Option, Rejoining the EEA as an Alternative Membership of the European Union*, The Bruges Group, November 2013.
[10] EFTA, 'The European Economic Area and the Single Market 20 Years On', Bulletin, 2012.
[11] WTO website, 'Understanding the WTO Agreement on Sanitary and Phytosanitary Measures'.
[12] *Daily Express*, 17 September 2013, 'Fury at EU plan to ban Union Flag from British meat packs'. The report also appeared in the *Daily Telegraph*, *Daily Mail* and many other newspapers.
[13] *Codex* Stan 1-1985 on country of origin labelling for packaged foods.

regulation, thus assuming the identity of EU law.[14] Even then, the *Codex* standard relied for its legal base on the WTO Agreement on Rules of Origin. Yet neither was identified in the regulation text – there was no distinction made between international and EU law.

In a similar vein, there was the episode of Michelle 'Clippy' McKenna, a small business in Sale, Manchester, selling jams made from home-grown Bramley apples. Because her products did not conform to British regulations, she was prevented from labelling them as jam.[15] The regulations, however, implemented EU law, so there was a classic EU 'red tape' story in the making, to be exploited by the media.[16, 17] Yet the originator of the standard was not the EU but the *Codex*, a fact not mentioned by the EU.[18] McKenna's problems arose because an exemption written into the original standard, and permitted by EU law, had not been transposed into the British regulations.

A more egregious example came in July 2018 when Boris Johnson resigned as foreign secretary, complaining in his resignation letter to Theresa May of frustrations, as mayor of London, in trying to protect cyclists from juggernauts. 'We had wanted to lower the cabin windows to improve visibility', he wrote, 'and even though such designs were already on the market, and even though there had been a horrific spate of deaths, mainly of female cyclists, we were told that we had to wait for the EU to legislate on the matter.' He concluded by saying: 'If a country cannot pass a law to save the lives of female cyclists ... then I don't see how that country can truly be called independent.'[19]

What he failed to remark upon was the role of UNECE, which in 1958 had concluded an Agreement on 'harmonised technical UN Regulations for the approval and certification of new wheeled vehicles, their equipment and parts'. Administering a global body known as the World Forum for Harmonisation of Vehicle Regulations (WP.29), this was the first attempt – pre-dating any activity by the then EEC in the field – to create a single market in automobile manufacture, and on a global scale.[20] In 1998, the

---

[14] European Commission, Regulation (EU) No. 1169/2011 of 25 October 2011 on the provision of food information to consumers.

[15] Jam and Similar Products Regulations 2003.

[16] Council Directive 2001/113/EC of 20 December 2001 relating to fruit jams, jellies and marmalades and sweetened chestnut purée intended for human consumption.

[17] *Daily Telegraph*, 22 February 2012, 'Couple left in a jam by EU regulations'; *Daily Mail*, 23 February 2013, 'When is a jam not a jam? Preserve maker in a pickle after EU jobsworths tell her apple spread doesn't qualify'.

[18] *Codex* Standard for Jams (Fruit Preserves) and Jellies – Stan 79-1981.

[19] BBC News, 9 July 2018, 'Boris Johnson's resignation letter and May's reply in full'.

[20] Economic Commission for Europe, 'World Forum for Harmonisation of Vehicle Regulations (WP.29): How It Works'.

European Union had become a 'contracting party' to UNECE, and, from 2007 onwards, had 'outsourced' its vehicle regulation to WP.29, adopting 'UN regulations' into EU law.[21] Thus, the originator of vehicle construction standards was no longer the EU but UNECE.

Under the direction of Johnson as London mayor, Transport for London (TfL) sponsored a preliminary study for improving the 'direct vision' in heavy goods vehicles.[22] However, UNECE found that proposed standards would have had the effect of banning 28 of 51 current vehicle models available in the EU. Furthermore, the core principle of UN regulations was that they should be 'technology neutral', allowing manufacturers flexibility in achieving the desired outcome. And when it came to improving direct vision, researchers categorised five different ways of making improvements, from changing cab designs to fitting additional windows, with no single solution applicable to all types of vehicle. To add to the complexity, methodologies for assessing compliance also had to be developed and agreed.[23]

Given that the UK no longer produced heavy goods vehicles on any scale, it was therefore dependent on the national authorities of supplier states, spread throughout the world, to develop new safety standards. The agreed mechanism for this was WP.29. The organisation is in the process of delivering various instruments.[24] When produced, these are automatically adopted by the EU. Yet, from Johnson, there was no understanding of this regulatory system. But what was equally striking was that two so-called 'fact-checker' websites weighed into the debate to dispute Johnson's claim that the issue illustrated problems with EU regulation.[25] Neither mentioned the role of UNECE, thus perpetuating public (and their own) ignorance.

A final example is the law on the classification, packaging and labelling of dangerous substances, which was originally defined by the EU for its own member states.[26] In 1992, the legislative lead was transferred to the UN

[21] Directive 2007/46/EC of 5 September 2007 establishing a framework for the approval of motor vehicles and their trailers, and of systems, components and separate technical units intended for such vehicles. Repealed by Regulation (EU) 2018/858 of 30 May 2018 on the approval and market surveillance of motor vehicles and their trailers, and of systems, components and separate technical units intended for such vehicles.
[22] Loughborough University, *The Design of Category N3 Vehicles for Improved Driver Direct Vision: Final Report*, August 2014.
[23] Composite, from multiple UNECE and related documents.
[24] For instance, see UNECE press release, 16 October 2018, 'Draft regulation will aim to reduce cyclist and pedestrian deaths caused by trucks' blind spots'.
[25] Channel 4 News, 10 July 2018, 'Boris Johnson lied about EU safety regulation in his resignation letter'; *Full Fact*, 10 July 2018, 'Do EU rules prevent safer lorries?'
[26] Council Directive 67/548/EEC of 27 June 1967 on the approximation of laws, regulations and administrative provisions relating to the classification, packaging and labelling of dangerous substances.

Conference on Environment and Development (UNCED), through which eventually emerged the Globally Harmonised System of Classification and Labelling of Chemicals (GHS), which is now administered by UNECE. The first version of the code was formally approved in December 2002 and published in 2003.[27] This, plus revisions, has been adopted as EU law.[28]

This regulation acknowledged that trade in such goods related not only to the internal market, but also to the global market. In many respects, it represented a legislative *tour de force* in introducing a single global code for hazard marking on chemical products. Predictably, as the regulation came into force, applying to a wide range of consumer products, the UK media launched into complaint mode about 'EU bureaucrats', one newspaper wrongly claiming that Fairy Liquid household detergent would have to be marked as 'corrosive'.[29] Not once was the true origin of the law mentioned.

THE DOUBLE COFFIN LID

What Johnson and his government did in early 2020, when they formally started the process of negotiating the UK's 'future relationship' with the EU, was, in regulatory terms, akin to a horror movie scene, where the hapless victim is trapped alive in an as yet unburied coffin. Having broken through the lid in a bid to escape, he finds to his consternation that there is another lid over the first.

So it was with the EU's regulatory code – and especially its Single Market *acquis*. In attempting to implement the 'Vote Leave' mantra of 'taking back control' and the oft-expressed ambition of making 'our own laws when we leave the EU', Johnson would find that once we had dispensed with EU laws in many areas, we would have to implement many of the same provisions. In the field of vehicle regulation, for instance, while the UK would no longer be required to adopt EU regulation, as full members of UNECE and contracting parties to the WP.29 Agreements, we would be bound by exactly the same codes.

The range of these standards-setting organisations is extraordinary. In the food and related fields, for instance, *Codex* is by no means unique. It is part of the UN Food and Agriculture Organization (FAO), and is one of three recognised by the SPS Agreement. The other two are the International

---

[27] United Nations ST/SG/AC.1/30/Rev 4 (4th revised edition).
[28] Regulation (EC) No. 1272/2008 of 16 December 2008 on classification, labelling and packaging of substances and mixtures.
[29] *Daily Express*, 15 July 2015, 'Now EU bureaucrats claim Fairy Liquid is "DANGEROUS" – and needs a warning label'; *Daily Telegraph*, 15 July 2015, 'Mild, green "Fairy" labelled "corrosive" by the EU'. The *Express* subsequently deleted its report.

Plant Protection Convention (IPPC) and the Office International des Epizooties, the international organisation for animal health. These 'three sisters' account for 28 per cent of the Single Market *acquis*. Outside the EU, as a member of the FAO and its subsidiary organisations, the UK would still be bound by its provisions.

Some standards are generated by single issue, or sector-specific, organisations (or groups of organisations). One such is the convention on transboundary movements of hazardous waste, created by an ad hoc body set up in response to a public outcry over exports of toxic waste to Africa and other developing countries. The convention was agreed in March 1989, entered into force in 1992 and its provisions were adopted into EU law in 1993.[30]

The more important examples of the 'double coffin lid' phenomenon lie in the financial sector, where in the wake of the 2008 financial crisis a huge raft of legislation was implemented, such as the EU's measures on the adequacy of banking capital, known as the CR IV Package. But, like much of the financial law of the period, this had been 'downloaded' from elsewhere, in this case from the Basel Committee on Banking Supervision (BCBS) in the form of the Basel III agreement.[31]

The BCBS itself is a committee of the Bank for International Settlements (BIS), the latter established in 1930 as a bank under Swiss law. Its share capital is owned by 63 central banks, representing countries from around the world that together account for about 95 per cent of world GDP. It is not, therefore, a governmental organisation and has no supranational powers. The authority of the BCBS stems from a 1996 report by the G7 finance ministers that called for effective supervision in all important financial marketplaces, including those of emerging market economies. It works alongside the G7 and the 'top tier' organisations such as the Financial Stability Board (FSB), together with the IMF, the World Bank and the OECD, to provide the template for banking law of global application.[32]

In an evaluation of post-crisis regulation in 2013, a House of Lords Committee found that when it came to EU banking laws, 'it is likely that the UK would have implemented the vast bulk of the financial sector regulatory framework had it acted unilaterally, not least because it was closely engaged

---

[30] Council Regulation (EEC) No. 259/93 of 1 February 1993 on the supervision and control of shipments of waste within, into and out of the European Community.

[31] European Banking Authority website, 'Implementing Basel III in Europe'. Implemented as Directive 2013/36/EU of 26 June 2013 on access to the activity of credit institutions and the prudential supervision of credit institutions and investment firms.

[32] Statutes of the Bank for International Settlements; multiple BIS websites.

in the development of the international standards from which much EU legislation derives'.[33] Equally, in a post-Brexit environment, the UK would be implementing the same regulatory framework. The idea that it could 'take back control' and make its own laws to govern an industry that operates on a global scale is not realistic.

Perhaps of even more importance than financial services law, certainly in terms of overall cost, are the many measures directed at combating climate change, together with the related measures on energy. The UK has been bound by the EU's Renewable Energy Strategy and the Climate and Energy Package, but this implemented the UN Framework Convention on Climate Change, the Kyoto Protocol, and subsequent agreements.[34] Furthermore, EU law is largely irrelevant. The UK's own 2008 Climate Change Act not only takes in the Kyoto commitments; it expands upon them, exceeding EU requirements. Post-Brexit, the Johnson administration has already committed to upholding the UK's climate change commitments, and is going further with 'net zero', bringing forward a ban on the sale of new diesel and petrol cars, and introducing a 'green industrial revolution'.[35]

THE BRUSSELS EFFECT

To add still further to post-Brexit complications, there is yet another phenomenon that will have a considerable impact on the regulatory environment. This is 'The Brussels effect', a term coined by academic Anu Bradford in her book of the same name describing 'a deeply underestimated aspect of European power that the discussion on globalisation and power politics overlooks: Europe's unilateral power to regulate global markets'.[36]

The basis of the effect is 'unilateral regulatory globalisation', a process that occurs when a single state is able to extend the reach of its laws and regulations beyond its borders through market mechanisms, resulting in the globalisation of standards. The phenomenon has been noted in the context of what has been dubbed the 'California effect', where, due to its large market and preference for strict consumer and environmental regulations, the state of California has been able to set the regulatory standards for other states. Businesses willing to export to California must meet its standards, and the

---

[33] House of Lords European Union Committee, *5th Report of Session 2014–15*, op. cit.
[34] Council Decision 94/69/EC of 15 December 1993 concerning the conclusion of the United Nations Framework Convention on Climate Change.
[35] Gov.uk, 18 November 2020, 'PM outlines his Ten Point Plan for a Green Industrial Revolution for 250,000 jobs'.
[36] Oxford University Press, 2020.

economies of scale from production to uniform standards gives firms an incentive to apply the same (strict) standards to their entire production.

This expands to become the Brussels effect, when firms trading internationally find that it is not legally or technically feasible, or economically viable, to produce to different standards for different markets. When trading with the EU requires foreign companies to adjust their conduct or production to EU standards – which often represent the most stringent standards – they tend to adopt them uniformly throughout their entire enterprises, even in areas not covered by EU law. On that basis, the ability of the UK to repatriate its technical law, and undergo a programme of deregulation, would be of little value. Dominated by the Brussels effect, UK-based manufacturers trading internationally would still maintain conformity with EU law.

THE DEMOCRATIC IDEA

The changes that were to come and are still shaping events have profound effects on the nature of our societies. But in the early days of the European *projet*, the issues were so much simpler, and were to remain so until the last decade of the twentieth century and the first decades of the twenty-first. But, in a sense, Monnet and his successors redefined international territory, creating a unique, supranational structure that, to this day, stands unique. Nowhere has it been replicated in the form that has emerged.

But, in post-war Europe, where fragile new democracies were struggling to emerge, the one thing above all that the *projet* could never be, because by definition it had never been intended to be, was in the remotest sense democratic. The whole purpose of a supranational body is to stand above the wishes of individual nations and peoples. When Monnet and Salter first conceived their idea of a supranational 'United States of Europe', it never entered their minds that people should be consulted. They were technocrats who thought that the future of Europe would best be served by placing it under the role of a government of technocrats like themselves, men whose only interest was efficient co-operation to pursue a common goal, unsullied by any need to resort to all the messy, unpredictable business of elections and the other, untidy components of democracy.

Nowhere more than in Britain, however – except perhaps Norway, which has rejected in two separate referendums the idea of membership – has the dominance of an alien, supranational authority been so continually, and ultimately successfully challenged. In theory, Brexit has restored to the United Kingdom – for as long as it remains intact – its long-lost sovereignty, the ability to control its own borders and to make its own laws. The nation that gave to the world the idea that democracy relies on the right of the people to dismiss a government that has failed them, has shrugged off a form of government that was essentially a one-party state, in which the same unaccountable ruling elite would be permitted to remain in power for ever.

However, no sooner were the so-called 'Brexiteers' revelling in their victory, insisting that their new-found sovereignty should not be compromised, than the very object of their desire was fading, rather like the rainbow that disappears as one approaches its end. The problem, in a practical sense, is the ambiguity over the meaning of sovereignty. Traditionally, this has been assumed to be the *right* to govern, with a sovereign being a person on whom was conferred a divine, i.e., God-given, right to rule. Although sovereignty is often elided with power, the concept works better if it is treated as an absolute, distinct from power. Where sovereignty stands alone, it requires power in order to exercise it. And the latter is relative and variable – and can be delegated. A 'sovereign' can have power in some areas but not in others.[37]

Within that framework, even as a member of the European Union, the UK had kept its sovereignty intact – evidenced by the right to withdraw, which had existed before Article 50.[38] Thus, when Edward Heath claimed that joining the EEC meant 'no essential loss of sovereignty', he was not entirely incorrect, although more than a little disingenuous. It would have been better – and more honest – had he stated that there had been an essential loss of *power*, which would increase over time. Mostly, when sovereign states conclude treaties, they do not cede their inherent rights to govern.[39] Where trade and like agreements give treaty organisations that they create powers to frame regulations or standards, the nations are simply delegating their powers. Sovereignty is preserved as long as states reserve the right to end the agreements and to recover their powers.

The differences between the supranational and the intergovernmental are several. In the EU, power is ceded to the Commission, which makes the regulatory proposals that, in most instances, are approved by majority decision. In the intergovernmental scenario, the power to propose is retained by the states, and measures are largely approved by unanimity,

---

[37] A sovereign can even be devoid of power, such as when they are a minor or incapacitated and the power is exercised by a regent. The term 'regent' itself helps to illustrate the distinction between sovereignty and power. Derived from the Latin *regens*, meaning ruling or governing, it implies a separation between the person and the power, especially when a fully empowered sovereign might be termed the *regnant* monarch.

[38] As in the Vienna Convention on the Law of Treaties.

[39] An example of an exception being the 1706 Treaty of Union between England and Scotland.

or states will often have to opt in before they take effect. However, the outcome of each process can be the same. Once adopted, states are bound by their decisions – even where the routes taken are different. In each case, sovereignty is retained. What changes in each system is the balance of power.

With Brexit, and the expiry of the transition period, the UK is now committed to an intergovernmental path, with its trading arrangements managed through the medium of free trade agreements. This has been done in the name of democracy, on the basis that the country is no longer subordinate to the essentially anti-democratic European Union. But there is an inherent flaw in the assumption that distancing the nation from the EU is necessarily an improvement. In many respects, the transfer of powers from the Commission and EU institutions has empowered the executive without noticeably enhancing democracy.

In the UK, as a constitutional monarchy, the sovereignty of the British people is not formally acknowledged. It remains with the Crown but the power is split between the executive, which acts in the name of the Crown, and parliament, which has limited power of approval and scrutiny. Talk of parliament being 'sovereign' should be qualified. Effectively, it is sovereign only in its own house. It has certain prescribed rights exercisable within its own institutional context, but those rights are limited by statute and convention. But, as is all too painfully evident, with a weak parliament in thrall to the party-political system, power in the post-Brexit period has passed from one largely unaccountable body to another. The *kratos* that is the essential part of democracy, as a complement to the *demos*, shows no sign of being closer to the people than it has ever been.

In that context, there is nothing intrinsically democratic about intergovernmentalism, and some will argue that a fully democratic society is incompatible with globalisation, regardless of the means by which it is brought about.[40] Thus, while one can rail against the lack of democracy in the EU, it has to be said that its commitment to transparency, manifest in the accessibility of information via its websites, is a model that the UK could do well to emulate. By contrast, the proceedings of UNECE are opaque, with its website difficult to navigate and its meetings poorly reported. When it comes to the *Codex* and the other 'sisters', mere opacity would be a distinct improvement, while the BCBS, the FSB and the alphabet soup of acronyms that identify the galaxy of financial standards institutions could hardly be less transparent if they relocated themselves on the far side of the moon.

---

[40] See, for instance, Rodrik, Dani (2012), *The Globalization Paradox: Why Global Markets, States, and Democracy Can't Coexist* (Oxford University Press).

While EU institutions might strive to be transparent, and the British government continues to pay lip-service to keeping its citizens informed, there is little point in sketching out details of legislative proposals, or inviting consultation and debate, if the issues at hand were decided years earlier at global level by often peripatetic committees from obscure institutions and handed down for implementation by unknowing ministers advised by anonymous officials. In terms of outcome, it makes little difference to the British public what route the final instrument takes. The effect will be the same, with not the slightest concession to the democratic process.

THE FINAL ACT

The largely unrecognised background of globalisation had not only permeated the EU's legislative *acquis*. So fundamental had it become to the Union's way of working that it defined the structure and content of its more recent 'next generation' trade agreements. These encompassed the treaties with South Korea, Canada and, latterly, Japan. Unlike the Free Trade Agreement signed with Norway in 1974 in the wake of its rejection of EEC membership, which ran to 19 pages including the annex, these were monster documents: the South Korean Agreement took 1,338 pages, while the Comprehensive Economic and Trade Agreement (CETA) with Canada comprised 1,598. It was inevitable, therefore, that the EU–UK Trade and Cooperation Agreement (TCA) signed on 30 December 2020, the final act of Britain's tortuous membership of the EU, would be more of the same. And indeed it was.

Stretching to 1,246 pages, structure and content followed a similar pattern. Johnson's much vaunted 'zero tariff, zero quota deal' was the least part of it, with the pride of place reserved for a comprehensive institutional structure built round a Partnership Council. This supported a Trade Partnership Committee, which in turn supported a network of ten 'Trade Specialised Committees' and three working groups. Directly reporting to the Council were eight subject-specific 'Specialised Committees' and one additional working group, the whole matrix amounting to 20 functional bodies. The purpose of these was to deal with the ongoing performance of the agreement, and to manage its development, expanding its scope over time. Far from being the end point – a 'fire and forget' agreement, so to speak – this set the framework for a future relationship that was intended to deepen and mature.

As to Johnson's claim to have 'ensured the UK's full control of our laws and our regulations', which he had repeated when opening the Commons debate on 30 December, this was more in his imagination than a reflection of reality. As it had with its other comprehensive agreements, the EU had built into the TCA a wide range of international standards-setting bodies, where common adoption of standards was a mandatory element.

Thus, while the UK had 'broken free' of EU law, it was still – for instance – bound by the UNECE/WP.29 vehicle regulations, the only difference being that, instead of implementing them via the EU, the British government could adopt them directly, without the 'middle man'. Nevertheless, via the institutional structure of the agreement, the EU was able to monitor the implementation of the standards and commence proceedings (and sanctions) in the event of default. From climate change and environmental standards, to labour standards, food, animal welfare, plant health, manufacturing standards, intellectual property and much else, the UK was bound in lockstep to EU standards that all originated from the same sources. Having broken through the first 'coffin lid', the UK was confronting the second. The legislative independence was largely illusionary.

THE ULTIMATE DECEPTION

In the earlier editions of our book, we examined the question of whether the driving force behind the European Union was more self-deception than deception. But with the clarity and perspective of nearly twenty years on, as a new chapter in history is being written, that question can be addressed anew, in a way that was hardly possible when there was so much unfinished business those 20 years ago.

If one accepts that deception played a part in the establishment of the EEC and its subsequent development (and many do not), the further question arises as to the level at which that deception arose, and its location. It has been observed, for instance, that politicians from most if not all nations can be two-faced, saying one thing to their counterparts in the councils of 'Europe' and different things to their domestic audiences. In that context, the deception stems from the highest level but is localised – tailored to specific audiences.

However, deception is undoubtedly more effective when combined with self-deception on the part of recipients. It is this combination that was seen in the 1975 UK referendum, where the advocates of political integration did not rush to display their enthusiasm for their cause, while the majority of the British nation was not particularly interested in that message.

On the other hand, deception is perhaps at its most powerful when self-deception and the willingness to deceive are combined in one person or group. On reflection, that seems to have been the dynamic that first drove Macmillan and Heath into believing that membership of the EEC was the answer to Britain's post-colonial problems, and then motivated them to convince the rest of the nation that theirs was the correct path to follow, using deception where argument failed to convince, or reality might have tarnished the vision.

It is here that we can draw a parallel between those who sought to take us into the EEC and some of those who, many years later, strove to remove us from the European Union. In the first instance, membership was seen as the (or an) answer to Britain's structural problems, and, more importantly, as defining for the political classes a role that could fill the political vacuum caused by loss of Empire. At the other end, there were those who would attribute most or many of Britain's structural problems to membership of the EU, whence leaving was seen as the solution. In neither case were the protagonists correct. Joining the EEC was no more a cure for Britain's problems than was leaving the EU. Specifically, of the nostrums offered by the Conservatives in their 2019 manifesto, the assertion that the UK could 'take back control of our laws' defies reality. If not the 'double coffin lid', then the 'Brussels effect' will ensure that there can be very little substantive change to those laws that hitherto had been decided by Brussels.

Intriguingly, after Theresa May had delivered her Lancaster House speech in January 2017, Christoph Scheurmann, writing for *Der Spiegel*, described her as *realitätsblind*, which can be loosely translate as 'in cloud cuckoo land'.[41] Self-evidently, there was a significant element of self-deception, verging on the delusional, in a prime minister who believed she could broker 'a bold and ambitious Free Trade Agreement' that would mimic the UK's membership of the Single Market, while walking away from its obligations.

As for Boris Johnson, this was the man who was described by his former boss, Max Hastings, as 'a cavorting charlatan' who would be 'an unfunny joke' as prime minister, 'unfit for national office, because it seems he cares for no interest save his own fame and gratification'.[42] This was the same man who, having rejected May's Withdrawal Agreement, went on to sign up to an agreement that was infinitely worse, describing it as a 'fantastic deal'. Having then refused to extend the post-Brexit transition period, he ran the 'future relationship' talks to the wire, and then presented a lengthy treaty of 1,246 pages to Parliament, demanding that the implementing European Union (Future Relationship) Bill be passed in one day. This brought a whole new meaning to parliamentary democracy.

[41] 16 January 2017, '*Ich will, ich will, ich will*'.
[42] *Daily Mirror*, 26 June 2019.

But it was there, in that debate, that the prime minister opened a new chapter on a tale of deception that has spanned a century. While he claimed that, in leaving the Single Market, 'British exporters will not face a sudden thicket of trade barriers, but rather, for the first time in the history of EU agreements, zero tariffs and zero quotas', the leader of the Opposition, Kier Starmer, countered:

> The truth is this: there will be an avalanche of checks, bureaucracy and red tape for British businesses. Every business I have spoken to knows this; every business any Member has spoken to knows this. That is what they are talking about. It is there in black and white in the treaty.[43]

That was the truth. While the treaty did address tariffs and quotas, it did little to mitigate the effects of the 'non-tariff barriers' that protected the Single Market, or for that matter, provide access to the all-important services market. It was Britain's misfortune, therefore, that she entered a crucial period in her history guided by a leader whose lack of a grasp of the issues and the needs of the country was matched by self-deception of epic proportions. Understandably, at the end of the transition period, there were many who argued that Brexit should be reversed, although there was an unfortunate tendency to talk in generic terms, heedless of the fact that there were many different versions of Brexit. Yet only Johnson's version had been experienced, many considering it to have been a 'botch'.

However, nothing could change the fact that Britain, nearly fifty years previously, had been taken into a supranational construct without the informed consent of the people, imperfectly 'ratified' by the 1975 referendum and then extended, treaty by treaty, until even David Cameron had to concede that the people once again had to be consulted. When they were, the world – and in particular, the trading environment – had changed beyond all recognition from the 1970s, but the core, structural problems of the United Kingdom had not. Membership of the European Union had simply put them on hold, leaving our demons unsated.

This is essentially why the UK had to leave the EU. Having lost an empire and failed to find a role, as Dean Acheson had so perceptively put it, it had taken refuge in the then-EEC as a means of avoiding having to confront its new status. It is significant, therefore, that when it came to the campaign to leave the EU, none of the main protagonists sought out an exit plan that would have defined our role, other than the vaguest aspirations of a 'Global

---

[43] HC Deb, 30 December 2020, c524.

Britain', based on obsolete and unrealistic notions of 'free trade' that harped back to days of empire.

What was hardly explored was that, once out of the EU, Britain would have to confront that self-same issue that it had been avoiding for so long. And, while there are those who seek material gains from Brexit, the essential benefit from leaving the EU is that it paves the way for a debate on who we are as a nation, and how we define our role. To that extent, Brexit was never an answer to anything. It is simply the precursor to something bigger and more important, creating an opportunity better to define ourselves.

In particular, we might address what it means to be a democracy and whether, even, that form of government is viable in this crowded nation where the communications revolution has fractured any sense of a *demos*, the United Kingdom has never seemed so divided, and where our regulation is increasingly defined by globalisation. Without the stress of dealing with the divisive and contentious issue of our membership of the European Union, our nations might be better equipped to undertake that debate. But, if our membership has taught us anything at all, it is that single fact that, temperamentally, ideologically and by any other measure, the EU is an organisation to which we do not belong. That our leaders had to resort to deception to take us in, and then keep us there, tells its own story.

The difficulties that the UK found in negotiating a 'future relationship' with the EU reflect those same difficulties we had in being a fully committed member. And with many matters of detail as yet unresolved, it is probably the case that, before we are ever going to relate properly to our neighbours, we must define who we are. For the moment, though, even despite the extraordinary mess that has been made of the Brexit process, the great deception has come to an end. Even if it is only the beginning of the next one, that is a start.

INDEX

9/11, terrorist attack 392

Aachen, 'spirit of Charlemagne' 191
Academics, views of 207, 298, use of, 298, to
promote integration, 388
Abattoirs, closure of 307, slaughterhouse
crisis, 403, horsemeat, 531–532
Accession treaty 147–148, vote (EEC entry),
collaboration, 149, triumph for Heath, 150
Acheson, Dean 20, 27, 29, 42, Schuman Plan
'mistake', 47, 633
Acquis Communautaire 124, 192, 295
Action Committee for the United States
of Europe 61, 65, 66, 69, 76, in favour of
British entry, 118
Actions ponctuelles 242
Adenauer, Konrad 6, 10, 33, 36, 39, 40,
salvation of Europe, 41, 53, 56, 58, favours
customs union, 64, welcomes Euratom, 68,
84, meets de Gaulle, 96, state visit to France,
101, retirement, 112, funeral, 117
Adonnino, Pietro 217
Afghanistan 392, 393, 466, 497, 591 fn
Afriyie, Adam 544
Agencies, European 418
Agenda 2000 200 fn, 344, 358, 360, 362
Agnelli, Giovanni 5
Agriculture (see also CAP), and Nazis 14,
German concessions, 63, importance to
France, 67, 97–98
Ahern, Bertie 383, 387, 418, 419, 420, 421,
422, 424, 425, 430
Al Q'aeda 392, 420
Algeria, French war 73, 77
Allason, Rupert, MP 288
Allied Maritime Transport Council 11
Altafaj, Amadeu 518
Amato, Giuliano 474
American Committee on United Europe
(ACUE) 37 fn, 61
Amsterdam, Treaty of 337–338, 339, 340,
342, leftovers, 365, 376, 399
Anderson, Anne 424
Anderson, John 11
Andreotti, Giulio 220
Andrew Marr Show 514, 528, 529, 554, 561,
570, 580, 582, 589
Andriessen, Frans, 256
Anthem, European 6 fn, 203 fn, 342, 361, 474
Arab Spring 503–504
Archbishop of Canterbury (Michael
Ramsey) 170
Article 50 402, 536, leverage, 556, invoke
'straight away', 559, 569, no negotiations
without, 575, legal challenge, 576, deal
in two years, 577, notification, 578, 579,
extension to, 593, additional extension, 594,
Johnson's refusal to extend, 596, right to
withdraw, 628
Ashton, Catherine Margaret (Baroness) 492,
504, 547
Ashton, Joe 169
Atomic Energy Authority (UK) 64
Attali, Jacques 222
Attlee, Clement 44
Audibert, Jacques 578
Australia, as law-taker 620
Awkward partner 176 *et seq* 191
Azarov, Mykola 546
Aznar, José María 362, 392, 419, 421

Bach, Christian Friis 572
Baker, Steve 589
Balance of competences 540–541, 563

Baldry, Tony 328
Balfe, Richard. MEP 206
Balkenende, Jan Peter 442, 470, 475
Ball, George 31, 88, 202
Bananas, concessions 130, bendy, 570–571
Bangemann, Martin 207
Bank of England 231, 235, 245, 283, 338,
484 fn
Bank of International Settlements 245
Banks, Arron 570
Barroso, José Manuel 413, EU president,
430, 432, 434, rounds on France, 435,
financial framework, 436, 437, 440, 441,
right to an opinion, 442, 446, 451, reshuffle,
452, 'Sheriff of Nottingham', 454, 455, 'Who
Runs Britain?', 460, 461, 462, Pittsburgh
speech, 463, 'more Europe', 464, 467,
argues against word 'constitution', 468,
470, mini-summit, 471, tribute to Merkel,
473, 'dimensions of an empire', 474, 'not
a constitution', 475, treaty still 'alive', 480,
482, 484, second term, 487, 'marathon of
hurdles', 488, 495, 'painful reforms', 509,
510, debt crisis, 511, 'banking union',
519, promised treaty 'blueprint', 523, deal
on MFF, 535, 543, Humboldt University
speech, 553
Barber, Anthony 124, 125
Barclay, Sir Roderick 86
Barker, Alex 548
Barnier, Michel 376, 385, 397, 434, heads
Brexit taskforce, 575, sets out stall, 576,
meets May, 579, urges 'negotiating
seriously', 581, stresses need for 'unique
solution', 582, no announcements, 583,
'choreography' of deal, 584, colour-coded
version, 587, instructed to continue, 592,
596, trade talks, 599, UK 'going much
further', 601, 'disappointed', 602, deadline,
603, EP deadline; team tests positive for
coronavirus, 604, pressure to conclude, 605,
'little chance' of deal, 606
Baron, John, MP 526
Barrot, Jacques 460
Barteling, Simon 390
Basel Committee (on Banking
Supervision) 484
BBC, *That Was The Week That Was*
show 104, 'nobbling', 141, documentary
Poisoned Chalice, 147, 'fair balance', 165,
EU competences, misunderstand Single
European Act, 228, receptive to 'Europeanists',
259, Norwegian referendum result, 321,
disproportionate airtime, 345, CBI bias, 353,
361, report on EU jobs, 373–374, 425, 'Who
Runs Britain?' poll, 460, Solberg prominently
reported, 535, reports parties favouring EU
membership, 539, 541, misreports speech,
559, trots out 'received wisdom' on Norway,
540–541, documentary *Who Really Rules Us?*,
571, referendum result, 572
Beckett, Margaret 468
Belka, Marek 422, 423
Beneficial crisis 187, 264, BSE, 368, 9/11,
392–393, 421, euro, 492–493, 611
Benelux Memorandum 59, 60, 67
Benn, Tony 158, 169, 170
Benyon, Tom 151
Berlaymont building, opening 115, asbestos,
271, 482
Berlin, blockade 44, 84, wall, 95, fall of wall,
251, Declaration, 469
Berlusconi, Silvio 362 fn, 393, 399, 500, 511,
resigns, 514

Berthelot, René 356
Bertelsmann Stiftung 544, 617
Beveridge, William 18
Beyen, Johan, proposes customs union 58, 59
Bevin, Ernest 37
Biffen, John 231
Bisignani, Giovanni 497
Black Wednesday 282
Blair, Tony ix, 209, Labour leader, 318, BSE,
332, 336, EU mini-summit, 337, prime
minister, 338, European tour, 339, sets
position for Amsterdam, 340, quota-hoppers,
341, 'leading role in Europe', 345, presidency
preview, 346, limited options on euro, 347,
censured by EP, 348, presidency, 349, 352,
353, 358, St Malo, 359–360, rebate row,
362–362, 363, Toulouse, 364, 'what sort of
Europe?', 367, obsessed with euro, 369, calls
for debate, 370, beef ban, 371, path to Nice,
372, discredited claims, 374, new agenda,
375, ignorance on European Council, 380,
381, Nice, 382–384, meets Prodi in London,
385, re-elected, 386, 9/11, 392, 393, stranded,
394, 'very rude', 406, 'coalition of the willing',
408, 409, rules out euro referendum, 410,
red lines, 415–416,' nothing is agreed until
everything is agreed', 419, Rome, 420, loses
ally, 421, with Chirac, 423, constitution
agreed, 425, refuses referendum, 426,
constitution not 'constitutionally significant',
427, offers referendum, 428, announces
timing, 431, third term, 439, 'given up on
Europe', 442, budget row, 443 *et seq*, 'war
with France', 446, 'lacking political will',
447, 'strong man of Europe', 448, 'blowing
the trumpets', 449, EU presidency, 449,
Hampton Court, 452, budget dance, 452 *et
seq*, showdown, 456, promise on referendum,
459, Oxford speech, 462, 463, 'no consensus',
466, collision course, 469, joins forces, 470,
denies new treaty 'constitutional', 471, resigns
Labour leadership, 471, 472, perpetuates
deceit, 473, stands down, 473–474, 'last act',
475, speculation on president of European
Council, 477, warns 'economic suicide' to
leave EU, 542, 614, 615
Bloody British Question (BBQ) 192 *et seq*
Blum, Léon 36
Bolkestein, Frits 434
Bookerism 304 fn
Boothroyd, Betty 288
Bonino, Emma 324, 332, 341, 356, 366
Bono, José 419
Borg, Tonio 531
Borges, António 485
Bot, Bernard 461
Bovine Spongiform Encephalopathy
(BSE) 330–333, 348, 368, 458
Bradford, Anu 626
Brandt, Willy 120, 153, 154, retires, 156, 206
Bratteli, Trygve 145, 146
Bretherton, Russell 62, announces Britain's
withdrawal, 64
Brexit, milestone 516, name in circulation,
542, 551, implications of exit plan, 552, IEA
prize, 552, 557, no-deal, 574, 'Brexit means
Brexit'; new department, 575, 'massive
opportunity'; attempt to block, 576,
countdown, 578, bill, 578–579, May tries
for a stronger mandate, 579, 'war' over form
to take, 580, 'soft' vs 'hard', 581, internal
Irish border, 583, new barriers, 585, 588,
589, Raab takes portfolio, 590, Johnson's
'better Brexit', 591, resignations, 592,

Parliament's indicative votes, 593–594, not been able to deliver, 594, 'dead in a ditch', 596, Parliament instructs delay, 597, 'oven-ready deal', 597, extraordinary mess, 634
Briand, Aristide 1, 4, 7, 8, 13
BRINO 580
Britain in Europe 168, 170
Britain Stronger in Europe 569
British Air Line Pilots Association (BALPA) 543
British National Party (BNP) 486, 498, 565
Brittan, Leon 240, 254, 320, 324, 334, 345, 353
Brokenshire, James 589
Brown, Fred, Professor 390
Brown, George 116
Brown, Gordon, chancellor 330, 338, 347, Socialist manifesto for Europe, 354, on Today, 374, Stability and Growth Pact, 406, five tests, 410, 'federal state', 413, attacks Commission, 416, 'hard line' on CAP, 443, referendum, 459, 'embarrassing reprimand', 461, determined to block new treaty changes, 469, poisoned chalice, 472, prime minister, 474, resiles on referendum, 475, 'two-finger salute', 476, ratification Bill, 477, financial rescue, 481–482, loses election, 497
Brown, Nick 362
Brown, Roger 289
Brugmans, Dr Henri 32
Brussels, headquarters of EEC 75
Brussels effect 626 et seq
Brussels Treaty Organisation (BTO) 32, 34, 36
Budget, UK contribution 128, agreement on, 130, UK's 'massive disadvantage', 131, renegotiation, 166, Thatcher, 194 et seq, revisions to formula, 200
Bulgaria 369, 479, 483
Bundesbank 189, 190, 239, 240, 245, 250, 282, 314, 334, 339, 430, 505, 520, 533
Bush, George 237 fn, 255
Bush, George W. 407, 408, 409, re-elected, 431, 449
Business for New Europe 538
Business for Sterling 353
Butler, Sir Michael 172
Butler, R. A. 18
Byrne, David 372, 391

Cable, Vince 592
Callaghan, Jim 141, foreign secretary, 159, 160, memorandum on renegotiations, 161, discussion with Giscard d'Estaing, 162, 164, 167, 'Yes' campaign, 172, 173, 179, energy conference, 180, prime minister, 183, European Parliament, 183–184, policy on EEC, 186, 189, refuses to join EMS, 190, budget contributions, 192, vote of confidence, 192, rear-view mirrors, 202, 204 fn, 612
Callanan, Martin, MEP 519
Cameron, David ix, leadership contest, 439, 455, opposition leader, 458, broad policy on 'Europe', 461, demands constitution 'null and void', 466, stresses need for referendum, 472, quotes Blair on constitution, 473, 'cast-iron guarantee', 476, 485, backs away from referendum, 486, 488, can't hold a referendum; pledges renegotiation, 488–489, hung parliament, 497, coalition, 498, 'constructive approach' to Europe, 499, turn to immigration, 500, 'Canute moment' on budget, 500–501, introduces EU Referendum Bill, 501, supports treaty change, 505, annual budget ritual, 506, blocks use of EFSM, 509, seeks to remove UK from ESM, 510, told must call referendum, 511, 512, suggests repatriating powers; vote on referendum, 513, links treaty change to repatriation of powers, 514, called to identify powers; 'vetoes' new treaty, 515, conforms reality of two-speed Europe, 516, safety of cruise ships, 517, 'balance of competences', 521, ignores 'Fresh Start'; Commons demands budget reduction, 522, referendum 'happened regardless', 525, affirms support for referendum, 526, extolls merits of referendum, 527, demolition of 'Norway', 528–529, Bloomberg speech, 529–530, plans on migrants, 534, 'Plan for Britain's success', 537, moots Libya action, 541, 542, little headway on repatriating powers, 543, private member's Bill, 544, 545, discusses EU enlargement, 546, strategy appears assured; appearance deceptive, 548, fate sealed, 549, timing problems, 550, sets out renegotiation changes, 551, treaty change timetable 'impossible', 553, doubts on winning election, 554, 'humiliating defeat' on new president, 555, hints at exit, 556, turns again to immigration, 557, 'emergency brake', 558, demand for more contributions, 558–559, speech on immigration, 560, continues to argue for treaty change, 561, repeats promise of referendum, 562, asserts Europe 'isn't working properly', 563, wins election, 564, renegotiations started, 565, accepts no treaty change, 566, claims outcome of renegotiation 'legally binding', 567, announces referendum, 568, leads 'Remain' campaign, 569, complains of 'lies', 570, reflects on criticism, 573, resigns as prime minister, 574
Camps, Miriam 67, 79, 80, 81
Canada, loan from 27, OEEC, 79–80, concern over UK in EEC, 93, de Gaulle's complaint, 107, no concessions, 130, security conference, 178, Estai affair, 324, trade deal, 573, 580, 581, 586, 591, 598, 601, 603, EU deal, 630
CAP 86, idea of, myth of, 97 fn, 98, funding, 99, Agriculture Regulation, 113, Pompidou discusses with George Brown, 116–117, reason for rejecting British entry, 119, out of control, 120, new funding agreed, 121, UK payments, 125, cost of, 131, spending row, 197, 90 percent of budget, 203, runaway spending, 235, reform, 305, new constitution, 377, MacSharry reforms, 317, 'one-size-fits-all', 343
Carmichael, Alistair 557
Carrington, Lord 196, 207
Carswell, Douglas, MP 556, 557, 562, 564
Casetta, Louise 435
Cash, Bill 278, 286, 480, 513
Cassis de Dijon case 204
Castle, Barbara 116, 169
Catholic Herald 15
CBI 78, 140, 170, 255, Scottish, 282, 320, 345, membership poll, 353, 537, 538, 540, 545, 551, 586, 588
CE Mark 289, 303
CEEC 30, 31
CFP, see fisheries
Chalmers, Professor Damian 558
Chamberlain, Tom 290
Charlemagne prize 364
Charter of Fundamental Rights 369, 375, call for inclusion in treaty, 377, no more legal significance than Beano or Sun, 380, Blair 'at odds', 381, Blair refuses Nice declaration, 382, included in draft constitution, 398, new status accorded, 473, included in treaty, 473, 'concession' to Czech Republic, 488, return powers agenda, 499
Château Val-Duchesse 68
Chatham House 16, 17, 18, 187, 245
Cheney, Dick 405
Chirac, Jacques 220 fn, calls Thatcher 'housewife', 237, difficult to predict, 238, president, 325, anticipating enlargement, 334, election, 337, cohabitation, 338, Iraq, 348, meets Schröder, 359, St Malo, 359–360, opposition to Anglo-American axis, 361, Toulouse, 364, concert of nations, 378, core group, 379, 381, nightmare, 382, Nice, 383–384, threat of impeachment, 386, mini-summit, 392, 393, misdemeanours, 402, row, 'l'escroc' election victory, 404, 406, Élysée Treaty anniversary, 407, UN resolution, 407, 408, 409, 410, 411, breaches Stability and Growth Pact, 412, 414, 'big three', 419, 421, 423, 425, agrees referendum, 430, scandal, 433, corruption, 434–435, TV debate, 436–437, constitution poll, 440–441, emergency summit, 442, versus Blair, 443 et seq, 446, budget row, 447, 449, 451, domestic crisis, 452, attacks Blair, 453, 454, 456, 457, 461, deal with Merkel, 465, presidency ends, 471
Christian heritage 417
Churchill, Winston 4, 6, New York Saturday Evening Post, 7, Zurich speech, 24–25, Albert Hall, 25–26 Hague, 25, Strasbourg, 37, EDC, 54, dies, 113
Ciampi, Carlo 420
Citizens, of the European Union 213
Clark, Alan 262
Clarke, Kenneth 271, 276 fn, 321, 345, 352, 353, 369, 374
Clarke, Richard 71
Clayton, Will 28
Clegg, Nick 478, coalition, 498, deputy prime minister, 499, rift with Cameron, 510, resigns as Lib-Dem leader, 565
Climate change 395, 469, 470, 471, 482, 490, 626, 631
Coal and Steel Community 10, 50, 52, 55, 115, 183, 374, 610, 614
Cockfield, Arthur 221, 226, 233, replaced, 240
Codex Alimentarius Commission (CAC) 538–539, 571, 572, 621, 622, 624, 625
Cohesion fund 274
Collaborators 21–22
Comitology 298
Commission, in League of Nations 13, supranational character, 57, 67, 73, combined executive and civil service, 75, financed, 76, OECD, 80, dilution of powers, 96, CAP proposals, 98, Britain's application, 111, empty chair, 113, 114, Berlaymont, 115, 121, proposal for CFP, 133–135, 138, European Movement, 140, Heath's advice on, 146, role in Paris Summit, 153, European Council, 156, rejects notion of 'renegotiation', 160, UK contributions, stance on, 166, support for 'Yes' campaign, 170, warns on 'additionality', 178–179, 180, on fishing resource, 182, pig meat, 185–186, study group on EMU, 187, proposal to replace, 188, ERM 'vital', 191, budget question, 193–194, correction mechanism, 200–201, low politics, 203, Cassis de Dijon, 204, 209, TAC allocations, 210, new treaty, 223, role in IGC, 225–226, immigration policy, 226, 13th government, 233, 234, budgetary situation, 235, CAP spending, 236, own resources, 238, power over money transfers, 239, pushing frontiers of competences, 242, political role, 248, Social Charter, 252, trade powers, 256, Thatcher's response, 258, confirmed as executive, 261, question on right of initiative, 262, core activities, 265, climax at Maastricht, 268–269, no role in defence policy, 270, single institutional framework, 271, extended competences, 274, Major's claims, 275, admits right of initiative remains, 276, more powers not ruled out, 278, attempt to set limits, 279, 280, gesture, 285, no laws withdrawn, 290, continued border controls, 291, White Paper on internal market, 292–293, officials, 297, origin of proposals, 298, 302, scrapping forms, 303, effect of CAP reforms, 305, vegetable 'directives', 306, slaughterhouses, 306–307, failure of fishing policy, 308–309, 'military junta', 312, control over research and development, 315, 318, 323, 324, greater intrusiveness, 326, internal workings, 327, IGC proposals, 328–329, beef

ban, 330–331, 332, sabotage, 333, gloomy picture, 334, 343, 345, agreement on euro, 347, withholding tax, 347, regional policy, 352, tax harmonisation, 354, fraud crisis, 355–358, 'den of vipers', 357, *Concours* exams cheating, 356, *Corpus Juris*, 359, 'college' resigns, 362, new Commission, 366–367, lifts beef ban, 371, IGC proposals, 372, 'strategic objectives' 373, rivalry with Council, 375, draft constitution, 376, Chirac's response, 377, counter-attack, 378–380, Blair's view, 382, summit squabble, 383, Schröder Plan, 386, governance white paper, 388, role in FMD, 390–391, 'waning influence', 393, 9/11 response, 394, role in constitutional convention, 397, Andreasen affair, 403, caves in on deficits, 404, lacks powers, 406, turning point, 410, more fraud, 412, call for change to economic policy, 413, humiliated, 416, illegal suspension of rules, 419, reduced size, 423, proposals on deficit enforcement, 430, row over Services Directive, 435, financial framework, 436, Plan-D on constitution, 452, delivery failures, 464, recession forecast, 482, high-level group, 483, financial regulation, 487, criticises Greece, 489, 493, budget, 500, migration crisis, 503, cruise ship standards, 517–518, treaty change 'blueprint', 523, deal on budget, 535, state of union address, 542, demands budget top-up, 543, Five Presidents Report
Commission on Security and Cooperation in Europe (CSCE) 266
Committee of Permanent Representatives (Coreper) 76, 298, 299, 300
Committee of the Regions 274
Committee for European Economic Co-operation. See CEEC
Common Agricultural Policy. See: CAP
Common currency, not possible without common government 19
Common energy policy 413
Common Fisheries Policy. See Fisheries
Common Market 73, British cabinet votes for entry, 90, second application, 115, Wilson's cabinet votes, 118, final application, 124 *et seq*, 'brutally and dangerously re-opened', 161
Commonwealth, preferences 70, 88, 'problem', response to Britain's EEC talks, 93, de Gaulle, 118
Community preference 129
Completing the Internal Market (report) 222
Concorde 82
Conditionality 505, 520, 521
Confederation of British Industry. See CBI
Conference on Security and Co-operation in Europe 178
Connolly, Bernard 191 fn, 231 fn, 327, 403
Constitution (European), Blair enthusiastic for ix, federal, 16–17, Spinelli, 23, Hague Congress, 34, Europe's first, 55, Treaty of Rome as, 73, ECJ confirms, 204, calls for, 261, Commission argues for, 328, Fischer promotes, 355, 361, existing treaties amounting to, 369, Hague 'hell-bent' remark, 372, Fischer repeats, 376, University Institute in Florence draft, 376, Schröder and Chirac propose, 377, Blair rejects idea, 380, 381, 382, proposed by 2005, 385, decision at Laeken, 385, Schröder Plan, 386, 387, Prodi announces, 393, Blair 'stranded', 394, Laeken Declaration, 395, Spinelli 'crowning dream', 396, Convention, 396–402, 409, summit plan, 414, is it necessary?, 417, 418, positions 'deadlocked', 419, work unlikely to resume, 420, accelerated adoption, 421, warnings about rejection, 422, treaty agreed, 425, Blair refuses referendum, 426, not ' constitutionally significant', 427, agrees vote, 428, text not complete,

429, new members 'bribe'; France agrees referendum, 430, leaders sign; Howard promises referendum, 431, Lithuania first to ratify, 432, Spanish referendum, 433, becomes best-seller in France, 436, French and Dutch vote 'No', 441, ratification 'dance', 442, kicked into long grass, 444, 'pause for reflection', 446, Plan D for dialogue, 448, Commission publishes, 452, 'covered in snow', 460, treaty 'dead', 461, 'Sound of Europe' conference, 462, 'back door' implementation, 464, rebranding; 'mistake to call it a constitution', 465, Merkel 'firmly convinced' of need, 467, decision to revive, 468, transformed into 'reform' treaty, 468–469, Britain on 'collision course', 469, new treaty by 2008; Blair and Balkenende join forces against, 470, new treaty being assembled, 470; 'presentational changes', 471, Blair passes 'poisoned chalice' to Brown; 'substance' of original preserved, 472; IGC convened, 472–473, constitutional concept 'abandoned', 473, leaders decide document to be 'unreadable', 474 (Continues as: Lisbon Treaty)
Conservative Party 91, 156, 189, 220, 245, 246, 250, 258, 259, in tatters, 283, wreckage of, 288, 352, 455, 543, 544, 551, 555, 556, avoid long-term damage, 569, 576, state of war, 580, 582
Cook, Robin 336, 338, 349
Cooper, Duff 17
Cooper, Yvette 588
Corbyn, Jeremy 594, 597
Corpus Juris 359
Costa Concordia 516
Coudenhove-Kalergi, Count Richard 5, 16, 36, 51
Coulson, John, letter on Messina 60–61
Council of Europe 32, 39, decision to establish, 36, Strasbourg, seat of, 37, EDC, 54
Court of Auditors 274, 321, 355, 357, 358, 394, 403
Copenhagen criteria (enlargement) 313
Council of European Municipalities and Regions (CEMR) 351
Council of Ministers 13, 31, 35, genesis of (EEC), 49, 52, 73, staff for, 76, 79, 86, 96, 105, 121, 131, fisheries policy, 136, 156, 159, 161, takes all important decision, 172, 179, 188, 204, impotence, 205, 215, 224 fn, 232, as senate, 258, 261, 282, 297, 'democratic', 299, 300, 379, 382, 386, 397, 400, 415, 553
Council on Foreign Relations 16, 28
Couve de Murville, Maurice 97, 102, 113, 116
Cowen, Brian 323, 480
Cowgill, Brigadier Anthony 277 fn
Cox, Pat 399, 423
Craxi, Bettino 206, 223, calls vote at Council, 224
Creagh, Mary 530–531, 533
Credit Lyonnais bank 409
Cresson, Édith 356, 357
Creutzfeldt-Jakob Disease (CJD) 330
Cridland, John 538, 540, 546
Crimea 547
Cripps, Sir Stafford 44
Crosland, Anthony 183, death, 192
Cruise ship safety 517
Cuban Missile Crisis 106
Cucumber rule 571, UNECE, 572
Cummings, Dominic 568, campaign director, 569, slogan, 570, 'genius', 573. Johnson recruits, 596, departs from No.10, 604
Currie, Edwina 244
Curry, W. B., The Case for Federal Union (book) 17
Curtis, Lionel 16, 17
Customs union 5, 8, 10, 30, 35, 58, 65, 69, 70,

71, 78, 105, 166, EEC reduced to, 203, effect of, 291, Moscow-led, 541, breaking from, 576, 580, 581, 583, 586, 587, 588, 608, 618
Cyprus, applies to join EU 254, 'big bang' enlargement, 294, allowed to join, 322, negotiations, 344, 439 fn, 468, bailout, 519–520, horsemeat, 531
Czech Republic 344, 368, floods, 405, joins EU, 410, 412, 430, 436, referendum, 440, 444, car production, 484, 485, 487, 488

D'Aubert, François 321
Daily Mail, '*Toppled*' 408, 'blueprint for tyranny', 425, 'Blair's surrender', 457
Dante Alighieri (De Monarchia) 9
Darling, Alistair 498, 557
Davis, David, leadership contest 439, chief negotiator, 575, White Paper, 577–578, tries to link cash settlement with trade deal, 579, boast of by-passing Brussels, 580, urges talks on future relationship, 582, complains about Notices to Stakeholders; misconceptions, 585, 589, 'max fac'; resigns, 589
Davison, Ian 180
Davignon, Étienne 122, Report, 125, adopted, 127, 128
Debré, Michel 94, 220 fn
De Clercq, Willy, *Comité des Sages* 312
De Gasperi, Alcide 33, 48, 53, 220
De Gaulle, Charles 19, 20–21, 77, 84, opposition to EDC, 56, president, 78, obstacle to UK entry, 91, view of 'European Communities', 93, *Europe des Etats*, 94, meets Macmillan, 100, state visit to Germany, 103, decides on veto, 107, delivers 1st veto, 108, 'Treaties are like maidens and roses', 112, veto on QMV, meets Wilson, 117, *Le Grand Non*, 118, holds referendum, 120
De Guindos, Luis 519
De Jong, Piet 121
De Larosière, Jacques 483, 484
De Manio, Jack 141
De Michelis, Gianni 266
De Pange, Comte Jean 17, 18
De Rougemont, Denis 33
De Silguy, Yves-Thibault 220 fn, 311, 346, 354, 360
De Villepin, Dominique 407, 441
De Villiers, Phillipe 434, 438
Deception, Monnet's strategy 57
Dehaene, Jean-Luc 318, 368, 392, 395, 425
Dehousse, Fernand 118
Delamuraz, Jean-Pascal 294
Delors, Jacques 205, commission president, 219–220, single market, 222, 223, 224, defines agenda for IGC, 225, includes EMU in treaty, 226, 'white stones', 227, 228, 'humiliation' by Thatcher, 232–233, annoys Thatcher, 233–234, budget 'package', 235, parlous state of finances, 236, structural funds, achievement, 239, committee of wise men, 240–241, addresses EP, 242, TUC congress, 242–243, 245, Report, 246–247, Social Charter, 249, sets out agenda for IGC, 252, 'true federation', 252–253, *Acte Unique Bis*, 253, blocks enlargement, 254, distrust of GATT, 255–256, support of Soviet Union, 257, 'Up Yours', 258, Thatcher downfall, 259, common foreign and security policy, 261, expects draft treaty welcome, 262, Europe 'rather ineffectual', 263, draft treaty 'unworkable', 271, brooding, 272, major success, 273, speech on subsidiarity, 280, 'big idea', 284 *et seq*, regional aid, 285, 'visionary speech', 293, 'European village', 293–294, 'big bang' enlargement, 294, resiles on Efta promise, 295, appoints 'wise men', 312, complains of 'back-sliding', 313, crows on ERM, 314, white paper on jobs, 315, road map, 316, buys fishing rights, 316, *Daily Mail*, 317, due to retire, 318, attacks Lamont, 321, last Council, 322, ambitions for

Europe, 328, Trans-European Network, 333, re-floating the EU, 392, warns of 'political cataclysm', 435, 618
Democratic deficit 343
Democratic idea 627 *et seq*
Democratic Ulster Unionist Party 562
Democratic Unionist Party (DUP) 580, 583
Denman, Sir Roy 52
Denmark 23, 37, EFTA, 78, 121, applies to join EEC, 133, 137, 138, 146, 187, industrial fishing, 211, 219, 221 fn, 223, 226 fn, 256, referendum on Maastricht, 278–279, 284, 285, 308, referendum on single currency, 379, 382, 408, 433, 436, 440, 442, 446, 479, 502
Denning, Lord 175, 564
Deregulation 305, 310, 322, horsemeat, 531, 533, 627
Destructive embrace, Britain's 69–72
Dien Bien Phu, battle 56
Dillon, Douglas 79, 80
Dimbleby, David, mars historic moment 572
Directive 91/497 290
Directive, effluent discharges into rivers 178
Discards (fish) 211, 309
Dioxin 291, food scandal, 368
Dixon, Sir Pierson 100
Dooge Committee 216 *et seq*, meeting in Bonn, 217, interim report, 219, final report, 220–221, 231
Dooge, James 217
Dorrell, Stephen 330
Double coffin lid 624 *et seq*
Douglas-Home, Alec 124, 159
Douste-Blazy, Philippe 445, sanctimonious, 453, 'Britain is isolated', 456
Dover, queues of lorries 607, unable to cross Channel, 607, 'eerily quiet', 608
Draft Treaty Establishing a European Union 213
Draghi, Mario 520, 521
Driver and Vehicle Licensing Agency 350
Driving licence, community model 350
Drummond, Sir Eric 12, 88
Dublin Convention 273
Duisenberg, Wim 347, 409
Duncan Smith, Iain 278, leader, 386, 426
Dulles, John Foster 12, 56, 79

Eastleigh by-election 534
ECJ 74, subordination to, 86–87, pig subsidies, 186, Community 'supreme court', 203–204, Treaty of Rome 'internal constitution', 204, upholds fishing claim, 211, power to levy fines, 274, Factortame, 308, Air France subsidies, 323, 'curb powers', 329, beef ban, 331–332, 333, call to enforce Charter of Fundamental Rights, 375–376, Monti's wish to strengthen, 378, primacy over members' law, 400, deficit rules referred, 419, 520, ruling on ESM, 523, Single Market means 'accepting ECJ jurisdiction', 577, under jurisdiction during negotiations, 581–582
Ecofin Council 282, 346, 493, 506
Economic Steering (Europe) Committee 83
Economist 18, 228, 337, on Greek rescue plan, 507
EDC 52, 54, Anglo-American guarantee, 55, French opposition to, 55–57
Eden, Anthony 54, 62, 70, 77
Edlinger, Rudolf 347, 354
EEA 292 *et seq*, Agreement, 295, 559
Egypt, invasion of 72
Eide, Espen 528, 539
Eisenhower, President 65, 68, 79, three power meeting, 84, 88
Electoral Commission ruling 566
Electromagnetic Compatibility Directive 289
Elliott, Matthew 569
Ellis-Rees, Hugh 62
Élysée Treaty 112
Emmanuelli, Henri 434
Empty chair crisis 113–114

Enarques 220 fn
Encounter, magazine 103
Engrénage 74–75
Enlargement, admission of Spain and Portugal 212, 'widening' and 'deepening', 254
Erhard, Ludwig 39, 58, support for free trade area, 59, 77, opposition to common market, 65, 68, 69, at loggerheads with Adenauer, 70, support for Plan G, 71, 72, 78, retires, 112
ERM 189, start, 191, Thatcher's doubts, 193, 195, Lawson's support, 226, mistakes role, 230, Howe, 231, Thatcher pressed to join, 240, 245, Lawson's continued misunderstanding, 246, attempt to convince Thatcher, 247, 'sincerity', 248, ambush before Madrid, 248–249, intention to join, 249, Lawson favours entry, 251, Major's conversion, 254, Thatcher accepts, 255, high interest rates, 260, recession, 277, Black Wednesday, 281–283, paying the price, 287, Delors crows, 314, 'confidence trick', 327, effect on Tories, 337
Escalator clause 411
Estai (trawler) 324
Euratom 58, 63, study by European Parliament, 68, 73
Eureka programme 227
Euro crisis (see also Greece) 498 *et seq*, bailout instrument, 498, ominous phase, 501
Euro Plus Pact 505, 512
Euro-sillies 290
Eurocontrol 81
Eurocorps 364
Eurocrats 75, 297 fn, 422
Eurogroup 346, 489, 493, 495, 506, 509, 510, 513, 520, 525 fn, 566
Euromaidan 547
Europa Begeisterung (Euro-fanaticism) 190
Europäische Wirtschaftsgemeinschaft 18
Europe à la carte 188
Europe Day 423, 438, 507
Europe, visions of 5
European Agricultural Guidance and Guarantee Fund (FEOGA) 99
European Army 9, 52, 53, 66, 264, 355, 363, 366, 371, 'Mary-Ann', 373, 480
European Assembly, call for 34, established, 73, 76
European Banking Authority (EBA) 487
European Central Bank (ECB) 126, 240, 241, 245, 246, opens for business, 349, 502, 516 Securities Markets Programme 511
European Centre for Disease Prevention and Control (ECDC) 600
European Civil Aviation Conference 81
European Coal and Steel Community 50, 52, UK agreement of association, 57
European Commission. See Commission.
European Communities Act 148, amended, 228
European Community (EC), formal creation of 227
European Community Humanitarian Office (ECHO) 356
European Council, genesis of 155–157, named, 163, Dublin 1975, 166, Brussels 1976, 177, Copenhagen 1978, 189, Bremen, 190, Brussels, 191, Dublin 1979, 193, Luxembourg, 1980, 195, Stuttgart 1983, 196, Athens 1983, 197, Brussels 1984, 198, Fontainebleau 1984, 199, Brussels 1985, 220, Brussels, 1988, 200, Milan 1985, 223, Brussels 1987, 236, Copenhagen, 1987, 237, Brussels 1988, 238, Hanover 1988, 240, Madrid 1989, 248–249, Strasbourg 1989, 252, Dublin 1990, 253, Rome 1990 (October), 260, December, 262, Luxembourg 1991, 269, Lisbon, 1992, Edinburgh 1992, 281, Fontainebleau 1984, 291, Copenhagen 1993, 313, 'Extraordinary' Council, Brussels Oct 1993, 315, Dec 1993, 315, Corfu 1994, 318, Essen 1994, 321, Cannes 1994, 325, Majorca

1995, 325, Madrid 1995, 326, Amsterdam 1997, 333, 341, Luxembourg 1997, 346, Cardiff 1998, 349, Vienna 1998, 360, Berlin 1999, 362, Cologne 1999, 364, Tampere 1999, 369, Helsinki 1999, 371, Lisbon 2000, 375, Santa Maria da Feira 2000, 376–377, Biarritz 2000, 381, Nice 2000, 384, Göteborg 2001, 387, Ghent 2001, 392, Laeken 2001, 394–395, Porto Carras 2003, 399, Seville 2002, 403–404, Copenhagen 2002, 407, 408, Thessalonika 2003, 409, Rome 2003, 412, 419, 420, 427, 430, 434, 435, 440, 442, 443, 444, Brussels 2005, 445, 449, Dec 2005, 456–458, 464, Brussels 2006, 466, 468, Brussels March 2007, 469, June 2007, 472, 473, Dec 2007, 477, Dec 2008, 482, special meeting March 2009, 484, June 2009, 487, Oct 2010, 500–501, Dec 2010, 502, March 2011, 505, June 2011, 509, Oct 2011, 512, 513, Dec 2011, 515–516, June 2012, 520, 522, Dec 2012, 523, 525, 526, Feb 2013, 533, June 2013, 535, Dec 2013, 547, 549, June 2014, 555, 558, 561, informal meeting, June 2016, negotiating guidelines, 579, rules out separate negotiations, 581, decision on talks, 582, informal meeting Gothenburg Nov 2017, 583, Dec 2017, 584, March 2018, 587, June 2018, 588, Sep 2018, 591, Oct 2018, 592, Oct 2019, 597, 602, 603, Dec 2020, 605, 606
European Court of Human Rights (ECHR) 376, 551, 567
European Court of Justice. See ECJ
European Defence Agency 419
European Defence Community. See EDC
European Defence Identity, Mitterrand plans 219, 280, 322, consigned to invisibility, 467
European Defence Treaty 55
European Economic Area. See EEA
European Economic Association Committee 83
European Economic Community 74, 84
European Economic Space (EES) 292, 294
European Exchange Rate Agreement (snake) 187
European External Action Service 477
European Federation or League of Nations (book) 5
European Financial Stabilisation Mechanism (EFSM) 498
European Financial Stability Facility (EFSF) 499, 501, 502, replacement, 505, in play, 509
European Food Safety Authority 372, Parma, 418
European Free Trade Association (EFTA) 78, *coup de grâce*, 81, 82, 88, 92, 171, 292
European Monetary System (EMS) 189
European Movement 36, 37, 168, 170, assists Spinelli, 207, Congress 1984, 214
European Parliament, bicameral proposal 9, 33, 34, 35, 105, discusses UK application, 118, 122, 134, 155, 177, direct elections proposed, 183, need for elections, 184, 186, Tindemans proposal, 188, direct elections, 193, 205, 206, Genscher – Colombo plan, 208, 209, 213, adopts Spinelli's draft, 214, low turnout, 217, 220, 223, extension to role, 226, Alterio Spinelli Building, 229, Thatcher's 'right of reply', 233, new drive, 235, Delors, 242, 244, 252, 253, 256, Thatcher's rejection, 258, hybris structure proposed, 261, 263, 271, official seat, 286, Efta, 293, 295, co-decision, 299 fn, scrutiny, 300, 313, elections delayed, 318, Goldsmith, 329, 333, 335, Blair censured, 348, fraud accusations, 355, threatens discharge delay, 356, dossier, 358, censure motion, 361, Prodi 'vision', 363, proportional representation, 366, new building, 367, convention plan, 369, 370, new powers proposed, 376, 378, second chamber, 380, convention opens, 396, not 'power grab',

397, constitution unveiled, 398, 399, limit powers, 415, 423, 424, elections, 427, Barroso approved, 430, 432, no politics in, 433, Blair 'missing', 452, 461, 465, 468, 469, 470, 474, corruption, 479, increased allowances, 490, 500, Barroso address, 509, Van Rompuy, 516, 519, budget 'veto', 533, deal, 535, 547, treaty change procedure, 549–550, *Spitzenkandidaten*, 550, Cameron 'digging', 560, 566, 581, 598, 601, 602, 604, deadline, 606, ratification of UK deal, 607
European Peoples' Party (EPP) 206, 208, 356, Cameron's withdrawal, 461
European Political Community (EPC) 55
European Political Co-operation 184
European Reform Group 278
European Research Group (ERG) 587
European Resistance Movements, draft Declaration of 22
European Security and Defence Policy (ESDP) 365
European Stability Mechanism (ESM) 505, 511, 515, 518, 519, 521, ECJ ruling, 523
European Union 155, 156, moves towards, 186, officially named, 315
European Union of Federalists 32
European University Institute in Florence 376, 398, 429
Europol 280, 325, 531
Eurosclerosis 204
Eurostat, 'vast enterprise of looting' 409, 412, 414, estimate on deficit, 451, scrutiny of Greece, 491
Eustice, George 522
Evans Pritchard, Ambrose 492
Ever closer union viii, 73, 202, 203, 208, 342, 'get rid of', 505, 551, 554, 555, 563, 567, 611, 613
Exchange Rate Mechanism. See ERM
Exit plan, absence of 557, Cummings, 568–569
Eyjafjallajökull eruption 496–497

Factortame 308, 327, 322
Fairbairn, Carolyn 586
Falklands War 196
Fanfare for Europe 151
Farage, Nigel 513, 515, Westminster strategy, 552, 553 fn, 554, 557, 558, 562, 564, 565, 570, 572, 575, 586
Fascists 21–22
Faure, Edgar 58
Faure, Maurice 217
Federal Union 19
Federation of British Industries 78
Fiennes, John 148
Financial crash (2008) 481 *et seq*
Financial Stability Board (FSB) 484
Fischer, Joschka 376, 378
Fisheries 132, equal access, 133, *actes préparatoires*, 134, Dutch role, 135, damaging to UK interests, 136, Norway, 136, 12-mile limit, 145–146, legal basis of, 137, the lie direct, 144, Rippon lies, 147, 200-mile limit, 181, Cod wars; Fisheries Limits Act, 182, Total Allowable Catch, 182, CFP rules, 209, Hague preferences, 210, national quotas, 210–211, Rippon's lie exposed, 212, Spanish and Portuguese access to Community waters, 212–213, 'considerable dowry', 218, Sea Fish (Conservation) Bill, 'flag boats', 308, decommissioning, 309, ecological crisis, 310, fishing rights from Russia, 316, 'Irish Box', 322, Factortame, 327, boat numbers; 'too many people chasing too few fish', 328, further cuts, 332, register drops by third, 348, Spanish 'equal access', 403, capital of illegal fishing, 418, Whitby skippers fined, 455, Brexit talks, 600, 'long-term solution' on fishing, 601, breakthrough 'close', 605, 'gone backwards', 606, last minute haggling, 607
Fischler, Frans 211 fn, 331, 333, CAP reform, 404–405, 410

Food and Veterinary Office 390
Flight time limits 543
Floods Directive 563
Food safety 368, 372, 395, 530, 531, 540, 621
Food Safety Authority of Ireland 530
Food Standards Agency 372, 541
Foot, Michael 116, 169, 209, cod quota, 211
Foot and Mouth Disease 389 *et seq*
Ford Foundation 61
Ford, President 179
Foreign Office, implications of Werner Report 126–127, paper on sovereignty, 132 fn, fails to focus on fishing, 137
Foreign policy, intergovernmental treaty 227
Forsyth, Michael 328
Fortuyn, Pym 403
Foster, Arlene, no special status for NI 583, NI 'must leave on same terms', 584, threatens to withhold votes; accuses Johnson of betrayal, 597
Fotyga, Anna 469
Fouchet Committee 94–95, 96, proposals, 99
Foundation myth 51, 522, 619
Four freedoms 74, 575
Fox, Liam 526, 575, 576, 581
France, draft Act of Perpetual Association 18, Fourth Republic, 77, 'The wrecker' (*Times*), 78, agricultural crisis, 97–98, 1968 student unrest, 120, bureaucracy, 190, 'birthright', 239
Franco-German axis 100, treaty, 112
Frankfurter, Justice Felix 20
Franks, Oliver 30
Fraud, VAT 152, CAP, 235, allegations, 313–314, HoL committee, 320, Court of Auditors, 321, European Parliament, 355–356, Santer policy, 361, 'wise men', 362, Andreasen affair, 403, ' vast enterprise of looting', 409, Eurostat, 412, horsemeat, 531–532
Free Trade Area, British proposal 71
Freitas do Amaral, Diogo 436
Fresh Meat (Hygiene and Inspection) Regulations 290
Fresh Start Group 278, 284, 286, 288
Fresh Start Project 522, 554
Friedman, Milton 508
Friedmann, Bernhard 357
Fundamental Law of the European Union 544, 617
Funk, Walther 14
Füzes, Oszkár 454

Gaillard, Félix 77
Gaitskell, Hugh 104–106, 'thousand years of history', 105, death of, 112, 115
Garel-Jones, Tristan 277
Gaspar, Vítor 506
GATT 116 fn, 255, 256, 257, 258, 261, 264, Uruguay Round, 317, Doha Round, 410, 620
Gauweiler, Peter 483
Gaymard, Hervé 433
Genscher – Colombo Plan 207, 208
Genscher, Hans-Dietrich 240
George, Stephen 177, 180, 184, 191, 198
Gilmour, Ian 196
Giscard d'Estaing, Valéry, premier 120, monetary union, 121, president, 157, discussions with Callaghan, 162, 'summit is dead', 163, 164, 'compulsion for independence and self-esteem', 179–180, EP elections, 183, 184, backs Jenkins, 189, 190, 'spirit of Charlemagne', 191, 193, 194, treatment of Thatcher, 195, Monnet's funeral, 202–203, expands Delors' 'vision', 294, 'concentrate on EMU', 320, speech, 339, president, CEMR, 351, 'regroup' around Six, 386, choice for convention president, 394, appointed, 395, task 'to seek consensus', 396, Giscard decides, 397, unveils 'skeleton' draft, 398, hands over draft, 399, 400, retains an essential ambiguity, 401, nothing for

national parliaments, 402, negotiations 'for show', 409, complete text, 411–412, 413, objections, 414–415, Italian revision, 416, 420, 'torrent' of amendments, 422, '*c'est un bon texte*', 425, architecture remains, 429, hopes on ratification, 440, 442, Blair comments, 462, Lisbon Treaty 'substantially equivalent'
Globalisation 464, 484, 518, 529, 568, 591, 619, *et seq*, 630, 634
Globally Harmonised System of Classification and Labelling of Chemicals (GHS) 624
Goebbels 15, 374
Gold plating (regulation) 303, 305, 619
Golden Dawn 519
Goldman Sachs 494, 514
Goldsmith, Sir James 329, 337, 424
Gonzales, Felipe 324
Good Friday Agreement 579
Goodman, Lord 151
Goodwin, Matthew 562
Gorbach, Hubert 460
Gorman, Teresa 284, 286
Gorse, Georges 118
Gove, Michael 570, 'betrays' Johnson, 575
Grade, Lew 169
Grant, Charles 508
Grasser, Karl-Heinz 434
Greece, euro crisis (part 1) 489 *et seq*, 494–496, crisis resurgent, 507 *et seq*, 'haircut, 512, debt write-off, 518
Greek Loan Facility (GLF) 495
Green, Pauline 358, 361
Greenland 308
Grimmond, Jo 138, 169
Gummer, John Selwyn 170, 250, 307, 309, 352
Guterres, António 375
Gymnich-type meetings 207

Hague Congress 33, 35, 41
Hague Summit 121, 125, 220
Hague, William 345, 353, 366, 372, resigns as leader, 386, competences, 521, Article 50, 536
Hain, Peter 381, 397, 426, 427
Halifax, Lord 19
Hall, Katja 537
Hallstein, Walter 75, 76, 79, 82, Doctrine, 84, CAP talks, 98, own resources proposal, 113, new and independent legal system, 296
Hammond, Philip 581, 583, 585
Hänsch, Klaus 333, 335
Hankey, Maurice 19
Hannibalsson, Jón Baldvin 294
Hart, Judith 158
Hartlepool, by-election 431
Hastings, Max 632
Hattersley, Roy 173
Hazard Analysis and Critical Control Points (HACCP) 532, 540
Healey, Denis 106, 116, Common Market, 142, 147, 176, 204 fn
Heath, Edward 47, 85, visits Hallstein, 86, 91, begins entry negotiations, 92, Grocer, 104 fn, recognises importance of French agriculture, 110, 1970 general election, 123, on UK contributions, 125, meets Pompidou, 129, 'favourable compromise', 130, no loss of essential sovereignty, 132, writes to Norway on fishing, 145–146, sign accession treaty, 147, regional development fund, 154, meets Monnet at Chequers, 155, general election, 157, resigns, 157, attacks Labour's plans, 160, opposes Referendum Bill, 168, 171, jubilant, 174, attacks Thatcher, 244
Heathcoat-Amory, David, MP 397 fn, 398, 426 fn
Heaton-Harris, Chris 522
Helsinki agenda/goals 371, 466
Herron, Neil 389
Heseltine, Michael 104 fn, Defence secretary, 219, Westland, 231–232,

leadership bid, 259, deregulation, 305, supports Major, 325, 345, 352, 353, Benefits of Europe, 369, 374
Hidden hand 621 *et seq*
High Representative 491
Hitchhiker's Guide to the Galaxy 611
Hitler, Adolf 4, 8, 14
Hogg, Douglas 331, 333
Hollande, François 434, president, 519, revising treaties 'not a priority', 550, 561, 575, 577, 578
Horsemeat scandal 530 *et seq*, 540
Howard, Michael 315 fn, 424, 428, 431, resigns as leader, 439, 462
Howe, Geoffrey, drafts European Communities Bill 148, accused of imposing 'alien system of law', 149, joining EEC 'a triumph', 150, budget settlement comment, 197, French 'ideal negotiating partners', 198, 199, foreign secretary, 209, enjoyable day in Germany, 218, *Europe Tomorrow* (book), 218, 219, Milan 'ambush' fail, 220, confirms Delors' fears, 222, intent to block IGC, 223, only simple majority needed, 224, circulates proposals on political cooperation, 224, announces IGC, 225, supports ERM, 230, aware of real purpose; 'downcast' by Thatcher rejection, 231, 'notable achievement' in 'enlargement of Community authority', 232, Delors 'offence', 232–233, Brussels Council 'war', 236, Chirac 'difficult'; 'gruelling and bafflingly complex' negotiation, 238, rebate settlement, 239, 'outrage' at Bruges speech, 244, ERM membership 'desirable', 246, suggests 'joint analysis' on ERM, 247, request meet with Thatcher, 248, 'ambush before Madrid', 248–249, 'brittle and businesslike'; identifies with Delors, 249, demoted, 250, speech 'calculated malice', 251, sniping in background, 254, drafts resignation, 258
Huhne, Chris 534
Hungary 27, 72, accession negotiations, 344, support declining, 368, 382, 405, votes 'Yes' to constitution, 410, ratifies, 432, 454, 478
Hunt, Jeremy 590
Hurd, Douglas 188 fn, foreign secretary, 250, hard ecu, 251, influence on Major, 254, reading Maastricht, 260, 261, 265, 267 fn, 268, 271, 272, 274 fn, 276, signs treaty, 278, 279, 304 fn, 'level killing field', 315 fn, 317, benefits of EU membership, 323, replaced as foreign secretary, 325, 334, 353, 371, on Heath, 450
Hussein, Saddam 262, 348, disintegrator, 407, 408

Immigration, Commission powers 226, Major refuses control, 226, Schengen, 340, Germans worried, 381, Pym Fortuyn, 403, Berlusconi, 411, Howard election issue, 439, BNP election success, 486, Cameron announced 'cap', 500, renegotiation, 551, Australian points system; emergency brake, 558, attracts headlines, 559–560, Cameron's 'radical changes', 560, pressure on Hollande, 561, Cameron's 'welfare rules' commitment, 562–563, 'safeguard mechanism', 567, attraction of Australian points system, 570, Turkey accession claim, 570, Johnson insists return of controls, 576, May 'not giving up control', 576
IMF 176, 190, 334, troika, 346, 413, 483, 494, Greece 495–496, 'bazooka', 498, 502, 506, 508, 509, 510, 511, Greek bailout, 518, global governance, 625
Information society 318
Integrated Administration and Control System (IACS) 305
Intergovernmental conference (IGC) 217, agreed at Milan, 224
Intergovernmentalism, triumph of 57
Independent League for Economic Co-operation (ELEC) 32

International Air Transport Association 497
International Authority for the Ruhr. 40
International Civil Aviation Organisation (ICAO) 496
International Committee of the Movements for European Unity (ICMEU) 33, 35
International law of the sea 135
International Maritime Organisation (IMO) 517
International Monetary Fund. See: IMF
International Steel Cartel 9
Iraq 15, 263, 265, 299, 348, 361, 381, 405, 407, 408, 421, 422, 468, 497
Ireland 37, applicant, 121, 124, refuses fishery proposal, 144, 146, 'snake', 187, 226 fn, support for Spinelli, 235, structural funds, 236, European Council, 253, IACS, 305, response to cuts, 344, benefits from CAP, 358, 383, spending, 385, rejects Nice Treaty, 387, 389, second referendum, 406, immigration, 411, harmonising criminal law, 415, 416, 419, 423, constitution, 430, 440, 'sent to bed without supper', 441, 'No' camp, 445, 452, 457, opening labour markets, 463, referendum Bill, 479, secret plan, 480, guarantees, 482, votes yes, 487–488, liquidators, 491, Greek Loan Facility, 495, bailout, 502, at risk, 507, 511, horsemeat, 530, budget, 535, border, 583, common regulatory area, 586, Ireland first, 587

James, Diane 534
Janša, Janez 471
Jay, Douglas 116
Jebb, Gladwyn 70
Jenkins, Roy 116, 141, 143, 158, 169, 173, Commission president, 188–191, 192, 194, 195, 196, 269
Jobert, Michel 129
Jospin, Lionel 338, 344, 371, 375, 381, 398
Johnson, Boris xi, Brussels correspondent, 271, 'inchoate', 527, offers alternatives to EU, 528, challenges Johnson, 555, denies ideas impossible to deliver, 556, referendum as leverage, 569, bananas, 570–571, personality contest, 571, victory speech, 574, 'betrayed' by Gove, 575, joins forces, 576, cakeism, 577, 'punishment beatings', 578, 'fuck business'; resigns, 589, Trump endorses, 590, 'suicide vest', 591, no-deal 'million-to-one against', 594, kipper, 595, prime minister, 596, renegotiation, 596–597, 'get Brexit done', 597, signs Withdrawal Agreement, 598, White Paper, 598–599, suffers Covid, 601, imposes deadline, 602, accuses EU, 603, 'pause talks', 605, talks with von der Leyen, 606, 'now for the sprouts', 607, speech to House; signs agreement, 608, thrust of approach, 619, cyclist protection, 622–623, 624, net zero, 626, 'full control of laws', 630, ' cavorting charlatan', 632, 'botch', 633
Johnson, Stanley 206
Judicial co-operation 463
June Movement 278
Juncker, Jean-Claude 429, 435, 440, 441, 443, 446, Europe 'in deep crisis', 447, 448, 'Britain is different', 474, 480, 489, Greek crisis, 493–494, nominated as Commission president, 555, 'doomed romance', 562–562, promises to help Cameron, 565, Five Presidents Report, 566, 'they don 't have it [a plan]', 574, 575, meets Cameron, 579, May 'upstaged', 582, agree 'choreography', 584, 598
Junktim 58, central feature of talks, 67
Justice and Home Affairs 274, 318, community framework, 328, 400, 421
Justus Lipsius (Council HQ) 415, 446

Kaczyński, Jarosław 472, refuses to sign Lisbon Treaty, 486
Kaczyński, Lech 472, 481, 488
Karamanlis, Kostas 489

Karlsruhe (and German constitutional court) 39, 315, 347, 481, 483, 487, 511, 520, 523
Kavanagh, Trevor 426
Kellogg – Briand Pact 6
Kellner, Peter 525
Kennedy, Charles 428
Kennedy, John F 88
Kennan, George 28, 31
Kent, lorry parks 605
Kerr, Philip (Lord Lothian) 15, 18
Kerr, Sir John 396, 398, 442
Keynes, John Maynard 18, 26
Kiesinger, Kurt 117
Kilmuir, Lord 38, loss of sovereignty, 86–87
Kilroy-Silk, Robert 424
Kinnock, Neil 241, 257, 277, 283, 412, 414
Kirk, Kent 211
Kirkhope, Timothy 472
Kissinger, Dr Henry 179, 180
Klassen, Karl 190
Klaus, Václav 412, 414, 479, 485, 486 fn, signs treaty, 488
Knudsen, Bjørn 538–539
Kohl, Helmut, at Verdun 1, chancellor, 196, 197, at No.10, 198, Brussels Council, 198–199, rebate, 200, 203 fn, pressure for new treaty, 216, New Year message, 220, 311, determined on new treaty, 223, 224, 226–227, 237, 240, German reunification, 251, 252, call for political union, 253, aid for Soviet Union, 254, meets Major, 264, climax, 269, Maastricht, 272, reassurance on 'superstate', 280, secret visit to Bundesbank, 282, response to referendum, 283, economic union, 311, back Jean-Luc Dehaene, 318, 319, last Council, 321, 325, 333, anticipating next enlargement, 334, driving force, 335, 338, budget hole, 339, rescues single currency, 340, 346, election defeat, 354, Honorary Citizen of Europe, 360, manifesto for Europe, 392, 450
Kohnstamm, Max 60
Kok, Wim 338, 393
Korean War 47, 52, 53
Kosovo 348, 361, 363, 364, 365, 535
Khrushchev, Nikita 84, 96
Krebs, Sir John 372
Krichbaum, Günther 554
Kuwait, Iraqi invasion 255, 260, 262, 263, 264, 409
Kwaśniewski, Aleksander 443

Labouchère, George 63, 65
Labour Party, opposes accession Bill 149, conference, 162, conference 1976, 184
Lampedusa, migrant crisis 503
Lamy, Pascal 422, 436
Laeken 384, 385, Declaration, 387 and 395, prelude, 393 *et seq*, intentions, 401, timing, 550
Lafontaine, Oskar 354, 355, 360
Laitenberger, Johannes 454
Lamers, Karl 319
Lamont, Norman, ERM crisis 281–283, 311, 320, 321
Lamoureaux, François 225
Lamy, Pascal 220 fn, 422, 436
Lange, Erwin 206
Laniel, Joseph 56
Languages, official 76
Laski, Harold 16
Lavergne, Professor Bernard 42
Lawson, Nigel 115, 128 fn, 226, chancellor, 230, obsession with ERM, 231, 'boom', 234, shadows deutschmark, 235, 239, 240, 241, 242, 243, 244, prepares ground for ERM, 245, fails to understand role of ERM, 246, persists in delusion, 247, meets with Thatcher, 248, threatens to resign, 249, savaged by *Daily Mail*, 250, resigns, 250, Howe praises, 251, Cameron's renegotiation 'likely to fail', 536, IEA competition, 552

Layton, Walter 18
Le Pen, Jean-Marie 403
Leadsom, Andrea 522
League of Nations 3, 7, 10, 12, 17, German admission to, 4, talking shop, 8
Leave campaign (Vote Leave), fails to exploit strongest weapon 569, red battle bus; lies, 570, victory speech, 574, failed to formulate exit plan, 616, 'take back control', 624, 'vaguest aspirations', 633
Lee, Sir Frank 83, 88
Legal framework 296 et seq
Lehmann Brothers 481
Leigh-Pemberton, Robin 231, 245
Leinen, Jo 471
Level playing field 178, 303, 523, 543, 599, 601, 619
Lewandowski, Janusz 500
Lewis, Brandon 602
Liberal Party 138, 149, 157, 169
Liechtenstein 295, 538
Likaanen, Erkki 358 fn
Lilley, Peter 315
Lindh, Anna, murder 413
Lisbon Treaty 474, Giscard d'Estaing attests to similarity with constitution, 475, Cameron promises referendum; final draft signed; 476, calls for swift ratification, 477, not a 'fundamental constitutional change'; motion for referendum defeated, 478, Irish referendum: 'No', 479, Irish have to vote again, 480, UK ratifies, 481, German constitutional court, 483, Cameron: 'not let matters rest', 486, Commission's first task, 487, Irish voters say 'Yes', 487–488, Václav Klaus signs, 488, treaty comes into force, 488, Cameron pledges renegotiation, 489, MEPs allowances increased, 490, comes to the rescue, 502
Lithuania 253, 369, 432, 479, 483, 546
Lobbyists 298
Locarno, Treaty of 4, 5
Loucheur, Louis 2, 5, 9, 10, 51
Loughton, Tim, MP 553, 554
Low, David, cartoon 43
Lubbers, Ruud 247
Luxembourg, refusal to accept more Eurocrats 75
Luxembourg Agreement 128
Luxembourg Declaration (1984) 292
Luxembourg Treaty 122
Lyons, Dr Gerard 556

Maastricht 216, treaty summit, 271–275, treaty signing, 276, 'too complicated', 312
MacDougall, Sir Donald 187, 189
Mackay, Richard, MP 37
MacKinnon, Neil 508
Macleod, Iain 125
Mackinlay, Craig 565
Maclennan, MP, Robert 138
Macmillan, Harold 20, 33, 37, 49, Messina, 61, becomes foreign secretary, 62, 71, 82, 84, 87, becomes prime minister, 77, 'Supermac', 83, 'wind of change', 83, considers joining EEC, 84–85, Kennedy talks, 88–90, ridicules Gaitskell, 106, meets de Gaulle, 106–107, acquisition of Polaris, 107, underestimates France's agricultural interests, 108, observations on veto, 110, Anglocentric perspective, 111
Madrid, bomb 420
Major, John, foreign secretary 250, chancellor, 250, conversion to ERM, 254, announces joining, 255, prime minister, 259, 'heart of Europe', 260, first cabinet, 261, maximise influence, 262, 'hard ecu', 262, UN peace initiative, 262, meets Kohl, 264, Iraq 'safe haven', 265, Yugoslavia, 267, object to treaty draft, 269, Commons debate, 270, Maastricht, 271–275, press reaction, 275, cabinet. 275–276, 'Roman triumph', 276,

snap general election, 277, subsidiarity, 278, postpones committee stage, 279, 'big idea', 280, ERM crisis, 281–283, policies for Britain, 283, offers debate on Maastricht, 283–284, stresses subsidiarity, 284, effects, 285, parades 'successes', 286, 'old maids bicycling' speech, 287, vote of confidence, 288, celebrates launch of Single Market, 301, burden of regulation, 304, unemployment, 311, meditating on 'Europe', 314, 'bastards', 315 fn, Trans-European Network, 315–316, 'poodle of Brussels', 316, cartoon, 317, Santer, 318, Leiden speech, 319, pressure from party, 320, 321, fisheries, 322, Estai, 324, resigns as party leader, 324–325, re-election, 325, 326, challenged by Heath, 329, Goldsmith, 329, concedes referendum on currency, 330, BSE beef ban, 330, cull plan, 331, 'bunch of shits', 332, 'humiliation', 332, abandons cull, 333, champions 'flexibility', 335, dissolution of parliament, 337, benefits of 'Europe', 370
Mallaby, Sir Christopher 216
Malta, applies to join EU 254, 294, 322, invited to negotiate, 369, referendum, 408, 422, 430, 439 fn, 478
Manchuria, Japanese invasion of 8
Mandela, Nelson 349
Mandelson, Peter 431, 437, 445
Mansholt, Sicco 76, Plan, 98, disturbed by CAP, 120, on common fisheries policy, 132
Marcinkiewicz, Kazimierz 457
Marjolin, Robert 30, 31, study group, 187, report, 189, beneficial crisis, 492
Marković, Ante 266
Marlow, Tony 317
Marshall Plan 26–28, 32
Martin, David, MEP 253
Martino, Gaetano 59
Maude, Francis 276
May, Theresa 574, runs for leadership, 575, holds firm om Article 50, Lancaster House speech, 577, meets Juncker, 579, general election, 579–580, 'strong and stable', 580, Florence speech, 581, informal Council at Tallinn; party conference, 582, Gothenburg; no special status for NI, 583, Brussels, 583–584; Foster disowns deal, 584, difficulty understanding, 585, trapped by 'deep and special partnership', 586, rejects Commission proposal, 586–587, ultimation to May, 587, no room to manoeuvre, 588, problem with cabinet; Chequers, 589, reshuffle, 590; participation in agencies, 590–591; Salzburg, 591, three-corner fight, 591–592, 'Dancing Queen', 592, Westminster blocks progress, 592–593, enlists help from Tusk; Strasbourg agreement, 593, reaches out to Labour; steps down, 594, 597, May's approach, 619, realitätsblind, 632
Mayer, René 56
Mayrisch, Emil 9
Maxwell Fyfe, Sir David. See: Kilmuir, Lord
McAlpine, Alistair 170
McCoy, John 44
McCreevy, Charlie 479
McDermott, John 552
McKenna, Michelle 'Clippy' 622
Meat Hygiene Service 301 fn, Sefra, 304
Mendès-France, Pierre 56, 58, 73
Merchant Shipping Act 327
Merger Treaty 57, 115
Merkel, Angela, chancellor 450–451, rescues Blair, 453, first speech, 454, first European Council, 457, 459, 464, agreement with Chirac, 465, 467, meets Barroso, 467, presidency programme, 468, 469, drops constitution label, 470, no change to legal substance, 471, 472, Barroso's tribute, 473, euro warning, 491, denies bailout, harsh terms for Greece, 495, defends

euro, 498, 499, need to change treaties, 501, EU budget, 506, possibility of treaty change, 511, intergovernmental option, 515, defends Draghi, 521, urges treaty change, 547, doubt about intentions, 548, 550, dismisses EU treaty change, 551, 554, new Commission president, 555, 559, need to avoid treaty negotiations, 561, denies need for treaty change, 567, warns against 'cherry-picking', 576, warns UK about rights, 578, 581
Méry, Jean-Claude 435
Messina 59–62, communiqué, 60
Metric, measures, compulsory 372, martyrs, 389
Meyer, Henning 516
Michel, Charles 596, 601
Middleton, Jeremy 431
Migrant workers 463
Migration Watch UK. 411
Mikardo, Ian 169
Miliband, David 477, 478, 501, 512, taunts Cameron, 515, 551, 565
Millan, Bruce 352
Millennium Declaration 371
Miller, Leszek 406
Milner group 15
Milošević, Slobodan 266, 348, 365
Miners' strike 149, 220
Minford, Patrick 231
Ministry of Agriculture, Fisheries and Food (MAFF) 137, 290, 307
Mitterrand, François 1, 35, 114, president, 196, open to new treaty, 215, recommends split, 215, 216, guiding hand, 217, prioritises Single Market, 222, meets Delors, 223, insists of IGC, 252
Mollet, Guy 66, 68, 72
Monetary union, Saar 30, Monnet excited by, 77, 121, 122, 125, 126, 131, 132, 142, Paris summit, 153–155, renegotiation 'shopping list', 152, 159, 186, 187, 189, 203, EMS as a precursor, 214, Franco-German agreement, 227, Delors, 'white stones', 228, 239, committee of wise men, 240, Thatcher 'first step', 241, Pöhl, 245, 'glidepath', 246, Delors report, 246, Lawson, 247, Madrid Council, 249, 'hard ecu', 251, Mitterrand demands IGC, 252, Thatcher capitulates, 252–3, 257, Labour support, 261, no compulsion, 269, Thatcher's referendum call, 270, 'back-sliding', 313, 314, 326, Connolly, 327, 336, Tindermans Report, 363, Schröder, 354, 371, Greek exit from, 509, Stability treaty, 516, 523, 542, Five Presidents Report, 566, Heath, 612–613
Monnet, Jean 10–12, 13, 18, 20, 21, 41, 51, Franco-British Union, 19, Marshall Plan, 26, 30–31, Council of Europe, 38, Schuman Plan 41–48, first government of Europe, 50, beginning of Europe, 52, EDC, 54–55, resigns from ECSC, 57, re-launch (relancer) of 'European idea', 58, destroys OEEC, 78–79, 'Monnet effect', 90, Paris Summit, 153, provisional government, 163, Honorary Citizen of Europe, 164, dies, 202, questioned work, 203
Monnet Professors 177
Monopoly right of proposal 203
Montgomery, Field Marshall, opposition to EDC 54
Monti, Mario 354, 378, 514, 518, 523
Moratinos, Miguel Ángel 469
Mordaunt, Penny 570
Mori International 173
Morrison, Herbert, 'Durham miners won't wear it' 44, EDC, 53
Mugabe, Robert 407
Mutual recognition 204, 326, of vehicle type approval, 590, of standards, 590, May proposes, 591, agreement on conformity assessment, 603

Naish, David 331
Nasser, Colonel Gamal, Abdul 72
National Institute for Economic and Social Research 374
National Referendum Campaign 170
NATO 53, 54, 73, 80, 81, 84, 95, 207, 218, 219, 245, 253, 261, 264, 280, 323, 359, 365, 371, 381, 382, 415, 615, France threat to withdraw, 85, Kosovo, 361, Libya, 503, Cameron, 537
Natura 2000 programme 563
Nazis 18, 21, origins of EU, 14–15, Europe for the Europeans, 15
Negotiations, Britain's entry, success 130
New Zealand 92, dairy products, 130, 166
Newbury by-election 287–288
Nicolaï, Atzo 416
Nobel Peace Prize, award to EU 523
Noël, Emile 225
Non-tariff barriers 203, 585, 607, 633
North Sea oil 179
Northern Ireland 276, region, 351, 352, border, 583, 584, Johnson rejects 'backstop', 591, to remain aligned, 597
Norway, resistance 23, Council of Europe, 37, Efta, 78, joining EEC, 121, applies to join, 124, CFP, 133, alive to CFP implications, 137, passes law on vessel size, 144, access to waters, 144 fn, intransigent, 145, unmoved by concessions, 147, first referendum, 147, 200–mile limit, 182, participation in 'snake', 187, Delors considers new application, 286, accession date set, 313, second referendum, 321
Notices to Stakeholders 584

O'Neill, Sir Con 124, on fishery negotiations, 133–135, Chairman, BiE, 169, 617
Observer, BSE 330, 'Goodbye Xenophobia', 338, Blair 'in the cold', 371, horsemeat, 533
OEEC 31, 35, 38, Spaak Committee, 62, 65, 71, destruction of, 78–80
Office International des Epizooties 625
Officials, number of (in EU) 297, nexus, 297–298
Ombudsman, parliamentary 274
OPEC 179, 180
Opinion polls, Gallup, on EEC entry 123, 1st referendum, 165
Ordóñez, Miguel 434
Organisation for Economic Co-operation and Development (OECD) 80
Organisation for European Economic Cooperation. See OEEC.
Osborne, George 559
Oslo Declaration 293
Outright Monetary Transactions (OMTs) 520
Owen, David 184, 185, 192
Own resources 238

Palazzo dei Congressi 414
Palliser, Michael 116
Papaconstantinou, George 493, 496
Papademos, Lucas 514
Papandreou, Andreas 197, 213
Papandreou, George 489, 514
Pan Europa (book) 5
Paris Peace Conference 3, 9
Paris Summit 152 et seq, Wilson, 159, 163, EMU affirmed, 164, 220
Paris, Treaty of 50
Passports Union 178, 181
Paterson, Owen 533, speech, 559
Paxman, Jeremy 563, BBC documentary, 571, 572
People's Europe 188, 217
Peoples' Vote 586
Persson, Göran 442, 446
Pétain, General Philippe 1, 19
Petersberg Declaration 280

Peyrefitte, Alain 108
Peyton, John 166
Philadelphia Congress 339
Pig meat subsidies 186
Pinay, Antoine 55, 56, 58, 60, 61, 72
Pineau, Christian 66, 67
Pioneer group 377
Piris, Jean-Claude 553
Plan G 71, 78
Plassnik, Ursula 458, 461
Pleven Plan 52
Plumb, Sir Henry 169
Pöhl, Karl Otto 240, 245
Poland, resistance 22, 23, farmers, 343, accession negotiations, 344, 368, 372, voting, 383–384, 386, 406, 409, emigration, 411, 414, 416, 417, 419, 420, 421, 422, 422, European elections, 424, 426, 430, 439 fn, 440, 443, 457, UK visitors, 463, 469, 476, 479, hold-outs on Lisbon, 486–487, president signs treaty, 488, horsemeat, 531
Polaris 87
Polish plumber 434
Political co-operation 207, 224, 252
Pompidou, Georges 116, president, 120, 'humorous stage', 128, meets Heath, 129, agreement will be reached, 130, fears on Paris Summit, 152, dies, 157
Poos, Jacques 266, 267
Pope Benedict XVI 470
Portillo, Michael 271, 315 fn, 360 fn
Portugal, Efta 78, 178, 186, admission to EU, 212, structural funds, 213, voting, 226 fn, 236, IACS forms, 305, 314, 322, fishing rights, 332, 344, 375, 397, budget deficit, 404, 'angry', 413, referendum, 430, 436, 'dance', 442, labour barriers, 463, 471, 476, ratifies Lisbon Treaty, 479, GLF, 495, at risk, 502, in firing line, 504, economy crumbles, 506, 507, 511
Pöttering, Hans-Gert 470, 471, 474, 477
Powell, Enoch 148, 149, despairs, 150, 170
Prayers for Europe 170
Prescott, John 350, regions, 351, 352, 432
Price, Matthew 539
Pritchard, Mark 511
Private Eye 104
Prodi, Romano 357, acclaimed as president, 362, 'Mr Clean', 363, presents new Commission, 366, 'coronation', 367, concern for 'democratic deficit', 368, enlargement, 368–369, tax package, 370, accession negotiations, 371, proposals for IGC, 372, European Army – 'Mary-Ann', 373, losing ground, 375, warns on undermining democracy, 379, shopping list, 381, urges 'frank and fundamental appraisal' of the EU's ultimate purpose, 385, need to explain Europe, 387, European governance, 388, calls for 'international solidarity', 392, demands Europe speaks with one voice, 393, 'Community method' crucial to security, 394, money also identity, 395, wants 'European democracy', 396, 'not enough Europe', 403, offers flood cash, 405, national vetoes 'destroy harmony', 412, Eurostat scandal, 414, blames decline in support on 'squabbling', 417, fight to salvage constitution, 418–419, calls for 'joint action', 421, catching up 'a chimera', 422, successor chosen, 430, bows out, 432, heads coalition in Italy, 450, supports EU constitution, 465
Project fear 542, 546
Pym, Francis 148, 149, 150

Qualified majority voting 9, 49, 78, 86, 114, 225, extension of, 226, 242, 256, 274, defining characteristic of supranationalism, 316, 335, 336, 372, 376, 401, 414, 416, 498, 512, 628
Quatraro, Antonio 313
Quisling, Vidkun 22
Quota hoppers 308, 341

Raab, Dominic 590, resigned, 592
Raffarin, Jean-Pierre 404, 421, 441
Rake, Mike 537, 538
Ramadier, Paul 34
Rapid Reaction Force 280
Rasmussen, Poul Nyrup 332
Ratification, of Britain's entry to EEC 147
Rau, Johannes 420
REACH 418
Reagan, President Ronald 219
Rebate, Thatcher agrees 200, formula changed, 200–201, 'Fontainebleau effect', 348
Reckless, Mark, MP 557, 559, 562, 564
Red tape 291, 296, 305, 325, 326, 449, 545, 551, 562, 563, 588, 622
Redwood, John 325
Rees-Mogg, Jacob 587
Referendum Bill 501
Referendum (UK) 1975, question 151, Labour pledge, 157, 158, Labour manifesto, 161–162, Labour decision of expenditure, 165, grants to campaigners; Callaghan reports, 167, Cabinet votes, 168, financing of, 170, leaflets, 171–172, 'not really about Europe', 173, result, 174
Referendum (UK) 2016, campaign already begun 391, Lib-Dem offer, 497, call or face rebellion, 511, petition, 513, poll, 521, UKIP role 'overstated', 525, Cameron supports, 526–527, Bloomberg speech, 529–530, draft Bill, 535, low-key campaigning, 541–542, private member's Bill, 544, opinion polls, 544–545, 'settle the issue', 545, countdown started, 548, timing, 550, 'central plan' of election campaign, 551, IEA competition, 552, Cameron's guarantee, 554, UKIP 'surge', 557, Paterson speech, 559, promise by end of 2017, general election, 565, renegotiation, 565–566, question, 566, date announced, 568, absence of exit plan, 568–569, Cummings defines 'Vote Leave' issues; protest at 'lies' 570, 'trivial' debate; media treats as personality contest, 570–572, result, 572; country 'unprepared'
Referendum Party 329, 337, 338, 424, 543
Regional development agencies 351
Regional policy 131, 154, rules agreed, 166, first grants approved, 178, additionality, 179
Regulatory union 301
Renegotiation, EEC 157, Council of Ministers, 158, shopping list, 159
Luxembourg statement, 159
Reste à liquider (RAL) 578
Retinger, Józef 32, 33
Reynaud, Paul 19–20, 33
Reynolds, Emma 543
Rhineland, French evacuation of 7
Rifkind, Malcolm 221, 280, foreign secretary, 325, 329 fn, 334, footprints, 342, 478
Rippon, Geoffrey 125, Werner Report, 127, denies existence of CFP, 137, statement on negotiations, 146
Robertson, George 237
Robbins, Olly 580
Robinson, Nick 527
Robinson, Robert 141
Rocard, Michel 251
Roche, Dick 419
Rogers, Sir Ivan, 'muddled thinking' 577
Rogoff, Kenneth 413
Romania 27, 369, 478, horsemeat, 531
Rome, Treaty of 73, 74, 82, not a 'frozen document', 89, 291
Roper, John 150
Roscow, Walt 29
Rotfeld, Adam 443
Round Table (journal) 15
Roussin, Michel 435
Royal Institute of International Affairs. See Chatham House.
Royal Prerogative 147

Ruhr, French occupation of 3–4, argument over, 39–40
Rumsfeld, Donald 407
Rusk, Dean 100

Saar region 9, 30, conventions, 40–41, cartoon, 43
Saarbrücken Agreement 291, 292, 618
Salter, Arthur 1, 10–11, 12–13, 14, 17, 18, 20, 34, 51, EEC structure, 73, 124 fn
Sandys, Duncan 32, 33, 35, 85, 92
Sanitary and Phytosanitary (SPS) checks 590, 621
Santer, Jacques 267, 318, 329 fn, 331, 336, 340, 341, 344, 345, 349, 354, ECHO scandal, 356, 357, 361, fatally weakened, 362, 366, 369
Sapir, André 413
Sarkozy, Nicolas 421, 451, 461, 467, president, 471, pledges end to EU 'paralysis', 472, 475, 478, 'France is back', 479, 'Irish will have to vote again', 480, 484, street violence, 498, 499, 506, 511, 'sick of you', 512, 'incandescent', 514, 515, deposed, 519, 561
Sassoli, David 601
Sauvagnargues, Jean 162
Schäffer, Hans 63
Schäuble, Wolfgang 319, 506
Schengen Agreement 292, 320 fn, 328, 340, 503, 504, 618
Scheurmann, Christoph 632
Schlüter, Poul 279
Schmidt, Helmut 157, 162, 181, 190, ERM and sterling, 193
Schmidt, Stefan 356, forced from post, 403
Schönfelder, Wilhelm 468
Schröder, Gerhard 354, 'frenzy', 355, 359, 360, 361, accepts Eurocorps, 364, 370, IGC to follow Nice, 377, agrees on 'joint efforts; with France, 379, 381, 'utter chaos', 384, 385, Plan, 386, mini-summit, 392, 394, rejects subsidy cut, 404, floods 'godsend', 405, 406, 407, public works, 414, voting rights, 419, election defeat, 421, contemplates Britain's failure to ratify constitution, 423, backs Verhofstadt for Commission president, 425, loses strongholds, 440, vows to continue with ratification, 442, 443, accused of making Britain 'bad boy', 444, 445, one of 'worst political crises', 447, 449, loses general election, 450
Schulz, Martin 411, 533, 549, 550
Schuman, Maurice, on CFP 146
Schuman Plan 41–44, UK rejection of, 45–46, 614
Schuman, Robert 33, 36, 40, 42–43, 52, EDC, 54, president of European Assembly, 76, beatification, 420
Schüssel, Wolfgang 450, 459, 460, 461
Scottish government, exit plan 557
Scrutiny, of community legislation 132 fn, 186, 300, 475
Séguéla, Jacques 437
Sequencing 580
Serbia, ethnic cleansing 361, applies to join EU, 535
Services Directive 434, 435
Shanks, Michael 103
Shepherd, Richard 276
Sherpas 225
Shinwell, Manny 46
Shonfield, Andrew 187
Shore, Peter 115, 116, 119, 147, 169, 181, 243
Short, Clare 357, 358
Short, Ted 165, 166, 181
Sick man of Europe 176
Silkin, John 169, 185, 186, 204
Simplified revision procedure 502, 515, 550
Sinclaire, Nikki, MEP 513
Single currency (European) ix, 14, 17, Werner report, 125, Jenkins, 188, nest

stage on agenda, 239, German 'merit', 240, Thatcher 'not on the cards', 241, Howe keen to join, 246, claim of savings, 256, Thatcher rejection, 257, Major's concerns, 260, European Parliament calls for, 261, Delors starts process, 262, Major refuses, 269, chief preoccupation, 270, British unveil opt-out, 272, Delors 'success', 273, role of structural funds, 274, retain right to opt-in, 276, Labour and Lib-Dem support, 277, Black Wednesday, 281, Danes refuse, 265, 'like building the mediaeval cathedrals', 311, Major's 'fork in the road', 314, pressure to join, 320, 1999 set for launch, 322, named 'euro'; 'rock for Europe', 326, 328, Stability and Growth Pact, 333, problems with preparations; Rifkind exploits gloom, 334, backbenchers oppose, 336, timing 'shaky', 340, Brown rules out joining; Heseltine, 'only issue when', 345, Euro XI, 346, 11 members to join, 347, important step on way to European integration, 354, Britain not survive as serious international power unless joins, 360, launch, 360–361 beginning of political integration, 361, 'theme of 90s', 363, Blair Ghent speech, 374, 'quantum leap' towards federalism, 378, Danish referendum, 379, Blair pledges to join by 2007, 419, Prodi complains, 432, euro crises 492, et seq
Single European Act, genesis 216, 225 et seq, treaty signed, 227, 'smiling mouse', 228, 239, regionalisation, 351
Single Market (also internal market) ix, completion of, 222–223, 225–226, directives, 232, 238, 239, 249, 254, 289 et seq, regulation, 291, enlargement, 294, EFTA/EEA, 296, launch, 301, as regulatory union, 301, statutory instruments, 302, theory and practice, 303, gold plating, 303, 310, 319, 321, law decided by QMV, 487, Norway, 514, Johnson, 527, Norway option, 527–530, horsemeat, 532–533, EEA, 537, balance of competences, 540, IEA competition, 552, Cameron, 562, renegotiation, 575, breaking away, 576, cherry-picking, 576–577, preserving, 579, BRINO, 592, leaving, 581, Northern Ireland, 583, misconception, 585, interim solution, 586, confusion over terms, 588, mutual recognition, 590, undermining, 591, Northern Ireland Protocol, 597, ecosystem of rules, 601, departure, 608, dilemma, 618 et seq, new normal, 619, globalisation, 621, UNECE, 622, realitätsblind, 632, new chapter of deception, 633
Sked, Dr Alan 287
Slaughterhouses 306 et seq. See also: Abattoirs
Slovakia 369, floods, 405, 410, 424, 463, 478, 479, drops out of GLF, 495
Smith, John 277, 316, 317, death, 318
Smuts, Jan 1
'Snatch' Land Rovers 466
Soames, Christopher 85, 129
Social Chapter (and Charter) 249, 250, 252, 260, 269, 272, 273, 277, 288, 314, 326, 329 fn, 338, 340, 374, 505
Sócrates, José 456, 471, 476, 506
Solana, Javier 365, 379, 393, 402, 408, 419
Solberg, Erna 535–535, used by BBC, 540
Solbes, Pedro 385, 412, 414, 419
Solemn Declaration on European Union 208, purpose of, 209, 215
Somerset Levels flooding 563
Soros, George 282–283
Soustelle, Jacques, Schuman Plan 'anti-European' 50
Sovereignty, League of Nations 8, supranational authority overrules, 21, dogma, 23, no violation of, 30, limits on, 31, delegation of, 34, Monnet, 38, German, restoration of, 55, French concerns, 60, UK

preservation of, 82, considerable loss of, 86, surrenders, 87, respect of national, 95, strong feelings about, 126, ultimate stage, 127, no loss of essential national sovereignty, 132, FCO 30/1048, 132 fn, Enoch Powell, 142, 150, Tony Benn, 150, transition from, 155, transfer to EU, 163–164, debate on, 172–3, raising the flag for, 236, perforated, 239 fn, reasons for retention, 244, avoiding loss of, 251, delegate to the centre, 253, giving up to Hitler (Nicholas Ridley), 254, mentions of, 270, new legal framework, 296, over taxation, 348, adopting the euro, effect of, 378, opinion poll, 384, Blair signing away, 426, Junker admits transfer, 474, EEA, 538, Brexit, 627–628, and power, 628, of the British people, 629
Spaak, Paul-Henri 20, 35, 55, president of Council of Europe, 37, EDC, 56, fronts Monnet's proposals for a relaunch, 58, emphasises 'economic community', 59, political will, 130
Spaak Committee 62–66
Spaak II Committee 217. See also Dooge.
Spain 186, admission of, 212, fishing fleet, 212, 213, 226 fn, structural funds, 236, 244, ERM, 281, fruit payments, 305–306, vets, 307, registering fishing boats, 308, jobs, 311 & 333, fishing 'ransom', 316, cuckoo, 321 et seq, 332, budget deficit, 334, spending cuts, 335, structural payments, 344, CAP, 358, regional aid, 381, 383, votes, 384, pressures commissioner, 403, 404, 414, Christian heritage, 417, Fisheries Control Agency, 418, 419, 420, 421, voting rights, 423, referendum, 430, EU constitution, 433, net receipts, 434, rejects budget deal, 448, labour barriers, 463, euro crisis, 502, in firing line, 504, 507, bonds, 511, unemployment, 518, credit rating, 518–519, contagion, 519, 521
Special relationship, USA 87
Spectator 115
Spicer, Michael 278
Spinelli, Altiero 22, 23, 52, 202 et seq, Crocodile Club, 205–206, works on draft treaty, 213, EP adopts draft, 214, seeks Mitterrand's aid, 214, 223, dies, 229
Spinelli Group 544, 617
Spierenburg, Dirk 49
Spongiform Encephalopathy Advisory Committee (SEAC) 330
Stability and Growth Pact 333, regulations, 341, not enough, 394, 'stupid', 406, pressure to review, 412, 413, 417, 455, 512, 516 fn
Stability, Coordination and Governance in the Economic and Monetary Union, Treaty 516
Standard & Poor's (S&P) 511, 516, 519
Standing Veterinary Committee (SVC) 330
Starmer, Kier 633
Steinbrück, Peer 455
Sterling, effect of Suez 72, Heath undermines, 131, court judgement, 175, crisis, 190, Schmidt ERM linkage, 193, 195, exchange rate, 231, shadows deutschmark, 235, membership of ERM, 247, ERM crisis, 281–283
St Malo, Blair meets Chirac 359, 363, 364, 415
Stockholm Convention 78
Stoiber, Edmund 386, 405
Strategic Defence Initiative (SDI) 219
Strauss-Kahn, Dominique 340
Straw, Jack (foreign secretary) 399, 400, 417, 420, no fundamental change in relationship, 427, 428, 431, decide on ratification, 442, 'withering assault', 444, 446, 'cunning plan', 453, 'Sherwood Forest', 454, 'negotiate with our money', 456, treaty 'in limbo', 461, replaced, euro 'cannot last', 508, 569
Straw, Will, heads 'Remain' campaign
Structural funds, genesis 154–155, 213, 226, 235, 236, 237, 238, 239, 274, 309, 313, 344, 352

Streit, Clarence K. 16
Stresemann, Gustav 4, 5, 9
Stewart, Marshall 140
Subsidiary 226, 274, 278, to the rescue, 279 et seq, 'big idea', 284 et seq, study group, 298, 323, 326, 384
Suez 72 77, 83, loss of national self-confidence, 616
Sun, newspaper 114, 251, 'Up Yours, Delors', 258, 349, 335, 380, 442, 426, poll, 428, 476, 576 fn, Trump interview, 590, 597 fn, 604 fn
Sunderland 389
Supranationalism 12, 49, 54, 57, of Euratom, 65, 66, 67, 81, 85, 94, 97, 264, 316, 412, 616, 617
'Swallow it whole', entry negotiations 124, 617
Syria 503, diaspora, 503–504, refugees, 504, chemical attack, 541
Szamuely, Dr Helen 488

Tampere programme 369, 392
Tapsell, Peter 228
Tariffs 13, 49, common external, 58, 59, 63, 67, 69, walls, 74, programme for harmonising, 82, 86, 88, 92, French demands, 102, 103, 166, 167, 200, removal of, 203, Uruguay Round, 255, abolition, 291, Brexit, 577, 588, 589, zero tariff deal, 620, 633
Taverne, Dick, Lord 553
Tebbit, Norman 231
Thatcher, Margaret 168, launches 'Yes' campaign, 169, prime minister, 193, disagrees at first European Council, 194, compared with de Gaulle, 195, rejects offer, 196, blocks 'own resource' increase, 197, discussions with Mitterrand, 198, rejects 'half-baked' offer, 199, agrees rebate, 200, dismisses Declaration on European Union, 209, Dublin Council, 213, pressure for new treaty, 216, IRA bomb, Avignon speech, 220, nominates Cockfield, 221, 222, Milan, 223–224, 226, considers veto, 227, unaware of political union agenda, 228, deceived, 229, seeds of downfall, 230, disagrees on EMU, 231, weakened by Heseltine, 232, alienates Delors, 233–234, economic transformation, 234, EMS, 235–235, budgetary crisis, 235, 236, Chirac, 'isolated and alone', 237, Brussels 1988, 238, crisis over, 239, at odds with everyone, 239 et seq, pressed to join ERM, 240, rejects idea of European central bank, 241, outraged by Delors, 242, Bruges speech, 243–244, Heath launches attack, 244–245, worst fears, 246, battle of wills on ERM, 247–248, Lawson/Howe meeting, 248–249, announces intent to join ERM, 249, dismisses 'social charter', 249–250, reshuffles cabinet, 250, capitulates on political union, 252–254, poll tax, 254, joins ERM, 255, Rome 'ambush', 257, 'No! No! No!', 258, the end, 258–259, calls for referendum, 270, Maastricht 'a treaty too far', 284, dies, 535
Thoburn, Steve 389, ghost of, 572
Thomson, George 178
Thorpe, Jeremy 157
Tickell, Crispin 127 fn, 146
Tietmeyer, Hans 339, 347
Tindemans, Leo, Report 188, 351
Tobin, Brian 324
Todd, Ron 243
Topolánek, Mirek 484
Toynbee, Arnold 17, 18
Trade Agreement 630
Trade and Cooperation Agreement (TCA) 607, 630
Trade Union leaders 176
Trans-European Network (TEN) 274, 315, 333
Translation, cost of 76

Treaty on European Union, genesis 216
Trend, Burke 70
Trethowan, Ian 140
Trichet, Jean-Claude 347, 409, 502
Troika, structure established 207, 266, 267, 268, 271, eurozone troika, 346, Merkel, 474, 518
Truman Doctrine 27
Trump, President Donald, state visit 590, presidential elections, 603
Tsunami, Indian Ocean 432
Tucholsky, Karl 6, fn
Turkey 27, 90 fn, 263, entry talks, 430, fear of, 434, overstretch, 450, 464, 467, clash over, 477, riots, 485, Cameron to fight for entry, 500, refugees, 504, talks resume, 547, immigration, 570
Turner, Adair 486
Tuomioja, Erkki 465
Tusk, Donald, Council president 555, no '*à la carte*', 575, visits May, 582, no Irish hard border, 583, 'sufficient progress', 584, losing patience, 587, dismisses May's initiative, 591, 'special place in hell', 593, delay 'deeply corrosive', 597
Tuthill, John 79
Tvinnereim, Anne 539
Two-speed Europe 216
Twohig, Colman 289

U-2 'spy plane' 84
UCLAF (anti-fraud unit) 355, 357
Ukraine 272, 450, 454, 541, Partnership and Cooperation Agreement, 546, protest, 547
Ulster Unionists 288
UK Independence Party (UKIP) 287, success of, 424, 431, effect, 439, 462, 486, 498, 513, 525, 534, 535, 551, 552, 553, 554, 556, 557, 559, 560, 562, 564, 565, 568, 575
UK Internal Market Bill 602, 605, controversial clauses abandoned, 606
UN Conference on the Law of the Sea (UNCLOS) 181
UN Economic Commission for Europe (UNECE) 29, 30, 571, 572, 620, Harmonisation of Vehicle Regulations, 622, 623, GHS, 624, proceedings, 629, WP.29, 631
UN Food and Agriculture Organization (FAO) 624
UN Security Council 268, 407, 408
United Europe Movement 33
United States of Europe (book) 1, 12

Value added tax. See VAT
Van Agt, Andries 194
Van Buitenen, Paul 355, 358, 361, 362, 403
Van den Broek, Hans 266, 267
Van Gogh, Theo 431
Van Rompuy, Herman 492, 509, 510, 'interim report' on treaty change, 513, leaked, 515, intergovernmental route, 516, debate, 520, budget, 523, replaced, 555
Van Zeeland, Paul 33, 48
Vanhanen, Matti 462
Vansittart, Sir Robert 19
Varadkar, Leo 583, ultimatum to May, 587, 593, meets Johnson, 596
VAT 115, arrival of, 152, budget ceiling, 197, 6th VAT Directive, 204
Vatican 285, 420
Vaz, Keith 380
Vehicle Type Approvals 590
Venizelos, Evangelos 514
Ventotene Manifesto 22
Verdun 1–2, 219, 613–614
Verheugen, Günther 358, 416, 436, 445
Verhofstadt, Guy 386, 387, 398, 419, 425, 581
Veritas 424 fn, 439
Verros, Costas 312
Versailles, Treaty of 3, 4, 8

Vienna, European Congress 6
Vietnam War 116 fn
Vitorino, António 397
Vittori, Roberto 436
Volcanic Ash Advisory Centre (VAAC) 496
Von der Leyen, Ursula 596, meets Johnson in London, 598, video conference, 601, 'significant gaps', 602, explains to MEPs, 604, 'quite helpful', 605, direct dialogue, 605–606, 'no progress', 606, imminent deal, 607
Vote Leave. See: Leave campaign

Waigel, Theo 339, 345, 416
Wakeham, John 231
Waldegrave, William 322, 323
Wall, Stephen, on common fisheries policy 133
Wall Street crash 8
Wallström, Margot 438, 442, 477
Walters, Professor Alan 231
Watson, Graham 425
Watt, Dougal 403
Weale, Dr Martin 374
Weil, Christoph 521
Weimar Triangle 443
Wellink, Nout 413
Werner, Pierre 121, Report, 122, 125–126, 241
Western European Union. See WEU.
Western Union. See: Brussels Treaty Organisation
Westland Affair 232
WEU 57, 219
Wharton, James, private member's Bill 544
What's Wrong with Britain School 103
White Paper, 1971 British entry 131, on renegotiations, 160, A Partnership of Nations, 329
Whitelaw, William 169, 231
Whitney, Nick 419
Williams, Shirley 149, 172
Wilson, Harold 91, Labour leader, 112, election victory, 115, 2nd term, 157, 'theology', 163, budget 'correction mechanism', 164, EMU 'distant goal', 165, in Brussels, 177, resigns, 183
Wilson, Dr Nigel 556
Wilson, Woodrow 2, Fourteen Point Declaration, 3
Wirtschaftwunder 69
Withdrawal Agreement, first draft 586, colour-coded, 587, NI Protocol, 588, not without legally binding backstop, 591, new draft, 592, May loses votes, 593–594, Johnson signals new agreement, 594, revised, 596–597, passed by Parliament, 597, signed: 'fantastic moment', 596, infinitely worse, 632
Wolfson, Simon, Lord 542
Wolridge-Gordon MP, Patrick 138
Worcester, Bob 173, 353
World Health Organization 599
Wulf-Mathies, Monika 357

Xenophobia 318, year against, 336, goodbye, 337–338, 418

Yanukovich, Viktor 547
Yeltsin, Boris 272
Yes, Prime Minister 612
Yom Kippur War 156, 179
Young, Hugo 52, concedes Council 'rude', 195
Young, Lord 239
Younger, Kenneth 45
Yugoslavia, resistance 22, 23, break-up, 266–268, 348, 504

Zalm, Gerrit 443
Zapatero, José Luis Rodríguez 421
Zimmern, Sir Alfred 18, 19
Zollverein 13